CICERO AS EVIDE[

For my grandchildren

CICERO AS EVIDENCE

A HISTORIAN'S COMPANION

ANDREW LINTOTT

OXFORD
UNIVERSITY PRESS

OXFORD
UNIVERSITY PRESS

Great Clarendon Street, Oxford OX2 6DP

Oxford University Press is a department of the University of Oxford.
It furthers the University's objective of excellence in research, scholarship,
and education by publishing worldwide in

Oxford New York

Auckland Cape Town Dar es Salaam Hong Kong Karachi
Kuala Lumpur Madrid Melbourne Mexico City Nairobi
New Delhi Shanghai Taipei Toronto

With offices in

Argentina Austria Brazil Chile Czech Republic France Greece
Guatemala Hungary Italy Japan Poland Portugal Singapore
South Korea Switzerland Thailand Turkey Ukraine Vietnam

Oxford is a registered trade mark of Oxford University Press
in the UK and in certain other countries

Published in the United States
by Oxford University Press Inc., New York

© Andrew Lintott 2008

The moral rights of the author have been asserted
Database right Oxford University Press (maker)

First published 2008
First published in paperback 2010

All rights reserved. No part of this publication may be reproduced,
stored in a retrieval system, or transmitted, in any form or by any means,
without the prior permission in writing of Oxford University Press,
or as expressly permitted by law, or under terms agreed with the appropriate
reprographics rights organization. Enquiries concerning reproduction
outside the scope of the above should be sent to the Rights Department,
Oxford University Press, at the address above

You must not circulate this book in any other binding or cover
and you must impose the same condition on any acquirer

British Library Cataloguing in Publication Data
Data available

Library of Congress Cataloging in Publication Data
Data available

Typeset by SPI Publisher Services, Pondicherry, India

ISBN 978–0–19–921644–4 (Hbk.)
ISBN 978–0–19–959972–1 (Pbk.)

Preface

The aim of this book is to assist those who study late-Republican history to read Cicero, to introduce them to the variety of evidence available in the whole range of his writings and to suggest the kind of critical approach that is necessary if this evidence is to be given its proper value. It is this second aim that guides the first two parts of the book in particular. Here I seek to show how the historian must handle evidence that at first sight may seem both attractively immediate and transparent, but on further inspection proves to be far otherwise. The surviving texts of Cicero's speeches present special difficulties. Chapter 2 is unashamedly technical and will be best appreciated by those who are already grappling with the problem of the speeches as historical evidence. Chapters 4 to 6 are equally technical about matters of private law, but that is inevitable, if one is to do justice to this aspect of Cicero's writing and work. It is often neglected by philologists and historians, but one cannot judge Cicero as an orator or as a member of Roman society without taking it into account. Parts 3 and 4 follow a general path well trodden in Ciceronian biography, but will be found to differ considerably in their emphases from the majority of such works. Because my text focuses on Ciceronian writing it will be more of an intellectual history of the man than a history of his actions. In so far as it is biographical, it will for the most part neglect the tradition created by contemporary and later writers about Cicero. Because the latter, though sometimes perceptive, is also sometimes misleading, it is important to clarify the vision to be found in Cicero's own works.

Readers may be frustrated by not finding a narrative interpretation of Cicero's career before the beginning of his correspondence. The discussion of his advocacy in private law suits may seem a dry substitute. However, it should be remembered that this advocacy was both his chief achievement and how he must have presented himself to the rest of Roman society in this period—a rather different picture from the romantic vision of the young defender of liberty often constructed on the basis of the speech for Sextus Roscius but now under question (see Appendix 1). His life during the civil wars of the eighties remains enigmatic. Our best clues do not emerge until we read his correspondence during the war between Caesar and Pompey and the determinedly laconic account of his forensic apprenticeship in the *Brutus*: they will be considered in their place there. If this book is not to be considered a Cicero biography, it is even less to be treated as a history of the late Republic. That, I believe, can only be achieved by knowing the Ciceronian evidence but standing a long way back from it. Scholars have had difficulty in finding a satisfactory approach to writing the history of this complex period and have frequently turned to biography of one of the great men, perhaps as a substitute. When Cicero is the subject of such a work, the danger is that it becomes more of a history of the late Republic than a life of Cicero: many valuable insights into Cicero himself have to be sacrificed in order to tell the bigger story. I hope that the present work may provide some compensation for that tendency.

For the author the work is the product of teaching Cicero and the history of the late Republic to undergraduates for over forty years. Its range may be in part ascribed to the special needs of the Cicero special subject in the Ancient and Modern history syllabus at Oxford, which has provided me with some of the most exciting teaching hours in my career. The book has as background a mountain of Ciceronian scholarship, whose more recent peaks are the biography by Matthias Gelzer and the commentaries of D. R. Shackleton Bailey. My debts to my own teachers, colleagues, and pupils are beyond enumeration. I should, however, mention in particular my tutor as an undergraduate, Dacre Balsdon, who combined a highly critical attitude to Cicero's statements about himself with considerable sympathy for the man, and John Crook, whose work has stimulated interest in forensic advocacy and who gently encouraged me in this project over dinner in Cambridge some ten years ago. It is my pleasure to thank those who have read all or parts of the work while it has been in preparation—Arnd Kerkhecker, Doreen Innes, Michael Winterbottom, Miriam Griffin, and the readers of the Oxford University Press—and Hilary O'Shea for continuing to be my publisher.

A.L.

Worcester College, Oxford
October 2006

Contents

Abbreviations   ix

PART A. READING CICERO

I. Reading Events   3
II. The Texts of the Speeches   15
III. Truth and Fiction in the Speeches   33

PART B. READING ORATORY

IV. Cicero's Forensic Baptism: The *Pro Quinctio*   43
V. More Problems of Partnership: The *Pro Quinto Roscio Comoedo*   60
VI. Property and Violence: The *Pro Tullio* and *Pro Caecina*   68
VII. Cicero and the Citadel of the Allies   81
VIII. The Defence of Good Men (1): The Other Side of the *Quaestio de Repetundis*   101
IX. The Defence of Good Men (2): Treason and Other Crimes against the Roman People   111

PART C. HISTORY IN SPEECHES AND LETTERS

X. Candidature and Consulship   129
XI. The Aftermath of the Consulship   149
XII. The Gang of Three and Clodius   167
XIII. After the Return   183

PART D. HISTORY AND IDEAS

XIV. The Search for *Otium*   215
XV. The Governor and the Approach of Civil War   253
XVI. The Mediator and the Partisans   281

XVII.	Living with Dictatorship	301
XVIII.	The Ides of March and After	339
XIX.	Answering the Republic's Call	374
XX.	Epilogue	408

APPENDICES

1.	The *Pro Sexto Roscio*	425
2.	The *De Imperio Gnaei Pompeii* (*Pro Lege Manilia*)	427
3.	Further Notes on the *Pro Caelio*	430
4.	The End of Caesar's Command in Gaul	433
5.	The *De Legibus*	436
6.	The *De Senectute*	438
7.	Events after Caesar's Murder	440
8.	Antonius' Letter (CIC. *Phil.* 13. 22 ff.)	445

Bibliography	448
Index	457

Abbreviations

Abbreviations of periodicals in general follow the system of *L'Année Philologique*, with one important exception: *ZSS* for *Zeitschrift der Savigny-Stiftung für Rechtsgeschichte, romanistische Abteilung*.

ANRW	*Aufstieg und Niedergang der römischen Welt*, Festschrift J. Vogt, ed. H. Temporini and W. Haase (Berlin and New York, 1972–)
CAH	*Cambridge Ancient History*
CRR	A. Lintott, *The Constitution of the Roman Republic* (Oxford, 1999)
EJ²	V. Ehrenberg and A. H. M. Jones, *Documents Illustrating the Reigns of Augustus and Tiberius*, 2nd edn. with addenda (Oxford, 1975)
FGH	F. Jacoby, *Die Fragmente der Griechischen Historiker*, 3 parts, 11 vols. (Berlin and Leiden, 1923–58)
FIRA	S. Riccobono, *Fontes Iuris Romani Anteiustiniani*, 2nd edn. (Florence, 1968)
GC	A. H. M. Greenidge and A. M. Clay, *Sources for Roman History 133–70 BC*, 2nd edn. rev. E. W. Gray, corrected and augmented (Oxford, 1986)
How	W. W. How, *Cicero Select Letters*, ii: *Notes* (Oxford, 1926)
HRR	H. Peter, *Historicorum Romanorum Reliquiae*, 2 vols., 2nd edn. (Stuttgart, repr. 1993)
IGRR	R. Cagnat *et al.*, *Inscriptiones Graecae ad Res Romanas Pertinentes*, 3 vols. (Paris, 1906–27)
ILLRP	A. Degrassi, *Inscriptiones Latinae Liberae Rei Publicae*, 2 vols. (2nd. edn. Florence, 1966)
Imp. Rom.	A. Lintott, *Imperium Romanum: Politics and Administration* (London and New York, 1993)
Inscr.Ital.	A. Degrassi, *Inscriptiones Italiae, xiii: Fasti et Elogia*, 3 vols. (Rome, 1947–63)
JRLR	A. Lintott, *Judicial Reform and Land Reform in the Roman Republic* (Cambridge, 1992)
LTUR	E. M. Steinby (ed.), *Lexicon topographicum urbis Romae*, 6 vols. (Rome, 1993–2000)
MRR	T. R. S. Broughton, *The Magistrates of the Roman Republic*, vols. i–ii (2nd edn., New York, 1960), vol. iii (Atlanta, 1987)
OGIS	W. Dittenberger, *Orientis Graeci Inscriptiones Selectae*, 4 vols. (Leipzig, 1903, repr. Hildesheim, 1960)

ORF	H. Malcovati, *Oratorum Romanorum Fragmenta*, 2 vols. (4th edn., Turin, 1976–9)
Puccioni	G. Puccioni, *M. Tulli Ciceronis Orationum Deperditarum Fragmenta* (Verona, 1963)
RE	Pauly–Wissowa, *Real-Encyclopaedie der classischen Altertumswissenschaft*
RDGE	R. K. Sherk, *Roman Documents from the Greek East* (Baltimore, 1964)
RRC	M. H. Crawford, *Roman Republican Coinage*, 2 vols. (Cambridge, 1974)
RS	M. H. Crawford (ed.), *Roman Statutes*, 2 vols. (London, 1996)
SB *Att*	D. R. Shackleton Bailey, *Cicero's Letters to Atticus*, 6 vols. (Cambridge, 1965–70)
SB *Fam*	D. R. Shackleton Bailey, *Cicero: Epistulae ad Familiares*, 2 vols. (Cambridge, 1977)
SB *QFBrut*	D. R. Shackleton Bailey, *Cicero: Epistulae ad Quintum Fratrem et M. Brutum* (Cambridge, 1980)
Syll^3	W. Dittenberger, *Sylloge Inscriptionum Graecarum*, 4 vols., 3rd edn. (Leipzig, 1915; repr. Hildesheim, 1960)
THerc	*Tabulae Herculanenses*, ap. G. Rowe, *SCI* 20 (2001), 235–42
TP	*Tabulae Pompeianae*, ap. L. Bove, *Documenti processuali dalle Tabulae Pompeianae di Murecine* (Naples, 1979)
TPSulp	G. Camodeca, *Tabulae Pompeianae Sulpiciorum* (Vetera, 12; Rome, 1999)
VRR	A. Lintott, *Violence in Republican Rome*, 2nd edn. (Oxford, 1999)

Part A

Reading Cicero

I

Reading Events

TEXTS AS EVENTS

ONE of the first things that students of late-Republican Roman history have to learn is that they cannot treat Ciceronian texts as authentic records of history. They must realize not only that the statements about his own lifetime, especially in his speeches, contain bias and misrepresentation, if not at times downright fantasy, but that most accounts of past history in his works have a persuasive element that tends to overshadow his devotion to the truth as he knows it. Cicero knew the 'laws of history', that one should neither venture to say anything false nor fail to venture to say anything true.[1] However, that did not apply to the stories told in speeches: in his dialogue dedicated to Brutus, he puts in Atticus' mouth the comment that orators had a licence to lie in order to make a point more emphatically.[2] This last point should not surprise us. In the courts of the Roman Republic an orator's duty was to his client, not the court, and Cicero stressed the importance of adapting the *narratio*, the account of the 'facts of the case', to the later argument.[3] The same is true of the historical *exempla* he introduces. Cicero is not a detached and impartial narrator of either the world in which he himself moved or the past history of Rome.

Some of what follows in this work will be an elaboration of this theme in relation to specific texts and problems. However, there is another complementary aspect of Cicero's writings that is less often stressed: they were themselves events in history with causes and effects. Some of the works on philosophy and rhetoric may have been trivial events historically: others, such as *De Oratore* and *De Re Publica*, deserve a fuller integration in the political history of their time than they normally receive.[4] Even the *Brutus*, which for

---

[1] *De Or.* 2. 62; *Fam.* 5. 12. 3.
[2] *Brut.* 42, arising from Cicero's professed preference for the more poetic account of Coriolanus' death—suicide, rather than assassination or death in old age as in Livy 2. 40. 10–11; Plut. *Cor.* 39. 1–9; Dion. Hal. *AR* 8. 59.
[3] *Inv.* 1. 30; *Off.* 2. 51. See on the principles of advocacy in the Ciceronian period Crook, 1995, 119 ff.
[4] On *Rep.* see Lintott, 'The Theory of the Mixed Constitution at Rome', in Barnes and Griffin, 1997, 71–85 at 81 ff.; *CRR* 220–32.

the most part seems a nostalgic exercise in recreating the oratory of the Republic at a time when the conditions of public speaking had been significantly changed by Caesar's dictatorship—with an obvious cause, that is, but apparently in a historical cul-de-sac—has in its conclusion the wish that Brutus may have that state of public affairs (*res publica*) in which he can renew and magnify the renown of two outstanding families. These were the Iunii Bruti and the Servilii Ahalae, both famed as enemies of tyrants. Hence he was making a none too discreet suggestion that Caesar should be murdered.[5]

The speeches, both those spoken and those only published, are obviously events, some more important historically than others. They document Cicero's progress in rhetoric and reveal to us more generally the oratorical techniques of the time. However, when we seek Cicero's aims in a speech, even a forensic speech, there is more scope for detecting 'hidden agenda' than is sometimes appreciated and this will often explain the apparent irrelevance of sections of speeches to the issue being discussed or the case being tried. When a speech is published some time after delivery, this is an event in itself and frequently signifies a purpose different from that of its delivered counterpart. As for the letters, many were written with a specific object, to recommend one friend of Cicero's to another, to seek a favour, to console, to conciliate friends or placate enemies, often too in the expectation that they would be shown to others than the recipient. What may be less obvious is how many letters written to his brother Quintus, to Atticus, or to other close friends are carefully constructed with an aim in view. Gregory Hutchinson has pointed out the elaborate structure of certain letters from a literary point of view.[6] I would wish to stress first the persuasive element that lurks even in the most apparently casual letters, secondly how recognition of this both helps us to grasp the historical significance of the letter itself as an event and suggests how we should interpret the information that the letter contains.

Letters as Events

The surviving correspondence of Cicero with his close friend Atticus begins in 67 BC, the year when he was elected praetor for 66. We have no letters from the year of his praetorship, only his first political speech advocating the bill of Manilius, which assigned to Pompey the command against Mithridates (see Appendix 2). However, one of the most read letters of Cicero is the account of

---

[5] *Brut.* 331; cf. *VRR* 55–6. Cicero denies being an instigator of the assassination in *Phil.* 2. 25–6, but in an oblique way that suggests the opposite.

[6] Hutchinson, 1998.

his consular canvass in the year 65 (*Att.* 1. 1). Or is this the correct description of the letter? Certainly, at the opening Cicero writes, 'the balance-sheet of my canvass, which I know to be of supreme concern to you, is roughly this, as far as can be forecast from the signs up to this point.' Thirty-six lines of the Oxford text review the position in a generally positive fashion. Then, 'but there is a point over which I would wish your forgiveness' and thirty-one further lines describe an embarrassing difficulty that has arisen and threatens to damage relations between Cicero and Atticus (1. 1. 3–4). After this the letter concludes in about two lines. As soon as one begins to ask why Cicero wrote this letter, the importance of the second main section stands out.

The letter is presented as a progress report, but for both writer and recipient the request made in the latter part of the letter was the nub. Cicero had refused to give forensic help to Atticus' uncle Q. Caecilius and a group of creditors, including Atticus' close friend L. Lucullus,[7] because Caninius Satyrus, the man from whom they were seeking to extract money, was an election agent whom Cicero and Quintus had been using. He was also a devoted supporter of L. Domitius Ahenobarbus, not only a great noble but immensely wealthy.[8] Cicero had given offence to Caecilius by this breach of the normal rules of friendship. He suggests in the letter that he had done this to avoid an offence against another friend who had conferred on him many services. If Atticus would not accept this excuse and ascribed the decision to his friend's desire for office, Cicero still thought that he should be forgiven. In an election campaign he could not afford to lose Atticus' friendship either.

And that is what the first half of the letter is about (1. 1–2). Cicero races through notes on other likely candidates and a few brief comments on his own plans. The competition is not as serious as it might be; he himself will put all he can into it, even to the extent of canvassing in Cisalpine Gaul. 'When I have got a clear view of the attitudes of the *nobiles*, I will write to you. The rest I hope will be straightforward, at least with these competitors from the city.' He concedes that there is a potential problem with the attitudes of the *nobiles*: this anticipates his emphasis on the importance of Domitius Ahenobarbus in the second half of the letter and is also relevant to the fact that he has been forced to disappoint Atticus' friend Lucullus. Atticus is not only expected to forgive Cicero himself but to see that Lucullus and his friends forgive him also. Cicero returns to this subject in the brief letter from later in this year, where he says that he needs Atticus' presence soon, since his noble friends are said to be hostile to Cicero's attaining the consulship (*Att.* 1. 2. 2).

---

[7] Mentioned in the same sentence as Caecilius by Nepos, *Att.* 5. 1.
[8] Note his role of advocate for the *publicani* against the Oropians in 73 BC (*RGDE*, no. 23, l. 24).

Was Atticus expected to help with Pompey? 'See that you provide me with that support of my (*nostri*) friend Pompey, since you are not so far away from him; tell him that I will not be angry if he doesn't come to my elections' (1. 1. 2). It sounds like a joke, especially if we compare it to the more serious requests relating to the Caecilius affair. If it had been a serious request, it ought to have been postponed until he had placated Atticus over Caecilius. In any case Atticus was in Epirus, about two weeks' journey away from Rome, but about two months' journey away from Pompey, who was probably in the Caucasus. Should we even conclude that Atticus was a friend of Pompey, assuming that *nostri amici* really means 'our friend', not 'my friend', and is not ironical? Pompey's great command in the East had entailed the final replacement of Lucullus there and created enmity between the two. However, Atticus was of course well known for cultivating simultaneously people who were enemies of each other:[9] so his friendship with Lucullus is not necessarily an objection. On the other hand, if we look ahead to how Cicero defended in his letters to Atticus his new political alignment with Pompey in 61–60, it becomes apparent that Atticus can hardly have been Pompey's friend, since Cicero took pains to justify himself: indeed Atticus actually mildly criticized this alignment.[10] We therefore should not draw any inferences about Atticus' relationship to Pompey from *Att.* 1. 1. 2, nor regard this sentence as an important element in the letter for Cicero.

Four year later Cicero was at the height of his political influence, having held the consulship in 63 and taken the lead in the suppression of the Catilinarian conspiracy. His authority received a rebuff when he gave evidence against Clodius in the latter's trial for sacrilege (the Bona Dea affair) and Clodius was nevertheless acquitted. The letter describing the trial (*Att.* 1. 16) seems to have been written a little before the normal time of the consular elections in the late Republic (1.16.12), that is early to mid-July. There had been a significant interval since the trial. The bill establishing the court had been passed before the middle of March and the trial was over by 15 May. It was a matter of some urgency since Clodius was quaestor at the time and appointed to the Sicilian province.[11] Atticus had to ask Cicero for an account of the trial (1. 16. 1). This suggests that Cicero was embarrassed by what had

---

[9] Nep. *Att.* 11.

[10] See *Att.* 1. 19. 6–7, where Pompey is an alternative to the *piscinarii* Lucullus and Hortensius; 2. 1. 6, the reply to Atticus' criticism. There is no reason to suppose that Atticus' friend in 1. 13. 4 is Pompey, just because the man is duplicitous. Cicero's evasions in describing the relationship are in direct contrast with the blunt statement about Pompey in 1. 12. 3.

[11] *Att.* 1. 14. 5, 15. 1: the allotment of praetorian provinces had been postponed until after this bill was passed but was over by the Ides of March. Ides of May: *Att.* 1. 16. 9. For Clodius' quaestorship see Asc. 52–3 C; *Schol. Bob.* 87 St. On the Bona Dea affair see Tatum, 1999, 64–71; Balsdon, 1966.

happened and was reluctant to tell the story to Atticus until he had found a satisfactory way of presenting it in a positive light.

The preliminaries and the trial itself occupy about three pages of Oxford text; almost the same amount is devoted to Cicero's subsequent political position, and there is a long coda on other political news and some private business. Cicero begins by describing his attacks on Clodius and his friends before the passage of the bill of Fufius Calenus establishing the court, at which point, according to the letter, he mistrusted the likely jury and modified his attitude (1–2). The story of what must have been a sensational trial is in the letter largely the story of the jury. Cicero says nothing about either the procedure or the evidence presented (did the women present at the ceremony allegedly violated by Clodius give evidence?), except that he himself only said what was well known and attested by other sources (2), nor does he mention the quality of advocacy. The jurors are presented as debt-ridden and disreputable. Surprisingly, they turn out to be highly respectful and protective of Cicero in face of the catcalls of Clodius' supporters when he comes to give evidence (3–5). However, in the end a majority, albeit a small one, succumbs to lavish bribery 'by the bald man from the Nanneian estates, that panegyrist of mine, about whose celebratory speech regarding me I wrote to you' (5).[12]

Cicero concludes that the stability of the political order (*res publica*) created by his consulship has been overthrown, indeed the bad men hoped to exploit this in taking reprisals against all the best men for the grief they had suffered from Cicero's consulship.[13] (6–7) Yet there is a ray of light, provided by none other than Cicero himself, in so far as he has counterattacked with speeches in the senate denouncing the jury, the consul Piso, and Clodius himself, the last leading to an exchange of insulting witticisms (*altercatio*) with Clodius (8–10). The speech published by Cicero as *In Clodium et Curionem* is his version of this last broadside: according to the scholiast it was a reaction to Clodius' threats to transfer to the plebs and attack Cicero for his execution of the leading Catilinarians.[14] In the letter, after describing this debate Cicero concludes that his own political status is unshaken among the *boni*, but is better now among the plebs because of his association with Pompey. The

---

[12] Note that an open allegation of bribery was made by Catulus: it is not just Cicero who is being excessively suspicious. The traditional view, based on the identification of the source of the corruption with the man who delivered a eulogy of Cicero (cf. 1. 14. 3–4), that the bald man is M. Crassus still seems the best. I cannot share Wiseman's powerfully argued view (1974, 147–51), that the man actually is a Calvus, C. Licinius Calvus, for the simple reason that Cicero's evasive allusiveness in referring to the man would have been completely subverted by the open use of his *cognomen*.

[13] *Att.* 1. 16. 6–7 is the earliest Ciceronian text that reveals anxiety, as opposed to indignation, about a reaction against the measures of 63, but the anxiety is not yet focused on his own danger.

[14] *Schol. Bob.* 85–6 St.

subsequent excursus on the corruption attending the consular elections thanks to Pompey's money leads to an ironical comment that his own consulship will seem worthless, if Afranius is elected, and the only course will be to abandon political ambition like Atticus (13).

It is not the place here to argue how much the trial of Clodius was decided by bribes and how much by other factors, including honest doubt about what happened on that night in December the previous year. It is sufficient for my present purpose to point out that this letter is for the most part very poor evidence for anything except Cicero's reaction to what happened at the trial. If Atticus had really wanted information about the events of the trial and its whys and wherefores, he must have been disappointed. Rather, the letter was an attempt to reassure him that nothing disastrous had happened to Cicero, even if the *res publica* was in bad shape. Cicero was claiming that he was continuing to fight for his optimate vision of politics, but, if that failed, he was ready for academic detachment. He had already, perhaps unwisely, worked out his bitterness in speeches in the senate and this letter was an extension of the process.

Speeches as Events

By contrast let us look at two speeches. Clodius' acquittal at the Bona Dea trial created a menace for Cicero that was only finally banished when he returned to Rome in quasi-triumph in September 57.[15] The day after his return (5 September) he came in to the senate and gave a speech of thanks, whose text we possess, *Cum Senatui Gratias Egit* or *Post Reditum in Senatu Habita*. Two days later, after demonstrations orchestrated by Clodius over the price of grain and claims that Cicero had created the shortage, Cicero spoke again in the senate advocating negotiations with Pompey over a bill that would entrust him with managing the corn-supply. The resulting decree of the senate was read out to the crowd assembled outside the temple of Jupiter on the Capitol and then Cicero was granted an opportunity to address the people (*contio*) by the great majority of the magistrates present.[16]

We might expect the speech to the people whose text we possess, entitled *Cum Populo Gratias Egit* or *Post Reditum ad Quirites* to be this last speech. Yet there are grave objections. The second speech should have mentioned Cicero's efforts that day to safeguard the city's corn-supply by his proposal. But there is no trace of this: rather, he suggests that the immortal gods were contributing their approval to his return by the rich abundance and cheapness of the fruits

---

[15] *Att.* 4. 1. 5. [16] *Att.* 4. 1. 6; cf. *Dom.* 15.

of the earth (*Red. Quir.* 18)—hardly a proposition that would have found favour with the crowd. What we have is a speech of thanks, in many ways parallel to that delivered in the senate, one complimentary to Pompey but in no wise suggesting that he was Cicero's candidate for the new supreme authority over grain.[17]

The speech to the senate was delivered, unusually for Cicero, *ex scripto*, from a prepared text.[18] Cicero later claimed that he did so because of the importance of the matter, but we may also wonder if this was an insurance against oratorical failure when he had been out of practice for about eighteen months. It is best to take the speech to the people as a text similarly prepared with care against the occasion. It ought to have been delivered on 5 September: it is easy to see why amid the agitation among the plebs Cicero himself may have hesitated to ask a magistrate for the opportunity to deliver it.

In the speech to the senate Cicero begins by thanking the senate for restoring to him his family, rank, fortunes, and fatherland. He owed these originally to his parents, the immortal gods, the Roman people, and the senate, but it is the senate that has restored them to him. He then turns to individuals in the order in which they gave him support, so providing a narrative of his downfall and recovery that gives colour to what otherwise might have been a catalogue. This is further thrown into relief by the excursus (10–18) on two select villains—not Clodius himself, who is not highlighted but mentioned either obliquely or simply as 'my enemy' (*meus inimicus*) (4)—but the two consuls of 58 BC, Gabinius and Piso. They are pilloried for betraying their office and the orders of society, the senate and the *equites*, which they should have defended. Cicero explains this as a result of their bargaining over their provinces, their devotion to Catiline and Cethegus (10), and their mode of life—Gabinius a flagrant libertine (12–13), Piso a devotee of secret vices justified by a crass Epicureanism and concealed by his gloomy and boorish demeanour in public (13–15). Cicero thus avoided picking a fight with Clodius directly but vented his bitterness on two men who were not there to reply.

Among the heroes L. Ninnius, tribune in 58, has the first place as the pathfinder for the mission to get Cicero restored (3). More important are the consuls of 57, P. Lentulus Spinther in particular (5, 8–9, 18, 25–7). Second in importance are eight of the tribunes of 57, headed by Milo and Sestius. Seven

---

[17] Nor can we easily construe *Red.Quir.* as a forgery. The style is convincing. It resembles at many points but is at the same time strikingly different from the speech to the senate and contains interesting points of detail, not found in other speeches after the return. A useful comparison from a literary point of view was made by Mack, 1937, 18–47.

[18] *Planc.* 74. For other examples of speeches in the senate *ex scripto* see *Phil.* 10. 6 (Fufius Calenus) and *Fam.* 10. 13 (Cicero), both in 43 BC.

of the praetors of 57 are also briefly mentioned, and there are special thanks to Cn. Plancius for his help while quaestor in Macedonia (35).[19] Only two other senators are commended, P. Servilius Vatia Isauricus for his speech persuading Q. Metellus Nepos, Lentulus Spinther's colleague, to abandon his hostility to Cicero. In this Servilius apparently resurrected the shades of dead Metelli, including Nepos' brother Celer and Metellus Numidicus who had been driven into exile by the popular tribune Saturninus (25). The other is Pompey, whose treatment is somewhat ambiguous. He is complimented as the greatest commander of all time, but is first presented as someone who thought he could only come to the senate in safety when the consuls of 57 entered office. He is not mentioned again until Cicero singles out four people who specifically contributed to the method by which he was recalled: Lentulus Spinther, Pompey, Milo, and Sestius. There, in the encomium of Pompey, Cicero returns to the unfortunate picture, describing him at the time when he was asking the tribunes of 58 to promote a bill for Cicero's recall as 'living in retreat at his home through fear of conflict and blood'—undignified demeanour for an incomparable general.[20] These then were the leaders; behind them came the representatives of the towns and countryside throughout Italy whom the senate, on Spinther's prompting, had summoned to support the cause (22–3).

Cicero stated in the speech that he was readily passing over the sins of several people against him (23). He later justified the comparatively short list of those he mentioned favourably, by saying that it would have been impossible to mention everybody and he therefore had concentrated on the leaders and standard-bearers.[21] It is true that two new names, Cn. Oppius and L. Gellius, appear in the text of the speech to the people (*Red. Quir.* 12, 17). However, it is hard to resist the conclusion that many of the *boni* are not mentioned in the speech to the senate, because they were either collaborators with Clodius, pusillanimous, or lukewarm in their sympathies for Cicero (33). He did not want to attack them directly as he did Gabinius and Piso: he needed to integrate himself once again in senatorial society and it would have been unwise to offend an important group of senators. Neither, however, did he want to humiliate himself by flattering them undeservedly.

Other sections of the speech deal more directly with his *dignitas*—those which justify his withdrawal into exile in the first place (6–7, 32–5). Cicero later admitted that he had been advised by people of similar political sympathies to stay and fight in 58.[22] One of these was apparently L. Lucullus,[23] another perhaps

---

[19] Cf. *Planc.* 74.
[20] *Red. Sen.* 4–5; 29; Mack, 1937, 40. See also *Mil.* 37, 40 for Pompey as a passive recipient of Clodius' violence.
[21] *Planc.* 74.   [22] *Dom.* 63; *Sest.* 39.   [23] Plut. *Cic.* 31. 5.

Cato, although the latter, to judge from his own career, was more likely to have advised passive resistance.[24] On his return Cicero was to be attacked for the cowardice of his withdrawal, particularly, no doubt, by those, like Plancius' prosecutor Iuventius Laterensis, who had not liked his return under a Pompeian umbrella.[25] In his speech for Sestius he effectively admitted that he had been accused of cowardice (36, 45); at the moment of his return he was eager to rebut this charge in advance by stressing the forces that had been massed against him and the consequent risk of unnecessary bloodshed. He also stressed the humiliation of others, the senate and equestrian order as a whole (12, 31) and, as we have seen, Pompey himself. In the *epilogus* (37–8) he contrasts his return with those of other *consulares* driven into exile by tribunes, Popilius Laenas and Metellus Numidicus. Unlike them, he had not had great support from relatives, but more support from the senate as a whole. As for Marius, a third consular driven into exile, his return not only received no support from the senate but almost led to the destruction of the senate (38).

Like so many of Cicero's speeches, though on the surface directed towards other people, this speech to the senate is about himself. It reasserts his old political alignments, both with the *optima causa*, the authority of the senate, and with Pompey; it reclaims his former *dignitas*, and it gives notice that he has not forgiven certain of those who in his view have betrayed him.

The speech prepared for delivery to the people does not need to devote time to thanking individuals. However, in other respects many themes are similar and much of the same material is reused with an interesting difference of balance in a speech that is more loosely constructed.[26] The theme of the *exordium* is similar (1–5): Cicero has recovered the benefits conferred on him originally by his parents, the immortal gods, and the Roman people. The credit for this, however, is not given here to the senate but to the Roman people as whole: indeed for a moment they are made to seem more important than the immortal gods (5). This sentiment is worked out in a deliberately grand and elaborate style. The first period, a little over sixteen lines of Oxford text, expresses Cicero's joy that he has successfully sacrificed his own fortunes for the safety of the Roman people. It exploits the concept of *devotio*, according to which heroes of the past, P. Decius Mus and his son of the same name, had formally prayed to the gods to accept their lives as the price of the success of the Roman army.[27]

In the following section (6–11) Cicero reworks the theme of the *epilogus* to the speech to the senate, the comparison with Popilius Laenas, Metellus

---

[24] *Att.* 3. 15. 2; *VRR* 60–1. [25] *Vat.* 6–8; *Pis.*, 19–20, 31–2; *Planc.* 83–90.
[26] Mack, 1937, 29.
[27] Cf. *Sest.* 48 and on the story of Decius Livy, 8. 9–10, 28. 12 – 29. 4; *Fin.* 2. 61; *Tusc.* 1. 89.

Numidicus, and C. Marius: unlike those who previously were brought back from exile, he had had few relatives to assist him, but more public support. Here the authority of the senate and the agitation in the *municipia* and *coloniae* find a brief mention (10). When he compares the attitude of the consuls of the time to Popilius and Metellus with what happened to him, he soft-pedals his bitterness towards Piso and Gabinius in a brief passage of heavy irony. They were asked to bring up his recall, but were afraid that they might be thought to do so as a personal favour, since one was his relative by marriage and the other had been defended by him on a capital charge; in fact they resisted all appeals because they were bridled by the pact over their provinces (11). The contrast with the speech to the senate is striking. Certainly, there would have been nothing generally inappropriate in using invective in a *contio*:[28] it seems more a matter of tactics. In the speech to the senate there was no direct attack on Clodius, and only Gabinius and Piso were singled out for denunciation. In this way Cicero refrained from being excessively provocative, while showing that he still had some teeth. Here he presents himself in an even more pacific mode, ready to sacrifice himself, unwilling to damage the republic by personal feuds.

This image is preserved in what follows. Cicero now reviews the circumstances of his recall, highlighting the importance of the attitude of the people in assembly (11–17). The tribunes would have recalled him at the beginning of 57, had it not been for a veto from an ungrateful tribune (Atilius Serranus), who ignored his father-in-law Cn. Oppius when the latter threw himself weeping at his feet. Moreover, while Cicero in 58 had been reluctant to see good men die in his cause, his opponents had resorted to violence, leaving no place for the *res publica*, as they had previously left no place for Cicero (13–14). The efforts to resist this violence by Lentulus Spinther, Milo, Sestius, and Pompey are placed in a framework of a consensus of the magistrates, senate, the *municipia, coloniae*, and all of Italy; they are also represented as bearing on the final decision of the assembly and culminating in this. In particular Cicero focuses on the speeches made by Pompey, Servilius Isauricus, and L. Gellius Publicola (cos.72) in the *contiones* leading up to the decision. Cicero continues with what might have been the conclusion of the speech, a promise of continued loyalty to the Roman people (a *pietas* that he compares directly with that of religious men to the gods) and a promise to continue his former political life, maintaining his principles (18–19).[29]

He might well have stopped there, but then, seemingly, he allows the self-restraint to slip. He brings back the figure of Marius, not to criticize his

---

[28] As suggested by Mack, 1937, 32–3.   [29] Mack, 1937, 44.

methods, but to recall how he was unbowed on his return from exile and had not lost his spirit for battle.[30] Marius took revenge on his enemies by arms and thought of nothing else; Cicero would use words, and only when the *res publica* permitted. The orator then lists four types of his enemies (it recalls the catalogue of six types of villain in the second Catilinarian, also spoken to the people in a *contio*[31]). No names are provided; first mentioned are the self-confessed political enemies (in other words Clodius and his like), then the false friends (presumably certain of the *boni*), thirdly the feeble and jealous (perhaps other less important members of the *boni*); last the guardians of the *res publica* who had deserted their post and sold their office (clearly Gabinius and Piso). The latter Cicero promises to have brought back from their provinces and prosecuted (21). Finally, he recalls himself from revenge by arguing that repaying benefits is more difficult and rendering the Roman people their due will be his prime concern (22–5).

By comparison with the speech to the senate we have the impression of a less organized harangue, in which the orator has indulged himself and even moved capriciously from one topic to another. However, there is a strong element of calculation. Cicero is resuming his relationship with the Roman people by serving the popular audience with what it likes to hear. It is the assembly itself that is the focus of the narrative of Cicero's struggle to return. The recall of the figure of Marius is a similar tactic.[32] Cicero reminds his hearers that he is a fellow-townsman of one of the greatest *populares* of the Republic, a man whose name and memory, even after the ugliness of the last year of his life, clearly retained its appeal to the plebs of Rome. Caesar had played on this during his early political career in his funeral speech for his aunt and in restoring Marius' trophies.[33] About the time of Caesar's death a Greek doctor was to achieve instant and sensational celebrity among the plebs by claiming to be Marius' grandson.[34] By setting himself beside Marius, Cicero could produce the fighting talk of revenge. At the same time he left largely unclear the persons against whom revenge was to be directed and committed himself to no specific policy except towards Gabinius and Piso (21).

In discussing the two letters as historical events this chapter has not uncovered a concealed meaning, rather it has sought to stress the importance for Cicero and Atticus of the parts of the letter that historians themselves do not often stress—a redressing of the balance. One of the speeches on inspection proves not to have been delivered, a non-event. However, this does not mean that that the speech to the people has lost its historical context, linked,

---

[30] This seems to be the particular sense of *virtutem animi* in §20.   [31] *Cat.* 2. 18–23.
[32] Mack, 1937, 26–7.   [33] Plut. *Caes.* 5. 2; 6. 1–2; Suet. *Jul.* 11.
[34] Yavetz, 1969, 58–62, 70–72.

as it is, as a project to the parallel speech to the senate. Cicero's aim of reintegrating himself into Roman politics can best be understood by taking the two together and comparing the tactics used in each. At the same time we can appreciate the irony of the fact that on 7 September 57 BC Cicero was forced before the people to substitute for a speech with himself at the centre one that presumably had Pompey at the centre—in effect a second *De Imperio Cn. Pompei*.

II

The Texts of the Speeches

Our texts of the works on philosophy and rhetoric represent, allowing for the flaws in manuscript transmission, what was read at their respective publications. As for the letters, although Cicero was contemplating an edition of a selection (somewhat above 70 letters) in July 44, apparently mainly from those to his friends, there is no evidence that he was able to carry out any of this plan.[1] In any case the revision would not have covered the bulk of the letters, and we can be generally confident that we are reading what Cicero actually wrote at the time. The speeches present a far greater problem. In particular there is a major controversy over what the texts of the forensic speeches represent. The chief contributors to this have been scholars of Latin literature, in particular Jules Humbert and Wilfried Stroh,[2] whose primary concern is how we should judge the speeches as examples of rhetoric. However, the controversy has obvious historical implications, especially when we are studying the speeches as historical events and not merely as sources.

PUBLISHED, BUT NOT AS IT WAS SPOKEN

It is common knowledge that some of the texts of speeches we possess were not delivered. The convention of pretending that a published exhortation or invective had been actually delivered was an inheritance from the Greek world, probably as old as the fifth-century sophists.[3] The example of *Post Reditum ad Quirites* has been discussed in the last chapter. Asconius contrasted the text of *pro Milone* on which he wrote a commentary with that which was actually taken down in April 52 BC by shorthand writers. We can see Cicero lovingly composing the insults of the *Second Philippic* after its

---

[1] *Att.* 16. 5. 5; cf. *Fam.* 16. 17. 1; SB *Att* i. 59–60.
[2] Humbert, 1925; Stroh, 1975. See also Classen, 1998, 20 ff., stressing the gap between performance and text.
[3] Thrasymachos' *peri politeias* (DK B1) preceded in this genre Lysias 34 and Isocrates' *Plataikos* and *Archidamos*.

purported time of delivery, thanks to a letter to Atticus of October 44.[4] According to his letter to Ser. Sulpicius Rufus, Cicero had not intended to deliver a speech in the senate on the day in 46 when Caesar pardoned M. Marcellus, but he was so moved by the occasion that he changed his mind and delivered a long oration of thanks.[5] We may be sure that this was a polished oratorical performance (we know how fifteen years earlier Cicero could improvise a speech full of rhetorical tropes and syntactical devices);[6] what is totally uncertain is the relationship of the speech in the senate in 46 to the published *pro Marcello*.[7]

The five speeches of the *actio secunda* of the *Verrines*—which in theory would have occurred in September–October 70 (see Ch. 7) after the compulsory repetition of the process through *comperendinatio*)—were not needed to secure the conviction. What the texts do represent remains an interesting question. They are largely composed of sections of narrative supported by statements of evidence with emotional *amplificatio* at the ends of sections. This may be regarded as reproducing what Cicero had elicited from his witnesses in the first *actio*.[8] Hence they may be treated as imaginative, but plausible reconstructions of what the orator would have said. But we should not forget that even with Verres' departure, the trial was not over. The praetor would have pronounced a condemnation after consultation with the jury, and then would have followed the *litis aestimatio*, the investigation of what damages precisely were owed to each wronged party.[9] Much of what is detailed in the five speeches of the second action would have fitted well with such an investigation. The speeches, therefore, though they did not occur as Cicero presented them, may have had a relationship to what actually happened in court. By contrast, the *exordium* of the *In Vatinium* seems to present the text as the cross-questioning of a witness, but we have in fact a

---

[4] Asc. 42 C, cf. *Fam.* 8. 1. 1–2 for professional shorthand-writers; *Att.* 16. 11. 1–2, cf. 13. 1.

[5] *Fam.* 4. 4. 3–4.

[6] *Att.* 1. 14. 4–though it must be admitted that the themes of this speech of 61 were, according to Cicero, well worn.

[7] *Pro Marcello* 20–32 is a brief speech of advice to a ruler (*sumbouleutikon*) rather than a speech of thanks. For Cicero's unsuccessful attempts in 45 BC to write an acceptable *sumbouleutikon* to Caesar see *Att.* 12. 40. 2, 13. 27. 1, 13, 28. 2–3. A major disjunction between the delivered and the published *pro Marcello* (which he takes to be disguised attack on Caesar) is maintained by Dyer, 1990.

[8] *2Verr.* 1. 1–24 is a transparent pretence that Verres has returned, cf. *Orat.* 129; PsAsc. 205, 224 St. Note that Quintilian (6. 3. 4) thought that Cicero deliberately ascribed the inferior jokes he used against Verres in the *actio secunda* to witnesses as if this had been part of their testimony.

[9] *Lex rep.* (*RS* i. 1), ll. 58–68; *JRLR* 23–4, 140–8. According to Plutarch (*Cic.* 8. 1), Cicero was criticized for underestimating the damages to be sought from Verres at a mere 3 million sesterces (contrast 40 million in *Verr.* 1. 40 and 100 million in *Div. Caec.* 19, though this first claim was made before the *inquisitio*). However, 3 million may represent what was actually recovered through the sale of Verres' surviving real estate.

continuous oration in which the questions are largely rhetorical and are not designed to establish facts. We will return to this problem later.

The Catilinarian orations we know to have been carefully edited with the rest of the consular speeches.[10] There is nothing in the first three inconsistent with actual delivery on the occasion. However, the fourth is manifestly a cento. The *exordium* introduces the subject of the punishment of the leading Catilinarians, culminating in the passage: 'I have decided to consult you (*referre ad vos*), senators, as if it is still an open question, both about your judgement on the facts of the case and your opinion about the penalty. I shall make the preliminary remarks appropriate for a consul.' There follows a request for a quick decision in view of the seriousness of the crime and the danger that revolution may spread, ending in the sentence, 'By whatever means you decide you must act swiftly to exact retribution.'[11] The speech so far evidently represents a consular *relatio*—what would have been summarized in the text of a *senatus consultum* by the words 'quod M. Tullius consul verba fecit de coniuratis, quo modo in eos vindicari oporteret'. This was the preliminary to a formal consultation of the senate, that is, the request for members' opinions in order of seniority, one which defined the topic to be decided but did not require a lengthy expression of opinion from the presiding magistrate. By normal standards even the first six paragraphs of *In Catilinam* 4 were probably somewhat excessive.[12]

The text continues: 'I see that up to now that there are two proposals, one of Decimus Silanus, who urges that those who attempted to destroy these things should be punished by death, the other of Gaius Caesar, who removes the death penalty but brings together all the harshness of penalties of other kinds.'[13] The debate has now moved forward to a point after the consultation of the consul-designate and ex-consuls and after that of at least one praetor-elect. Can this part of the speech have a basis in fact? As an intervention by the consul it was not totally implausible: those who had spoken were allowed to return to the debate in what was technically called an *interrogatio* to rebut objections made to the view that they had given,[14] and the same may have been true of the president of the senate. However, whether its elements are genuine or invented, *In Catilinam* 4 as a whole is fiction—a combination of an introductory *relatio* with an *interrogatio* in the course of a debate. In fact, it may be plausibly argued that the speech from §7 onwards is *ex post facto* invention, whether Cicero had intervened to ask the senate to choose between

---

[10] *Att.* 2. 1. 3.   [11] *Cat.* 4. 6.
[12] *CRR* 77–8. For Cicero's later claim that he had indicated in the *relatio* which way he expected the senate to vote, see *Att.* 12. 21. 1.
[13] *Cat.* 4. 7.   [14] *Schol. Bob.* 170 St.; *CRR* 81–2.

the motions of Silanus and Caesar or not.[15] Much later Cicero sought to recover for himself part of the credit for proposing the execution of the Catilinarians, complaining to Atticus about the version in Brutus' *Cato*: 'This man praises me for having put the matter to the senate, not for having made the matter plain, for having exhorted, for in short having made my own judgement *before* consulting (my italics).'[16] Here Cicero did not claim to have made an intervention in the debate.

Another example of patching can be detected from the fragments of the speech in the senate with which Cicero sought to recover his authority after Clodius' acquittal (see Ch. I), the *In Clodium et Curionem*.[17] Fortunately, in addition to the fragments preserved in the *Scholia Bobiensia*, Cicero included in a letter to Atticus a summary of the theme, a purple passage, and an account of the subsequent *altercatio* with Clodius.[18] Clodius asked Cicero in his rebuttal what an Arpinate (that is, implicitly a boorish man from the hills) was doing with the hot springs of Baiae, and Cicero made a rejoinder referring to the purchase of Marius' villa by the elder Curio, Clodius' *patronus*. From the fragments preserved in the scholia it appears that this was worked up to form part of the main speech, on the assumption that Clodius had already made this attack: 'In the first place the tough, old-fashioned man (presumably an ironical reference to Clodius) inveighed against those who were at Baiae in April ... a man who does not allow the elderly even to be in their own property attending to their health, when there is no business at Rome.' In the published speech there followed a reference to 'that *patronus* of his (Clodius') immorality', which the scholiast, knowing the whole speech, could interpret as a reference to Curio, who had bought the former estate of C. Marius in Campania.[19]

Later in the speech we find a discussion of Clodius' acquittal. In the description of the *altercatio* to Atticus, Cicero reported this exchange: 'You bought a house.' 'You might imagine that the phrase was "You bought a jury."' 'The jury did not believe your sworn testimony.' 'Twenty-five jurors believed me; thirty-one, to judge from their previous receipt of bribes, put no trust in you.'[20] In the speech Cicero says, 'Am I really not content, that twenty-five jurors believed me?' A lacuna follows with clearly a reference to the thirty-one who acquitted, described as 'those who received from you financially

---

[15] Plutarch (*Cic.* 21. 3–4) interpreted *Cat.* 4 as an intervention in mid-debate but stated that after this it was in fact Catulus who then responded to Caesar's new proposal, before the debate reached Cato. Gelzer, 1969, 97–9, believed that *Cat.* 4 was a cento but that the later intervention by Cicero had been genuinely made. In any case the discussion of the *inimicitiae* that would result for Cicero (*Cat.* 4. 20 ff.) is surely an *ex post facto* creation.
[16] *Att.* 12. 21. 1.   [17] Puccioni, pp. 88 ff.
[18] *Schol. Bob.* 85–91 St.; *Att.* 1. 16. 9–10.   [19] Ibid. 88–9 St.   [20] *Att.* 1. 16. 10.

sound deposit-holders (*sequestres*) (that is men to retain the bribes until after the verdict).'[21] It is just possible that this was in the real speech and was repeated in the *altercatio*, but the whole point of such a joke was its spontaneity.[22] It is far more probable that this element in the *altercatio* was also moved by Cicero into the continuous speech for publication.[23]

THE PROBLEM OF THE FORENSIC SPEECHES

We know that, when pleading before *quaestiones*, Cicero was frequently only one of a team of orators, often speaking last when emotional appeal was more important than argument from evidence. We, therefore, have to make allowance for the fact that we do not know all the arguments on his side, let alone what was said by the opposition—except in so far as we can infer this from Cicero's speech. Furthermore, the single forensic oration that usually survives cannot fully represent trials that had more than one action, whether this was through *comperendinatio*, the compulsory division of a hearing *de repetundis*, introduced by Servilius Glaucia, or through *ampliatio* (a further hearing in a civil or a criminal case resulting from a pronouncement by the judge or president on account of either his own indecision or that of a section of the jury).[24]

An important part of Humbert's original case against the authenticity of the forensic speeches as speeches was that for many of Cicero's cases no speech was preserved, only a *commentarium* or *principium* (beginning). He cited Asconius' comment on a passage in the *In Toga Candida*, that he could find no 'commentarium aut principium' of a defence of Catiline in the *commentarii* of Cicero's cases, and Quintilian's comment that Cicero's *commentarii* bore out the conclusion that busy orators usually improvised the greater part of their speeches, only writing the beginnings and the most essential parts.[25] This of course does not exclude that some speeches were written and memorized. As for the preparation of speeches for publication, apart from obvious

---

[21] *Schol. Bob.* 90 St.   [22] *De Or.* 2. 220–5.

[23] Humbert, 1925, 43 argues for the creation of the speech from the *altercatio*, though he seems to ellipse the original speech in the senate. J. W. Crawford, 1994, 235 derives the published speech from a mixture of speech and *altercatio*, but believes that this was not done by Cicero, though remarking that 'the set speech would have been a more likely source for an unauthorized copy'.

[24] On the division of labour between orators see e.g. *Cael.* 23; *Sull.* 12–13; on trials with more than one action *2Verr.* 1. 26, 74; *Scaur.* 29; *Caec.* 4–6, 29; *lex rep.* 46–9 with commentary in *JRLR*—where a further hearing requires a request from more than a third of the jury.

[25] Asc. 87 C; Quint. *Inst. Or.* 10. 7. 30–1; Humbert, 1925, 1 ff.; Fantham, 2004, 288–9.

examples such as the second *pro Milone*, Humbert pointed out the evidence for revising speeches in the letters. In 61 BC Atticus had apparently requested that he should include a geographical excursus on Puteoli and Misenum in a speech he was publishing, and he promised to comply.[26] He also talked of having added certain things to his *oratio Metellina*, evidently his reply to the *contio* of Metellus Nepos in late 63.[27] In 45 Atticus suggested that Cicero should incorporate in the published *pro Ligario* some apparently derogatory remarks about the prosecutor Tubero's wife and stepdaughter, but Cicero did not want to offend Tubero and anyhow it was too late: the speech had already been published.[28]

Humbert went on to argue first that the published forensic speech could not do justice to what actually happened in court because of the complexities and peculiarities of Roman legal procedure; secondly, that in the course of edition for publication Cicero sought to remedy this defect by inserting elements, drawn especially from the examination of witnesses, that had not been part of one continuous spoken oration.[29] Apart from speeches by the prosecutors and defendants themselves, if the latter wished, and the defendants' counsel, Roman trials included the examination of witnesses (*testimonia*) and arguments arising from this testimony (*altercatio*). Whereas Attic orators either called witnesses (the original procedure) or had testimony read in the course of their speeches, Roman orators in *quaestiones* (criminal tribunals) spoke before the witnesses on either side were called,[30] except in the special *quaestiones de vi* and *de ambitu* set up by Pompey in 52 BC.[31] The same seems to have applied both to private trials before a single judge (*iudex*) and to those before a small jury of *recuperatores*.[32] However, orators were not arguing completely blind, as evidence had to be delivered beforehand under oath in writing, probably in sealed groups of tablets with the testimony reproduced on the exterior.[33] While delivering his speech in defence of

---

[26] *Att.* 1. 13. 5. *Pace* SB *Att* i. 305–6, this speech seems to be distinct from the Metellus speech. Nor do Puteoli and Misenum seem appropriate there. Perhaps the reference was to *De Lege Agraria* 1 or 3.
[27] *Att.* loc. cit. The fragments of *in Metellum* are in Puccioni, pp. 83–6.
[28] *Att.* 13. 20. 2.
[29] Humbert, 1925, 13 ff.
[30] *Rosc. Am.* 82, 102; *Flacc.* 21; *I Verr.* 51; PsAsc. 223 St.
[31] Asc. 36, 39, 53 C.
[32] The references to witnesses in *Tull.* 23–4, *Caec.* 24–8, 31, 44 can be explained by the previous hearings, see the reference to an earlier speech in *Tull.* 6 and to *ampliationes* in *Caec.* 4 and 6.
[33] *Cael.* 19–20, 66; *Flacc.* 21, cf. *lex rep.* 33–4 with commentary in *JRLR* 126–7. For later examples of sealed and sworn testimony with exterior copies see *Tabulae Herculanenses* 16–25 in Arangio-Ruiz and Pugliese Carratelli, 1948; and for a similar document on papyrus *FIRA* iii,

Cluentius Cicero apparently not only invoked the testimony of a certain witness but asked him to stand up in court.[34]

The actual examination and cross-examination of witnesses were, according to Quintilian,[35] followed by an *altercatio*, in which the orators debated the merits of the evidence. Humbert believed Quintilian's evidence could not be applied to Republican practice: there were only brief introductions of witnesses, followed by the interrogations themselves over which counsel might argue.[36] However, one passage in the *Verrines*, discounted by Humbert,[37] seems to suggest argument and speeches as well as questioning at this point in the trial. Admittedly, Cicero talks here about the novelty of his procedure:

I shall do in one respect what is not new, but has been done before by those who are leaders (*principes*) of our community, by making use of witnesses immediately. In another respect you will discover a novelty in my action, members of the jury, in that I shall so organize the witnesses as to unfold the whole charge, when I have supported it by questions (*interrogando*), proofs (*argumentis*), and pleading (*oratione*). Further, I will so adapt the testimony to the charge that there will be no difference between the usual form of accusation and this new one, except that in the traditional one the witnesses are produced after all the pleas have been made, here they will be produced for individual items, in such a way that the other side may also have the same opportunity for question, proof, and pleading.[38]

The novelty, however, that Cicero seems to be claiming is not that he is introducing argument and pleading on the basis of the witness statements and replies—it is hard to see how earlier *principes*, who proceeded directly to their witnesses, could have failed to argue from what their witnesses said—but that he will be so efficient in organizing testimony that the jury will miss nothing by comparison with the usual practice of long speeches. Nor can he be arguing that the defence did not usually have the chance to discuss what the witnesses

---

no. 188. An exception to this would have occurred when a witness was forced to give evidence against his will through *testimonii denuntiatio*, cf. Quint. 5. 7. 15–25.

[34] *Clu.* 168. Humbert, 1925, 40–1, believes this moment in the published speech was imagined, but invention of the impossible would not have added vividness or conviction to the published speech.

[35] *Inst. Or.* 6. 4. 1 ff. Exchanges that seem to drive from Cicero's *altercationes*, presumably preserved in the collection of Cicero's aphorisms by Tiro (ibid. 6. 3. 5), are in ibid. 6. 3. 49, 86 (J. W. Crawford, 1984, *pro Fundanio* T5), and perhaps 6. 3. 98 (see below Ch. VII). See also Macr. 2. 1. 13 with Alexander, 2002, 288–9 for the joke that saved Cicero's client Valerius Flaccus—not part of the published speech, but retailed by Furius Bibaculus, so probably made during the examination of witnesses or the *altercatio*.

[36] Humbert 1925, 60 ff.

[37] Ibid. 64–5; 1*Verr.* 55.

[38] Humbert, 1925, 64, following Madvig's suggestion, wished to delete *interrogando* as an interpolation. However, what matters for the present argument is that proofs and pleading follow the witnesses.

said, only that the discussion here will take place after each witness has been questioned. In fact, Humbert went on to suppose that in general there was considerable debate over the evidence of the witnesses, which might lead to a peroration.[39]

Humbert's basic thesis about the limitations of our Cicero texts as evidence for the work of a Roman orator can hardly be contested. Clearly, the successful examination of witnesses was a vital part of the orator's craft that the surviving speeches can hardly display. Nevertheless, it remains a question how far the limitations of the texts are disabling for our studies. The conflict between the views of Humbert and Stroh relates principally not to the question whether the texts of the forensic speeches we possess were actually delivered, but to whether the texts are such that they could and would have been delivered in a Roman court, that is, whether they are fair examples of Roman oratory as it was spoken.[40] Stroh takes them to represent satisfactorily one element in any set of spoken pleadings, Humbert to represent in an artificial, and hence ultimately misleading way, the totality of the contribution of the orator to a particular case.

Thus the controversy is more about the validity of treating Cicero's forensic speeches in the form we possess them as a coherent oratorical genre than about their validity as evidence of what actually happened in court. The argument nonetheless is also of considerable importance to the historian who is concerned with the tactics employed by Cicero on a particular occasion, not just with the fact of the trial and the factuality of the statements found in the speeches. In some ways a speech that is a conflation of the orator's actual contributions to the case may be more useful for historical purposes, simply because it is fuller and may reflect to some extent the investigation of testimony; on the other hand, the more remote the text is from what was actually said at one time, the less is our immediate grasp of that particular event itself.

Sometimes Humbert pressed his argument too hard. Stroh's most effective criticisms arise from the treatment of certain speeches. As a first example, Humbert had sought to prove that the second published speech for the former tribune C. Cornelius, known only from a few fragments, was a conflation by Cicero from the examination of witnesses,[41] in spite of Cicero's

---

[39] Humbert, 1925, 216, 226. So dismissal of the *altercatio* is more a matter of terminology. Humbert was influenced by the fact that in Quintilian's experience this part of the case was often neglected by the chief orator, wrongly in view of its importance (*Inst. Or.* 6. 4. 6–7), but this may reflect the compression of procedure under the Principate and the vanity of leading orators: Quintilian notes that the crowd would be drifting away, probably because it was evening.

[40] See esp. Stroh, 1975, 51–2.

[41] Humbert, 1925, 42 ff.; Stroh, 1975, 36 ff. J. W. Crawford 1994, 67–148 at 141, follows Humbert without considering Stroh's arguments.

own reference later to a second speech for Cornelius.[42] Could Cicero have had the opportunity to speak twice? Although there is no evidence that *comperendinatio*, a compulsory adjournment, was prescribed for trials *de maiestate*, as in Cornelius' case, it is clear from Asconius' description of the trial that it was hotly contested and thus could have caused considerable indecision among the jury.[43] Hence it is perfectly possible that this should have led to a demand for further hearing (*ampliatio*).[44] Humbert argued that the *lex Aurelia* of 70 BC abolished *ampliatio*,[45] but this strange suggestion was based on his own reinterpretation of the fragments of *pro Cornelio II*. In fact there is no evidence that the *lex Aurelia* dealt with anything but jury-selection. Nor can we imagine any Roman statute completely forbidding jurymen to say *non liquet* ('the matter is not clear') thus causing *ampliatio*, if they did so in sufficient numbers.[46]

In a lemma, surviving in Asconius under the title *pro Cornelio*, towards the end of that commentary,[47] we find:

Surely you are not in doubt about who these witnesses are? I will declare them to you. The two remaining ones are enemies of the tribunician power, drawn from the ranks of the consulars. Besides these, a few of their devotees and hangers-on follow in their train.

Asconius comments:

He means M. Lucullus and M. [probably Mam(ercus)] Lepidus.[48] For five consulars, as we have already said,[49] gave evidence against Cornelius: Q. Catulus, Q. Hortensius, Q. Metellus Pius the *pontifex maximus*, whom he discusses in this second speech, and two who had not yet spoken whom he now indicates, Lucullus and Lepidus.

As it stands, the lemma makes perfect sense as part of a second speech, delivered before the second hearing of witnesses. Even if we grant for the sake of argument that Cicero in fact invented *pro Cornelio II* out of the investigation of the witnesses, though referring to it later as a speech in the *Orator*, it is hard to see why, on that supposition, he chose to treat the evidence of two witnesses as something in the future. If, as Humbert suggests,[50] this lemma was a deliberate evocation of the moment between the examination of Catulus,

---

[42] *Orat.* 225.   [43] Asc. 60–1 C.
[44] It is true that only one speech of the accuser, Cominius, survived (Asc. 61–2 C), but that may have been because the orator, like Cicero in *repetundae* cases, only chose to publish one.
[45] Humbert 1925, 59.
[46] In *lex rep.* 47–8, a law of 122 BC associated with C. Gracchus, *ampliatio* is permitted, but jurymen are penalized for causing excessive rehearings. That *ampliatio* was provided for later in Sulla's *lex Cornelia de veneficis* is clear from *Caec.* 29, *Clu.* 55.
[47] Asc. 79 C.   [48] Cf. Sumner, 1964 and see below, Ch. IX with n. 26.
[49] Asc. 60 C.   [50] Humbert 1925, 46.

Hortensius, and Metellus Pius and that of Lucullus and Lepidus, it is strange the subsequent lemmata refer only to the evidence of Catulus.

The end of the defence of Fonteius is presented by Cicero as that delivered in the second part of a trial *de repetundis*, after the *comperendinatio* (39).[51] Earlier in the speech (21) Cicero represents Gallic witnesses as contradicting his own previous responses (only recorded by titles in the text) to the prosecution's charges regarding the tax on wine, the war with the Vocontii, and the allocation of winter-quarters. I assume that our text here reproduces what Cicero had actually published. If so, it shows how the publication was not just a display of rhetorical virtuosity but a record of successful forensic activity. Even if Cicero did not wish to publish everything he said in a particular speech, he wanted to show how his oratory had functioned in court at the time. In the first *actio* Cicero would have responded to the charges made in the first prosecution speech. The Gallic witnesses had then supported the prosecution's construction. In *pro Fonteio* Cicero returned to this argument and then went on to denounce Gallic witnesses by comparison with Roman ones. There is nothing in the published text inconsistent with delivery in the second *actio* after the first examination of witnesses, when the Gauls denied the propositions Cicero put to them, but before any further testimony. The same is true of what survives of the earlier part of the speech. It is clear from this that Cicero harped on the lack of Roman testimony on the side of the prosecution (3, 5–14, 16), but that does not require us to assume a contamination between two speeches.[52]

Elsewhere, however, Humbert's case for contamination is difficult to refute. One of the most striking parts of *pro Plancio* is Cicero's reply to the personal attack that the prosecutor Iuventius Laterensis had made on him.[53] Laterensis claimed that Cicero had been lying to suit the occasion when he was explaining how he was discharging an obligation to Plancius (72). The prosecutor went on to make some jibes whose humour Cicero did not appreciate, including the suggestion that Cicero had made exile the penalty for electoral bribery in his *lex de ambitu*, in order that he might have the chance to deliver more tear-jerking perorations (83). Laterensis also apparently mentioned Cicero's propensity to make bad jokes. 'You even gave me advice', Cicero says, 'that, because you had been in Crete, a witticism could have been made

---

[51] Humbert 1925, 32, 216 ff.

[52] Humbert, 1925, 216 ff., believed that the speech as far as paragraph 17 was from the first action, and explained the lack of expansion of the headings, *De bello Vocontiorum* and *De dispositione hibernorum* (20) reflected the fact that in the second action the accuser had not included these topics in his speech but reserved them for witnesses. This seems over-imaginative. See Stroh, 1975, 45.

[53] *Planc.* 72 ff.; Humbert, 1925, 176 ff. See Chap. XIV with n. 31.

against your candidature; I had missed the chance.[54] Which of us is more greedy for a witticism? I, because I did not say what could have been said, or you who made the joke against yourself?' (85).

As far as we know, there was no *comperendinatio* in trials under the *lex Licinia de sodaliciis*, the law of 55 under which Plancius was tried. So normally Cicero would not have already delivered a speech when the prosecutor delivered his. We might, however, explain the passage by assuming that there had been *ampliatio* as a result of indecision by the jury. Stroh thought that the prosecutor was referring to a speech by Cicero in an election battle (72),[55] but it is not clear why Cicero should have been called upon to make a speech on behalf of Plancius at that time. The only earlier public mention by Cicero of Plancius that we know, a brief one, was in his speech to the senate on his return.[56] In any case, Laterensis seems to have been speaking at this point about Cicero's performance at the trial, suggesting that his whole defence was hackneyed and factitious. If we accept that the texts of published Ciceronian forensic orations may be conflated, as Humbert suggests, the whole speech from §68 onwards may be seen as Cicero's contribution to a final *altercatio* between the orators, one that passes smoothly into the *epilogus* that sought to elicit pity for Plancius (95 ff.).

Two speeches in trials *de repetundis* also raise potential problems. That for Scaurus, of whose text we possess about half, was on its own evidence delivered in the second part of the trial. 'You adjourned until the third day' (*comperendinasti*), Cicero rebukes Triarius, 'after only producing one witness' (29). However, earlier in the speech Cicero claims that Triarius had questioned (*interrogavit*) every Sardinian about the charge of demanding grain improperly and had obtained identical testimony from them all (21). This evidence must have been brought to Rome, since Triarius had not undertaken a tour of investigation (*inquisitio*) himself (so 'every Sardinian' is extreme rhetorical hyperbole). Equally the reference to 'one compact (*foedus*) and consensus of testimony' shows that this evidence had been submitted to the court and was now known to the defence.

Humbert concluded that this section of what survives of the text represents the investigation of evidence following the speeches in the second part of the trial, an investigation in which topics were taken separately[57]—a somewhat strained interpretation that ignores the fact that the division between the one witness and the rest of the evidence is associated by Cicero with the break provided by *comperendinatio*. Stroh argued that Valerius Triarius had tried to

---

[54] Presumably of this kind: 'You went to Creta to get chalk-white (*creta*) in anticipation of your candidature (standing in whitened garments)'. *Creta* was also used for seals in Asia (*Flacc.* 37), but that does not seem relevant here.

[55] Stroh, 1975, 44.   [56] *Red. Sen.* 35.   [57] Humbert, 1925, 235 ff.

accelerate the proceedings by submitting to examination in person only one of his declared witnesses in the first part of the trial.[58] Hence the text, as we possess it, was that of the speech delivered in the second action after *comperendinatio*, where Cicero could discuss the one witness, Valerius Aris, questioned in the first action.[59] This is plausible, but we may wonder if there were still prosecution witnesses to be heard in person. The repetitive testimony of Sardinians about grain (20–1) may have been merely submitted in writing, and this would have been enough for Cicero to dismiss it as perjured, without referring to the witnesses individually.[60]

The greatest part of the surviving text of *pro Flacco* is devoted to the dissection of witnesses, for the most part Asiatic Greeks. In one section Cicero portrays these Greeks as living in the prosecutor Laelius' house and sitting next to him at the trial with carefully prepared testimony (21–2).[61] They are *legati*, envoys of their cities, who were entrusted with pursuing the claims of their fellow-citizens, as becomes clearer when Cicero describes the embassy from Temnos—Heraclides, Nicomedes, Lysanias, Philippus, and Hermobius (42–3). In fact these *legati* made the same sort of contribution to Flaccus' trial as men like Dio of Halaesa or Sthenius of Thermae made to Cicero's own prosecution of Verres.[62] In the central section of *pro Flacco* (21–66) it appears that the Greeks had already given evidence with the exception of Lysanias, who was yet to be heard (51). Indeed one ambassador from Dorylaeum had died since he had given evidence—from overeating at Laelius' house, Cicero suggests (41). By contrast, the restraint in court of three Roman witnesses used by Laelius is praised (10–11). All this is consistent with the text representing Cicero's speech in the second action after the regular *comperendinatio*.

However, in the Milan fragment, apparently to be located near the beginning of the surviving text, Cicero speaks as if the evidence of the Greeks as a whole is yet to come: 'When you have branded his youth, when you have spattered the rest of his life with the stains of turpitude, when you have produced blots on the family, infamous conduct in the city, vices and debauchery in Spain, Gaul, Cilicia, and Crete, provinces in which he had a high

---

[58] Stroh, 1975, 47.
[59] *Planc.* 9–13, 29; given Roman citizenship by Triarius' father and hence a guest-friend of the family.
[60] The concentration on the witnesses conforms to the principle (*de Or.* 2. 105) ascribed to M. Antonius (*cos.* 99) that in most criminal cases, including those *de repetundis* and *de ambitu*, the defence strategy had necessarily to be based on denial of the facts alleged.
[61] Humbert's inference (1925, 222 ff.) from *Flacc.* 21 that Laelius had adopted the tactic of dispensing with a full-scale oration in the first *actio* does not seem secure: Cicero's somewhat feeble point here is that it was obvious from the start that the witnesses would support the prosecution claims.
[62] *2Verr.* 1. 27–8; 2. 83.

profile, then finally we shall hear what the people of Tmolus and Dorylaeum think about L. Flaccus.' This sounds as if Cicero in the first speech of the trial is looking forward to the first production of evidence. Not long afterwards, in the main text deriving from the Paris manuscript and its family, after Cicero has denied that there are in fact any signs of cupidity in Flaccus' earlier life, he asks the jury rhetorically, 'By what witnesses can I then refute them but you? Is that villager from Tmolus, a man not only unknown to us but even among his own people, going to teach you about Flaccus' character?', and a little later, 'Are you going to listen to the evidence of others concerning those for whom you should be witnesses to others?' (7–9) Immediately after this (10–11) Cicero contrasts the Greeks with the restrained evidence of Roman witnesses who were enemies of Flaccus.

Humbert argued that the speech as far as §27 belonged to Cicero's main plea in the second action; after this it was an edition of the examination of the witnesses.[63] But this does not do justice to the contrast drawn by Cicero between the Greek witnesses already heard and Lysanias, who was yet to speak (51), or to the witness who had died (41). Could the whole transmitted oration represent Cicero's speech in the second action? The appeal to the jury as better witnesses than the villager from Tmolus (7–9) is consistent with the possibility that the man from Tmolus and other Greeks had already appeared as witnesses,[64] but it is a weak point, when compared with the systematic demolition of the evidence actually given by Asclepiades of Acmonia, the Dorylenses, and Heraclides of Temnos later and is equally plausible as part of an anticipatory attack in the first *actio*. Moreover, the passage in the Milan fragment clearly looks forward to the production of witnesses from Flaccus' earlier provinces and from Tmolus and Dorylaeum: it is indeed the sort of point that an orator might make in the first action when he had as yet no detailed criticisms to make of the prosecution testimony. It seems therefore likely that two speeches for Flaccus have been collapsed into one, though we cannot be certain where the dividing-line between them lay or indeed if there was a clear dividing-line.

What Cicero published as the *In Vatinium* is unique among surviving oratorical texts. When Cicero described the trial of Sestius in a letter to Quintus,[65] he commented, 'By defending a peevish man I gave him the most abundant satisfaction, and, something that he especially desired, I cut to pieces Vatinius, by whom he was being openly attacked, just as I pleased amidst the applause of gods and men.' It is not clear from this whether Cicero is referring to cross-examination, a subsequent argument with the prosecution in the *altercatio* or both. He went on to write of the threats made to prosecute Vatinius. The charge would presumably have been about Vatinius'

---

[63] Humbert, 1925, 226.   [64] Stroh, 1975, 46.   [65] *QF* 2. 4. 1.

obstruction of his own trial under the *lex Licinia Iunia* in 58, or for electoral malpractice under the *lex Tullia de ambitu* on account of the timing of his gladiatorial show.[66]

Cicero also refers to the rebuttal of Vatinius in the *apologia pro recenti vita sua* that he despatched to Lentulus Spinther in late 54 on the eve of the latter's return from Cilicia. There it is claimed that, after Vatinius had alleged in his testimony that Cicero had begun to be Caesar's friend, Cicero had replied, in full view of Pompey, that he preferred the fate of Bibulus to anyone's triumphs; later he said that the same people were behind Bibulus' imprisonment in his house and his own exile.[67] From this it would appear that Cicero used the cross-examination of Vatinius as an occasion for making a personal political statement. What relation have these reports of events to the published text of *In Vatinium* that we possess? There is no reason to doubt that Vatinius had pointed to a new friendship of Cicero with Caesar. However, although Cicero mentions in *In Vatinium* (22) the treatment of Bibulus by Vatinius in 59, we do not find any downright expression of a political position, such as he claims in the letter.[68]

In the prooemium to the preserved speech itself Cicero claims to be cross-questioning in rebuttal (*interrogare*) the testimony that Vatinius gave the previous day (1–3). There follow a series of questions, pointed either by the verb *quaero*,[69] or by the phrases *volo ut mihi respondeas*,[70] *scire ex te cupio*, and *audire de te cupio*.[71] Most of these questions amount to a derogatory review of Vatinius' political career, where the basic facts were not in doubt, but Cicero's hostile interpretation would have been fiercely contested by Vatinius. In conclusion, Cicero says that he will actually ask Vatinius a few things about the case itself (40). These are two: why he had now begun to praise Milo, given that the latter had been Sestius' ally, and why he had accused Albinovanus of *praevaricatio*, when he had also stated that it was inappropriate to accuse Sestius of violence (40–1).

The repeated formula of questioning makes it plain that Cicero is representing the examination of a witness. No doubt the phrases we find in the text

---

[66] *Vat.* 33–4, 37; Pocock, 1926, 34.   [67] *Fam.* 1. 9. 7.

[68] By contrast, *Vat.* 15 shows Cicero seeking to separate Vatinius from Caesar. Nor is the charge that Caesar and Vatinius engineered Cicero's exile made elsewhere in the texts of the speeches after his return. Pocock, 1926, 6–8 pointed to the discrepancy between the letter and the speech, arguing that the speech was a truer reflection of what was said and that it was hostile to Caesar by implication only. The problem with the veracity of *Fam.* 1. 9 is that it was written to justify Cicero to Spinther, and probably to other former allies among the *boni*, on account of behaviour that they may have regarded as cowardice and desertion.

[69] *Vat.* 5, 10, 11, 13, 15, 19, 20, 22, 27, 33, 34, 40, 41.
[70] Ibid. 14, 17, 18, 21, 28, cf. 41 *extremum illud est quod mihi abs te responderi velim*.
[71] Ibid. 30, 37.

were those customarily used in such interrogation. It is uncertain how far a Roman orator would normally use questions designed not to elicit information about the case but to blacken the character of the witness and so destroy his testimony. However, Cicero's statement in the letter to Quintus may be best understood as suggesting that he had done precisely this, and it would have been a natural tactic for an orator. On the other hand, it was the function of a witness to give evidence. and it is hard to imagine that in court an orator would have been permitted to assemble so many questions, whether strictly relevant to the case or not, without permitting the witness to reply.[72]

The text we have, then, is probably an artificial composition. Humbert held it to be an adaptation of an *altercation réelle*. Is the matter genuine? An early section (5–9) deals with criticisms made by Vatinius of Cicero himself, perhaps in the context of Vatinius' denunciation of Albinovanus for undertaking a collusive prosecution (*praevaricatio*) (3, cf. 41).[73] Here Vatinius seems to have used the fact that one of the supporting prosecutors was C. Cornelius, whom Cicero had formerly defended, when accused *de maiestate* (5). This section can only be explained on the supposition that Vatinius had actually made these criticisms in his testimony. The subject was otherwise unimportant. There is, then, some connection between text and event, but how far does it go?

Macrobius knew of a speech by Vatinius against Cicero, in which he called him a consular comedian.[74] This speech was presumably Vatinius' version of his testimony and exchanges with Cicero. Macrobius also retails Vatinius' retort to a remark by Cicero that the *res publica* had carried him back from exile on its shoulders: 'How then did you get your varicose veins?'[75] To judge from the published version of *pro Sestio*, Cicero had dwelt on his own exile and return in that speech.[76] The likelihood is that the joke about varicose veins also occurred in one of the exchanges during Vatinius' testimony at this trial. In the text of *in Vatinium*, by contrast, we find Cicero rather pompously defending himself against criticisms about his return from exile, concentrating on an alleged suggestions of Vatinius that people had worked for Cicero's return, not in Cicero's interests but in those of the *res publica* (6–9). This passage is surely Cicero's more dignified rendering of what had

---

[72] See *Ad Her.* 4. 47 for the distribution of functions in a criminal court.
[73] Humbert, 1925, 175 ff.; cf. Stroh, 1975, 48.
[74] *Consularis scurra*, Macr. 2. 1. 12.
[75] Ibid. 2. 3. 5; Macrobius regards Cicero's later jokes about Vatinius' consulship of 47 BC as revenge for this.
[76] *Sest.* 15–55, 117–31. It may be thought that the published *pro Sestio* is totally implausible as a defence in court. However, it was not irrelevant to a claim that Sestius' violence had been justified and in the public interest, to argue that Clodius' violence and Cicero's exile had been unjustified and against the public interest.

passed between him and Vatinius on this point. 'If the *res publica* had carried Cicero back on its shoulders', Vatinius might have added, 'it did so by necessity, not through any love for Cicero.' The *in Vatinium*, then, is better interpreted as the edition of the question and answer of a cross-examination, that is, on the lines suggested by Humbert, than as the publication of a real or largely fictitious speech. We should allow, however, for more editing in order to create the impression of an oration than Humbert was prepared to acknowledge.[77]

Humbert regarded the interruptions indicated in the texts of Cicero's speeches as genuine,[78] and it is attractive to believe this. It would entail that both the interruption and the reply were recreated from memory after the event, as would have been any examination of witnesses or discussion of their evidence. An interesting example can be found in the *pro Sulla*. This trial *de vi* would have normally had a single *actio*. Cicero was speaking last, after Hortensius (12–14). The prosecution's allegations did not derive so much from witness statements yet to be heard as from the evidence given during the investigation of the Catilinarian conspiracy (17, 36–9), that of C. Cornelius transmitted through his son as prosecutor, together with documents such as a letter of Faustus Sulla (45) and Cicero's own letter to Pompey (67). The testimony of the colonists of Pompeii (61) and the possible extraction of evidence from slaves under torture (78) were yet to come.

The core of this speech is a point-by-point refutation of charges by the prosecutor, the younger L. Manlius Torquatus, charges that are directed as much against Cicero himself as the defendant. There is at times a resemblance to the technique used in the speech against Vatinius, where questions are underlined with the verb *quaero* (3, 36, 44). At one point, after Cicero has refuted Torquatus over what the Allobroges had learnt from Cassius, he says, 'Cut off as he is from this charge, Torquatus assaults me again, accuses me, claims that I have placed in the public records something other than what was said' (40). If this genuinely occurred during Cicero's speech, it was a highly significant interruption, a point that Torquatus could not have made unless he knew what Cicero had replied to his first point, and is an important datum for the historian.

D. M. Berry, in a critique of Humbert,[79] has taken this charge of forgery not to be an interruption in Cicero's speech but an element in Torquatus' original argument. However, the charge could only be made if Cicero did not accept that the Allobroges had named Sulla as a conspirator and cited the record of the senate hearing as support. Torquatus would not have admitted that possibility too soon, even if he anticipated it (the accusation of forgery

---

[77] Stroh, 1975, 48–50.   [78] Humbert, 1925, 93.   [79] Berry, 1996, 57–8.

affected not only Cicero but other senators).[80] We should, however, leave open the possibility that Torquatus' intervention derived from the *altercatio*, the discussion of the testimony, and that it has been neatly inserted here.[81] Humbert also plausibly suggested that Torquatus' attack on the consulars who had delivered *laudationes* (formal testimony to character) at Catiline's trial in 65, but had failed to defend other accused Catilinarians later, and who were now supporting Sulla (81–2, cf.7) was made as a reaction to their *laudationes* in Sulla's trial. Torquatus would have been saying 'What is this evidence worth, when these same men were character-witnesses for Catiline?'[82]

Humbert's argument that the texts of Cicero's forensic speeches contain material from the subsequent examination of witnesses and the discussion of their evidence cannot, then, be dismissed. Once this door has been opened, a further perspective offers itself. Given that orators debated evidence both with the witnesses and each other, can we imagine that, above all in a major criminal trial, the two sides refrained from any concluding statement? Would not the defence have made some emotional appeal to the jury, perhaps on a smaller scale than that found in the main speeches, but more pointed since this was the last opportunity?

There can be no proof of this, given our lack of knowledge of the latter part of trials. However, one passage in a letter is perhaps an indication. On 7 July 54 Cicero described to Atticus the outcome of some recent court-cases: C. Cato and Nonius Sufenas had been acquitted on charges relating to their tribunates of 56 and the obstruction of the elections, Procilius had been condemned. Cicero comments:

From which it was deduced that the supreme Areopagites cared not a straw for bribery, elections, the interregnum, the majesty of the Roman people, in a word the whole of public affairs, but disapproved of the head of a family being killed in his own home, and not even that by much. For twenty-two acquitted, twenty-eight condemned. Publius (Clodius) in what was, to be sure, an eloquent peroration (*epilogus*) had influenced the minds of the jurymen by his charges (*criminans*).[83]

There is no need to emend *criminans* to *lacrimans*, as Shackleton Bailey suggested:[84] the arousal of indignation against the prosecution was as much a regular part of the *epilogus* as eliciting pity for the defendant.[85] What is

---

[80] By contrast Cicero's dialogue with Cornelius in *Sull.* 54–5 is perfectly explicable as an imagined debate in the light of Cornelius' speech.
[81] Humbert, 1925, 146–9 thought this section an 'altercation prolongée'.
[82] Ibid. 145.
[83] *Att.* 4. 15. 4.
[84] SB *Att* ii. 90, ad loc., who is right, however, to argue on historical grounds that Clodius must be defending.
[85] For *indignatio* see *Inv.* 1. 98 ff.; a textbook illustration in *Quinct.* 91 ff.

important here is the impression Cicero gives that the *epilogus* had an immediate influence on the jury's decision, in spite of the clear evidence given beforehand. This is not to suggest that the main speeches in a lawsuit lacked perorations, but that orators would have taken an opportunity to reinforce them at a later stage in the trial, if this was available. If so, the concluding appeals that we find in published speeches may owe as much to what was said at the last gasp in trials, as to the ends of the formal speeches.

III

Truth and Fiction in the Speeches

The historian must not only be cautious about what the texts of speeches actually represent; allowance must also be made for the orator's preference for persuasiveness over veracity. In the speeches there are no obvious warning signs: Cicero does not signal possible inventions by any marks of diffidence. On the contrary, caution seems designed to suggest to the jury a reluctance to appear pedantically omniscient. 'It is now the hundredth and, I think, second day since the death of P. Clodius', remarks Cicero in the peroration of the published *pro Milone*, set on 8 April 52.[1] In fact, Cicero must have lovingly computed the days that had elapsed, to judge from the way over a year later he dated a letter by a new era—that of 'the Battle of Bovillae'.[2] Similarly, historians do not doubt the statement in the first oration of the second action against Verres, 'However, in my opinion, it was Glaucia who first legislated that a defendant should be adjourned to the third day (*comperendinari*)'.[3] Cicero, who pursued his apprenticeship in the forum (*tirocinium fori*) in the nineties BC, should have been well informed about the then current *lex de repetundis* passed no more than a decade earlier. The same kind of modest hesitation, this time over his knowledge of Greek art, can be seen when he mentions the names of the Greek masters at the beginning of the account of Verres' theft of works of art.[4]

The best-attested example of falsehood in a forensic speech is Cicero's account in his defence of Milo of the death of Clodius at Bovillae. Here the relevant part of the published *pro Milone* is taken by Asconius to follow the line actually used in court and is exposed by him as misrepresenting the event in important ways.[5] The murder in fact arose from a fortuitous brawl and was unplanned,[6] but nevertheless deliberate, since Milo believed that it was dangerous to leave Clodius wounded but alive.[7] In Cicero's speech the actual murder was passed over briefly as a reprisal by Milo's slaves when they

---

[1] *Mil.* 98. This is a correct calculation of the time since 18 January, if the intercalation was 23 days. See Lintott, 1974, 73, n. 132.
[2] *Att.* 5. 13. 1.   [3] *2Verr.* 1. 26.
[4] *2Verr.* 4. 4–5.   [5] Asc. 31–2, 34–5, 41–2 C and see Lintott, 1974, 69, 75.
[6] Asc. 41 C, cf. Quint. *Inst. Or.* 6. 5. 10.   [7] Asc. 32 C.

thought their master was dead.[8] Instead Cicero concentrated on intention: using the unproved assumption that one must have plotted to kill the other, he argued that Milo's behaviour on the day in question was not consistent with such a plan, but that Clodius' was.[9] This is largely deceit by evasion, but in order to make this plausible he had to make one transparently false claim, altering the time of the fight from the ninth hour of the day to the eleventh hour.[10]

When seeking to evade the young Torquatus' attacks on his allegedly corrupt behaviour in *pro Sulla*, Cicero was driven to lie about himself. Torquatus argued that Cicero must know that Sulla had participated in a conspiracy in 66–65 BC as well as in 63. Cicero replied that not only did he have no close contact with Torquatus' father, who was held to be the target of the earlier conspiracy and cause of its exposure, but that he knew nothing of events of that time or the rumours circulating.[11] Certainly, Cicero was not an intimate of the Torquatus family like Hortensius. However, if we consider that in 66 Cicero was praetor in charge of the *quaestio de repetundis*, that he defended C. Cornelius against an accusation *de maiestate* which was postponed from 66 to 65 (see Ch. II), and that C. Manilius, whom he was asked to defend at the end of 66, sought to obstruct his own trial by violence about the time of the alleged conspiracy,[12] his second claim was blatantly misleading.

The validity of his early civil plea for Quinctius hinged to a great extent on whether his client had failed to meet his opponent Naevius in the forum according to a *vadimonium*. Cicero first claims that Quinctius had postponed all his *vadimonia* (*Quinct.* 23); next he suggests that the document, drawn up and sealed with the names of distinguished witnesses, declaring that his client had failed to appear, was a piece of false testimony (25). In effect he is charging Naevius with forging either a *vadimonium* or a declaration of non-appearance or both. Yet we hear suspiciously little about this later in the speech. To be sure, he does seek to show that his client was not at Rome on the day of the *vadimonium*, according to a statement by Naevius, was drawn up (57–8). However, this is in a brief passage following an argument largely devoted to showing that Naevius had pursued his former partner for a debt in

---

[8] *Mil.* 29.
[9] *Mil.* 23, 31 ff.; for a similar dichotomy in an earlier speech see *Clu.* 64. Cicero's claim (*Mil.* 14) that the senate had judged that there had been a plot (*insidiae*) seems to be a forced interpretation of the decree of 27 Intercalary that the murder on the via Appia, the burning of the senate-house, and the attack on the house of the *interrex* were against the public interest (Asc. 44 C). However, the prosecutors had claimed that there had been a plot by Milo (Asc. 41 C) and this gave Cicero his opportunity. For a possible explanation of why the prosecution claimed more than they could prove see Lintott, 1974, 74–5.
[10] Asc. 31 C, cf. Quint. *Inst. Or.* 6. 3. 49; contrast *Mil.* 29.
[11] *Sull.* 11–14. [12] Asc. 66 C.

an improper fashion and in particular had been indecently strict about Quinctius' non-appearance (42–56). A conclusion that will be developed in a later chapter is that Quinctius had indeed made a *vadimonium* with Naevius, but that document was no longer available, only the declaration of non-appearance. Cicero could, therefore, claim that the *vadimonium* had never existed and he did so with apparent confidence, but the time that he devoted to other, less compelling, arguments must cast grave doubts of the reliability of his claim.[13]

The technique we have examined so far is to insert a relatively brief and unadorned lie into a mass of other narrative or argument which may itself be a misrepresentation of the facts. More common is the falsehood by implication through tendentious description. In *pro Caecina* Cicero wished to prove that his client had been violently expelled from a property that was his, the *fundus Fulcinianus*. This farm had been in fact bought by Caecina's opponent Aebutius with money from the widow Caesennia to whom Caecina was the chief heir. Aebutius seems also at the time of the expulsion to have been in possession of the farm. Hence, although Aebutius probably owed money to the widow's estate, he had a strong claim to the farm itself. Cicero admitted Aebutius' original purchase, but immediately went on to suggest that in fact ownership or at least possession had been transferred by Aebutius to Caesennia: everyone, he claimed, knew that it had been bought to be passed on to her; furthermore, Caesennia took possession and rented the farm out—a point which was a neat misrepresentation of the fact that Caesennia already had usufruct during her lifetime over the farm as a result of an earlier will.[14]

In the second speech against Rullus' agrarian law, made to the people in January 63, Cicero argued against the foundation of a colony at Capua. There was a fair point to be made on his side, that this would lead to loss of the rents from the existing tenants of the *ager Campanus* (80–5).[15] But this was not enough for the orator. He claimed that the 5,000 colonists chosen would be the worst sort of men and that in any case they would soon have their

---

[13] It may also be that this claim had been made on behalf of Quinctius in earlier hearings but had been shown to be dubious. Cicero would have been reluctant to abandon it completely, since this amounted to an admission that his client had previously lied, but equally reluctant to press it on account of its weakness. There are also clear examples of the lie direct in political speeches, for example Cicero's claim in *Phil*. 11. 10 that he was ignorant of Dolabella's unscrupulousness while he was his father-in-law or his praise of the members of Pompey's staff at Pharsalus (*Phil*. 13. 40) which is in complete contrast with the views he expressed in his correspondence.

[14] *Caec*. 16–17, 94–5, see further Ch. VI and Nicosia, 1965, 41 ff.; Frier, 1985, 105 ff. Note especially Frier, pp. xii, 178–9 on the invalidity of Stroh's argument, based on an inadequate treatment by Nicosia of this topic, that Cicero misrepresented the *interdictum de vi armata*.

[15] He maintained this view in 59 BC (*Att*. 2. 16. 1).

allotments illegally bought up by rich men based in Cumae and Puteoli; worse still, men from rural tribes would have preference over those from the city (77–9). So far this is mere unproved speculation and anti-rural prejudice. Cicero also appealed to tradition. After its revolt and recapture in the second Punic War, the Romans feared it as potential rival to Rome (86 ff.). There was a recent precedent for Rullus' plans, the colony projected by M. Brutus, the Marian tribune of 83 BC: his project was duly denounced at length (89, 92–4, 98). On his side Cicero enlisted figures from the opposite ends of the political spectrum—the Gracchi and Sulla (81): neither the devotees of the plebs nor the man who had no conscience about confiscation and redistribution dared to touch the *ager Campanus*. Regarding Sulla, this was strictly true in so far as the 'Campanian land' was the territory of Capua, not the whole of Campania.[16] Sulla's activities had been apparently restricted to Pompeii and Nola. However, we still possess a Gracchan *terminus* from the Monte Tifata above Capua.[17] Unsatisfactory efforts have been made to save the truth of Cicero's claim,[18] but any such attempts are probably a waste of time. Either Cicero did not know much about Gracchan land-assignment here or he was prepared to sacrifice veracity to make a rhetorical point. Interestingly, in his preceding speech to the senate the same claim is less absolute, 'the land which in its own right had resisted the domination of Sulla and the largesse (*largitio*) of the Gracchi'.[19]

Perhaps the classic example of Cicero's skill in tendentious description is his speech for Cluentius in 66, in which he threw a smokescreen over the jury—his own description of the case, according to Quintilian.[20] Cicero's skill lay in destroying the authority of Cluentius' mother Sassia, in transferring the guilt for the corruption of the court that had tried the elder Oppianicus from Cluentius to Oppianicus himself (rather than denying the well-established fact of the corruption), and in leaving to last the technical argument that Cluentius, as an *eques*, was not liable under the law.[21] The accuser, T. Attius of Pisaurum, had alleged that in 74 Cluentius had conspired to have the elder Oppianicus condemned on a capital charge by accusing him of murder and bribing the jury (9, 148 ff.). He added three charges of poisoning (conveniently, as the first charge was incorporated in Sulla's statute about poisoners, the *lex Cornelia de veneficis*), one relating to Oppianicus senior, another to

---

[16] The towns listed in *Leg. Agr.* 2. 86 seem to be chosen as those neighbouring the territories called *ager Campanus* and *ager Stellas*.
[17] *ILLRP* 467.
[18] See my account of these in *JRLR* 202–3.
[19] *Leg. Agr.* 1. 21.
[20] *Inst. Or.* 2. 17. 21. He had himself denounced in 70 BC the corruption of the jury four years earlier by both Oppianicus and his present client (*1Verr.* 39). On the case see especially Stroh, 1975, 194 ff.
[21] Quint. *Inst. Or.* 6. 5. 9.

C. Vibius Capax, a third to Oppianicus junior, charges which do not seem to have been serious enough for Cicero to have devoted much time to them (165 ff.).

In reply, Cicero related the intermarriages of what must have been the leading families of Larinum in the era of Sullan domination. His aim was to highlight the machinations of Sassia in changing husbands and argue that this was a major contribution to Cluentius' accusation of Oppianicus senior for poisoning him (12 ff.). When he came to the trial of Oppianicus, Cicero posed a false dichotomy, similar to that used later in *pro Milone*: either Cluentius or Oppianicus had bribed the jurors (64, 81); no mention of the possibility that both did. He then proceeded to a brilliant and witty narrative placing the blame for the condemnation on the unscrupulous C. Staienus, who, he alleged, had been the banker of Oppianicus' bribes for the jurors and chosen to keep them for himself (67 ff., esp. 72). Conveniently, there was evidence for Oppianicus transferring money to Staienus (82–7). In this narrative and the following argument Cicero probably made no statement that could have been shown to be false in itself, but operated by stress and omission. Cluentius may have had a strong case against Oppianicus (59–60, 81), especially in the light of the earlier condemnation of Scamander (in spite of Cicero's own efforts to defend him) (50–5) and that of Fabricius (56–9). Nevertheless, amid the corruption of the senatorial courts (61), it can be easily understood Cluentius should have chosen to reinforce his case with money.

We have already discussed two of Cicero's apologies for fleeing into exile in face of Clodius' threats (ch. I, pp. 8–14). There is no reason to dispute the potential threat from Clodius himself in 58 or the embarrassing lack of support for Cicero from certain eminent men. However, Cicero gives this a further dimension. In the speech to the senate after his return[22] he claimed that, if he had stayed, he would have had to fight against the same 'army' (*exercitus*) that he had defeated not by arms but with the senate's authority. The current equivalent in 58 of the former Catilinarians in the city was of course Clodius and his gangs. During the struggle over the Bona Dea prosecution Cicero had identified Clodius' supporters with Catilinarians, and Clodius himself as a successor to Catiline and Lentulus. Even Clodius' supporters, Cicero alleged, called Clodius 'the lucky Catiline'.[23] In *Post Reditum in Senatu* he reinforces this identification of Clodius and Catiline by claiming that at that time L. Piso had sought to punish the *equites* for their protection of Cicero in 63 'on the Capitoline slope', that is, by mounting guard round the temple of Concord.[24]

---

[22] *Red. Sen.* 32.　　[23] *Att.* 1. 14. 5, 1. 16. 9; *Dom.* 72 *felicem Catilinam*. Cf. Lintott, 1967.

[24] *Red. Sen.* 32. This was Cicero's *exercitus*: compare *Att.* 2. 1. 7, the *equites* on the Capitoline with ibid. 1. 19. 4; 2. 19. 4, the (*consularis*) *exercitus*. Cf. Ch. X n. 3.

So far, the threat to Cicero in 58 is compared to the threat to the Republic in 63, though the two 'armies' only merit the title metaphorically. However, 'there was another at the gates with *imperium* for many years and a great army, who I do not say was my personal enemy (*inimicus*), but I do say remained silent, when he was alleged to be my enemy'.[25] Cicero implies, without stating unequivocally, that not only Caesar but his great army were at the gates of Rome. Caesar indeed had four legions, but three were at Aquileia at the head of the Adriatic and one was in Transalpine Gaul. On arrival at the Rhône Caesar had, moreover, to recruit vigorously on both sides of the Alps.[26] He may well have started from Rome with some recruits as reinforcements, but these would hardly have been a great army.

In the speech for Sestius of March 56 Cicero's own allegation about Caesar is attributed to Clodius.[27] According to Cicero Clodius was openly stating in his speeches to the people that he had Pompey, Crassus, and Caesar behind him, 'of whom one had a very large army in Italy and the two, who were then private citizens, could and would raise armies, if they wanted'. Apart from the exaggeration about Caesar (one could even question whether Caesar's Cisalpine province was part of 'Italia' at this time), the allegation runs counter to what we know of Pompey's behaviour and that of Crassus since Sulla's dictatorship. They had not in fact raised armies without public authorization and were most unlikely to have wanted it stated that they would. Did Clodius really state this without encountering a denial? Or did Clodius merely claim that he has the support of the three, the remarks about the armies being a Ciceronian gloss? Two months later in *De Haruspicum Responso*, with some results of the compact between Caesar, Pompey, and Crassus at Luca already visible, the claim about Clodius has been watered down. Clodius would never have been able to harry Cicero and the *res publica* so viciously,

> had he not been threatening to send Caesar's army with standards at the ready into the senate-house (he was lying about this, but no one tried to refute him), had he not been screaming that he was doing this with the aid of Cn. Pompeius and the authority of M. Crassus, had he not been giving assurances that the consuls had joined their cause with his—the one point on which he was not mendacious.[28]

In the end Cicero was compelled, in face of the *force majeure* of the gang of three, to suppress any reference to Crassus and Pompey's armies and to argue that Clodius' alleged claim about Caesar's army was false. But the reason for

---

[25] *Red. Sen.* 32; Caes. *BG* 1. 6. 4–7. 1.   [26] *BG* 1. 7. 2, 1. 10. 3.   [27] *Sest.* 40.
[28] *Har. Resp.* 47. I take *de Haruspicum Responso* to have been delivered in the latter part of May 56, after senate-sittings resumed, following Courtney, 1963, who combined *Har. Resp.* 15 and Dio 39. 20. 3 with *Att.* 4. 7. 3.

his change of tactic does not make his own original insinuations about the three any more true.

The danger for the historian in using statements in Ciceronian speeches out of context is apparent. However, the varying forms of argument and the rhetorical techniques used are themselves important data for history and for Cicero's biography. In the following chapters I want to explore this in more detail in relation to different types of forensic case, beginning with the civil cases that made a great contribution to Cicero's early success.

Part B

Reading Oratory

IV

Cicero's Forensic Baptism: The *Pro Quinctio*

PROOEMIUM: HOW CICERO CAME TO TAKE THE CASE

When Gellius criticized Cornelius Nepos for saying that Cicero pleaded his first public case for Sextus Roscius at the age of 23, he pointed out that in fact the orator had pleaded a private case for Quinctius the year before in the consulship of Tullius and Dolabella (81 BC), 26 years after his birth by the Roman method of calculation.[1] It is thus the first Ciceronian speech that we can identify. An admirable commentary on this speech was published by T. E. Kinsey, which comprised a determined effort to straighten out the legal tangles with a close examination of its rhetorical technique. This work portrayed the speech as a technically adept but laboured effort in a lost cause. Kinsey's estimate of the speech as oratory still seems fair. Subsequently, J. Platschek and E. Metzger have produced a careful studies of the legal issues.[2] The legal aspects merit further consideration (especially in relation to *vadimonium*, where new evidence is available), and an interpretation of the speech is possible which, while not making Cicero's client a more sympathetic character, makes his position in law seem stronger. This in turn has implications for Cicero's oratorical strategy.

We tend to think of the *pro Quinctio* as Cicero's first sortie into forensic oratory, made, like the *pro Sexto Roscio*, under the shadow of Sulla's domination and the proscription of his opponents. However, in the *exordium* to the *pro Quinctio* (4) Cicero refers to his previous cases—presumably private cases, like Quinctius', and apparently undertaken earlier under Sulla's dictatorship, if we trust his own account of his early career.[3] He must have performed well enough in these to impress Sulla's friend, the actor Quintus Roscius, who, as

---

[1] Gellius 15. 28. 1–3; Cornelius Nepos 1P.
[2] Kinsey, 1971; Platschek, 2005; Metzger, 2005, esp. 27 ff. See also Mette, 1965, 16 ff.; Bethmann-Hollweg, 1864–6, ii. 783–804; Arangio-Ruiz, 1964; Costa, 1899.
[3] *Brut.* 311.

Quinctius' brother-in-law, was the intermediary in arranging that Cicero took over this case when the previous advocate M. Iunius was called away as a *legatus* (77–9, cf. 3).[4] Nevertheless, Cicero was at best second choice and still something of a debutant.

The judge was C. Aquilius, already a jurisconsult, later Cicero's colleague as praetor in 66 and one of the canon of Republican jurists. Cicero treats him not only with great respect but also with gratitude as an asset to Quinctius' cause (5, 10, 33, 47). However, his previous involvement with Quinctius as an arbiter in a matter of debt (17), which is evidence of familiarity, may not have been entirely to Quinctius' advantage. At most we can conclude from his appointment now that both Quinctius and his opponent regarded him as fair choice for their case. We are not told why the previous hearings (3) had not led to a verdict. A civil judge had the power to adjourn a hearing by 'dividing the day' (*diei diffisio*), with the implicit promise to reconvene and pursue the matter to a verdict.[5] However, Hortensius' alleged complaints (34) that the long-winded speaking of Iunius had curtailed the time for his own peroration (Cicero's emphasis on the peroration is surely ironical) suggest that the previous hearings had in fact been concluded, but that the judge had been unable to reach a decision and requested further hearings by declaring *non liquet* and/or *amplius*.[6] It may be that at this point too the technical procedure used was also *diei diffisio*.

This would have made Cicero's task both easier, in that certain matters of fact had already been cleared up, and harder, since the scope for concealment of points unfavourable to his side was also reduced. Moreover, there was at least one point in his client's original case whose weakness the earlier hearings would have exposed—the claim that Naevius had invented a non-existent summons (*vadimonium*) and hence that the seizure (*missio in possessionem*) decreed by the praetor Burrienus was unsound (below, pp. 50–3). To abandon this completely would suggest that his client had lied; to stress it now would be imprudent. A final problem lay in the form of the action, which meant that he had to speak before the opposing advocates—he claimed with some justification that this was

---

[4] *Pace* Kinsey, 1971, 54 and Platschek 2005, 6–7, it is hard to identify him with the Marian tribune M. Iunius Brutus referred to as 'M. Brutus' in *Quinct.* 65, where he plays an important part in the story, when Cicero never hints at the identification and this would have had some bearing on the conduct of the case.

[5] *XII Tab.* ii. 2 (*Dig.* 2. 11. 2. 3; Festus, 336 L); *Lex Irnitana* (González, 1986), chap. 91; *PAnt.*, no. 22; Metzger, 1997, 91 ff.; Kinsey's acceptance (1971, 104–7) of the traditional view that the hearing of a Roman civil case by a *iudex* was expected to be over in a calendar day (*contra* Metzger) influences his belief that Iunius was filibustering; the lemma from the Twelve Tables (i. 8) in Gell. 17. 2. 10, used to support this view is better applied to procedure before the praetor *in iure*, see *RS* ii. 592 ff.

[6] On *ampliatio* see Chap. II with nn. 29 and 45.

unfair since his client was in reality the defendant[7]—and this entailed that he needed to anticipate the points that they would emphasize.

THE NATURE OF THE CASE

The case arose from the dissolution of a partnership, where one partner, Sextus Naevius, was seeking to extract what he was due from the dissolution. The question was whether Naevius' seizure of property in accordance with a praetor's edict had taken place—thus primarily a question of fact (*causa coniecturalis*) but with an element of legal interpretation (*legitima*), in so far as Cicero was to argue from the meaning of the phrase *ex edicto* ('in accordance with the edict'). In a matter that rested on the correct and effective performance of a legal procedure, it was not strictly an issue whether the partners had behaved equitably towards one another, but Cicero spent much of his speech arguing that Quinctius' opponent, Naevius, should never have taken this action, normally the first step in making someone bankrupt. This gave him the opportunity to stress the depravity, brutality, and lack of good faith of Naevius (no doubt Hortensius, speaking for Naevius, did the same about Quinctius).

From the first sentences in the *exordium* Cicero also tried to exploit his own position and that of his client as underdogs, when confronted by a client of *nobiles* who were also outstanding orators, that is, Q. Hortensius and L. Philippus (7, 72). However, he was cautious in presenting his client as disadvantaged politically under Sulla's dictatorship, perhaps because that would have suggested that he had had an unfair advantage before in 83, under the Marian domination, when the events occurred out of which the case arose. He rapidly discounted his client's connection with leading Marians (69) and the fact that Quinctius' former agent, Sextus Alfenus, had been proscribed by Sulla (70, 76), arguing that the connection was shared by Naevius (cf.21). He later pointed out that Naevius had bought Alfenus' property at the auction following his proscription, citing Quinctius as his partner (76). This gave the impression that both the partners were good Sullans now, like Cicero himself—in spite of his connection by marriage with the Marian family.

Nonetheless, in the *exordium* Cicero associated the influence (*gratia*) of his opponents with violence (*vis*),[8] suggesting that there was a danger that truth

---

[7] *Quinct.* 8–9, 33, 43, 71, 95.

[8] *Quinct.* 5. Cf. 10 for the *vis adversariorum*; Hinard, 1985, 149–51 for the sinister language used in *Quinct.* 51. Bannon, 2000, 71–94, has plausibly argued that Naevius' actions are

(*veritas*) might be driven into exile by this violence. A similar sinister impression is conveyed in subsequent passages, where he claims that his opponent's action for bankruptcy was a form of capital accusation (33, 72, 95). In this way the atmosphere of the proscriptions and the seamy side of the Sullan regime is evoked, even though on the evidence stated they are irrelevant to this case.

THE ORGANIZATION OF THE SPEECH

The speech is carefully structured in accordance with what was by then current practice and the boundaries between the sections are signalled. Cicero concludes the *exordium* and introduces the *narratio* with a plea to the judge and assessors to defend equity, adding 'So that you can do this the more easily, I will see to it that you understand the story of this matter and how it became an issue' (11). The *narratio* in turn ends with Quinctius making the legal wager (*sponsio*) that his opponent's earlier seizure of his property was invalid and this is said to be the issue in the case (*in hoc summa iudici causaque tota consistit*, 32)—the *constitutio causae*. After a digression denouncing the unfairness of the form given to the case by the praetor and the impropriety of the request by the opposing advocates to the praetor that he should restrict the length of Cicero's speech (33–4), Cicero highlights his *partitio*, his organization of argument, saying (with blatant irony) that he is dividing the case into well-defined parts in order to shorten the time taken by the hearing (34–5). It is, he avers, the sort of thing that Hortensius always does because he is naturally clever; he, Cicero, can do it only because the case is now well known. This *partitio* involves no concessions to the opposition about common ground. Cicero's own claims are that his opponent had no reason for demanding the seizure of Quinctius' property, that he could not have seized it according to the praetor's edict (hence, not legally), and that he did not in fact seize it.[9]

The claims of the *partitio* are sustained in the following argumentation (*reprehensio/confirmatio*)[10] in the order in which they were made: after the first section (37–59) Cicero underlines the transition: 'docui quod primum pollicitus sum causam omnino cur postularet non fuisse...attende nunc ex

---

presented in general by Cicero as improper self-help rather than proper legal procedure (83 ff.). Her treatment of the legal aspects of the case should, however, be treated with caution.

[9] On the *constitutio causae* see *Ad Her.* 1. 18 ff. On *partitio* see *Inv.* 1. 31 ff. For the theory concerning *status* = *stasis*, deriving from Greek rhetorical theory, see Quint. *Inst. Or.* 3. 6.

[10] Cf. *Inv.* 1. 34; 78; *Ad Her.* 1. 18.

edicto nullo modo potuisse' ('have explained what I promised first, that there was no reason at all why he should have demanded [the seizure of the property] ..., mark now the point that he was in no way able to according to the edict') (60). The second long section ends in the lacuna that must be postulated in paragraph 85; the third survives only in the excerpts of the rhetorician Iulius Severianus, but its sense can be seen in the summary of arguments in the *conclusio* or *epilogus*. We do not have the beginning of this peroration, but, to judge from what we do possess, this was an extremely elaborate *enumeratio*, summary of the argument (85–90), followed by an *indignatio*, complaint about the injustice of the accusation, and *conquestio*, appeal for sympathy, that were heavily loaded with rhetorical devices.

THE ORIGIN OF THE DISPUTE

Naevius had been the partner (*socius*) of Publius Quinctius' brother Gaius in a stockbreeding enterprise in Gaul—one which also may have involved trading in slaves (12, 24). According to Cicero he was the son of a freedman of no great property who was a herald by profession, and the orator not surprisingly suggests that he took rather more from the partnership than he put in, since all he had was his voice and wit (11–13). It is clear from a conflict of juristic opinion between Cicero's teacher, Quintus Mucius Scaevola, and Servius Sulpicius Rufus, recorded first for us by the jurist Gaius,[11] that by the time of our case partners did not need to make contributions of the same value or of the same kind, nor were the shares in the profits and losses of a partnership necessarily either proportionate to each other or determined by the capital each contributed, since a person's labour might be the critical contribution. This last point arises in Cicero's later speech for the actor Quintus Roscius.[12] One could indeed have a situation where one partner received some of the profits but suffered none of the losses (for example a freedman agent)—an arrangement which Quintus Mucius thought was against the nature of partnership, but Servius Sulpicius perfectly acceptable. Cicero has therefore to argue that Naevius' rewards were merited by neither his financial contribution nor his talents.

After a number of years Gaius Quinctius had died and by his will Publius became his heir (14). This death would have legally terminated the original partnership according to later 'classical law'.[13] Watson, however, has suggested

---

[11] Gai. 3. 149, supplemented in the light of Just. *Inst.* 3. 25. 2, see Watson, 1965, 137.
[12] *Rosc. Com.* 27 ff.; *Dig.* 17. 2. 5, 29 (both Ulpian).
[13] Gai. 3. 152; *Dig.* 17. 2. 35, 59 (the exception were the *societates vectigalium*), 60 pr.

on the evidence of this speech that in the late Republic there was an 'automatic partnership of heirs'.[14] His arguments are, first, that Cicero never hints that the partnership between Publius Quinctius and Naevius was the result of an agreement reached by them, and, secondly, that the reference to the link being by 'choice or chance', *voluntas* or *fortuna* (52) is a feeble concession by Cicero, if he could actually point to Naevius having deliberately entered into the current partnership. However, as Watson himself has stated, 'since *societas* was consensual' (that is, created by the consent implicit in behaviour), 'there was no need for any formalities for the conclusion of the contract'.[15] Moreover, the terms might remain unspecified.[16] In fact, it may not have suited Cicero to stress that a new partnership had been created in which the relationship between the two had not been clearly defined and, as it appears, dissatisfied Naevius more than Quinctius. It is true that at one point Cicero calls this a *societas hereditaria* and contrasts it with a later freely undertaken *societas* (69), but it would be rash to extract any technical legal meaning from this phrase: it means simply a partnership that has resulted from an inheritance.

A division of the assets might have taken place on C. Quinctius' death. Instead, we are told that Publius joined Naevius in Gaul and lived with him in friendship for about a year (it was not merely a business relationship, since Naevius was married to Publius' cousin). It is implicit in Cicero's description of the behaviour of Naevius and Publius Quinctius here (14 ff.) and it is plainly asserted later in the speech (48, 53, 69) that they were themselves partners in exploiting the Gallic estate. Hence, because there was no attempt to separate the assets and the estate continued to be jointly managed, it followed that a new partnership legally came into being, even if there was no detailed, written agreement. Thus it could be called *hereditaria*, because inherited *de facto* rather than *de iure*. Cicero's silence on the terms of this partnership suggests that they were indeed left vague (if they had been clear, he would have either exploited them in his own interest or sought to rebut in advance any unfavourable conclusions his opponent might draw). Any vagueness would have contributed to the problems, when there was a move to terminate the partnership.[17]

According to Cicero, problems arose, when Publius Quinctius was faced with the necessity of paying off debts incurred by his brother Gaius apparently

---

[14] Watson, 1965, 131 ff. [15] Ibid. 128. Cf. Gai. 3. 135–6; *Dig.* 17. 2. 4 *pr.*
[16] *Dig.* 17. 2. 7, 29 *pr.*
[17] Kinsey, 1971, 70—more cautiously, to allow for the view of Watson, 1965, 131 ff.—says that a new partnership may have come into being, if the original one came to an end with Gaius Quinctius' death. Platschek, 2005, 21–30, while noting that technically the old *societas* with Gaius should have been wound up so that the new could begin (*Dig.* 17. 2. 37), believes that Naevius and Publius were *socii*, whether this had happened or not.

outside the partnership. He accordingly prepared to sell of some of his own private property in Gaul, but was deterred by Naevius, who offered instead to lend him the necessary sum until he could sell at a more advantageous time. The two came to Rome, and Quinctius settled through an arbitration by C. Aquilius—the jurist who happened to be the *iudex* in this very case—the amount he was to pay to the children of P. Scapula (15–17).[18] The distinction between what was owed and what should be paid may relate to the alteration in debt repayments made by the *lex Valeria* of 86 (the question perhaps being how long this alteration was in effect); Kinsey[19] prefers to relate it to the contracting of debts in foreign currency, but it is hard to see why Roman lenders should formulate a loan or purchase in anything but sesterces.[20] However, Naevius refused to provide the money until there was a settlement about the affairs of the partnership.[21] So Quinctius was compelled to sell personal property in Gaul after all. He and Naevius then appointed *amici*, Marcus Trebellius and Sextus Alfenus, to negotiate a settlement between them, but in vain. From that time on the issue began to be *in vadimonium*, a matter of security for appearance in court (22). It appears from what follows that the two parties were instituting each against the other actions *pro socio* for the receipt of what was owed to the plaintiff from the partnership—actions either of which brought a partnership to the end merely by virtue of its occurrence,[22] but which presumably still related to the old partnership.

At this point the story becomes complex and Cicero's account (22–9) is alternately explicit and opaque. According to this, Naevius appeared in accordance with the *vadimonia* he had exchanged with Quinctius,[23] but

---

[18] Kinsey, 1971, 73 plausibly identifies him with the P. Quinctius Scapula who died, according to Pliny *HN* 7. 183, while dining with Aquilius Gallus. This would be the family to which T. Quinctius Scapula, perhaps the man from whose estate Cicero hoped to purchase *horti* much later, belonged: *Att.* 12. 37. 2; *Fam.* 9. 13. 1; *Bell. Hisp.* 33; Dio 43. 29. 3–30. 2.

[19] Loc. cit.

[20] The temple of Castor, where Aquilius conducted an investigation, was a repository of weights and measures and safe–deposits of the *argentarii*, see *LTUR* i. 242–3.

[21] The *societas* in §19 may be interpreted as the now defunct one with Gaius Quinctius, which Naevius was seeking to wind up in order to give the new partnership a clear start; see n. 17.

[22] *Dig.* 17. 2. 65 pr.

[23] The *vadimonia* would have been for appearance in the neighbourhood of the praetor's tribunal, whence the formal summons (*in ius vocatio*) would have taken place, see below, n. 25 and esp. *TPSulp.* 15, 19; *THerc* 15 for locations clearly near, but not actually at, the urban praetor's tribunal under the Principate—at that time in the Forum Augusti. For *ad vadimonium venire* see *TPSulp.* 28 = *TP* 10 (a *iusiurandum in iure*), 'cum ad vadimonum ventum esset'. I have assumed with most scholars that these were 'extrajudicial' *vadimonia*, as we hear nothing of the appointment of a judge and I find it difficult to conceive the praetor making a series of postponements in proceedings *in iure*. For a contrary view see Metzger 2005, 27 ff., whose general argument (ibid. 19–44) is that there is no clear evidence for the existence of extrajudicial *vadimonia*. He has a point (35) that the bankruptcy order (*missio*) was more justifiable if Quinctius' appearance had been ordered by the praetor, but it could still have seemed to

then said he was abandoning his action: he had sold part of the partnership's property in Gaul to ensure that he was not owed anything by the partnership; he was neither demanding or promising a *vadimonium*; if Quinctius wanted to sue him (sc. on the ground that he, Naevius, had taken too much and hence was now himself in debt to the former partnership), he was ready, that is, ready to defend an action there and then. Cicero at this point records no reply of Quinctius to the proposal, but says that he did not demand a *vadimonium* for the present (it appears that he was undecided about the offer): instead Quinctius spent about a month in Rome deferring other *vadimonia* before setting out to revisit the Gallic property. We may presume that he wished to see for himself how much of this had been disposed of by Naevius. Our understanding about Naevius' offer is now improved by a document from suburban Pompeii (Murecine) attesting the out-of-court conclusion of a dispute (*conventio finiendae controversiae*) between Faenius Eumenes and Sulpicius Faustus. In this *vadimonia* are remitted, with the plaintiff promising to take no action against the defendant's representative, should the latter fail to appear.[24] The importance of this evidence will be soon apparent and we shall return to the issue.

After a delay of about a month Quinctius set out on 29 January 83 BC, passing on the journey, at Vada Volaterrana in Etruria, a close friend of Naevius', L. Publicius, who was bringing from Gaul some slaves for sale in Italy (24, cf. 57). When Naevius learnt of this, on the following day at the second hour he met friends of his at the 'picture of Sextius',[25] presumably a location in the area of the Forum, used as a rendezvous in *vadimonia*, and before them he bore witness that he had responded to a *vadimonium*, but Quinctius had not.[26] On this basis Naevius later successfully requested from the praetor Burrienus *bonorum possessio ex edicto*—permission to seize

---

Burrienus a reasonable way to treat a debtor who was apparently refusing to do business with a creditor and was outside Italy.

[24] *TPSulp* 27 = *TP* 66+113.

[25] *Quinct.* 25. Kinsey 1971, 84, cites Pocock 1926, 180 f. for the *tabulae Valeriae* and *Sextiae* both being pictures of *triumphatores* but has doubts himself, believing that they might be banks. However, all that is needed here is a convenient location for a *vadimonium* near the Forum, cf. Camodeca, 1999, 49–51. For the *tabula Valeria* set up by M′. Valerius Messalla (*cos.* 263) see Cic. *Fam.* 14. 4. 2; Pliny, *HN* 35. 22. It was at the side of the *curia Hostilia*; Cicero's wife Terentia was taken there in 58, presumably in consequence of the seizure of Cicero's property after his exile. Platschek, 2005, 64–70 believes the *tabula Sextia* was a monument at the south-west corner of the Forum near the site of the tribunal of the *praetor urbanus*, citing Hor. *Sat.* 2. 6. 34–5 (for a meeting at the Puteal Libonis) and the altar dedicated to 'sei deo sei divae' by C. Sextius Calvinus found at the north-east corner of the Palatine (*ILLRP* 291).

[26] Kinsey's preference for the reading of inferior MSS, *maximae*, for *maxime* in 'tabulae maxime signis hominum nobilium consignantur' (25) is hardly justified. It would have been grotesque to carry around outsize versions of standard pairs of tablets.

Quinctius' property as a defaulting debtor. He had got no further, according to Cicero, than seizing one unimportant slave, when Sextus Alfenus, Quinctius' agent (*procurator*) tore down the placards (*libelli*) advertising the imminent seizure and sought to prevent this proceeding any further.[27]

There were further hearings before the praetor, where Naevius requested that Alfenus should give security for the payment of the judgement, as a preliminary to a lawsuit about the dispute. Alfenus refused, allegedly claiming that this would have been inappropriate even for Quinctius.[28] However, as Kinsey pointed out, since the man who sues the agent is not subsequently entitled to sue the principal, if Naevius was to sue Alfenus as Quinctius' *procurator*, he needed security to be furnished that Quinctius would accept the judgement and this was a matter for the *procurator* himself, that is, Alfenus.[29] Not surprisingly, Alfenus was reluctant. There was an appeal to the tribunes, presumably against the praetor's decree, and finally Alfenus managed to escape from the situation by a *vadimonium* promising Quinctius' appearance on 13 September. Meanwhile, Quinctius was expelled from the jointly owned estate in Gaul by the slaves of the partnership. He consequently obtained aid from C. Valerius Flaccus, the proconsul of Gaul and Spain—presumably in the form of an interdict ordering his restitution (28).

Some further detail was reserved by Cicero for the arguments in the *confirmatio*. Naevius allegedly told Quinctius on his return to Rome that the *vadimonium* that he had failed to meet was drawn up on 5 February, that is, five days after Quinctius had set out for Gaul, according to Quinctius' own story (57). The day of Burrienus' edict granting Naevius *bonorum possessio* was *ante diem V Kalendas intercalaris*, 20 or 21 February (79); Quinctius' expulsion from his property in Gaul took place on 23 or 24 February—after Burrienus' edict, but before those expelling Quinctius could possibly have known that this edict had been given (78–80). Thus the events of February 83 BC are presented in the *narratio* as a dastardly plot by Naevius to ruin his partner by depriving him of all his property, and this is developed in the first

---

[27] *Quinct.* 27. Kinsey, 1971, 87, interpreted these as advertisements of the sale, but this would have been premature. Quinctius had to be granted thirty days' grace, first prescribed for those condemned as debtors in the Twelve Tables (30, cf. *Tab.* iii. 1 = Gell. 15. 13. 11). The creditors had then to assemble and appoint a *magister bonorum*, who would register the property and prepare for the sale. *Libelli* are mentioned again in §50 as a general feature of bankruptcy and in that passage these could include sale-advertisements.

[28] Perhaps on the ground used later by Quinctius (31), that Naevius should have been bringing an *actio pro socio*, which was *in personam*. This would not normally have required the defendant to give security, whereas security was required from those subject to *bonorum possessio* (bankrupts) and those being sued for the performance of a judgement (cf. Gai. 4. 102) Hence for Quinctius to provide security implied that he was admitting the validity of the bankruptcy.

[29] Kinsey, 1971, 88, following Gai. 4. 84, 90, 97–8, 101 and de Zulueta, 1953, 274–6.

part of the *confirmatio* (37 ff.), where Cicero asks 'Is this the behaviour one would expect from one partner to another?' This is a plausible conclusion from the story Cicero has told, but there are problems with the story.

VADIMONIA *AND* ACTIONES

Naevius is unlikely to have obtained the decree for *bonorum possessio* from the praetor on 20 February without offering as evidence not only the *testatio*, that he had appeared and that his opponent had not—specifically mentioned by Cicero as 'sealed most particularly with the seals of noble men' (25) (see n. 26)—but also his *vadimonium* documents. We possess documents of this kind in various states of preservation from the archives of first-century-AD Pompeii (Murecine) and Herculaneum. The *testationes* from Pompeii[30] record that in different cases a person 'stood' (*stetit*) in a certain place at a certain date and time. Cicero does not challenge the *testatio* made by Naevius, but the prior existence of *vadimonia*. However, he does the latter only indirectly by arguing that his client could not have been in Rome to make a *vadimonium* on the date alleged. This date depended on the verbal testimony of Quinctius about a question he put to Naevius on his return to Rome, perhaps at proceedings before a magistrate *in iure* (57).[31] The *vadimonium* documents from Pompeii and Herculaneum begin with the date, time, and place for which the *vadimonium* was made, that is, when and where the parties were to meet for their lawsuit.[32] These are extra-judicial, created by the agreement of the parties without the authority of the praetor;[33] at the end of the text, where this survives, is the date on which the documents themselves were drawn up.[34] Thus, if *vadimonium* documents of this kind survived, they would have been essential evidence about the truth or falsity of Naevius' claims in 83 and Quinctius' claims in 81.

It is a fair inference from Cicero's dismissal of the *vadimonium* of February 83 and the way that Naevius' case had been conducted that the relevant document was no longer available. Hence the date on which it was made was open to doubt and Cicero's argument from it may simply depend on an

---

[30] *TPSulp.* 16–21, edited earlier as *TP* 37, 56, 56*bis*, 71, 84, 101; noted by Platschek, 2005, 71.

[31] Kinsey, 1971, 146 inferred that the question was put *in iure*—probably rightly. Platschek, 2005, 83–9 concludes that Naevius must have made a slip here. Metzger, 2005, 34 believes that Naevius' claim was correct but that the *vadimonium* was for Quinctius' *procurator* Alfenus to appear. However, if true, this must have emerged from earlier hearings even in the absence of the document itself and Cicero could not have ignored it.

[32] *TPSulp.* 1–15, 1*bis* = *TP* 1, 2, 3, 4, 11, 32, 33, 36, 38, 41, 42, 70; *THerc.* 14, 15.

[33] Camodeca, 1999, 151.   [34] *TPSulp.* 1, 3, 4, 1*bis*; *THerc.* 14, 15.

unprepared or misunderstood answer by Naevius in the confrontation on 13 September 83. In the *confirmatio* Cicero does not accuse Naevius immediately of forging a *vadimonium*; indeed he argues at some length on the assumption it was valid, before finally raising the possibility of a case created by malice—not a direct charge of forging documents (56)—and supporting this with the argument from the date for the creation of *vadimonium*, once given by Naevius (57–8). The *vadimonium* convinced the praetor at the time and the probability must be that it was genuine, presumably drawn up by Naevius and Quinctius before the latter left Rome. Why then did Quinctius leave Rome without covering himself in this respect? He may simply have been careless with his diary. It may also be that he in fact expected his procurator Alfenus to appear on the due date and postpone the hearing, but that the latter failed for some reason to operate as he should.

Another, in my view more plausible, explanation is that he was misled by Naevius into thinking that the latter was not going to use the *vadimonium*. A pair of tablets from the Sulpicius archive at Pompeii (Murecine) record an agreement to end a dispute between Faenius Eumenes and Sulpicius Faustus. In this Faenius formally remits *vadimonia* made by his representative (*cognitor*) to meet his opponent's representative at Rome. The promises, however, made in these by the respondent cannot be directly cancelled: instead Faenius himself formally promises in a *sponsio* to take no action, if his opponent's representative fails to appear on the due date in the due place, as originally promised in the latter's *sponsio*.[35] No doubt this is what Naevius would have been expected to do, if Quinctus had accepted his offer to end the dispute, but there had been apparently no agreement and hence any outstanding *vadimonia* between the two were in fact still valid in the absence of formal promises by Naevius. It may be that Quinctius naively either disregarded his former partner's *vadimonium* or trusted him not to act on it. Against this explanation it can be argued that Cicero failed to stress Naevius' sharp practice in this respect. However, it was within the letter of the law and Cicero was hampered by the defence earlier adopted by his client, to deny the existence of the *vadimonium* entirely.

Another interesting question concerns the suit that Naevius was intending to bring at this juncture. At first sight, if we believe Cicero's statement that on the day that they did meet after a *vadimonium* Naevius told Quinctius that he had taken steps to ensure that the partnership owed him nothing, no further action to wind up the former partnership was to be expected. Could there have been a debt of Quinctius to Naevius outside the partnership? The picture

---

[35] *TPSulp.* 27. Eumenes also makes a *sponsio*, following a *stipulatio* of Sulpicius Faustus, that he will pay damages for the value of any breach of this agreement.

that Cicero provides of Naevius refusing at the last to lend Quinctius money (16–19) would then be misleading. However, if the issue had been a private debt, for which documentary evidence would have been provided, it would have been an enormous and blatant gap in his case for Cicero to have ignored it completely, since unchallenged it tended to justify the *bonorum possessio* decreed by the praetor. It is true that at one point Cicero denied that Quinctius had a private debt to Naevius: 'There was no reason for the demand. How can this be concluded? Because Quinctius did not owe anything to Sextus Naevius either in relation to the partnership or privately' (37), but he felt no need to discuss any evidence brought by Naevius on this score.

An alternative explanation, which only requires us to assume some obfuscation by Cicero in order to heighten the apparent impropriety of Naevius' behaviour, is that the affairs of the partnership were not yet settled. Here the treatment of Quinctius in Gaul is relevant: he was thrown off the common property by the partnership's slaves on Naevius' orders (28, 81–2, cf. 90). I would suggest that, while Naevius had ensured that he had in his estimation a reasonable monetary return from some at least of the business of the former partnership (I am thinking here particularly of the slave-trading), he wished now for a share of the common property. Indeed, if there were no strict terms about the proportions in the partnership, he was entitled to 50% of it.[36]

Although Cicero is able to score points by arguing that the slaves on the estate who ejected Quinctius anticipated any news of the granting of the *bonorum possessio*, it is clear that a praetorian decree of this kind cannot have been in Naevius' mind when he originally sent them instructions. They were indeed acting in advance of a judgement, but may have been doing no more than managing that part of the estate that Naevius was claiming as his share from the partnership. Cicero points out later that Naevius expelled, hence did not seize as his property, the private slaves of Quinctius on the Gallic estate (90). This is consistent with my hypothesis that Naevius was bringing a second form of action to disentangle a partnership—an *actio communi dividundo*.[37] To that end he had secured a new *vadimonium* from Quinctius. When Quinctius failed to appear, Naevius employed the same procedure that would be used against a debtor who failed to come to court. Cicero would have us believe that such behaviour was unthinkable between

---

[36] *Dig.* 17. 2. 29 *pr.*

[37] *Dig.* 10. 3. Platschek, 2005, 58 notes that there is no mention of division of common property in *Quinct.* 23. This is good evidence that it had not already taken place but not good evidence that Naevius was not now pursuing this, since it was in Cicero's interest to suppress a justifiable cause for Naevius' actions. Platschek also argues (23–4) that, as long as the two did have common property, they could be regarded as *socii*, even without a new agreement between them.

socii, who were breaking up their partnership, but it would no doubt have depended on the degree of hostility and the status relationship between the partners: in any event in the long section of the *confirmatio* (37–59) he cannot show that Naevius' demand for *bonorum possessio*, however unusual, was legally incorrect.

THE CONTINUATION OF THE DISPUTE

The next act of the story, before civil war brought an intermission, had two scenes in different locations. In Gaul Quinctius responded to his ejection from the estate by taking the matter before the provincial governor, C. Valerius Flaccus. He probably asked for restitution according to the interdict against violent expulsion, *unde vi* (see Ch. VI), and if he achieved this, he would have been in effective control of at least part of the Gallic estate, though still with unresolved obligations to his partner (28). Kinsey argued that he did not in fact achieve this, on the basis of the vagueness of Cicero's language ('Flaccus thought he should take vigorous reprisals') and the later reference to Quinctius' expulsion 'from an excellently equipped farm (*fundus*)' in the final *conquestio*.[38] However, Cicero also refers to the estate as a *saltus* (79), and a *fundus* would be but one element within a *saltus* that comprised a number of properties. Moreover, if, through the agency of the staff loyal to him, Naevius in 81 BC was in possession of the whole Gallic *saltus*, it is not clear why he was pressing this case. It therefore seems more likely that Quinctius had been restored in 83 BC to what at the time he was deemed to possess in Gaul, that is, part of the original estate.

At Rome, Alfenus appealed to the tribunes—principally M. Iunius Brutus, the father of the later tyrannicide—in support of his plea not to give security for his principal before trial (29, 63–5). It appears from Cicero's involved arguments about this in the *confirmatio* that the tribunes did not actually rescind the praetor's decree. Brutus allegedly threatened he would do so, if there was no agreement between Alfenus fand Naevius about future procedure (65). Alfenus promised to accept any form of lawsuit that Naevius proposed and to produce Quinctius on the day fixed in the new *vadimonium*, 23 September.[39] Cicero says that this promise was made 'with Quinctius' property neither advertised nor seized': he does not say 'with Burrienus'

---

[38] In *Quinct.* 98, *inter alia*, Cicero seeks sympathy for Quinctius, 'ornatissimo e fundo eiectus', cf. 81 for expulsion from a *fundus* by slaves. See Kinsey, 1971, 90–1.

[39] As Kinsey, 1971, 93 notes, the day following the beginning of the *ludi Romani*.

decree cancelled' (29, 66–7). We are not told what form of suit was planned, but perhaps it was one to be brought by Naevius against Quinctius. Thus at this point Naevius would have had lost ground both in Gaul and at Rome. Naevius' advocates in the present case in 81 were suggesting that the state of the dispute at Rome owed much to pressure from leading Marians. Cicero points out in reply that Burrienus and Brutus had acted in different directions and that Alfenus had been a protégé of Naevius himself (69). However, it may not have been so much a Marian combination against Naevius as an attempt among Marians to ensure that private differences did not divide them on the eve of another civil war.

No action was taken for a year and six months following September 83.[40] This was hardly caused entirely by Naevius' tergiversation, as Cicero suggests. However, when the matter was finally brought to court, it was Quinctius who had been ordered by the praetor to bring an action. This was because he refused to accept a formula as defendant, whereby he gave security for the payment of the judgement on the ground that he had been made bankrupt— that is, that his property had been seized for thirty days (the period of delay before the execution of judgement on debtors attested in the rules of the Twelve Tables) (30). The praetor Dolabella accordingly ordered him to make a *sponsio* (judicial wager) that his property had not been seized according to the edict of Burrienus. Quinctius claimed that the formula originally offered prejudged the case (this is what I suggest may have been claimed by Alfenus in 83), while, if he was required to make a *sponsio* that he had not been made bankrupt, this put him unfairly in the position of plaintiff in a matter which might ruin him. Dolabella stuck to his position and ordered Quinctius' legal advisers to move away from the tribunal. After a time, Quinctius returned to the praetor and agreed to make the *sponsio* (31–2).

During the period of over two years that had intervened since the alleged failure to meet a *vadimonium*, the affairs of the partnership had remained unsettled and Quinctius had apparently remained in control of much of the Gallic estate. There had been no attempt by Naevius to distrain on Quinctius' private property (89–90, cf. 85). Naevius' citation of Quinctius as his partner, when he bought up the estate of Alfenus at the proscriptions (76, cf.70), suggests at least a limited reconciliation, whether this purchase was in pursuit of profit or a favour to Alfenus' family from his former friends. It may be that there was by now an understanding between Naevius and Quinctius that this old issue between them had to be settled. However, each remained determined to give himself the best chance of winning the case: hence the tactical infighting. Cicero in his *conclusio* suggests that a case only concerned with

---

[40] *Quinct.* 30, cf. 67 for Naevius' allegedly making bogus excuses for two years.

financial compensation (*pecuniaria*)—that is one not involving *infamia*—could be finished in one day: his client was prepared to give security for the judgement, if Naevius was prepared to sue for money and provided that Quinctius could sue on the same terms for anything he himself believed he was owed (85, cf. 33). He is presumably contemplating *actiones pro socio* or *communi dividundo*. By contrast he suggests that Naevius' lawyers had been spending the adjournment thinking up a recherché legal action (67). In fact the matter had probably become something of a lawyers' case with the legal advisers on both sides interested in the issues of procedure and substance that it had raised, an appropriate case also for a juriconsult like Aquilius Gallus to judge.

THE RELATIVE STRENGTHS OF THE CASES

If our earlier argument is correct, the strength of Naevius' case in law was that the praetor Burrienus had in fact decided that Quinctius had failed to meet his *vadimonium* and had granted Naevius *bonorum possessio*. The form given to the current action derived from the view of another praetor, Cn. Dolabella, that the earlier decree was valid and in effect. This in turn implied that by his failure to appear Quinctius had been deemed to have lost the action that Naevius had been bringing against him in early 83.

Cicero's arguments about the *vadimonium* were weak, as we have seen, although his position was improved by the apparent failure of the document to survive. He also tried to argue that the praetor's decree was improper, contesting the ground that must have been actually invoked for it—that Quinctius had not been defended in his absence—by referring to Alfenus' later efforts.[41] The best point in his case was that a tribune of 83, M. Brutus, had prevented Naevius putting Burrienus' decree into effect by the threat of veto on the decree and that in consequence Quinctius' property had not in fact been seized for thirty days. It seems likely that in an earlier hearing Naevius' advocates, when faced with that argument, had cited the seizure of the property in Gaul, overturned (on their view improperly) by Valerius Flaccus. But in so doing they had fallen into a trap, as Cicero's friend, the actor Quintus Roscius, had spotted, since it was easy to show from the timing of the act that that seizure had not been a consequence of Burrienus' edict

---

[41] *Quinct.* 60, cf. Kinsey, 1971, 153–4. Platschek, 2005, 127 ff. discusses at length whether the *missio in possessionem* was appropriate, pointing out that the normal penalty for failing to appear was to lose the amount of the *vadimonium*.

(78–83). Furthermore, even if the seizure had been in consequence of Burrienus' decree, the violent expulsion of Quinctius by the slaves from the Gallic estate would have been improper under the conditions imposed by the praetor on the *missio in possessionem* (84). Finally, Cicero could point to other creditors of Quinctius, who had not tried to take advantage of the praetor's decree to seize Quinctius' property (73, 80). By contrast, Cicero's arguments that Burrienus' decree had been improper were of little value in law. The argument from the *vadimonium* was, as we have seen, dubious and the claim that *bonorum possessio* was unwarranted in a dispute between partners was at best an argument from morality and a plea for sympathy.

It seems in the end that Cicero had a strong case by the letter of the law, that Burrienus' decree of *bonorum possessio* had not taken effect and in fact become void, whatever the justification for it in the first place. However, the time he spends on seeking to prove that Quinctius had behaved uprightly throughout and had been a victim of a plot by an unprincipled rascal may indicate that in the previous hearings his client had not appeared in as sympathetic a light as his opponent and that this needed redress. It certainly shows that arguments from character were not inappropriate in a case full of legal technicalities heard by a jurisconsult (particularly the inventor of the *actio de dolo*). In the speech Naevius is what you would expect from a *praeco*—a smart city-slicker with the gift of the gab (11–13, 92–3), while Quinctius, Cicero in effect admits, is a mean and boorish countryman who is something of a recluse (59, 92). However, Cicero cannot evade the fact that they are relatives by marriage and have friends in common, in particular Sextus Alfenus: in fact he highlights this and uses it as an argument for Naevius' treachery.[42] It is further implied that Naevius brought less money and fewer services into the partnership, that he was the poor relation who tried to exploit his richer partners (12–14). This may have been true, but equally his commercial skills may have in fact been important for the partnership's success. Cicero by contrast cannot cite any special status for Quinctius that places him at a higher level than Naevius: it is Alfenus whose equestrian status is stressed (62, 87). Indeed, from the Quinctii and Naevius—not to mention Quintus Roscius—we get a general impression of a milieu of hard-headed, acquisitive, upwardly mobile men, who relied on their better-educated social superiors to protect their interests in the Forum.

Was Cicero successful? The publication of his speech at this stage in his career is more likely to have been an advertisement of success than failure. Even if some of his arguments are unlikely to have impressed Aquilius, he still had technically a strong case in the terms of his client's *sponsio*. However, if

[42] *Quinct.* 16, 21, 38, 54, 87.

Quinctius had succeeded in this action, the likely consequence would have been that Naevius resorted to suing for what he believed was owed him from the partnership, or returned to the arbitration that had been attempted three years or more before.[43] For Cicero himself, the speech is an interesting exhibition of a wide range of forensic techniques. The blackening of Naevius' character served to nullify any impression in the minds of the judge and his assessors that Cicero's client had in fact tricked his partner. Nevertheless, the ultimate strength of Cicero's case lay in close argument about the proper legal interpretation of certain actions. In this respect it was to resemble the speeches for Roscius the actor and for Caecina. The latter speech has been argued to mark the rise of the Roman jurist.[44] This speech can well be described in the same terms.

---

[43] Bethmann-Hollweg, 1864–6, ii. 804 thought that Aquilius would decide for Quinctius in order to allow him to contest a subsequent *actio pro socio* on even terms.

[44] Frier, 1985.

V

More Problems of Partnership: The *Pro Quinto Roscio Comoedo*

THE year after *pro Quinctio* Cicero undertook his first criminal defence—that of Sextus Roscius of Ameria (see App. I)—and from then on he seems to have had a regular practice in both private and criminal cases, broken only by a study-trip to the East in the early seventies and his time in Sicily as quaestor (*Brut.* 312–15, 318–19). The speech for the actor Quintus Roscius relates to another private suit arising from a partnership (*societas*). It was delivered some time after Sulla's dictatorship (for the likely date see below) and is rhetorically more sophisticated. However, the issue stemmed from events of the eighties BC and relates to people of similar status to those in *pro Quinctio*. Roscius himself is a link, since he was the person who originally asked Cicero to take on Quinctius' case. Like *pro Quinctio* the speech is valuable evidence for private law procedure in the late Republic and for the law of partnership. It also reveals the types of argument an orator needed to deal with these legal issues.

The text we possess is unfortunately defective. We only have some, probably most, of the argumentation about the evidence, the *confirmatio* and *reprehensio*; nothing of the introduction (*exordium*), *narratio*, or *conclusio*.[1] In the text that survives Cicero seems to be deliberately making matters as confused as he can.[2] In so far as we can discern the structure created by the *partitio*, Cicero moves from arguments drawn strictly from law to arguments from equity, derived from Roscius' character and the history of the partnership.[3] In this later section he called into question allegations made by the prosecution, which involved the legal interpretation of more than one point of fact from the past, largely damaging to Roscius. Cicero seems indeed to have tried to rewrite the legal history behind the case.

---

[1] It has indeed been argued that Cicero dispensed with a *narratio*, see Stroh, 1975, 137, also Mette, 1965, 16–19. On the legal issues in the case see Bethmann-Hollweg, 1864–6, ii. 804–13; Costa, 1927–8, i. 166 ff.; Robbe, 1941, 54–70.

[2] Stroh, 1975, 146.

[3] On the usual interpretation of the issue, this latter section was strictly irrelevant, see ibid. 139–40.

RECONSTRUCTING THE NARRATIVE

Quintus Roscius and C. Fannius Chaerea had been partners in the financial exploitation of a slave actor called Panurgus, owned by Fannius, trained by Roscius in his home (27–8). After some appearances on the stage (how many is unclear, but he had not acquired a reputation in his own right) he was killed by Q. Flavius Tarquiniensis (29–32). Roscius started an action against Flavius, using Fannius as his formally appointed legal representative (*cognitor*), for *damnum iniuria datum*, loss caused unlawfully (according to the *lex Aquilia*). This reached *litis contestatio*—the authoritative acceptance by the parties of the formula for the action given by the praetor and the judge appointed by him. However, Roscius, apparently without consulting Fannius, came to an out-of-court settlement with Flavius (32), by which he received as compensation a country estate. This is said in the present case to have happened 'fifteen years ago' (37), allegedly at a time when land-prices were low and the estate itself was uncultivated and without a villa. It is possible that the estate was originally either forest or undrained wetland near the coast. At the time of the present case, however, it was 'extensively cultivated with an excellent villa' (33).

The date of the speech and the consequent date of these events have been much debated.[4] Although we should not draw too strict inferences from Cicero's mention of his own *adulescentia* (44), Cicero is unlikely to have talked in this way when he was praetor in 66 BC.[5] Low land-prices fit any time between 90 and 80 BC and hence there is a wide time-bracket for the original settlement. The fifteen years alleged to have passed between settlement and lawsuit may be a slight exaggeration. Cicero mentions that Roscius had declined to receive fees for acting for ten years (23), probably since Sulla made him an *eques* in 81 or 80 BC.[6] This makes the date of 76, traditionally assigned, unlikely, but leaves *c.*72–68 open; 66 BC[7] is impossible as the judge, C. Calpurnius Piso (*cos.* 67) was the proconsul of Cisalpine Gaul in 66–64. Stroh's argued that the suit against Flavius could not have taken place until *c.*81, because Roscius could not have appointed a *cognitor* (representative) until he ceased to be *infamis* through taking pay for acting.[8] However, this rule was not necessarily extant in the late Republic.[9] If we accept a date of *c.*72 BC

---

[4] Ibid. 149 ff.

[5] *Contra* ibid. 154 ff. It was another matter when he looked back on the sixties BC in the *Philippics* (2. 118).

[6] Macr. *Sat.* 3. 14. 3.

[7] Stroh's date (1975, 152).

[8] See *Dig.* 3. 2. 1, 3. 2. 2. 3; Paul. *Sent.* 1. 2. 1.

[9] e.g. actors are not among those treated as *infames* in the municipal regulations from Heraclea (*RS* i, no. 24), ll. 104–5, 122–3.

for the speech as compatible with Cicero's claimed *adulescentia*, that will mean that the origin of the quarrel belonged to the years when Rome was first in Sulla's hands and later recaptured by the Marians.

The matter seems to have lapsed for ten years or more after 88–86 BC (8 and 37). Roscius in the meantime had received the gold-ring of an *eques* from Sulla and no longer appeared on the stage for money. The Flavian estate had become much more valuable. The *societas* in relation to the exploitation of Panurgus had clearly lapsed. Fannius was conceivably Roscius' partner in another acting enterprise,[10] but we have no evidence for this: he was certainly not a partner in the Flavian estate. He might have brought an *actio pro socio* arising out of the partnership. Instead, however, Fannius first essayed to bring an action for theft (26), presumably on the ground that Roscius had stolen his share of Flavius' compensation.[11] This action completed the stage *in iure* before a magistrate (since the judge had to be informed that he was not needed), but was abandoned either before it came before the judge, or before he delivered a verdict, apparently because there was a compact (*pactio*) between the parties.

In this agreement Fannius appears to have agreed not to resume the action for theft—'you gave security, you said that you would not appear',[12] provided that Roscius submitted to an *arbitrium ex compromisso*—that is, a private arbitration not established by a magistrate. 'You made a joint promise concerning this money, concerning these very 50,000 sesterces (sc. those at stake in the case for which Cicero is speaking), you took up an arbitrator to decide how much it was juster and fairer that it should be given you or promised in return, if the verdict was in your favour' (12).[13] The arbitrator was C. Piso (12, cf.7, 22), who was later the judge when Cicero was speaking.

The arbitration took place three years before the *pro Roscio* (37). Piso's decision—only cited by Cicero, in what survives, as an argument that his client had originally settled with Flavius on his own behalf, not on behalf of the partnership—was that Roscius should pay Fannius 100,000 sesterces (on the simplest correction of the MSS), but at the same time stipulate that

---

[10] One might draw this inference from the present tense in 6 (16, 25 are ambiguous).

[11] 'Tamen fraudis ac furti mentionem facere audes', 'furtum erat apertum'. See Stroh, 1975, 117–18, following Arangio-Ruiz, 1964, 308–9.

[12] 'Satis fecisti...te adfuturum negasti' (26). This must have been a similar procedure to that used to nullify the effect of a pre-trial *vadimonium* in *TPSulp*.27.

[13] 'De hac pecunia, de his ipsis HS IↃↃↃ, de tuarum tabularum fide compromissum feceris, arbitrum sumpseris quantum aequius et melius sit dari repromittique si pareat' (12). For examples of *arbitrium ex compromisso* from Puteoli see *TPSulp.* 34–9. Stroh, 1975, 115 believes that there was in fact another agreement, suppressed by Cicero here, specifically to pay 50,000 HS compensation to Fannius—which Roscius in fact paid (51, described as *prima pensio*), but there is no need for this hazardous conjecture and it renders the speech even more confusing.

Fannius should promise to pay Roscius half of any money he should recover from Flavius (37–9). At some point after this Roscius did in fact pay Fannius a 'first contribution' of 50,000 sesterces (51). In the same period, so Cicero claimed, Fannius sued Flavius and was paid 100,000 sesterces, but the testimony for this was hearsay, depending on what two senators, T. Manilius and C. Luscius Ocrea, said that the judge, Cluvius, told them. Cicero alleges that this suit took place 'after this recent stipulation of Roscius' (sc. at the arbitration).[14] Fannius did not admit it and Flavius had died some time before this final trial (41–5). Stroh[15] argues rightly that the payment must have been an out-of-court settlement, if anything, but less convincingly that there could not have been a lawsuit between Fannius and Flavius at this point. When Fannius sued as Roscius' *cognitor*, he would not have sued in his own name and was thus not debarred from undertaking another action on the same matter: indeed this possibility was implicit in Piso's judgement as arbiter.

THE LEGAL ARGUMENT

Fannius' third action against Roscius was one for the payment of a fixed sum of money owed, *actio certae creditae pecuniae*, to wit, 50,000 sesterces. The assumption normally made by scholars is that this was for the second payment still due to Fannius from Piso's arbitration. The difficulty is that, if Piso's judgement as arbiter was as we have supposed, the case would seem to have been open and shut and Cicero's advocacy a waste of breath. Cicero in the first part of the surviving argument seeks to show that Fannius has no acceptable evidence for the exact sum being owed to him, which was essential for the success of an *actio certae creditae pecuniae* (11). Normally a debt had to be substantiated by evidence of either a money transaction, or a written entry in accounts, or a stipulation (cf. 13). In this case the first form of evidence could not be expected. As for the second, Cicero makes play with the fact that Fannius could not produce an entry in his accounts to substantiate the debt, only in his notebooks (1–9), but this distinction is not only invalid, but irrelevant, given that the conclusion of the arbitration was the source of the obligation.[16] However, it might not have been plain to what the entry in the notebooks referred.

---

[14] 'Post hanc recentem stipulationem Rosci' (41). [15] Stroh, 1975, 132 ff.
[16] Ibid. 119–20.

Hence we must consider the third possibility, a stipulation, and this is what does in fact seem to have been the origin of Fannius' claim—his stipulation and Roscius' promise (*sponsio*) at the conclusion of the arbitration. Cicero carefully does not directly use these words about Piso's requirement to Roscius when he is discussing the arbitration, he merely says 'You, Piso, asked Roscius that he should give Fannius 100,000 sesterces', but they are implicit in the *restipulatio* made by Roscius and the *repromissio* made by Fannius that the latter would pay over half of any money extracted from Flavius to Roscius (38–9). Cicero, however, in his discussion of the legal grounds for Fannius' claim briefly and baldly denies that there was any stipulation justifying Fannius' present case (13). Apart from sheer oratorical trickery, how could he do so?

Stroh conveniently listed the various solutions propounded up to his time of writing.[17] The first is that there was no stipulation by Fannius and no *sponsio* by Roscius at the time: Roscius' payment was only a condition for the fulfilment of Fannius' promise.[18] However, Cicero does not say that Roscius' payment was conditioned by Fannius' payment, only by a possible payment by Fannius (i.e. by a promise by Fannius)—and the terms *repromissio* and *restipulatio* used in relation to the latter are surely significant. The second solution is that Roscius' actual *sponsio* was formulated to include the condition that Fannius should have paid half of anything he might have received from Flavius, hence it was not the basis for an action, unless this condition could be proved to have been fulfilled.[19] If that was so—and the formulation seems improbable and unfair, since it would have been hard for Fannius, if he had not been already compensated by Flavius, to show that he would never be so compensated—Cicero failed to exploit this point in support of his case. Moreover, it is strange that, to judge from Cicero, Fannius seem to have been uninterested in the suit against Flavius that was vital to his present case.

A third explanation is that Roscius did not promise money to Fannius in a legally binding form. Against this is the intrinsic improbability that one side of the outcome of an arbitration should have been formulated in a *sponsio* and the other not. Furthermore, the phraseology (*restipulatio*, *repromisse*) used of Fannius' promise suggests that Roscius made a *sponsio*. Fourthly, it has been suggested that Roscius did make a legally binding *sponsio*, but that Fannius had no evidence to prove this. This too seems improbable, especially as the

---

[17] Stroh, 1975, 107 ff.

[18] See Bethman-Hollweg, 1864–6, ii. 812. He thought that, if there had been a *stipulatio*, Fannius' advocate Saturius would have made more of it. However, if the *stipulatio* was not for the sum now being claimed in the *actio certae creditae pecuniae*, it was of dubious value to Fannius.

[19] Costa 1927–8, i. 168–9; Robbe, 1941, 57.

arbiter Piso was judge in this case. Finally, Stroh himself, faced with all these implausibilities, suggested that the money sought in the present *actio certae creditae pecuniae* had nothing to do with the arbitration judgement but derived from a separate debt contracted before the arbitration. However, this means that Cicero is being totally misleading when he identifies the matter of the arbitration and the present trial (12). Moreover, if this debt was between the two as partners, it should have formed part of the arbitration; if it was a separate, private debt, most of the speech we have is irrelevant.

It seems rash to offer yet another explanation, but it may be tried. Thanks to the tablets found at Pompeii and Herculaneum, we know much more about the documentation of *stipulationes* and *sponsiones*, when money was owed. A particular point arises from those relating to business at Puteoli between Hesicus, an imperial slave, and C. Novius Eunus. We can partially trace the story of a loan made by the former to the latter against security in Alexandrian grain and legumes. When the sum in question changed, perhaps through interest accumulating, a new *stipulatio* and *sponsio* were made.[20] Perhaps Fannius failed to extract by a new *stipulatio* a new accurate *sponsio* from Roscius, when Roscius paid him 50,000 sesterces—half the sum adjudged in the arbitration (51, cf. 37). The best that Fannius could have done was to produce an entry for the money he had received—interestingly we now have a document of this type from Herculaneum[21]—together with the original *sponsio*. But the original *sponsio* could no longer be used in an *actio certae creditae pecuniae* and there was no substitute *sponsio*. Hence Roscius had a point in strict law deriving from his opponent's procedure.

It is apparent from the speech that in the last few years at least, relations between Fannius and Roscius had been poor, while both Roscius' conduct and Cicero's line of defence suggest that Roscius was far from happy with the result of Piso's arbitration. No evidence is given of any agreement about the proportion of profits and losses to be borne by the partners and, in default of this, we must assume that they should have been shared equally.[22] This in fact seems to be implied by Cicero's imaginary dialogue between Fannius and Roscius (32): 'You settled your half share at a high price.' 'Settle your own share at a high price too.' Even if we assume that Cicero's account is fair, neither Fannius' contribution of all the original capital (27) nor Roscius' contribution of all the training (28–30) was legally significant. Piso's judgement that Fannius should give Roscius half of any money extracted from Flavius suggests that he was operating a 50–50 distribution of the assets of the

---

[20] *TPSulp* 51, 52, 67, and 68.
[21] *TH* 52 + 90, 5 + *ined.*, according to the reconstruction of Camodeca, 1993, 115 ff.
[22] *Dig.* 17. 2. 29 pr.

partnership: his award to Fannius of 100,000 sesterces from Roscius in respect of the latter's receipt of the Flavian farm in settlement no doubt was meant to represent half of its value at transfer plus half the value that Roscius had derived from it over the previous ten years.[23]

If Roscius was dissatisfied with Piso's arbitration and only able to pay in instalments, we can see why he might have neglected to make the second payment of 50,000 sesterces—especially if there were rumours about a settlement between Fannius and Flavius, in respect of which he would have been due to receive back 50,000 sesterces himself. When Roscius was challenged over failure to pay, it suited his case for Cicero to widen the issue to cover the general equity of the settlement between partners and, in particular, to raise the matter of the alleged settlement between Fannius and Flavius. Fannius for his part seems to have thought that the evidence of his notebooks about payment and non-payment was adequate, when backed with the story of the dispute, to support the claim for an exact sum. He might not have wanted to revive the old arguments about an equitable settlement of the partnership, brought up in the arbitration, by bringing an *actio pro socio*. He decided, therefore, for an *actio certae creditae pecuniae*. This, however, seems to have played into Cicero's hands by providing him with a simple point from legal procedure, assuming that Fannius lacked an appropriate *sponsio* from Roscius, in addition to bringing into question the general fairness of Fannius' claim.

Cicero's arguments about that claim are (i) that Roscius was the chief contributor to the partnership and morally deserved most of the proceeds (22–32); (ii) that Roscius settled for himself, not for the partnership, and so Fannius could have claimed against Flavius in a separate action, while Roscius was not liable to give Fannius a share of what he had himself obtained (32–9, 52–6); (iii) that Fannius had anyhow obtained such compensation without disclosing it to Roscius (40–51). Of these arguments (i) was legally invalid and had not impressed the arbitrator; (ii) was largely invalid legally—even if Roscius had not given Flavius a guarantee that his partner would not sue, the proceeds of the settlement were due to the partnership. However, although Roscius could not sue Flavius again nor could Fannius as Roscius' *cognitor*, Fannius should have been able to sue for himself and duly deliver a proportion of the proceeds, as the arbitration of Piso suggested. (iii) depended on uncertain evidence. Cicero's insistence on these secondary arguments, which at best were an attempt to rewrite the arbitrator's previous judgement, seems somewhat desperate, especially since the former arbitrator C. Piso was now the judge in the case, and suggests a belief that the procedural argument might not stand up.

[23] *Rosc. Com.* 37, cf. 32–3; it is not clear what figure should be restored at the end of 32.

The plaintiff and defendant came from a similar milieu to those in the *pro Quinctio* and neither seems to have been a particularly attractive character. Cicero's efforts were more likely to receive applause from the *cognoscenti* for their legal ingenuity than create public favour for himself, but they are still an interesting example of the techniques of an advocate in a far from admirable cause. It was by taking up cases like this that Cicero could create the network of connections among members of the new rich in the society of the late Roman republic, that stood him in such good stead as he pursued his political career.

VI

Property and Violence: The *Pro Tullio* and *Pro Caecina*

'Who will put up with those immense volumes about an exception and a formula, delivered for Marcus Tullius or Aulus Caecina, which we read?'

(Tacitus, *Dialogus* 20. 1.)

THE suits about partnerships have shown Cicero using considerable legal ingenuity in causes that were far from sound. In order to reconstruct plausibly the events that gave rise to the suit we have to supply material that he is likely to have suppressed or so played down that it has become almost invisible. Occasionally, but not often, his statements must be completely discounted. Usually he proceeds not by assertions that it would be easy to refute directly, but by diverting the attention of the jury to arguments that show his client in a more favourable light, whether or not they are strictly relevant to the issue being tried. In the cases we are about to consider, Cicero seems to have had a reasonable case on a strict interpretation of the law, but as in *pro Roscio Comoedo* he needed to reinforce it by presenting his client in a better light than perhaps his character justified.

The two lawsuits arose from property disputes involving violence. In each case Cicero's client claimed to have suffered violence, in *pro Tullio* (*Tull.* 21–5) to his slaves, in *pro Caecina* (21–2) to his own person and those of his friends and supporters. The aims of the suits, however, were different: in the first it was a matter of obtaining damages for the loss (*Tull.* 7); in the second the winning of a judicial wager which in due course should have led to taking possession of a disputed piece of real estate (*Caec.* 23). Both cases were controversial. In the *pro Tullio* it is clear that there already had been one complete hearing with arguments and witnesses (*Tull.* 1, 6); in *pro Caecina* (6) we are told specifically in the *exordium* that the judges (*recuperatores*) had already been unable to deliver a verdict twice: that is, they had declared *non liquet* ('the issue is not clear') and the action had been renewed as in the *pro Quinctio*. Here Cicero is at pains to argue that there should be no reason for doubt and that the matter should be decided quickly.

PRO TULLIO

The *pro Tullio* is fragmentary. There are small lacunae in the *exordium*, considerable gaps in the *narratio* and *argumenta*; the conclusion is missing except for one or two brief citations. Nevertheless, the issue and the main lines of Cicero's argument are clear. Cicero's client, M. Tullius, owned an ancestral farm in the centuriated territory of Thurii, that is, the formally measured and distributed land of the Roman colony. He had recently acquired a new neighbour, P. Fabius, who had bought the neighbouring property in conjunction with a partner, Cn. Acerronius. According to Cicero, Fabius had made a bad bargain, since he had paid half as much again as his predecessor had paid for the farm, although at the time of Fabius' purchase the estate was a wilderness with its villas burnt out—most probably the result of the Social War (*Tull.* 13–16). Cicero's explanation is that he was eager to sink in the farm some ill-gotten gains that he had embezzled from a consular governor of Macedonia and Asia (*Tull.* 15), presumably L. Valerius Flaccus (*cos.* 86), who would have held both these provinces for the conduct of the Mithridatic War.[1] Fabius at first tried to resell his property and this led to a dispute about the exact boundaries of the estates, Fabius laying claim to the *centuria Populiana*, which Tullius maintained to be his. Violence followed with Fabius' armed gangs wandering everywhere (*Tull.* 17–19).[2] At a certain point Fabius, noticing that Tullius' slave Philinus was occupying a building in the *centuria* in question, took his partner and confronted Tullius at his villa. In consequence, Cicero alleges, Tullius promised to make a formal expulsion of Fabius from the disputed area and become the defendant in a lawsuit at Rome (*Tull.* 19–20). However, the following night, before this could take place, an armed gang of Fabius' slaves attacked the building in the *centuria Populiana* and killed a number of Tullius' slaves who were occupying it, though not Philinus, who managed to escape and bring the news to his master (*Tull.* 21–2).

Tullius sued, not about the disputed property, which seems to have remained in his hands, but about the loss he had sustained through the assault on his slaves, using a new legal remedy invented by M. (Terentius Varro) Lucullus (*cos.* 73), when he was *praetor peregrinus* in 76 (*Tull.* 7–8).

---

[1] Without this passage it would have been equally plausible to explain the devastation by Spartacus' uprising.

[2] This violence is probably Cicero's construction of part of Spartacus' uprising. The *centuria Populiana* would have been one of the squares in the allotment grid, 200 *iugera* in size, which probably took its name from a former owner, Populius/Popilius.

This used a jury of *recuperatores*, before whom procedure was more rapid, thanks to fixed time-limits and restrictions on the number of witnesses.³ The jury were required to condemn Fabius to pay four times the cash value of whatever loss (*damnum*) he was proved to have caused Tullius by the violence of organized or armed men (*vi hominibus armatis coactisve*) through the *dolus malus* of his slaves (*familia*) (*Tull.* 7, 41).⁴

Cicero says in the fragments of the *exordium* that in the previous action(s) he had worked hard to prove that Fabius' slaves had perpetrated the slaughter of those of Tullius, but in the event the defence-counsel, L. Quinctius, admitted the fact (*Tull.* 1–2, cf. 24–5). Quinctius was arguing instead that, since there had been no *dolus malus* by Fabius' *familia*, the facts did not match the *formula* (*Tull.* 25–36) and, furthermore, that Tullius' slaves had not been killed unjustly (*iniuria*) (38–56). For him the issues established in the hearings were about the meaning of the *formula* created by Lucullus' edict (a *constitutio legitima*) and whether the action of Fabius' slaves was just or unjust (a *constitutio iuridicialis*).⁵

Cicero's initial move in countering the first of Quinctius' contentions comes at the end of the *exordium*, when he describes the origin of, and intention behind, the action devised by M. Lucullus. It arose, he argues, to deal with the danger caused to private and public interest by the gangs of slaves in remote estates and pastures. For this reason Lucullus focussed the action on the *familia* and eliminated the concept of loss caused unjustly (*damnum iniuria*) characteristic of the fundamental law in this field, the *lex Aquilia* of the third century BC (*Tull.* 8–12). The importance of the word *familia* in the *formula* is shown by Quinctius' argument (35); the absence of the word *iniuria* must also be accepted, since otherwise Cicero would have been blatantly and futilely misrepresenting the *formula*. Whether Lucullus had consciously sought to eliminate the use of arms by slave-gangs in self-defence, as Cicero states (8), cannot be absolutely certain, but this seems to have been the effect of his new action.⁶

After the *narratio* Cicero's argument begins with the meaning of *dolus malus*. The conventional meaning of *dolo malo* seems to have been 'with premeditation, with unlawful purpose'.⁷ Quinctius had clearly argued that there had been no premeditation—to judge from Cicero's response, in which

---

³ Lintott, 1990*b*, with earlier bibliography; Schmidlin, 1963.
⁴ On the Lucullus edict see *VRR*, 2nd edn., 128–9; Serrao, 1954, 74 ff.
⁵ *Ad Her.* 1. 19, 24; Cic. *Inv.* 1. 17–18.
⁶ Contrast the exception clause introduced by the end of the Republic into the later interdict *de vi armata*, found in Cic. *Fam.* 7. 13. 2 but not in the interdict at the time of the *pro Caecina* (23, 62), which permitted armed violence in response to previous armed violence.
⁷ See the examples indexed in *RS* ii. 823.

he claims that an action presupposes an intention (*Tull.* 32)[8]—and further that Fabius' slaves acted in defence of property or even in self-defence (47–8; 54–5). Cicero alleges that the presence of the words *dolo malo* in Lucullus' *formula* merely extends it to cover persons planning an enterprise that they do not themselves carry out: when gangs of armed men are concerned there can be no question of lack of intent (25–8).[9] Moreover, he develops a convincing argument from the current *formula* of the interdict *unde vi*, which dealt with restitution to property after violent expulsion—circumstances similar to those at issue in this case—to support his view that *dolo malo* may be used to embrace planners as well as perpetrators. What he does not allow for in the speech is that both he and Quinctius may be right and that the phrase may have alternative meanings and functions.

Quinctius also apparently argued that one could not apply the phrase *dolus malus* to slaves. His ground would have been that in law a gang of slaves could have no purpose of its own, only that of its master. He would then have been able to point to the pacific intentions of their master manifested in his willingness to go to court. What we possess of Cicero's reply to this point is that, if this defence is valid, all cases under Lucullus' *formula* will fail (*Tull.* 35–6). In fact, we are told that Quinctius had sought to block the action from the beginning by appealing to the tribunes against the *formula*, when it was decreed by the praetor Metellus (*Tull.* 38), though the grounds given by Cicero for this relate to the other aspect of Quinctius' case, the issue of whether the violence was unjust.

Quinctius' third argument seems to have been that the violence, even though it brought about deaths, was not wrong. He cited the clauses from the Twelve Tables that allowed the killing of a thief who came by night and the thief who came by day who defended himself with a weapon, also the law granting immunity to the killer of someone who had struck a tribune of the plebs (*Tull.* 38 ff., esp. 47–8). His argument would have been that the violence of Fabius' slaves was either a legitimate reprisal to an invasion of property, or a response to violent provocation (54–5). Cicero alleged in the *narratio* that Tullius' slaves had not resisted Fabius' *familia* when they entered the building

---

[8] 'Nisi putamus eum <in iudi>cium venire qui consilium fecerit, illum qui fecerit non venire, cum consilium sine facto intellegi possi, factum sine consilio non possit.'

[9] Mette, 1965, 19–20 quotes Ulpian (*Ad edict.* 37) in *Dig.* 47. 2. 50. 2–3: 'recte Pedius ait, sicut nemo furtum facit sine dolo malo, ita nec consilium nec opem ferre sine dolo malo posse: consilium autem dare videtur, qui persuadet et impellit atque instruit consilio ad furtum faciendum, opem fert, qui ministerium atque adiutorium ad subripiendas res praebet.' This provides some support for Cicero' argument about the use of the phrase *dolo malo*, since *dolus* in relation to assistance implies only intention, not premeditation. See also Stroh, 1975, 163–4, 167–9.

(*Tull.* 21). It seems likely that they were completely outnumbered, as Cicero says, and surprised. Hence the casualties were on their side alone (Cicero is likely to be right about this as he would have needed to have taken notice in this speech of any counter-claim about losses by his opponent). However, it would have been hard to prove that they themselves had offered no violence, especially as the majority of them were dead and could not give evidence.

Cicero prepared the ground for his answer to this by his interpretation of the introduction of the new Lucullan action (*Tull.* 7–12). At the end of the *exordium* he pointed out that the word *iniuria*, found in the *lex Aquilia*, was deliberately omitted in Lucullus' edict in order, he said, to discourage armed violence. In the *argumenta* he took his stand on that omission, claiming that by appeal to the tribunes Quinctius had tried to alter the *formula* to be used in the case so that he could use that defence, but had failed (*Tull.* 38–9). Here he drew a clear distinction between this action and that under the *lex Aquilia*—the latter before a single judge for a double penalty and concerning loss suffered *iniuria*.

He also contrasted the present action with the interdicts about violent expulsion (*unde vi*) which contained exception clauses requiring the plaintiff to have had possession that had not been obtained by violence, stealth, or on sufferance (*Tull.* 41–6). It is indeed possible that, if Cicero's client either had performed the formal expulsion that had been planned and had been sued by Fabius under the interdict *unde vi*, or had himself sued under this interdict after the violent expulsion of his *familia*, he would have lost the case because of faulty title. In fact, exploitation of the Lucullan *formula* gave him a good chance of compensation. Moreover, success in this suit would have provided useful ammunition for his advocate in any future lawsuit about the disputed property.

The foundation of Cicero's strategy in this speech was the fact that in the light of the apparent purpose of the *formula* of Lucullus he had a strong case. It was uncontested that Tullius' men had been killed. He had to counter Quinctius' arguments that the *formula* was inappropriate since the killings were unintentional and that the wording of the *formula* was itself improper. Fortunately perhaps, the rights of possession to the disputed *centuria* were irrelevant and he could neatly leave them aside, while putting his client in a good light by his claim that Tullius had agreed with Fabius to go to law (*Tull.* 20). Tullius' character of course may have been vulnerable to attacks. From the fragments of the *exordium* it seems that Cicero had avoided slinging mud at the character of Fabius in his first speech, allegedly because it seemed inappropriate in a suit about money (the *pro Quinctio* suggests the opposite), but perhaps because he did not want a reply in kind. In fact Quinctius had attacked Tullius' character in his reply, and in our speech Cicero asks the jury's forgiveness for introducing aspersions against Fabius in return, restrained though these will be (*Tull.* 3–5).

In the speech rhetorical strategy and legal strategy seem neatly amalgamated. The argumentation is technical, as it must be, but forceful; rhetorical skill is to be seen, however, as much in the presentation of the dispute in the narrative and in the description of the nature of the Lucullan action, which prepare the ground. Cicero appears sure-footed and confident, as in *pro Roscio Comoedo*. He is in fact more experienced and he knows that confidence makes an important contribution to his effect on the jury. For the historian the wider background to the case, that is, the violence bedevilling post-Sullan Italy, is more visible than the backgrounds to the *pro Quinctio* and *pro Roscio Comoedo*. There Cicero is at pains to suppress the politics that were contemporaneous with the disputes; here the need to restore order in Italy is part of his argument. What is, however, common to all three speeches is the nature of the *dramatis personae*—wealthy landowners of equestrian and sub-equestrian rank riding the waves of political turmoil without ceasing their efforts to conserve or increase their wealth.[10]

PRO CAECINA: THE FORM OF LITIGATION

We possess the text of the *pro Caecina* effectively complete, unlike that of the preceding speech, and we can see in their full glory the technical arguments which were later found rebarbative by the *persona* of M. Aper in Tacitus' *Dialogus*. Cicero's client Aulus Caecina of Volaterrae was suing Sextus Aebutius in consequence of a *sponsio* (solemn wager) made by Aebutius, when challenged by Caecina after failing to comply with a decree of the praetor Dolabella. This decree had taken the form of the *interdictum de vi armata* and ordered Aebutius to restore Caecina to the *fundus Fulcinianus* in the *ager Tarquiniensis*, from which Caecina had been allegedly expelled (*Caec.* 23).

If Aebutius had complied with the decree originally, there would have been no further action. As it was, Caecina was challenging Aebutius with having disobeyed the interdict, by requiring him to make a wager of a considerable sum

---

[10] *Pro Tullio* must have been delivered after the praetorship of M. Lucullus in 76 BC and in the praetorship of the Metellus mentioned in §39, either Q. Metellus (*cos.* 69 and therefore praetor 72 at the latest), or L. Metellus (*cos.* 68, *pr.* 71). Cicero's treatment of M. Lucullus in the speech suggests that his praetorship was comparatively distant; 75 and 74 BC are therefore unlikely. Moreover, in 74 Quinctius was tribune and unlikely to have the time for advocacy in private cases. In 73 M. Lucullus was consul and this would have surely been mentioned. We are left with 72 and 71, of which the latter is more likely, since the lawsuit can be placed in the aftermath of Spartacus' revolt. Cf. Stroh, 1975, 160.

that he had not, a form of *sponsione provocare*.[11] According to the procedure later described by Gaius,[12] Aebutius would have balanced the action by requiring Caecina to wager a similar sum that Aebutius was in the wrong. If Caecina had succeeded in the action, he would have prepared the ground for the recovery of the farm by an action defined by a third *formula*, one that entitled him to damages, if the defendant was condemned, unless the latter made the restitution required in the opinion of a judge—a *formula arbitraria*.[13] If this were successful, the judge would condemn Aebutius to pay Caecina the value of the farm, should he not have restored it to him.[14] It was later the rule that—perhaps at the time when the *sponsiones* were made—the temporary possession of the disputed property was assigned in the interim to the party who bid highest in an auction. The sum represented the assumed profits from the estate that he would pay to his adversary if he lost.[15] This may not have been the practice in Cicero's day. In any event the impression given by the speech is that the farm was in Aebutius' hands at the time of the trial.

The Backgound to the Lawsuit

Caesennia, the woman whose estate caused the controversy, was the widow of M. Fulcinius, a man of decent, but not aristocratic, ancestry from Tarquinii who had become a respectable, rather than an outstandingly important, banker at Rome (*Caec.* 10 ff.); Caesennia was in fact superior to him in birth. Fulcinius had sold her a farm in Tarquinian territory, at a time when he was short of cash, in order to use her dowry to support his bank without injuring her interests. Later with the money obtained from winding up his banking operations he bought farms adjacent to it. Fulcinius died leaving his only son, also a M. Fulcinius, his heir, but with Caesennia having usufruct—life interest—in all his property jointly with his son.

[11] On *sponsione provocare* see Crook, 1976.
[12] Gai. 4. 161–70, esp. 165; de Zulueta, 1953, 295 ff.
[13] Gai. 4.163–5.
[14] Aebutius could have resorted to this legal mechanism directly in place of the action by wager but on one view, according to Gaius 4. 163, this amounted to a confession of liability.
[15] Gai. 4. 166–7. On the *pro Caecina* the most important discussions are now those of Nicosia, 1965, and Frier, 1985. Note also Labruna, 1970, 160 ff., who, however, overemphasizes the distinction drawn later by Ulpian (*Dig.* 43. 17. 1. 2–3) between actions under the interdicts about possession and disputes about ownership. Because, as here, ownership could be used as an argument against the claim of valid possession by another (on the ground that this possession was *vi vel clam vel precario*), actions under the interdicts could serve to settle a dispute about ownership. See *Ad Her.* 4. 40 and in general on the parallel use of *legis actiones in rem* and the interdicts the metaphor in *de Or.* 1. 41: '... qui aut interdicto tecum contenderent aut te ex iure manum consertum vocarent, quod in alienas possessiones tam temere inruisses.' The *legis actio sacramento* image is developed ibid. 42.

The son died too. Under the younger Fulcinius' will his heir was P. Caesennius, his wife received a great amount of money, and his mother the greater part of his property. This will would have violated the *lex Voconia* of 169 BC, inasmuch as a single legatee received more than the heir.[16] Frier has plausibly argued that the loophole permitting its acceptance by the praetor was that the testator was *incensus*, not yet formally registered as a Roman citizen.[17] In order to distribute the shares owed to the women there was an auction at Rome of the estate. On Aebutius' advice Caesennia lent him money to purchase out of it the property next to her existing farm. She then entered into possession of this, the subject of the present dispute, and rented it out. A little later she married Caecina, but soon died herself, leaving him heir to 23/24 of her property, with Aebutius getting 1/36 and a freedman of her first husband Fulcinius getting 1/72.

Aebutius apparently contested Caecina's inheritance on the ground that he was not a Roman citizen with full rights on account of the penalty imposed by Sulla on the people of Volaterrae (as on those of Arretium) (18, cf. 95–100). When this failed, Caecina was granted *bonorum possessio* by the urban praetor and requested an arbiter to preside over the division of the inheritance. Aebutius in response claimed the *fundus Fulcinianus* he had purchased as his own and outside the division.[18] Aebutius seems now to have been treating the farm as his, whether he was in actual occupation of it or not.[19] After Caecina had taken advice from friends, by agreement of both parties it was resolved to meet on a particular date at the farm so that Caecina could be removed from it 'in the traditional fashion' (*moribus deduceretur*), that is, that he should be formally expelled before witnesses and the basis thus laid for an appeal to the praetor through the interdicts about possession (20, 22, cf. *Tull.* 20).

On the day in question, after assembling with his friends at the Castellum Axia (a few miles west of modern Viterbo), Caecina was not even allowed to set foot on the *fundus Fulcinianus* from the neighbouring estate by a gang of armed slaves under Aebutius' orders. Caecina and his friends fled, and in consequence subsequently obtained from the praetor Dolabella an interdict *de vi armata*, ordering his restitution. When Aebutius in response claimed that Caecina had in fact been restored, resort was made to *sponsiones* in order to generate a lawsuit (23).

[16] *2Verr.* 1. 110, cf. 104 ff.   [17] Frier, 1985, 15 n. 38.
[18] 'In foro' (19) perhaps means during the arbitration or the proceedings *in iure* before it.
[19] Frier, 1985, 18 has taken Caecina's visit to the farm while on a circuit of the properties, mentioned in *Caec.* 94, to fall in this period. If so, it is strange that Cicero does not mention this in the *narratio* at the appropriate point, as this would have been useful argument for his client. The tour could equally well have occurred when Caesennia was alive: Caecina would have been acting as his wife's bailiff.

The Issue

Cicero presents Aebutius as someone who had tried to exploit an inexperienced widow by running her affairs for her (13–15). There may been some truth in this. He was probably disappointed that he had done no better out of her will: hence his attempt to upset it by the allegation that Caecina was disqualified from inheriting. However, this did not mean that he had no right to possess the farm.

The Fulcinian farm had been auctioned to raise cash for the younger Fulcinius' estate. Aebutius had bought it and legally he could only buy it in his own person.[20] He may not have paid back Caesennia's loan (17)—in which case he was a debtor to her estate and could be proceeded against on that ground. Nevertheless, he was still the owner of the farm, since there is no evidence that he had legally transferred it to Caesennia (as the elder Fulcinius had transferred a farm to his wife in respect of her dowry).[21] It is true that Caesennia had been in possession of it throughout her lifetime, but, as Aebutius correctly pointed out (19), this was because she had part-usufruct for life of this property, as of all her late husband's property, by virtue of his will, irrespective of any change of ownership. (11).

Hence, if Caecina had brought either an *actio in rem* claiming the ownership of the property or an action *ex sponsione* for possession arising from the regular interdict for restitution (*unde vi*), it is doubtful whether he would have succeeded. Even had he been in possession of the farm physically, this possession would have been legally defective in face of an entry by the owner, since, in the absence of any legal agreement for the enjoyment of the farm, it would have come under one of the headings (*vi, clam, precario*), that disqualified possession from praetorian protection. An exemplary argument in the treatise *Ad Herennium*[22] shows an advocate pleading that his opponent's inability to contest ownership of a property shows that his right to possess was invalid and amounted to expulsion (*deicere*) by force.[23] It is not, therefore, surprising that Aebutius had originally acceded to the request for a *deductio moribus*. It may be asked why Caecina was trying to get the farm, rather than the repayment of the loan, if in fact this was due. It seems that it was attractive to combine the Fulcinian farm with the farm of Caesennia's

---

[20] Cf. *Caec.*16 *fundus addicitur Aebutio*.   [21] Cf. Nicosia, 1965, 55 with n. 131.

[22] *Ad Her.* 4. 40.

[23] Frier has pointed out (1985, 180) that, while later law disqualified those with a usufruct or tenancy as possessors from the point of view of the praetor, this was not true in 69 BC (*Caec.* 19). So Caesennia was a possessor. Caecina, however, had no status, unless he was in fact the owner. *Contra* Bethmann-Hollweg, 1864–6, ii. 840, who seems to have thought that Caecina had acquired *possessio* with his inheritance.

already in Caecina's possession (cf. 15). Moreover, the farm had probably increased in value since its purchase.

Aebutius' use of armed slaves to expel Caecina, if we follow Cicero's argument, changed the situation, because it enabled Caecina to have recourse to the interdict *de vi armata*. The question, much debated by scholars, is whether this was really so. In Cicero's day the standard interdict for restitution (*unde vi*) ran '[I order you] to restore him to that place from which you or your agent or your slaves have expelled him or his agent or his slaves by violence in this year, when he was in possession, in so far as he was possessing neither through violence nor by stealth nor on sufferance.'[24] According to this the interdict only applied to someone in possession.[25] Thus immediately after Caesennia's death, if we are right to assume that Aebutius had taken over the property, it was open for him to use it to protect his position against Caecina but not for Caecina to use it against Aebutius. What precisely the planned *deductio* involved is not clear. It would have helped Aebutius if Caecina had formally expelled him, as he then had obvious access to the interdict *unde vi*, as the possessor at the time. However, according to Cicero, Caecina was planning to be expelled.[26] This implied that he wanted to become (apparently) the possessor himself, a position which might have diminished Aebutius' legal advantage. If this was the case, it is not surprising that Aebutius resisted his move onto the farm.

If we follow Cicero's account,[27] the decree of the interdict *de vi armata* would have run: 'From where you or your slaves or your procurator by the violence of men organized in a gang or under arms (have expelled him) ...: it did not contain the clause 'while he was in possession'.[28] It cannot either, though Cicero does not mention this, have contained the clause *quod nec vi nec clam nec precario*... ('in so far as he possessed neither through violence nor by stealth nor on sufferance'), which was consequent on the possession clause. Hence, according to Cicero's main argument, the absence of the clause about possession in the interdict *de vi armata*, when contrasted with its presence in *unde vi*, showed that it was unnecessary for Caecina to prove

---

[24] 'Unde tu aut familia aut procurator tuus illum aut familiam aut procuratorem illius in hoc anno vi deiecisti, cum ille possideret, quod nec vi nec clam nec precario possideret, <eo illum restituas>' (*Tull.* 44).

[25] Possession was identical neither with ownership, nor with mere physical control, since it could be exercised from a distance, as by Caesennia: it was perhaps equivalent to having the capacity to control a piece of property or an object.

[26] *Caec.* 20: *de fundo Caecina moribus deduceretur.*

[27] 'Unde tu aut familia aut procurator tuus <vi> hominibus coactis armatisve <illum deiecisti>...' (see *Caec.* 23, 89–91, cf. *Fam.*15. 16. 3). See also *Tull.* 7 for the parallel phraseology of Lucullus' formula.

[28] 'Cum ille possideret', transposed in the speech as 'cum ego possiderem' (*Caec.* 91).

possession.²⁹ Some scholars have accepted the main argument as at least a plausible legal interpretation; others, in particular Nicosia and Stroh, have seen it as a mere rhetorical device, ingeniously adopted by Cicero. Nicosia in particular has proposed that the words *deicere* and *deiectio* implied in themselves expulsion from possession;³⁰ *cum ille possideret* was in the interdict *unde vi*, simply to introduce the clause *quod nec vi nec clam*...³¹

Frier, however, has more plausibly maintained that, irrespective of whether possession, or at least physical control, was assumed by the drafters of the interdict, there was a genuine argument from its text for Cicero.³² The drafting of the chapter in the *lex agraria* of 111 BC (l. 18), which provides an earlier formulation of the matter in the interdict *unde vi* of Cicero's time, runs 'si quis...]...ex possessione vi eiectus est, quod eius quei eiectus est possederit, quod neque vi neque clam neque precario possederit ab eo, quei eum ea possessione vi eiecerit'.³³ *Possessio* is stressed four times and thus clearly is not implicit in the verb for expulsion, while the parallel *quod* clauses apparently contain two equally important definitions, the second narrower than the first. It is hard to see in the later change of *eicere* into *deicere* a means of eliminating the need for further qualification about possession.³⁴ The omission of the qualifying clauses found in the interdict *unde vi* from that *de vi armata*, therefore, gave Cicero a loophole—and in fact perhaps one that was intended by the praetor who drafted the relevant edict. For it is possible that it was intended to discourage any use of armed force in property disputes, even when the man expelled had no claim to possession beyond his physical presence. That certainly is what is implied by the exception later cited by Cicero jokingly in a letter to his lawyer friend Trebatius, 'in so far as you did not arrive first with armed men'.³⁵

---

²⁹ At one point Cicero rather desperately tries to argue that Caecina had inherited possession from Caesennia, but only briefly (*Caec.* 94).

³⁰ Nicosia, 1965, 12 ff.

³¹ Note that even on Nicosia's view vitiated possession would have been protected against armed violence because of the absence of *quod nec vi nec clam*..., but this might have been understandable, if praetors had been eager to discourage the use of armed violence to settle disputes.

³² Frier, 1985, pp. xii, 53–4.

³³ '[If any of those whose] land is mentioned above, is ejected by violence from possession, in so far as he, who was ejected, was in possession of it, and he was in possession of it neither through violence nor by stealth nor on sufferance from the man who ejected him by violence from that possession': *JRLR* 180, 220–1; *RS* i. no. 2, p. 164. Frier, 1985, 178–9 rightly refers to this text, of which Nicosia failed to take proper account. Bethmann-Hollweg, 1864–6, ii. 839 believed that Cicero's account of *possessio* was correct.

³⁴ In *Ad Her.* 4. 40 *deiecisti* is used of a possessor having expelled an owner.

³⁵ 'Quod tu prior vi hominibus armatis non veneris' (*Fam.*7. 13. 2).

The Advocates' Strategies

The *recuperatores* evidently found it difficult to reach a decision, since there had been already two adjournments (*ampliationes*) and the balance of the advocates' arguments had probably changed over the three actions.

Piso had sought to wrongfoot Cicero, as Quinctius had done in the *pro Tullio*, by admitting the violence and claiming justification (24 ff.). He actually called distinguished witnesses, presumably local landowners, who admitted that they came with armed men. Two even admitted hearing Caecina's request for a *deductio moribus* (27).[36] He used P. Caesennius and the banker Sex. Clodius Phormio to testify to the purchase of the farm (27, cf. 17), thus claiming that Aebutius owned the property. Aebutius' possession was implicit in the story of the defence of his property and his recognition by his neighbours. When it appeared that Aebutius might yet be liable under the interdict because he used the violence of an armed gang, although not himself confronted with violence, Piso sought support in the letter of the interdict, arguing that Caecina could not have been *deiectus* from a property where he had never set foot in the first place and which he could not be said to possess (48 ff.).

Cicero knew that his client's claim to ownership was hard to substantiate in law. Hence his best hope was to shift his ground towards general equity, by suggesting that Caesennia had wanted Caecina to have the farm, that it had been hers *de facto* and therefore was now his (16, 19, 94–5). It is unlikely that he had made much headway with the judges on these lines. He further argued that by his mere use of violence Aebutius had disqualified himself from being a victor in law (32–47). As to the niceties of the wording of the interdict *de vi armata*, he sought to refute Piso by arguing that one could in fact be *deiectus* from a place that one had not reached (48–89), and in return devised a helpful argument of his own from the language of the interdict, based on the omission of any reference there to possession (90–5). This led back to his primary argument that it was wrong for Aebutius to get away with using a gang for violence. Aebutius had the better legal claim to the property; Caecina was technically in the right by a strict interpretation of the interdict and perhaps had a moral claim to the property. Judging by Cicero's pride in the speech and his later good relations with Caecina, his arguments eventually seem to have prevailed.

As Frier has persuasively argued, this speech is excellent evidence for the rise of jurisprudence in the late Roman Republic. True, the law is not yet a

---

[36] See Frier, 1985, 25–6 who notes that their names are Italic (for the most part indeed Roman), not Etruscan, but they do appear in records of local magistrates and in Latin funerary inscriptions from the region.

profession with schools and a hierarchy of practitioners, as it was to become in the Principate. Knowledge of the law, however, has become an expertise, which only relatively few people could master. These are not organized in some official structure but operate, as it were, from corner-shops. If you know the sort of help you need, you can find it.[37] At the time of the *pro Caecina* Cicero is one of these recognized practitioners and is not ashamed of it, for all his well-known later burlesque of lawyers in *pro Murena*.

A NOTE ON THE DATE OF PRO CAECINA

See Frier, 1985, 45, and 1983.

The praetor who decreed the interdict and the consequent action was P. Dolabella, later proconsul of Asia (Val. Max. 8. 1. *amb*. 2; Gell. 12. 7 (who wrongly calls him Cn.); *IGRR* iv. 422). Counsel for the respondent was C. Piso (*cos*. 67), at the time of the speech unlikely to be a consular and certainly not in office as praetor or consul. We can in addition rule out 66–5, when C. Piso was governor of Gaul. Hence a date before 67 is almost inevitable. This allows Cicero in *Orator* 102 to be dealing with speeches in chronological order, first *pro Caecina*, second *pro Lege Manilia* (*de Imperio Cn. Pompei*), third *pro Rabirio Perduellionis Reo*.

However, Dolabella cannot have become governor of Asia until the province was removed from L. Lucullus. Broughton, who has a high dating for Lucullus' arrival in the East to fight the third Mithridatic War (spring rather than autumn 74) and hence the chronology of the war, still dates the senate's action over this province to 69 (*MRR* ii. 109, 133, cf. iii. 121–2). It can hardly be in 70, when in any case it is probable that M. Mummius was urban praetor (*Verr*. 3. 123). Hence the earliest the senate could have opened the door for Dolabella to go out to Asia would have been after a praetorship in 69, so that he went out at the beginning of 68.

Stroh, 1975, 100 followed Nicosia, 1965, 147 ff., who argued for an earlier date, on the ground that *Caec*. 36, where Cicero enumerates praetorian duties, contains no direct reference to Piso's having held the office. However, this weak argument from silence cannot stand against the impossibility of Dolabella's going from his praetorship to govern Asia while Lucullus was its proconsul. Nicosia was forcing the evidence because he wanted to date *pro Caecina* to the same year as *pro Tullio* (71 BC) or earlier, as part of an argument that the interdict *de vi armata* did not change its formulation in this period.

---

[37] Cf. *Balb*. 45 on the property-experts (*praediatores*), Furius and (A.) Cascellius (cf. *RDGE* no. 23, l. 13; *Dig*.1. 2. 2. 45), and M. Tugio, the expert on water.

VII

Cicero and the Citadel of the Allies

THE COURT AND THE PROSECUTORS

THE *quaestio de repetundis* was the first permanent criminal tribunal (*quaestio perpetua*) to be established (149 BC) and in many ways the model for the later tribunals of this kind established during the Republic. Originally designed, as its name makes clear, to allow the pursuit and recovery of what had been illegally taken by Romans in authority, the court developed into a general tribunal for the prosecution of corrupt behaviour by magistrates in office and their subordinates and for the receipt of bribes by senatorial jurymen.[1] We are better informed about the workings of this tribunal than others of its kind thanks to the survival on bronze fragments of an important part of a statute reforming the *quaestio*, which, we must infer, formed part of the legislation of Gaius Gracchus in 123/2.[2] However, the nature of the court changed considerably during Cicero's lifetime. Cicero's speeches in the court and the comments of Asconius cast light on these changes and, in conjunction with the statute, are important evidence for the legal historian. These speeches also constitute almost a separate branch of Cicero's forensic activity with its own special problems to overcome and frequently with an accompanying political agenda. Cicero's one prosecution, that of Verres, is perhaps studied more now as a political contest than a trial, but there is still value to be derived from examining it as forensic process. It may appear frustrating that the bulk of the texts, the second action, do not represent speeches actually delivered in court. However, apart from being a mine of historical information, they lead to conclusions about Cicero's forensic strategy and performance throughout the trial, many of which are of general application to prosecutions in this court.

Under the earliest statute *de repetundis*, the *lex Calpurnia* of 149, Roman patrons must have prosecuted on behalf of non-Roman plaintiffs.[3] The

---

[1] *JRLR* 10–29; Lintott, 1981; Venturini, 1979.
[2] See the state of the question summaries in *JRLR* 166–9, *RS* i, 51–2.
[3] *JRLR* 14–16; Lintott, 1981, 172–5; Serrao, 1956; Venturini, 1969, 79 ff. A dissenting voice is that of Richardson, 1987, who believes that the law only permitted Romans to prosecute on their own behalf.

Gracchan statute transferred the initiative to the wronged allies themselves, who could, however, be granted a Roman *patronus* to assist them, if they so desired.[4] Probably with the law of Servilius Caepio of 106, the procedure was changed so that a jury was asked to select a prosecutor from among those who presented themselves, and it seems that subsequently *de facto*, but not *de iure*, cases tended to be entrusted to Roman citizens.[5] Before the Gracchan statute prosecutors had been eminent men acting as patrons for the injured parties (*Div. Caec.* 69); after Caepio's *lex Servilia* the element of patronage of the allies was still present on occasion (*Div. Caec.* 64, 67), but, Cicero could claim, accusation was normally a matter for young nobles or professional accusers (*quadruplatores*): this assertion forms part of a jibe at Hortensius, who is said to fear that his domination of the courts in general would be threatened if accusing passed to courageous and experienced men.[6] Furthermore, Cicero implies that it was thought extraordinary for him to be prosecuting Verres, when he was not moved by some personal feud or injury (*2Verr.* 3. 6): indeed he was provoking a feud with the nobility by his action (*2Verr.* 5. 180–2). His answers to these criticisms are, first, that he was reviving the ancient tradition of patronage of the friends and allies of the Roman people (*2Verr.* 1. 15), secondly, that he was an enemy of an enemy of the Roman people (*2Verr.* 3. 7), and, thirdly, that the nobility was in any case hostile to a hard-working new man (*2Verr.* 5. 181–2). Once he had performed his duty to the Sicilians and the Roman people over Verres in one court or another, he planned to cease accusing bad men and turn to defending good men (*2Verr.* 5. 183, 189).

Cicero suggested in the speech with which he claimed the right to prosecute Verres (*Divinatio in Caecilium*) that it was beyond doubt that the whole statute concerning the recovery of money (*de pecuniis repetundis*) was established for the sake of the allies: when money was seized from Roman citizens, this was generally pursued by civil action and private law (17–18). This somewhat misrepresents the legal position. It is true that a simplified private law action was available in the Gracchan statute and we know of one private action in the seventies BC,[7] but this was not apparently confined to Roman citizen prosecutors. In fact even in the Gracchan statute, where prosecution was a matter for the injured parties or their delegated

---

[4] *Lex rep.* (*RS* i, no. 1) 9–12; cf. 19, showing that the person suing for the money performed *nominis delatio*, 76 ff. on potential rewards.

[5] *JRLR* 28; Lintott, 1980. *Contra* Venturini, 1979, 422, who believes in a legal restriction.

[6] *Div. Caec.* 24; Cicero as an ex-quaestor and, by the time of the trial itself, aedile elect, had about ten years' more experience than the young men to whom he refers.

[7] *Lex rep.* 7–8; Asc. 84 C.

representatives, it appears that Roman citizens could prosecute under the main provisions of the law.[8] In the accusation of Verres the complaints of Roman citizens in Sicily and elsewhere formed an important part of the prosecution case. Nevertheless, even if his premiss is dubious, Cicero's conclusion that 'this is the statute for the allies, this is the law of foreign nations, they have this as a citadel'—a point reiterated in the later *Verrine* speeches[9]—remains true. The court was the chief countervailing force against the all-powerful Roman magistrate and his companions in the military field and provincial government.[10]

Cicero can therefore present his prosecution of Verres in a number of ways that bring him glory and thus mitigate the enmities he is creating for himself. Nor is this presentation misleading about the actual advantages that were accruing to him. In the first place he could display patronage to the people of Sicily, the one province in which, as quaestor in 75 BC, he had exercised public authority.[11] This was not something that was easily available to a new man with no inherited *clientelae*, who chose to eschew military and provincial service in favour of a career in the forum. He could even extend this patronage by incorporating in the charges offences committed by Verres earlier in the provinces of Asia and Cilicia (*2Verr.* 1. 44–102). Secondly, he could exploit the fact that some of Verres' offences were against Roman citizens. In particular the flogging and execution without trial of men who claimed the privileges of Roman citizenship could be denounced as offences against the *provocatio* laws and the liberty of the Roman people.[12] Even Verres' conduct as urban praetor could be brought in to the indictment and described as 'arrogance and cruelty against the Roman *plebs*' (*2Verr.* 1. 122). Cicero could thus from time to time adopt a *popularis* stance to reinforce his self-portrayal as a new man fighting against a conspiracy of the nobility (*2Verr.* 5. 180–2). Finally, this public position could add lustre to Cicero's frankly confessed personal rivalry with Hortensius: his attempt to defeat Hortensius in this court was not merely a professional contest but a fight against the corruption rife among Hortensius and his like.[13]

---

[8] This is implied in *lex. rep.* 22, 76; l. 87 is best interpreted as providing rewards for Roman citizen prosecutors, as does the later statute partially preserved on the *fragmentum Tarentinum* (*RS* i. no. 8, ll. 7–12).

[9] *Div. Caec.* 18; cf. *2Verr.* 2. 15, 3. 218, 4. 17.

[10] The court of course by now also covered matters that allies could not pursue themselves, such as the bribery of senatorial jurymen.

[11] This patronage was alluded to by Clodius in 61 (*Att.* 1. 19. 5) and still asserted by Cicero in 44 (*Att.* 14. 12. 1).

[12] *2Verr.* 1. 13–14; 5. 69–74; 140–73. esp. 163.

[13] *Div. Caec.* 24; *1Verr.* 33; *2Verr.* 5. 174–7; cf. *1Verr.* 18–19, 25.

THE MOUNTING OF THE PROSECUTION

Cicero's involvement in the opposition to Verres began before the latter left his governorship. In 72 BC Sthenius of Thermae, a former guest-friend of Verres, became his enemy when he resisted the removal of bronze statues from his city and was consequently indicted at Verres' instigation for the corruption of public documents at Thermae. Verres decided to judge the case himself and Sthenius fled to Rome. The case was now made capital by Verres; the legitimacy of Sthenius' being tried in his absence was discussed in the senate, but in the end he was condemned, still absent, by Verres on 1 December of that year. His case was taken up by Lollius Palicanus, one of the tribunes who entered office on 10 December 72. Subsequently, probably early in 71, Cicero himself successfully defended Sthenius before this college of tribunes, who had to decide whether to apply to Sthenius their edict forbidding anyone condemned on a capital charge to reside in Rome.[14] Sthenius was to be one of Cicero's chief assistants from the province (*2Verr.* 2. 83) and it is clear that from this time onwards the orator was well briefed on Verres' offences.

Among Sthenius' former guests were Pompey and C. Marcellus, praetor in 80 BC and afterwards governor of Sicily.[15] Cicero never ascribes any direct interest in the case to Pompey and, whatever the great man's concern for his Sicilian clients—such as Sex. Pompeius Chlorus and Cn. Pompeius Theodorus (*2Verr.* 2. 23, 102)—he may not have wanted to involve himself openly in the controversy over Verres. It was different with the Claudii Marcelli, traditional patrons of Sicily. In the *Divinatio in Caecilium* Cicero appeals to C. Marcellus and Cn. Cornelius Lentulus Marcellinus as witnesses to the pressure brought to bear on him by the injured Sicilians—the former was actually on the jury for the *divinatio*, the latter is claimed to be present (13–14). In the published second action of the main trial C. Marcellus is again invoked as a juror and Cicero appeals to him about the appropriate procedure for governors of the province (4. 90, 3. 42, 212). As for Lentulus Marcellinus, he was a witness for Cicero in the first action (*2Verr.* 2. 103). The elder M. Marcellus (*aed.* 91) had himself been treated unjustly by Verres as urban praetor in 74, but was apparently not available as a witness. By contrast, Verres had sought to involve in his defence about a certain charge the young M. Marcellus

---

[14] *2Verr.* 2. 86–101; Cicero's defence 100. J. W. Crawford, 1984, no. 6, p. 49 dates the speech to 72 without argument. Obviously, the matter was urgent for Sthenius, but there was not much time for the college of tribunes to be brought together for a hearing in the last 20 days of December, some of which were unavailable through festivals.

[15] *2Verr.* 2. 110; also C. Marius and L. Cornelius Sisenna.

Aeserninus—described by Cicero as 'a young man born to that (high) station, a patron of Sicily'—but the attempt had been futile.[16]

We have no reason to reject Cicero's picture of himself as the preferred accuser of Verres for a number of Sicilians and their patrons, one who had been sought after for some time before proceedings actually started.[17] This could not take place until Verres' return to Rome. The chronology of the early stages of the accusation cannot be fixed with complete precision, but, in the light of Cicero's comments on the chronology of subsequent procedure (see below), the first move can hardly be later than the middle of January 70 BC, the year when Pompey and Marcus Crassus had their first consulships and the praetor Manius Acilius Glabrio had been allotted the presidency of the *quaestio de repetundis* (*Verr.* 1. 4, 51).

Under the procedure laid down in the Gracchan law an accuser used to proceed immediately to formal denunciation (*nominis delatio*), whereupon, if the charge was accepted, he was offered a *patronus*, if he wished, and facilities to collect evidence in Italy. It seems to have been assumed that any witnesses from abroad had already arrived. Meanwhile, a process was set in motion for selecting the jury, that involved a delay of over 70 days.[18] By the nineties BC a new form of procedure had been introduced that was still in force in the post-Sullan period. The prosecutor was selected by *divinatio*. This meant that the summons (*postulare*) of the accused by an accuser was in a sense provisional, since he might not in fact be assigned the task of prosecution. Moreover, the, usually Roman, accuser was afforded, once selected, an opportunity to conduct an *inquisitio*, that is an investigatory tour to collect evidence, abroad as well as in Italy.[19]

Cicero had a rival—Q. Caecilius Niger, a former quaestor of Verres', probably at Lilybaeum. He had been educated in Sicily and is alleged by Plutarch to have been a freedman and a Judaizer.[20] He claimed to have been treated unjustly by Verres, but his quaestorship had involved a degree of cooperation with the governor and complicity in his acts, which provided Cicero with a useful argument against his being permitted to accuse.[21] Cicero could also argue that there was a quasi-parental connection between a governor and his quaestor, which made such an accusation an impiety: former quaestors had tried to accuse their governors but their claims had been

---

[16] *2Verr.* 1. 135, 143, 153; contrast 4. 91.
[17] The scepticism of Stroh, 1975, 181 ff. goes too far.
[18] *Lex rep.* 9–12, 19–24, 31.
[19] Cic. *Scaur.* 23 ff; Asc. 19 C, cf. *JRLR* 28–9.
[20] *Div. Caec.* 4, 39, 56; Plut. *Cic.* 7. 6. Perhaps a *libertinus* (of freedman descent), rather than a manumitted *libertus*.
[21] *Div. Caec.* 29 ff.; cf. *2Verr.* 1. 15.

rejected.[22] In fact we do not know of a case where a quaestor obtained the right to prosecute his governor under the Republic. The first, ill-omened, example we have is that of Granius Marcellus by Caepio Crispinus under Tiberius.[23]

If we combine in a calculation first Cicero's statement that the trial had been postponed for three months, secondly the period allotted for his *inquisitio* (*2Verr.* 1. 30), and thirdly the actual trial date, 5 August (*Verr.* 1. 31), the *divinatio* should have been over by the beginning of February. February was traditionally the climax of the period in which foreign embassies petitioned the senate, and some of the communities who later supported Cicero at the trial may have already sent delegations to Rome.[24] After success in the *divinatio* Cicero denounced Verres and asked for a period of 110 days for *inquisitio* (*2Verr.* 1. 30). At about the same time another prosecutor going to Achaea was awarded 108 days and was placed higher in the order of cases.

Cicero claims to have spent in fact only 50 days on his tour of Sicily (*Verr.* 1. 6), where he was supported by his cousin Lucius, probably his *subscriptor*, assistant accuser.[25] He also relates that he had made a hasty and dangerous return journey from Vibo Valentia up the toe of Italy to Velia, through the midst of the pirates (*2Verr.* 2. 99). Vibo was not a necessary stopping-place on his route back to Rome, but he must have gone there to collect evidence about P. Gavius of Consa, whom Verres executed (*2Verr.* 5. 158 ff.). The tour of Sicily and southern Italy provided him with a mass of documentary evidence and a great number of witnesses. Some of these were not used in the first action in August but deliberately deferred. In particular he was supported by embassies from most of Sicily and from Vibo, Consa, and Regium in Italy (see below). Cicero also seems to have investigated at least one house of Verres' in Italy in search of the looted works of art and in order to collect witness statements. He claimed that he saw the pictures and statues taken from the Greek cities of the Aegean and Asia Minor in Verres' porticoes and in his ornamental grove: after the first part of the trial all but two were no longer there, but he planned to use the testimony of Verres' household about them.[26]

---

[22] *Div. Caec.* 60–3; impiety 62; precedents 63; on the dates of these precedents (and a problem of nomenclature) see Badian, 1984*a*.

[23] Tac. *Ann.* 1. 74. See Thompson, 1962, 339–55 for an investigation of this quasi-parental relationship.

[24] By a later *lex Gabinia* the senate's agenda in February was confined to hearing embassies until these had all been sent home (*Fam.* 1. 4. 1; *QF* 2. 12. 3).

[25] *2Verr.* 4. 145; PsAsc. 213 St.

[26] *2Verr.* 1. 50–1. See *Flacc.* 21 for the phrase *obsignandi gratia* referring to witness statements (the seals of the jury on these were required by the later *lex Iulia*); for the collection of evidence in Italy see *lex rep.* 31.

If we allow time for Cicero's journeys to and from Sicily, including the visit to Vibo, and for his pursuit of evidence in the neighbourhood of Rome from Verres' house and from Romans wronged by Verres as urban praetor in 74, then the total time he spent collecting evidence will not have been so far short of the 110 days he was granted. He would not have been ready to proceed to jury selection before early May—that is, assuming his Sicilian witnesses had arrived—and, had he then prosecuted, the trial would have coincided with the last two months of his candidature for the aedileship, which, as he admits, in the event considerably distracted him from preparing the case (*Verr.* 1. 24). The problems he had in the management of the prosecution to a great extent resulted from the complexity of the case and his own pursuit of a magistracy.

Before Cicero's election as aedile in late July, probably earlier that month, the jury was selected.[27] Jury-panels under Sulla's *lex Cornelia* were no longer created according to the prescriptions of the Gracchan law, where the prosecutor, after being informed of any members of the (non-senatorial) album who were connected by the defendant with him, offered a hundred names of those unconnected by kinship or association with himself, which were in turn reduced to fifty by the defendant. The jurors now were allotted from the album, which consisted entirely of senators, and then subject to a process of rejection, probably alternately between prosecution and defence.[28] Cicero took the opportunity to make forensic capital out of this process by alluding to Verres' bribery and suggesting that foreign embassies should go to the senate requesting the repeal of the *lex de repetundis*, since then Roman magistrates would only take what they needed for themselves and their families: at present they extorted extra money to pay their defence counsel and legal advisers and to bribe the presiding praetor and the jury.[29]

We have the names of a number of the jury: Q. Manlius, Q. Cornificius, P. Sulpicius, M. Crepereius, L. Cassius, Cn. Tremellius, M. Metellus (*Verr.* 1. 30); M. Lucretius (*2Verr.* 1. 18); C. Marcellus (*2Verr.* 4. 90); and the consulars, Q. Lutatius Catulus (*2Verr.* 4. 69) and P. Servilius Isauricus (*2Verr.* 4. 82). An almost certain addition, although the text may be thought ambiguous, is L. Octavius Balbus.[30] Among the names of the rejected are: P. Galba; Sex.

---

[27] *2Verr.* 1. 18–19; cf. *1Verr.* 29–31.

[28] See esp. *1Verr.* 10, 16, 41; *2Verr.* 1. 17 ff. On procedure under the Gracchan law see *lex rep.* 19–27.

[29] *Verr.* 1. 41; cf. 40, where he rehearses an alleged dictum of Verres that he had allocated the profits of one year for himself, one for his *patroni* and defence counsel, and the third, most profitable year for the jury.

[30] *2Verr.* 2. 31. Here Balbus is referred to as a *iudex*, a learned and high-principled one, in a context where he is being also imagined as the judge appointed under one of Verres' tendentious formulae. Since the two other men named in the legal formula, Q. Catulus and P. Servilius, are also on the trial-jury, Cicero is clearly using three members of the jury as his examples.

Peducaeus, Q. Considius, Q. Iunius, P. Cervius, and the consular C. Cassius Longinus.[31] Cicero's statement that almost the whole jury would be changed the following year though the enforced resignation of seven members is an obvious exaggeration (*Verr.* 1. 30), but it must be allowed vestigial plausibility. It is possible that the final panel contained no more than the twelve names we know and it is unlikely to have exceeded fifteen members. The jurors originally allotted to the panel were no less than eighteen and may have numbered considerably more.[32]

STRATEGY AND TIMING

The trial proper began on 5 *Sextilis* (August) at the eighth hour—with most of that day already lost. As Cicero explains, there were then ten clear days before Pompey's votive games on 16 August, which effectively postponed further proceedings till 2 September. The *ludi Romani* followed, from 4 to 19 September. Verres, Cicero claims, did not expect to have to reply to the charge until after these games, almost forty days from the start of the trial.[33] After 19 September there were thirty-five days available (which, according to Cicero, Verres would have liked to eliminate) before the *ludi victoriae Sullae* on 26 October. These constituted the chief period remaining for the trial before the end of the year, since the *ludi victoriae Sullae* ended on 1 November and the *ludi plebeii* then followed from the 4th to the 17th.[34]

McDermott, 1977, correctly counts the names mentioned in the text but develops a strained argument from a comparison with the trial of Oppianicus—where the voting jury numbered 32 (*Clu.* 74)—to the effect that a *repetundae* trial required a greater number of jurors because of the greater *dignitas* of the defendants—he opts eventually for 50. I would suggest that in the thinking of Sulla a senator would be better tried by a small jury of high calibre (including former curule magistrates) than by a large jury dominated by *parvi senatores*.

[31] *2Verr.* 1. 18, 5. 114, 3. 97. Cicero talks of a restriction of rejection to three potential jurors (presumably applied to both sides) under the *leges Corneliae* (ibid. 2. 77), but in the context this applies only to trials of non-senators. Senators, it is implied, were allowed more.

[32] For the reduction by rejection of a panel of *recuperatores* from 45 to 15 see *lex prov. praet.* (*RS* i, no. 12), Cnidos V, 6–22.

[33] *1Verr.* 31—the 'almost 40 days' must be counted from 16 Aug. onwards. Under the Republic *Sextilis* (and September) had 29 days. I have counted the fifteen days eliminated by Pompey's games inclusively from the 16th.

[34] *2Verr.* 2. 130; *1Verr.* 31. In *2Verr.* 2. 130 I read *XXXV*, the reading of the fragments of the vetus Cluniacensis, which is an approximately accurate rendering of the time available. *XXXXV* or *XLV* in other MSS seems to be a repetition of the number of days in the extended intercalary month at Cephaloedium, mentioned in the previous sentence. There is no point in retaining this reading as a deliberate echo by Cicero as he would then be echoing an increase in time, not a subtraction.

Cicero accelerated the trial by using a brief speech in the first action and then calling his witnesses (*Verr.* 1. 55; *2Verr.* 1. 25). After three days of witnesses, he later alleged, their cumulative effect was so overwhelming that Verres effected an adjournment by pleading illness—probably a form of *intertium* adjournment to the third day, that is the day after next, since otherwise the first action would not have finished before Pompey's games.[35] We are in fact told elsewhere that the first part of the trial before the compulsory adjournment (*comperendinatio*) was over in nine days (*2Verr.* 1. 156).

Hortensius contributed to the speed of the process by refraining for the most part from questioning Cicero's witnesses (*2Verr.* 1. 71, 3. 41). We hear of only a few interventions. Hortensius interrupted Tettius' evidence about the trial of Philodamus of Lampsacus, pointing out that Philodamus and his son had been condemned; he also complained about Cicero's production of the boy Iunius in court during the evidence of his uncle and guardian M. Iunius: it was directed merely towards creating odium for Verres (*2Verr.* 1. 71, 151). In addition there was an exchange between the orators recorded by Quintilian (6. 3. 98): while Cicero was examining a witness, Hortensius said to him, 'I do not understand these riddles'; 'you should do', Cicero retorted, 'as you have a Sphinx at home' (a bronze Sphinx, a present from Verres). However, in general there is no reason to disbelieve Cicero that Hortensius on the whole gave his opponent's witnesses a clear run. Moreover, if he did not on the whole cross-examine, as Cicero alleges, it is hard to see how he could have argued at length in an *altercatio* (Ch. 2 with n. 35). He did, nevertheless, have witnesses of his own, such as the embassy from Messana (*2Verr.* 5. 47, cf. 4. 15), and he did deliver at the beginning of the trial an oration: a published version of Hortensius' speech for Verres was still available in Quintilian's time.[36]

After the first action Verres does not seem to have abandoned the case immediately. Cicero in fact portrays him as still in Rome, *comperendinatus*, that is with an adjourned trial hanging over him, on the morning of the circus day of the *ludi Romani*—the last day (19 September). He is said to have showed excessive interest in the silver displayed by his friend, the historian Sisenna, on that occasion.[37] Although the interpretation of the event may be

---

[35] *2Verr.* 1. 20; cf. *lex Irnitana* (González, 1986), chs. 90–2; cf. *TPSulp.* 32–3; Camodeca, 1999, i. 100–2 with earlier bibliography; Metzger, 1997, 9 ff.; Rodger, 1996; Wolff, 1997. Alexander, 1976, 47 also interprets Cicero to mean a one-day interval.

[36] Quint. 10. 1. 23. Cf. Alexander, 1976. Gelzer, 1962–4, ii, 169 thought his speech might have held during the *litis aestimatio*, but we know nothing of formal speeches by advocates being held on this occasion. Note that Quintilian 5. 7. 6 advised against cross-examining solid witnesses and Cicero himself admitted the dangers of cross-examination (*Font.* 22).

[37] *2Verr.* 4. 33; cf. *2Verr.* 1. 20 for Verres being *comperendinatus* during 'these intervening days of games'. The chronology is set out correctly by Gelzer, 1962–4, ii, 168–70; cf. Alexander, 1976,

Cicero's and only Cicero's, it is hard to imagine Cicero gratuitously inventing Verres' presence at Sisenna's home on that day. We must conclude that it only became clear that Verres had abandoned the case when the trial was due to restart at some point after 19 September.[38] Even in Verres' absence, it was not all over. The second action would have been a formality, but it would still have been necessary for the praetor presiding to pronounce a verdict of 'guilty', probably after consulting the jury. Moreover, the third part of the trial, the *litis aestimatio*, would still have been required to assess the damages due to the various plaintiffs.[39] The large number of these would have necessitated a long and complex process and it is easy to imagine the *litis aestimatio* lasting as many days as the first action.

The trial took place under Sulla's *lex Cornelia* before a senatorial jury, but an important part of the background was the controversy over the staffing of the courts. In the first action Cicero alludes to this more than once. He portrays the aristocracy saying to each other 'Verres will be acquitted, but we shall lose control of the courts because of his acquittal' (*Verr.* 1. 20), He then threatens to conduct prosecutions for judicial bribery in his aedileship, in which he will denounce the corruption of the senatorial courts in the ten years since Sulla's judicial laws and compare this unfavourably with the previous near-fifty-year reign of equestrian jurors (*Verr.* 1. 36–40). He refers both to a speech by Q. Catulus, in which the latter ascribed the desire for the restoration of tribunician powers to the senate's mismanagement of the courts, and to a *contio* by Pompey about the same subject, where he denounced the plundering of the provinces and judicial corruption (*Verr.* 1. 44–5). This culminates in an appeal to the jury to erase the blot on the reputation of senatorial juries by condemning Verres (*Verr.* 1. 46–9) and an appeal to Glabrio to remember his father's law and the stern (equestrian) jurors of that era (*Verr.* 1. 51–2).

We know that in 70 the basis for selecting juries was changed by a *lex Aurelia* of L. Cotta (Asc. 17 C). In the first *Verrine* this is simply on the horizon. In Cicero's imaginary scene-setting for the second action the law is

---

51–2. The account of Frazell, 2004, 130–3 is confusing in appearing to argue that only the prosecution case was heard before the *comperendinatio* (this was not the purpose of the institution), nor does he notice that Cicero claimed ample precedent for his procedure.

[38] His departure into exile is noted but not dated in the scholia to the speeches, PsAsc. 205, 223 St. See Gelzer 1962–4, ii. 168 n. 124 for a refutation of the view that the second action actually took place.

[39] Cf. *lex rep.* 29 for the pursuit of charges when a man who had gone into exile or (probably) died before the end of a trial. Mommsen, followed by Lintott in *JRLR* ad loc., took the fragmentary text ('ea]m rem ab eis item quaerito[...]') to refer to the pursuit of money from connections of the accused; *RS* i, no. 1, ad loc. prefers investigation of the matter with the jury. Both would have in fact been necessary.

described as not promulgated at the time of the first action, unmentioned during the period when it was thought that Verres would abandon the case, and only finally promulgated, when Verres seemed to recover strength.(*2Verr.* 2. 174–5; 5. 177–8) It does of course suit Cicero to present the *lex Aurelia* as called into being by Verres ('a law which was not promulgated by the man under whose name you see it published, but by this defendant'), but the plausibility of the presentation depends on the timing of the law being accurately portrayed. We should conclude that it was promulgated close to the end of the *ludi Romani* and discussed and voted on in the period when Verres was condemned in his absence and the *litis aestimatio* took place, that is, the thirty-five days before the games of Sulla's victory on 26 October. Cicero elsewhere pictures the praetor (Cotta) holding *contiones* every day during what would have been the period of the second action, and claiming that public affairs at Rome could only remain on their feet, if the courts were returned to the equestrian order (*2Verr.* 3. 223).[40] Cicero, until recently an equestrian himself, can show admiration for the jurymen of former times, who may soon be returning, but simultaneously urge the current senatorial jurymen to free their own order, now his, from the odium which it has been suffering by condemning Verres (*Verr.* 1. 43).

TACTICS

The first *Verrine* is not so much a prosecution speech as an extended prooemium. The orator seeks to win sympathy for himself in the battle he is having with the money of Verres (*Verr.* 1. 3–17, 22–3) and the authority of Hortensius and the Metelli (*Verr.* 1. 18–37), and to secure in advance the support of both jury and presiding magistrate. The meat of the action was to be in the evidence. However, this must have been a feature of most prosecutions *de repetundis*, whose function was to bring forward the pleas of the plaintiffs and whose strength lay more in the clear delineation of the crimes committed than in any refined argument about whether the actions constituted a crime in law. One important function of the *quaestio* was to give the provincials their day in

---

[40] The importance of the trial of Verres as motivation for the *lex Aurelia* has been firmly denied by T. N. Mitchell, 1979, 107–49; cf. Butler, 2002, 78–9. Whatever view one takes of the seriousness of senatorial corruption—and it is clear that it was serious enough to be admitted by a loyal supporter of Sulla such as Catulus—the bill was hardly a reaction to Verres' trial, which was up to a point a vindication of a senatorial jury, and the probability is that it was planned some time in advance. It needed to be passed by the end of October to give time for the new jury panels to be drawn up for the following year. This to some extent would have been contingent on the progress of the censors of 70 in classifying *equites* and *tribuni aerarii*.

court and so provide a safety-valve for provincial indignation over what were inevitably numerous grievances. As for Cicero, he needed to make enough of his evidence stick as to make acquittal impossible. Condemnation was not itemized under particular counts in a *quaestio* under the Republic: the defendant was either guilty under the law or not. Once Verres was condemned, the validity of the particular charges could be re-examined in the *litis aestimatio*.

Cicero says in his introductory speech that his policy of moving immediately to his witnesses is not a new one, but one used by many who were now leaders in the community (*Verr.* 1. 55). Such people, now in their forties or older, would have prosecuted as young men before the Social War. It is likely that the impetus towards this practice was provided by Glaucia's introduction of *comperendinatio* shortly before 100 BC.[41] With the certainty of an other action to follow, in which he could display his oratorical skills, a prosecutor might well judge it best to get the bulk of his evidence heard first and reserve a long oration until he had discovered the line of defence that would be pursued against it.

Thanks to the evidence from the texts of the second action we are well informed about Cicero's witnesses. Moreover, Cicero usually indicates whether these had been already heard in the first action or were yet to be called in the second action, should it occur (they might well have also a part to play in the *litis aestimatio*). The sheer number of these was formidable. Thirty-two Roman citizens can be counted (including one anonymous Roman *eques* from Messana and the wife and mother of the dead quaestor C. Malleolus).[42] Of these, twenty-six certainly gave evidence in the first action, while three were to give evidence in the second and there are a further three men who probably either gave evidence or were about to give it.[43] At least

---

[41] *2Verr.* 1. 26. On the dispute over the precise date see Lintott, 1981, 189; Gruen, 1968, 85 ff.; Sumner, 1973, 101.

[42] Butler, 2002, 27 ff. correctly stresses the importance of written testimony but misguidedly seems to minimize the amount of oral testimony actually given in court. In the second *Actio* it is not calls for new testimony that are especially relevant but references to testimony given earlier in the first *Actio*.

[43] *2Verr.* 1. 14, 71, 93, 139, 151; 2. 23, 69, 80, 102–3, 119; 3. 36–7, 61, 97, 148, 166–7; 4. 62, 70; 5. 15, 73–4, 147, 154–6, 158, 163, 165. I take it that when Cicero refers in the second action to someone 'having spoken' this is evidence that the person concerned was actually a witness, as are references to someone as a past or future *testis*. When he claims that someone 'says' in the present tense, this may be simply a reference to written testimony that may or may not be supported in person in court. On this basis we find that L. Suettius, L. Flavius, M. Annius, C. Matrinius, P. Tettius, P. Titius, M. Iunius, L. Domitius (Ahenobarbus), L. Caecilius, L. (Aelius) Ligus, T. Manilius, L. (Fufius) Calenus, M. (Terentius Varro) Lucullus, Q. Minucius, Sex. Pompeius Chlorus, Cn. Pompeius Theodorus, Cn. Cornelius Lentulus Marcellinus, Q. Varius, C. Licinius Sacerdos, Cn. Sertius, M. Modius, M. Lollius (on behalf of his infirm father Q. Lollius), C. Numitorius, the mother and grandmother of the boy Malleolus and an

thirteen embassies gave evidence for the prosecution in the first action, eleven from Sicily and two from Italy. Seventeen more were to follow in the second action.⁴⁴ Fifteen individual *peregrini* (non-Romans) are named, and one mentioned anonymously, who certainly spoke in Cicero's interest in the first action; three more are attested as being ready to speak in the second action. In addition three named citizens from Centuripae are likely to have spoken with their embassy in the first action.⁴⁵ We should also allow for a contribution from Sthenius of Thermae, who was seeking to overturn his condemnation and assisting Cicero with the case (*2Verr.* 2. 83, 5. 128), but whose own evidence is not specifically mentioned by Cicero.

Of the named non-Roman witnesses who spoke for Cicero in the first action, eleven can be associated with embassies who appeared then; Posides Macro from Soluntium spoke, although the Soluntine embassy was reserved for the second action (*2Verr.* 2. 102, 3. 103); Diodorus of Melita spoke on his own behalf (*2Verr.* 4.38); Heius of Messana was persuaded to give evidence against Verres, although the Mamertine embassy had officially been sent to support him (*2Verr.* 2. 13, 5. 47).⁴⁶ There were also documents other than witness-statements, taken from the records of an earlier prosecution, from the tax-collectors (*publicani*), and from various Greek cities. Cicero imagines these being read during his speech in the second action.⁴⁷ He never refers there to the previous recitation of documents in the first action, but it is possible that some of these needed to be read to elucidate the evidence of witnesses.

---

anonymous *eques* from Messana spoke in the first action. C. Cassius Longinus, P. Vettius Chilo, and P. Granius were expected to speak in the second action. To these we may add M. and P. Cottius and Q. Lucceius who also are described as *testes* (*2Verr.* 5. 165). As for C. (Visellius) Varro (*2Verr.* 1. 71) and Cn. Cornelius Lentulus Clodianus, censor in 70, (*2Verr.* 5. 15) it seems to me that *dicat/dicit* leaves it uncertain whether they appeared in court. Alexander, 2002, 26–8; cf. his app. 2, 253–62, has rightly argued that we should take seriously Cicero's representation of his witnesses and documents, most of which reflects what actually happened in the first *actio*. Our criteria for deciding precisely who appeared and when differ somewhat.

⁴⁴ *2Verr.* 2. 120, 123, 128, 156; 3. 103, 120; 4. 84, 91, 113–14; 5. 108, 158, 164.

⁴⁵ First action: Dio of Halaesa (2. 23–4); Heraclius of Centuripae (2. 66); Posides Macro of Soluntium (2. 102); Artemon, Andron, and Nympho of Centuripae (2. 156; 3. 53, 114); Eubulidas Grospus of Centuripae (3. 56; 5. 128); Apollodorus Pyragrus of Agyrium (3. 74); Mnesistratus of Leontini (3. 109); Heius of Messana (4. 15; 5. 47); Phylarchus of Centuripae (4. 29, 50); Diodorus of Melita (4. 38); Poleas and Demetrius the gymnasiarch of Tyndaris (4. 92); Theodorus, Numerius, and Nicasio of Henna (4. 113); an anonymous Syracusan (4. 125); Onasius of Segesta (5. 120). Second action: Sositheus of Entella (3. 200), about to give testimony; Phylarchus of Haluntium and Phalacrus of Centuripae (5. 122), said to be present and speaking in the present, not past tense.

⁴⁶ Heraclius of Syracuse gave written testimony against Verres, allegedly because he had been prevented from obeying Cicero's summons, although the city council had under pressure given written testimony for Verres (*2Verr.* 2. 15, 65; 4. 125; 141–4).

⁴⁷ *2Verr.* 1. 96, 99; 2. 182–3; 3. 83, 85, 87, 89, 99–100; 4. 92, 140; 5. 148, 164, cf. 5. 10.

All the non-Roman witnesses gave evidence about injuries to themselves or their own communities. As for the Romans, two testified to Verres' early misconduct at Lampsacus (*2 Verr.* 1. 71), two about the estate of Malleolus (*2 Verr.* 1. 93), three about Verres' treatment of the ward Iunius during his praetorship (*2 Verr.* 1. 139, 151), the rest about Verres' conduct in Sicily. Many of these were Roman citizens resident in Sicily. However, we also find two consular witnesses, C. Cassius Longinus, M. Terentius Varro Lucullus, and one who submitted evidence, Cn. Cornelius Lentulus Clodianus, currently censor, as well as the former praetor and governor of Sicily, C. Licinius Sacerdos.[48] The young aristocracy were represented by L. Domitius Ahenobarbus and one of the patrons of Sicily, Cn. Cornelius Lentulus Marcellinus (*2 Verr.* 1. 139, 2. 103).

Any attempt to gauge the time occupied by Cicero's witnesses must be speculative. We do not necessarily know all of them. If the non-Roman witnesses knew little Latin, no more might be expected of them than to give brief verbal confirmation to previously provided written testimony. However, given the richness of the available resources and the powerful Roman influence in Sicily, it is likely that Cicero could deliberately choose witnesses who spoke Latin effectively. For each Roman witness a minimum average of half an hour seems reasonable, hence a minimum of thirteen hours in the first action. Where witnesses formed part of an embassy, it is perhaps better to calculate from the time occupied by that group. Here a minimum of one hour for each embassy seems reasonable, hence a minimum of thirteen hours in the first action. To this we must add time for allied witnesses not belonging to embassies—another four hours. Compared with this, any other element in the first part of the trial was small.

THE RHETORIC OF THE SECOND ACTION

The published second action was not needed to convict Verres. However, it was not merely an oratorical exercise *in vacuo*. Although usually regarded as an exhibition of Cicero's oratorical ability, it must equally have been aimed at Cicero's Sicilian clients, to acknowledge their contribution to the case and to publicize their complaints. Moreover, a Roman reader would recognize a political agenda that was forward-looking but would not have been inappropriate in the actual trial.

The *exordium* of the first speech of the second action is much what we would have expected, had in fact Verres reappeared. The orator expresses

---

[48] *2Verr.* 2. 23, 119; 3. 97; 5. 15.

surprise that he has dared to do so in the light of his offences (1–3, 7–9) and argues that this will be a splendid occasion for this senatorial jury to restore the public image of the morals of the order and for Cicero to restore confidence in the courts (4–6, 22). The breadth of Verres' offences is stressed: if he cannot be convicted in this court, Cicero claims, he could be convicted in various others, including a trial before the people conducted by Cicero himself as aedile (11–14). He then justifies his compression of the first part of the trial against the potential criticism—perhaps actually made by Hortensius in the first action—that he had provided no case to answer. His first point is that the single action that operated before Servilius Glaucia was kinder to the defendant, since the accuser had no chance to rebut the defence case (24–6). However, he then argues that he had in fact made a case, on the ground that evidence is more impressive from the horse's mouth, as the example of Dio of Halaesa showed (27–9). Moreover, he had then been forced into compressing the trial by the time-factor (30–2). All this is convincing as an introduction to a speech delivered in court, if on a generous scale.

An extended account of Verres' offences now begins—from his quaestorship under Cn. Carbo in 84 BC onwards—and this dominates the rest of the corpus of the oration. The quaestorship does not detain Cicero long (34–40): he moves on to the proquaestorship in Cilicia (41–102) and the urban praetorship (103–58). The case is put by pointed narrative. The condemnation by C. Claudius Nero of Verres' enemies Philodamus of Lampsacus and his son—Hortensius' one strong point (71)—is explained by the corruption of Dolabella and Verres. Only at one point does Cicero develop an elaborate argument when he asks why, if the Lampsacenes had really raised an unjustified riot, there were no reprisals against the city as a whole (78–85).

This is the pattern for the subsequent orations. Essentially they are a parade of witnesses with Cicero retelling or occasionally anticipating their stories in a way that was most likely to engage the sympathies of a reader or juror. Sometimes he needs to set some background. Sicily is praised at the outset of the Sicilian narrative, its importance to Rome, its loyalty, its un-Hellenic character which resembled traditional Roman virtue (*2Verr.* 2. 2–11). Cicero explains the Sicilian judicial system under the decree of P. Rupilius, but briefly (*2Verr.* 2. 32). He would have needed to do no less in the first action to give point to the evidence of some of his witnesses. A rather longer explanation is given of Sicilian taxation under the *lex Hieronica* and its retention by the consuls of 75 BC when they let the contracts, which has the additional function of stressing the part played by Sthenius in resisting alterations to it.[49] Later in

---

[49] *2Verr.* 3. 12–20 (on Sthenius see above with nn. 14–15). Sthenius would surely have been called to bear witness to this, unless he was regarded as disabled from giving evidence.

the same oration Cicero has a brief introduction to the terms under which Verres was required to buy grain under the *lex Terentia Cassia* (*2Verr.* 3. 163). Regarding the thefts of works of art, Cicero carefully distinguishes this from the borrowings made by other Roman magistrates (*2Verr.* 4. 6) and notes that an ancient law forbade purchases by magistrates in provinces absolutely (*2Verr.* 4. 9–10), but his chief point is to demonstrate in the narratives that Verres' acquisitions never came about in fact with the consent of the previous owners.

We may reasonably wonder whether Cicero would have dwelt so long on these stories in court, when the evidence had already been given or was about to be given, especially as the account of Verres' manipulations of grain-taxation was boringly repetitive, as Cicero himself admitted (*2Verr.* 3. 10). What may be more illuminating about the speech that Cicero actually would have given is to notice special pieces of argumentation. Four items are of interest here: first, appeals to the text of the relevant law; secondly, financial calculations; thirdly, anticipations of Hortensius' defence; fourthly, general arguments about the nature of Roman provincial government.

Cicero does not cite formally the text of the current *lex de repetundis*, as he cites, for example, the *lex Cornelia de veneficis* when defending Cluentius (*Clu.* 148). Arguably, a jury familar with trials in this court would not need citations of those parts of the law that were most relevant for them, those that defined the crime and the classes of persons liable to be charged. However, Cicero does allude to the language of the law when he wants to make a point. In the middle of the section on the tithe-collection he exclaims, 'quid est aliud capere et conciliare pecunias, in quo te lex tenet, si hoc non est, vi atque imperio cogere invitos lucrum dare alteri, hoc est pecuniam dare?'[50] In *capere et conciliare* we have clear reference to the phraseology known to us through the epigraphic *lex repetundarum* (ll. 3, 59). Cicero returns to this allusion at the end of the oration, when he asks the jury whether, seeing that they are a jury *de pecunia capta conciliata*, they can overlook so much money taken (*2Verr.* 3. 218). Interestingly, the one occasion when we know that Cicero did read out the law was not in court but when he was seeking to compel the governor of Sicily, L. Metellus, to lift his veto on the supply to Cicero of a decree of the Syracusan senate: at this point he read out the *sanctio* (enforcement clause) of the law and its penalty.[51]

---

[50] 'What else is stealing and procuring money, the act in which the law holds you liable, if it is not this, to compel people by the force of *imperium* to give a profit to another against their will, that is, to give money?' (*2Verr.* 3. 71).

[51] *2Verr.* 4. 149. A further possible reference is in *2Verr.* 5. 126 *non argentum, non aurum, non vestem, non mancipia repetunt, non ornamenta*. The catalogue of objects of theft may have formed part of the current law.

Cicero had plentiful evidence of Verres' extortionate practices in relation to Sicilian grain, but largely from one side, that of the Sicilian complainants. He had apparently no access to Verres' accounts before or during the first part of the trial.[52] Apronius, Verres' agent, refused to produce any accounts when formally requested to do so before the magistrate, on the ground that he had kept none (*2Verr.* 3. 112). In order to make plain Verres' excessive profits, Cicero calculates the maximum product of the *ager Leontinus* in the light of the quantity of land (in *iugera*) declared to be under seed and compares this with the quantity of *medimni* for which the contractor had bought the right to collect the tithe. This last sum was vastly more than a tenth of the maximum possible harvest in an excellent year.[53] Verres had also made money out of the sums assigned him to buy grain for the *res publica*. He had not only been mean about his payments to the cities but had profited from the interest accruing to the money, while it was deposited with the *publicani* at Syracuse. The relevant documentation had largely disappeared, deliberately weeded, Cicero claims, following a decree of the tax-collectors. Nevertheless, Cicero found two copies of a letter from the executives (*magistri*) of the company to their colleague L. Carpinatius in Sicily, saying that they were going to see whether Verres was going to declare this profit in his accounts and return it to the public treasury: if he did not so return it, they were intending to claim it for the company.[54]

There are two main lines of defence that Cicero anticipates, apart from the demand that he should back his claims with evidence and the assignation of responsibility to Verres' subordinates[55]—first, that Verres' behaviour was not unusual, secondly, that any harsh actions could be ascribed to the needs of the *res publica*. Early in the account of the thefts of works of art Cicero mentions that a marble Eros stolen by Verres from Messana had previously been lent for exhibition in the forum to C. Claudius Pulcher during his aedileship, but the latter had duly returned it. Other nobles had adorned the forum and the basilicas with similar works of art—temporarily (*2Verr.* 4. 5–6). Verres, by contrast had taken and kept. But Verres had bought his pieces: so Cicero imagines the counter-argument. There was in fact an old law forbidding purchases by a Roman magistrate abroad, that seems, at least in part, to have been in force at the time of the *lex agraria* of 111 BC.[56] However, Cicero

---

[52] *2Verr.* 1. 98–9; 4. 36. Verres apparently stated in the senate that he was waiting on the accounts of his quaestor.

[53] *2Verr.* 3. 112–13, rightly highlighted by Butler 2002, 44.

[54] *2Verr.* 3. 165–8, esp. 167; cf. 2. 177; Butler 2002, 47–8.

[55] The first is explicit at *2Verr.* 2. 177–8. The weak argument that Verres was not responsible for what his subordinates did is put forward more cautiously at *2Verr.* 2. 27—to be dismissed. On this see Alexander, 2002, 69–70, in relation to *Font.* 19.

[56] *2Verr.* 4. 9–10; cf. *lex agraria* (*RS* i. no. 2), 54–5; *Dig.* 49. 16. 9; Lintott, 1981, 176; M. H. Crawford, 1977, 51, n. 4.

accepts the objection that this is now outmoded. He will cease to question Verres' intentions in the purchase, if he can show that he bought the statues at the vendor's price (*2Verr.* 4. 10).

At the beginning of the fifth *Verrine* Cicero assumes that Verres' wholesale depredations are manifest, but he may be still defended as a man who saved Sicily in a military crisis (*2Verr.* 5. 1). The volume that follows is thus presented not only as a denunciation of Verres' corruption and cruelty as evils in themselves, but as a move to subvert the defence that he was a good governor in the respect that concerned Romans most, military effectiveness. Cicero goes on: 'I know the *topos* (*locus*); I see where Hortensius is likely to make an exhibition of himself. He will recall the perils of war, the political situation, the shortage of commanders; at one moment he will seek your indulgence, at another he will even argue from his own legal standpoint (*pro suo iure*) that you should not allow such a commander to be snatched from the Roman people by the testimonies of Sicilians, that you should not consent to the lustre of a commander's glory being rubbed away by charges of greed' (*2Verr.* 5. 2).

Later, when dealing with the case of Apollonius of Panhormus, he anticipates a response by the defence to his charges: 'I am not going to act so roughly, I will not follow that tradition among accusers of denouncing any act of clemency as lax, of extracting the odium of cruelty from any strict punishment.' His point is that Verres had acted arbitrarily: the defendant should have been tried by a jury under oath.[57] There follows an emotional appeal by *praeteritio* to the misery of Apollonius. This Cicero swiftly leaves aside: 'I foresee the line of defence Hortensius will take; he will admit that neither the age of the father nor the youth of the son nor the tears of both were more important to Verres than the interests and survival of the province; he will say that public affairs cannot be managed without the threat of stern punishment; he will ask why the rods are carried before praetors, why axes are given them, why the prison was built, why so many penalties have been established by our ancestors for bad men.' Cicero has of course an answer. After this stern and impressive diatribe, he will ask why Verres suddenly let Apollonius out of gaol (*2Verr.* 5. 21–2).

The sentiments Cicero ascribed to the defence seem in context a pastiche of rhetorical commonplaces, but the point was surely that, however trite, they were used to good effect in other cases. Cicero had no doubt heard them used in the *repetundae* court before. He used a similar argument from public interest in the *pro Fonteio*, which on its likely date of 69 BC was delivered when the written *Verrines* were circulating. Fonteius is portrayed there as a

---

[57] *2Verr.* 5. 19; cf. 18 *indicta causa.*

defender of the province, supported by the most reliable elements in it—the colony of Narbo Martius, the allied city of Massilia, the mass of resident Romans—attacked by the Gauls whom he had forced to pay their proper dues to the Roman people.[58] The important differences between him and Verres were that the Roman citizens were on his side and that the threat to Gaul was more serious than that to Sicily.

Cicero also portrays Hortensius resorting to the argument that Verres was no different from the average provincial governor. This comes after the elaborate exposé of his profiteering over the grain (*2Verr.* 3. 205–6). Cicero's response is to pick up this very point and dilate on the misery of allies everywhere: 'The provinces are all in mourning, the free peoples are all crying in distress, to cap it all, even the kings are protesting about our greed and injuries.' This distress, Cicero maintains, is worse than armed rebellion and the Roman people cannot stand against it (*2Verr.* 3. 207). The same theme recurs in an appeal to the jury during the examination of Verres' military conduct in the fifth Verrine. Where, asks Cicero, can the allies find help? This is no longer the practice of the senate. The people have provided this court, the citadel of the allies. The allies no longer resort to it as they used to. They assume that the Roman people expect them to be robbed of their gold, silver, clothing, slaves, and the works of art from their shrines. 'For it is for many years now we have been tolerating it in silence, when we see the wealth of all nations has passed into the hands of a few men ... Where do you think the wealth of the foreign nations is, who are all now in poverty, when you see Athens, Pergamum, Cyzicus, Miletus, Chios, Samos, in short the whole of Asia, Achaia, Greece, and Sicily behind the doors of so few villas (*2Verr.* 5. 126–7)?' As a depiction of the iniquities of the Roman empire, these passages are more powerful than the much-quoted passage from *de imperio Cn. Pompeii* (68), when Cicero tells the people that that it is hard to describe how much the Roman people are hated.

What we cannot tell, of course, is how far such expostulations were the stock-in-trade of representatives of allies in the *quaestio de repetundis*. We have no parallel in the speeches of other Roman orators of the time. However, other material suggests that Cicero may be part of a long tradition. Before the era of the *quaestio* Cato the Censor made a practice of denouncing the greed and corruption of his contemporaries in the courts and on other public platforms.[59] A further parallel is the words put in the mouths of foreigners by Roman historians. The letter of Mithridates inserted by Sallust in his *Histories*, set in the same period as Cicero's *Verrines*, is a reprise of Cicero's

---

[58] *Font.* 11–15, 21, 26, 32, 46. On the Fonteius case see Alexander, 2002, 59–77.
[59] *ORF* no. 8, frr. 58–61, 69–71, 132, 154, 173–4 (204), 177, 224.

sentiments, and from this we can look onwards to the famous speech given by Tacitus to the Briton Calgacus.[60] We should therefore be cautious about ascribing to Cicero a heartfelt identification with the allies. Such passages were demanded by his duty to his clients—and this would have been a convenient excuse, should anyone have suggested that he was being excessively *popularis* and subversive.

The same defence was available, if anyone suggested that his passionate appeal to the *provocatio* laws (*2Verr.* 5. 163 ff.) was demagogic to excess: it was the appropriate argument for this part of the case. What Cicero's real sentiments were in this period can at best be roughly gauged by considering a great deal of other evidence. The important thing was that he could appear *popularis* in a text like this, while having a retreat ready prepared from this position. At the same time he could appear deferential to the senatorial order, as in earlier speeches in the corpus (1. 43–50, cf. *2 Verr.* 1. 21–3).

Caution is therefore required in using the Verrines as evidence for Cicero's politics. With later speeches the evidence of the Letters is often a useful corrective. The texts are, nonetheless, better evidence than might be thought for the conduct of a *repetundae* prosecution. Curiously enough, the mass of published rhetoric demonstrates clearly the paramount importance of witnesses and evidence. This is reflected in Cicero's later defence speeches in this court: most of what we possess is concerned with the demolition of prosecution witnesses. The 'defence of good men', to which Cicero promised he would turn at the end of the *Verrines* largely depended on destroying the character and reliability of those who suggested in their testimony that his clients were not good.

[60] Sall. *Hist.* 4. 69. 5–9, 17; Tac. *Agric.* 30. 4–31. 2.

VIII

The Defence of Good Men (1): The Other Side of the *Quaestio de Repetundis*

RECENT chapters have followed the course of Cicero's forensic career from private speeches to a public criminal prosecution. The two following seek to give an overview of his subsequent activity as a defence advocate in criminal cases and the oratorical techniques this entailed. Some aspects of these cases are best considered later in the book in conjunction with the politics of their time. The object of the present investigation is the working of the courts in their own right. It is convenient to begin with the *quaestio de repetundis*, in order to complement the investigation of the accusation of Verres.

PRO FONTEIO

The first defence speech that we possess in any quantity is that for M. Fonteius, whom Cicero may have already promised to defend at the time of the trial of Verres.[1] Fonteius had been governor of Transalpine Gaul in the late 70s, but Cicero is probably addressing a jury with a significant equestrian component (cf. 32, 46). Hence the usually assigned date of 69.[2] The text appears to represent a speech delivered in the second action following *comperendinatio*, after the prosecution evidence had been heard for the first time (40). There is no evidence of contamination with material from the first action, though that cannot be completely ruled out on principle (see Ch. 2 with nn. 51–2). Although the Roman province of Transalpine Gaul was at present at peace, there had been a major revolt in its western part (Aquitania) in 77 BC,[3] and

---

[1] For the Fonteius case see Alexander 2002, 59–77. On a fragment of Iulius Victor referring to the argument that the question in the case was the obedience of the allies to Roman *imperium* see Riggsby, 1999*a*.

[2] For a tenure of Gaul for three years from 74 see Badian, 1966, 911–12. For his tenure from 75 see *MRR* iii. 93. On Badian's chronology Fonteius would have returned home in 71 and there may well have been a leisurely *inquisitio*.

[3] *Leg. Man.* 30; Caes. *BG* 3. 20. 1; cf. Sall. *Hist.* 2. 22 M.

later, while not itself in the front line against Sertorius, it was an important supply base for the armies in Spain fighting him.[4] It was therefore easy for Cicero to denounce Gallic witnesses as disloyal and unreliable and to appeal to Fonteius' services as defender of the province and the empire. Although Pompey's activities in Spain (6, 8) and his use of the province for winter-quarters (16) are mentioned, as is the provisioning of armies in Spain from Gaul (8, 13), there is no sign that Pompey gave specific support to Fonteius at his trial. The Sertorian war did, however, provide a context in which the defence of the empire could appear to have been in crisis.

Fonteius had been a moneyer,[5] a treasury-quaestor at Rome under the Marians, and later legate to a Marian-appointed quaestor in Spain. Before his praetorship he had been legate in Macedonia (1–6, 44–5). He was accused of financial irregularities in the first two offices, in particular for cutting the interest on debts at Rome, but direct testimony for corruption was apparently lacking (2–7). As governor in Transalpine Gaul, it was claimed, Fonteius had allowed the Gauls to become deeply indebted to moneylenders, was corrupt in letting contracts for road-building, and had imposed extortionate taxes on the import of Italian wine into Gaul (11, 17–19, 19–20).

Cicero's answer to these last charges is at bottom very simple. The allegations are made by untrustworthy Gauls (14, 21, 26–33), many of whom had suffered at Fonteius' hands for their previous disloyalty to Rome (13, 26). With disarming ingenuousness Cicero admits that on each charge his best course is only to cross-examine a Gallic witness once and briefly, often not even cross-examine at all, in order to avoid giving opportunities to an embittered witness for damaging testimony or importance to one eager to establish his authority (22). This is similar to Hortensius' tactics when defending Verres (*2Verr*.1. 71, 3. 41). No evidence, we are scarcely surprised to discover, was forthcoming for the prosecution from the Roman citizens who were moneylenders, nor from the other Romans involved in the province as tax-collectors, farmers, stock-raisers, businessmen, colonists of Narbo Martius, nor from the free allies from Massilia (11–15, 45–6): indeed such men had given character-testimony for the defendant (32).

Cicero's positive line of defence is to appeal to the security of the empire. He stresses Fonteius' services in defending the province and supporting the war in Spain (13–14, 27, 45–6). However, it is not only important to save Fonteius, but to resist and discourage the Gauls, the traditional enemies of the Roman empire (12–13, 27–36). The Gauls of the province are portrayed as men with a grievance over their previous humiliation in defeat, their loss of

---

[4] *Font*.1 3, cf. e.g. Sall. *Hist*. 2. 98. 9 M; Plut. *Sert*. 21.

[5] *RRC* i, no. 347. No coins of his survive, though we do possess those of M'. Fonteius, moneyer in 85 BC (ibid. no. 353), perhaps his brother.

liberty, loss of land, and loss of centres of civilization. Some of them in particular have been defeated by Fonteius, when they rebelled and attacked Narbo (13, 46). Moreover, it was Gallic peoples (30) who were responsible for sacking Delphi and capturing the Roman Capitol (these two, almost legendary, events, seem to have been standard sources of prejudice). As for the leading witness, Indutiomarus (27, 29, 36), who must have been a chief of the Allobroges, and probably gave evidence about Fonteius' conduct in his war against the Vocontii and subsequent billeting of his troops (20), Cicero presents him as a potential leader of a revolt. If Fonteius is condemned, the Gauls will ascribe this to Roman fear of the threat they pose, not to the honesty of their evidence, and the Romans will need to raise their former commanders from the dead to suppress them (36).

PRO FLACCO

Another elaborate attack on prosecution witnesses is to be found in Cicero's defence of L. Valerius Flaccus—spoken ten years later in Caesar's first consulship some time after the trial of C. Antonius in March (5, 95) and shortly after the passage of Caesar's own *lex de repetundis*.[6] The accusation had been made under Sulla's *lex Cornelia* and the trial presumably was taking place under the provisions of that law. When referring to the regulations governing the trial, Cicero simply says 'lex iubet', 'lex dedit', by contrast to his description of the *lex Iulia* as 'lege hac recenti ac nova' (21, 82, cf. 13). Cicero had a political debt to Flaccus: he had been praetor in Cicero's consulship and had played an important part in the suppression of the Catilinarians, action specifically evoked by Cicero (102–3). He had subsequently governed the province of Asia in 62, probably only handing over to Quintus Cicero in the midsummer of 61.[7]

The importance of the prosecution witnesses was accentuated by the elaborate *inquisitio* conducted by the prosecutor, D. Laelius, in the province. The size of Laelius' entourage and the expenditure made on the expedition was specifically attacked by Cicero (13). During this period, thanks to his brother's governorship of the province, Cicero had access to a great deal of information about it, apart from what he had learnt from his client, including

---

[6] *Flacc.* 13, referring to the limit placed in that law on the number of *comites* the accuser could use in his *inquisitio*. On the case against Flaccus see Alexander 2002, 78–97.

[7] See *Att.* 1. 15. 1 on the allotment of Quintus to the province shortly before the Ides of March 61. Assuming that the denunciation of Flaccus had taken place early in 60, the case had taken a long time to come to trial.

a useful stock of scandal about the witnesses themselves and the assistant (*subscriptor*) to the prosecution, Appuleius Decianus.[8] Decianus' treatment of Amyntas' pregnant wife had been reported to Cicero by his brother in a letter. Laelius requested the production of this letter, but, it seems, did not include it in his evidence, as it is Cicero who had it read out (78–9, cf. 72–4).[9] Heraclidas' conviction as a debtor had been brought to Quintus' attention, when Heraclidas sought to contest the previous judgement by appealing to the new governor (49).

As has been argued earlier (Ch. II with n. 61 ff.), although one section of the speech seems to be a contamination from the first action, the *pro Flacco* is for the most part presented as Cicero's speech after the *comperendinatio*, when the evidence from most of the witnesses was already known from the first action, indeed one witness from Dorylaeum had died in the interval (41), but Lysanias of Temnos was yet to speak (51). Apart from the delegations from Dorylaeum and Temnos (*frag. Med.* 39–43), we hear of at least one delegate from Tmolus (*frag. Med.* 8); Pergamum was probably only represented by Mithridates (17, 41), while Acmonia and Tralles each sent a single delegate, Asclepiades and Maeandrius (34, 52). Appuleius Decianus, the *subscriptor*, is treated by Cicero as the chief Roman complainant (70); others were M. Lurco, P. Septimius, and M. Caelius (10–11).

We should not assume that this was the total of Laelius' witnesses. However, it is unlikely that he had brought to Rome as many as Cicero did against Verres. The distance and expenditure required by the delegates would have militated against that. Nevertheless, Cicero included a comparison with his own prosecution of Verres, when discussing the way Laelius collected evidence. He denounced the votes of the assemblies in Greek cities, comparing them to a Roman *contio* (mass meeting) which had been given powers of decision, without any time for reflection or the distribution of votes into tribes or centuries: the Greeks were even more undisciplined in that they voted in a sitting position. On this basis he belittled the decrees that Laelius and Athenagoras had extracted from Cyme and Mithridates from Pergamum. He himself had brought witnesses from Sicily at public expense but their evidence was not that of an inflamed mass meeting but of a senate under oath (15–18).[10] The end of this passage seems to be a reply to an objection. Was this imagined or anticipated, or had it actually occurred?

---

[8] See e.g. 46–50, 52–4, 72–4. For Decianus as *subscriptor* see 51, 81–2.

[9] For the demand for the production of documents see *lex rep.* 34; *2Verr.* 4. 36; Butler, 2002, 57.

[10] A briefer attack on a Greek assembly may be found in *Flacc.* 57. On Cicero's exploitation of ethnic prejudice against Asiatic Greeks and on Romans, like Decianus, who imitated their ways see Steel, 2001, 53 ff.

It does not seem a wise tactical move for Cicero to have spontaneously introduced a comparison with his own successful prosecution of Verres. That would have reminded the jury of similarities between the cases. It is more likely that the prosecutor had used the parallel in his second speech as a rebuttal of Cicero's earlier attacks on his witnesses. In fact, the close relationship that Laelius had with Greek witnesses, who were living at his house (22),[11] had an obvious resemblance to Cicero's relationship with Sthenius of Thermae (*2Verr*. 2. 83). Again, Cicero's sneer at Laelius' involvement with the assembly at Cyme reminds us of L. Metellus' reaction to Cicero's participation in the business of the Syracusan senate (17, cf. *2Verr*. 4. 137–47). Cicero was speaking from the position occupied by Hortensius in 70 BC. The difference was that he was not the only defence counsel in 59: Hortensius himself spoke before him (41).

What was the case against Flaccus? One charge was of brutality. He had had Athenagoras of Cyme flogged for exporting grain in a famine (17). However, as was appropriate in the *quaestio de repetundis*, the main burden of the prosecution was Flaccus' self-enrichment through administrative and judicial decisions. He had demanded money for oarsmen from the cities in order to mobilize a fleet to combat piracy. It had not achieved anything, and Cicero's brother had subsequently remitted the levy (27–33). Asclepiades of Acmonia claimed that he had given 206,000 drachmas to Flaccus on behalf of a certain A. Sestullius and his brothers, presumably as a bribe for a favourable decision (34–8). This contrasted with the official laudatory decree sent by Acmonia (36–7)—just as the testimonies of Heius of Messana and Heraclius of Syracuse had conflicted with the official honorific decrees provided by their cities for Verres (*2Verr*. 2. 15; 4. 125, 141–4). A similar charge to Asclepiades' was made by a man from Dorylaeum (39–40). The embassy from Temnos complained that they had been forced to give 17,000 drachmas openly to Flaccus and a far greater sum in secret towards the rebuilding of a temple (43–4).

The representatives of Tralles complained about a debt that the praetor had forced them to repay to a certain Castricius and, more importantly, that Flaccus had deprived them of the money that had been collected to celebrate a festival in honour of his father, the consul of 86 (54–7). Flaccus had also seized the gold that the Jews sent as the temple-tax to Jerusalem from Asia and confiscated it for the treasury, something which, Cicero is at pains to point out, was not a matter of private profit. It might yet have been an illegal exaction, since, even if at that time there was a ban on such contributions by the Jews, it did not follow that the gold in question could be seized by the Romans.[12]

---

[11] Cf. *Flacc*. 41 *contubernalis*.   [12] *Flacc*. 67–9; cf. Jos. *AJ* 16. 167–71.

Finally, there were the complaints deriving from Roman citizens. Decianus himself had an interest in a case. He had apparently taken over the wife and unborn daughter of a Pergamene, Amyntas, together with the property of Amyntas' mother-in-law, in suspicious circumstances. The *tutor* of these women, Polemocrates, had been condemned for fraudulent behaviour in his guardianship, and the property transactions he had authorized (presumably allowing Decianus to become owner of the estates vested in his new wife and her mother) had been declared void. Decianus had appealed to successive governors over this and Flaccus had decreed against him (72–80).

M. Lurco had a more serious charge about Flaccus' making a decree in a case in which he himself had an interest (84–9). A certain Sestullius Andro, who is called Lurco's freedman—perhaps formerly a slave jointly owned by his sister and her husband Sestullius (see 88–9)—had married a Valeria after her father's death, when she was in the wardship of a number of guardians (*tutores*), including Valerius Flaccus. She had then died intestate. Sestullius then had claimed her estate on the ground that she had come into his *potestas* or *manus* (legal power) when she married. Flaccus also had claimed the estate, presumably as either the closest agnate (somewhat unlikely, as it would have helped Cicero to stress this) or a member of the *gens Valeria*, on the ground that her marriage had not been with *manus* and she was independent (*sui iuris*).[13] Flaccus had apparently already made this claim before he became the supreme magistrate in Asia (85), but it was decided in his favour in an arbitration under his authority, and he then ceded the money to a young relative. M. Lurco seems to have argued that the governor had improperly enriched himself; against this Cicero, citing L. Lucullus' behaviour as precedent, claimed that to receive inheritances when a governor was not against the law (85–6).

We hear briefly about the wrath of another Roman witness, P. Septimius, over a letter written by Flaccus about a homicide committed by his bailiff (88). A further charge was supported by a letter from a certain Falcidius, who after considerable competition with the locals had bought the rights to collect the taxes of Tralles for 900,000 sesterces. The auction had happened under the previous praetor Servilius Globulus, but Falcidius had claimed that he had paid Flaccus 50 talents, that is about 1,200,000 sesterces, in order to keep the contract (90–3). A complaint relating to Mithridates of Pergamum is only mentioned in passing as answered by Hortensius (41, cf. 17); there were no doubt others of which we hear nothing.

---

[13] On the legal technicalities see Watson, 1967, 20 ff., 132 ff.; 1971, 181. For the name Sestullius in the best manuscripts of *Flacc.* 84, in *Schol. Bob.* 106 St, and appearing as Sextullius in *Flacc.* 35 and 89, see S. Mitchell, 1979; 1993, i. 158; Badian, 1980.

Even in Cicero's presentation it appears that the prosecution had evidence of some flagrant wrongdoing and some questionable behaviour. It was not as massive as the case against Verres, but sufficient to justify a conviction. It must be remembered that even before Caesar's *lex Iulia* the statutes *de repetundis* were tightly drafted and most of those accused would have been technically guilty under the law. However, the very strictness of the law left it open to the defence to present the accused as someone who had not done anything really wrong, someone who was fundamentally a good man. This is Cicero's approach, where he deals with behaviour by Flaccus that was questionable, but not incontestably illegal, such as the demands for ship-money and the receipt of an inheritance. More serious charges about receiving money are countered by denying validity to the testimony, either by impugning the credibility of the individual witness or by generic denunciations of Greek assemblies (15–18, 57) and Asiatic witnesses (65–6), where he employs a crude appeal to chauvinistic proverbs.

Asia was at peace during Flaccus' governorship. So Cicero could not praise the military achievements of Flaccus and present him as a bulwark of the empire. However, the threat of piracy could be used to justify his raising of a fleet (27–32). Furthermore, Cicero could appeal to the past military achievements of Flaccus (*frag. Bob.* 6) and link them to the military service of his father and other members of the *gens Valeria*. In response to the complaints of the people of Tralles he evoked the memory of their complicity in the slaughter of Romans during the first Mithridatic War (60–1) and their resistance to the recapture of Asia by Flaccus' father, the consul of 86 BC.

Flaccus himself had not served in Asia before his governorship. His military career had begun under his uncle, Gaius Valerius Flaccus, during the latter's long tenure of Spain and then both Spain and Gaul in the eighties;[14] later he was tribune of the soldiers in Cilicia under Servilius Isauricus, quaestor in Spain under M. Pupius Piso,[15] and legate under Q. Metellus in the Cretan war. This last service allowed his defence to deploy character witnesses 'from the true and untainted Greece' on his behalf—from Athens, Sparta, Achaea, Boeotia, Thessaly, and Massilia.[16] This last city must have become a client of the Valerii. As for the peoples of old Greece, we may infer that Flaccus had earned their gratitude by his restraint in requiring military aid for Metellus.[17]

---

[14] *Frag. Bob.* = *Schol.Bob.* 96 St.; *Flacc.* 63, where the manuscripts' reading *militem quaestoremque* is surely right. Gaius Flaccus' command seems to have begun in 92 in Spain with Gaul added perhaps in 85 (*MRR* iii. 211–12).

[15] *Flacc. Frag. Bob.* 6, 63.

[16] *Flacc.* 61–3. He would have been able to visit Massilia again on the way to Spain.

[17] This sort of exchange of services is exemplified in the decree of Gytheion for the brothers Cloatii who negotiated with a series of Roman commanders over their demands for material and military assistance in the same period (*Syll*³ 748).

It is also possible that the connections were an inheritance from his father. In portraying their support, Cicero forgets his previous generic denunciation of Greek witnesses and Greek assemblies (13) in favour of distinguishing between the original Ionians, Dorians, and Aeolians and the area they conquered and blockaded with their colonies (64).

Finally, Cicero appealed to what was for some a reason for prejudice against Flaccus, his services against Catiline in 63–2. Here the condemnation earlier in the year of C. Antonius, Cicero's fellow consul in 63, provided an unfortunate precedent.[18] Cicero dismisses Antonius as a disgraced man who nevertheless would not have been condemned by the present jury. His condemnation was a funeral offering for Catiline (95). As for the threat to Flaccus, Cicero confronts it directly: he numbers himself among those in danger of prosecution and says he is prepared to meet it, even before an ignorant popular assembly: a threat of this kind was more tolerable than to be assailed in a court staffed by the senators and *equites* who shared the resistance to Catiline.[19] Courts in the past had always been able to forgive offences against the laws by people who had defended the *res publica*.[20] The jury would be voting not just about Flaccus but the survival of the community and the empire (99–100). In short, Cicero's plea is: 'On the evidence the man is guilty. But acquit him!'

PRO SCAURO

The imperfect survival of this speech makes it hard to appreciate as a piece of forensic oratory. Nor, if it had survived intact, would it have been easy to judge its contribution to Scaurus' defence in view of the number of *patroni* used by Scaurus—six, apart from Scaurus' own contribution (Asc. 20 C). It does, however, provide useful confirmation of Cicero's method in defending cases *de repetundis*. The speech is presented as delivered in the second part of the trial. If, as argued earlier, we accept Cicero's statement that the prosecutor had only called one witness before *comperendinatio* (29), this limited Cicero's scope for impugning prosecution witnesses.

---

[18] *Flacc.* 1–5; *Frag. Bob.* 95–7, 102–3. See Ch. XII with nn. 7–11.

[19] Cicero was at this point anticipating that Clodius might either prosecute him before an assembly or use violence against him (*Att.* 2. 22. 1; *QF* 1. 2. 16).

[20] *Flacc.* 98. Interestingly, Cicero implies by his parallel with the flagrantly guilty M'. Aquillius here that C. Piso, L. Murena, and even A. Thermus, though qualified by him as *innocens et bonus*, were technically guilty when acquitted. On Flaccus' acquittal thanks to a Ciceronian joke, not in the published speech, see Macr. *Sat.* 2. 1. 13; Alexander 2002, 78.

Cicero in fact devoted a considerable section of the speech to that one witness, Valerius Aris.[21] It appears that Aris had suggested that this wife had been driven to suicide through Scaurus' activities, to which Cicero's sensational and defamatory rejoinder was to claim it was more probable either that she had hanged herself in despair over Aris' planned marriage to his mistress or that Aris had arranged to have her put out of the way (1–13). Cicero argues that the prosecution's charges have been totally refuted over the death of Aris' wife, because they did not depend on a witness, but on matter that a juryman could weigh up by himself. An unknown witness could lie, even if he was more scrupulous and respectful of his oath than an African or Sardinian. An argument, however, belonged to the nature of things: it was the voice of the facts which was taken over by the orator, not invented (14–16).

In effect, Cicero is saying that the jury should trust an argument from probability, not a witness. But he presents his position as privileging the certainty of reasoning against the uncertainty and flexibility of human testimony. Triarius had also collected a great deal of written testimony regarding misbehaviour in exacting corn, but Cicero claims that the uniformity of that evidence was a sign of conspiracy among the Sardinians and that testimony of this kind could not compare with accounts, which in themselves showed the progress of a commercial contract (18–22). This is reinforced by his strictures about Triarius' failure to execute a proper investigation (*inquisitio*) in the province. He contrasts this with his own energy in traversing Sicily in 70 BC (23–6); unlike the comparison with the Verres case in *pro Flacco*, this seems to have been a spontaneous move by Cicero, since the parallel was entirely to his advantage. In *pro Flacco* (65–6) Cicero had quoted proverbs to prove the unreliability of Asiatic Greeks; here he pointed to the traditional reputation of Phoenicians (42) and argued that the Sardinians were trying to please their patron Appius Claudius who had an interest in the election of his brother Gaius (31–7). Even in its truncated state, the speech shows how the evidence of plaintiffs could be dismissed, much of it before it was given on the witness-stand.

What survives of these defence speeches shows on a smaller scale Cicero wrestling with the problem that faced Hortensius when he defended Verres. Each of the defendants had almost certainly committed offences against the *lex de repetundis*, even if some of them were more in the nature of improprieties than gross violations of its norms. The prosecution had witnesses and evidence, most of which was not worth fighting point by point: as Cicero

---

[21] *Scaur.* 9–13, 29; given citizenship by Triarius' father and hence a guest-friend of his family. On the case against Scaurus see Alexander 2002, 98–109.

himself admitted in *pro Fonteio* (22), contesting the evidence reinforced the impression it had made in the jury's minds. Accordingly, Cicero dismisses prosecution witnesses and their evidence, rather than arguing with them. Instead, he appeals to the general achievement of the defendants in promoting the interest of Rome's empire and to their basic decency. This was the 'defence of good men' which at the end of the fifth *Verrine* (189) he programmatically claimed as his new *métier*.

IX

The Defence of Good Men (2): Treason and Other Crimes against the Roman People

OTHER crimes handled by the permanent tribunals did not have the element of compensating wronged individuals, but directly concerned the Roman people as a whole. Treason indeed, traditionally, had been prosecuted, not before a jury, but before an assembly of the people. Cicero's method when defending in the *repetundae* court was, as we have seen, to discount testimony rather than to examine evidence. Positively, he sought to portray his client as a good man defending Rome's empire against hostile foreigners. The cases we are about to consider required a different approach. The facts were often well known, at least in general terms, and the prosecution supported by Roman witnesses whose character could not be casually denigrated. On the other hand there was more scope for arguing about the interpretation of the law and of the defendants' actions in relation to the law. The difference between rhetorical strategies in different public courts has been well characterized by Andrew Riggsby.[1] It was not just a question of variation in the quantity and quality of evidence for different charges: it arose from the nature of the offence. In cases where the political element was stronger, the definition of the offence had been left vague, even ambiguous, by the legislator—probably deliberately, because the judgement was expected to be political, rather than purely criminal.[2] Here there was more opportunity for defending counsel to argue, not merely that his client was a 'good man', but that the actions of his that were being prosecuted were justifiable.

The context of speeches in these other *quaestiones*, moreover, differed in an important respect from a trial *de repetundis* in that, unless enough of the jury were unwilling to deliver a verdict on the basis of what they had so far heard

---

[1] See Riggsby, 1999b, especially 151 ff.
[2] Riggsby, 1999b, 161 contrasts the Roman republican system of public courts with the dual system in the United States of impeachment on the one hand (loosely defined and purely political both in the offences embraced and penalties consequent on conviction) and, on the other, criminal prosecution of politicians for actions that happen to be criminal offences.

(something which could not be forecast), the trial would have but a single action. The main speeches of both prosecution and defence, therefore, came before any examination of witnesses. This did not mean that it was not known beforehand what evidence the witnesses were going to give. T. E. Kinsey mistakenly tried to explain the lack of discussion of evidence in the *pro Sexto Roscio* by Cicero's ignorance of what Erucius' witnesses would say.[3] There is indeed a puzzle about why the *pro Sexto Roscio* is so little concerned with the circumstances of the murder and the evidence directly pointing to Roscius' guilt. However, this is best explained by the traditional supposition that the charge against Roscius was speculative and relied on the political influence of his accusers.[4] Similarly, Cicero's brief treatment of two of the poisoning charges in *pro Cluentio* (165 ff.) suggests that no specific testimony was offered about them. The third (169 ff.), backed by the testimony of slaves, about which Cicero was well informed, required more rebuttal. In general, testimony had to be delivered under oath and deposited in writing beforehand, probably in sealed packages of tablets with the text reproduced on the exterior, such as those found at Herculaneum.[5] These would have given at least the gist of what the witness would say in court and allowed the orator to shape his argument accordingly. However, a speech largely devoted to destroying the credibility of witnesses who had not yet been either heard or cross-examined risked seeming misdirected and redundant.

One of Cicero's most interesting defences in a political case has a special problem, in that it is only known from fragments, viz. *lemmata* from the commentary of Asconius and from writers on oratory. The commentary of Asconius, however, gives sufficient background to the trial for us to grasp Cicero's argumentation, even if we cannot appreciate his oratory properly. The *pro Cornelio* is a defence of a *popularis* tribune, who had sought to legislate in defiance of the senate. We have already seen in the discussion of the *Verrines* how Cicero could assume *popularis* clothes, where it assisted his case and where such self-representation suited his current political strategy. What is important for the present discussion is not Cicero's sincerity but the line of argument with which he defended conduct that *prima facie* appeared an offence against the constitution and unlikely to elicit sympathy from many of the jury.

[3] Kinsey, 1985. Note that Quint. 6. 4. 14, cited by Kinsey, refers to the concealing of points in a main speech in order to produce them suddenly in the *altercatio*, not to the concealing of evidence. See Appendix 1 on historical aspects of the Sextus Roscius case.
[4] See, however, Stroh, 1975, 61 ff. for a convincing argument that the accusers expected Sex. Roscius to accept the loophole provided by the argument that this was no murder, because his father had been either proscribed or in a Marian camp and thus could be killed with impunity, and in this way buy his own life at the cost of his inheritance.
[5] *Cael.* 19–20, 66; *Clu.* 168, 184 (here records of the torture of slaves); cf. *Flacc.* 21; *lex rep.* 33–4 with commentary in *JRLR* 126–7; *THerc.* 16–25 in Arangio-Ruiz and Pugliese Carratelli, 1948.

C. Cornelius had been an active tribune in 67 and clearly had cooperated with A. Gabinius, the proposer of the statute conferring an extraordinary command against the pirates on Pompey. Cornelius' first proposed bill forbade the lending of money to provincial embassies. This was rejected by the senate, but a similar bill was subsequently passed by Gabinius,[6] probably in that same year. Cornelius next proposed that the granting of exemption from the laws (*privilegia*) should be reserved for the popular assembly, not, as the practice was at the time, decided by the senate often without reference to the people. This bill met fierce resistance from the most powerful members of the senate, who found another tribune, Servilius Globulus, to veto it. When on the day of voting Globulus prevented the scribe from proffering the text of the bill and the herald from reading it out, Cornelius read the bill himself. The consul Piso protested against the disregard of the veto and this provoked a riot and the stoning of the consul. Cornelius in consequence dismissed the assembly and the bill was abandoned in that form. He subsequently secured the acceptance of a bill which required a quorum of 200 senators for a decision about a *privilegium*, followed by a reference to the assembly which was to be free of veto.[7]

This was not his only successful piece of legislation. A second law required praetors to abide by their edicts, when issuing decisions during their jurisdiction (58–9 C). Furthermore a proposal of his about electoral bribery led to a less drastic law being passed by the consul C. Piso.[8] The year following (66 BC) he was accused first *de pecuniis repetundis* and then *de maiestate*, of infringing the majesty of the Roman people, but on the day he was due to appear before the appropriate praetor on the second charge, this magistrate failed to appear and his accusers, the Cominii, were chased away by gangs. The Cominii abandoned their accusation for the time being, but Publius Cominius returned to it in 65 BC,[9] by which time another *popularis* tribune, one who had legislated in Pompey's interest, C. Manilius, had also been accused and Cicero had undertaken his defence.[10] The Manilius trial was broken up by violence and it is not certain whether it ever reached a verdict.[11]

In the *exordium* of the first speech for Cornelius Cicero sought first to pinpoint the charge of infringing the majesty of the Roman people for the purposes of the case. In principle *maiestas minuta* could be argued to cover a great range of political crimes, and no doubt the prosecutors wished to

---

[6] Asc. 57 C, cf. Cic. *Att.* 5. 21. 12; 6. 1. 5, 2. 7.
[7] Asc. 57–9 C. On the superiority of Asconius' narrative to that in Dio Cassius 36. 38–40. 2 see Griffin, 1973.
[8] Asc. 69, 75, 88 C; Dio 36. 38–39. 1; Griffin, 1973, 197–201.
[9] Asc. 60–2 C, *Brut.* 271, cf. perhaps *Corn.* 1. 61 P with Griffin 1973, 213.
[10] Asc. 59–60, 62, 65–6 C.   [11] Asc. 66 C; *Corn.* 1. 19 P; Dio 36. 44. 1–2.

exploit a perception of Cornelius as a generally turbulent demagogue, while basing their case technically on his disregard of a veto. Cicero admitted that Cornelius seized and read the text of the bill about *privilegia* himself.[12] At the same time he apparently questioned whether this amounted to violent sedition,[13] and probably also whether seeking to enact a popular proposal by force could in any case be a diminution of the majesty of the people.[14] He also criticized the persistence of Cominius in his accusation,[15] and sought to remove any prejudice that might arise from allegations that Cornelius and Manilius were connected:[16] Cornelius had not passed on to Manilius the bill about freedmen's votes, which in any case was not ratified by the assembly, nor was Cornelius involved in the violence at Manilius' trial.

Cicero then moved on to the bill about *privilegia* itself. First, he, seemingly, tried to respond to accusations that that the bill itself was bad on Cornelius' own admission, since he had modified it under pressure from the senate. He listed examples from history of distinguished men changing their mind about legislation or wishing that they had,[17] pointing out at the same time the established role of the senate in monitoring legislation and declaring either that it was technically invalid or that it needed to be modified. Next he reviewed Cornelius' action on the day of the critical assembly, trying to minimize the impropriety of his behaviour. In particular, he compared it with that of Gabinius, who had successfully removed an interceding colleague, Trebellius, from office on the way to enacting the appointment of Pompey to supreme command against the pirates.[18] He appealed to the utility of Cornelius' legislation in general: the importance of the restriction on *privilegia*, especially when otherwise the senate would have interfered with the courts;[19] the importance of the restriction on the arbitrary behaviour of praetors,[20] the value of the bribery proposal, and Cornelius' innocence in relation to the violent resistance to the consular law that followed it.[21]

By this time Cornelius had been presented as not so much a turbulent tribune, but a good man whose good intentions for the *res publica* had involved him in turbulence. Cicero's next move was to broaden the issue: the accusation against Cornelius, he claimed, was in reality an attack on the restoration of full powers to the tribunes and on those who had restored them in 70 BC, Pompey and Crassus—a convenient opportunity for a digression in

[12] *Corn.* 1. 7, 29 P, cf. Quint. 5. 13. 18.   [13] *Corn.* 1. 6 P; Quint. 7. 3. 35.
[14] Cf. *Part. Or.* 105, discussing the Norbanus case, on which see below.
[15] *Corn.* 1. 8–9 P, cf. 13–16 P, 61 P. Kumaniecki, 1970 would place 13–16 P immediately after 8–9 P.
[16] Asc. 64–6 C; *Corn.* 1. 10–12, 18–9 P = 15–19 Kumaniecki.
[17] Asc. 66–70 C; *Corn.* 1. 20–27 P.
[18] Asc. 71–2 C; *Corn.* 1. 28–33 P.   [19] Asc. 73–4 C; *Corn.* 1. 34, 36 P= 35 K.
[20] Asc. 74 C; *Corn.* 1. 37–8 P =36–7 K.   [21] Asc. 74–6 C; *Corn.* 1. 39–46 P = 38–45 K.

Treason and Other Crimes against the People   115

praise of Pompey.[22] This in turn led to a panegyric on the history of the tribunate and those who had advanced the popular cause, whose function was not merely to set Cornelius among this gallery of heroes, but also to show that the history of the plebs had been a matter of violent struggles.[23] The last fragments that we can interpret are concerned with the mutual opposition of the nobility and the plebs and perhaps a pious aspiration for cooperation rather than conflict, exemplified in the *lex Plotia iudiciaria* of 89, a plebiscite supported by the nobility, which led to both senators and members of the plebs judging together in the same court.[24]

Not much survives of the second speech for Cornelius. We have already seen that there is no reason to doubt that Cicero spoke twice, the most plausible explanation for the unusual procedure in this court being the jury's refusal to give a verdict without a further hearing (Ch. 2 with nn. 41–50). The second action gave Cicero an opportunity to attack the prosecution witnesses.[25] Three eminent consulars, we are told, by Asconius—Q. Catulus, Q. Hortensius, and Q. Metellus Pius—had given evidence in the first action: they not only stated that they had seen Cornelius reading the text of the law himself from the rostra, but that this was unprecedented (60–1, 79 C). The implication would have been that Cornelius' disregard of the veto was a breach of the traditions of the constitution and hence an offence against the majesty of the people. Cicero referred to them and two further consulars who were yet to speak—according to Asconius, M. Lucullus and (?) Mamercus Lepidus. There were also further supporters of the consulars to be called.[26]

Cicero attacked the consulars as entrenched enemies of tribunician power and therefore prejudiced (*Corn.* 2. 3–4 P). He pointed to an inconsistency in this attitude among the nobility, in that many of the plebeian nobility had not only held the tribunate but pursued *popularis* policies during this

---

[22] Asc. 76 C; *Corn.* 1. 47–8 P = 46–7 K; Quint. 4. 3. 13; 9. 2. 55.

[23] Asc. 76–8 C; *Corn.* 1. 49–51 P = 48–50 K. Cicero follows a version (50 P) in which the plebs seized the Capitol under arms from the *decemviri*, in effect a *coup d'état*—a much more violent story than we find in Livy 3. 52–4. See Lintott, 2006.

[24] Asc. 78–9 C; *Corn.* 1. 52–4 P. It seems unlikely that 55 P concerning the exile of an innocent man should be associated, as Kumaniecki, 1970 believes, with the condemnation of a man hated by the gods and the nobility, Cn. Pompeius or Pomponius (on the emendation 'Pomponius', see *MRR* iii. 166, following Badian, 1969, 482).

[25] Asc. 79–80 C; *Corn.* 2. 1–3 P.

[26] *Corn.* 2. 3 P; Asc. 79 C. The MSS of Asc. 60 and 79 C have M. (= Marcus) Lepidus, usually emended into M'. (= Manius), i.e. one of the consuls of 66. But the latter are said by Asconius to have been legal advisers (*advocati*) to Cornelius in 66 (60 C). Hence Sumner (1964, 41–8) proposed the attractive alternative emendation, 'Mam. Lepidus' (*cos.* 77), already made in 81 C, l. 6 (where Clark's text follows Sigonius). This is questioned by Griffin, 1973, 213, on the ground that M'. Lepidus was a weak and flexible character who could easily have changed sides (a hint of this, she argues, in *Corn.* 1. 16 P). However, there is no sign of this *volte-face* in either the lemma here or Asconius' comment.

magistracy. Catulus' maternal uncle Cn. Domitius Ahenobarbus had in 104 successfully proposed that priests for the chief colleges should be chosen by election from seventeen tribes rather than by cooption. He had also prosecuted before the assembly M. Iunius Silanus (*cos.* 109) for starting a war with the Cimbri without popular approval and then being defeated. Was not Domitius more seditious than Cornelius? Or was Catulus' ideal tribune M. Terpolius, a nonentity of 77 BC, elected in the period when the tribunate was hamstrung by Sulla's legislation?[27] Of the remaining fragments one seems to be a reply to attacks on Cornelius' wealth, claiming that former slaves and eunuchs now had greater riches and more elaborate villas than the great men who had expanded Rome's empire in the past;[28] others appealed to the conflict between the domination of the few and the defence of liberty, in which it ought to be no crime to summon the populace to battle.[29]

We can see in outline that the two speeches in outline probably contain more *popularis* argument than any other Ciceronian texts. In combination with Cicero's other support for Pompeian tribunes they may be regarded as reflecting the political position that Cicero himself was adopting, at least temporarily, in his pursuit of the consulship. However, he himself has supplied us with a corrective in one of his works on oratory. In the second book of *De Oratore* the persona of M. Antonius (*cos.* 99), one of Cicero's mentors, plays an important role and the orator's achievement is also reviewed by another character in the dialogue. In particular Antonius had successfully defended on a charge of damaging the majesty of the Roman people a former tribune, C. Norbanus. The latter had been one of the tribunes of 104 or 103 BC who harried Q. Servilius Caepio (*cos.* 106) on account of his defeat by the Cimbri and his seizure of Gallic gold from Toulouse, eventually driving him into exile.[30] One meeting of the plebeian assembly, either that which voted to deprive Caepio of his *imperium*, or that which set up the tribunal to investigate the theft of the gold, had led to a riot in which two tribunes had been prevented by violence from vetoing the bill.[31]

Some time later, probably in 95 BC, Norbanus was accused by P. Sulpicius under the law of Saturninus *de maiestate minuta*.[32] Antonius defended him by

---

[27] Asc. 79–80 C; *Corn.* 2. 5–8. *Corn.* 2. 15 P seems to be also a reference to a tribune who paid only lip-service to his duty to look after the welfare (*commoda*) of the people.

[28] *Corn.* 2. 9 P; *Orat.* 232.

[29] *Corn.* 2. 11–14 P.

[30] *Ad Herenn.* 1. 24; Livy, *Per.* 67; Val. Max. 4. 7. 3; Licinianus 13 F; Dio frr. 90–1; Oros. 5. 15.

[31] Cic. *de Or.* 2. 197; cf. *ND.* 3. 74; Asc. 78 C; Livy, *Per.* 67.

[32] On the timing of the trial see Badian, 1964, 35. It should not be thought that Norbanus could not have been accused of an offence committed before the passing of the *lex Appuleia de maiestate* in 103. The Romans had no strict objection to retrospective legislation, especially in

admitting the facts alleged, as Cicero did with Cornelius, but denying that this amounted to the diminution of the majesty of the people. It was the man who handed over the army of the Roman people to the enemy who diminished the people's majesty, not the man who handed over the delinquent to the power of the Roman people (*de Or.* 2. 107, 164). 'If a magistrate should be in the power of the Roman people, why accuse Norbanus, whose tribunate served the will of the community?' (ibid. 167). Furthermore, he argued in an encomiastic review of past seditions that many had been justified and in the public interest, such as at the time of the expulsion of the kings and the creation of the tribunate.³³ A similar excursus was used by Cicero.³⁴

However, Cicero's imitation of Antonius' tactics in the Norbanus case seems to have gone beyond the borrowing of arguments. The discourse given to the character Antonius in *de Oratore* (2. 104 ff.) begins by discussing the importance of defining the issue in the case; it goes on to discuss how the orator commends himself or his client to the jury, how he instructs them in his interpretation of the case, and how he arouses the jury's emotions. It is the mastery of these forms of persuasion that is regarded as Antonius' special skill.³⁵

In the Norbanus case, Antonius had to respond to a passionate speech by the young Publius Sulpicius, who dwelt on the violence, in which the leader of the senate had been struck by the stone and the tribunes driven from the temple that was the focus of the voting, and on the pitiful humiliation of the former consul Caepio. It seemed scarcely honourable for a man of censorial status like Antonius to be protecting such a ruthless man, even if Norbanus had been his quaestor.³⁶ Antonius' response was, first, to develop the argument that we have mentioned—that seditions, however uncomfortable, were often just and almost necessary; then to point out that the expulsion of the kings, the creation of tribunes, the diminution of consular power, and the creation of *provocatio*, the protector of liberty, could not have happened without conflict among the nobility. Hence, instigation of a riot was not

---

political matters where legal procedure was being provided to deal with offences that were already recognized to be injurious to the Roman people.

³³ *De Or.* 2. 124—which derives not from a speech of 'Antonius' but an interjection from 'L. Crassus'; 2. 199.

³⁴ *Corn.* 1. 49–51 P; Asc. 76–8 C.

³⁵ *De Or.* 2. 104–14, 121; for 'Crassus'' view of Antonius, 128 ff. While the exposition of oratory by 'Antonius' no doubt owes much to Cicero himself, as does the judgment on Antonius' actual achievement as an orator, there is no reason to disbelieve Cicero's exposition of a *cause célèbre* from his youth.

³⁶ Ibid. 2. 197–8. Norbanus was presumably Antonius' quaestor during his Cilician command against the pirates. This perhaps explains why eventually in 82 BC he went into exile in Rhodes (App. *BCiv.* 1. 91. 422).

self-evidently a capital offence and no juster cause could be found for a riot than that of Norbanus (*de Or.* 2. 199). Interestingly, Antonius is defending Norbanus here not only against the charge of being a rabble-rouser but against that of betraying his own class by the measures he used against his political opponents.

Having thus defused the jury's wrath against Norbanus, Antonius swung his speech round into the attack, lamenting the loss of Caepio's army and deploring the general's own flight. There were people grieving for their own lost relatives, and the equestrian jury had no love for Caepio on account of his judiciary law. Antonius was now in command of the high ground of moral indignation through fierce and aggressive oratory. He finally appealed to the tenderer emotions of the jury by alluding to his own position, pleading for a comrade, who as a former quaestor, ought to be like a son to him. It would be disgraceful should the orator, who had saved so many unconnected with him, at an advanced age and the height of distinction, fail to help someone as close to him as Norbanus (ibid. 2. 199–201).

Obviously, it is hard to recover the passion from the debris of the speeches *pro Cornelio*. Nevertheless, there are sufficient hints for us to see how Cicero could put his own construction not only on the crucial assembly in 67 but on Cornelius' whole tribunate. The first indication is Cicero's invocation of Gabinius' more drastic conduct as tribune, when 'he was bringing salvation to the Roman people and to the peoples of the world an end to their long-standing humiliation and servitude' (*Corn.* 1. 31). What he had done was to ask the plebeian assembly to strip the tribune Trebellius of his office, when the latter vetoed his bill—just as Tiberius Gracchus had deposed M. Octavius in 133 BC (Asc. 72 C). This, Cicero implied, was a just and necessary cause for violence. The indignation of Cornelius' jury was aroused against the corruption of the magistrates and the senate over both praetors' edicts and electoral bribery (*Corn.* 1. 36–41 P). Later, the theme of the importance of tribunician power allowed Cicero to remind the jury of the glorious episodes of popular history which had brought liberty to the Roman people (*Corn.* 1. 49–52 P). Cicero could not seek sympathy from the jury for his own position, like Antonius. Instead, we can see a trace of a more conventional *commiseratio*: 'a poor and innocent man is being snatched from the Roman people, driven from his fatherland, wrenched from his own family (*Corn.* 1. 55 P)'.

In the second speech Cicero returned to the theme of defending the tribunate against its enemies, stressing that the active tribunes were frequently members of the nobility (*Corn.* 2. 3–8 P). This reminds us of Antonius' argument that the republic and popular liberty could never have been achieved without dissension among the nobility (*de Or.* 2. 199). The climax of the speech is likely to have been Cicero's appeal to the jury to defend the defenders of liberty against the domination of the few: 'If you subject this man's fortunes to the hatred of the few...Are you to allow him to be surrendered to the most painful and cruel tyranny?...how devoted protectors of liberty you should be...that the man who summons the people to a conflict may come to no harm.'[37]

If we seek a difference between Antonius' technique and Cicero's, it lies in the structure of their respective speeches. Antonius developed his technical argument about the application of Saturninus' *lex Appuleia de maiestate* to Norbanus' conduct comparatively briefly; the majority of his speech was devoted to seeking sympathy for seditious behaviour and, subsequently, to attacking Caepio, there being a major change of tone between these two sections; finally, he appealed to the jury in his own person. Cicero after a similar technical argument about *maiestas* and general defence of seditious behaviour, seems to have oscillated between defending Cornelius and attacking his opponents more than once.[38] There is also no trace of the orator exploiting his own relationship to the defendant in the conclusion of either speech. Cicero's speeches are, moreover, more dialectical, having the nature of a dialogue with the opposition.[39] The resemblance lies in the focus of the two orators. Antonius early on in his discourse in *de Oratore* points out that criminal cases are frequently not about matters of fact, but of interpretation; 'qualis sit quaeritur'.[40] What both he and Cicero tried to do in these speeches was to impose their own construction on the events, not only by legal argument, but morally, and emotionally.

We can see something of the same technique illustrated later on in Cicero's *pro Milone*. There Cicero was to portray the affray at Bovillae as Clodius' attack on Milo, and Clodius' death as Milo's self-defence (*Mil.* 24–60). This involved both manipulation of the facts[41] and extracting the maximum emotional effect from his construction. Clodius is portrayed forecasting Milo's journey to Lanuvium and laying an ambush, into which Milo innocently wanders while impeded with a wife and other unwarlike members of his *familia* (no mention of Milo's vast superiority in numbers of armed men).

---

[37] *Corn.* 2. 11 P 'si vos huius fortunas paucorum odio adiudicaveritis'; 12 P 'ad miserrimum crudelissimumque dominatum dedi patiamini'; 13 P 'quam diligentes libertatis vos oportet esse'; 14 P 'ne fraudi sit ei qui populum ad contentionem vocarit', the last perhaps contrasted with the *faux popularis* (15 P) 'qui commodis populi Romani lingua dumtaxat ac voluntate consuluit'.

[38] *De Or.* 2. 201, cf. 199; contrast *Corn.* 1. 34–36 P; 42–3 P; 46–8 P; 51–2 P.

[39] Asc. 64, 66, 72, 75 C; *Corn.* 1. 10, 20–1, 32, 45–6 P.

[40] *De Or.* 2. 106; a *constitutio* either *legitima*, interpreting statute, or *iuridicialis*, interpreting what is just and equitable, according to the terminology of *Ad Her.* 1. 19–24, *definitiva* or *generalis*, according to the parallel terminology of Cic. *Inv.* 1. 10.

[41] See Ch. III with nn. 5–10 and Lintott, 1974, 68–9, 75.

The actual murder in the *taverna* is omitted: Clodius is said to have been killed in the middle of a pitched battle on the road while proclaiming that he had killed Milo.[42] However, with this approach the scope for moral justification was restricted. Certainly, one could portray self-defence as a law of nature (*Mil.* 9–11), but, logically, Cicero could hardly claim the justification of acting in the public interest for an action that was forced unwittingly on Milo, not undertaken voluntarily. He did this in the published speech (72 ff.) but, in my view unsurprisingly, not in court (Asc. 41 C).

A more useful contrast to the *pro Cornelio* is a speech delivered in Cicero's consulship two years later, not in a *quaestio* but in a trial before an assembly—one which unfortunately, only survives in a mutilated state but at least for the most part as continuous text. Cicero's defence of C. Rabirius before the people has been studied more for the odd historical circumstances in which it was delivered than for its forensic skills. C. Rabirius, an elderly senator,[43] was accused of treason (*perduellio*) before the assembly by the tribune T. Labienus on the ground that in 100 BC he had been involved in the illegal homicide of the tribune Saturninus and his followers, one of whom had been the prosecutor's uncle Q. Labienus. This had occurred after the violence of Saturninus and his supporters at the consular elections and their subsequent occupation of the Capitol had provoked the 'last decree' from the senate, ordering the consuls to save the *res publica*.[44]

It appears that before this trial in the assembly, Labienus had sought to revive, presumably through a plebiscite, an antique form of trial before the *duumviri perduellionis*, whereby these two officials were selected by the urban praetor precisely to condemn Rabirius to death without his being granted the right to defend himself or to have his sentence voted on by the people.[45] Rabirius in fact employed *provocatio* and this appeal to the people brought to an end the activities of the *duumviri*.[46] Instead Labienus resorted to a capital prosecution before the assembly, in which treason was combined with a number of capital and non-capital charges—violation of sacred precincts and groves, embezzlement, the murder of his nephew, and offences against the *lex Fabia* about runaway slaves and the *lex Porcia de provocatione*.[47]

---

[42] *Mil.* 27–9; 53–5. Contrast Asc. 31–2 C; 34–5 C.

[43] His senatorial status is specifically mentioned in Dio 37. 26. 3; *Vir. Ill.* 73. 12.

[44] *Rab. Perd.* 20–1, 35, (20 for Q. Labienus); App. *BCiv.* 1. 32. 142–33. 146.

[45] *Rab. Perd.* 10–13, 15–16; Suet. *Iul.* 12; Dio 37. 27. 2. It is significant that Labienus in his accusation of Rabirius had accused Cicero of eliminating a trial for *perduellio* (*Rab. Perd.* 10). For the interpretation here see e. g. Lintott, 1972a, 261–2; Strachan–Davidson, 1912, i. 188 ff.; Bleicken, 1959, 338 ff.

[46] Suet. *Iul.* 12; Dio, 37. 27. 3; Cicero's support: *Rab. Perd.* 10, 17.

[47] Capital charge *Rab. Perd.* 5, 36–7; other offences ibid. 7–8.

The trial involved three *contiones* in which the prosecution and defence made their cases, followed after the interval of a *trinundinum* by a fourth before a formal meeting of the *comitia centuriata*, which ended with the people delivering their verdict. Rabirius was defended by Hortensius as well as by Cicero (*Rab. Perd.* 18). The latter complains that he has only half an hour to speak (*Rab. Perd.* 6, 9), probably because he was speaking at the very end of the trial before the call to the assembly to vote.[48] Witnesses had already been heard in previous meetings of the assembly (*Rab. Perd.* 18). The defence had claimed that Rabirius had not actually killed Saturninus (ibid.)—not implausibly since the death of the tribune had occurred in a form of lynch-justice, when the mob had pelted Saturninus and his followers with tiles from the senate-house,[49] and it would have been difficult to prove Rabirius' personal responsibility. However, the prosecution may have argued that Rabirius had actually claimed responsibility himself, if it is true that he had subsequently carried about Saturninus' head at parties.[50]

Cicero's own speech is not concerned with matters of fact but of interpretation, as in Cornelius' case. He admitted that Rabirius had taken up arms to kill Saturninus, but as a preparation for a claim of justification, on the ground that Saturninus was an enemy of the Roman people (*Rab. Perd.* 18–19). The prosecution had clearly set this trial in motion in order to question the implications of the senate's passing of the 'last decree' and to dispute the optimate interpretation, according to which it created a state of war against the seditious which disabled them from claiming the protection of the *provocatio* laws. Cicero wished to confront Labienus on this point. He argued that, if the prosecution conceded that it was right to take up arms, they at the same time conceded that it was right to kill Saturninus. Labienus had clearly sought to separate the actions of Rabirius from those of Marius, the latter a *popularis* hero. In particular, he had argued time and again that when Saturninus had surrendered to Marius, the latter had given him a guarantee (*fides*), presumably that he would not be put to death arbitrarily on the spot.[51] Cicero answers this sophistically, first by saying that it was not Rabirius who broke faith, but Marius, if he did not stand by his promise, secondly by arguing that such a guarantee could not be given without a decree of the senate—an allegation palpably false in the light of the discretion accorded by the 'last decree' to holders of supreme *imperium*.[52]

So far Cicero's reasoning, but it is embedded in an evocation of the context of Saturninus' death, that portrays Rabirius as not some lawless thug but part

---

[48] The last day of the trial is suggested by *Rab. Perd.* 5 'precorque ab eis ut hodiernum diem et ad huius salutem conservandam et ad rem publicam constituendam inluxisse patiantur.'
[49] App. *BCiv.* 1. 32. 145.   [50] *Vir. Ill.* 73. 12.
[51] *Rab. Perd.* 28 *frequentissime*.   [52] See *VRR* 132–74, esp. 159–60, 168–9; *CRR* 92, 95–9.

of a community of people from all classes who answered the consul's summons to defend the *res publica*. This is set against the barbaric conduct of the present prosecutor. In the *prooemium* Cicero claims that the issue is not the guilt of a weak old man but whether the authority of the senate, the *imperium* of the consul, and the common action (*consensio*) of good men should prevail against those who threatened the community.[53] He turns the prosecutor's complaint, that the process before the *duumviri* had been abolished, into a charge of 'regal' cruelty against the prosecutor, in that he had sought to revive primitive forms of justice which had been banished in company with the kings and now needed to be hunted up in the records of the annals and the commentaries of the kings.[54] This allows him to contrast Labienus, who wished, after duly taking the auspices for the *comitia centuriata*, to set up a cross for the execution of citizens in the Campus Martius, unfavourably with himself, who wished to keep the assemblies of the Roman people uncontaminated by such crimes and the liberty enshrined in *provocatio* unimpaired: which of them was *popularis* (*Rab. Perd.* 11)? Labienus' credentials as a *popularis* are also questioned by contrasting him with the proposer of the *lex Porcia* about *provocatio* and with C. Gracchus, the author of the law forbidding capital condemnations without the authority of the Roman people. Gracchus never tried to avenge his brother by an execution; Labienus takes sadistic satisfaction in the ritual formulae ordering the covering of the condemned man's head and the hanging of his body from an unlucky tree (*Rab. Perd.* 12–16).

Antonius defending Norbanus and Cicero defending Cornelius sought to rescue their client's reputation before attacking the opposition. Here Cicero commences his retaliation in the *prooemium* with his attacks on Labienus' cruelty. He says little about his client himself, perhaps because there was not much good that could be said. The centrepiece of the speech is the narrative of the events of 100. Cicero recalls the 'last' decree of the senate directed at the consul Marius and Valerius Flaccus, their enlisting of the help of the praetors and tribunes, Glaucia and Saturninus excepted, and the formal declaration of an emergency levy: all those who wished the *res publica* secure should take up arms and follow them.[55] On the Capitol there were Saturninus, Glaucia, Saufeius, the *soi-disant* son of C. Gracchus, and Labienus' uncle. In the

---

[53] *Rab. Perd.* 2, cf. 4. See ibid. 34 for Cicero's appeal to the jury to support the continued use of the consul's cry to arms.

[54] *Rab. Perd.* 10, 15. Because the duumviral process is tyrannical, Cicero associates it with Tarquin the Proud (ibid. 13), not with Tullus Hostilius, as annalists apparently did (Livy 1. 26; Dion. Hal. *AR* 3. 22). In Dionysius of Halicarnassus (ibid. 6) there is a popular vote about Horatius but no trace of the *duumviri* or the ritual formulae that Livy (ibid.) and Cicero (*Rab. Perd.* 13) highlight.

[55] *Rab. Perd.* 20 cf. 21, 34.

forum were the whole senate, the equestrian order, then at the height of their influence in the courts, and everyone of every rank who believed his safety depended on that of the *res publica*.

The leading men (*principes*) are enumerated: the arthritic *princeps senatus*, M. Scaurus, in the *comitium*; Q. Scaevola, aged, disease-ridden, and near-paralysed; consulars, including L. Metellus, C. Atilius Serranus, P. Rutilius Rufus, C. Flavius Fimbria, and Q. Lutatius Catulus; after them a rollcall of aristocratic families, ending with the then young men who were still alive in Rome in 63. Which side, Cicero asks rhetorically, should Rabirius have chosen (*Rab. Perd*. 20–1)? In the same way that he inserted Cornelius in a catalogue of the heroes of the plebs, Rabirius is shown as part of an army of defenders of Rome, indeed an army that was Rome. By contrast, if Labienus had been there to join his uncle, he would have joined a group of criminals, who 'took refuge in death because of the baseness of their life'. Even those of Saturninus' supporters who survived the conflict in 100, like Sextus Titius and Gaius Appuleius Decianus, were soon condemned (*Rab. Perd*. 22–5). Labienus' cause was dead before he was born. His prosecution was an accusation of the outstanding men of that time—Catulus, Scaurus, the Mucii, Crassus, Antonius. With them were the *equites*, then at the height of their importance through their command of the courts, the *tribuni aerarii*, and men from all ranks who took up arms.[56]

In the conclusion there was the customary *commiseratio*, evoking the fate of the defendant, should he be condemned (*Rab. Perd*. 36–8). But this was linked with a greater issue. In the *pro Cornelio* Cicero called on the jury to defend the tribunate; here he focused on the preservation of the immortality of Rome and her empire. Rome was no longer threatened from outside, especially since the convenient suicide of Rome's long-term enemy, King Mithridates VI of Pontus, but it had to be saved from sedition and internal threats.[57] This meant defending the consul's right to call the people to arms. Cicero claims that he would have imitated Marius in 63, had there been the need, but the threat now was not the occupation of the Capitol but a pernicious accusation that needed to be resisted by votes, because it was an attack on the majesty of the Roman people (ibid. 35). Here he sought neatly to steal the clothes of the prosecution by appropriating for his own side the concept of *maiestas populi*

---

[56] Ibid. 27, cf. 20, 31. Another example of Cicero highlighting the event that was the subject of a case in such a way as to obscure the dubious activities of his client in the general glow of a glorious occasion, can be found in another speech of the same year, the *pro Murena*. Here the centrepiece is the consular election of 63 (*Mur*. 49–53), when Catiline, surrounded by his young men from Rome and settlers from Etruria, had been making dire threats against those who would oppose him but was defeated by a presiding consul wearing a breastplate and an assembly that reacted against Catiline's threats by choosing Murena.

[57] *Rab. Perd*. 32–4. Note 'nullus est reliquus rex...' (33).

Romani, used by Saturninus to found a *quaestio* in the *popularis* interest. It was an inversion of his method in *pro Cornelio*, where the prosecution had used the concept to attack a seditious tribune and Cicero had relocated it—where Norbanus and Saturninus would have wanted it—in the tribune's promotion of the demands and the freedom of the plebs.

The *pro Rabirio* was one of the consular speeches published by Cicero in 60 BC, as models for young orators (*Att*. 2. 1. 3). The question arises whether the text we possess of the *pro Rabirio* was modified in the light of the later Catilinarian conspiracy and Cicero's desire to present his own actions at that time in the best possible light. The 'last decree' provides an obvious potential bridge. However, Cicero's defence of the decree and its implications is directed precisely towards the events of 100, not those of November and December 63. The procedure that Cicero wants to defend is the consul's universal call to arms in an emergency, something which he himself did not have to use in late 63, because there was in fact no violence in the city requiring this remedy, no occupation of the Capitol by a tribune.[58] In 63 the consuls held a levy after Catiline left Rome, but this was to produce an army for C. Antonius to command in Etruria.[59] Furthermore, the lynching of Saturninus and Glaucia in the aftermath of military action only provided a relevant comparison to Cicero's execution of the leading urban conspirators in so far as both actions were justified by the claim that the victims were enemies (*hostes*) of the Roman people. Cicero does indeed call Saturninus an enemy in *pro Rabirio* but only once in the text that survives, and he does not labour the point (*Rab. Perd.* 18). We should conclude that the text of *pro Rabirio* preserves Cicero's view of the political situation about midsummer 63, when he might fear some future uprising but could not know the form it would take.[60]

In both these trials Cicero was facing a prosecution that had a plausible case. Cornelius had disregarded a sacrosanct tribune's veto and had stirred up violence, both in his tribunate and in 66 at the time of the first attempted accusation. Even if Scaeva, the slave of Q. Croton, had actually killed Saturninus,[61] Rabirius had been deeply involved in the death of the sacrosanct tribune, not to mention his companions.[62] It was true that Rabirius had been

---

[58] *Rab. Perd.* 34–5; cf. 20.   [59] Sall. *Cat.* 36. 3.

[60] It is worth remarking by way of comparison that in the published *De Lege Agraria* 3. 3 ff. Cicero was happy to present an attack on Sullan land-assignations, which conflicted with his current policy of respecting them, stated in the speech he made on Flavius' agrarian bill (*Att.* 1. 19. 4; the date of this speech is about three months earlier than the letter referring to the circulation of his consular orations, *Att.* 2. 1. 3).

[61] *Rab. Perd.* 31; the grant of freedom as a reward for this action presumably came from the master and was not necessarily the result of official recognition.

[62] It is not clear to me that Appian, *B.Civ.* 1. 33. 142 was right to place the affair on 10 Dec. 100, the first day of Saturninus' new tribunate and of that of L. Equitius, the *soi-disant* Gracchus. See Gabba's (1958) commentary *ad loc.* and Badian, 1984.

summoned to arms by the consuls, but Saturninus had surrendered and entrusted himself to the *fides* of Marius. Neither Cornelius nor Rabirius appears to have been a particularly sympathetic character. Cornelius was prepared to see his trial disrupted by the use of gangs and may well have deployed his wealth to buy off an accusation.[63] It is not surprising that he was only acquitted after a second hearing. Rabirius had delighted in the violence against the seditious, but probably acquired sympathy in 63 as a result of the savage punishment proposed for him. Nevertheless, the prosecution took the assembly trial almost to the point of voting before the praetor Metellus Celer used the device of lowering the flag on the Ianiculum to bring it to an end.[64]

There were good political reasons for Cicero to undertake both defences. How far that of Cornelius would have ingratiated him with Pompey is hard to say. Though associated with Gabinius and Manilius, Cornelius had no direct claims on Pompey's gratitude. Nevertheless, Cornelius was wealthy and influential. The author of the letter on electioneering ascribed to Quintus Cicero mentions the *sodalitas* of C. Cornelius as one of those Cicero had usefully brought on his side thanks to his advocacy.[65] Equally, Rabirius was not without connections. Cicero refers to the wealthy C. Curtius Postumus, the father of Caesar's later friend and Cicero's client C. Rabirius Postumus; also to Rabirius' support from Apulia and Campania, which reminds us of Cicero's accumulation of connections throughout Italy in the pursuit of his consulship.[66] Defending Cornelius gave Cicero the opportunity to deliver a *popularis* oration, which was required in the service of his client and for that very reason could be conveniently dissociated from his personal sentiments, should that prove necessary. In the case of Rabirius Cicero had the opportunity to articulate genuinely felt sentiments that reflected the optimate political position he had adopted as consul.[67] Both cases are part of the political history of the period, but both are also excellent examples of Cicero's forensic technique, when he was required to argue a case and not simply dismiss the statements of witnesses.

---

[63] Asc. 59–60, cf. 75; *Corn.* 1. 42–3, 2. 9 P.

[64] Dio 37. 27. 3, believing that Rabirius would have been convicted. There seems no good reason to think that Celer was cooperating with Labienus and Caesar. Since the flag terminated the normal assembly-trial, not the earlier duumviral prosecution, it was not needed to protect Rabirius from execution: he could have gone into exile.

[65] *Commentariolum Petitionis* 19.

[66] *Rab. Perd.* 8; cf. Wiseman, 1971, 136 ff.

[67] Notice his recollection of the repudiation of Rullus' agrarian bill with the cooperation of the assembly, *Rab. Perd.* 32. The classic exposition of scepticism regarding Cicero's *popularis* statements is that of Heinze, 1909. They certainly did not reflect the principles he enunciated later. How far he believed them at the moment of delivery is another matter.

Part C

History in Speeches and Letters

X

Candidature and Consulship

CANDIDATURE

This book began by considering a famous letter of summer 65 BC on Cicero's consular candidature. About this time evidence from speeches and correspondence combine to produce a historical picture of Cicero's life and political career. Before, his speeches are on the whole more illustrative of rhetorical and forensic technique than political attitude or personal views. Now they can be viewed and need to be viewed in conjunction with the evidence of the letters. The Cicero we find in the letters is an entity that justifies Heraclitus' dictum. He fluctuates not only from year to year, but from month to month, even from day to day. A more narrative structure is the only way to do justice to the flow and to place the varied evidence in context.

The candidature is an important historical topic in its own right because it illustrates for us how a 'new man' such as Cicero could reach his supreme ambition of consular dignity and because it raises questions about Cicero's relationship to other politicians—Pompey, Catiline, and the men Cicero describes in another letter to Atticus as 'your friends, noble persons' (*Att.* 1. 2. 2). Cicero is referring here to men like the orator Q. Hortensius, L. Lucullus, L. Manlius Torquatus, M. Cato, and the young M. Brutus (Q. Servilius Caepio Brutus).[1] This second letter from 65 BC shows, like the first, how important at this stage of the canvass Cicero judged the support from men at the summit of the political establishment to be.

Its most sensational item is the revelation that at this point Cicero was considering defending Catiline *de repetundis*. In the previous letter Cicero had compared the likelihood of Catiline's acquittal to that of a verdict that it was dark at midday (*Att.* 1.1.1). Nevertheless, as we have seen (Ch. VIII above), even men palpably guilty could be defended as 'good men'. Much later, when defending Caelius, Cicero was to claim that he had once almost been deceived by Catiline, 'when he seemed to me a good citizen and a supporter of all the best men and a firm and loyal friend' (*Cael.* 14). It is clear that in summer

---

[1] *Att.* 1. 18. 6, 1. 19. 6, 2. 25. 1; Nepos, *Att.* 5. 1, 15. 3, 16. 1. For Cicero's cultivation of Pompey see Ch. IX with n. 22 on *Pro Cornelio* and App. 2 on *De Imperio Gnaei Pompeii*.

65 BC there was no thought of Catiline having conspired to overthrow the *res publica*. If Cicero had defended him, he would have been standing shoulder to shoulder with men like L. Manlius Torquatus—legal adviser (*advocatus*) to Catiline at the trial and one of the consuls of 65, later alleged to have been one of those whom Catiline conspired to assassinate about the beginning of his consular year[2]—and a number of consulars who gave character-testimony (*laudationes*) for the defendant (*Sull.* 81).

Cicero would have had the jury that he wanted thanks to the full cooperation of the prosecutor (*summa accusatoris voluntate*), P. Clodius. In other words, during the alternate rejection of jurymen by prosecution and defence (see Ch. VII with n. 28), Clodius had not excluded friends of Catiline—this must have occurred with someone other than Cicero acting as Catiline's chief defence counsel. Clodius was evidently not yet Cicero's enemy.[3] Later Cicero was to allege that Clodius was practising *praevaricatio*, collusive prosecution intended to fail—conveniently ignoring that he himself might have profited (*Har. Resp.* 42). Most commentators have assumed that this is what Cicero meant by the phrase in the letter, but at the time he may have been simply referring jokingly to Clodius' carelessness in this respect. Asconius was cautious about believing that there was *praevaricatio* (87 C). Asconius must also be right in arguing that in practice Cicero cannot have joined Catiline's defence team; on this point he criticized Fenestella, a historian of the Augustan period (85–7 C). There is no mention of such a defence in Cicero's attack on Catiline in the speech *In Toga Candida* of the next year; it would also have featured in the younger Torquatus' attack on Cicero when he prosecuted and Cicero defended Sulla in 62.

By the eve of the consular elections in 64 attitudes to Catiline had changed. One piece of evidence is the fragmentary *In Toga Candida*, a speech originally delivered shortly before the election and probably published almost immediately; another, at least potentially, is what purports to be a letter of Quintus to Marcus Cicero, attached to almost all the manuscripts of the latter books of *Ad Familiares*, which contains a lengthy briefing on how Marcus' consular election campaign should be conducted.[4] The authenticity of this work, described in its last sentence as 'commentariolum petitionis', has been much

---

[2] *Sull.* 12, 49, 81; cf. Sall. *Cat.* 18. 5. The authenticity of the story of a conspiracy to massacre the consuls and other leading men is now generally discredited among scholars. Pathfinders in this direction were Frisch, 1948; Syme, 1964, 88–99; Seager, 1964.

[3] See Plut. *Cic.* 29. 1 for Cicero's previous friendship with Clodius and the latter's support for Cicero in 63 as a bodyguard (probably on 5 December on the Capitol). Clodius probably also assisted Murena by organizing bribery at the consular elections of 63. See Cicero's general denunciation of his behaviour on his return from membership of Murena's staff in Gaul (*Har. Resp.* 42; Tatum, 1999, 55–7). On the alleged *praevaricatio* see Gruen, 1971, 59–62.

[4] See especially Balsdon, 1963; Nardo, 1970; Richardson, 1971.

disputed. It has been alleged that this is the work of a later rhetorician who used Cicero's speeches *In Toga Candida* and *pro Murena* to create a pamphlet of advice. None of the alleged errors of detail or anachronisms in the *Commentariolum* turn out on inspection to be decisive.[5] Resemblances between passages from the *Commentariolum* and from *In Toga Candida* or *pro Murena* can be explained as Marcus Cicero's improvement on material in his brother's, stylistically inferior, work. The fundamental problem is to explain why the *Commentariolum* was created, if genuine. Here it must be recognized that there was no question of Marcus needing his brother's advice on electoral campaigning at the apparent time of the composition of the work in the immediate run-up to the elections in 64. The campaign was already well-developed, as we can see from the letters to Atticus in 65. However, by the same token Marcus' letter of advice to Quintus (*QF* 1. 1), written at the earliest in 60, after Quintus had already administered his province for a year, was equally superfluous. In fact, both can be interpreted as works written for discreet circulation, intended to create or confirm support for the ostensible recipient.[6]

The author of the *Commentariolum* confronts Marcus' problems under two heads, Marcus's 'newness' (*novitas*) and the immensity of the task of campaigning amid the vast electorate of Rome (*Comm. Pet.* 2). These could be regarded as two aspects of the same problem. Cicero was short of inherited connections and this enhanced the difficulty of communicating with the large number of people he needed to reach: *novitas* also raised questions about merit. The compensations for *novitas* were, first, Cicero's eloquence (2), then his wide range of friendships (3–5), finally the inadequacy of the opposition from the nobility (7–12), who were either feeble (Galba and Cassius Longinus) or criminal (Antonius and Catiline). Cicero's existing support among the *publicani*, the *equester ordo* in general, the *municipia* in Italy, the *collegia* at Rome, and the young men interested in rhetoric needed to be reinforced by appeal to the nobles, including the younger generation, and especially consulars (4–6)—essentially Cicero's own theme in *Ad Atticum* 1. 1 and 2. In particular the nobles needed to be persuaded that Cicero had always thought

---

[5] Objections conveniently summarized by Nisbet, 1961*b*. See also Henderson, 1950. Among the disappearing problems, (i) the defence of Gallius (*Comm. Pet.* 19) would have taken place in late 66 after Gallius' election to the praetorship of 65 (Asc. 62 C) and after (*postea*) Catiline had bought Gallius' gladiators (Asc. 88 C); (ii) as Nisbet (1961*b*, 85) recognizes, though he finds it forced, Cicero could well have already been chosen as defence counsel by C. Piso on his return from Gaul in 64 before the consular elections (cf. *Comm. Pet.* 2): the time taken in *repetundae* cases by the *inquisitio* in the province and the difficulty in completing trials within the calendar year would account for the trial not taking place till 63.

[6] Essentially the conclusions of Nardo (1970) and Richardson (1971), though the latter believed that *Comm. Pet.* would have been dangerous to Cicero, if it fell into the wrong hands.

like an optimate: any *popularis* sentiments had been designed to gain goodwill or nullify opposition from Pompey (5), a clear reference to *De Imperio Cn. Pompeii* and *Pro Cornelio*. The good repute of Cicero's friends was implicitly contrasted with the low-grade support for Catiline and Antonius and their dubious political records (8–10). Interestingly, the list here of Catiline's victims in the proscriptions is not identical with that which appears in *In Toga Candida*.[7]

The main section of the *Commentariolum* (13 ff.) is devoted to winning friends and influencing people, with a preliminary warning about his detractors (*invidi*)—some jealous rivals, others who had suffered in the courts from Cicero's eloquence, yet others who disliked his support of Pompey (13–15). Cicero had simultaneously to cultivate friends and acquire the general favour of the public. Friendships here are not limited to the ideal friendships later praised in *De Amicitia* (15, 20, 31), but include those described there as 'vulgar and mediocre' (*Amic.* 26), created by benefits (*beneficia*), services (*officia*), long acquaintance, and natural affability (*Comm. Pet.* 16). Indeed, although those who have some genuine connection with Cicero through family or social ties are to be treated with particular affection, in an election the term friend could be stretched to cover almost anyone who offered support of some kind. On the one hand there were members of the household and genuine intimates, fellow-tribesmen, neighbours, clients, freedmen, even slaves. On the other there were those who were or should be attached because they either reflected distinction on the candidate or brought influence in a particular section of the electorate—the voting districts (*tribus*), centuries, clubs of the wealthy (*sodalitates*), the *municipia* in the countryside, and the quarters in the city (17–24, 29–32). The author moves on to techniques—manipulating the attendance of those who performed the morning greeting (*salutatores*), those who escorted Cicero to the forum (*deductores*) and those who formed his permanent entourage in public (*adsectatores*) (33–8). Finally, the discussion is of how to treat the apparently uncommitted part of the electorate, where the essentials are to remember names, to be benign and obliging, and to promise anything that could be decently promised (41–53).[8]

The reader of this little treatise comes away with the impression that Cicero's campaign is well-informed, streetwise, and only as scrupulous as it needs to be. The potential breadth of his support is emphasized, not least in any branch of the equestrian order, including tax-collectors and the cadet

---

[7] In *Comm. Pet.* 9, apart from M. Marius and Q. Caecilius, we hear of the Titinii, Nanneii, and Tanusii; in *In Toga Candida* Cicero mentioned Marius, Caecilius, Tanusius, and Volumnius (Asc. 84 C).

[8] On electoral practice and malpractice in this period see Taylor, 1961, 50 ff.; Wiseman, 1971; Lintott, 1990*a*.

members of the nobility. It is implied that Cicero is a winner in ways that were unlikely to offend anyone except those who were his enemies from the start or of particularly strict ethical principles.

The *Commentariolum* is more about friends than enemies; *In Toga Candida* is the converse. We possess it only through the *lemmata* in Asconius' commentary. It is chronologically the second speech known to us that Cicero delivered in the senate, the first being the *De Rege Alexandrino* of 65 against the project of Crassus and Caesar to intervene in Egypt.[9] Until his praetorship Cicero, as a junior senator who would not have been called to speak until late in the debate, would have had few, if any, opportunities of making significant contributions to senate discussion. *In Toga Candida* was classified by Quintilian with *In Clodium et Curionem* and *In Pisonem* as a vehicle for *vituperatio*, though delivered as a *sententia*, that is a response to a question put by the magistrate presiding over the senate.[10] It was not usual at Rome for candidates to debate with one another before elections or even to employ invective against their competitors. Moreover, debate in the senate was in principle determined by the terms of its president's introduction (*relatio*): hence the *curia* was an even more unlikely venue for any such attack on a fellow-candidate. In 64 the opportunity was provided by a motion in the senate urging that a new law against electoral bribery with a harsher penalty should be passed: this was approved but vetoed by the tribune Q. Mucius Orestinus (the attempt was in fact repeated in 63 and led to the law of Cicero himself and Antonius).[11]

Our reconstruction of the speech is made more difficult, as Kumaniecki pointed out, by the fact that Asconius has not recorded the *lemmata* strictly in the order in which they appear in the speech. Fragment 8 P ('Why should I proclaim to the world how you violated your province?...', addressed to

---

[9] Crassus had proposed to intervene in Egypt on the ground that the kingdom had been left to Rome. Cicero's speech opposing this survives in a few fragments, mainly preserved in the Bobbio scholia. That it was a speech to the senate appears from the phrase 'quae sunt nostra iudicia', referring to previous judgments on this topic that can only have been made in the senate, and from the scholiast's comment on the *lemma* following, 'debent esse modestissima,,' 'nam vult orator intellegi paene inpudenter senatum de causa sua iudicare voluisse' (*Schol. Bob.* 92 St.; frr. 3–4 P). The intervention would have been in theory on behalf of Ptolemy Neos Dionusios, but would have allowed the designated commander, Caesar (Suet. *Iul.* 11), to make money for the treasury from selling land that Rome claimed as hers (*Leg. Agr.* 2. 43–4), and, no doubt, privately for himself from Ptolemy. I am grateful to Dr M. T. Griffin for advice on this point.

[10] *Inst. Or.* 3. 7. 2.

[11] Asc. 83 C; cf. *Mur.* 3, 46–7, 67; Dio 37. 29. 1 (further refs in *MRR* ii. 166). Curiously enough, the closest parallel to the *In Toga Candida* is the speech that Catiline delivered in 63 after Cicero had postponed the holding of the elections in order, so he alleges, to extract a comment from Catiline on the revolutionary statements that he had been reported to Cicero as having made to his friends (*Mur.* 50–1).

Catiline) appears more briefly later in the speech (21 P), where it seems more appropriate in a chronological list of Catiline's misdeeds. It was mentioned by Asconius (85 C) in anticipation in order to contribute to a refutation of the historian Fenestella's view that Cicero had actually defended Catiline in his trial *de repetundis* in 65 as he had planned (*Att.* 1. 2. 1). Asconius argues that Cicero could not have failed to reproach Catiline for ignoring this *beneficium*. For the same reason Kumaniecki inferred that the fragment about Antonius being elected to the praetorship, allegedly through Cicero's generosity (5 P), should belong with the other fragment about his election (23 P), and further that 6 P, a reproach to Mucius Orestinus for ignoring Cicero's services to him as defence counsel—which, according to Asconius (85 C), followed closely on 5 P—also belonged to the latter part of the speech.[12]

If this is taken into account, a comparatively simple pattern emerges. Cicero begins by claiming that massive bribery was being engineered by an unnamed *nobilis* on behalf of Catiline and Antonius (1 P)—Asconius inferred (83 C) that this man was either Crassus or Caesar, but his identity is uncertain. Cicero then explains Catiline and Antonius' need for bribery by their lack of clients and friends resulting from their disgraceful lives (2 P), and their readiness to use bribery by their lack of respect for either the senate, the courts (3–4 P), or the Roman people (10 P). In particular they underestimated Cicero himself (11 P). Ultimately they were prepared to defend their corruption by force, either with slave herdsmen or with bought gladiators (12–13 P). In fact there was no need for a new bribery law when two consuls-designate had been condemned in 66 under the *lex Calpurnia* (14 P)—passed in 67 by the consul Piso under pressure from Cornelius (Ch. X with n. 8). Cicero then dismisses Antonius as a lightweight villain in order to concentrate on Catiline (15 P). Catiline's weaknesses as a candidate are first analysed by considering those he has offended—the leading men (*principes*), the senators, the order of knights (*ordo equester*), and the plebs (16 P). Cicero later shifts to a chronological approach, beginning with Catiline's crimes under Sulla's dictatorship, then adducing his alleged intercourse with a Vestal Virgin, adultery and marriage to his bastard daughter, his plundering of the province of Africa, and finally his plot with Cn. Piso as accomplice to murder *optimates*—the so-called 'first Catilinarian conspiracy' (7–10 P, 17–22 P).

'I pass over that nefarious enterprise of yours and the day that nearly brought grief and misery to the *res publica*, when with Gnaeus Piso as your accomplice, not to mention anyone else, you intended to make a slaughter of *optimates*' (22 P). The *praeteritio* is, as often (cf. 15 P; *2Verr.* 5. 51–2), a means

[12] Kumaniecki, 1961.

of emphasis. Equally emphatic, potentially, is the position of the charge at the end of the list of Catiline's crimes. This is the earliest mention of the so-called 'first conspiracy' in a surviving Ciceronian text; it is, however, clear that the story of a conspiracy was already in circulation. It had, one may conjecture, surfaced after Catiline's acquittal in the *quaestio de repetundis* in 65, as the election campaign warmed up. Nevertheless, Cicero's remark is brief and allusive, which is remarkable, given that the conspiracy charge, if true, was more serious than any other levelled at Catiline. Thus Cicero uses the story while apparently reluctant to make much of it—a contrast to his treatment of Catiline's behaviour under Sulla. Certainly, it enables him to leave the conspiracy mistily hanging in the air without the need for substantiation. However, the minimal reference may also reflect Cicero's own estimate at that time of the veracity of the charge.

More important than Catiline's own behaviour as a revolutionary in 66–65 is the hint at the shadowy figures behind him: Asconius seems to assume that they were Crassus and Caesar, as Cicero claimed in the secret *ex post facto* memoir *De Consiliis Suis* (92 C, cf. 83 C).[13] Some time later in the speech Cicero refers to anonymous persons (24 P; Asc. 93 C) who first tried to use the 'little Spanish stiletto' and were now trying to draw two daggers at once. Asconius plausibly takes the stiletto to be Piso and the daggers to be Catiline and Antonius, but offers no opinion here on the identity of the nameless men he calls 'bad citizens'. It is likely that he thought this another reference to Caesar and Crassus.[14] Whether he was right to follow Cicero's memoir in this way is another matter. The source of electoral corruption, which he consequently took to be either Crassus or Caesar (83 C), could well have been Autronius or Sulla. What is in any case important is Cicero's vision in this speech of Catiline and Antonius as dangerous, not just in themselves, but more importantly as front men for more powerful figures. This is not a theme of the *Commentariolum*, but that work, on the view argued here, was designed not to offend the powerful figures whose support Cicero was trying to draw to himself. In the *In Toga Candida* Catiline is dangerous as the tool of other men; in the *Commentariolum* Catiline is not a present threat to the *res publica* at all.

---

[13] Brunt, 1957, 195, followed by Gruen, 1974, 138, raised doubts about Asconius' acceptance of Cicero's later allegation that Crassus and Caesar were behind the campaign of Catiline and Antonius in 64. Marshall, 1985, 285–7 was prepared to believe the *De Consiliis Suis*. The identity of the house of the bribe manager must in any case remain uncertain.

[14] The emendation of the paradosis of Asc. 92 C, *quos nominet intelligitis*, to *quos non nominet intelligitis* (Kiessling–Schoell) gives plausible sense to what would otherwise be an otiose and (since only one person is named by Cicero) inaccurate comment by Asconius.

CONSULSHIP

Cicero was elected consul by the unanimous vote of all the centuries required to give him the necessary majority; C. Antonius was chosen as his colleague. Unfortunately we do not possess any correspondence for his consular year. He left a public record of that year in the form of a commentary written in both Latin and Greek which unfortunately no longer survives (*Att.* 2. 1. 1–2). Furthermore, in the middle of 60 BC he wrote up a number of his consular speeches for publication. He explained to Atticus that he wished to have a corpus of orations like Demosthenes' *Philippics*, which were more grand and political than the argumentative forensic variety, and hence had collected a group of speeches to be named 'consular' (ibid. 3). The first two were the speech to the senate on 1 January and that to the people on the agrarian law; the third one supporting the praetor Otho over the segregation of the *equites* in the theatre; the fourth the defence of C. Rabirius against the treason charge (discussed in Chapter IX); the fifth a speech in opposition to the restoration of privileges to those proscribed by Sulla; the sixth Cicero's address to the people when he surrendered the right to go to a province. There followed four *Catilinarian Orations* and an appendix of two brief speeches on the agrarian law. Judicial speeches, such as the *pro Murena* and the *pro C. Pisone*, were thus excluded; the exception made for the *pro Rabirio* was presumably because of the importance of the political issue it handled. Of these we possess the four *Catilinarians*, the whole of the speech to the people on the agrarian law, part of the preceding speech to the senate on 1 January, another brief speech on the same topic, and a fragmentary text of the *pro Rabirio*.

The gaps in the tradition make it difficult to analyse the corpus as whole. Nevertheless, it seems that these speeches, like Demosthenes' *Philippics*, were united not only by style and tone but by theme. Essentially they were about the defence of the present *res publica* against those who sought to subvert it, hence optimate and conservative in theme, but also popular in that they appealed to a consensus of good men in support of the consuls and senate. This is clear in the agrarian speeches, the *pro Rabirio*, and the *Catilinarians*; it is not difficult to see how the speeches about equestrian privilege, the maintenance of political disability for the children of the proscribed, and Cicero's compact with his fellow consul, could have fitted into the same pattern. The relation of the texts to what was actually said at the time varies from speech to speech. At best, there was an editorial element in the writing up of the orations delivered; at worst, Cicero may have made a fresh start: we have noticed earlier (Ch. II) how the published fourth Catilinarian was a cento, probably involving free composition.

In fact, the information the speeches provide the historian about the events of Cicero's consulship is somewhat limited: Cicero's commentary on his consulship,[15] however rhetorically elaborated, would have been more helpful to us, had it survived. Nevertheless, the speeches do reflect the particular circumstances in which they were delivered and were doubtless intended to create a narrative effect, conducting the reader of the corpus though the vicissitudes of Cicero's consulship. Moreover, they are immensely important as a guide to Cicero's attitudes and self-perception.

CICERO AND RULLUS

An agrarian bill, under the names of the new college of tribunes who entered office on 10 December 64, had been announced in a public meeting on 12 December by its leading proponent, P. Servilius Rullus and published before the year was out (*Leg. Agr.* 2. 11–13). This was a major event. Agrarian legislation had been common in the period from the Gracchi to Sulla, whether concerned with the reorganization and reassignment of public land in Italy or with settlement in the provinces. Sulla's victory had led to an enormous convulsion of land-holdings in Italy and a large programme of allotment to Sulla's veteran soldiers, whose inequities were at the same time a source of vested interest and a cause of bitterness for those who had suffered thereby. From the period between 80 and 63 BC only one, obscure, agrarian bill is known to us, the *rogatio Plotia*, whose ratification by the people is in doubt and whose implementation was certainly ineffective. For the proposal of the tribune Flavius in 60 was, according to Cicero, to a great extent a revival of this bill. The *rogatio Plotia*, therefore, must have involved an investigation of public land improperly made private, including that seized by Sullan supporters, and the acquisition of further land with a view to new allotments.[16]

Rullus' bill was different. We can extract from Cicero's quotations and descriptions, albeit tendentious, a fairly full outline of the bill's contents. It began by providing for the creation of a ten-man land-commission by a form of popular election, involving seventeen out of the thirty-five tribes. These commissioners were to hold office for five years with praetorian powers, the

---

[15] *Att.* 2. 1. 1–2; Plut. *Crass.* 13. 5.
[16] *Att.* 1. 18. 6, 1. 19. 4; the bill most plausibly assigned to 70–69 BC, see *MRR* ii Supp. 46, iii. 158, following Smith, 1957. On the context of Rullus' bill in the story of land-tenure in the late Republic see *JRLR* 55–8.; on its likely contents *RS* ii, no. 52 and Ferrary, 1988.

right to take the auspices, and a large staff of attendants and equipment.[17] They were given the right both to sell public land in order to raise money and to buy land for distribution with the proceeds. Sales would have affected land in Italy confiscated by Sulla but not sold, land outside Italy acquired since 88 BC, and the surviving public land in and outside Italy currently rented out. This would have privatized much provincial land, but to judge from the precedent of the agrarian law of 111 BC, it would not have removed the right of the Roman people to tax the land so sold.[18] There was also to be an increase in rent on lands retained in the public sector.[19] With this money and with further sums realized from booty handed over to the treasury,[20] cultivable land was to be bought in Italy for distribution. In particular, a colony was to be founded on the site of Capua.[21] However, any public assignments of the right to exploit land or water since the demise of the Marian regime in 82 BC were to be maintained, including all those that resulted from the Sullan proscriptions and confiscations.[22]

From what remains of the first speech in the senate on 1 January, it appears that Cicero's criticisms in the senate and before the people were essentially the same: the bill would involve the privatization of important public assets, the concession of arbitrary and tyrannical powers to the commission, and the creation of a military threat to the liberty of the *res publica* from the settlement of soldiers in Italy.[23] In the conclusion to the first speech he urges the senate to defend the authority of their order and asks the tribunes to desert their colleagues and join the 'good men' (*boni*), at the same time promising popular support (*Leg. Agr.* 1. 26–7). In the speech to the people he has to make good this promise by appearing 'popular' and thus stealing the clothes of the proposers of the bill: he cannot sincerely appeal to traditional plebeian political instinct.

---

[17] *Leg. Agr.* 2. 16, 24, 26, 28–9, 32. Election by less than half of the tribes was the procedure used to elect the *pontifex maximus* (24). The *potestas praetoria* (32) was not a military command but power, which would have enabled the commission to ensure their orders were obeyed and gave them jurisdiction.

[18] *Leg. Ag.* 2. 35, 38, 48, 50–1, cf. 1. 3–6. The foreign land acquired included acquisitions in Pamphylia, Bithynia, the former kingdom of Mithridates of Pontus, the Thracian Chersonese, Macedonia, Corinth, Cyrene, Spain, and the province of Africa (2. 50–1). For selling provincial land that would remain *vectigalis* see *lex agraria* (*RS* i. no. 2; *JRLR* 177 ff.), ll. 46 ff.; 48 ff.; 70 ff.; 96 ff.; *Imp. Rom.* 80–3.

[19] *Leg. Agr.* 1. 10, 2. 56–8.

[20] *Leg. Agr.* 1. 12–13, 2. 59. The commission was to take over judicial investigations of money which commanders had failed to pass on to the treasury, as they should have done.

[21] *Leg. Agr.* 1. 17–18, 2. 73–5, 76–97.

[22] *Leg. Agr.* 3. 4, 7, 11.

[23] Compare *Leg. Agr.* 1. 2–6 with 2. 36–56; 1. 7–10 with 2. 55–8; 1. 14–22 (esp. 17) with 2. 63–90 (esp. 75).

His first speech to the people had been the advocacy of Manilius' bill about Pompey's Mithridatic command in 66 (App. 2) There he gave his resounding success in the much-obstructed praetorian elections as a justification for venturing to address them in a *contio* (*Leg. Man.* 2). However, this did not lead to any further identification with the common people and their interests. The classes for whom Cicero requested especial sympathy then were the tax-collectors (*publicani*) and the businessmen, both those actually operating in Asia and those in Rome with money invested in the province (*Leg. Man.* 17–19). In the conclusion he did refer to the mass of people who had come to support the bill (69), but his own endorsement of the bill was cool and measured: it had other distinguished supporters (68), nor was he himself seeking influence with Pompey but only to lend his support to the will of the people, the dignity of the *res publica*, and the safety of the provinces and allies (70–1).

Cicero begins his speech to the people on Rullus' bill by appealing to a tradition that those who had achieved or renewed nobility by being elected consuls should thank the people for their choice and recall the glory of their ancestors. The speech Sallust gives C. Marius in his *Jugurtha* (85) after his election to the consulship of 107 BC is an interesting variant on this genre, in that, while implicitly thanking the people for 'maxumo vostro beneficio', he stresses his lack of ancestry.[24] Cicero for his part asserts that all he owed to his ancestors was birth and education, and this allows him to dwell instead on his, he claims, unparalleled success in reaching the consulship as a new man at the first attempt and *suo anno*, at the earliest age possible. His overwhelming election as a new man was an invasion of the fortress of the nobility.[25] The consequence was that he could not count on support from that quarter and 'certain men' would pounce on his mistakes as a criticism of not only himself but the electorate. In this way he sides up to the audience in the *contio* and prepared the way for the claim that he would be a 'popular consul', genuinely, not in name alone (*Leg. Ag.* 2. 5–7).[26]

Cicero sums up his case against the bill by saying that land will only be waved before the eyes of the Roman people: instead, everything will be handed over to 'certain men' who will make fortunes at the public expense

---

[24] Sall. *Jug.* 85. 3, cf. 8, 26 *beneficium*; ibid. 4, 14, 17, 24–5, lack of ancestry.

[25] *Leg. Agr.* 2. 1–4. Sallust's Marius is equally self-made: all that he has learnt 'ex parente meo et aliis sanctis viris' is that the refinements of living suit women, hard work men (85. 40).

[26] His claim (*Leg. Agr.* 2. 6) that he declared in the senate on 1 Jan. that he would be a *popularis* consul cannot be verified in what survives of that speech. In its peroration he argues that his promise that the peace ensuing from his frustration of the dangerous innovations of Rullus would be more popular than Rullus' bill, while referring to Rullus and his colleagues as *populares tribuni plebis* (1. 24–5), a less dramatic claim.

and tyranny will be established in place of the traditional plebeian right to liberty (2. 15–16). The diminution of *libertas* is a thread that runs through the rest of the speech. Liberty is destroyed by the bizarre system of election that Rullus has devised for his *decemviri* (16, 20, 24–5); moreover, the powers of the commission, once established, will create a *regnum* (32–5). A well-known characteristic of tyranny was that it seized private property—not usually a particular concern to the poor. However, the Rullan bill offered Cicero a magnificent alternative: the commission had powers to sell the public land of the Roman people (36 ff.).[27] One type of tyrannical action would be complemented by another, the implicit confirmation of the acts of a previous tyrant by providing maximum opportunity for Sullan profiteers to exploit their former gains (68 ff., 98).

At the same time the urban plebs would lose the privileges of Rome by being settled on an unsavoury and insanitary site in the Gargano or Apulia. Here Cicero claims that Rullus argued in the senate that he would thus 'drain off the urban plebs', implying that they were some kind of sewage (70–1).[28] After suggesting that the discretion granted the commission to plant colonies where it wished would permit them to place a military settlement on the Janiculum (74), Cicero reinforces this evocation of tyranny in lengthy and outraged denunciation of the project to refound Capua as a colony. This would not only deprive the people of public land that was theirs—yielding valuable taxation and occupied by the best kind of *plebs*—but would recreate the former rival to Rome under a new tyrannical oligarchy.[29] The spectre of tyranny was given further substance by Cicero's recalling the Marian attempt to found a colony at Capua in 83 BC.[30]

He also imputed a hostility to Pompey to the backers of the bill, in particular to those that wished to raise money from sales in Egypt (43–4)—the project of Crassus and Caesar in 65.[31] He stressed heavily that the prospective sale by the commission of the royal land of Mithridates, which was in fact legally unobjectionable, was an insult to Pompey (53–4). As for the sale of the gold and silver from booty and the *aurum coronarium*, he noted that Pompey was excused from liability under this chapter but treated this too as an insult (60–1). The view that the bill was in reality intended to undermine Pompey's power and influence is little favoured now. One problem is

---

[27] Note 'quod publicum populi Romani factum sit' (38); 'Mytilenae, quae certe vestrae, Quirites, belli lege ac victoriae iure factae sunt' (40); 'de populi Romani hereditate' (44), 'populi Romani auctionem' (47); 'haec P. Servili imperio...vestra facta sunt' (50).

[28] He himself was to use this terminology more explicitly in later private letters, *Att.* 1. 16. 11, 19. 4.

[29] *Leg. Agr.* 2. 76–98, esp. 80–4, 92–8.

[30] *Leg. Agr.* 2. 92–3, 98.   [31] Cf. *Leg. Agr.* 1. 1 and see above with n. 9.

that two of the tribunes, T. Labienus and T. Ampius Balbus, were on other evidence supporters of Pompey.[32] In fact, it was probably a compromise between a number of different interests, as one might have expected from a bill supported by the whole tribunician college. It may well have been backed by men with Marian sympathies like Caesar, but it was also in the interest of the possessors of land confiscated and distributed under Sulla's regime (67, 98).

Cicero's revival of the spectre of Marianism provided an opening for a counter-attack by the proposers of the bill, which in turn provoked Cicero's third speech. The proposers of the bill had held a *contio* in reply, portraying Cicero as a man working for the interests of Sullan *possessores* and an enemy of the welfare (*commoda*) of the plebs, hence by implication no *popularis*.[33] He faced a hostile audience. (*Leg. Agr.* 3. 2) His reply centred on ch. 40 of the bill (4 ff.), which, as he reproduced it, declared all land, buildings, inland waters, and other sites publicly assigned and possessed since 82 BC to be 'private land with as good title as any private land'. Thus the Sullan assignations had been confirmed by the bill. Cicero does his best to ridicule the phrase 'with as good title as any private land ('ut quae optimo iure privata sunt'). However, it had a perfectly acceptable legal meaning as 'not being subject to servitudes (such as liability to provide access to neighbours or water-rights) or special conditions'.[34] Moreover, to judge from the text Cicero actually quotes, the bill did not confirm possession effected without public authority, although later Cicero suggests that the unofficial holders of land formerly confiscated but left undistributed were hoping to make a financial killing from the bill.[35]

Where Cicero was on better ground was to point out the connection between Rullus and his father-in-law, C. Quinctius Valgus—since Sulla's dictatorship a land-owner near Casinum and in the *ager Hirpinus* and a magistrate in three Campanian towns, including Pompeii, where his name appears on both the theatre and amphitheatre.[36] It may well have been these accusations of personal interest that enabled Cicero to block the bill, whether

---

[32] Vell. 2. 40. 4; Dio 37. 21. 3–4. See for example Gruen 1974, 389–94; Seager, 2002, 68–9; contrast Gelzer, 1969, 73; Stockton, 1971, 88–91.

[33] *Leg. Agr.* 3. 1–3. For *popularis* concern with the welfare (*commodum/a*) of the people cf. ibid. 2. 78, 81; *Corn.* 2. 15 P; *Sest.* 103. The tradition goes back at least to Gaius Gracchus (*ORF* no. 48, fr. 44 = Gell. 11. 10. 3).

[34] See *JRLR* 229–30 on *lex agr.* 27.

[35] *Leg. Agr.* 3. 12: the word 'possessa' introduced after 'data, donata, concessa, vendita' in 11 should surely refer to the implementation of the means of transfer previously listed, which would have had implicitly the qualification 'publice', though the law could not have used the phrase 'publice possessa' here, since this would have meant 'confiscated'. See Ferrary, 1988, 158–60 on the problems in reconstructing the present passage.

[36] *Leg. Agr.* 3. 3, 8, 13–14; cf. *ILLRP* 523, 598, 645–6.

or not it was actually voted down as the elder Pliny claims.[37] In any case Pliny is right to see the second and third speeches, like the speech for Otho and that against the children of the proscribed, as testimony to Cicero's remarkable control over the people in *contiones*. This was the part of the *Consular Orations* that impressed Pliny. He does not mention the *Catilinarians*.

At the end of the second speech Cicero pointed to his common purpose with his fellow consul Antonius as a potential deterrent to any turbulent behaviour by tribunes (101–3). The situation imagined to some extent reflects that in 60 BC, when the consul Metellus Celer was imprisoned by the tribune Flavius (101). It also perhaps anticipates the common front Cicero formed with Antonius against Catiline later in 63. However, there is no doubt that *popularis* tribunes in the past had profited from division among the consuls. One sign of Cicero's success at this time was that Rullus saw no point in delaying the bill until February, when Cicero's colleague would be in possession of the *fasces* and the leader of the *res publica*.

THE CATILINARIAN SPEECHES

'Then Marcus Tullius the consul, whether fearing his presence or beside himself with rage, delivered a brilliant speech in the public interest, which he afterwards wrote out and published.' In this sentence Sallust stresses the impromptu nature of the *First Catilinarian* and perhaps also implicitly its oddity. By 8 November the Catilinarian crisis was almost twenty days old.[38] Cicero, as senior consul,[39] held the *fasces* in January and alternate months thereafter—hence in July (when the elections did not occur as they should have, but the *ludi Apollinares* and his defence of Otho did), September, when the elections are likely to have actually occurred, and in November. Accordingly in October, although his intelligence reports would have been important,

---

[37] Pliny, *HN* 7. 116; contrast *Rab. Perd.* 32, where there is no mention of *suffragia*, and *Sull.* 65 (threatened veto of L. Caecilius).

[38] Sall. *Cat.* 31. 6; Cic. *Cat.* 1. 4, the 'twentieth day' is corrected by Asconius to 'eighteenth' (*Pis.* 6 C), which, calculated in the Roman fashion from 8 November, would place the 'last decree' on 22 October, though Cicero's announcement about Manlius' uprising occurred a day earlier (*Cat.* 1. 7).

[39] On the meaning of *consul prior* see *CRR* 100 n. 29 with further references. The elections were postponed to enable the consuls to pass a new law against electoral bribery and Cicero sought to block Catiline's candidature in view of an alleged threat of violence from Catiline's supporters (*Mur.* 49–52). The elections were probably held about the time of the birth of the future emperor Augustus, 22 September by the Republican calendar (Suet. *Aug.* 5 and 94. 5, with an otherwise inexplicable reference to a debate about the Catilinarian conspiracy).

he did not preside over the initial responses of the senate to the announced uprising. In November he held the initiative in public business which he retained until the end of the consular year, since his colleague Antonius left Rome in the latter half of the month.[40]

This did not mean, however, that he had an excuse for speeches like Demosthenes' *Philippics* at every senate-meeting. As president, his task was to introduce subjects for discussion. This might entail a speech, but a long oration on each occasion would have been irritating to senior senators who were waiting to be consulted.[41] In fact on 8 November the formal consultation of the senate had not begun at the time of the *First Catilinarian*, since Cicero portrays Catiline as intervening and asking for a formal reference to the senate about him, one that would culminate in a vote and perhaps a decree—something which never in fact happened (*Cat.* 1. 20). The speech, therefore, belongs to the period of informal discussion that regularly occurred when information was received or audience granted to foreign representatives.[42] Invectives against individuals were of course nothing strange in the senate, but one delivered by the presiding magistrate outside any formal *relatio* was a remarkable event in itself.

Cicero's first speech against Catiline from one point of view is straightforward: it is a performative oration expelling Catiline from the city. However, its theme has an inbuilt contradiction. On the one hand, it is an argument that Catiline could and should be killed as an enemy (*hostis*) of the *res publica* at any moment: he should therefore withdraw for his own good. On the other hand, it is a piece of self-exculpation by the consul for his failure to have Catiline killed on those grounds. While the first argument assumes that his summary execution, or indeed his assassination, would be both just and expedient, the second points to the problems this would raise for those who undertook it. If it had been a forensic speech, it would have violated the principle that a prosecutor should not confuse the jury. The question immediately arises whether Cicero sharpened this contradiction in publication in order to cover himself against later accusations that he had acted improperly in 63.

---

[40] Sall. *Cat.* 36. 3.

[41] See chap. II for the suggestion that *Cat.* 4. 1–6 represents what Cicero might have said introducing the debate on 5 December.

[42] *CRR* 77, 80–1. The *senatus consultum* recorded by Dio 37. 33. 1 at this point is totally at variance with the evidence of the *First Catilinarian* and Sallust and should be rejected (it would have been convenient support for Cicero to cite). Probably *ben trovato*, but consistent with the Ciceronian tradition, is the story in Diodorus 40. 5 that Cicero exploited the silence greeting his verbal expulsion of Catiline by proposing as a contrast the expulsion of Catulus from the city and using the cries of disapproval at that proposal as yardstick to interpret the earlier silence.

In the first six sections he develops the *hostis* argument and, by citing the examples of the almost legendary killing of Maelius and the more recent historical examples of the two Gracchi, Glaucia, and Saturninus, he seeks to show that the summary killing of alleged public enemies had been accepted practice both before and after the institution of the so-called 'last decree' in 121.[43] He then points out that Catiline's complicity in the rebellion in Etruria is not obvious to everyone and summary action against him may be regarded as 'crudelius' (*Cat.* 1. 5). This word does not admit of simple translation. It would have suggested to the senate excessively violent action under the influence of emotion against a man of rank: it was indeed the complaint voiced by the consul L. Piso against Cicero in 58 just before the latter was forced into exile.[44] Cicero's solution is, therefore a 'graduated response', whereby Catiline will be so carefully watched that he can do no harm.

The speech could stop there, if its object were simple denunciation. Instead, it develops into an expulsion of Catiline from Rome. Cicero first urges Catiline to leave in his own interest. Catiline's actions have been, he argues, an open book right up to the meeting at the house of Porcius Laeca on 6 November when the assassination of Cicero himself was planned (*Cat.* 1. 8–10). He will not order Catiline's execution, because this will leave a residue of conspirators in the city: if, however, Catiline leaves voluntarily, this will drain away the sewage of his companions (ibid. 12). At this point Cicero changes course and actually orders Catiline to leave the city (ibid. 13). This power of *relegatio* consuls could exercise in the public interest: it was to be used by Piso and Gabinius against Cicero's friend L. Aelius Lamia in 58.[45] By saying 'exire ex urbe iubet consul hostem' ('the consul orders an enemy to leave the city') Cicero commits himself to exercising his consular authority in one direction, though not the most drastic one. It is not, Cicero hastily adds here, tantamount to a decree of exile: Cicero could advise this but it is beyond his consular power to enforce.

Once again, the speech could stop, but Cicero, not content with his order, proceeds to argue a second time that Catiline should leave voluntarily. He takes the opportunity to revive the old charges of *In Toga Candida* about Catiline's private life and about the 'first conspiracy' (see above) and adds a vague reference to the times Catiline has tried to kill him as consul designate

---

[43] On the killing of the tyrant-demagogues in the early Republic see Lintott, 1970 and 2006; *VRR* 55–8; on the relationship improperly claimed between the 'last decree' and *hostes VRR* 155–80; *CRR* 91–2 with further bibliography. Habicht, 1990, 37–8 with n. 9 rightly stresses the unsoundness of Cicero's argument.

[44] *Pis.* 14, 17, cf. *Red. Sen.* 17 for Piso claiming himself to be *misericors*. On the Roman concept of cruelty see *VRR* 44 ff.

[45] *Red. Sen.* 12; *Sest.* 29; *Pis.* 23; Asc. 9 C.

and consul. Catiline should go because there is no hope for him in the city (*Cat.* 1. 13–20). Indeed there is danger that he will suffer physical violence from young men such as the quaestor P. Sestius, the former quaestor M. Marcellus, and the *equites Romani* who stand round the senate (*Cat.*1.21). Cicero here seems to be exploiting the tradition in the annals of early Rome according to which the cadet members of the aristocracy, who belonged to the equestrian order, were the strong arm of the senate and its weapon against turbulent demagogues.[46]

The last part of the speech is the least convincing in context. After at first imagining that Catiline would disobey—which would have in fact left the consul with no choice but to use force on him—Cicero then offers Catiline the choice between exile and heading a rebellion. The former would be invidious for Cicero, the latter would suit Catiline's own temperament better. Cicero rejects the formal reference to the senate demanded by Catiline without giving a reason (*Cat.* 1. 20). One justification might have been that the consul has already acted. However, Catiline's departure, desirable as it is, raises the question whether Cicero is right to let him go. Here Cicero returns to the alleged right to kill enemies of the republic, granted even to private citizens such as Scipio Nasica and Ahala (*Cat.* 1. 28). The proposition that rebels have lost citizen-rights anticipates the argument to be set out in the *Fourth Catilinarian* (10). Cicero appears to disdain the *invidia* that would have arisen from direct action against Catiline, but then points that there are several senators who are either blind to Catiline's threat or are his accomplices: they will convince a wider public that Cicero's action was unnecessarily violent and tyrannical (*crudeliter et regie factum*).[47] It is better, therefore, for Catiline to reveal himself and for his other supporters in the city to do the same. The slight feeling of bathos is finally relieved by an appeal to Jupiter Stator to punish the traitors and criminals.[48]

What in the text can we believe to have been actually delivered on 8 November? First, Cicero must have ordered Catiline to leave the city on the ground of constituting a public danger and cited evidence in justification. Secondly, it is unlikely that Cicero inserted *post eventum* the threats that Catiline could be killed on the spot (ibid. 2–4): at the time, as the *pro Rabirio* shows, he was a 'hawk' on public security. And it would have been pointless to add in 60 BC material which could be used by his enemies as evidence of his *crudelitas*. Rather, Cicero left these arguments in, because he was known to have used them, but perhaps tempered them in the published speech with an

---

[46] *VRR* 59–60; Lintott, 1970, 24–9.

[47] *Cat.* 1. 30. This is of course what did happen after 5 December and must have been written with an eye on those events.

[48] Ibid. 33, cf. 11, an earlier invocation.

elaborate display of caution regarding what would have appeared justifiable to a wider public under the influence of secret Catilinarian sympathizers. The reference to people believing his actions to be 'tyrannical' and 'cruel' reflect the reaction after the executions on 5 December.

The *Second Catilinarian*, delivered on 9 November, is a reassurance to the people that everything is under control. Catiline has gone (at one point Cicero rebuts the charge that he has ejected Catiline, on the ground that Catiline is not the sort of man simply to obey the order of a consul, but he admits the order (12)). Cronies remain, who are at first dismissed as worthless (4, 7 ff.) and urged to follow, later are subjected to an extended analysis ranging them from debt-ridden aristocrats to common criminals and debauchees (18–22). In the field there is no question but that the strength of the republic is superior. In the city the citizens are to defend their own houses while Cicero is to maintain overall control of the city (26). By the end the speech has come to resemble a general's exhortation before battle, decrying the enemy, and expressing confidence in his own forces. This is a conscious development, as Cicero shows when he predicts 'that the greatest and most cruel civil and domestic war in the memory of man will be brought to a peaceful end with me alone and in a toga as *dux* and *imperator*' (28). We can see here the beginnings of Cicero's self-praise, which soon would lead to *invidia* and misfortune.[49]

There are, however, signs of uncertainty: first in Cicero's self-justification for allowing Catiline to escape (3), where he does not elaborate on the precedents for summary execution or assassination, secondly in the more detailed defence of Catiline's ejection (12 ff.), which initially seeks to argue that this was a voluntary departure by someone bent on war and, later, that even so this will be used to evoke odium for Cicero by Catiline's sympathizers. What would such men have said, had Catiline been killed? This last argument is so much at variance with Cicero's general claim to full responsibility for what happened that we may suspect revision for publication. We can infer, however, from Cicero's repeated apologetics in the *Third Catilinarian* that he was nervous at the time about reactions to his ejection of Catiline.

If the *Second Catilinarian* can be compared to a speech before a battle, then the *Third* is the report of a victory with Cicero at its centre. Even the charge of ejecting Catiline is now happily admitted (*Cat.* 3. 3). Cicero stresses that he is the source of the evidence that unmasked the conspiracy; he was awake and made provisions, he saw, he discovered, he instructed the praetors, and so on... until at the end we find that he is going to make provision that the citizens could live in perpetual peace (3–5, 29). At one point he shifts the

---

[49] Note the earlier consecutive first person verbs in 5–6, 12–13.

responsibility and credit to the immortal gods (18 ff.)—remembering the lightning-strike of 65 and the subsequent relocation of the statue of Jupiter on the Capitol—but after this excursus, he returns to exult over this peaceful victory which the citizens in togas have won with Cicero alone and in a toga as their *dux* and *imperator* (3. 23, recalling 2. 28).

For the historian it is the most informative piece of narrative in the corpus of consular speeches, containing the story of the arrest at the Mulvian bridge, the investigation of the conspirators, and finally the decree of the senate that singled out nine major conspirators and praised the magistrates involved in their arrest—including Cicero's colleague Antonius—for distancing himself from Catiline's men (Cicero could conveniently mediate his own self-glorification through an impartial senatorial verdict). We also already have hints of later Ciceronian rhetoric on the subject. The 'fire and steel' from which the commonwealth was rescued had by early 61 BC become a Ciceronian *topos*.[50] At the end of the speech he compares his achievements in the city to Pompey's abroad, which we shall find as a theme in the letters of the following years.[51] This might of course be a later addition, but the search for reflected glory from Pompey's achievements was nothing new for Cicero.

We have already discussed (Ch. II above) how the *Fourth Catilinarian* is at best a cento of Cicero's introduction to the debate on 5 December and of a subsequent intervention, but it may be largely a fiction. The first six paragraphs set the subject of the debate—the penalty to be imposed on the leading conspirators. Cicero stresses the heinousness of the crime and argues that since the prisoners have confessed to soliciting the Allobroges to revolt, they should be treated as condemned men.[52] The second section (7–13) weighs in the balance the proposals of Silanus and Caesar—the one for execution, the other for imprisonment in Italian *municipia* combined with confiscation of property. There is no mention of Claudius Nero's proposal for an adjournment or of the fact that Silanus abandoned his proposal in order to side with Nero after hearing Caesar's speech.[53] Cicero calls Caesar a true *popularis* who is perfectly prepared to pass what is in effect a capital sentence in the senate, even if it is one that it will be less invidious to execute (9–11). He ascribes to Caesar his own view that *hostes* cannot be *cives* and so are outside the protection of C. Gracchus' *lex Sempronia*.[54] We also find the argument that there can be nothing cruel in punishing men who were contemplating the worst of crimes (12–13).

---

[50] *Cat.* 3. 1; cf. *Att.* 1. 14. 3, there taken over by Crassus.
[51] *Cat.* 3. 26–7. The phrases 'earum rerum quas ego gessi' and 'ea quae gessi in consulatu' (29) are echoed in the letter to Pompey (*Fam.* 5. 7. 3 'res eas gessi').
[52] *Cat.* 4. 5, an argument that appears in the speech Sallust attributes to Cato (*Cat.* 52. 36).
[53] Sall. *Cat.* 50. 4.   [54] *Cat.* 4. 10, see *VRR* 169–71.

The speech continues with an evocation of the support at the consul's disposal to enforce the senate's will. Cicero's ideal of *concordia ordinum*, briefly alluded to in *Pro Cluentio*, recalled as an *exemplum* from the past in *pro Rabirio*, emerges now as a living fact.[55] Not only the *equites Romani*, but the *tribuni aerarii*, the scribes, the free-born poor, the freedmen, even the slaves are for resisting the conspirators.[56] Cicero himself is prepared to risk his life for the glory of resisting depraved citizens: in place of all the power and glory he might have achieved by other means, he wants only that the memory of his consulship should remain fixed in senators' minds. If he should succumb in the struggle, he commends his small son to the senate's care (20–4). The spirit of the heroic *aristeia* seems hardly appropriate on 5 December 63, especially as Cicero was seeking at the time to underplay his own leadership by comparison with the authority of the senate. It reflects better Cicero's attitude, when he became embattled by criticism after the event. In any case it is clear that the *Fourth Catilinarian* is most useful as evidence of the themes that were to figure regularly in his speeches in the aftermath of the conspiracy.[57] In these his self-praise is in part a reaction to the attacks on his actions, in part an attempt to ensure that the events in Rome in December 63 were not eclipsed by their sequel—the military victory over Catiline the next year and the conflict between the senate and those who agitated on Pompey's behalf, Metellus Nepos and Caesar (see Ch. XI).

---

[55] *Clu.* 152; *Rab. Perd.* 27.

[56] *Cat.* 4. 14–17, cf. 22 'coniunctionem vestram equitumque Romanorum et tantam conspirationem bonorum omnium'.

[57] See *Sull.* 2 for the opportunities given to Cicero of speaking about his own glory in 62 BC; *Att.* 1. 14. 3–4 for his performances being known to Atticus.

XI

The Aftermath of the Consulship

RECRIMINATIONS AND THE RETURN OF POMPEY

A FEW days only elapsed between the execution of the leading conspirators and the entry into office of the new tribunes of the plebs on 10 December. Rullus and his colleagues had apparently done nothing to obstruct Cicero. Two, however, of the new college became his critics—L. Calpurnius Bestia[1] and Q. Metellus Nepos. The latter in particular obstructed Cicero's attempt to deliver a *contio* on his last day of office. The consul had to be satisfied with swearing an oath—not the usual oath, which was presumably that he had obeyed the laws, but a grander one, that he alone had saved the *res publica*.[2]

It is unfortunate that our knowledge of the political crisis that was created at the turn of the consular year is barely known to us from Cicero's writings. According to secondary sources, complaints about the repression of the conspiracy were combined with an attempt to entrust military operations against Catiline to Pompey. This last was proposed in a bill of Metellus Nepos as tribune, supported by Caesar as praetor, and was obstructed by Cato and Minucius Thermus. There was conflict between a gang supporting Nepos and a force led by the consul Murena. The 'last decree' was again passed and the senate decreed that both Nepos and Caesar should be suspended from their office.[3] More direct evidence is provided, however, by some brief citations from a *contio* delivered by Cicero in self-defence against Nepos[4] and an interesting exchange of correspondence with Metellus Celer, Nepos' brother.

Celer wrote to Cicero some time in early 62, when he was in the field against the Catilinarians, complaining that, in spite of the good relations and reconciliation between Cicero and himself, Cicero had made fun of him and had caused his brother Nepos to be threatened with the loss of life and fortune, the latter presumably a reference to the passing of the 'last decree' in 62. (*Fam.* 5. 1). In reply Cicero pronounced himself puzzled. The joke had

---

[1] *Ad Brut.* 25. 1; Sall. *Cat.* 43. 1, cf. *Mur.* 83 for suspicions of the incoming tribunes.
[2] *Pis.* 6; Asc. 6 C; *Fam.* 5. 2. 7; Plut. *Cic.* 23. 3.
[3] Dio 37. 43–44. 2; Plut. *Cato mi.* 26–9; Suet. *Jul.* 16; cf. *Sest.* 62.
[4] Pp. 83–5 in Puccioni's edition, see esp. Gell. 18. 7. 7; Quint. 9. 3. 50.

been rather on him. When Celer had returned to Rome for a senate-meeting, apparently at the end of 63, Cicero had expected an encomium from him, but was disappointed. When he explained this in conversation, people found it funny. He himself felt that Celer had not made an adequate return for helping him obtain the province of Cisalpina (ibid. 5. 2. 1–4). As for his attack on Nepos, that was in response to Nepos' attacks on him, which he had tried to avert by using the influence of Celer's wife, Claudia, and his sister Mucia, who was Pompey's wife. Nepos had prevented him from delivering a *contio* on 29 December, arguing that he had executed men without allowing them a hearing. Further private negotiations having failed, he opposed Nepos in the senate on 1 January and in a *contio* to the people on the 3rd (ibid. 6–8)

Cicero's reply made no concessions to Metellus' protest. He was clearly indignant about Nepos' behaviour towards him, while stressing that he had neither advocated nor supported the most drastic measures that were being urged against the tribune (ibid. 9). We know nothing about Celer's reaction to this letter. By the time he became consul in 60, he was held in high esteem by Cicero, who thought him then his friend.[5] What is clear from the exchange is that in early 62 men like Celer regarded the threat in the city as insignificant, compared with the conflict with Catiline, Manlius, and the other insurgents in the field. The executions of the leading conspirators without due legal process were held to be improper and unnecessary by those sympathetic to Caesar's view in the senate. Cicero had been forced to defend himself against this charge by the same token that he had claimed glory for his action. His future reiteration of his own praises was driven not only by vainglory but by insecurity in face of criticism.

Two other Ciceronian texts cast light on his position in 62. One, his defence of P. Sulla on a charge of violence (*vis*), we have already briefly discussed in relation to its representation of court-proceedings (Ch. II). Sulla had been accused in the *quaestio de vi*, the regular forum now for charges of violence against the *res publica*, as had the other leading Catilinarians not executed on 5 December 63.[6] It was in this court that both Catiline and Cethegus had been accused in 63, before Catiline left Rome.[7] Cicero spoke last for Sulla after a division of labour with Hortensius whereby the latter concentrated on charges relating to the so-called 'first conspiracy', while Cicero dealt with events of 63.[8] Most of the evidence seems not to have been new but had surfaced earlier in the investigation of the conspiracy of 63.[9] Cicero argued that the evidence was not relevant to his client, but the form in which he did so was determined

---

[5] *Att.* 1. 18. 5, cf. 1. 17. 9, respectful without affection. [6] *Sull.* 6, 7, 18, cf. *VRR* 107 ff.
[7] Sall. *Cat.* 31. 4; *Schol. Bob.* 149 St; Dio 37. 31. 3.
[8] *Sull.* 12–14.   [9] Ibid. 17, 36–9, 51–2.

by the attack that the chief prosecutor, the young L. Torquatus, had mounted on Cicero himself. Whether the text we have of the speech has been contaminated by material from the *altercatio* or not, it is to a great extent a debate about Cicero's own conduct.

Torquatus had contrasted the way in which Cicero and other *principes* had given adverse testimony about earlier defendants, Autronius in particular, but now were defending Sulla.[10] This culminated in a charge of *regnum* (tyranny): Torquatus suggested that Cicero was the third foreign *rex*, after Numa Pompilius the Sabine and Tarquinius Priscus the Etruscan, thus making him a substitute for another Tullius—Servius Tullius, son of a captive slave-girl.[11] That might have been just a good joke, had it not recalled Catiline's jibe the previous year that Cicero was a resident alien (*inquilinus*),[12] and had not Torquatus amplified it by declaring that Cicero was from a *municipium*.[13] We need not doubt that Cicero recorded sneers that were actually made: they were too uncomfortable to be invented. His riposte was to compare himself to other famous 'new men' and to point out that the majority of citizens were now municipal men ('they can't all be patricians; to tell the truth, they don't even want to be'): as for Torquatus, he should not be making this charge, as his mother was from Asculum (*Sull*. 23–5).

Torquatus is perhaps the first orator to oppose Cicero who can be seen to have got under his skin. As we have seen earlier (Chap. III), he forced him into evasiveness and indeed a lie over his claims that there had been a 'first Catilinarian conspiracy' (ibid. 11–12), especially as he was able to quote a letter that Cicero had written to Pompey about his achievements as consul (67). His charge of tyranny was amplified by an emotional exposition of the execution of the leading conspirators, which provoked from Cicero a purple passage about how he had saved Rome, Italy, and the world without military force by the punishment of five mad and desperate men (30, 33). A major point in the prosecution case was that the Allobroges had named Sulla in their evidence. According to Cicero, they simply questioned Cassius about Sulla's participation and received no clear reply. Torquatus then accused Cicero of registering false evidence in public records.[14] I have already argued that Cicero is representing here either an incident from the *altercatio* or a genuine intervention in Cicero's main speech, since Torquatus' allegation was only

---

[10] Ibid. 3–10, 81–2.   [11] Ibid. 21–2; cf. Livy 1. 39. 5 with Ogilvie, 1965, ad loc.
[12] Sall. *Cat*. 31. 7.
[13] *Sull*. 23. Much later, Tacitus, himself probably of provincial family, could write how Livia Julia had stained herself *municipali adulterio* with Seianus (*Ann*. 4. 3).
[14] *Sull*. 40–4; cf. *Dom*. 50 for Clodius' later charge that Cicero had forged a decree of the senate.

necessary if Cicero chose to argue from the letter of the documentation about the Allobroges. In any case, this was a very serious charge, inasmuch as Cicero had taken pains both to record in the senate and to circulate widely this dossier of evidence.[15] Cicero was not the prosecutor's only target: he also denounced the consulars who were now giving character testimony for Sulla for having earlier supported Catiline at his trial *de repetundis* in 65.[16] Sulla, however, was acquitted. He had shown Cicero his gratitude in advance with a loan of 2 million sesterces for the purchase of a house on the Palatine from Crassus.[17]

The letter to Pompey which young Torquatus mentioned and whose contents must have become widely known was another embarrassment to Cicero. In his earlier attempts to negotiate with Nepos' relatives, he had tried to stress his Pompeian connection (*Fam.* 5. 2. 6), with no apparent effect. This first letter to Pompey had either been intercepted and copied on its journey or circulated by its recipient. Nor had Cicero had an acknowledgement. Cicero protests about this in a second, uncomfortably tortuous, letter by pretending not to protest (*Fam.* 5. 7). He first congratulates Pompey on his official letter (*publice*), that is to the magistrates and senate, especially for the *otium* he offered—peace abroad of course and implicitly also in Italy. There follows a sentence that has much exercised scholars. 'But be assured of this, your ancient enemies (*hostes*), new friends, have received a severe shock from the letter and are prostrate, cast down from their great expectations.' We seem to have a reference to those who hoped to exploit the return of Pompey to Italy in a military capacity, but it is not clear why someone like Nepos should be regarded as an ancient enemy and a new friend. The term *hostis* suggests an enemy in civil war, hence a Marian, and that might point to Caesar, except that he had displayed no recent change of attitude to Pompey. Cicero's precise meaning remains obscure and it is possible that it would have puzzled Pompey too.[18]

Cicero goes on to refer to the traditional glue of political *amicitia*, services (*officia*): if Pompey has not made a return for Cicero's services to him, he is

---

[15] *Sull.* 41–3; a rough parallel is the circulation of the *senatus consultum de Cn. Pisone* in AD 20 (Eck, Caballos, and Fernández, 1996, 169–73).

[16] *Sull.* 81–2. Cicero's answer to this in fact casts doubt on the whole story of the first conspiracy.

[17] *Fam.* 5. 6. 2; Gell. 12. 12. 2.

[18] Gruen, 1970 and 1974, 84–5, followed by Seager, 2002, 63, argues for those dispossessed by Sulla and indebted people who hoped for something from Catiline, which makes sense, did not the oblique reference suggest that Cicero had specific persons in mind. The former standard view that this refers to Crassus and Caesar can be found in the commentaries of How and Shackleton Bailey ad loc. Gelzer, 1969, 108 refers generally to *populares*, but not all *populares* would have been Pompey's enemies in Cicero's view.

happy that the balance of credit is on his side. In any event they will find themselves on the same side in politics (*Fam.* 5. 7. 2). What had Cicero expected in return? Only one guess is needed—praise for his achievements. Pompey, Cicero imagines, passed over these to avoid giving offence (he must have known that they were controversial). However, the verdict of the world is in favour of Cicero's actions in defence of the fatherland ('ea, quae nos pro salute patriae gessimus'). Once Pompey realizes this, he will be happy to allow Cicero to play the Laelius to Pompey's Scipio Africanus (ibid. 3). It is hard to avoid reading this passage in the light of two of Cicero's later philosophical dialogues, the *Laelius de Amicitia*, and the *De Re Publica*, where the younger Scipio Africanus (Aemilianus) and his friend Laelius are interlocutors. Certainly, Cicero may he harking back to an idealized state of Roman politics in the middle Republic, but it would be unwise to ascribe to him in 62 the theories of the *De Re Publica*, in particular that which comprised the requirement for a *moderator rei publicae*.[19] The dialogue on friendship is more relevant. There Cicero scorns *amicitia* that is merely based on *utilitas*: only the true friendship that is pursued for its own sake as the natural outcome of two generous characters is worth pursuing.[20] In this letter he in effect passes over a more mundane relationship, while aspiring to a much higher one. What Pompey's reaction to this would have been is hard to assess. Cicero must have hoped that the *fausse naïveté* would appeal, but it might have appeared presumptuously intrusive, even condescending. It is, however, clear that Cicero, for all his earlier claims to a relationship with Pompey, could not yet claim one, however zealously he so desired.

We do not know if Pompey replied to this letter either. Publicly, Cicero displayed support for Pompey by proposing in response to his letter to the senate a further ten days of *supplicationes* to the gods—in addition to those already decreed in Cicero's consulship.[21] He also helped a rival of Pompey: when the Greek poet Archias, who was a friend of Lucius Lucullus and had commemorated his Mithridatic victories, had his Roman citizenship challenged, Cicero defended him and took the opportunity to stress the value of the Mithridatic poem (*Arch.* 21). Nevertheless, he managed to introduce as a supporting parallel Pompey's grant of citizenship to his own pet historian, Theophanes of Mytilene (ibid. 24). Pompey returned towards the end of the year. On 1 January 61, Cicero wrote to Atticus, 'It is generally understood that Pompey is very well disposed to me' (*Att.* 1. 12. 3), but it does not seem yet to have been a matter of Cicero's own experience.

---

[19] See *CRR* 220–5 with further references; Stockton, 1971, 144 ff.
[20] *Amic.* 26 ff., esp. 31–2. See further Ch. XVIII with nn. 94 ff. [21] *Prov. Cos.* 27.

THE BONA DEA DRAMA

Pompey had disbanded his army until the day of his triumph. This was in fact not to occur until the last two days of September 61, almost a year after his return to Italy.[22] It was indeed going to be 'the greatest show on earth' and the length of preparations needed must be the chief explanation for the delay. Meanwhile Pompey could not enter the inner circle of the city inside the *pomerium*. He could only attend a meeting of the senate if this was in a temple in the southern Campus Martius, such as those of Bellona or Apollo, or a meeting of the people, if in the Saepta or the Circus Flaminius. By the time we can follow events from Cicero's letters to Atticus of 61, Pompey's return had ceased to be the centre of public attention, its place usurped by a scandal involving sex and religion—one that Cicero came to treat as a kind of pendant to the Catilinarian conspiracy and found that his attitude in turn provoked others to discover a political identity in pursuing revenge for Catiline.

Cicero's letters to Atticus in this period are a rich source of information, but must be handled with caution in case they mislead. Cicero is preoccupied with himself in his new status as a consular. In a letter of late January 61, he is more immediately concerned with the fact that he was not asked his opinion first of the consulars by the new consul, M. Pupius Piso, than with the Bona Dea scandal; by contrast he thought Piso's colleague Valerius Messalla to be outstanding, a devotee and imitator of him (*Att.* 1. 13. 2, 1. 14. 6). We have already noticed the inadequacies of the account of the trial of Clodius (Chap. I) His subsequent discussion of the state of politics (*status rerum*) is closely tied to his own *status* (*Att.* 1. 16. 6, 11). When a decree of the senate was passed in 60 concerning the recovery of money lent to provincials, which impeded Atticus' attempts to get money from the people of Sicyon, Cicero apologized by saying that it was passed thanks to massive support from the *pedarii* (the low-ranking footsoldiers of the senate) with no backing from any of *us*, that is the consulars.[23]

'I believe you have already heard that Publius Clodius, son of Appius, was caught in woman's clothing at the house of Gaius Caesar when the sacrifice for the people (i.e. for the Bona Dea) was taking place; he was saved and led outside though the agency of a slave-girl. The matter is a sensational scandal, and I am sure you are shocked' (*Att.*1. 12. 3). The 'good goddess' was a divinity worshipped only by women, concerned primarily with female health. The rites were well established and respectable, though the principle of exclusion of anything male was taken to bizarre lengths and lent itself to

---

[22] Pliny, *HN* 7. 98–9; Plut. *Pomp.* 45.   [23] *Att.* 1. 19. 9, cf. 1. 13. 4 for 'one of us'.

satire.²⁴ There is a Republican temple to the Bona Dea at Ostia, where Octavia, wife of Lucilius Gamala, had the portico cleaned, seats made, and a roof put on the *culina*, where food-offerings were laid out.²⁵ The public rite at Rome, however, was held in the house of a magistrate with *imperium*. In 63 it had actually taken place in Cicero's house on the night of 3–4 December and a portent occurred which his wife Terentia apparently used to encourage her husband to take a strong line with the Catilinarians.²⁶

In the letter following Cicero describes how the matter was raised first in the senate by the ex-praetor Cornificius, 'in case you think it was one of us', then referred to a joint committee of the *pontifices* and Vestal Virgins and judged to be sacrilege, and finally made the subject of a consular bill proposing a special court. Caesar, meanwhile, had divorced his wife Pompeia on the ground, presumably, that the *pontifex maximus* could not retain his authority in a matter like this, if his own wife was compromised.²⁷ However, the initial desire for severity was weakened through Clodius' influence with 'good men', including the consul Piso; gangs were being prepared to oppose the bill; even Cicero was relenting from his original stern line, though Messala and Cato were still on the warpath (*Att*.1. 13. 3).

Cicero breaks off describing the political crisis to talk of the behaviour of 'your friend (do you know whom I mean?), about whom you wrote to me that after he did not dare to criticize me, he began to praise me'. This man displays a degree of affection for Cicero and openly praises him, but his secret jealousy is such that it is obvious. Commentators have tended to assume that this must be Pompey, because the description seems to match later accounts of Pompey's well-known *simulatio*. However, there are good reasons to reject this identification. As has been pointed out earlier, Pompey was not Atticus' friend (Ch. I with nn. 9–10). This friend is someone who talked with Atticus about Cicero in Cicero's absence. In the immediately following letter Pompey is found carefully avoiding praising Cicero in the senate and embarrassed when Crassus takes the opportunity instead. We should therefore look elsewhere and one of Atticus' noble friends, such as Hortensius and Lucullus, is an obvious candidate.²⁸

The importance of the issue concerning Clodius' trial becomes clearer in the next letter. Here Cicero first describes a *contio* held by the tribune Fufius

---

²⁴ They have a place in Cicero's religious code (*Leg*. 2. 21, 35–6). For the details of the rite see Sen. *Ep*. 97. 2; Plut. *Mor*. 268 c; Lact. 1. 29. 9; Macr. 1. 12. 25, burlesqued in Juv. 6. 314 ff.
²⁵ *AE* 1973, no. 12, Reg. V. x. 4.
²⁶ Plut. *Cic*. 19. 4–20. 3.
²⁷ This seems the most plausible origin of the *mot*, 'Caesar's wife must be above suspicion' (Plut. *Caes*. 10. 9). When giving a judgement about his own family in his official religious capacity Caesar would have striven to be objective.
²⁸ *Att*. 1. 2. 2; 18. 6; 19. 6; Nepos, *Att*. 5. 1.

Calenus in which he questioned Pompey on the matter, in particular over the proposal that the presiding praetor should elect his own jury. Pompey replied like a true optimate that he had now and always the greatest respect for the senate's authority, and at some length—raising no doubt the eyebrows of those who remembered the struggle over the *lex Gabinia* (*Att.* 1. 14. 1–2). The sacrilege and the proposed bill about the trial were then put to him again in the senate by the consul Messalla. Pompey once again approved the consular bill by appealing to the wisdom of the senate's decisions as a whole. Then, as he sat down beside Cicero, he remarked to him that he had also said enough 'de istis rebus'. This seems to refer to the decrees in 63 and 62, which his supporters had opposed.[29]

The speech was naturally well received. Cicero believed that this was because it implied approval of his efforts as consul. At this point Crassus took the opportunity to deliver an effusive panegyric of Cicero's achievement on lines already familiar to the senate from Cicero's own speeches: he owed it to Cicero that he was a senator, that he was a Roman citizen, that he was free, that he was alive; whenever he saw his wife, his home, his fatherland, at each and every time he saw the gift of Cicero (ibid. 2–3). The latter happily accepted the compliments in whatever spirit they were given. Seated as he was next to Pompey, he was conscious that the man was disconcerted. Cicero was not sure whether it was because Crassus had seized the chance to do him a favour that Pompey had passed over or because Cicero's achievements were so important that the senate happily heard a speech in their praise. At all events he could not resist the chance of ramming the point home by an extravagant display of extempore rhetorical virtuosity (ibid. 3–4).

This vignette of senate business is wonderfully revealing. We see Pompey keeping Cicero firmly in his place, then finding himself outmanoeuvred by Crassus, who seems to have been deliberately trying to irritate Pompey by his panegyric and perhaps had anticipated also that he would provoke Cicero into another speech about himself, so intensifying Pompey's irritation. Cicero thought he had achieved the appreciation he had hoped for in his letter to Pompey, but it is far from clear that he had actually advanced his cause. The reader must also ask what this had to do with Clodius' trial for sacrilege. One response is 'nothing': this is simply an instance of senators

---

[29] *Att.* 1. 14. 2. I follow the manuscript reading, but believe it has to refer to the controversial decrees that were still an issue. How (ii. 71) goes perhaps too far in equating *de istis rebus* with *de nostro consulatu*. SB *Att* i. 307 and Seager, 2002, 216–17, following Reid, believe that the phrase simply refers to the Bona Dea affair, but that surely was the main subject of the reply and Bailey is forced to emend *etiam* to *iam*. Tatum (1999, 277, n. 114), interprets *de istis rebus* as 'such things as you characteristically talk about', cf. Tyrrell and Purser (1904–33, i, 199), 'those exploits of yours'. The decrees of late 63 were indeed Cicero's affair.

using their traditional right to leave the subject for discussion, *egredi relatione*.³⁰ However, it is clear that others than Cicero thought that the senate's authority, which had prevailed in 63 and 62, should remain dominant on principle. Trials for sacrilege had been an important part of the political process before, notably those arising from the alleged unchastity (*incestum*) of Vestal Virgins. In 73 both Catiline and Crassus had been accused, as had Fabia the half-sister of Cicero's wife Terentia.³¹ The Roman attitude to religious subversion had been illustrated supremely in the repression of the 'conspiracy' of the Bacchanals in 186 BC.³² Religious subversion was regarded in itself as political subversion, even if it was not connected with those who were held to be politically subversive on other grounds. We see this in Cicero's comment that Piso's behaviour owed not so much to his friendship with Clodius as his support for desperate causes and desperate movements (*Att.* 1. 14. 6). Hence for many senators now the Bona Dea affair would have been a test of the authority gained by the senate in the last two years.

Yet we still need to ask why Cicero himself became so deeply involved in the campaign against Clodius, especially after admitting that his severity was wearing off (*Att.* 1. 13. 3). There is no evidence, apart from his carelessness as Catiline's prosecutor in 65, that Clodius had supported Catiline or was previously Cicero's enemy. Plutarch indeed talks of Clodius' support for Cicero in 63. In that year, it has been plausibly suggested, he may have actually worked against Catiline by supporting the candidature of Murena, under whom he had served in Gaul.³³ His sister, the wife of Metellus Celer, had been used as a go-between by Cicero in an attempt to defuse the hostility of Nepos. Scandal even alleged that Terentia made Cicero attack Clodius to compensate her for his visits to Claudia (Clodia) and this lady's attempts to marry him in place of Celer.³⁴ This is perhaps best taken as evidence for the puzzlement Cicero's behaviour caused some of his contemporaries.

There is a clue to an explanation in the letter we have been considering. After the account of the senate-meeting Cicero goes on to describe how the Clodian gangs successfully obstructed the legislative assembly, where the consular bill was to be put to the vote. 'The young men with little beards, all that flock of Catiline, with Curio's little daughter as their leader, rushed about in a mob and asked the people to say no. The consul Piso who was the proposer of the bill was also its opponent. The Clodian gangs seized the voting

---

³⁰ *CRR* 80.
³¹ *Cat.* 3. 9; *Brut.* 336; Asc. 91 C; Sall. *Cat.* 15. 1; 35. 1; Oros. 6. 3. 1; Plut. *Crass.* 1. 4.
³² Livy, 39. 8–19; *FIRA* i, no. 30; Paillier, 1988.
³³ Plut. *Cic.* 29. 1–2; *Har. Resp.* 42; Tatum, 1999, 56–7.
³⁴ *Fam.* 5. 2. 6. Plut. *Cic.* 29. 3. Clodia was still on visiting terms with Atticus in 59 (*Att.* 2. 9. 1; 12. 2; 14. 1).

galleries (*pontes*); tablets were handed out with none saying "aye".' Cicero identifies Clodius' supporters with the effeminate and debauched young men who (in his view as a class) had found Catiline attractive.[35] Thus Clodius has become associated with Catiline and with those who kept his cause alive by criticizing Cicero. Indeed, Clodius himself contributed to that impression by accusing Cicero of having detected everything, a charge that reflected Cicero's own claims about the conspiracy in the third Catilinarian.[36] When this is combined with Clodius' mockery of the ceremony that had been so significant for Cicero in the crisis of December 63, it is easier to see why Cicero came to think that he had been challenged personally. More positively, he took the incident as an opportunity to 'prune immorality and bring discipline to Roman youth' (*Att.* 1. 18. 2).

We do not know when Clodius first defended himself by alleging an alibi or when Cicero first argued that the alibi was unsound. Clodius' comment on Cicero's detective work might be taken to indicate that this had already occurred by the time of the attempt to pass the consular bill, but it may simply refer to a Ciceronian claim in a speech to knowledge about the event at Caesar's house. Clodius' alibi was that he was at Interamna that night, but Cicero apparently argued that he would have only three hours to reach Interamna after a call he had made on Cicero himself. If Cicero's argument had any plausibility, this was clearly not a morning *salutatio*, but a visit made towards the end of the working day.[37] Whenever Cicero made clear that he could be used as a witness to break Clodius' alibi and denounce him, it was a step of great significance. As has become clear in the earlier discussions of forensic oratory, witnesses did not confine themselves to giving relevant information but pronounced on the guilt or innocence of the accused. Moreover, Cicero and other consulars had recently given important evidence in the trials of the less important Catilinarian conspirators. Clodius and his friends could thus have presented his trial as an extension of that process, a witchhunt organized by the *principes* in the senate.[38]

---

[35] *Cat.* 2. 22–3; Catiline's friendships with young men are treated more soberly by Sallust (*Cat.* 14. 5–7).

[36] *Att.* 1. 14. 5; *Cat.* 3. 3 'quae quoniam in senatu inlustrata, patefacta, comperta sunt per me'; cf. the fragment in Quint. 9. 3. 49. See also *Fam.* 5. 2. 6 for the detection of Nepos' designs and Torquatus' jibe (*Sull.* 12) about Cicero's failure to detect the first Catilinarian conspiracy.

[37] *Att* 2. 1. 5; *Dom.* 80; Quint. 4. 2. 88; *Schol. Bob.* 85. 29 ff. Which Interamna is not stated. The Bobbio scholiast cites the distance from Rome as 90 Roman miles, which implies Interamna Lirenas (near Pignataro Interamna) in southern Latium. Interamna Nahars (Terni) in Sabine country (*c.*60 miles) would have been marginally more plausible.

[38] *Sull.* 4–10. For the actual prosecution, as so many political trials, being undertaken by personal enemies of the accused see Balsdon, 1966, 68–9, Tatum, 1999, 73–4.

We have already seen (Ch. I) that Cicero took time to inform Atticus about what happened, and then very inadequately. We only learn of events that had occurred before 15 May in a letter written on the eve of the July elections. Under the bill proposed by the tribune Fufius Calenus, the jury was selected in the normal way by sortition and rejection.[39] It is interesting that Cicero tells us that he deliberately restrained his testimony, only stating things that were so well known and attested that he could not omit them. This implies that his evidence was not confined to breaking the alibi by describing Clodius' visit to him, but shows that he avoided the fulminations against the youth of Rome that he elsewhere claimed to have discharged (*Att.* 1. 18. 3). Bribery may not be a sufficient explanation of the acquittal. The friends and connections of the Claudii no doubt played their part; some jurors may have felt Clodius' guilt inadequately proven; other may have felt uncomfortable about the decision to treat the affair as sacrilege—to be penalized by exile.[40] However, Clodius' opponents were convinced that there had been bribery. This was manifest from Catulus' comments to a juror at the time and from the later proposal to subject equestrian jurors to trials for judicial corruption (*Att.* 1. 16. 5, 1. 17. 8).

Cicero had been late in involving himself personally in the prosecution of Clodius and we cannot tell how significant his evidence was at the trial. However, both Cicero and Clodius believed in its importance. Afterwards Cicero thought that his authority and that of the senate had both been shaken: the secure state of the *res publica* created by the 'alliance of good men' had slipped from their grasp.[41] Hence his attack on Clodius in the senate and subsequent *altercatio*, subsequently developed and published as the *In Clodium et Curionem* (see Ch. I), which entrenched his enmity with Clodius perhaps even more deeply than his evidence. He saw the cause of Catiline surviving (*Att.* 1. 16. 9) and the perception was to be self-fulfilling.

THE GENESIS OF CAESAR'S FIRST CONSULSHIP

A consolation for the acquittal of Clodius in Cicero's eyes was the public perception that he was close to Pompey (*Att.* 1. 16. 11). It is not clear how this had been achieved, perhaps because Cicero had been carefully combining praise of Pompey's achievements in the East with those of his consulship. However, Pompey's return created a new political conflict, in relation to

---

[39] *Att.* 1. 16. 2. See Asc. 45 C with Moreau, 1982, 125 ff., for the division of an issue in the senate.
[40] Cf. *Att.* 1. 16. 9 for the penalty in the bill.
[41] *Att.* 1. 16. 6; cf. *Cat.* 4. 22, Ch. IX with nn. 55–6.

which Cicero had to take a position. His correspondence with Atticus of late 61 and 60 is important evidence for this, whilst leaving the reader with tantalising gaps.

Atticus was abroad in Greece and Illyricum, but Cicero did not write to him as often as he might, as he admits. If he had written as short letters as Atticus, there would have been more of his letters than Atticus'. As it was, he was immensely busy and did not like to send a letter without a proper subject and theme (*Att.* 1. 19. 1). He needed to explain to Atticus his political stance, not least because the estrangement of his brother Quintus from his wife, Atticus' daughter Pomponia, had apparently led Atticus to question his whole relationship with Cicero himself.[42] Atticus must have been conscious that Cicero as a *consularis* was now a grandee, not least from reading Cicero's letters, and seems to have been suspicious that the new political friendships that Cicero was cultivating would exclude him. Cicero has to reassure him that a mass of morning callers and the train of friends that escorted him to the forum were no substitute for a real intimate with whom one could share a joke—another anticipation of one of the themes in his later work on friendship.[43] In particular, he took pains to justify his attitude to the leading men that Atticus admired, to the equestrian order, and above all to Pompey. This agenda helps to explain the selection of events that form the public themes of Cicero's letters.

In the latter part of the letter describing Clodius' trial, he pairs his comment on the perception of his closeness to Pompey among the plebs with a description of the electoral corruption used by Pompey to get his candidate, L. Afranius, the consulship (the consul M. Pupius Piso was acting as his leading agent in this). A new *lex de ambitu* was being proposed by the tribune Lurco with the support of the senate that sought to expose the electoral bribery that was claimed to be normal patronage of fellow tribesmen. However, the law was not passed and Afranius was elected.[44] A law was similarly proposed for a criminal tribunal to investigate bribe-taking by jurors. This caused such disquiet among *equites* that Cicero took up their 'far from respectable' cause in the senate. Again, when the company that had contracted for the Asiatic taxation wanted the sum due to be written down, Cicero joined Crassus in supporting what he regarded as an unpopular and disgraceful claim.[45] Cicero's object was to 'protect the *concordia* that he had glued

---

[42] *Att.* 1. 17. 1–7, esp. 5–7 on Cicero's own friendship with Atticus.
[43] *Att.* 1. 18. 1, cf. n. 20 above.
[44] *Att.* 1. 16. 12–13, 1. 18. 3; on Lurco's law see Lintott, 1990, 8.
[45] *Att.* 1. 17. 8–9, written on 5 Dec. 61. I have argued that the contract in question was that let in 65, on which final payment would be due in March 60 (*Imp. Rom.* 89–90). A leading figure in the *societas* was Cn. Plancius, the father of the man who was to shelter Cicero in exile and later be

together'. This was not purely in the general interest: Cicero needed the *equites* as a source of political support. However, he did not think that they would be sufficient and this was why, he told Atticus, he was paving an alternative route: he was keeping very close to Pompey but, he hastened to reassure him, was taking all necessary precautions in so doing (*Att.* 1. 17. 10).

The contrast between his treatment of the *equites* and Pompey is striking. He is exasperated with the former, but does not have to defend his policy to Atticus, who would assume it. Rather, he stresses the cost to his principles. By contrast he always needs to justify his alliance with Pompey to Atticus. In the following letter (of 20 January 60) he complains of the general lack of statesmen: 'Pompey, my *familiaris* (for so he is, I want you to know), who could be a statesman, looks at that nice little triumphal toga of his in silence.' This cool appreciation is immediately matched by two others. 'Crassus says not a word that might damage his personal connections (*gratia*). You already know the others; they are so stupid that that they appear to hope that their fishponds will be secure when the republic is lost to us.' So Cicero's friendship with Pompey gains in plausibility as best of the bad options. The dismissal of the *piscinarii* (fishpondmen) is especially pointed in view of Atticus' friendship with two of them, Hortensius and L. Lucullus.[46] This letter also reveals more threatening clouds on the horizon. The tribune C. Herennius is trying to transfer Clodius to the plebs by ordering a vote in the *comitia centuriata*—with the support of the consul Metellus Celer, and a new agrarian bill like the *rogatio Plotia* was being proposed by Flavius.[47] Cicero is worried about the stability of the *res publica*, but not least because his own stability is involved. He needs to manoeuvre and wants Atticus to be his partner in the process.

By 15 March the agrarian proposal had crystallized but everything had temporarily been eclipsed by a dual threat from Transalpine Gaul. Rome's allies the Aedui in Burgundy had been defeated by the Suebian chief Ariovistus from across the Rhine and the Sequani, and, furthermore, the Helvetii had been making sorties from what is now Switzerland into Rome's Transalpine province. The senate treated this as a *tumultus*, a military crisis, with an immediate allocation of the Gallic provinces to the consuls and emergency levies. Cicero and Pompey were selected by lot as ambassadors to the Gallic communities who might be approached by the Helvetii, but then released

---

defended by him on a charge of *sodalicia*. The plea was also supported by the censor of 61–60, L. Caesar (*Planc.* 31–2; *Schol. Bob.* 157 St.; cf. *Lex de Delo, RS* i, no. 22, 21–2 for L. Caesar's censorship).

[46] *Att.* 1. 18. 6; cf. Nepos, *Att.* 5. 1, 5. 4, 15. 3, 16. 1; Varro, *RR* 3. 3. 3, 9–10.

[47] *Att.* 1. 18. 4–6, cf. Ch. X with n. 16 on the *rogatio Plotia, Att.* 1. 19. 5, 2. 1. 4–5; *Har. Resp.* 45 on Herennius.

from their selection (*Att.* 1. 19. 2–3). Cicero is laconic on the Gallic threat here. We have to reconstruct events from the early chapters of Caesar's *De Bello Gallico*, which tells us of a senate decree the previous year urging proconsuls to protect the Aedui, and a chance reference in Cicero's work on divination revealing that the leading Aeduan druid, Diviciacus, stayed with him in Rome—presumably when on an embassy—and discussed augury with him.[48]

Cicero next continues the story of the Flavian agrarian bill, revealed now as backed by Pompey, who, Cicero comments, was the only *popularis* element in the bill. This reaction mirrors Cicero's treatment of Rullus' bill.[49] However, two elements of the Flavian bill were substantially different, as we discover from Cicero's account of the objections that he made at a *contio* summoned to discuss it. (*Att.*1. 19. 4) Flavius wished to investigate the tenure of all land that that had been public in 133, the year of Ti. Gracchus' tribunate, in other words to establish whether land now claimed to be private had improperly changed status; he further wished to check the legality of holdings of Sulla's supporters. On the other hand, like Rullus, he wished to exploit land confiscated by Sulla but left to its original holders. This last element affected Cicero's friends in Volaterrae and Arretium.[50] Finally, he also had a scheme for buying land for distribution, but this was to be financed not from the sale of public land but from the new revenues created by Pompey in the East.[51]

Cicero opposed all the measures except the last, which he believed would clean out the sewage of Rome and populate the empty spaces of Italy—a striking contrast to his words to the people about the Rullan bill.[52] For the rest he was against anything that threatened the tenure of private property—an attitude that won him friends among the landowners. 'For this', he tells Atticus, 'is my army (*exercitus*) of men who are rich, as you well know.' This is a reference to the men of equestrian rank who cordoned the Capitol in December 63. He was to complain to Atticus later that 'the cavalry formation which I deployed on the Capitoline slope with you as their standard-bearer and leader has deserted the senate'. The wealthy landowners, like Atticus, are

---

[48] Caes. *BG* 1. 2–6; 31; 35. 4 on *s.c.* of 61; *tumultus* procedure *VRR* 153–4; Diviciacus *Div.* 1. 90: the discussions were probably in Greek, the language learnt by elite Gauls at Massilia (Strabo, 4. 181 C).

[49] Ch. X with nn. 26, 27, 33.

[50] Cf. *Leg. Agr.* 1. 3–4, 2. 35–6; also *Fam.* 13. 4. 2–3 for Cicero's continued patronage of Volaterrae under Caesar's dictatorship. He retained his friendship with A. Caecina, whom he defended in 69 (*Fam.* 6. 6).

[51] According to Plut. *Pomp.* 45. 4, based on the tableaux displayed at Pompey's triumph, Pompey had addded 85 million denarii (= 340 million sesterces) to the former revenues of 50 million. Note Plut. *Cato mi.* 31. 2 for Cato's opposition to the agrarian scheme.

[52] *Leg. Agr.* 2. 70–1; Ch. IX with n. 28.

those whose who provided the consul and senate with physical protection in 63—and later in 62.[53]

The Flavian bill cooled off, thanks to the interruption provided by the Gallic crisis. Meanwhile, Herennius' attempt to transfer Clodius to the plebs was being vetoed. However, Cicero was still in search of powerful friends. Once again he contrasts the attitude of Atticus' 'fishpond friends' who are jealous of him with Pompey's complimentary speeches. He is also using his charm on the debauched and luxurious young men (*Att.* 1. 19. 5–8). Atticus had meanwhile written him a letter on 13 February that he received on 12 May. It was a letter of reconciliation but clearly contained warnings about Cicero attaching himself too closely to Pompey. Cicero agrees: he should not enter someone else's fortress without his own forces. Pompey has nothing grand and lofty; he humiliates himself in the pursuit of popular favour. Cicero, accordingly, will not desert the optimate cause, the 'Sparta' that is his lot, however useless its other supporters are, now that Catulus is dead.[54]

In the following letter of June discussion of literary works—their commentaries on Cicero's consulship and Cicero's collection of consular speeches—takes first place. Political business, including the agrarian law, has frozen. Clodius is no further forward in his plans: Cicero is exchanging jokes with him (one very dubious), he is also trying to render Pompey less *popularis* and has hopes of making Caesar 'better' (the latter was now on his way back from Spain).[55] Once again he defends himself to Atticus. If he was not the subject of envy, if everyone was on his side, as would have been fair, even so it was as justifiable to use a medicine to cure the diseased parts of the commonwealth as to excise them surgically.[56] He then turns on Atticus' regiment of *equites* for deserting the senate and, once again on the fishfarming *principes* for lack of interest. As for Cato, Cicero has as much affection for him as Atticus has, but Cato is behaving as if he were in Plato's *Republic*, not Romulus' cesspool.[57]

Cicero then quickly reviews the elements of the current political *impasse*. Cato had wanted the *equites* brought to trial for judicial corruption, the senate

---

[53] *Att.* 2. 1. 7, cf. 8 'quorum ego concursu itemque ii consules qui post me fuerunt rem publicam defendere solebant'. When threatened by Clodius in 59, he would still see his safety resting in the hands of the *consularis exercitus*, otherwise styled 'the old-fashioned band of good men', *antiqua manus bonorum* (*Att.* 2. 19. 4; *QF* 1. 2. 5. 16).

[54] *Att.* 1. 20. 2–3, another reference to the *piscinarii*.

[55] *Att.* 2. 1. 1–6, cf. 8 for Caesar being expected to arrive in two days.

[56] *Att.* 2. 1. 7. The image is found again in writings after his return, where the contrast between physic (diplomacy) and surgery (violence) fits the context even better: *Att.* 4. 3. 3 'ipse occidi potuit, sed ego diaeta curare incipio, chirurgiae taedet'. Contrast *Sest.* 43, where killing is the only *medicina*. For the later use of this metaphor see Livy, *Praef.* 9; Lucan, 2. 141–3 on Sulla's proscriptions—'excessit medicina modum'. See also Syme, 1986, 448–9.

[57] *Att.* 2. 1. 8; cf. Nepos, *Att.* 15. 3 for Atticus looking after Cato's business interests. In *de Or.* 1. 230–3 Socrates is said to have spoken as if he were in Plato's fictitious state.

agreed; which started a war between the *equites* and the *curia*. The repudiation of their contract by the *publicani* was shameless, but the loss should have been accepted in order to keep the order on side. Cato resisted and won his point (his obstruction had begun in November 61) (*Att*.1. 18. 7). Hence—Cicero here briefly alludes to the later struggles over Flavius' agrarian bill—when the consul was shut up in prison and during the frequent riots, the people who had supported Cicero and his consular successors with their *concursus* (i.e. an armed rally) had not stirred. It is Dio who tells us that, faced with obstruction from Celer, Flavius had led him off to gaol and sat on his bench outside the door, whereupon the consul ordered some of the wall to be pulled down so that the senate could join him.[58]

Cicero's descriptions of the political crisis are mainly deployed in order to justify his policy of cultivating Pompey. The *principes* are largely worthless and the *concordia* of 63 has been broken by the alienation of senate and *equites*. Cato has made the crisis worse by his obstruction over the revision of the tax-contract. One major political event of the last year, which was to have serious consequences, is never directly mentioned in these letters—the debates over Pompey's settlements in the East. After his victories Pompey had not used a senatorial commission to advise him over the disposition of his conquests. He had on his own authority created or reorganized provinces, imposed taxes, and assigned territories to allied kings and dynasts,[59] to some extent apparently revising the settlement created by Lucullus and his commission in 71–70. However sensible and in the Roman interest his measures may have been, it is clear that they were also calculated to secure him patronage and kickbacks.[60] Not surprisingly, senators were reluctant to endorse the settlement en bloc, in particular Lucullus himself. According to the secondary sources, he was backed by Cato, Crassus, and Metellus Celer.[61] The complexity of the arrangements would have required a large number of senate-meetings and were a gift for those who wished to obstruct.

---

[58] *Att*. 2. 1. 8; Dio 37. 50. 1–3. Cf. *Leg. Agr.* 2. 101 for a reference to the possibility of a tribune imprisoning a consul. This may have been inserted in the published speech after the incident with Metellus Celer. For *concurrere* referring to a gathering of men to provide emergency defence see *Verr*. 4. 95–6; Verg. *Aen*. 7. 520 with *VRR* 15; Lintott, 1972*a*, 229.

[59] Later evidence in *Att*. 2. 9. 1, 2. 16. 2; *QF* 2. 11. 1.

[60] Notoriously discernible in the 800,000 sesterces a month interest Ariobarzanes of Cappadocia still owed Pompey in 51 (*Att*. 6. 1. 15). On the settlement in general see App. *Mith*. 114–15; Sherwin White in *CAH* ix², 265–70; Seager, 2002, 60–2. For money paid to Pompey and his subordinate commanders during operations in Palestine and Nabataea see Jos. *AJ* 14. 37, 39, 80–1. Note also *OGIS* 383 ff. for the inscriptions on the Nemrud Dağ monument commemorating another beneficiary, Antiochus I of Commagene.

[61] Dio 37. 49. 4–50. 1; App. *BCiv*. 2. 9. 32; Plut. *Pomp*. 46. 5–6; *Cato mi*. 31. 1; *Luc*. 42. 4–5. The last passage argues that Lucullus left the open opposition to Cato and Crassus.

Cicero says nothing about the part he took in these many debates, unless the removal of the province of Syria from the consul M. Pupius Piso (*Att.* 1. 16. 8) can be regarded as a result of them (it could have been argued that the appointment of a proconsul to the province improperly anticipated the senate's verdict on that part of the settlement). However, it is unlikely that he remained entirely silent, and it is tempting to deduce that his increasingly good relations with Pompey arose from his support for the settlement in the debates at this time. This cannot have improved his standing in the eyes of Atticus' friends Lucullus and Cato or with Lucullus' friends. It is not surprising that Atticus was suspicious of Cicero's overtures to Pompey and that Cicero took such pains to defend his position.

By July Atticus was in Rome (*Att.* 2. 1. 11) and the correspondence stops just when we would like to know about the consular elections at which Caesar was planning to stand in conjunction with L. Lucceius—probably Pompey's candidate[62]—but was in fact elected with Bibulus. When the correspondence briefly resumes in December, we find that Cicero is being forced to face the consequences of his earlier manoeuvrings. Balbus has come to Cicero claiming that Caesar will use Pompey's and Cicero's advice in his consulship and is about to forge a link between Pompey and Crassus. Caesar expects Cicero's support over his agrarian law (no mention is yet made of other legislation) (*Att.* 2. 3. 3). There is no reason to doubt that we have a glimpse here of the process by which the notorious political alliance of the 'Gang of Three' was formed.[63] It is evident that Cicero was wanted and could have become a fourth member. It was not simply that his oratory would have presented Caesar's legislation in the best possible light. He still retained from his consular canvass and his consulship a considerable amount of support, especially his 'consular army'. Caesar's bill was essentially a resumption of the element in the Flavian bill that Cicero had not opposed: so it would have been consistent for Cicero to support it.[64]

Cicero has no doubt that this would have provided him with a strong alliance with Pompey and even with Caesar; it would have reconciled him with his enemies (he seems to mean here those created by his actions over the Catilinarians as well as Clodius and his friends) and the plebs, so allowing him a peaceful old age. He could have achieved what, to judge from the earlier letters since the Bona Dea affair, he had been seeking for the last eighteen months. Nevertheless, Cicero is conscious that this will be a change of course

---

[62] *Att.* 1. 17. 11, 2. 1. 9, cf. Caes. *BCiv.* 3. 18. 3.
[63] Some later sources place the formation of this alliance at the time of the elections—App. *BCiv.* 2. 9. 31–4; Dio 37. 54, arguing that the three concealed their intentions from everyone but Cato; Plut. *Caes.* 13. 3–4 (less clearly). Suet. *Jul.* 19. 2 places it afterwards.
[64] App. *BCiv.* 2. 10. 31, 3. 2. 5; Dio 38. 1. 4–6; cf. *Att.* 1. 19. 4.

and lose him his reputation among 'good men'. There is no firm decision in the letter, but his conservative 'optimate' sympathies clearly now weigh more heavily with him: he quotes both lines from his own poem on his consulship, in which Calliope speaks to him 'aristocratically', and Hector's dismissal of Polydamas' omens from the Iliad.[65] Atticus is expected to approve, as no doubt are the 'good men', such as Lucullus and Cato, who are Atticus' friends. We have no evidence that Cicero actually spoke against Caesar's bill, but the violence over it must have alienated him and in the end he could not restrain himself from open criticisms of what was happening in Caesar's consulship. So once again he exposed himself to his enemies.

[65] *Att.* 2. 3. 4; Hom. *Il.* 12. 243. He resorts to Homer again next year when faced with a choice of political alignment in *Att.* 2. 5. 1 (*Il.* 6. 442; 22. 100—to be used again in late 50, *Att.* 7. 1. 4).

XII

The Gang of Three and Clodius

CAESAR'S FIRST CONSULSHIP

WE do not have any letters of Cicero from the critical first three months of Caesar's consulship. By the time the correspondence resumes in April he is taking his spring holiday first at Antium and then at Formiae.[1] One letter, to which we shall return, reviews Caesar's legislation up to that point and Pompey's attitude to it—the agrarian law, the recognition of the Egyptian king, the remission of the sums owed by the tax-collectors in Asia—with an allusion to Pompey' eastern taxation (*Att.* 2. 16. 2). There are also allusions elsewhere to the implementation of the eastern settlement, the recognition of Ptolemy, and the agrarian legislation.[2] Other April letters deal with Clodius' transfer to the plebs by a *lex curiata* and his planned tribunate.[3]

The agrarian law, as we have seen, seems to have been a cut-down version of Flavius' bill. (Chap. XI with n. 64) Our secondary sources depict a great struggle over it with opposition led by Bibulus, Cato, Lucullus, and three tribunes, Cn. Domitius Calvinus, Q. Ancharius, and C. Fannius.[4] Caesar failed to get senatorial approval for the bill owing to Cato's delaying tactics; when he took the bill to the assembly, Pompey provided him with a force of armed men, which enabled him to ignore religious obstruction and override vetoes by the tribunes through violence. Bibulus tried unsuccessfully to get the senate to annul the law.[5] Instead, all the senators eventually took an oath to observe it, except Metellus Celer, Cato, and Favonius; Bibulus meanwhile retired to his house to watch for omens (*servare de caelo*) which, he hoped, would vitiate the legality of what was being enacted.[6]

---

[1] For the vacation in the courts, *res prolatae*, which was normally taken as an opportunity for senators to take a holiday, see *Att.* 14. 5. 2; *Cael.* 1.

[2] *Att.* 2. 4. 2, 2. 5. 1, 2. 7. 2–4, 2. 9. 1.

[3] *Att.* 2. 7. 2, 2. 9. 1, 2. 12. 1, especially for Pompey acting as augur; cf. 8. 3. 3.

[4] Dio 38. 1–7; App. *BCiv.* 2. 10–12; Suet. *Jul.* 20; Plut. *Cato mi.* 32–3; *Pomp.* 47–8; *Caes.* 14; *Luc.* 42. Later Ciceronian references to this opposition are in *Att.* 2. 20. 4; 21. 4; *Vat.* 5, 16, 21–3; *Sest.* 135.

[5] Dio 38. 6. 4–5.

[6] Ibid. 6. 5, 7. 1–2, cf. *Att.* 2. 19. 4 for the later oath in the law about the Campanian land. Bellemore, 2005 has exposed the confusions in Plutarch and Appian and cast some doubt on the

We must leave aside here the many major issues raised by Caesar's first consulship, concentrating on the light shed by the Ciceronian evidence upon what happened and Cicero's own reaction. The previous December, when invited by Balbus to join the three, he believed he had three choices—to oppose, to do nothing, or to join (*Att.* 2. 3. 3). It seems that in the event he chose the second. He never claims to have spoken against the legislation while it was being proposed. He would have had difficulty in opposing the agrarian law after his reaction to Flavius' bill; he had supported in 61 the bid of the Asiatic *publicani* for the remission of their contract; he seems not to have joined in the criticism of Pompey's eastern settlement in 61–60. These were bridges towards the programme of the three that could hardly be broken, even though Cicero was now reluctant to walk over them. However, an opportunity for a political statement occurred when he found himself defending his former consular colleague C. Antonius, accused of damaging the majesty of the Roman people in his governorship of Macedonia.[7]

Antonius had not only been extortionate but was also accused of undertaking ill-judged and unsuccessful campaigns. His accuser, the young M. Caelius Rufus, was remembered for a purple passage portraying Antonius' failure to respond to an enemy threat through drunkenness and preoccupation with his mistresses.[8] Cicero was obliged by the *beneficium* of Antonius' change of allegiance in 63 and by the help he had given to Atticus and perhaps to Cicero privately.[9] After previously avoiding public criticism of Caesar's measures, Cicero protested in his defence speech that the accusation had been engineered by unrepentant supporters of Catiline and denounced the current state of politics. Nevertheless, Antonius was condemned: in Cicero's later speech for Flaccus this was interpreted as a funerary offering to Catiline.[10] On the same day as the condemnation, three hours later, Clodius' adoption was carried out in the symbolic assembly of 30 lictors representing the *curiae* under Caesar's presidency with Pompey officiating as augur.[11] Cicero himself interpreted the sequence of events as *post hoc, propter hoc*. However, the

---

veracity of the tradition of Cato's resistance. However, the narrative in Dio about the agrarian law is consistent and more difficult to discard. Nor can I believe that the *sanctio* in the original *lex Iulia agraria* did not incorporate an oath, when Caesar incorporated one in the later law.

[7] This defence speech was probably in March. The trial was being prepared at the turn of the year: *Att.* 2. 2. 3.

[8] Dio 38. 10. 1–3; see *ORF* no. 162, fr. 17 = Quint. 4. 2. 123.

[9] Dio 38. 10. 4; *Att.* 1. 13. 1, 1. 16. 16; cf. 1. 12. 1 for Cicero's original reluctance to defend him; 12. 2 for Antonius' alleged claim that he was being extortionate in order to pay Cicero; 14. 7, on the usual interpretation, for a sign that Cicero had received some financial help from Antonius.

[10] *Dom.* 41; *Flacc.* 95; Suet. *Jul.* 20. 4; Dio 38. 10. 4, claiming direct criticism of Caesar, possibly tendentiously in order to ground the historian's next moralizing chapter.

[11] *Dom.* 41; *Att.* 2. 12. 1, 8. 3. 3; Dio ibid.

transition of Clodius to the plebs must surely have been planned by the three beforehand. Whatever their attitude to Cicero was, their primary interest was to bind a promising and potentially dangerous politician to themselves. The pressure put on Cicero was a bonus.[12]

In his letters of April he claims to have had enough of Roman politics, even to the extent of being prepared to go on an embassy to Alexandria—presumably to reconcile the citizens to Rome's recognition of Ptolemy Auletes (*Att.* 2. 5. 1). He has also been offered a *libera legatio*—in principle a private mission to fulfil a vow at a foreign shrine, in practice a senator's justification for leaving Italy when not sent on public business, a source of corruption that Cicero had tried to eliminate in his consulship.[13] It becomes clear that this is related to the threat from Clodius when he argues that, if the latter goes on an embassy to Tigranes of Armenia, this will allow him to postpone the journey to a more convenient time.[14] He continues to be anxiously interested in Clodius' potential behaviour.[15] The story that he hears from the younger Curio about disagreements over policy between Clodius and the three and Clodius' threats to rescind Caesar's legislation probably had a basis in fact, but is less encouraging than he hopes, since it suggests hard-nosed negotiation rather than outright antagonism between Clodius and his new allies.[16]

What has dramatically changed is Cicero's attitude to Pompey. He was prepared to make excuses for him to Atticus in the two years after he came back to Rome. Now Pompey's transfer of Clodius to the plebs is a disgraceful return for the compliments Cicero has been paying him in speeches.[17] He is not referred to as 'Pompeius', but as 'the transferrer to the plebs of Jerusalem origins', 'my friend Gnaeus', 'my friend Magnus' and 'Sampsiceramus.'[18] Cicero's most extensive comment in the letters on the events of early 59 comes in a response to a letter of Atticus' informing him of the promulgation of Caesar's second agrarian law dealing with the *ager Campanus* (*Att.* 2. 16. 1–2). Here he portrays Pompey defending the legislation of Caesar and Vatinius on the principle that he approved the result but the means employed were Caesar's responsibility:

---

[12] VRR 190–3; Lintott, 1967, 162–3. Tatum, 1999, 102 ff. takes the view that irritation with Cicero precipitated the action but does not see the likelihood of the three planning an alliance with Clodius.

[13] *Att.* 2. 4. 2, cf. 2. 18. 3; *Leg.* 3. 9, 18; *CRR* 74.

[14] *Att.* 2. 4. 2. Clodius had family connections and interests in the East (Rawson, 1991, 102–24), and was no doubt genuinely interested in such an embassy. The question was, when he should go.

[15] *Att.* 2. 5. 3, 2. 7. 2–3, 2. 8. 1.

[16] *Att.* 2. 12. 2; cf. 2. 7. 2, 2. 15. 2; Tatum, 1999, 109 ff.; Seager, 2002, 94 and 1965, 521–2.

[17] *Att.* 2. 9. 1; cf. 2. 12. 1, 2. 16. 1.   [18] *Att.* 2. 9. 1, 2. 12. 1, 2. 13. 2, 2. 14. 1, 2. 16. 2.

He approved of the agrarian law, whether it had been possible for a veto to be made or not was not his concern; he approved that at last something was being done about the Alexandrian king, it had not been for him to ask whether Bibulus had been then observing the heavens; as for the *publicani*, he had wanted to oblige the order, what would have happened if Bibulus had then descended into the forum, he had not been able to forecast. What will you say now, Sampsiceramus? That you have instituted a tax for us on the Antilebanon, while removing one on the *ager Campanus*? Well? How will you secure this? 'I will keep you in subjection', he says, 'by means of Caesar's army (*exercitus*).' You will not do this to me, by Hercules, so much by that army as by the ungrateful hearts of those men called *boni*, who have never repaid me with the enjoyment of any rewards or even of kind words or thanks.

This passage is important in more than one way. It casts light on the obstruction offered to Caesar's legislation. Over the agrarian law the tribunes' vetoes were critical; the later legislation was passed, probably in March, after Bibulus had already retired to his house. Pompey is imagined declaring in his augural capacity that Bibulus' *servatio* was irrelevant, since it had not been brought to his notice. One could not base augury on reports that had not occurred.[19]

The reference to Caesar's *exercitus* has frequently been taken to refer to the army of Cisalpine Gaul, which was conferred on Caesar by the *lex Vatinia*. However, this conclusion is far from automatic. Firstly, as we have found when Cicero is referring to his own source of physical support,[20] *exercitus* can be used for political muscle: in Caesar's case it would have been particularly appropriate since his men would have been largely Pompey's veteran soldiers[21] (Pompey of course, as imagined by Cicero, would disclaim direct responsibility by calling the force Caesar's.) Secondly, there is no other reference in the letters of April to Vatinius' proposal about Caesar's province: the first reference to it comes after the passing of the *lex de agro Campano*, when Cicero says that he has been offered a post as *legatus* to Caesar (*Att.* 2. 18. 3). Moreover, there is also the general improbability of Cicero imagining that Pompey would request and succeed in the request that Caesar should commit treason and occupy Rome with the proconsular army of Cisalpine

---

[19] Pompey's excuses over past legislation are given as those he actually made. Note that *futurum fuerit* is grammatically the result of the apodosis of an impossible condition in past time forming an indirect question (cf. *Pis.* 14). It should not be translated as if Bibulus actually did go down to the forum to oppose the legislation about the *publicani* (so Shackleton Bailey, with unsound historical inferences drawn: SB *Att* i. 407, cf. *VRR* 144–5). On the timing of the legislation see Taylor, 1951; Meier, 1961; Lintott, 1968, 194–5. Caesar's first law could have been passed on 28 or 29 January without violating the *trinundinum* regulation.

[20] Ch. X with n. 53; see also *Mur.* 49; *Sest.* 88; *Flacc.* 13; Livy 3. 14. 4; Gelzer, 1962–4, ii. 208–9, with further examples. Pompey's statement about the Campanian bill is of course, by contrast to the previous excuses, a Ciceronian fantasy.

[21] Plut. *Caes.* 14. 4–5, 10; *Pomp.* 47. 7; 48. 1.

Gaul. Could the remark be a deliberately ridiculous fantasy? The problem then is that this would weaken the comparison Cicero then makes with his failure to get support from the *boni*, which may seem laughable to us but for him was deadly serious. The seizure of power by the three through Caesar's use of force was in his eyes the outcome of the collapse of the *concordia* of 63, largely produced by the jealousy and stupidity of the old aristocracy.

The coalition of the year 59 was to be marked out by Cicero and Cato, before the civil war actually broke out in 49, as the prelude to disaster, and this interpretation was seized on happily under the Principate by authors wanting to explain the downfall of the Republic.[22] It is not the place here to discuss the validity of this view, but to issue a warning against using *Ad Atticum* 2. 16 as an argument that civil war was already being contemplated. The same may be said about the texts in which Cicero laments the grip the three dynasts hold over the *res publica*—especially in the letter of the end of July where he claims that the whole *res publica* has perished, because the three were now at loggerheads with the mass of the population—and in his letter to Quintus late in the year.[23] Certainly, Caesar's consulship was a year of *dominatio* by a group working through the consul and one tribune in particular, Vatinius. However, it was not entirely unprecedented—apart from the period of civil wars in the eighties, Marius' sixth consulship of 100 was in many ways similar—nor is there good evidence that it was intended to be permanent.[24] The powerful immediate impression made on Cicero should not mislead the historian.

In the letters from May onwards the theme of the domination of the three is one main thread, the coming battle with Clodius another. Cicero finds consolation in the damage to Pompey's reputation: he used to be jealous that distant posterity would regard the services to the fatherland of Sampsiceramus greater than his own, but is no longer (*Att.* 2. 17. 2). The younger Curio, who spoke openly against the three, was especially responsible for the damage to Pompey's public image. It is not made clear how he was given the opportunity to speak. He was too young to hold any of the magistracies of the *cursus* (his quaestorship is perhaps of 55).[25] One may suppose that he was conducting a prosecution of someone associated with Pompey and used the occasion to denounce Pompey's current activities. Alternatively, he may have taken advantage of the rule that in discussions of legislation private citizens had to be given a chance to speak before it was either voted on or vetoed.[26] Curio's speeches led to him being given a rousing reception at the *ludi*

---

[22] See Lintott, 1971, 493–4; Syme, 1986, 442.
[23] See e. g. *Att.* 2. 17. 1, 2. 18. 2, 2. 19. 2, 2. 20. 3, 2. 21. 1; *QF* 1. 2. 15.   [24] *VRR* 189–96.
[25] *Att.* 2. 18. 1, 2. 19. 3; quaestorship *MRR* iii. 186.   [26] *CRR* 45–6.

Apollinares in July, above all from the *equites*, an event at which the theatre audience shouted its approval of lines that could be interpreted to Pompey's disadvantage.[27] The other source of verbal opposition to the three was the edicts produced by Bibulus from the safety of his house. The purpose of these seems ostensibly to have been the announcement of unfavourable omens to delay meetings of the assemblies,[28] but this was soon combined with general 'Archilochian' attacks on the three, including the earlier careers of Caesar and Crassus, which made the edicts popular reading.[29] Eventually Bibulus succeeded in deferring the elections of magistrates until October 18—perhaps in the hope that by then Caesar would have had to leave for his province and could no longer influence them directly.[30]

The threatening conflict with Clodius produces a complex reaction from Cicero. He was invited to be Caesar's *legatus*, an alternative to the *libera legatio* already on the table. The problem with the latter was that Cicero had to leave, since *ex hypothesi* he had made a vow to a divinity so to do, and this meant that he would be away from Rome when his brother returned from Asia; he would also be vulnerable to recall by a tribune. If he were Caesar's *legatus*, he could return to Rome when he wanted, but he would be beyond recall, at least when in the province. He was therefore keeping this option open.[31] However, he did not think he would use it: 'I don't like running away: I long to fight; I have great support from people.'

This theme continues in subsequent letters. Atticus clearly was warning him of the dangers of confronting Clodius. He believes he can resist without losing dignity because of the backing of the *consularis exercitus omnium bonorum*; he even has the support of Pompey, who thinks (falsely) that Clodius will do nothing. Another escape route had been offered in the shape of a post on Caesar's land-commission in place of the dead Cosconius, but that would have been humiliating. He still is not against being *legatus* to Caesar (there were no doubt agreeable postings in Cisalpina, a province with

---

[27] *Att.* 2. 19. 3. For other theatrical demonstrations see *Sest.* 117–23; *Att.* 4. 15. 6 and Cameron, 1976, 157 ff.

[28] *Att.* 2. 15. 2 doubting their effectiveness, on which see *VRR* 144–5.

[29] *Att.* 2. 19. 5, 2, 20. 4, 6, 2. 21. 4; cf. Suet. *Iul.* 9. 2; 10. Cicero also mentions the copying and reading of *contiones* (2. 20. 4), presumably Bibulus' earlier speeches.

[30] *Att.* 2. 20. 6, 2. 21. 5, 2. 23. 3. We do not know how, perhaps by adding days of prayer, *supplicationes*, see *VRR* 144 n. 2. The obstruction affected the curule, as well as the plebeian, elections.

[31] *Att.* 2. 18. 3, where *hanc* in *hanc ego teneo* must refer to the last mentioned option in the preceding sentence, the post with Caesar (which is there *illa* because it is the first mentioned in that sentence), cf. How ii. 109; *SB Att* i. 387. See n. 13 above on the *libera legatio*; *Att.* 4. 2. 6 on its inflexibility, cf. ibid. and *Att.* 15. 11. 4 on the flexibility available to the *legatus* of a magistrate. Messius was recalled to trial in 54 when appointed as a *legatus* to Caesar (*Att.* 4. 15. 9), but was at the time in range of the power of a praetor (cf. Tac. *Ann.* 13. 28).

which he was already acquainted thanks to his consular canvass). He prefers to fight but has not made up his mind (*Att.* 2. 19. 2, 4–5). In subsequent letters we read again about both Clodius' hostility and reassurances from Pompey that Cicero does not trust. No one expected Pompey to be Cicero's friend after his business with Clodius, but Cicero could not help feeling grief and affection at the pathetic figure Pompey cut at a *contio* about Bibulus' edicts. Clodius threatened sometimes violence, sometimes a trial. Pompey claimed that Clodius and his brother Appius Claudius had made him promises to leave Cicero alone, since an attack would look like treachery by Pompey himself. This did not lead to any moderation in Clodius' language. In consequence Cicero's appeals for Atticus' presence and support became more and more urgent.[32]

Meanwhile he devoted himself to forensic work in order to build up friendships. This included the defence of Flaccus, which he exploited to recall the events of December 63 and speak of his own present peril (on the defence in general see Ch. VIII).[33] Cicero links the prosecution of Flaccus to that of C. Antonius—who had his faults, he admits, but would not have been convicted by the present jury. If Antonius' condemnation was a funerary offering to Catiline, this trial was an attempt to recompense Lentulus (Sura). It was intolerable that informers should be now be seeking to exile and reduce to beggary the leaders of the repression of the Catilinarians by means of a jury of senators and *equites* who had themselves participated in that same repression. As for the Roman people, Cicero himself is ready to submit to their judgement, provided that there are no gangs and violence (*Flacc.* 95–7). Cicero was pleased to relate to Atticus that Hortensius, his colleague in the defence, had also spoken about Flaccus' praetorship and had been fulsome in Cicero's praises (*Att.* 2. 25. 1).

Before Atticus actually arrived, there was a bizarre event that may have had important consequences for Cicero's future, to which Cicero seems to be alluding when he talks of the attacks of informers in the *pro Flacco* (96). Vettius, a man who had been an important, and probably none too scrupulous, informer against the Catilinarians, was brought before the senate after allegedly trying to involve young Curio in a plot to assassinate Pompey. Curio's father had warned Pompey about this. Vettius sought immunity in return for turning state's evidence, was denied it, but still declared that Curio was the leader of a band of young men, including L. Aemilius Paulus, Q. Caepio Brutus (that is Marcus Brutus), and the young Lentulus Niger. Niger's father was also an accomplice, as was Bibulus, who had sent Vettius

---

[32] *Att.* 2. 20. 2, 2. 21. 3–4, 6, 2. 22. 1–2, 2. 23. 3, 2. 24. 4.
[33] Ibid. 2. 22. 3, 2. 23. 3; *Flacc.* 94–7, 102–3.

a dagger by the hand of the scribe C. Septimius. The last claim aroused mirth at the thought that Vettius need to be supplied with a dagger by the consul. Moreover, it turned out that Bibulus too had warned Pompey about a possible assassination. Vettius claimed that the young men under Paulus' leadership were planning to make the attack in the forum at the time of Gabinius' gladiatorial show. Unfortunately, as Curio pointed out, Paulus was in Macedonia at the time. The consequence was that Vettius was imprisoned on the senate's advice (presumably by the consul Caesar), because he had confessed to being in public with a weapon—an offence both against the *lex Cornelia de sicariis* and the *lex Plautia de vi* under which he was about to be accused.[34]

Cicero adhered to what seems to have been the general opinion in the senate that Vettius was contriving for Caesar's benefit to manufacture a charge against Curio by being caught with his slaves armed in the forum and then turning informer, but had been frustrated by the warning given to Pompey by the Curiones (*Att.* 2. 24. 2, 3). Caesar certainly was involved in what followed. He questioned Vettius on the *rostra* and elicited a different rollcall of guilty men. Brutus disappeared from the list—because, Cicero insinuates, of pillow talk by Servilia, Brutus' mother and Caesar's mistress: Vettius added instead L. Lucullus, C. Fannius, and L. Domitius Ahenobarbus. Further, without naming Cicero, Vettius remarked that an eloquent consular, who was a neighbour to the consul,[35] had said that a Servilius Ahala or a Brutus needed to be found, that is, one to kill or expel tyrants.[36] Recalled by Vatinius, he claimed that he had heard from Curio that Cicero's son-in-law, C. Piso, and M. Iuventius Laterensis were involved (ibid. 3; *Vat.* 25–6).

The relation of Caesar and Cicero to Vettius had been reversed since 62. Then Vettius, 'my informer' (ibid. 2), had improperly and unsuccessfully tried to incriminate Caesar, although he was at the time praetor, before the *quaestio de vi*, when Cicero was a dominant figure in that court.[37] Then too Vettius 'had a little list' to which he apparently made frequent additions. However, in spite of Cicero, it seems unlikely that Caesar had engineered from the beginning the plot in 59, since he would have exercised more control over Vettius' original list of guilty men and avoided Vettius' slipshod allegations. Vettius, who probably made a profession of informing, would have been

---

[34] *Att.* 2. 24. 2–4; *Vat.* 24–5; *Sest.* 132; *VRR* 109, 119–20 on the exact nature of the charge against Vettius. On informers in the late Republic see Lintott, 2001–3, esp. 111.

[35] The starting point must be the *domus publica*, the official residence of the *pontifex maximus* at the bottom of the north-east slope of the Palatine by the *via Sacra*. Cicero's house must have been somewhere higher up the slope, whether it should be identified with one of those excavated by Carandini (1986) or not. Hortensius' house later formed part of the *domus Augusti* at the north-west corner of the Palatine (Suet. *Iul.* 46, 72. 1). See *LTUR* ii. 116–17, 202–4.

[36] For Cicero's evocation of these legendary enemies of tyrants see *VRR* 54–8; Ch. X with n. 43.

[37] Dio 37. 41. 1–4; Suet. *Iul.* 17. 2; cf. *Sull.* 2–4, 9–10.

building up a dossier which he would make available to someone more powerful in return for money or some other favour. Nor would he have totally invented his charges. In 62 he used any Catilinarian connection he could find against Caesar. His list in 59 was probably based on loose talk about the assassination of tyrants, including remarks by Cicero himself. He no doubt expected it to be exploited by Caesar. Cicero for his part must have felt very uncomfortable at being targeted by a man like Vettius and by Caesar: hence the protest in the *pro Flacco* (96). Moreover, the event contributed to the suspicions Pompey had of Cicero. As for Vettius, he was mysteriously murdered in prison, probably to ensure his silence.[38]

Towards the end of the year, writing to his brother, Cicero was more explicit and confident. He had many offers of physical support: people promised themselves and their friends, clients, freedmen, slaves, and to cap it all their money. His old-fashioned band of good men was fired up. He had two scenarios in mind: if Clodius prosecuted him before the assembly, the whole of Italy would rally in support and Cicero would emerge with added glory; if on the other hand Clodius tried to use violence, he hoped the resources afforded by friends and strangers would give him sufficient muscle to resist by violence. There are also promises from Caesar and Pompey, which he did not trust enough to cut down his own preparations. He did, however, have friends among the designate tribunes and praetors, and the new consuls appeared very well disposed.[39] Cicero's forecast about an assembly trial was well calculated. A capital charge would have been voted on in the *comitia centuriata*, where the equestrians and the Italian elites dominated a disproportionate number of centuries. He was to be proved wrong about the value of the physical support offered, because, to be most effective, this required the legal cloak of a magistrate's authority and the consuls turned out to be his enemies.

CLODIUS' TRIBUNATE AND CICERO'S EXILE

As in the previous year we have no letters of Cicero for its most critical period, the early months when most of Clodius' legislation occurred and Cicero was banished from Rome by a clever combination of plebiscite and violence. The

---

[38] Dio 38. 9. 4; §2 for the historian's claim that Lucullus and Cicero actually had plotted to assassinate Pompey. For Pompey's suspicions in 58 that Cicero planned to murder him see *Pis.* 76; *Dom.* 28; *Sest.* 41; Dio 38. 17. 3; Plut. *Cic.* 31. 2–3.

[39] *QF* 1. 2. 5. 16. It is worth noting for the interpretation of the word *exercitus* in *Att.* 2. 16. 2 that Cicero did not anticipate here intervention from an army of a proconsul.

earliest letter to Atticus was written from somewhere outside Rome in March, when Cicero was already on his way into exile (*Att.* 3. 1). There are a few indications in subsequent letters about what went wrong. For the most part we have to rely on Cicero's rhetorical reconstructions of his exile after his return and on the secondary sources. We have already seen that the former have to be read in the light of their purpose at the time. The latter also propagate their own interpretations, but do preserve some plausible detail, which Ciceronian rhetoric would have been unlikely to mention.

Clodius as tribune embarked on a large programme of *popularis* legislation, comparable to that of C. Gracchus and Saturninus, in which his revenge on Cicero formed only one part, if a significant one.[40] Clodius' initial tranche of legislation must have been proposed within two or three days of his entry into office on 10 December 59—assuming my interpretation of the *trinundinum* regulation—and passed on 4 January 58.[41] This consisted of a bill granting citizens in the neighbourhood of Rome grain free of charge; a modification of the *leges Aelia* and *Fufia*, the laws regulating the modalities of assembly business;[42] the removal of restrictions on the public activities of *collegia*; the limitation of application of the *nota* (black mark) by the censors to those accused before the censors and condemned by both.[43]

The tribune L. Ninnius Quadratus, a particularly loyal supporter of Cicero's, did not veto any of these proposals. According to Dio, this was in reciprocation for Clodius' promises that he would not attack Cicero, but vetoing the measures may have seemed inappropriate or tactically unwise.[44] Cicero was to complain to Atticus in a letter from Thessalonica that Atticus should not have allowed him to be convinced that the passage of the *lex de collegiis* was in his interest: he says nothing about any deal with Clodius.[45] Then, some time after 4 January, Clodius simultaneously proposed that all those who had put a citizen to death without trial should be forbidden fire and water, that is driven into exile, and that the consuls Piso and Gabinius should have Macedonia and Cilicia respectively as their provinces.[46]

---

[40] See in general Tatum 1999, chs. 5–6; Lintott, 1967 and *VRR* 74–88, 190–8; Gruen, 1966 ; on the chronology Lintott 1965 and 1968, 192; Grimal, 1967; on Cato, Badian, 1965; Oost, 1955. For other recent work on Clodius see *VRR* 2nd edn., p. xxiv and the supplementary bibliography there, 227–32.

[41] Main sources Asc. 7–8 C; Cic. *Sest.* 33–4, 55–6; Dio 38. 13. 1–3, 6; see also *MRR* ii. 196. On *trinundinum* see Lintott, 1965.

[42] Astin, 1964; Sumner, 1963; Meier, 1966, 142.

[43] *CRR* 118–20.

[44] Dio 38. 14. 1–2; cf. *Red. Sen.* 3, where Ninnius is the first to be thanked in that speech.

[45] *Att.* 3. 15. 4. Tatum, 1999, 136–7 argues for a deal over the *lex de collegiis* which Cicero was too embarrassed to mention, but this is a private letter to Atticus, accusing Atticus as well as himself.

[46] Vell. 2. 45. 1; *Sest.* 25.

Cicero summed up the factors that drove him into exile in a letter to Quintus in August: 'the sudden defection of Pompey, the alienation of the consuls and of the praetors also, the panic of the *publicani*, arms' (*QF* 1. 4. 4). Clodius exploited the liberation of the *collegia* in order to recruit gangs both from existing and newly created organizations in the districts (*vici*) of Rome.[47] He won the support of the consuls in a manner that Cicero was to denounce as disgraceful. Gabinius was on the verge of bankruptcy (and so needed a profitable province): this, according to Cicero, was what the consul Lucius Piso told his relative, Cicero's son-in-law, Gaius Piso, when the latter came to ask for assistance.[48] In public L. Piso maintained, with an ironical twist to his eyebrows, that he did not approve of *crudelitas*, the improper use of physical violence.[49] Pompey was turned against Cicero by the allegation that Cicero was plotting to kill him; indeed Plutarch claims that he retired to his Alban villa and when Cicero came himself to plead with him, he escaped by a side door as Cicero approached.[50]

The danger for Cicero was that, whereas retreat would seem a confession of guilt, if he was in Rome when the bill was passed he would be treated immediately as an outlaw and liable to be killed on sight by one of Clodius' men.[51] He did get support from the equestrian order, but it seems to have been more a demonstration than a source of physical protection. Cicero claims that 20,000 men put on mourning on his behalf, a figure that presumably represents Cicero's estimate of the total number of senators and *equites* combined.[52] A demonstration in mourning was led by L. Aelius Lamia, the elder Curio, and Hortensius. It went first to the Capitol and then to the consul Piso's house but was dispersed by him with the threat that he would punish the *equites* for their behaviour on the Capitoline slope on 5 December 63. Further use of mourning was forbidden by the consuls.[53] The leading *eques*, L. Aelius Lamia, was relegated 200 miles from the city.[54]

We have already discussed Cicero's references to the importance of Caesar's army in 58. It does not figure in the complaints in the letters of 58—unless we so interpret the word *arma* in the letter to Quintus (1. 4. 4). In the one allusion in 57 Cicero merely says that the proconsul was silent when he was said to be

---

[47] *Red. Quir.* 13; *Dom.* 54, 79, 89, 129; *Sest.* 34, 55; *Pis.* 9, 11, 23; *Asc.* 8 C.
[48] *Red. Sen.* 11; *Red. Quir.* 13; *Dom.* 23, 55, 60; *Sest.* 18; *Pis.* 12–13.
[49] *Pis.* 14, 17; alternatively that he himself was a merciful man (*Red. Sen.* 17). Cf. *Dom.* 94; Dio 38. 16. 6 and on *crudelitas* see *VRR* 44 ff.
[50] *Dom.* 28; *Sest.* 41; *Pis.* 76; cf. *Att.* 3. 15. 4; 10. 4. 3; Dio 38. 17. 3; Plut. *Cic.* 31. 2–3.
[51] Lintott, 1967, 164.
[52] *Red. Quir.* 8; Plut. *Cic.* 31. 1. On the aggressive use of mourning see *VRR* 16–20.
[53] *Red. Sen.* 12, 32; *Red. Quir.* 13; *Dom.* 55; *Sest.* 28–9; Dio 38. 16. 2–6.
[54] *Sest.* 29; *Pis.* 23.

his enemy (*Red. Sen.* 32). As has been pointed out (Ch. III at nn. 25–6), the large army at the gates is a myth. According to Dio, Clodius held a *contio* outside the *pomerium*, so that the proconsul could attend, and asked him his view. Caesar's reply was that he did not approve of either the execution of the Catilinarians or retrospective legislation. Crassus openly supported Clodius, but is said to have sent his son Publius to promise help for Cicero (perhaps advocacy at a trial). It was Hortensius and Cato who dissuaded Cicero from using force. Plutarch maintains that (Lucius) Lucullus urged Cicero to stay.[55] Cicero was certainly bitter about Hortensius in exile, while praising Cato's good faith.[56] Other senators—L. Lentulus Crus, Q. Fabius Sanga, L. Manlius Torquatus, and M. Lucullus—approached Pompey at his Alban villa urging him to resist Clodius' violence, but he referred them back to the consuls, carefully pointing out the illegality of resisting an armed tribune of the plebs without official approval: 'if the consuls were to implement the defence of the *res publica* after a senate decree,' i.e. the 'last decree', 'he would take up arms' (*Pis.* 77; *Sest.* 41).

We cannot be sure about the chronology of this confrontation. However, it seems unlikely that Clodius would have wasted time before introducing the bill which threatened Cicero. If this was proposed soon after 4 January, we must then allow for the passage of about half January, February, probably an intercalation of 23 days,[57] and a week or so in March—over 70 days in total—before Cicero's departure, a period throughout which he would have been under pressure from Clodius' gangs. He probably tried to get support from Pompey and the consul Piso early on. Then, when a date had been set for a vote on the legislation, the demonstration by the *equites* was mounted—unsuccessfully—the final appeal to Pompey was made by the senators but failed. Cicero had an unofficial bodyguard of 'good men' in his home, but they would have been hopelessly outnumbered without wider support. Moreover, the consuls seem to have contributed to the menace by sending their friends round to Cicero's house to check up on the items that would be put up for sale, if Cicero was exiled and his property confiscated and proscribed (*Dom.* 55). In the end, following the advice of the majority of his friends—L. Lucullus perhaps advising a fight but Cato passive resistance, such as he himself had practised in 59—Cicero's own nerve failed and he left on the morning of the day on which Clodius passed both his general law exiling those who had executed citizens without trial and the law about the consular provinces (*Sest.* 53). After his departure Clodius drew up a bill about Cicero himself, which assumed that he was already a self-condemned exile and

---

[55] Dio 38. 17. 1–3–4; Plut. *Luc.* 31. 5.   [56] *QF* 1. 3. 8; *Att.* 3. 9. 2; cf. 15. 2.
[57] Lintott, 1968, 192.

consequently specified the terms of his exile and the modalities of the confiscation of his property.[58]

The exile imposed by Clodius was a capital penalty: Cicero lost his status as a senator and Roman citizen and the property that maintained his position in society. The early letters to Atticus betray as much shock as grief, admitted retrospectively (*Att.* 3. 8. 4); tears and sorrow form a refrain in the surviving letters to Terentia and his children, but there is more than a hint of artistic contrivance, suggesting that that this was a position adopted to deflect criticism.[59] In the earliest of these, full of almost operatic expressions of affection (Cicero regrets that he has not committed suicide already and then wishes to see Terentia for the last time and die in her embrace), although it is the end of life and prosperity, it is not vice but virtue that has struck Cicero down (*Fam.* 14. 4. 1, 5). Later letters express regret for the sufferings Cicero has inflicted on the family: he should have been less timid; his duty was either to avoid trouble by going away on a *legatio* or to resist with the forces he had or to die in the attempt. (*Fam.* 14. 1. 1, 14. 2. 1, 14. 3. 1) Terentia tells her husband to attribute the calamity to fate, but this may have been not so much her genuine opinion, as an attempt to extract her husband from the depths of self-pity into which he appeared to have fallen and as an encouragement for the future (*Fam.* 14. 1. 1). To Atticus Cicero writes from Brindisi that he has suffered an incomparable calamity to which death would have been a more honourable alternative (though that moment was now past). He regards the disaster as more the fault of jealous rivals than his enemies (*Att.* 3. 7. 2).

In subsequent letters the bitterness of betrayal is mixed with guilt over his lack of resolution and faulty decision, over which even loyal friends advised him badly. This is vaguely sketched in a letter of May. Atticus meanwhile was rebuking him for loss of moral fibre.[60] In June Cicero repeated the accusation about jealous rivals, after Atticus had suggested he should get Hortensius' support.[61] Atticus defended his friends against these accusations, among them Cato, to which Cicero replied in August that he did not include him in the accusation and particularly regretted that he had placed less reliance on his good faith than on the pretences of others.[62] By then Cicero was explicit over

---

[58] *Dom.* 47, 62, 81, 106–16; *Att.* 3. 4; *Fam.* 14. 4. 2; Plut. *Cic.* 32. 1; Dio 38. 17. 7.
[59] *Fam.* 14. 1–4. On the varieties of argument and tone in the early letters of exile see Hutchinson, 1998, 25–48.
[60] *Att.* 3. 8. 4, 3. 10. 2.
[61] *Att.* 3. 9. 2; cf. *QF* 1. 4. 4.
[62] *Att.* 3. 15. 2. For this reason I find it improbable that the defection of the *boni* from Cicero's cause can be ascribed to Clodius' grant of the commission to annex Cyprus to Cato—so Tatum (1999, 155–6), assuming this bill was proposed before Cicero's departure—as this would have been obvious to Cicero and influenced his view of Cato's attitude.

his guilt: he had been cowardly in not staying to face Clodius; if he had stayed he would have achieved honour or victory.[63] He had been betrayed, led by the nose, and cast into delusion, neglecting all his support and the readiness of the whole of Italy (*tota Italia*) to defend him.[64] It was only on his return that he was to discover a defence for his conduct: his withdrawal had saved the *res publica* from a civil war.[65]

Meanwhile hope for his return, although Cicero himself was reluctant to recognize it, was emerging from Clodius' conflict with Pompey[66] and the efforts of Ninnius.[67] Here Cicero begins to apply his intellect, if despairingly, because he cannot see how progress is possible while Clodius is tribune, especially if his enemy Metellus Nepos is consul designate.[68] His first view is that the important move is to abrogate the bill exiling him by name. The first general bill about those who had executed Roman citizens without trial should have been ignored, nay praised by him, as a harmless piece of *popularis* legislation. However, the problem with the second bill was that Clodius had attached to it an entrenchment clause (*sanctio*) forbidding even the proposal of its abrogation and prescribing a penalty (*Att.* 3. 15. 5–6).

At the end of November—by which time some moves had been made towards both Metellus Nepos and Caesar[69]—this was still a sticking point. Eight[70] of the tribunes designate for 57 had drafted a bill about Cicero's return, which Cicero was afraid would fall into the same errors as that previously proposed by tribunes from college of 58. The worst feature of this was that the tribunes had tried to secure impunity for themselves against the *sanctio* of Clodius' law by disclaiming any proposal that Clodius' law had made a penal offence, and in so doing they had let the baby out with the bathwater. Cicero feared that the college of 57 BC would regard this precedent as prescriptive, as Clodius himself had asserted they must (*Att.* 3. 23. 2–4). He points out that the tribunes of 58 were not bound by a law of their colleague anyhow and that when a law was abrogated, its *sanctio* was automatically abrogated at the same time. However, he does not take into account the

---

[63] *Att.* 3. 15. 4: the alternative to victory, missing in the MSS, was clearly honourable (cf. *a turpissimo consilio revocaret*): whether it was battle or death is not so certain.

[64] Ibid. 7: *proditus, inductus, coniectus in fraudem*; a similar triplet was to describe the effects of the conference of Luca, *inductus relictus proiectus* (4. 5. 1).

[65] *Red. Sen.* 32–4; *Dom.* 63, 91; *Sest.* 39, 42–6; *Planc.* 87–8; *VRR* 61–2.

[66] *Att.* 3. 8. 3; cf. 3. 18. 1, 3, 23. 1; *Sest.* 67, 69; *Red. Sen.* 29; Asc. 46–7 C.

[67] *Red. Sen.* 4; *Sest.* 68; *Att.* 3. 12. 1.

[68] *Att.* 3. 12. 1. He is also worried about losing the support of the elder Curio because of the appearance of his written version of the *In Clodium et Curionem* (§2; 3. 15. 3, cf. Ch. II with nn. 17 ff.).

[69] *Att.* 3. 22. 2; 23. 1; 24. 2; 18. 1; *Sest.* 71, Sestius' journey to Gaul.

[70] Not Q. Numerius Rufus or Sex. Atilius Serranus, cf. *Red. Sen.* 19–23; *Sest.* 68, 72, 74; Asc. 11 C; *MRR* ii. 201–2.

consequences of attempting to abrogate Clodius' law and then failing so to do, which would have rendered at least the college of tribunes in 57 BC liable to penalties.[71] He was also worried that the favourable tribunes of 58 were discouraged from putting pressure on both consuls of that year by threatening to veto the vote of money for their provinces.[72]

The following January discussion of Cicero's return in the senate was obstructed but eventually a decree recalling him from exile was passed. However, when Q. Fabricius brought a tribunician bill to the assembly on 23 January, the assembly was broken up by violence.[73] There follows an obscure period, in which two of the tribunes, T. Annius Milo and P. Sestius, set about acquiring gangs of their own,[74] and Milo tried to prosecute Clodius *de vi* but was prevented by a suspension of public business (*iustitium*) in which the two tribunes hostile to Cicero were supported by Metellus Nepos and Clodius' brother, Appius Claudius.[75] We have three short letters to Atticus, the second and third of which seem to show him first anticipating the legislation of 23 January and then losing hope again: in the second he even seems to contemplate returning to Italy on the basis of the senate decree alone, without the protection of a plebiscite (*Att.* 3. 25–7).

He did not in fact move yet. His friends set on foot a new plan, which would avoid the plebeian assembly of the tribes, where Clodius was still so influential, in favour of the military assembly of centuries, where the upper classes, especially the elites of rural Italy, were dominant. Accordingly, Pompey got moral support from the *municipia*: we know of decrees passed by Placentia and Capua.[76] It was nevertheless essential to dissuade Metellus Nepos from further obstruction. The situation did not change radically until July, the month of the consular elections and the *ludi Apollinares*. By then a corn-shortage was in prospect on account of the poor harvest (it is also likely that Clodius' law providing free corn had exhausted reserves in the city), which did nothing for Clodius' own prestige. There was a riot on the first day of the *ludi Apollinares*.[77] Three decrees were passed by the senate about this time. The first session met on the Capitol and on the proposal of the consuls voted for the recall of Cicero by 416 votes to 1 (Clodius).[78] In this the consul Metellus Nepos gave up his enmity to Cicero—apparently after a speech by

---

[71] On *sanctiones* see *CRR* 63 with n. 98; Bispham, 1997, and the bibliography cited there.

[72] *Att.* 3. 24. Piso and Gabinius had departed for their provinces some time before the entry in to office of the new tribunes, *Sest.* 71–2.

[73] *Red. Sen.* 22; *Red. Quir.* 12; *Sest.* 74–8; *Pis.* 34; *Att.* 3. 26.

[74] *Red. Sen.* 19–20; *Sest.* 75–8.

[75] *Sest.* 85, 89, 95; *Red. Sen.* 6, 19; Dio 39. 6. 2–7. 2.

[76] *Red. Sen.* 29, 31; *Dom.* 30; *Mil.* 39; Asc. 3 C.

[77] *Dom.* 11–12; Asc. 48 C.   [78] *Red. Sen.* 25–7; *Sest.* 129.

the elderly consular P. Servilius Isauricus, which had recalled to life the ghosts of dead Metelli, including Nepos' brother Celer and the great Numidicus who had been driven into exile by Saturninus in a similar fashion to Clodius' tactics with Cicero.[79] Cicero had already been informed by his brother and Atticus of Nepos' change of heart; when he learnt of Metellus' speech publicly acknowledging the change, he wrote him a delicate and dignified letter confirming his readiness to reciprocate should the hostility indeed cease.[80]

On the next day a further decree forbade obstruction by veto or religious means to the passage of a bill about Cicero (*Sest.* 129). A third followed, passed in the temple of Honos et Virtus during the *ludi Apollinares*, which urged the magistrates in the provinces to protect Cicero's life. News of this was brought to the games and added piquancy to lines delivered by the actor Aesopus from Accius' *Eurysaces*.[81] *Nundinae* (market-days) fell on 15, 23, and 31 July that year: so a bill proposed by the 15th could have been put to the vote on the first assembly day (*dies comitialis*) in August.[82] This duly happened on the second of those days, 4 August. 'The whole of Italy took its stand in that meeting.'[83] The municipal elites, who had apparently been thanked for their support of the original decree of the senate (*Red. Sen.* 27), would have been in Rome awaiting the bill and the elections, the latter presumably postponed to allow the passage of the bill.[84] Cicero had confidently crossed the Adriatic in anticipation and after he heard the news at Brindisi on August 11 began a quasi-triumphal return to Rome (*Att.* 4. 1. 4–5). Cicero was now deeply indebted, financially and for the services rendered him by so many people. How he interpreted this situation and how it was to restrict any future heroic posture was to emerge gradually in the years following.

[79] *Red. Sen.* 25; *Prov. Cos.* 22.
[80] *Fam.* 5. 4, normally dated earlier by editors, but it must follow Nepos' taking a public position on Cicero's return.
[81] *Sest.* 116, 120, 128.
[82] Lintott, 1968, 191 ff., cf. Lintott, 1965.
[83] *Sest.* 107; cf. *Att.* 4. 1. 4; *Red. Quir.* 16–17; *Sest.* 108; *Pis.* 35–6; Asc. 11 C.
[84] For the ban on proposing legislation in the period before the elections under the *leges Aelia et Fufia* see *Att.* 1. 16. 13. Cicero says nothing about the consuls' being freed from this regulation.

XIII

After the Return

THE correspondence from the period after Cicero's return to Rome is immensely rewarding, not so much by virtue of its sheer quantity, but because of the information it contains. In his letters to his brother Quintus and to Lentulus Spinther Cicero kept two fellow senators well informed on the current state of politics, because this affected their own prospects and a brother or devoted friend would have been expected to demonstrate his good will by ensuring that they were well informed. With Spinther the chief issue was that of the Egyptian commission and Pompey's attitude to it; the letters to Quintus are more general but are understandably concerned with Cicero's own relationship with Pompey and later with Caesar also, given that Quintus was *legatus* to the two men in succession and perhaps had hopes for further advancement from them.[1] However, even in the letters to Atticus, where he is more concerned to cement their friendship and exploit it to give expression to his own feelings, Cicero's letters show a greater interest in narrative for narrative's sake. It is not that he thinks that Atticus will be ignorant of the news, but that his version of events will illuminate for Atticus his own state of mind (*Att.* 4. 3. 1). The correspondence is unevenly distributed over the period. It is rich for the first nine months after his return, then a mere sprinkling, then rich again in 54, then almost non-existent until his own departure to his province in 51 led to a great increase. Compensation is provided to some extent by the survival of a relatively large number of Cicero's speeches, both political and forensic. Among them the speeches of 57–56, whatever their purpose, have a family likeness in that they all were spoken and published under the shadow of Cicero's earlier exile and for the most part incorporate Ciceronian self-justification on a greater or smaller scale, whether this was strictly required in the context or not. In the speeches Cicero is reconstructing a public persona: what is striking in the correspondence is that, perhaps for the first time, we can see a contrast between the public persona and the private one.

In the two speeches after his return—the one delivered to the senate on 5 September, the other not delivered to the people—that were examined in

[1] See Wiseman, 1966.

Chapter I, we see Cicero, with apparent confidence, creating once more a place for himself in the Roman political scene. He thanked his friends, he asserted his devotion both to the *optima causa* and (in *Post Reditum ad Quirites*) to the Roman people, and by the use of exemplars he inserted his own exile into the pattern of Roman history. As for his enemies, he showed himself unforgiving, but cautious about seeking reprisals.[2] Cicero's letters to Atticus by contrast betray his doubts and mistrust. Moreover, his excitement at being once more at Rome and the centre of political life remains shadowed by bitterness over his previous expulsion from it.

The letter to Atticus narrating his triumphant return to Rome has a carefully composed *exordium*, congratulating Atticus on this event and regretting his absence (4. 1. 1–2). In this Cicero once again stresses that Atticus was as guilty as he was himself for his exile: they both panicked. However, Atticus was distressed by their separation and made an enormous contribution to his return. Cicero goes on to contrast his recovery of his position in the senate and as a leading orator with his dismal financial position.[3] There follows a narrative comprising his return, the delivery of *Post Reditum in Senatu*, the demonstrations about the corn-supply, and his speeches in the senate and to the people on 7 September advocating the appointment of Pompey to administer the corn-supply (ibid. 4–6; cf. *Dom.* 5–16).

Cicero's proposal was put into effect in a fully attended senate-meeting on 8 September, when, after negotiations with Pompey, the consuls drafted proposals in the senate to be submitted to the assembly for ratification. Cicero was honoured by being nominated by Pompey as the first of his fifteen subordinate officers (*legati*). However, this satisfactory outcome was marred by the alternative proposal of the tribune Messius, granting Pompey full discretion over any money needed, an army and fleet, and superior power (*maius imperium*) than provincial governors—an echo of his powers against the pirates under Gabinius' law of 67.[4] Pompey claimed that he wanted the consuls' law, his friends said that he wanted Messius', which enraged Favonius and certain former consuls, no doubt because they suspected that Pompey's friends were right and this was another example of Pompey's disingenuousness. Cicero

---

[2] See above Ch. I with nn. 18–19. On the use of history in the speeches see Riggsby, 2002, 160 ff.

[3] *Att.* 4. 1. 3. SB *Att* ii. 166 believed that it was too early for Cicero to be referring to his position as an advocate, but one should not underestimate the boost given to his confidence by the delivery of at least three successful speeches, including one to the people, after eighteen months' enforced silence.

[4] *Att.* 4. 1. 7, cf. Vell. 2. 31. 2—*aequum imperium cum proconsulibus* up to the 50th milestone from the sea, though Tac. *Ann.* 15. 25 may be thought to suggest that Pompey's *imperium* in 67 was *maius*, on which see Seager, 2002, 45–6, 51. See also Plut. *Pomp.* 25. 6 for the permission to Pompey in 67 to draw as much as he wanted from provincial *fisci* and tax-collectors' deposits.

could say nothing, because he wished to offend neither Pompey nor the *boni*, whose support he needed if he was to get a favourable answer from the *pontifices* about the rebuilding of his house on the site that Clodius had consecrated as a shrine to Libertas.

This account illustrates well the new vulnerability of Cicero's position. To say nothing of the persisting enmity of Clodius, Cicero is not only in debt financially to those who have supported him since the confiscation of his property, but torn by conflicting obligations to Pompey and the *boni*, especially the consuls. The consequence of this can be seen at the very end of the letter, where Cicero remarks that some people who praised him in his absence are already secretly vexed and openly envious of him now he is at Rome (*Att.* 4. 1. 8). They are surely those *boni* who saw his return as a blow against the *populares* and the coalition of 59 and were offended that he should still appear Pompeian. The charge of servility, of in effect licking the boot that kicked him, was to be made publicly more than once in the future (*Dom.* 29; *Planc.* 91–3). Cicero's present balancing act between Pompey and the *boni* of course resembles that we found in the letters of his consular canvass and of the aftermath of his consulship. The difference is that now in his eyes both the *boni* and Pompey have betrayed him and cannot be entirely trusted. The letter about his return reveals both the pride that he expressed in his speeches and the persisting rancour.

DEFENDING PROPERTY

The next instalment of the story was sent to Atticus in October—an account of the restitution to Cicero of the sites of his Palatine house and other properties. The procedure resembled that used over the Bona Dea affair. The senate referred to the *pontifices* the problem of the religious objections to the restitution of the Palatine site, and, when they decreed that there was a fault in its dedication, took a decision itself. There had apparently been a preliminary discussion of the matter before Cicero's return.[5] However, the hearing before the *pontifices*, held on 29 September, was critical. Cicero was proud of the speech he delivered and planned to publish it quickly so that young orators could read it (*Att.* 4. 2. 2). From the text we possess, it appears that he spoke after Clodius, who used the opportunity not only to argue on behalf of his shrine to Libertas but to attack Cicero himself for his political position after his return. Clodius claimed that, whereas Cicero had been

---

[5] *Dom.* 3–4; *Har. Resp.* 12, cf. Stroh, 2004, 321–2.

summoned back because the senate could not do without him and the *boni* mourned his absence, he would now lose his case because he had turned *popularis* by advocating the grant of the corn-commission to Pompey: in so doing he had betrayed the authority of the senate (*Dom.* 3–4).

The published speech begins with a long excursus dealing with the *praeiudicia* raised by Clodius. Cicero argued that it was only natural that he should have responded as he did to the corn crisis—not just high prices, but a fear of genuine shortage (*Dom.* 11)—especially as Clodius' mobs had chanted demands outside his house at night (*Dom.* 14). Clodius could not complain about Cicero's solution to the problem on the ground that it conferred extraordinary *imperium*, when he had himself created such *imperia* in his tribunate for Cato (Cyprus) and the consuls (Macedonia and Syria). Cicero even cited a letter sent by Caesar to Clodius, congratulating him on having it made it impossible for Cato to complain convincingly about those *imperia* awarded to others (*Dom.* 21–2). As for Pompey, Cicero alluded to his own previous support for the *lex Manilia* and the Mithridatic command (*Dom.* 19) and then proceeded to complain that 'certain men' had brought about a division in the old alliance between Pompey and himself. Even now some people, he claimed, had been encouraging him to believe that his own *auctoritas* and *dignitas* had brought about his return. 'Why', they asked, 'does he praise the man who deserted him' (*Dom.* 29)? Cicero's response is to assign Pompey a greater part in engineering his return that he had in his first *Post Reditum* speech to the senate.[6]

The central portion of the speech deals with the technicalities of Clodius' consecration. Cicero asserted that he would not talk directly about religion (it was not for him, an outsider, to teach the *pontifices*), but about public law (*Dom.* 32). In fact at the end of the speech he did deal with religion, and it was one of those points that was critical for his success. What we find is one of the most closely argued cases that he ever made outside the realm of private law. First, he claimed that no one could lose his citizenship and his property without a trial by senate or people—here attributing to the senate a capital jurisdiction that it did not properly possess under the republic, in order to cover the procedure used against the Catilinarians in 63 (*Dom.* 33). Secondly, Clodius' adoption by a younger man was not only grotesque and of purely political motivation but invalid because it contravened the auspices: Clodius himself had provided evidence for that by his questioning of Bibulus in 58.[7]

---

[6] *Dom.* 30–31; cf. *Red. Sen.* 29; *Red. Quir.* 16. For a later exploitation of Pompey's desertion of Cicero in 58 see M. Antonius' phrase 'the man who did you first an injury so that he could do you a service' in a letter to Cicero of 49 (*Att.* 10. 8A. 2).

[7] *Dom.* 34–42, esp. 40, cf. *VRR* 146.

Thirdly, the law was a *privilegium* (a statute directed against a single individual).[8] Its form, referring to Cicero's prior banishment by the previous general bill,[9] was irregular; it alleged falsely as a ground that Cicero had drafted a forged *senatus consultum*,[10] it combined diverse matters in one bill contrary to the *lex Caecilia Didia*, and it was passed by violence.[11] This last point provided an easy transition to a passage of self-justification for his withdrawal, as a personal sacrifice for the survival of the 'good men' and the *res publica*, at the end of which he compared himself to the supreme exponents of self-sacrifice, the Decii Mures father and son.[12]

Lucius Cotta, continued Cicero, had argued that Clodius' law was invalid, and a further proof of this was that, Pompey, Lentulus Spinther, even Metellus Nepos had all proposed Cicero's return, which would have been contrary to Clodius' law.[13] Furthermore, he could not have lost his citizenship unwillingly, a doubtful point given that banishment (*aqua et igni interdictio*) was probably now a regular penalty under the *quaestiones*.[14] Better arguments were that Clodius had made no provision for removing him from the censors' lists nor had he been replaced on the list of jurors.[15] Cicero then diverts into a comparison of himself with heroes of old—Kaeso Quinctius, Ahala, Camillus, Popilius Laenas, and Metellus Numidicus—who had returned after condemnation and had recovered their full status. This slips into a contrast between the assembly of slaves, hired supporters, criminals, and the poor that exiled him with the one that contained the senate and the authority of all Italy, which recalled him: he could have resisted Clodius in 58 with a force like that.[16] Clodius had made a joke in his speech about Cicero's self-praise, that he claimed to be Jove and that Minerva was his sister (*Dom.* 92). He also, it seems, had argued that Cicero was in fact a bully and a coward.[17] In reply Cicero returns to his standard self-justification, even admitting his grief over what he had lost as proof of his self-sacrifice (96–9).

At last he comes to the subject of his speech, the house. Clodius claimed that his legislation had legitimised his dedication of Cicero's house to Liberty

---

[8] *Dom.* 43 ff.; cf. *CRR* 151.   [9] *Dom.* 47 ff.; Ch. XII,n. 58; Lintott, 1972a, 261–2.
[10] *Dom.* 50; cf. Fezzi, 2003, esp. 57 ff..   [11] *Dom.* 50–3; cf. *VRR* 140–6.
[12] *Dom.* 54–64, cf. *Red. Sen.* 32–4; *Red. Quir.* 13; Livy 8. 9. 4–12; 10. 28. 12–18.
[13] *Dom.* 68–71; cf. Ch. XII with n. 71.
[14] *Dom.* 77–80; cf. Sall. *Cat.* 51. 22, 40; *Rab. Perd.* 16; *Clu.* 170; *Sest.* 146; Lintott, 1972a, 252–3; Martin, 1970, 87–8.
[15] *Dom.* 82–5. Notice also the earlier identification of Clodius as a 'fortunate Catiline', allegedly made by Clodius' henchmen, cf. Lintott, 1967.
[16] *Dom.* 86–92, including (91) a complimentary reference to the force used by Scipio Nasica against Tiberius Gracchus.
[17] *Dom.* 93–5: 'crudelitas' (93); 'me mortem timuisse' (95). In reply Cicero returns to his standard self-justification, even admitting his grief over what he had lost as proof of his self-sacrifice (96–9).

(*Dom.* 106). Against this Cicero pointed to the invalidity of consecrations of property by tribunes without proper authority,[18] and cited a *lex Papiria* which forbade such dedications without the specific authorization of the assembly: in the light of this law C. Cassius Longinus, the censor of 154, had been forbidden by the college of *pontifices* to dedicate a statue of Concordia in the Curia, similarly the dedication in 123 of a shrine by the Vestal Virgin Licinia had been declared void (*Dom.* 127–30, 136). If of course some of Cicero's prior argumentation was sound and Clodius' law prescribing the consequences of his exile was no law, there would have been no religious problem. However, although some had denied the validity of Clodius' law, there had been no *senatus consultum* to this effect, merely an instruction to the consuls to reinstate Cicero in his former rights by legislation, which, inconveniently, could not in itself overrule the religious force of the consecration. Hence it was vital for Cicero to find some fault in the religious procedure. Clodius seems to have carefully avoided incorporating any reference to himself by name in his law in order to avoid offending against the *leges Licinia* and *Aebutia* which did not permit legislators to create directly official posts for themselves or their relatives in their bills.[19] He was now to be caught on the other prong of that fork in that it was arguable that he had not been specifically charged by plebiscite with the dedication of the shrine.[20]

This technical argument is critical, but Cicero envelops it with an appeal to religious principles and colours it with a new set of *exempla* from the past. How could he, the saviour of his country, be compared to others whose houses had been destroyed—Spurius Maelius, Marcus Manlius, the Latin rebel M. Vitruvius Vaccus, and the associate of C. Gracchus, M. Fulvius Flaccus?[21] It was a disgrace that a man who spurned religion like Clodius, should claim to inflict such a religious punishment with the aid of, at most, one inexperienced *pontifex*—his brother-in-law L. Pinarius Natta—when his real aim had been to expand the view from his own Palatine property and to provide a location for a dubious statue, acquired by his brother in Greece (*Dom.* 105, cf. 140; 111–19). Cicero goes so far as to suggest that Clodius and Natta could not have pronounced the formulae correctly—though even correct procedure could not legitimize such a crime (*Dom.* 138–40). The roll-call of great Romans invoked by contrast, many of them former *pontifices*, includes Q. Catulus, whose portico Clodius had also destroyed; M. Livius

---

[18] *Dom.* 117–26, including Clodius' consecration of Gabinius' property and Ninnius' consecration of that of Clodius.
[19] Cf. *Leg. Agr.* 2. 21; *Leg. Man.* 57.
[20] See now the full discussions of Stroh, 2004, 323–30, and Tatum, 1993, on the legal issues.
[21] *Dom.* 101–3. On the destruction of houses see Mustakallio, 1994, esp. 59–64 about Vitruvius Vaccus.

Drusus, the tribune of 91, and his enemy Q. Servilius Caepio; C. Atinius Labeo and Metellus Numidicus (*Dom.* 112–14, 120, 123, 137). In the *epilogus* Cicero reminds the *pontifices* that the senate, all Italy, and all good men are behind his cause and calls on the gods—the Capitoline triad and Vesta—in a prayer recalling a vow made when he went into exile (*Dom.* 142–5). The brief *commiseratio* (146–7) carefully minimizes his poverty but stresses his current ignominy.

The verdict of the *pontifices* was that, if the man who claimed to have made the dedication had not been charged with that act by name nor ordered to do it by decree of the *populus* or *plebs*, their judgement was that the relevant part of the site could be restored to Cicero. Clodius claimed success in a *contio* authorized by his brother Appius, but the matter was duly referred back to the senate and, after a filibuster by Clodius and an attempted veto by Atilius Serranus had been circumvented, the senate decreed on 2 October in favour of restoring Cicero his confiscated properties with compensation (and rebuilding the portico of Catulus) (*Att.* 4. 2. 3–5). The sums calculated by the consuls' committee for compensation were not generous. Cicero of course had underplayed his financial distress, but he told Atticus that this was not the reason for the calculation, rather the jealousy of those who had cut his pinions (by tacitly supporting Clodius in 58).[22] His dignity restored, he could now look forward to resuming his political career. It might have suited him financially to depart on a votive *legatio* to almost every shrine that existed, but for the opportunity of a temporary absence the position as Pompey's *legatus* sufficed. He had his eyes on possible censorial elections in 57 (*Att.* 4. 2. 6).

DEFENDING FRIENDS

The winter of 57–6 was the last time before the eve of the civil war that Cicero sought to play an important independent political role. The chief themes in his writings and utterances in this period were already presaged in the *De Domo*. There he had expressed approval for the use of force even by a private citizen in the optimate cause.[23] In a letter to Atticus of 23 November he describes the violence used by Clodius against himself and the rebuilding of his house. His comment is that he is beginning a cure by diet and is tired of

---

[22] *Att.* 4. 2. 5; cf. *Dom.* 146–7. The *pontifices* were authoritative on the matter of religion, but their decision required interpretation and it was for the senate to decree the measures that followed. On this issue see Thomas, 2005.

[23] Explicit in *Dom.* 91, Scipio Nasica; implicit in references to Kaeso Quinctius and Servilius Ahala (86).

surgery, but he takes great satisfaction in describing Clodius' defeat by Milo and his supporters (*Att.* 4. 3. 2–3). It is the same the next year, after Clodius had escaped trial to get elected aedile and was prosecuting Milo for violence.[24] Cicero recounts with pleasure how Milo's men won the conflict that resulted from the collective spitting of the Clodiani, though he admits that he himself took to his heels to avoid any personal harm. He also reacts favourably to Pompey's plans to reinforce Milo's gangs with recruits of his own from Picenum and the *ager Gallicus*.[25]

Politically, he sought to maintain an alliance with those who had helped him to return to Rome and recover his former dignity. A new and important ally was Lentulus Marcellinus, the consul elect for 57, who took the lead in the debate following the judgment of the *pontifices* and subsequently sought to help Milo to bring Clodius to trial before the aedilician elections.[26] Men like Spinther and Marcellinus would have been happy with the strictly optimate sentiments in the argumentation of the *De Domo*. However, loyalty had to be expressed in action. Here divisions among the *boni* created a problem for Cicero, and so did his simultaneous debt to Pompey.

Two issues are revealing. The first, the *ager Campanus*, was raised in the senate by Rutilius Lupus, one of the tribunes who came into office on 10 December 57 (*QF* 2. 1. 1). We do not know how far the distribution of this land had advanced since Caesar's law of 59. Certainly, Capua had been refounded as a colony with Pompey one of the commissioners.[27] However, the distribution of the rest of the territory may have been waiting on the lapse of the censorial contracts of the present tenants, probably in March 55.[28] Lupus was clearly proposing a derogation from Caesar's bill—probably not its repeal, as that would have been a direct insult to Pompey as well as Caesar. He included much from Cicero's own speeches, presumably those on Rullus' agrarian bill,[29] and was heard in total silence. However, he declined to ask for formal opinions in order, he said, not to impose a conflict on Cicero and men like him. To which Marcellinus rejoined that he should not interpret the

---

[24] *QF* 2. 3. 2–3. Cicero's language makes it clear that this was a prosecution before an assembly, not *contiones* made in anticipation of a *quaestio*, as Gruen, 1974, 298 n. 39 thought, followed by L. Garofalo, 1989, 107. See esp. *Sest.* 95; *Mil.* 40; *Vat.* 40; *QF* 2. 3. 1–2, 6. 4: Clodius *diem dixit* and *prodixit*; Milo is *reus*; Pompey is *advocatus*; Vatinius gave testimony. On aedilician prosecutions see *VRR* 95–9; *CRR* 131–3. Clodius may have justified his action by pointing to his general duty to preserve the wellbeing of the city (cf. *2Verr.* 5. 36).

[25] *QF* 2. 3. 3–4. On the insults to Pompey by question and response see *VRR* 9–10.

[26] *Att.* 4. 2. 4, 4. 3. 3, cf. *Har. Resp.* 15 for the decree declaring that attacks on Cicero's house were actionable under the *lex de vi* and their perpetrators were acting *contra rem publicam*.

[27] On Capua see *Red. Sen.* 29; *Sest.* 9–10; *Mil.* 39; *Pis.* 24–5 Asc. 10 C; cf. *Att.* 2. 16. 1, where Cicero's comment suggests that in April 59 he thought that the refoundation was the main provision of the bill (for the 5,000 settlers see *Leg. Agr.* 2. 76–7 on Rullus' proposal).

[28] *Att.* 4. 11. 1; *Imp. Rom.* 88–9.   [29] Cf. *Leg. Agr.* 1. 18–22; 2. 76–98.

senators' silence as approving or disapproving: the matter should be discussed in Pompey's presence.[30] Rutilius Lupus later cooperated with committed Pompeian tribunes (*Fam.* 1. 1. 3) but need not be thought to be a crypto-Pompeian here, rather a independent man who was bidding for political support from more than one group.[31] The issue was then dropped, to be revived the following April (*QF* 2. 6. 1). How far Cicero committed himself then to an attack on the law of 59 is a question to which we shall return.

A more complex division of loyalty arose over Egypt, where Lentulus Spinther, as the new proconsul of Cilicia, had originally been commissioned to restore Ptolemy XII Neos Dionusos (Auletes), recognized by Rome as the legitimate king in Caesar's consulship.[32] This had been thrown into uncertainty after the whole issue had been reopened by the discovery of a Sibylline oracle: 'If an Egyptian king asks for help, do not deny friendship, but do not help with a *multitudo* (*plêthos*) or you will have trouble.'[33] The scandal about the bribery and violence being employed by Ptolemy Auletes in Italy in order to ensure his reinstallation in his kingdom by the Romans was flagrant. First, the distinguished embassy of protest from Alexandria led by Dion was attacked; then, after the Sibylline oracle had put a brake on the senate's original decree that he should be restored by Spinther (*Fam.* 1. 1. 3, 1. 7. 4) and Ptolemy had left Italy, Dion himself was murdered at the house of T. Coponius.[34] A contract had been made between Ptolemy and the financier Rabirius Postumus at Pompey's Alban villa before the former's departure (*Rab. Post.* 6). In January the creditors of Ptolemy were still deploying bribes on Pompey's behalf as instructed by the king's agent Hammonius (*Fam.* 1. 1. 1, 1. 2. 3). In fact various Alexandrian supporters of the king were put on trial and another Roman, P. Asicius, was accused by Licinius Calvus and defended by Cicero (*Cael.* 24; Tac. *Dial.* 21. 2.). Asicius had acquired from Ptolemy a *lectica* (sedan) and an entourage of 100 swordbearers, which Cicero on one occasion borrowed (*QF* 2. 9. 2). It is not surprising that C. Cato attacked Ptolemy and Spinther in a speech shortly after his entry to the tribunate in December 57.[35]

Cicero sought to reassure Spinther about the efforts being made on his behalf in a series of letters. From the first, written on 13 January 57

---

[30] 'Onus simultatis nobis imponeret' (*QF* 2. 1. 1) is unlikely to be a reference to Cicero alone, as that would have been acutely embarrassing and Cicero would have commented further.
[31] On this issue and for the Pompeian interpretation see. Cary, 1923; Stockton, 1962; Seager, 2002, 110–11.
[32] *Fam.* 1. 1. 3, 7. 4; Dio 39. 12. 3; cf. *Att.* 2. 5. 1; 16. 2; *Vat.* 29; Suet. *Jul.* 54. 3; Dio 39. 12. 1 and for the treaty *Rab. Post.* 6; Caes. *BCiv.* 3. 107. 2.
[33] Dio 39. 15. 1, 39. 16. 2.
[34] *Cael.* 24, cf. 51–4; Dio 39. 14–16.   [35] Fenestella fr. 21 Peter.

(*Fam.* 1. 1. 1–3), we find that it was generally accepted in the senate that an army could not be used, but there were still five differing views among the consulars. Hortensius, Cicero, and M. Lucullus supported Spinther; Crassus preferred three *legati* (envoys), who might include holders of *imperium* such as Pompey, Bibulus three *legati* without *imperium*. One consular, Servilius Isauricus, did not wish Ptolemy restored at all. The consulars Volcatius Tullus and Afranius and the tribunes Plautius Hypsaeus and Scribonius Libo, with the backing of other friends of Pompey, supported giving the task to Pompey alone. Rutilius Lupus had introduced the debate when this proposal was made and has been supposed to be Pompeian on this account,[36] but Cicero seems to distinguish him from committed Pompeians like Hypsaeus and Libo. The vigour of canvassing on Pompey's behalf suggested that the great man was behind it. Unfortunately, Cicero informed Spinther, those against Pompey were also against Spinther, because he had promoted Pompey's corn-commission, As for Cicero himself, he had less *auctoritas*, because he was known to be obliged to Spinther, and his own *gratia* was ineffective, because people thought they would be doing Pompey a favour (*Fam.* 1. 1. 3–4; cf. 1. 7. 2).

Few passages show so neatly how *gratia* was not automatically encashable, and how others' knowledge of the obligations of a statesman might diminish his actual influence. This letter begins by referring to Cicero's duty (*officium*) to Spinther 'or rather *pietas*', a word that suggests duty to a parent or close relative. It ends with an assurance of Cicero's own affection (*amor*) and loyalty (*fides*) and an innuendo against those who had failed to display the *fides* that they should have done. Here Cicero is telling his own story, past and present, as he pointed out later (*Fam.* 1. 1. 4; cf. 1. 6. 2). His feelings are well illustrated by a passage in the letter to Atticus of the previous 23 November, where he was enthusing about Milo's open commitment to violence: 'I see that if he (Clodius) puts himself now in Milo's way in a fracas, he will be killed by the man himself. He has no hesitation, makes it obvious; he has no fear of what happened to me; for he will never follow the advice of someone jealous and treacherous nor put his trust in a noble who does nothing' (*Att.* 4. 3. 5). Milo's uninhibited direct action made a refreshing contrast to the slippery manoeuvrings of Cicero's fellow *consulares*.

The letter that followed two days later revealed the accuracy of Cicero's fears. After an inconclusive debate on 13 January, to which Cicero contributed a long speech but which was dominated by an argument between the consul Lentulus Marcellinus and the pro-Pompeian tribune Caninius Gallus,[37] the

---

[36] See the scholars cited in n. 31 above; Gruen, 1974, 107–8.
[37] *Fam.* 1. 2. 1; cf. *QF* 2. 2. 3; Plut. *Pomp.* 49. 10 for the proposal that Pompey accompanied by two lictors should restore Ptolemy, ascribed by the MSS of Plutarch to 'Kanidios'.

After the Return

senate resolved the following day that contributions to the discussion should be brief.[38] According to Cicero, Spinther's friends hoped to have a majority on their side in the light of reactions to Cicero's speech and personal canvassing. The same was no doubt true of the other groups. It soon came to a vote. Crassus had dropped his proposal, as had Servilius Isauricus. The consul ordered Bibulus' motion first, followed by that of Hortensius, and then that of Volcatius Tullus. The motion of Bibulus was taken in two parts in response to a demand of *divide*.[39] The acceptance of a religious ban on an army was approved; the appointment of three *legati* without *imperium* was rejected. Hortensius' motion was about to be taken when Rutilius Lupus intervened, claiming the right to hold a vote next because he had introduced the earlier debate about Pompey. It was clearly felt that the next motion taken was likely to prevail.[40] The tribune was met by countercheers and a debate on this point of order ensued, which the consuls, who had been for Bibulus' motion, allowed to proceed until nightfall. Cicero then happened to be dining with Pompey and used the occasion to canvass support for Spinther. Pompey's own reply reassured him that Pompey himself was not ambitious for the Egyptian command, but one look at Pompey's friends inside the senate and out convinced him that 'certain people' had fixed the matter with the support of the king himself and his advisers (*Fam.* 1. 2. 3, cf. 1. 1).

The matter dragged on without decision either in the senate or the assembly. The inactivity of the assembly was the result of effective obstruction by Spinther's friends, especially, it seems, the tribune L. Racilius. This was particularly necessary when Caninius promulgated his bill in favour of Pompey,[41] and when C. Cato proposed to abrogate Spinther's *imperium* (*QF* 2. 3. 1; *Fam.* 1. 5a. 2). Much later, in the summer, when the political situation had been completely transformed and the prolongation of Caesar's command in Transalpine Gaul had been comfortably achieved, Cicero wrote to Spinther telling him that he had discussed matters with Pompey and urging him to take advantage of the fact that the original *senatus consultum* in his favour had never been revoked: he should invade Egypt without the king, but

---

[38] Presumably they were to be mainly in the form *adsentior Quinto Hortensio*, cf. *CRR* 78–9. How (ii. 188) believes, in view of the following 'videbatur enim reconciliata nobis voluntas esse senatus', that this was a decision by Spinther's friends only. However, 'placuit' is technical language for a senate resolution, cf. *Fam.* 8. 8. 6–7, and it is hard to believe that the decision of 'us' in the sense of Spinther's friends would have been effective in a matter like this. The *enim* sentence is to explain to Spinther not the senate's decision as a whole but why his friends were happy to see the debate curtailed.

[39] On *divisio* see Asc. 43–5 C; *CRR* 84.

[40] Cf. Pol. 33. 1. 5–7; *CRR* 83–4.

[41] Racilius *Fam.* 1. 2. 4, 1. 4. 2–3, 1. 5a. 2, 1. 7. 2. Caninius *QF.* 2. 2. 3; *Fam.* 1. 7. 3; Plut. *Pomp.* 49. 10.

keep him in a convenient location nearby, so that he could later return in peace. Spinther had previously written a tactful letter to Pompey reassuring him of his friendship (*Fam.* 1. 7. 3–6, 10). Cicero of course had been arguing continually for Pompey's good will to Spinther, but it only became evident at this time. One turning point, noted by Cicero in an earlier letter, may have been the trial of Milo in February, where the unpopularity of Pompey's Egyptian entanglement came to the fore and this may have convinced Pompey to give up his own ambitions there (*Fam.* 1. 5b. 1–2).

Milo's trial is further evidence for the complexity of Cicero's relationships. In spite of Milo's attempts, supported by Marcellinus and the tribune Racilius, to get Clodius to court first, the latter had finally become aedile in elections on 20 January.[42] He now prosecuted Milo before the assembly, an unusual procedure in the late Republic and unusual for an aedile, though legitimate constitutionally—no doubt chosen because it was well suited to popular demonstrations. Moreover, Clodius would have had more success with a popular vote than with a senatorial–equestrian jury in a *quaestio*, as the later trial of Sestius showed.[43] Here Pompey' support for Milo allowed Clodius to deploy all the resentment over corn-supply problems and the Egyptian question against him and hence against Milo and the rest of his supporters. There was even a similar reaction in the senate. In the debate after the trial was broken up through violence Pompey was attacked by Bibulus, Curio, Favonius, and the younger Servilius Isauricus. Cicero comments that he did not attend himself in order that he did not have to choose between silence and offending 'good men' by defending Pompey.[44] The next day the senate was held outside the *pomerium* in the temple of Apollo, so that Pompey could attend. On this occasion it was C. Cato who inveighed against Pompey, while cleverly heaping compliments on Cicero and portraying him as one whom Pompey had betrayed. This would not have been reassuring to Cicero, as it recalled Clodius' less complimentary portrayal of Cicero as one who fawned on the man who had betrayed him (*QF* 2. 3. 3; cf.*Dom.* 29).

THE DEFENCE OF OPTIMATES

In the same latter to Quintus we hear of prosecutions being mounted against Sestius in the *quaestiones de ambitu* and *de vi*. The first charge of electoral bribery came to nothing; the second, made originally by a certain M. Tullius

---

[42] *QF* 2. 1. 2–3; *Att.* 4. 3. 3–5; Dio 39. 7. 2; *QF* 2. 2. 2; Dio 39. 18. 1.
[43] On aedilician prosecutions see above with n. 24.
[44] *QF* 2. 3. 2; on the form of demonstration see above with n. 25.

was taken over by P. Albinovanus, with T. Claudius and perhaps Tullius acting as assistant accusers (*subscriptores*) but with Vatinius and Clodius in the background.[45] Cicero found here an opportunity to repay Sestius for his services to him and to deliver an elaborate panegyric of the optimate cause. This is frequently regarded by scholars as a kind of political testament or at least a manifesto,[46] but it is perhaps better understood in its context simply as a piece of advocacy. Of course our chief information comes from the texts that Cicero eventually circulated—not only the speech for Sestius, but his cross-examination of Vatinius in the form of a continuous oration. As we have seen earlier (Ch. II with nn. 74–6), at the time Vatinius may have given as good as he got and this is conveniently airbrushed in Cicero's *In Vatinium*. Moreover, this published text does not correspond in two points with what Cicero was to claim in a letter of 54 to Spinther that he had said at the time.[47] We should, therefore, also allow for editing in the *pro Sestio*. Nevertheless, although at first sight it seems peculiar as a defence speech, it may be a fair reflection of what was actually said in court.

Cicero spoke after a distinguished group of defending counsel—Crassus, Calvus, and Hortensius. He asserts that after Hortensius' speech there was nothing left unsaid either in favour of the defendant or as a lament for the condition of the *res publica*.[48] From Cicero's speech it is clear that the defence advocates did not deny what Sestius had done but argued that it was not *contra rem publicam* (against the public interest): rather it was on behalf of the *res publica*.[49] It was a matter, as we saw in a different context in Chapter IX, of their imposing on the jury their own construction—not only legally, but morally and emotionally—on the events that formed the subject of the case.[50] Hortensius had also used his speech to provide a sermon to the young men of Rome on correct political conduct (*Sest.* 14). Cicero did the same, but since the justification of Sestius' actions logically involved the justification of his own return to Rome, he had an opportunity once more to provide an apologia for his exile.

After the *prooemium* there is a brief section on Sestius' earlier career, especially his services against the Catilinarians.[51] Cicero then argues that he cannot do justice to Sestius' tribunate without recounting the events of 58 as a

---

[45] *QF.* 2. 3. 5, 2. 4. 1; *Vat.* 3, 41; *Schol. Bob.* 125 St.
[46] See e.g. Gelzer, 1969, 157–8; Stockton, 1971, 213; T. N. Mitchell, 1991, 52–3.
[47] *Fam.* 1. 9. 7; Ch. II with nn. 65–77.
[48] *Sest.* 3, 14; *QF* 2. 4. 1; *Schol. Bob.* 125 St.
[49] See *Sest.* 78, 84, and, on the nature of the *lex de vi*, VRR 116–21.
[50] Technically a *constitutio iuridicialis* involving *relatio* or *translatio criminis*, see *Ad Her.* 1. 18, 24–5; *Inv.* 1. 14–15; 2. 78 ff.
[51] *Sest.* 6–13, of which 8–12 are on 63–2 BC.

background. The villains in the narrative are not named but painstakingly described—Clodius the monster, Piso the decadent noble and Epicurean voluptuary, Gabinius the depraved debauchee.[52] The heroes are the senate, the equestrian order, and Italy, especially the *equites* led by L. Aelius Lamia, who are described as 'most noble young men' (*nobilissimos adulescentis*), a term that recalls the young members of the nobility that the annals of the early Republic portrayed as the strong arm of the senate, and one to which Cicero would return in his later portrayal of the true optimate.[53]

Pompey, Caesar, and Crassus are kept in an interesting category of their own. They are held responsible for Cicero's exile not because of their activity but because of their inactivity. Pompey, it is said, believed that he had made an agreement with Clodius protecting Cicero (*Sest.* 15). He and Crassus asked for the consuls' help, Pompey promising to take action if they would (*Sest.* 41, cf. *Pis.* 77). However, Clodius claimed the support of the three dynasts and their actual or potential military support; indeed Caesar was at the gates with an army and Clodius' brother—probably C. Claudius Pulcher—as one of his *praefecti* or *legati* (*Sest.* 41). The three said nothing to give the lie to Clodius, because they were afraid that all their acts of the previous year would be overturned, if they alienated Clodius.[54] In *In Vatinium* similarly we find the confinement of Bibulus treated in the same way that Cicero's exile is in *pro Sestio*: it is blamed on Vatinius, not Caesar (*Vat.* 22). This presentation of the events contrasts with Cicero's later letter to Spinther, where he claims that during the examination of witnesses he stated that the same people who had prevented Bibulus leaving his house had also forced Cicero to leave his (*Fam.* 1. 9. 7).

We have already considered the refinement over time of Cicero's apologia for his conduct in 58 (Ch. III with nn. 25–7). Cicero has to explain why he yielded to Clodius, when he had so much backing. He does not want to magnify the threat posed by Clodius himself: indeed, he compares this with the menace to Metellus Numidicus from the combination of Saturninus and Marius to Clodius' disadvantage (*Sest.* 37–8). Instead he makes the alleged threat of military action by the dynasts critical and at the same time depicts them as cowards in face of Clodius: hence it was not he alone who was humiliated by Clodius but the three great men. It may seem that this theme in *pro Sestio* is more likely to have appeared first in a written version circulated after Cicero had made his peace with the dynasts. Strictly interpreted, it is not

---

[52] Respectively *Sest.* 15–16; 18–24; 20. See 23 on Piso's Epicureanism.
[53] *Sest.* 25–9, esp. 27; 51; 136; *Red. Sen.* 12; *VRR* 59–60; Lintott, 1970, 24 ff.
[54] *Sest.* 40.; cf. *Har. Resp.* 47; also *Sest.* 67 for Pompey finally recovering from his fears. For Clodius' threats see *Dom.* 40; *Har. Resp.* 47; *VRR* 146–7; Pocock, 1924, 59–64.

conducive to the line of defence Cicero was adopting. If the real strength of Clodius lay in the putative support of an army—something conspicuously absent in 57—why was it so necessary for Sestius to resort to violence? Nevertheless, the alleged military threat is integral to Cicero's apologia for himself, while the circumstances of the trial did not permit him to employ harsh condemnation of Pompey, or of Crassus who was participating in this same defence.

Cicero' self-exculpation is more elaborate here than in any other Cicero text. He saved the state by preventing civil war. How could he be afraid of death with such examples before him as the original Mucius Scaevola, P. Decius Mus, both father and son, and most recently Crassus' father? On the other hand, even Marius in the Minturnae marshes had chosen survival and revenge; he chose survival because his own death would have been the death of the *res publica* (*Sest.* 36–52, esp. 48, 50). The scene-setting of the background to Sestius' violence continues with a narrative of the rest of Clodius' activities after Cicero's departure, where Sestius at last makes a further appearance by virtue of his journey to Caesar and his entry to the tribunate on 10 December 58 (*Sest.* 71; *Att.* 3. 17–18). There follows a selective account of the efforts made for Cicero's recall in 57, concentrating on the violence used against the bill of Fabricius on 23 January and on Sestius himself later (*Sest.* 75–83). Here Cicero turns to the prosecutor's point that Sestius had hired a gang, when it was more appropriate to use the courts, as Milo sought to do—in fact ineffectively because of the obstruction from Metellus Nepos, Appius Claudius, and one of the tribunes (84–90). Cicero's answer is that a community can work either by the law or violence: the one excludes the other. He evokes a picture of the violent state of nature ('ita naturam rerum tulisse') before men outstanding in their virtue and wisdom created communities and urban settlements with walls.[55]

This philosophical contrast between *ius* and *vis* is repeated more practically by the following comparison between the desperate state of the *res publica* at the time of the trial, when Milo, after being prevented from prosecuting Clodius through a decision in the senate, had been himself brought to trial (93–5), and Cicero's ideal optimate Rome. The prosecutor had apparently made play with the failure of the senate to back Milo to the end, asking Cicero what was his 'tribe' (*natio*) of *optimates*: did they really exist as a group?[56] Cicero's reply occupies the rest of the speech until the *epilogus*. *Optimates*, he proclaims, are those who seek in high politics to please all the best men

---

[55] *Sest.* 91–2 with Lucretian resonances, see Lucr. 5. 955–61, 1019–20, 1105–12, 1143–50; Campbell, 2003, 273–5. There is another Lucretian echo in *De Or.* 1. 33, composed in 55 BC.

[56] *Sest.* 96. The term *natio* for the *optimates* had apparently been coined by Vatinius (132). On Cicero's use of the terms *optimates* and *optimus quique* see Stone, 2005, 59–94.

(*optimus quisque*); *populares* those who seek to please the masses. The best men come not only from the ranks of senators and *equites* but include municipal men, farmers, businessmen, even freedmen. They must be sound in character and property. The politicians who serve their interests aim for tranquillity and the maintenance of status (*cum dignitate otium*) (*Sest.* 98).[57] The *dignitas* belongs to all the best men, *optimus quisque* (*Sest.* 104). The stability of the community is founded on religion, the auspices, the various powers of the magistrates, the authority of the senate, statutes, ancestral tradition, the criminal courts, the jurisdiction of magistrates in private law, trust (*fides*)—especially, that is, financial confidence—the provinces, the allies, the glory of the empire, military strength, and the treasury (*Sest.* 98–9). Those who wish to overthrow it are either criminals already, seeking to hide their crimes, or deep in debt, or simply so insane that their existence depends on civil strife. Its defenders are men like M. Scaurus (*cos.* 115), Metellus Numidicus, and the recently dead Q. Catulus (*Sest.* 99–101).

Once, Cicero argues, the *populares* had a platform, since the welfare and perceived needs of the people conflicted with the public interest. He cites the ballot law of L. Cassius, Tiberius Gracchus' agrarian law, and Gaius' grain law. Now the *populus* and its leaders are at one; the seditious have to buy their support (*Sest.* 103–6). As evidence of this Cicero cites the assembly that recalled him in 57 (107–10), the recent praetorian elections (he ignores Clodius' election as aedile) (113–14), the reactions in the theatre at the *ludi Apollinares* of 57 to the senate decrees that proposed his recall (115–27),[58] and the general popularity of his return with the senate and people (127–31). An attack on Vatinius for his enmity to the tribe of *optimates* leads to a final appeal to the young men, including the young nobles, to support the cause he has described (132–43).[59] In this he asks them to understand the Roman constitution, as handed down by their ancestors, in particular the idea that the senate was the guardian of the *res publica* and that the magistrates should follow the authority of this order and view themselves as it were as the servants of a most weighty council (136–7). The final *commiseratio* not only invokes Sestius' misery but that which would befall Cicero, should his defender be exiled (144–7).

We may wonder how far in substance Cicero's discourse on *optimates* differed from that of Hortensius, apart from the obvious personal reminiscences. Much

---

[57] Cf. *Fam.* 1. 9. 21; *de Or.* 1. 1, where it is the condition of an individual rather than the community, but the former would depend on the latter. See Wirszubski, 1954; Balsdon, 1960. For *otium* as domestic peace see e.g. *Sest.* 5, 15, 104; *Dom.* 12–13; *Leg. Agr.* 2. 9; *Mur.* 83; *Fam.* 5. 7. 1.

[58] On political demonstrations in the theatre see Cameron, 1976, 157–63.

[59] See above with n. 53.

was no doubt banal, including the blatant defence of rank and property. Cicero may have been original, however, in stressing the existence of *optimates* throughout the ranks of society and throughout Italy (97). The subordination of the magistrates of the Republic to the senate (137) is also an extreme view of the constitution and unusual. It was certainly not a view generally accepted by members of the senate, even by those who were neither *populares* themselves nor, like Piso in 58 or Metellus Nepos in 57, cooperating with *popularis* politicians.[60] As for Cicero, he himself in his later theoretical works stressed the authority of both the senate and the magistrates. In *De Re Publica* (2. 56–7) the *auctoritas* of the leading men is balanced by the *potestas* of the magistrates (including that of the dictator) and the *libertas* of the people; in the *De Legibus* (3. 2–5, cf. 8) the powers of the magistrates are central to the constitution: the magistrate is a talking law, just as a law is a mute magistrate. In practical politics, as Cicero knew well, the senate did not always recommend a just policy, as when it did not permit Milo to prosecute Clodius (*Sest.* 95). What we have in *pro Sestio*, then, is hardly a realistic programme for the time, nor even a properly elaborated theory, but an ideal vision suited to the appeal that Cicero was making to a jury of senators and *equites*, especially as it might recall the histories of the early Republic where the cadet members of the elite were heroised for using violence on behalf of the senate.

In a letter to Quintus shortly after that in which he recorded Sestius' acquittal, written towards the end of March, Cicero finds many reasons for satisfaction. C. Cato is being prevented from legislating about Spinther by religious obstruction to the days available for assembly meetings; Marcellinus, however, with senatorial backing is hostile to Pompey, who is also deeply unpopular among the urban proletariat. So Cicero is keeping out of the senate. However, he is busy in the courts; his house is full of people paying their respects; his enemies are being condemned with the exception of Clodius' assistant Sextus Cloelius, who was marginally acquitted on a violence charge, Pompey's unpopularity once again being a factor. There are two straws in the wind: certain tribunes are making monstrous proposals about Caesar, and Appius Claudius has not yet returned from a visit to him.[61]

About the end of the month Cicero found himself defending against a charge of violence someone who had not been a friend for some time, M. Caelius Rufus. The charges were in part connected with the infamous affair of Dion and the other Alexandrian ambassadors. Here Cicero had the

---

[60] *CRR* 65–8.
[61] *QF* 2. 5. 2–4; cf. *Cael.* 78 on Cloelius. The '*monstra*' proposed for Caesar were perhaps the appointment of 10 *legati* (as subordinate commanders or as a commission to settle the new province) and pay for a greater number of legions, se *Fam.* 1. 7. 10; *Balb.* 61; *Prov. Cos.* 28; cf. Dio 39. 25. 1 on the *legati*.

advantage of having already defended P. Asicius on a similar charge. However, the greatest inducement was that it gave him a chance to reply to charges of procuring murder, deriving from Clodius' sister, against Caelius, a former friend of hers.[62] Caelius had undertaken his forensic education (*tirocinium fori*) under the supervision of Cicero and Crassus (*Cael.* 9–10). He then got to know Catiline and supported him in his second consular candidature in 63 (10–12). About Caelius' career from that time onwards Cicero says little— only the reference to his tour in Africa and his prosecutions (73–6, cf. 15, 78). It is a fair inference that they moved apart: certainly Caelius' prosecution of C. Antonius in 59 must have been painful for Cicero speaking on the other side and defending his former consular colleague. Caelius apparently used Antonius' complicity in the conspiracy as an accessory charge,[63] and both sides seem to have regarded the success of the prosecution as a kind of Catilinarian comeback: were flowers really placed and a memorial feast held at Catiline's tomb?[64]

Caelius' prosecution of L. Bestia earlier in 56 for *ambitus* (electoral bribery) also found Cicero as one of his opponents.[65] However, this is unlikely to have made relations worse. Bestia was a previous opponent of Cicero over the Catilinarian affair in 62, but in 56 the orator had a special reason to defend him. He had protected Sestius in one of his conflicts with the Clodiani in 57, while Sestius was supporting a bill for Cicero's recall from exile. Not only was Cicero's defence a repayment to Bestia but it conveniently allowed him to praise Sestius and refute in advance the charge of *vis* being prepared at the time against him. This for Cicero was what was important about that case. It would not have mattered that Caelius was apparently obsessively embittered towards Bestia, whose candidature for the praetorship he had earlier aided (76, 26). In any case the situation changed when Bestia's son, L. Sempronius Atratinus, counterattacked by accusing Caelius and used the support of the Claudii: it was more than business as usual for Rome's leading defence counsel to undertake the case, it was a pleasure. For Crassus (23), another experienced defence counsel, it would have been more a matter of business— and of keeping all political options open: as we have seen, he had recently defended Sestius when the Claudian family had attacked him, in spite of what was believed to be a political connection between himself and Clodius at the time.[66]

---

[62] See Appendix 3 on the charges and, on Caelius and Clodia, Wiseman, 1985, 15–90.
[63] *Cael.* 15; Dio 38. 10. 3.
[64] *Flacc.* 95–6, cf. Wiseman, 1985, 64.
[65] *Cael.* 1, 16, 76, 78; *QF* 2. 3. 6—Cicero spoke on 11 February.
[66] *Schol. Bob.* 125St; contrast *QF* 2. 3. 2–3.

Cicero had the advantage of speaking last after much of the work had been done by Caelius himself and Crassus.⁶⁷ The matter did not touch him personally and he had no reason to talk about himself, except in relation to Caelius' *tirocinium*. His comment on Catiline's positive qualities and how he himself had once mistaken him for a 'good man' is one of two political passages in the speech (12–14). The other, in the *epilogus*, is the presentation of Caelius as one of 'the good party, the good men', who should be preserved for the *res publica* (77–8): Caelius was portrayed in that respect as another Sestius. Cicero's relaxed and brilliant speech helped to secure Caelius' acquittal, a new friend for himself, and no doubt useful gratitude in the financial circles with which Caelius seems to have been connected (see App. 3).

CHANGING COURSE

The *pro Sestio* in a sense marks the close of an enormous parenthesis in Cicero's career. In December 60 he had decided to hold to his traditional line of optimate politics in spite of an invitation to join Caesar, Pompey, and Crassus (*Att.* 2. 3. 3–4). Refusal of the invitation had led to exposure to Clodius, exile, guilt, recovery of status, and a desperate attempt to expunge guilt by apologia and assertion of impeccable optimate credentials. This reached a climax in *pro Sestio*. It led nowhere, and Cicero found his debt to Pompey in particular requiring him to abandon the 'good men'. Two self-justificatory letters to Spinther and a letter to Atticus in particular show how important he viewed his change of course: Cicero portrays himself as leading the fight against the Republic's enemies but, as in 58, deserted by those who should have been his friends and, in contrast to that year, running for cover. Later invective was happy to describe him as a *perfuga* or *transfuga*, a deserter or turncoat, though not on account of what happened in 56. We can, however, find traces of this charge in the period immediately after his return.⁶⁸ Hence for many of his contemporaries his change of course in 56 would not have seemed so dramatic, given his existing devotion to Pompey and his refusal to lend his support to the attacks on Pompey in the senate.

In his letter to Spinther of late 54, after describing his rejoinders to Vatinius at the Sestius trial with their discreet criticism of Caesar, Cicero goes on to claim that the senate had agreed with his motion on 5 April, that the *ager*

---

⁶⁷ *Cael.* 23; Quint. 1. 5. 61, 4. 2. 27.
⁶⁸ Witness Clodius' remarks the previous autumn (*Dom.* 3–4) and those of Laterensis at the Plancius trial (*Planc.* 86–90). On the invective tradition see Lintott, 1997*a*, 2514–5.

Campanus should be discussed at a quorate meeting on 15 May: could he, he asks, have made a greater attack on the citadel of that cause or have forgotten more his circumstances and remembered his (past) actions?[69] An adjournment motion is not the most vicious of attacks. Indeed, when Cicero recounts the debate in a letter to Quintus close to the event, he says nothing of any contribution of his to it. On the day in question the senate voted to Pompey a vast sum, 40 million sesterces, for his corn-commission. There was then a noisy debate on the *ager Campanus*, prompted by the shortage of money and the high price of corn. No specific proposal emerged and Pompey did not seem worried on that count: on the 8th Cicero made a courtesy call on him after dinner, the evening before his departure to Pisa and thence Sardinia, and apparently nothing political was said (*QF* 2. 6. 1–3; cf. *Fam*. 1. 9. 9). It was by then too late to get Pompey's approval of any specific proposal and the latter seems to have been happy to let matters drift on, as they had been since December. Modern scholars have constructed out of this a subtle plot by Pompey to get Caesar's attention, but Caesar seems to have had sufficient problems of his own in Rome relating to his command in Gaul—finance and staffing for his legions, and prevention of any moves to succeed him in Transalpine Gaul.[70]

According to our secondary sources there was a great gathering at Luca—magistrates with a total of 120 *fasces*, 200 senators.[71] The majority of the magistrates can be readily attested or surmised: Caesar, Pompey, Appius Claudius (on his way to be governor of Sardinia, Metellus Nepos (on his way to Hispania Citerior), perhaps also Quinctilius Varus (governor of Hispania Ulterior) and, from among the praetors of 56, C. Claudius Pulcher and M. Aemilius Scaurus. The stream of senators in conveyances or on horseback moving north-west up the *via Aurelia* would have been a remarkable sight, particularly as it contrasted with the more usual move south-east down the *Appia* or *Latina* towards the seaside villas of Latium, the *ager Falernus*, or Campania. In the surviving correspondence Cicero shows no sign of having noticed the direction in which his fellow-senators were travelling.

During the legal vacation he had other problems to distract him. There were portents in Latium and Rome—a shrine to Hera revolved, there were thunderbolts, earth tremors, and a shooting star. These were referred by the senate to the college of *haruspices*, the experts in Etruscan divination, for interpretation. The college stated in part of its reply that sacred and religious sites were being treated as profane, which provided a convenient pretext for

---

[69] *Fam*. 1. 9. 8; cf. *QF* 2. 7. 2. The quorate meeting (ibid. 1) would have been necessary for the discussion of Gabinius' request for a *supplicatio*, see Balsdon 1957, 20.

[70] See above with n. 61; Balsdon, 1957, 18 ff. We should be very cautious about believing Cicero's later self-presentation to Spinther.

[71] Plut. *Caes*. 21. 5; *Pomp*. 51. 4; App. *BCiv*. 2. 17. 62.

Clodius to attack Cicero on account of his reoccupation of the once consecrated site of his house and to attempt to destroy it once more.[72] Cicero was advising Atticus about protection for his house while he was at Arpinum in the middle of April.[73] When he returned to Rome he made two successive raids on the Capitol, with the support of Milo and some tribunes, to tear down the tablets recording Clodius' law exiling him, the first of which was frustrated by the praetor C. Claudius but the second successful.[74]

When the senate met again on 15 May, Gabinius was not granted a thanksgiving (*supplicatio*) for his restoration of order in Judaea after the revolt by Alexander and Aristoboulos,[75] but nothing significant was done about the *ager Campanus* either on that day or the next; Cicero himself was absent. So he informs Quintus in an allusive letter whose text is corrupt. A much debated phrase, 'in hac causa mihi aqua haeret' (usually translated as 'my flow of water is blocked in this cause') indicates that, as far as Cicero is concerned, there is no progress over the issue of the *ager Campanus*. This is generally taken by scholars as the first sign of the Luca agreement taking effect. The attractive emendation of the preceding clause by Sternkopf, followed by Shackleton Bailey, <ab>eram autem (MSS ante) *quod Idibus et postridie fuerat dictum actum iri ut est actum* ('I was absent, however, because it had been said that the matter would be handled on the Ides and the day after, as it was handled') would imply that the obstruction of any emendation of the *lex Campana* had been organized beforehand, but that Cicero had not been instructed directly to absent himself.[76] It is true that in the elaborate apologia to Spinther at the end of 54 Cicero was to claim that Pompey sent Vibullius to tell him not to make a move in Pompey's absence (*Fam*. 1. 9. 10), but this may be a more dramatic presentation of a message simply informing him of the plan to obstruct any change to Caesar's law. If Cicero himself had not been at the centre of the *ager Campanus* issue earlier this year, he had more excuse for failing to attend the debates. As for the optimates attacking the *lex Campana*, they might not have been enthusiastic for Cicero's support. His physical attack on Clodius' law seems to have aroused opposition from M. Cato, who had by now returned from Cyprus.[77] It is in any case clear that for Cicero this was not a turning point in policy: his recantation was to come later.

[72] *Har. Resp.* 9; 20; Dio 39. 20.
[73] *Att.* 4. 7. 2; cf. *QF* 2. 6. 4 for his itinerary and see on the chronology Courtney, 1963.
[74] Dio 39. 21. 1–2.
[75] *QF* 2. 7. 1; cf. Jos. *AJ.* 14. 82–97; *BJ* 1. 160 ff.
[76] *QF* 2. 7. 1–2. Cf. SB *QF*, pp. 62, 185–6. The precise meaning of the apparently proverbial phrase, *aqua mihi haeret*, has been contested: it has even been suggested that it means that Cicero is in disgrace, but for most scholars its general sense is clear: Cicero is at a standstill. What analogy is being used, is less evident. See the debate in *LCM* 5 (1980), 107, 133–5, 157, 185.
[77] Dio 39. 22. 1.

Cicero was, however, in the senate for a debate about the Syrian *publicani*, in which Clodius was supporting a certain Publius Tullio against them and defending the policy of Gabinius.[78] Here he took the opportunity for a violent invective against Clodius, Gabinius, and Piso. The following day, when the agenda was apparently the reply of the *haruspices* about the portents (*de haruspicum responso*), he delivered a speech, of which we have a text, that is in part a repudiation of the suggestion that the rebuilding of his house had offended the gods, in part a denunciation of Clodius. After beginning by defending the violence of his speech the previous day (*Har. Resp.* 1–7), he turned to the charge Clodius had made in a *contio*, that the rebuilding of his house had provoked the prodigies. His claim at bottom was simple: his house had been freed from any religious bond by the decision of the *pontifices* and the subsequent decrees of the senate the previous year (8–17). The pronouncements of the *pontifices* were, on the contrary, a commentary on the sins of Clodius and Piso—the management of the games of the Great Mother by Clodius as aedile, the profanation of sacred places by him and his friends, the murder of ambassadors by Clodius and Piso, the violation of oaths by the Clodian jury in 61, and the careless execution and pollution of ancient and secret rites (18–39).

The final warning of the *haruspices* was of the danger to the leaders of the republic and to the senate from division among the *optimates* and the consequent rule of one man.[79] This brings Cicero back to a theme of the *pro Sestio*—the conflict between *optimates* and *populares*, but, whereas there he argued that there was no reason now for the people to differ from the best men, here he contrasted the great *populares* of the past with their present unworthy successor, who changed his political colours not through any respectable personal grievance but after becoming a transvestite (41–4). The assumption here, but not in *pro Sestio*, that one did not become a *popularis* in the interest of the people but to right a personal wrong, is made simply in order to provide a contrast that would be most disgraceful to Clodius. He himself was the first victim of the discord, Cicero argued, but it was currently to be found between Pompey and his opponents, who were fostering Clodius (45–51). And yet Clodius had in this last address to the people begun to praise Pompey (51). Cicero brushed this aside, but it overshadowed the rest of the speech, where he dilated on the danger of civil war and the threats to political stability (53–63).

---

[78] *Har. Resp.* 1–2. The debate was held under Marcellinus' presidency and therefore in May (Courtney, 1963). See *Prov. Cos.* 10–12; *Pis.* 41; *QF* 2. 12. 2; 3. 2. 2; Dio 39. 59. 2 for the conflict with the *publicani*, and ibid. 56. 6 for an imposition of tribute.

[79] *Har. Resp.* 40. Such warnings could be found as early as the poetry of Solon (frr. 4, esp. ll. 7–22, and 9 West).

In the letter to Quintus in May (2. 7) Cicero is cheerfully expecting the imminent return from Sardinia of his brother, regretful that there is no progress on the *ager Campanus*, but ecstatic over Gabinius' discomfiture. The *De Haruspicum Responso*, of about the same time, shows him confidently attacking Clodius but puzzled over the latter's compliments to Pompey. However, we possess a speech on the consular provinces in which Cicero explicitly renounced his hostility to Caesar, though not to Clodius, Gabinius, and Piso (*Prov. Cos.*, esp. 18 ff., 40 ff.). The retention of Caesar in his command in Transalpine Gaul was raised in the senate debate on the consular provinces, which under C. Gracchus' law had to be settled before the elections (normally in mid-July).[80] The proposed candidature of Pompey and Crassus for the consulship, of which there is no trace in *De Provinciis Consularibus*, did not become public until shortly before the expected date of the elections, when it was legally too late because within the *trinundinum* (three market-days) preceding them.[81] It appears that knowledge of the decisions of the three dynasts at Luca was disseminated gradually and piecemeal. Similarly, Cicero's actions amounted to a gradual realignment rather than a single dramatic change of direction. In the long apologetic letter to Spinther of 54 Cicero explained that he had first been urged by Pompey, through his brother as intermediary, not to attack Caesar's *dignitas*, if he could not defend it. This and a message through Vibullius had deterred him from getting involved in the issue of the *ager Campanus*. The decision to commit himself to Caesar openly was his, taken after some reflection and perhaps after a letter from Caesar himself, something not clearly attested but an obvious move for Caesar to make.[82]

De Provinciis Consularibus then falls some time between *De Haruspicum Responso* and the moment when Pompey and Crassus showed their hand about the consulship of 55. Cicero's speech, even in the written version we possess, betrays great embarrassment. From the first sentences he was apologetic: his fellow senators would realise that he had to speak in this vein and would pardon him, even if they disagreed. Conveniently, Servilius Isauricus, the senior consular present, had argued for the allocation of Syria and Macedonia to the consuls about to be elected, and Cicero could vent his bitterness on Gabinius and Piso without harm to the public interest (*Prov. Cos.* 1). Almost a third of the speech is devoted to denouncing them. However, Cicero maintained, even if they were excellent governors, this would not affect his judgement about

---

[80] *Dom.* 24; Sall. *Iug.* 27. 3.
[81] Dio 39. 27. 2–3; cf. *Fam.* 16. 12. 3; *Att.* 1. 16. 13; Macr. 1. 16. 34.
[82] *Fam.* 1. 9. 10–12. There is no clear time-frame for 'his humanity and generosity perceived and experienced by me within a short period through his correspondence and good offices' (§12).

Caesar: he willingly put aside personal enmity for the sake of the *res publica*, as L. Crassus, M. Scaurus, and the Metelli did, when it came to appointing Marius to the war in Gaul (18–19). Other precedents of reconciliation follow; Caesar's achievements and the religious celebrations they have merited are compared to those associated with Marius and Pompey (20–7). By contrast, we are told, Cicero's enmity with Clodius remained because it was necessary for the peace of the *res publica* (24).

Cicero now turns to the arguments over the Gallic command. He had already proposed the extraordinary *supplicationes* for Caesar's victories, pay for his army, and the appointment of a commission of ten *legati*. These motions had been passed without objection (27–8)—presumably in a debate shortly before his present speech. Objections, however, arose to the retention of Caesar in Gaul for a further significant period. Here Cicero argued that the full subjection of the implacable enemies of Rome in Transalpine Gaul required Caesar's lasting guardianship. One or two summers (the time before a consul of 55 BC could arrive there) were not enough (29–35).[83] As for the senator who wished to remove the peaceful part of Caesar's command, Cisalpine Gaul, he respected a law that he thought no law (i.e. the *lex Vatinia* of 59), which allowed no succession before 1 March 54 and enjoined a veto on any contrary proposal.[84] However, this would put a consul of 55 in a ridiculous position of being without a province at the time when his consulship ended (36–8). A final objection had to be answered: was not the retention of Caesar in Cisalpina a tacit approval of demagogic *populares* politics and an invitation to future appointments in that province like that of the *lex Vatinia*? This is neatly sandwiched between the reflection that no one could be a *princeps* if he preferred to remain a *popularis*, and the assertion that after these honours from the senate Caesar would never detract from its authority in the future (38–9).

Finally, Cicero returned to his own relationship to Caesar. They were friends in their youth. Caesar had offered him a position among the three 'most intimately connected consulars' (*coniunctissimi consulares*) and a series of posts, including that of *legatus*. This would have allowed Cicero to escape the threat of his enemy, whom Caesar had transferred to the *plebs*, either in irritation or through succumbing to (Clodius') pleading. When Cicero was threatened, Caesar feared for his own laws of 59, and at least lent his weight to the pleas for Cicero's recall (40–43). Cicero should not be reproached for this reconciliation by those who believed that Caesar's legislation was illegal but

---

[83] In *Prov. Cos.* 34, 'sed tamen una atque altera aestas...', we find the, surely genuine, view of those who wished to make Transalpine Gaul a consular province.

[84] On the tenure of Caesar's command in Gaul, see Appendix 4 to Ch. XV.

Clodius' legal, especially when it was being suggested to Caesar that his legislation could be resubmitted for approval without violating the auspices, while Clodius' laws amounted to the overthrow of the state.[85] In the brief summary that ends the speech Cicero goes so far as to claim that, if he felt enmity to Caesar, he would now be putting it aside in the public interest, but in fact he felt none. Meanwhile his motion combined honour for Caesar, respect for the consistency of senate policy and the needs of the Gallic war, and any requirement of private gratitude. He would not be moved by those who criticized his reconciliation with their enemy, but were happy to become reconciled with a man who was both his enemy and theirs, Clodius (47).

The speech is cleverly argued and defiant. The theme of reconciliation with Caesar was repeated shortly afterwards, when Cicero defended the right to Roman citizenship of Balbus, who was now an aide-de-camp to Caesar as his *praefectus fabrum*.[86] The prosecution for illegal exercise of citizenship, arising from the *lex Papia* of 65, was initiated by a former fellow-citizen of Balbus at Gades, but clearly supported by his enemies at Rome.[87] There were aspersions against Balbus' wealth, luxury, and profitable adoption by Pompey's friend Theophanes (*Balb*. 56 ff.). The technical arguments marshalled by Cicero were surely decisive from the point of view of Roman law: the Romans had traditionally been happy to reward foreigners with citizenship, while simultaneously plucking them out of their citizen obligations in their original home.[88]

This case was not the first attack on the citizenship of a friend of Pompey under the *lex Papia*, in which Cicero had appeared for the defence (*Balb*. 4). Here Cicero spoke after Pompey and Crassus and was more unctuous in his compliments to Pompey's rhetorical prowess and high principle than he had been about Caesar's generalship in *De Provinciis Consularibus* (2–4, 9–13). Cicero had no friendship at the time with Balbus and shared the suspicions of the man that he denounced in the speech.[89] The speech may have been distasteful, but, in so far as it was justified by the needs of defence advocacy,

---

[85] *Prov. Cos.* 44–6. It is not clear who would be suggesting to Caesar the re-enactment of his laws. This amounted to admitting the invalidity of the legislation, and one cannot imagine his allies of 59 doing so. Was it a genuine attempt at reconciliation by a neutral or perhaps a trap being laid by an opponent? If one dates the attempted prosecution of Caesar by L. Antistius (Suet. *Jul*. 23. 1) to 56 BC, with Badian (1974), it may be tempting to link the offer with this attempted prosecution.

[86] *Balb*. 61 refers to Cicero's proposals for Caesar in *Prov. Cos*.

[87] See *Balb*. 32, cf. 25 and 58 on the Gaditane accuser—presumably now a Roman resident, since he had left his community, but had been rejected by Roman laws.

[88] This was only to change decisively with Caesar Augustus, see Sherwin White, 1973, 295 ff.

[89] See his later expostulation about the adoption and Balbus' Tusculan villa in late 50 BC (*Att*. 7. 7. 6).

would not have been humiliating, especially when Cicero had been confessing his devotion to Pompey's interests for some time.

The *De Provinciis Consularibus* was another matter. It must be the publication of this speech that occasioned an apologetic letter to Atticus, who had complained about not receiving a copy. Cicero admitted that the 'recantation seemed to him a little shaming: but it was goodbye to upright, true, and honourable policies.' However, he rapidly blamed 'those princes of the republic (*principes*).' He had realised that he had been 'led up the garden path, abandoned, and cast away by them', the phrase echoing the language he used about his exile.[90] Nevertheless, he had wanted to be their political ally. At last, on Atticus' advice, he had recovered his senses. Atticus might be surprised at the distribution of a written version of this palinode, but Cicero wanted to impose on himself the necessity of the new alliance. He had at least been moderate in his divinification of Caesar. Meanwhile those who disparaged his ownership of a Tusculan villa but enjoyed his expression of optimate views—not because they approved of the sentiments, but because they were contrary to Pompey's wishes—would have their noses put out of joint (*Att.* 4. 5. 2). The published speech may have gone beyond what was delivered in elaborating his reconciliation with Caesar and self-justification for the new course. From the point of view of the 'good men', Cicero's proposals for Caesar were damning enough. Yet they could have been ascribed simply to servility to Pompey, had not Cicero expressly coloured the move as a gesture of friendship to Caesar, thus putting a positive gloss on the action but at the same time bringing greater reproach on himself from former allies.

In a letter to Lentulus Spinther of summer 56—discussed earlier for its evidence of a reconcilation between Spinther and Pompey and its recommendation to restore Ptolemy to Alexandria[91]—Cicero comments gloomily on how those who were superior in wealth, arms, and power had even prevailed in *auctoritas* thanks to the stupidity and inconsistency of their opponents. They had achieved through the senate what they thought they would be unable to achieve through the assembly without violence—the grant to Caesar of pay for his troops and the ten *legati*, and the frustration of any successor being appointed under the *lex Sempronia*.[92] He says nothing about his part in this: clearly it was embarrassing. However, we should allow for its being written before he had decided to write up *De Provinciis Consularibus* for publication and make a virtue out of what he had done. Spinther would not necessarily have found Caesar's success totally repugnant. His politics were of

---

[90] *Att.* 4. 5. 1 'inductus relictus proiectus ab iis'; cf. 3. 15. 7—'proditus, inductus, coniectus in fraudem'.
[91] See above with n. 41.
[92] *Fam.* 1. 7. 10: Cicero says he will be brief, because 'status hic rei publicae non delectat'.

course opposed to Caesar's, but he had been a friend in the past, as Spinther reminded Caesar at Corfinium in the civil war: he had helped him to be co-opted into the college of *pontifices*, to get his Spanish province in 61, and even to obtain his first consulship.[93]

We have little correspondence from the end of 56 and 55, but what there is is even gloomier. This was when Pompey and Crassus engineered by a mixture of political manoeuvring and violence their elections to the consulships of 55. In November 56 Cicero compared Domitius Ahenobarbus' fate in being frustrated in his pursuit of the consulship to his own (*Att.* 4. 8a. 2). We should probably assign to the next spring a lament about the state of politics: if Cicero takes a high moral line, he is thought mad; if he advises expediency, he is thought a slave; if he says nothing, a defeated prisoner of war. He is considering retirement or perhaps a post on a commander's staff.[94] By this time Caesar had had his command in Gaul extended for five years by means of a law passed jointly by the consuls (App.4), while Pompey and Crassus had received five-year commands in the Spanish provinces and Syria respectively under the *lex Trebonia* (n. 96).

In a letter to Spinther of roughly the same period the same situation is expressed differently. Everyone, maintains Cicero, should allow a man in his position either to defend Pompey's policies, or to say nothing, or to retire in order to devote himself to literature. The rewards that would naturally have fallen to a man of his rank—respect for his status in the formulation of policy, freedom in his handling of public affairs—have been totally removed, as they have from everyone (*Fam.* 1. 8. 3). In fact, he continues, because the whole nature of the senate, the courts, of public life has changed, he has to hope for retirement (*otium*), which those in power would grant, even if he cannot contemplate that consular dignity characteristic of a resolute and principled senator (ibid. 4). Nevertheless, he reassures Spinther, he will exploit his closeness to Pompey to secure Spinther's interests (ibid. 5–6). In the few letters that survive the picture of the second consulship of Pompey and Crassus is perhaps even more depressing than that portrayed in the richer correspondence of 59. The domination of the three dynasts is as powerful as it was then and worse for Cicero, as he is too closely tied to Pompey for him to resist, and indeed there is no alternative source of power for him to exploit.[95]

---

[93] Caes. *BCiv.* 1. 22. 3–4.

[94] *Att.* 4. 6. 2. On the date see SB *Att.* ii. 233–5. Both this letter (4) and *Att.* 4. 9. 2, dated 27 April, refer to Cicero's request to Lucceius for an excursus in his history on Cicero' career (*Fam.* 5. 12), on which see Ch. XIV with nn. 4–5. For similar despair over politics see a letter to Quintus of mid-February (*QF* 2. 8. 3).

[95] Note the usual lament about how some unnamed persons had alienated the senate from the *equites*, and Pompey (*Fam.* 1. 8. 4).

Out of this frustration sprang an invective that was, for all its rhetorical brilliance, politically an irrelevance. Macedonia had probably been made one of the provinces of the consuls of 55 after Cicero's *De Provinciis Consularibus* (*Prov. Cos.* 1). Although Pompey received the Spanish provinces instead under the *lex Trebonia*, Macedonia was assigned to one of the praetors of 56, Q. Ancharius.[96] On Piso's return a debate was held in the senate in which his governorship was discussed, in particular his reaction to the invasion of Macedonia by Thracian peoples (*Pis.* 37–41, 44–8, 83–97). We have to reconstruct this event from Cicero's *In Pisonem*, an oration composed at some time after the debate, which refers back to the exchanges at the time, and from the comments of Asconius on this oration. It was probably not the kind of senate-session, when a formal motion was discussed, but one where there was informal discussion after a report.[97] Either in his original speech or a subsequent response to the accusations made against him Piso blamed Cicero for his premature removal from the province and delivered a counter-attack to the accusations that Cicero had been making and publishing about him since returning from exile (Asc. *Pis.* 2 C). He neither sought a triumph nor made any appropriate claims about his victories (*Pis.* 39, 56, 62, 97). After Cicero used the occasion to denounce Piso, in the course of his response Piso challenged Cicero to a wager over a point of fact about his return (55) and invited him to mount a formal accusation over his conduct of the province (82). Piso was also attacked by L. Manlius Torquatus, in particular about the demobilization of at least part of his army, and made a reply to him (47, 92).[98]

The *In Pisonem*, as we possess it, is a comparison of the disreputable career of Piso with the decent, but infortunate career of the speaker, which develops (82 ff.) into a concentrated attack on Piso's governorship, intended to inspire a prosecution by someone else.[99] Piso is portrayed not only as politically sympathetic to Clodius' attack on Cicero—he did not like Cicero's 'cruelty' to the Catilinarians (14–17)[100]—but as a companion to Clodius and Gabinius in decadence and greed (18, 22, 26, 65). The treatment of what happened in 58 is familiar: the consuls had deliberately connived at Clodius' terrorization of the *res publica* (8–31). Piso had mischievously suggested that Cicero had alienated Pompey by his boastful verses (72–4), and had stressed Caesar's support for Clodius (78). Cicero explains away his desertion by Pompey (76–8) and

---

[96] *Pis.* 89; *Att.* 4. 9. 1; *MRR* ii. 217–18.
[97] *CRR* 80–1.
[98] The best general guide to the speech is Nisbet's edition (1961a). On the context see his introduction, pp. v ff. On the relation of the speech to Piso's practice of Epicurean precepts see Griffin, 2001.
[99] The deliberately casual invitation is in *Pis.* 82.
[100] See above, Ch. XII with n. 49.

points to Pompey's return to his defence and his own consequent reconciliation with Caesar (79–82); Piso by contrast had supported Clodius' attacks on Pompey (27–8). It is difficult to disentangle the truth of Piso' conduct in Macedonia. He clearly had problems defending the line of the *via Egnatia* (the main west–east route from the Adriatic to Byzantium) against the peoples of Thrace (*Pis.* 40, 84, *Prov. Cos.* 4); his own punitive operations, though they led to an imperatorial salutation for him after a victory by Q. Marcius Crispus and other legates (38, 54), were insufficient to encourage him to request a triumph (55–63). Cicero's attacks on his corrupt administration are vague and unsubstantiated. It is unlikely that Piso was blameless, but for all Cicero's claims he was never prosecuted for his conduct in Macedonia.[101]

The invective was clearly composed and circulated some time after the senate debate that gave it rise. It purported to be delivered shortly before the inaugural games in Pompey's new theatre, held in August 55.[102] However, the reference to Caesar's *supplicationes* suggests a date two months or so later—after the reaction to the news of Caesar's invasion of Britain.[103] It cannot be a reproduction of the speech that Cicero delivered in the debate about Piso, as it refers to a reply of Piso's to a remark of Cicero's on this occasion and includes a correction (55): it therefore purports to be a further reply to Piso consequent on the debate. However, it contains much material that could have appeared in Cicero's original speech. Politically, it was probably meaningless at the time when it became available to the reader. Both Cicero and his enemies were now under the single umbrella of a reunited coalition of three dynasts. The speech was a rhetorical *tour de force* that would have satisfied Cicero's acrimonious feelings towards Piso without doing Piso any significant harm. It marked the end of one chapter in his life.

---

[101] See on Piso's governorship Nisbet, 1961a, apps. I and II.

[102] *Pis.* 65, Asc. 1 C; Marshall, 1985, 1–2, adducing the *fasti Amiternini* and *Allifani* for the festival of Venus Victrix in the marble theatre on 12 August (*Inscr. It.* xiii/2, pp. 180–1, 190–1, 493–4). This also affects the date of Cicero's 'review' of Pompey's games in a letter to M. Marius (*Fam.* 7. 1).

[103] *Pis.* 59; Caes. *BG* 4. 38. 5; Nisbet, 1961a, 201; Gelzer, 1969, 180, n. 121, who does not, however, take into account the evidence of the *fasti* for Pompey's theatre. The composition no doubt provided some relief from Cicero's weariness over Pompey's games and the defences of Caninius Gallus and other disagreeable people that he was required to undertake. See the letter to M. Marius (*Fam.* 7. 1. 1–4).

Part D

History and Ideas

XIV

The Search for *Otium*

IN March 56, when speaking for Sestius (98), Cicero had claimed that the supreme aim for the helmsmen of the *res publica* was 'cum dignitate otium', the undisturbed enjoyment of their rank. A year later he was complaining in a letter to Spinther that, while those in power were likely to provide *otium*, a tranquil life, provided that certain persons could accept that power more submissively, there could be no longer any thought of that consular rank appropriate to a courageous and resolute senator.[1] Nevertheless, he did not abandon the ideal: it appears in the lengthy apologia he was to write to Spinther in 54 and in the introduction to his dialogue *De Oratore*, which he composed in 55.[2] Cicero certainly did not retire from public life: he could not avoid the political leadership appropriate to his consular status, though he found himself having to deploy it in ways which he did not approve. Moreover, he sought to maintain his status first by forensic oratory and the favour (*gratia*) this earned with others, secondly by expressing his political and philosophical views in writing, and thirdly by seeking to ensure that his past career was firmly embedded in Roman historiography.

THE LETTER TO LUCCEIUS

By the time of his last letter to Spinther Cicero had written three more books of verse autobiography 'de temporibus meis' but, perhaps fortunately, did not think they should be published.[3] Instead, we find him in the spring of 55 soliciting the historian L. Lucceius, who had already written on the Social and Civil Wars and was extending his work into the succeeding period, to write an anticipatory monograph on his political life from consulship to return from

---

[1] *Sest.* 98; *Fam.* 1. 8. 4; cf. Ch. XIII with n. 57.
[2] *Fam.* 1. 9. 21; *de Or.* 1. 1; cf. *Fam.* 1. 9. 23; *Att.* 4. 13. 2; *QF* 3. 5. 1 on *De Oratore*. In *Fam.* 1. 9. 21 Cicero refers to his repeated (*saepissime*) use of the phrase *otium cum dignitate*: it is unlikely he is exaggerating.
[3] *Fam.* 1. 9. 23; cf. *QF* 2. 8. 1.

exile (*Fam.* 5. 12).⁴ This letter is notorious as testimony to Cicero's willingness to bend the laws of history in what he believed to be a good cause (ibid. 3); more generally, it is important evidence of Roman consciousness of the sensational genre of Greek historiography, which originated in the latter part of the fourth century BC—often termed in modern scholarship 'tragic history'.⁵ Cicero's precedents for the project he is suggesting are the monographs written by Greek historians on specific wars, but he clearly wants a work that is essentially biographical and indeed an encomium on his life down to his return from exile (ibid. 2–3). His reference to the acquisition of favour (*gratia*), that Lucceius had already declared to be his preoccupation in the introduction to his existing work, suggests that the historian had already showered praise on significant figures in the Civil Wars still alive at his time of publication—perhaps Pompey or Lucullus.

The parallels for emotional accounts that Cicero cites from Greek history (ibid. 5) indicate how he wished his story to be treated—Epaminondas dying on the field of Mantinea and the exile and 'return' (so the manuscripts) of Themistocles. Themistocles' bones did return to Attica, but not his person, except according to a chronologically confused passage in the Aristotelian *Athenaion Politeia*, and editors have sought to emend.⁶ However, it is probably best to think that Cicero has been careless here, carried away by the potential parallel to his own career.⁷ Cicero was later to refer to the exiles of Themistocles and Coriolanus in an aside in the *Brutus*, where he states a preference for the versions in which both commit suicide to avoid venting on their countrymen their wrath over their unjust banishment. His interlocutor 'Atticus' comments that Greek writers chose to portray Themistocles dying through swallowing bull's blood because this could be presented in a rhetorical and 'tragic' fashion (*Brut.* 41–3).

It was not, however, essential to such history for exiles to commit suicide. A more recent exile, apt for sensational treatment, was that of C. Marius. In the published speech to the people after his return Cicero had evoked the story of Marius sinking himself in the marshes of Minturnae before escaping to Africa in a tiny boat, and he returned to this image in the *pro Sestio*.⁸ His own escape across the Adriatic was less dramatic in fact, but that need not have deterred an enthusiastic panegyrist. Here, as elsewhere, there would

---

⁴ See esp. 2 and 4; cf. *Att.* 4. 6. 4, 4. 9. 2.

⁵ See Diod. 19. 8. 4; Pol. 2. 56, 12. 24–6, 15. 34; Ullman, 1942; Walbank, 1955; 1957, 8–9; 1960; Fantham 2004, 153–9.

⁶ Either by changing *reditu* (return) to *interitu* or *exitu* (death) or by adding a reference to Coriolanus, see e.g. How, ii. 308.

⁷ So Watt in the 1982 OCT.

⁸ *Red. Quir.* 20; *Sest.* 50; more prosaically rendered in *Pis.* 43 and *Planc.* 26.

have been ample scope for pathos, sensational treatment, and meditation on the ingratitude of fellow countrymen.⁹ Cicero himself gives us a vignette of this material in *pro Plancio* (97–8). He was carefully deposited on a reliable ship with prayers and vows for his safe return by M. Laenius Flaccus, who was accompanied by his aged father, his brother, and two sons; Greece was packed with the most desperate villains, refugees from Cicero's consulship. Cicero therefore rushed to meet Plancius, who himself hastened to meet him, casting off the insignia of his office and putting on mourning. When they met, Plancius embraced him and could not speak for tears. It was, comments Cicero, a scene painful to hear described and beyond description for those who saw it.

THE NEW POLITICAL ALIGNMENT

The limitations on Cicero's activity in the senate and forum are well illustrated by a letter to Atticus of November 55 (*Att.* 4. 13). Some of the elections of 55 for 54 were still taking place then; Crassus had just left for his proconsular command in Syria in a humiliating fashion ('what a wicked man!' exclaims Cicero).¹⁰ Cicero himself was happy that had not attended an argumentative debate in the senate. 'For either I would have defended what I did not approve, or failed to support a man whom I should not have failed' (ibid. 2)—clearly either Crassus or Pompey (the latter would have been supporting his consular colleague). However, a letter to Crassus of the following year reveals that Cicero then had defended Crassus' interests in the senate, apparently over the financing of his command: indeed he asks Crassus to regard the letter as a treaty (*foedus*), guaranteeing his further support.¹¹

In the February of 54 he participated in the hearings granted in the senate to the representatives of foreign kings and communities, where he supported in vain the attempt of the people of Tenedos to retain their free status. He was more successful in hampering concessions to Antiochus I of Commagene, whose position depended on the law ratifying Pompey's eastern settlement

---

⁹ The phrases 'temporum varietates fortunaeque vicissitudines', and 'admirationem, exspectationem, laetitiam, molestiam, spem, timorem' (*Fam.* 5. 12. 4–5) recall the catchwords of the Hellenistic historians, παράδοξον, πάθος, ἐκπλήττειν, ψυχαγωγία, τερατεία, cf. Ullman, 1942, 41.

¹⁰ For the curses of Ateius Capito see *Div.* 1. 29; Dio 39. 39. 6; Plut. *Crass.* 16. 4–8; Lucan, 3. 126–7.

¹¹ *Fam.* 5. 8. 1, 5. His affection for Crassus' sons, especially Publius (ibid. 4) does seem genuine, cf. *Fam.* 13. 16.

and a *senatus consultum* of Caesar's consulship. Pompey was apparently not present at the time, but the consul Appius Claudius was acting in his interest, and Cicero was not pressing the matter too far in case Appius called in reinforcements.[12] A further discussion involving the people of Tyre and the Syrian tax-collectors required no participation from Cicero. The tax-collectors attacked Gabinius, while the consul Domitius Ahenobarbus attacked the tax-collectors for escorting Gabinius on horseback on his expedition to Egypt to restore Ptolemy.[13] In general, it was not so much that Cicero had lost his consular authority, as he had suggested to Spinther (*Fam.* 1. 8. 4), but that the way this was being deployed did not seem to him to be consular. 'My proposals in the senate are such that others agree with me rather than I agree with them myself' (*QF* 2. 14. 4).

Cicero was by now even more tied to Pompey. Although he was suspicious of his political manoeuvrings in 54–3 which seemed designed to lead to the creation of a dictatorship—especially in view of its implications for Milo, now Pompey's enemy—he could do nothing about them.[14] On the other hand he was making a virtue of his new link with Caesar. For the latter we have the evidence of only one surviving letter to Caesar himself from this period (*Fam.* 7. 5), a letter of commendation for the young jurist C. Trebatius Testa, but compensation is provided by the correspondence with Quintus, who had now become Caesar's *legatus*, and with Trebatius himself (*Fam.* 7. 6–18). Cicero's first letter to Caesar, which must have been written about the end of the year 55, got too wet for Caesar to read, but by February they were corresponding frequently in language that was familiar and laced with humour (*QF* 2. 11. 4–5). His commendation of Trebatius to Caesar—which preceded the letter of May to Quintus (*QF* 2. 13. 3)—was not his first approach of this kind (manuscript corruption makes the identity of the previous beneficiary uncertain) (*Fam.* 7. 5. 2); he later commended M. Curtius (*QF* 2. 14. 3, 3. 1. 10). However, the strongest evidence for the growth of this friendship is the fact that by July Cicero was partnering Oppius in buying land and letting contracts for Caesar's building projects—the Forum Iulium and the Saepta in the Campus Martius (*Att.* 4. 16. 8).[15] At the end of the year his friendship with Caesar was the one surviving plank from the shipwreck that gave him pleasure (*Att.* 4. 19. 2).

---

[12] *QF* 2. 10. 2, 11. 2–3; cf. *OGIS* 383.
[13] *QF* 2. 12. 2; cf. Dio 39. 56–8; Jos. *AJ* 14. 98.
[14] *QF* 3. 4. 1, 3. 6. 4–6, 3. 7. 3; *Att.* 4. 19. 1; App. *BCiv.* 2. 19. 71–20. 73; Plut. *Cato mi.* 45. 7; *Pomp.* 54. 4–5; *VRR* 199–200.
[15] They had already committed 60 million sesterces to the Forum project; the cost was later put at 100 million, see Suet. *Jul.* 26. 2; Pliny, *HN* 36. 103.

The multiplication of his friendships inevitably affected the side of public life where he was most in demand, his forensic activity. Although he could talk of tranquillity in the forum—'of a community growing old rather than calm'—in a letter to Quintus of June 54 (*QF* 2. 14. 5), the correspondence of the next months provides a different picture. At the beginning of July Cicero represented the people of Reate in an inquiry into their dispute with Interamnna Nahars over the diverted waters of the Veline lake (*Att.* 4. 15. 5); at the end of the month he was due to defend Pompey's supporter C. Messius, accused under the *lex Licinia de sodaliciis* (see below with n. 28)—probably on account of bribery in his election to the aedileship in 55; his next case was that of M. Livius Drusus Claudianus, charged with collusive prosecution (*praevaricatio*) (ibid. 9). The latter was acquitted at some time in August and on the same day Cicero went on to defend Vatinius *de sodaliciis*.[16] He conducted two other defences on this charge—of M. Cispius and Cn. Plancius, the second of which was completed in September.[17] In this period Cicero also joined the defence-team of the consular candidate Aemilius Scaurus, accused *de repetundis* and eventually acquitted on 2 September.[18]

PRO PLANCIO

We have discussed earlier what survives of the *pro Scauro*, which seems in many ways a typical example of a defence-speech *de repetundis* (Ch. III with nn. 57–9; Ch. VIII with n. 20). The *pro Plancio* is important, apart from its technical interest in that the published text seems to incorporate material from the *altercatio* (Ch. III with nn. 53–5), because it reveals the reaction among former optimate supporters of Cicero to his present alignment. Plancius, as quaestor in Macedonia, had protected Cicero when in exile.[19] Subsequently tribune in 56 (*QF* 2. 1. 3), he seems to have taken advantage of the exemption of the tribunate from the normal rules of the *lex annalis*, combined with the delay to the elections for 55 through the obstruction by Pompey and Crassus,[20] in order to get elected curule aedile for 55 at the beginning of that year.[21] There had no doubt been corruption in these

[16] *QF* 2. 16. 3; *Att.* 4. 17. 5; *Fam.* 1. 9. 4, 19; *Schol. Bob.* 40 St.
[17] *QF* 3. 1. 11; *Planc.* 75–6; *Schol. Bob.* 165 St.
[18] *Att.* 4. 17. 4; Asc. *Scaur., passim*, esp. 18 C.
[19] *Att.* 3. 14. 2; *Fam.* 14. 1. 3; *Planc.* 1, 28, 99–101; *Schol. Bob.* 153 St.
[20] *CRR* 146; Dio 39. 31; Plut. *Cato mi.* 41. 5–42. 1; *Pomp.* 52. 1; *Crass.* 15. 6; App. *BCiv.* 2. 17. 64.
[21] On the dating of this magistracy see *MRR* iii. 158, and the recent examination of the arguments by Alexander (2002, 131–2). In this period curule aediles in office were immune from prosecution, as Clodius' manoeuvres in 57–6 prove. Therefore Plancius cannot have been aedile

elections; there certainly had been violence, entailing the repeat of the election,[22] which had embittered the opponents of the dynasts, such as the prosecutor M. Iuventius Laterensis, an unsuccessful rival candidate.

We do not know how far the defence might have combated the evidence brought against Plancius (the reference to the earlier speech of Hortensius merely shows that orator making a procedural point that Cicero repeats, *Planc.* 37). In the text we possess Cicero deals not so much with the details of the case as with the prejudices deployed against the defendant, the prosecution tactics, and especially his own treatment by the prosecutors. Cicero claims that they had spoken almost more about him than about the defendant and the charge (*Planc.* 3). Laterensis had been linked with Cicero and his son-in-law Piso in Vettius' accusations of 59, perhaps because he had been conspicuous in opposition to the three dynasts, abandoning his candidature for the tribunate in order to avoid having to swear to abide by Caesar's agrarian laws.[23] He had apparently supported Cicero and his family at the time of the exile, but, unlike Plancius, had received no special thanks from him on his return (*Planc.* 1, 73–4). More recently, he had solicited Cicero's help for the defence of M. Cispius, for whom he was a witness and perhaps a legal adviser (*advocatus*)—unfortunately to no effect with the jury.[24]

Cicero argues in the *prooemium* that Plancius has a better claim on his services than Laterensis, carefully refusing to decide which of the two was superior in *dignitas* (1–6). This leads him to a further, specious, argument that popular election was no warrant of superior *dignitas*. The assembly, once it had been liberated during the Conflict of the Orders from the *patrum auctoritas* (ratification of its decisions by the senate—or patricians), wilfully distributed its favours to those who cultivated it most. One could not, he concludes, take its choices as a criterion of worth: rejection for high office by a group of ten men would have been much more serious for Laterensis (*Planc.* 7–13).[25] To say this was to reject a principle on which Cicero's own career had been based: status among the aristocracy at Rome did depend on tenure of high office: it was from this that Cicero himself derived his *dignitas consularis*.

---

in 54. Nor can he have been elected in 54, since the curule elections of that year were postponed deep into 53.

[22] Dio 39. 32. 2–3; Plut. *Cato mi.* 42. 2–5; *Pomp.* 52. 3, cf. *Planc.* 49 for the repeated election.
[23] *Att.* 2. 18. 3, 2. 24. 3.
[24] *Planc.* 75–7; *Schol. Bob.* 165 St; Alexander, 2002, 143–4.
[25] Cicero may have derived the notion that rejection by a few wise men is more serious a rebuff than rejection by the people from Thucydides' comment on the dissidents among the oligarchy of the 400 at Athens (8. 89. 3). On Cicero's reading of Thucydides, see below Ch. XV with nn. 65–6, Ch. XVI with nn. 72–4.

The next point is more plausible. Iuventius' noble origins did not guarantee his election over the son of an equestrian from Atina. Iuventius, comments Cicero, only came from another *municipium*, Tusculum, one whose members were less interested in the success of their local heroes than Cicero's Arpinum or Atina. These towns, moreover, benefited from a system of mutual support in the area, embracing Sora, Casinum, and Aquinum (*Planc.* 22).[26] Cicero himself had helped in Plancius' election campaign (*Planc.* 24–6). As for Plancius' father, he was indeed distinguished: an eminent *publicanus*, he had led the agitation for the writing down of the Asiatic tax-contract in 61 and was first to vote for the bill in 59.[27] Nor was there anything serious to the discredit of Plancius himself in his earlier career (27–31).

Cicero now claims to have reached at long last the case itself. However, what follows is a criticism of Iuventius' legal tactics in exploiting the provisions of Crassus' *lex Licinia de sodaliciis*, passsed the previous year. This law, which sought to repress organizations created for electoral corruption, had introduced a new form of jury-selection. Instead of allotment from a panel followed by rejection of those alleged unsuitable by prosecution and defence, the law ordered the prosecutor to select four tribal contingents from the panel from which the defence was required to reject one.[28] Laterensis, as the legislator presumably intended, had chosen four tribes which had no connection with the defendant and so would not have been corrupted by the same illegal groups that were the subject of the prosecution, thus neither the Teretina of Plancius nor the Voltinia, where he was also said to be influential (43). Cicero appeals to remarks by Hortensius in the senate when the bill was being originally debated in 55, to the effect that corrupters of the electorate would be best known to the tribes they corrupted—true, no doubt, but not conducive to successful prosecution. Hortensius had, perhaps disingenuously, used this as an argument for the jury-provisions in the bill in 55 and apparently repeated it in his earlier speech for Plancius (37). It is, in any case, clear that the prosecutor's procedure had been accepted by the president of the court and did not contravene the text of the law.

As for the evidence of corruption, Cicero claims, with what veracity we cannot tell, that there was no case to answer. Plancius was influential in a number of tribes but had not been involved in the organizing groups to distribute bribes. Alexander has argued that Cicero may have been in part

---

[26] For Cicero's particular connections in this area see Lomas, 2004, 102–4; Wiseman, 1971, 136–8.

[27] *Planc.* 24; 31–5; *Schol. Bob.* 157 St., cf. Ch. XI with n. 45.

[28] *Planc.* 36–40. It seems from §40 that at a previous trial the defendant was allowed to reject a further five individual jurors from the three remaining tribes (perhaps on the ground of close connection with the prosecution), but this was not permitted to Plancius.

relying on the distinctive requirements of the *lex Licinia*, where mere evidence of corruption was not enough to prove the case.[29] A further point of interest here is Laterensis' charge that the similarity of the votes delivered for Plancius and A. Plotius implied that they had made an electoral pact (*coitio*) (53–4). Cicero denies this, while apparently accepting that a *coitio* was a prima facie argument for corruption, even if not proscribed specifically under the *lex Licinia*. *Coitiones* were not regarded in 61 as criminal in themselves (*Att.* 1. 17. 11) and, even after Crassus' law, Laterensis could admit that Plancius conceded the Teretina tribe to him in the earlier fruitless election.[30]

The most fascinating part of the speech for Cicero's biography is the section when he replies to the accusers' criticisms of him. The *subscriptor* L. Cassius Longinus had apparently appealed to aristocratic prejudice against equestrian upstarts, especially those with very ordinary attainments, which he expected Cicero to share since his family was now consular (*Planc.* 59). Cicero's answer is that the majority of magistrates are of unremarkable talent: it is enough for the Roman people that they are decent and honest. He adds a story about his own return from his quaestorship in Sicily in order to show that the people prefer those who make themselves visible at Rome (60–7). Cassius finally appealed to Cicero's loyalty to the *boni* as a whole who had been concerned for his preservation, arguing that should have outweighed his personal loyalty to Plancius (68). We can see here the bitterness of those who supported Cicero's recall as a blow against the three dynasts and now found that their standard-bearer had joined the opposing ranks.

Laterensis was even more severe. He claimed that Cicero was lying about the extent of Plancius' services to him (72), especially by comparison with those of another tribune of 56, Racilius (77); he sneered at Cicero's recent unsuccessful attempt to arouse pity for M. Cispius, the man for whom he had been an *advocatus* (75–6); worse, he made fun of the purple passages used by Cicero in his defences of other aediles, suggesting that the purpose of the increase of the penalty for electoral bribery to exile in the *lex Tullia Antonia* of 63 was to enable Cicero to deliver more pathetic final appeals to juries. He even attacked the quality of Cicero's jokes, remarking that Cicero had lost the opportunity to make a pun on the time he himself had been in Crete, and added that he had been warned by Cicero's example against sending off accounts of his achievements (*res gestae*)—a reference to the failure of Cicero's letter to Pompey about his consulship.[31] Above all, Laterensis argued that

---

[29] Alexander, 2002, 136.
[30] *Planc.* 54, cf. Alexander, 2002, 137–8; Craig, 1990, 76.
[31] *Planc.* 83–5; *Schol. Bob.* 166–7. The joke about Crete would have been presumably of the form 'you went to "Creta" to get chalkwhite in anticipation of your candidacy'.

Cicero through fear of death had let down those who were prepared to support him in 58 (86, 90). This was a charge that Cicero had been wrestling with since the letters of his exile. The corollary was, of course, that he was loyal to those, like Pompey, who had betrayed him, and had thus lost his freedom.[32] Cicero tried to answer Laterensis' more humorous remarks in a deliberately humourless way (83–5). As for the accusation of political cowardice, he made his usual defence that he had sacrificed his own interest in order to preserve the lives of fellow countrymen (86–91) and claimed, not very convincingly, that he had not lost his liberty (91–4).

There can be no doubt that the charges were genuinely made by Laterensis: they were too disagreeable for Cicero to invent them in order to produce his answer. Whether they were made in his speech or later in the *altercatio*, where some must belong (for example, Iuventius could hardly accuse Cicero of missing the opportunity for a joke before he had heard his speech), they are vital in revealing the flavour of this case. When the passages in *pro Plancio* are read, it is hard to resist the conclusion that the prosecutor has got underneath Cicero's skin and the replies are, for an orator of Cicero's calibre, somewhat lame. He seems embarrassed, as he is over Laterensis' former friendship with him (2, 73, 77). Why then did Cicero include this material in what he published? The answer must be that he believed that he must defend himself against these attacks. The exchanges between the orators were known: he needed to put the best gloss on them that he could.

THE LAST LETTER TO SPINTHER

A few months after preparing *Pro Plancio* for circulation, Cicero composed an apologia for his recent life. The final letter to Lentulus Spinther (*Fam.* 1. 9) is easily recognizable as one intended for eyes others than that of its recipient. It is unusually long and written in a style that at times has more in common with Cicero's speeches than his regular correspondence. Cicero, as we have seen earlier, had expressed to Spinther in spring 55 his discontent over the new order of things since the election of Pompey and Crassus to their second consulship, but as something to which he was resigned, in so far as he was expected either to follow Pompey's wishes or to keep a low profile. He placed the blame squarely on those who had alienated Pompey and the *equites* from

---

[32] To be inferred from *Planc.* 91–4. Cf. Clodius' charge in the hearing before the *pontifices* (*Dom.* 29) and the remarks about Pompey in the senate in February 56 (*QF* 2. 3. 4).

the senate.[33] Spinther had apparently accepted some aspects of Cicero's recent realignment—his reconciliation with Caesar and Appius Claudius—but had clearly been disturbed by the news that Cicero had defended Vatinius (4).

In the *exordium* to the letter Cicero says that Spinther's absence, in spite of his successes in his province, has been a matter of regret to him, since he would have had greater experience of Cicero's loyalty and friendship, if they had been together, especially in resisting their mutual enemies (1–3). The identity of one of these, the 'perennial enemy of his own friends' (2) is unclear, as indeed it may have been to Spinther. The readers' immediate reaction, before they had absorbed the whole passage, would have been that it was Pompey. In fact, it must have been one of Spinther's open enemies who had 'directed his broken-backed violence' against Spinther and subsequently 'brought punishment on himself instead of us' by actions 'whose exposure deprived him not only of dignity but liberty'—perhaps C. Cato.[34] As it was, Cicero goes on, Spinther had experienced at a smaller cost the same sort of treachery that Cicero himself had experienced (3).[35] The letter was to be an explanation of Cicero's thinking in this matter, as well as a reply to Spinther's questions.

He argues first that he treated his restoration through Spinther's efforts as an inspiration to devote himself to the *res publica*, that is, to defend the optimate cause, even if it meant offending Pompey (4–8, esp. 6). We have already seen that his version of what happened in the senate over the *ager Campanus* on 5 April 56 is at best somewhat misleading.[36] However, Cicero claims here, Pompey reacted by putting pressure on him through his brother not to act against Caesar's interests (9–11). This is made more abrupt and dramatic than it was in fact.[37] Cicero represents himself apologizing to the *res publica* for his desertion of it in favour of maintaining his devotion to Pompey, adducing as a further justification the delight of certain people that he was making Pompey and Caesar his enemies: indeed these men were seeking to anger him by making Clodius their pet (10).[38] This automatically entailed that Cicero embraced Caesar's cause. One reason was his generosity to Cicero and his brother, another the disgraceful leadership of the *res publica* after Cicero's return (12–18). The defence of Vatinius was at Pompey's

---

[33] *Fam.* 1. 8. 3–5. Is the alienation of the equestrian order a reference to the earlier quarrel over the Asiatic tax-contract or does it refer to the issue of the restoration of Ptolemy XII to Egypt? The latter would be particularly relevant to Spinther.

[34] See Balsdon, 1957, 18–19 n. 29. C. Cato was by now no longer an opponent of the dynasts.

[35] Cf. *Fam.* 1. 5a. 1.

[36] *QF* 2. 6. 1; Ch. XIII with nn. 69–70.

[37] Ch. XIII with nn. 75–82.

[38] The language here—*amplexabantur, fovebant, osculabantur*—suits the treatment of a lover, pet animal, or child.

request, but also a reprisal for the support for Clodius among certain *nobiles*. It was Pompey again who demanded his reconciliation with Crassus after Cicero had attacked Crassus in the senate over his change of attitude to Gabinius (19–20).[39]

The conclusion of the apologia compares change of political course to prudent steering of a ship in face of adverse weather. *Cum dignitate otium*, the undisturbed enjoyment of one's position, was to be achieved by retaining the same aims but not always asserting them openly (21).[40] Cicero says that he would have found himself doing the same thing, even if Spinther had been present to advise him (22). The letter then slips away from political philosophy by way of references to Cicero's writing the *de Oratore* and the poems, to matters relevant to the province—Quintus' farm in Cilicia, Appius Claudius' succession to Spinther's command (he planned to come out, even if his formal *lex curiata* was blocked),[41] and the governor's problems with the *publicani* (23–6). The letter, we must conclude, succeeded with the ostensible recipient. Cicero's friendship with Spinther was still alive at the time of his own governorship of Cilicia and the eve of the civil war. He took Spinther's freedman Pausanias to Cilicia as his *accensus* (Ch. XV), and Spinther joined those canvassing support in favour of a *supplicatio* to the gods for Cicero's achievements there.[42] This letter, however, would hardly have convinced a man like Iuventius Laterensis or M. Cato.

DE ORATORE

If the last letter to Lentulus is an apology for Cicero's recent life, the *de Oratore*, which he had composed in 55, is a defence of his whole career. As an exposition of the orator's art, it is also a panegyric of that art and its greatest practitioners, in which ultimately the supreme orator becomes identified with the supreme statesman. The introduction (*De Or.* 1. 1–3) uses similar language to that of the letters to Lentulus. Cicero expresses admiration for eminent men who can so hold their course in life that they are free from peril when engaged in their business (*negotium*) and in their leisure (*otium*) can retain their rank in society (*dignitas*). He had hoped, he says, that the demands of his forensic and political careers would give him time to recall the

---

[39] Apparently Crassus moved from criticizing to supporting Gabinius, perhaps in reaction to the news that the invasion of Egypt had passed off quietly.
[40] See above with n. 1.
[41] On the long-debated and apparently insoluble question of the *lex curiata* see *CRR* 49–50.
[42] *Fam.* 3. 7. 4–5; 8. 11. 2. Spinther is still *Lentulus noster* in *Att.* 6. 1. 23 and later letters.

arts in which he and his brother had been educated as boys. However, early in his life the ancient discipline was thrown into confusion, his consulship threw him into the turmoil of politics, and he was still suffering from the tidal waves that had rebounded from the *res publica* onto his own person. Nonetheless, in spite of his present hardships and straitened circumstances, he would satisfy his brother's request.

It was not simply a matter of recalling precisely the precepts of teachers. Quintus had apparently asked for a more complete and elegant exposition of Cicero's views on oratory, on the ground that the juvenile volumes of *De Inventione* were inappropriate to someone of his age and standing. Hence Cicero's aim was to put down what the most distinguished and eloquent of men *thought* about oratory (1. 4–5). This seems to cover an imaginative recreation of their ideas on the basis of their conduct of cases as well as the advice they directly gave to their pupils. Clearly, what Cicero thought they thought would have contained many of his own ideas and have had his own authority as well as that of his teachers. The artificiality of the dialogue that he was creating would contribute to this impression. However, the work, with its historical setting just before the deaths of L. Crassus and the tribune M. Livius Drusus in 91 BC, remained a tribute to the great orators of his boyhood and to an apparently, but deceptively, more secure and civilized world before the Social and Civil Wars (1. 24, 3. 1–8).

The key to the dialogue is found in the praise of his subject that prefaces the dialogue proper. Cicero poses the question why there are comparatively few great orators, compared with the supreme exponents of other arts—philosophers, mathematicians, musicians, grammarians, poets (6–16). His answer is that oratory is a composite of many arts and branches of knowledge. 'In my view no one will be able to be an orator piled high with every form of distinction, unless he has achieved knowledge of all great matters and arts: for oratory must blossom and overflow from the understanding of things' (16–20). This was the opposite view to that of Quintus, who believed that oratory was a specialized skill, requiring a specific natural talent and training.[43] However, what follows is not a one-way argument in that direction, but a series of theses and antitheses, following the principle of arguing both sides of the case used by Aristotle and the New Academy.[44] Cicero initially limits the subject. It is too much to expect a practising orator to know about everything, and the Greeks have confined the art of rhetoric to forensic and deliberative speaking (21–2). He then sets the scene in L. Crassus' Tusculan

---

[43] 'Tu illam ab elegantia doctrinae segregandam putes et in quodam ingeni atque exercitationis genere ponendam' (1. 5).

[44] *De Or.* 2. 152; 3. 80; *Fin.* 5. 10; cf. *Fam.* 1. 9. 23.

villa at the time of the *ludi Romani* of September 91, where Crassus is entertaining his father-in-law Q. Mucius Scaevola (*cos.* 117), M. Antonius (*cos.* 99), and the young friends of Livius Drusus, P. Sulpicius, and C. Cotta (24–5). The following day they are joined by Q. Catulus and C. Iulius Caesar Strabo. Of these only Cotta was to survive the coming conflicts and is portrayed as Cicero's source for the dialogue (26, 29, cf. *Brut.* 311).

A brief summary cannot do justice to the all twists in the dialogue. Fortunately, these are now elegantly unravelled in the work of Elaine Fantham.[45] The ideal orator is the subject (1. 118), but the discussion springs from the practice of Roman oratory (1. 105–6), illustrated by a rich fund of anecdotes. The rules of the rhetorical schools, such as are deployed in Cicero's juvenile *De Inventione*, are mentioned only to be dismissed as obvious (1. 137–46), misleadingly pedantic (2. 76–82), or in need of simplification (2. 104–13). Antonius' argument in book 2 about forensic oratory is directed to winning in court even in doubtful causes, illustrated by his own defence of Norbanus.[46] However, at the start philosophical issues are raised about the status of oratory, which derive from Plato's discussions in the *Gorgias* and *Phaedrus*.[47]

Initially Crassus praises the orator as the man whose skill holds society together, this being essentially what separates man from the beasts.[48] Scaevola objects that the wisdom of great politicians and lawgivers of the past was not necessarily linked with eloquence, while their eloquent descendants lack political wisdom and understanding of the law (1. 35–40). Crassus' more general claim, that the orator was an expert in all public and private business, would be disputed by philosophers, physicists, mathematicians, grammarians, and musicians (1. 41–4). Antonius produces an argument, attributed to the Academic philosopher Charmadas, that oratory cannot be classed as an art (*ars*), since it is not a coherent body of knowledge deriving from objectively secure fundamental data (1. 92–3). A solution to this problem is offered by a less demanding definition of an art as something based on an organized and defined assembly of empirical evidence, as presented to skilled observers (1. 108–9). However, the more insidious implication of Charmadas was that oratory, as commonly understood, does not deal with the truth and has therefore nothing to do with wisdom. This is also the view ascribed to the Stoic Mnesarchus, who contrasted the 'journeymen'[49]

---

[45] Fantham, 2004.

[46] 2. 107–9, 197–201. See Ch. IX with nn. 30 ff. for Cicero's imitation of Antonius' strategy in his defence of Cornelius.

[47] Fantham, 2004, 52 ff. See esp. Plato, *Phaedrus* 260 E ff.

[48] *De Or.* 1. 30–4, esp. 32–3: perhaps an echo of Lucretius, cf. Lucr. 5. 1019 ff.

[49] The word *operarius* is also used by Crassus to describe Antonius' initial portrait of an orator (1. 263), though Antonius' portrait changes the next day (2. 40).

commonly called orators with the sage who possessed true eloquence as part of his virtue (1. 83).

During the discussion Crassus has introduced a further definition: the orator is the man who can speak wisely and elegantly about any matter than can occur, not forgetting what he has prepared and with an impressive delivery—after taking the necessary expert advice (1. 64). It is also agreed that, even if oratory requires more than natural talent, contrary to the view of some philosophers (89–91), natural talent is a *sine qua non* (113). However, Antonius laments that he had met many capable speakers, but never a man of real eloquence who could develop and elaborate anything that he wished in an awe-inspiring and amazing fashion. He was confident that such a man might yet emerge—either Crassus himself or someone with the same natural talent, who could better Crassus by virtue of his wider education through listening, reading, and writing (80–95). There can be no doubt that Cicero is thinking of himself.

When Crassus is finally persuaded to speak about the art of oratory, his theme is first the importance of exercise in speaking, writing, and dialectic, and secondly knowledge of the law. Those ignorant of the law might defeat the interests of their clients by pursuing the wrong action or demanding the wrong exception clause; the knowledgeable might find themselves in such cases as the *causa Curiana*, and would derive glory and position from their knowledge (1. 166–205). He includes a plea for the organisation of the Roman civil law as a science[50] and an encomium of the Twelve Tables as a source of moral education superior to philosophy (193–7). Against this Antonius presents himself as a plain man who cannot aspire to the range of knowledge prescribed by the philosophers or by Crassus himself in the field of civil law. He rejects ethical theory and philosophy of mind in favour of knowing his audience and how to move them even at the expense of self-humiliation, appealing to Crassus' own practice when advocating Caepio's *lex de repetundis* and contrasting this with the refusal of Rutilius Rufus and Socrates to make themselves suppliants to their juries (219–31). As to the civil law, one needed to know the mechanics of actions. The more refined aspects of legal interpretation were not needed in court even in the *causa Curiana*, where Crassus had successfully argued for equity and the intention of the testator against Scaevola's advocacy of the letter of the text of the will (234–45). Knowledge of law and history was helpful, but a busy advocate could not attain expertise and could always borrow from the expert (248–62).

---

[50] 1. 197–91. A work on this subject is attributed to Cicero by Gellius (1. 22. 7), conceivably one of the lost books of the *De Legibus*.

In the second book, set the following day, Antonius pursues this discourse. He cheerfully admits that for him oratory only dealt with men's opinions and therefore could not be a branch of knowledge (*scientia*) or an *ars* (2. 30). Nevertheless, he claims that the perfect orator is the most outstanding being (33). The encomium on oratory that follows has a section on its importance as vehicle for history (36), which is amplified in the following discussion (51–64). Antonius' aim is to simplify theory to a few basic principles and to concentrate on forensic oratory, whence the principles can be transferred to other forms of speech (69–70). He privileges forensic oratory because court cases are a battleground and the real test for a man (72).[51] In this field he urges his audience to abandon the categories of Greek rhetorical theory in favour of a few central precepts (99–120): understand the case, isolate the issue— whether it is a matter of fact or interpretation (104, 137)—discover proofs, and excogitate means of winning the jury's support and moving them to favour your client. Although he presents himself as the practical orator here, he is in fact at many points exploiting the recommendations of Aristotle's *Rhetoric*.[52]

Persuasion of the jury was Antonius' speciality (2. 128–9, cf. 114) and this subject is discussed and richly illustrated by him in the rest of the book, though Antonius yields to Caesar Strabo for a discussion of humour (217–90). Essentially he advises the budding orator to exploit every aspect of the matter and personalities in the case that can be turned to his advantage and to illuminate this by parallels and contrasts from outside. If the earlier part of the dialogue asserted the importance of the orator, this defines it more precisely as the impact of particular cases and even moments in court, where the ring-craft of one orator proved superior. Cicero is by implication defending the justice he achieved in court by a not always scrupulous use of his rhetorical talents, against the kind of justice that philosophers and lawyers approved. That message could be derived from the way Crassus defeated Scaevola in the case of Curius (1. 142–4, 2. 24, 140–1). More precisely, the stress on Antonius' defence of Norbanus (2. 107–9, 197–201) was by implication a reply to those who were critical of Cicero's choice of clients to defend.

The final book deals mainly with language and style (*ornatio*)—with a brief coda on *actio* (delivery)—but for the historian and biographer its value lies more in the scene-setting at the beginning of the book and the lament ascribed to Crassus over the schism between oratory and philosophy.[53] The

---

[51] We find the same assertion being made later by the character Marcus Aper, the *delator*, in Tac. *Dial.* 5.

[52] See esp. 1. 1355^b–1356^a; 1368^b–73^b; 2. 1378^a–1381^b; Fantham, 2004, 164 ff.

[53] Also greatly indebted to Peripatetic sources, see Fantham, 2004, 242 ff., following Innes, 1986.

introduction describes how within ten days of the last day of the dialogue Crassus returned to Rome. He had been deeply disturbed by a report of a speech to the people by the consul Philippus in which the consul had complained about the impossibility of doing business with the present senate. In response the tribune Livius Drusus summoned the senate to discuss the implications of this speech.

Here Crassus lamented how the senate had been left an orphan, in so far as the consul, who should have been like a good parent or trusty guardian, had been robbing it of its inheritance of *dignitas*, its respected place in the constitution: nor was it surprising that he was rejecting the senate in view of the damage he had inflicted on the *res publica*. This led to an altercation, in which the consul was so provoked that he attempted to silence Crassus by seizing pledges from him. He in turn stoutly defended his freedom of speech: Philippus could not be his consul, if he could not be his senator; the pledges that Philippus threatened to seize from him were nothing compared with the viciousness of the consul's attack on the authority of the whole senatorial order. In the end Crassus obtained the acceptance of his motion, that the consul should assure the Roman people that he had never claimed that he had found the good advice and loyalty of the senate wanting. This was drafted in the most impressive and elegant language with Crassus' own participation.

The speech was in Cicero's words Crassus' swan-song, since immediately afterwards he had fallen ill and died six days later.[54] The whole passage would have recalled to Cicero's readers more recent insults to the authority of the senate, but, although they may have admired Crassus' freedom of speech, they would have also recognized that in its historical context it was futile. Drusus himself would be murdered, his policies would lapse, and the Social War ensue, in its turn provoking a civil war, in which the authority of the senate was to be humiliated time and again. The only consolation was that Crassus' death, as Cicero points out in an eloquent passage, did spare him from the horrors of that conflict (3. 9–12). Oratory, it might be concluded following Antonius' panegyric in book 2, was magnificent. The nature of human affairs, however, entailed that its impact was short-lived.

Nevertheless, grand claims could be made for it on a higher level. The speech that Cicero now assigns Crassus reasserts a unity of oratory that transcends its many varieties and the differing personalities that are orators

---

[54] *De Or.* 3. 1–6. The motion was preserved in the senate records *in auctoritatibus perscriptis*, which should mean that it was recorded, although it did not attain the status of *consultum* through being vetoed (*CRR* 84–5, where I should have noted this evidence). The drafting of the decree after the motion must have had the cooperation of the consul and we must assume that the veto stemmed from a tribune.

(3. 19–37).⁵⁵ Style essentially amounted to lucidity in matter and language and a kind of rhythm. This was not to be found in the books of the so-called *rhetores*, but was derived from the whole of human life (3. 53–5). Practical politicians had always possessed oratorical skill and it was for them inseparable from right action, but, as the study of philosophy progressed from being a leisure pursuit of men versed in public affairs and became the pursuit of learning in its own right by men dedicated to this and nothing else, the practice of oratory came to be despised (56–73). It was Socrates who began this trend. He separated the science of wise reflection from that of effective speaking (60)—Cicero here appeals to the evidence of Plato's writings—and this divorce was maintained by later philosophers following the Socratic tradition. One could not find the man who was the object of the present discussion, the author of public policy and the leader in government and public eloquence, among their ranks.⁵⁶

We orators, says Crassus, will not reject philosophy, but it will take its leisure in its own little gardens, luxuriously reclining and tempting us away from the Rostra, the courts, and the senate-house—wisely perhaps, especially when the *res publica* is as it is (63). In fact, orators could make a good showing when it came to philosophical argument. However, if someone should combine the experience to be drawn from oratorical practice with the ability in the Aristotelian fashion to argue on both sides of the question like Arcesilas or Carneades, he would be the perfect orator, he alone would merit the name. For an orator could not be sufficiently vigorous and impressive without forensic sinews nor sufficiently polished and wise without the varied resources provided by philosophic learning (77–80).⁵⁷

Cicero has moved the discussion beyond the bounds of the law-court, in order to create a picture of an ideal statesman who had reunited philosophical wisdom with political needs—a return in effect to his position at the beginning of book 1. Antonius' discourses in books 1 and 2 are implicitly a defence of Cicero's way of life since his youth. Crassus in book 3 provides an aspiration, for which Cicero himself in his own opinion had surely the talent, but was frustrated by circumstances. The perfect orator required an appropriate *res publica*. It was logical that Cicero's next dialogue should be concerned precisely with that.

---

⁵⁵ Note the physical arguments and metaphor in 3. 20, 23–5, referred to (25) as *in naturis rerum*.

⁵⁶ 3. 63 'auctorem publici consili et regendae civitatis ducem et sententiae atque eloquentiae principem in senatu, in populo, in causis publicis'. Cf. the definition offered by Antonius in 1. 211, 'rei publicae rectorem et consili publici auctorem'.

⁵⁷ See Fantham, 2004, 94 on the combination of oratory and philosophy that was found in the Greek education of Cicero's own day.

DE RE PUBLICA

Cicero had begun this work by May 54, somewhat experimentally, with the aid of Atticus' and Varro's libraries.[58] We learn about its composition in a letter to Atticus of July and later in one to Quintus about the beginning of November.[59] Cicero had already used Plato's *Republic* as a model for the form of his previous dialogue;[60] he now undertook a work on the same subject as Plato's. Just as the *De Oratore* was set immediately before the death of its protagonist Crassus in 91, this dialogue is set in 129, shortly before the death of Scipio Aemilianus. The personalities are chosen from among the known friends of Scipio, but it is clear that the conversations are total invention, as are those of the *De Oratore*. Cicero was advised by his friend Sallustius that the work would have far more authority if presented as spoken in his own person: in the *De Oratore* the effect was charming and Cicero had ascribed the conversation to people he knew; the *De Re Publica* was obviously fictitious. Cicero acknowledged this objection and further admitted that it prevented him from using as material the great upheavals that came after the date of the dialogue. Nevertheless, he had achieved one object, that of avoiding any offence that would be caused by discussing his own lifetime (*QF* 3. 5. 1–2).

In fact he changed this policy to the extent of addressing his brother and talking about his own fortunes in the introduction to book 1 (*QF* 3. 5. 2; *Rep.* 1. 1–13). Here he also gives a veneer of historicity to the dialogue by the claim that it represented what he and his brother had learnt in their youth from P. Rutilius Rufus during his exile at Smyrna (*Rep.* 1. 13). Apart from Scipio and Rutilius, the personae Cicero uses are M'. Manilius (*cos.* 149), C. Laelius (*cos.* 140), L. Furius Philus (*cos.* 136), C. Fannius (*cos.* 122), Q. Scaevola (*cos.* 117), Q. Aelius Tubero, and Sp. Mummius. Both *De Oratore* and *De Re Publica* evoke a past that was more stable than what followed; the difference is that the former is on the eve of a crisis—the failure of Drusus' legislation and the Social War—while in the latter the crisis has already begun with the tribunate and death of Tiberius Gracchus.

Our knowledge of this work is painfully inadequate even after the discovery of the Vatican palimpsest. We have enough in the palimpsest and citations of books 1–3 in other authors to reconstruct most of their text; we also possess the *Dream of Scipio* from book 6 in a number of manuscripts. It is nonetheless

---

[58] *QF* 2. 13. 1–2; *Att.* 4. 14. 1. A helpful general introduction to *De Re Publica* can be found in Zetzel, 1995.

[59] *Att.* 4. 16. 2; *QF* 3. 5. 1.

[60] *Att.* 4. 16. 3, where the departure of Scaevola from the *De Oratore* is justified in the light of his age and the parallel of Cephalus' presence only in *Republic* Book 1.

hard to determine the balance of the work and its ultimate thrust on this basis. However, we know most of the theoretical discussion of constitutions in book 1 and the narrative of the evolution of Rome as a mixed constitution in book 2. For its contribution to the theory of the mixed constitution I must refer readers elsewhere.[61] I concentrate here on its importance in its historical context. The very fact that Cicero chose to set the dialogue outside his own lifetime in order to avoid offending anyone (*QF* 3. 5. 2) shows that the work was intended to have political implications for his own time. Even its model, Plato's *Republic*, though primarily an investigation of the concept of justice in the community and the individual, contained a critique of the operations and failure of democracy at Athens and Syracuse.

The introduction to the dialogue in book 1, expressed in Cicero's own voice, is a protreptic to participation in politics as the supreme field for displaying virtue in spite of its perils and disappointments (1–12). Cicero's own career is added to a list of traditional examples of devotion to the community at personal expense (5–8). In *De Oratore* (3. 60–3, 77–80) Cicero contrasts the present-day orator with the philosopher to the latter's disadvantage: the orator could participate adequately in philosophic discussion, but the philosopher deliberately avoided public life. Here he praises the man who seeks to benefit the community by participating in public life in comparison with the man who either pursues pleasure (*voluptas*) through leisure (*otium*) or who believes on philosophic grounds that one only should become involved in public life in an emergency (*Rep.* 1. 8–11).[62] In the opening part of the dialogue itself the recent appearance of the second sun is a taken as an analogy for the political division in 129. This is soon adopted as a more important matter for discussion (1. 15 ff., 31–2). Scipio is said by Laelius to have already argued—to Panaetius, with Polybius listening—that the traditional Roman *res publica* was by far the best constitution.[63] He is asked to explain this and so provide a basis for the solution of the problems present in 129 (1. 33–4). Thus theoretical and historical discussion in the dialogue is expected to produce in the end a dividend of practical advice for Scipio's interlocutors and, hence, for Cicero's readers.[64] The nature of the advice in the

---

[61] *CRR* 220–5 with further references.

[62] A reprise in *Rep.* 3. 7.

[63] Such a conversation may or may not have occurred, but in either case Cicero could have had no knowledge of it. Nor should we infer that Cicero is trying to represent in what he ascribes to Scipio the views of either Panaetius or Polybius. His version of the mixed constitution is certainly not the latter's. See *CRR* 220–1; Lintott, 1997*b*, 81–2.

[64] See also 1. 70–1, where, after Scipio has promised to expound the nature of the ancestral constitution and why it is best, he also promises to talk about the best condition of the constitution. This Laelius understands as involving a strategy for the future—'aut de consiliis in posterum providendis'.

dialogue can only be roughly discerned from the later books. What is sure—so it appears from the *Dream*—is that it involved Scipio himself.

The work then is in the first place a defence of Rome's republican constitution and those who undertake political life in it. The *res publica* is defined as *res populi*, the possession of the community, and its existence is regarded as men's natural instinct for living in community and justice, with an argument similar to that used by Aristotle in *Politics* 1 for the *polis* being a creation of nature (1. 39).[65] Equally Aristotelian is the view of changes in constitutions. Cicero does not believe in one unidirectional cycle, like Plato and Polybius, but in a variety of cycles (*orbes*). One of the simple constitutions, whether good or bad, can be followed by any other or indeed by the mixed constitution.[66] It follows that if a reader thought the Republic to be lost for ever, as Cicero had claimed in his letters, then he must conclude that this was a violation of nature. As for the mixed constitution, Scipio, taking his aim to be to create as long lasting a constitution as possible (1. 41, cf. 3. 7), praises it both because it was less liable to violent changes (1. 45) and because it enshrined a good form of *aequabilitas*, just organization, in which the best men (*optimates*) ruled by consent (1. 47–50, 69). This condition is meant to contrast with the biased oligarchic and democratic interpretations of justice.[67]

Scipio is also asked to comment on the simple constitutions, and here he expresses a clear preference for monarchy (1. 54 ff. cf. 2. 43). *Imperium* is the only way to control passions; rule by a single capable person—whether bailiff, steersman, or doctor—is what we choose in non-political matters. Monarchy at Rome became only hated because of the violence and arrogance of Tarquin the Proud. Its value was still recognized by the Roman people on military service in treating a magistrate like a king, indeed in concentrating *imperium* on one man, the 'dictator' or 'master of the people', in military crises. The expulsion of royal authority had brought with it danger from the people exulting in their new-found liberty, driving the innocent into exile, plundering property, humbling the power of *imperium*, and undertaking secession (1. 62–3). An aristocracy created on the fall of an evil tyrant was second best to monarchy; on the other hand nothing was worse than democracy created on the overthrow of a just king, especially if they had also tasted the blood of the *optimates* (1. 65).[68]

---

[65] Cf. Ar. *Pol.* 1. 1257^{b}27, 1253^{a}8.   [66] *Rep.* 1. 44–5, 65–9; 2. 45; *CRR* 221.

[67] See 1. 53 for Cicero's view of democratic justice, where the highest and lowest have equal respect, in other words Aristotle's democratic justice, which holds that, because men are equal in liberty, they should be equal in everything. Aristotle's oligarchic justice, where those who are unequal in birth and wealth should be unequal in everything, is described in 1. 51. Cf. Ar. *Pol.* 3. 1280^{a}23 ff.; 5. 1301^{a}25 ff.; Lintott, 2000, 165–6.

[68] The description that follows of extreme democracy and its generation of tyranny is essentially that of Plato, *Republic* 8.

There is a reprise of the favourable view of monarchy in Scipio's narrative of the development of the Roman constitution in book 2, as Scipio has promised (1. 62). The monarchs operate in ever increasing cooperation with their people, Romulus creating the senate, Numa Pompilius the ratification of the election of the king by the people (2. 15–17, 25). Servius Tullius, it is true, usurps power but immediately creates a broadly based assembly (though one in which the votes of the wealthy are dominant) (2. 37–40). However, after the second Tarquin usurped power by murdering his predecessor, he and his family became tyrannical through the fear of violent overthrow and the arrogance that derived from success in battle: instead of being a parent to his people, he became worse than the beasts (2. 45–8).

Scipio comments that, though the Romans first discovered through Tarquin about tyranny, they called it *regnum* and learnt to hate the name of king (2. 49–52). However, he contrasts Tarquin the subverter of kingship with another model, the good and wise man who understands the interests and dignity of citizens, who is like a guardian and protector (*tutor et procurator*) of the *res publica*. 'For this will be our term for whoever will be the director and pilot (*rector et gubernator*) of the community' (2. 51). He tells his listeners to make sure that they recognize this sort of man, whose title is not well established in the Latin language but who will be frequently mentioned in the following dialogue. The language would have been perfectly appropriate for a good king but it is evidently meant to designate someone who operates within a republican constitution.

The sketch of the early history of the Republic that follows continues to display monarchic preoccupations. The Tarquins are banished, even the innocent Collatinus; Valerius Publicola has to forestall suspicions of himself by lowering the *fasces*; he abandons his project to build a house high on the Velia on the site of the house of Tullus Hostilius; finally he passes a law entrenching *provocatio* against magistrates who ordered flogging or execution, in consequence of which he removed the axes from his own *fasces* (2. 53–5). Liberty is defined as a contrast to monarchy, but the now free people concede the majority of matters to senatorial authority, and a quasi-king, the dictator, is instituted to provide royal leadership in certain wars (2. 56, cf. 1. 63). The creation of the tribunes after plebeian secession and the legislation against debt-bondage[69] are justified by implication through Greek parallels—the institution of ephors by the Spartan king Theopompus and the debt-law of the Athenian Solon—and explicitly as the means to achieve a just balance (2. 57–9). However, the theme of monarchy or tyranny returns with

---

[69] Here Cicero antedates the *lex Poetelia*, which was placed in 326 BC in the tradition followed by Livy 8. 28 and in 313 by Varro (*LL* 7. 105).

the suppression of Spurius Cassius and the law-commission of *decemviri* in 451 (2. 60–3). The history of the *decemviri* runs parallel to that of the monarchy, but in miniature: at first, though they have absolute power, they rule justly, but when they seek to become a permanent oligarchy, passing unjust laws such as that banning intermarriage between patricians and plebeians, and when one of them behaves tyrannically, they are deposed. The last event of the Conflict of the Orders in the surviving text is the second secession of the plebs in 449 (2. 63).

When our text resumes, we find Tubero developing the question originally posed by Laelius at the start of the dialogue: granted the Romans have the best constitution possible, by what form of education, what customs, what laws can it be preserved (2. 64, cf. 1. 33)? At this point the reader who knew Plato's *Republic* might anticipate a discussion of education and social organization such as is found in *Republic* books 3–5. However, before we reach this, Scipio points out that he has illustrated the ideal constitution by an example: if his readers want a definition, he must use an image. This is of the mahout riding the elephant, of the weak but wise man controlling a huge and unmanageable beast—both a vision of the mind–body relationship and that between ruler and ruled in society (2. 67). This simile was clearly developed at some length (editors assign here a fragment referring to an inexperienced charioteer being dragged from his vehicle, 2. 68). The discussion then moves to the person who is to fulfil this ruling function. He is to be mirror for his fellow-citizens, an image, it seems, of justice, through which the discordant parts of the community are to be brought together in concord and harmony (2. 69). Thus the concept of monarchy is being reconciled with republican values by portraying this director of the community as ruling by example as much as, or more than, by force.

Before this idea can be taken further, the notion of justice itself as the core of the *res publica* is defended in book 3. This recalls the central theme of Plato's *Republic* and the more recent exhibition of philosophic argument by Carneades on his visit to Rome with an Athenian delegation in 155 BC, where on successive days he argued first the case of Plato and Aristotle for justice and then that, put by Socrates' interlocutors in Plato's *Republic* books 1–2, for injustice and the pursuit of natural self-interest.[70] Cicero introduces the book in his own person with a discourse describing human intellect as a vital gift of nature and praising those in history who had best exploited it (3. 1–7). He mentions in particular those at Rome who had combined traditional values with Greek learning, such as the participants in his dialogue—Scipio, Laelius, and Furius Philus (3. 5)—and once again asserts the superiority of those who

---

[70] 3. 9 ff.; 20 ff.; Aug. *Civ. Dei* 2. 21.

have applied their intellect to politics over those who have only devoted it to arts and sciences, on the ground that the former have contributed more to growth of the elements of nature (3. 7).

In the dialogue following Philus speaks first (3. 8 ff.). His theme is that justice is an unstable value, dependent on human perceptions, like sensations of heat and cold, bitterness or sweetness (3. 13). He illustrates this by the variety of attitudes and social customs throughout the world, and by the instability and arbitrariness of the law at Rome. The *lex Voconia* (of 169) had entailed that the juriconsult Manilius had to change his views on the rights of women to inherit. Moreover, this law was unfair to women: why should a woman not have money (3. 17)? Philus moves on to the basic injustice of imperial expansion and rule—an argument used by Carneades and pointed specifically at his Roman audience (3. 20–2, 24, 28)—and to the injustice that likewise existed under any simple constitution, whether monarchy, oligarchy, or democracy. Here he seems to be following the argument of Thrasymachus in Plato's *Republic* 1,[71] that all rulers or ruling groups pursue their own interests to the neglect of those of anyone else. Even the mixed constitution (which has been earlier defined as based on justice) is presented as arising from weakness, fear, and mistrust (3.23).[72] The potentially miserable fate of the just man is also compared with the praise and honour that may be received by the unjust.[73] The climax of Furius' discourse is that there is no community that does not prefer to rule unjustly than to be subject to another justly, no individual who does not prefer his own self-interest to just behaviour and in a crisis is not prepared to commit murder to save his own life (3. 28–30).

In reply Laelius begins by appealing to an apparently Stoic definition of law as right reason, applying to all peoples at all times.[74] He distinguishes between just and unjust wars—the former undertaken either in response to a pledge or for self-protection and formally declared after an attempt to secure compensation—and comments that the Romans got control of the world through defending allies (3. 34–5). Empire itself is justified by the argument that it is right for the best people to dominate inferiors, as it is right for masters to control slaves and the superior part of the mind to control baser instincts—an argument that recalls that of Aristotle for the naturalness of slavery (3. 36–7).[75] As for the individual, he claims that justice has been pursued contrary to men's best interests, at best giving in return honour rather than profit.

---

[71] 338 C–339 A, 343 B–344 C.   [72] Cf. Adeimantus' argument in Plato, *Rep.* 2. 366 CD.
[73] Following Glaukon in Plato, *Rep.* 2. 261 A–362 C.
[74] *Rep.* 3. 33, cf. *Leg.* 1. 33; Long and Sedley, 1987, i. 431–5.
[75] It includes the Aristotelian objection that some people are in fact slaves who are naturally their own masters (*Pol.* 1. 1254^{a}13 ff.).

Laelius' conclusion needs some elucidation. The figure of Tiberius Gracchus is introduced in a sentence without beginning, standing after a break in the palimpsest. Gracchus is said to have neglected the rights and treaties of the Latins and allies by contrast with his treatment of citizens. This is described as a degeneration of imperial rule from justice to violence and, if regularly imitated, a threat to the endurance of the Roman empire, one that could last for ever, if Romans lived according to their ancestral tradition (3. 41). Laelius was probably treating Gracchus as someone who disregarded justice in the empire because in all his conduct he sacrificed the interests of others to personal ambition and greed—a criticism applied by Cicero to Romans in general in *De Officiis* (2. 27). Gracchus' demagoguery would have been part of the same picture in that he was allowing his reason to be ruled by the desires of the masses rather than using it to rule them. This connection of demagoguery with aggressive exploitation of the empire was not new but is found in remarks by the philosopher-historian Poseidonius about Tiberius' brother Gaius.[76]

Laelius' defence of justice does not end the book. Instead we find a reiteration by Scipio (with some help from Spurius Mummius) of the importance of a 'bond of justice' (*vinculum iuris*) in the community they were discussing: its absence in the rule of tyrants, oligarchic juntas, and rule by the masses rendered all these three conditions unworthy of the name *res publica* (3. 43–5). There is a debate over which of the good simple constitutions is most worthy of this name. Mummius gives the preference to the rule of *optimates* over monarchy but Scipio once again asserts his view that a good king is the best simple constitution. The rule of *optimates* comes next. As for democracy, the constitution of the Rhodians is taken as its best representative, but even this is described as excessively subject to the masses (3.46–8).

The discussion of education and social organization, parallel to that in Plato's *Republic* books 3–5, finally appears in Cicero's fourth book. Essentially it seems to have asserted the superiority of Roman institutions over Greek, including those proposed by Plato. What survives is fragmentary and can be briefly summarized. Scipio approves Roman social stratification, their reluctance to impose by law what should be left to custom and the family, for example the education of children, the discipline of women, and the mild moral regime of the censor (4. 2–3, 6). He criticizes Greek homosexual love and the nudity in the gymnasium that contributed to it (4. 3–4). He denounces Plato's proposal for community of wives and children (4. 5), but is more in harmony with Plato in extolling parsimony and the simple life (4.7).

---

[76] See Diod. 34/5. 25 and, on the effects of the empire on morals, Strasburger, 1965; Lintott, 1972*b*, 634 ff.

Like Plato too, he is suspicious of music and the theatre, especially that of Old Comedy, which, he points out, would have been a contravention of a law of the Twelve Tables (4. 10–14). He does seem, however, to accept comedy that was a mirror of life (3. 13), presumably Roman *fabulae palliatae* and *togatae* (cf. 3. 11). This eulogy of Roman values, however, is undercut by the introduction to book 5, where Cicero in his own person laments the collapse of traditional morals, ascribing it to the disappearance of men who made it their business to represent these values (5. 1–2).

Most of what we possess of book 5 relates to the position and function of the *rector* (director) of the *res publica*, to whom Scipio first referred in book 2. The jurist Manilius is portrayed evoking the 'ancient custom of Greek kings', who are said to have been allocated generous and productive estates to be cultivated on their behalf by others, in order that they might devote their time not to war but to being universal judges and arbitrators (5. 3).[77] The Roman king Numa is adduced as a parallel and his function as a lawgiver in both religious and secular matters is said to be particularly appropriate to the man Cicero is discussing. However, the time of the *rector* is not to be spent perpetually in giving legal opinions and reading and writing the civil law. He must be an expert in the supreme law, while sufficiently knowledgeable about the civil law, as a steersman knows astronomy and a doctor physics. Only in this way can he be a just manager of the *res publica* (5. 3–5).[78] One of the speakers goes on to see the task of the *rector* as lying in the inculcation of good morals by his opinions and the social institutions he creates. Here the palimpsest ends, but its message can be amplified by a citation in a letter of Cicero himself of 49, where in a lament to Atticus he refers to his own words about the controller (*moderator*) of the *res publica*, that this man should have as his goal the happiness of the citizens, just as a steersman seeks a favourable course and a doctor health: 'this', he goes on to comment there, 'never entered the head of my friend Gnaeus; both (he and Caesar) sought domination' (*Att.* 8. 11. 1–2).[79]

---

[77] The origin of this notion of Cicero is not clear. The *basileus* at Athens retained his judicial functions after the monarchy; the same may have happened at Argos. Perhaps more relevant is the post of *aisumnetes*—held for example by Pittacus as an elected monarch at Mytilene—which Aristotle says existed among 'the ancient Greeks' (*Pol.* 3. 1285ᵃ29 ff.; Alcaeus in *LGS* 163).

[78] The rare word *responsitare* for the regular giving of legal opinions appears here and in *Leg.* 1. 14, where Cicero in his own person rejects this procedure in favour of discussing the general principles of law.

[79] The political governor as an exponent of an art, who seeks the good of those subject to him, is Socrates' vision, expounded in answer to Thrasymachus (Plato, *Rep.* 1. 339 D–342 E). One might also wish to see here the influence of Cicero's reading of Thucydides, whose portrait of Pericles is essentially one of a man who uses his superior intelligence to look after the interests of the masses while not yielding to their emotional demands. For Cicero's reading of Thucydides see above with n. 25, Ch. XV with n. 65, Ch. XVI with nn. 72–4.

There is more discussion of the *rector* in the citations we possess at the beginning of book 6. Indeed Cicero says himself in another letter to Atticus that this was where the man was portrayed (*Att.* 7. 3. 2). Here he appears not as a dispenser from on high of true justice but as defender of the *res publica* from sedition (*Rep.* 6. 1). This apparently leads to talk of tyrannicide and Laelius complains that there were no statues set up of Scipio Nasica to commemorate his killing of Tiberius Gracchus (6. 2). It is this that spurs Scipio to narrate his dream—Cicero's equivalent of Plato's myth of Er. While on a visit to king Masinissa at the beginning of the last war against Carthage in 149, he dreamed of his grandfather. The latter prophesied his future career down to his return from Numantia to the turmoil at Rome in the aftermath of Gracchus' death. At this point the eyes of everyone—the senate, the aristocracy, the Latins and allies—would be on him. On him alone would depend the safety of the community. He would be obliged to put the *res publica* in order as dictator, providing that he escaped the impious hands of his relatives (6. 11–12). His grandfather goes on to encourage him by pointing out the special place in heaven that the supreme god (*princeps deus*) had reserved for the directors and preservers (*rectores et conservatores*) of communities (6. 13 ff.).

The concept of the *rector* has given rise to a long controversy among scholars.[80] Scipio's dream makes it certain that this idea was the goal and conclusion of the book. Powell has argued against much of earlier scholarship that Cicero was doing no more than alluding to the function of leadership falling to the ideal republican statesman, who would be one among a number of *principes* in the senate. That is certainly the conclusion we would draw, if we only had the passages from *De Oratore* (1. 211, 3. 63). In the first of these a number of examples are given, including both Scipio Aemilianus and Laelius. However, in *De Re Publica* Cicero seems to have passed beyond this traditional notion. The *rector* is introduced as the diametrical opposite to the tyrant and the concept is said to be one little discussed (2. 51). There is said to be a shortage of those who could fulfil this position in the senate in general (2. 67). The *rector* is compared to ancient Greek monarchs and King Numa by virtue of being a superior kind of lawgiver (5. 3–6). He is also expected to assume supreme authority in a crisis, taking the position of dictator to restore stability to the *res publica* (6.1, 12). Thus the man is a republican statesman who is required generally to be supreme source of justice and to act as a temporary monarch when need arises. We should remember that in the past

---

[80] See P. L. Schmidt, 1973 for a review of this up to that date. More recent interpretations in Powell, 1994; Ferrary, 1995. See also *CRR* 224–5. For a reassertion of the political significance of the talk of Scipio's dictatorship in Book 6 see Stevenson, 2005, 140–52.

dictators were rarely appointed to repress civil unrest: the best example before Sulla is Q. Hortensius in 287. What we read, therefore, is not simply a banality of optimate thought.

Cicero's idea of the director of the *res publica* is, perhaps deliberately, a little confused. In book 5 he is the man of peace who establishes laws, justice, and morals without the distraction of fighting wars, a position eminently suited to Cicero's own view of himself at the present time.[81] In book 6 the task is to repress sedition and restore stability to the *res publica*, and it is given to the warrior Scipio. This undertaking is in theory not inappropriate for the man described in book 5 and one fulfilled to some extent by Cicero in 63, but now, as history had proved by the time the book appeared in 51, it was something that needed Pompey's use of military force. For us the two superimposed portraits, poorly preserved as they are, are somewhat blurred. It is possible that what was inevitably a long-term vision in book 5 gave place to a more immediate reflection of the present in book 6. This book would in any case deflect the reader from associating the plea for a republican quasi-monarch too closely with Cicero.

POMPEY AND THE RES PUBLICA

When Cicero started writing *De Re Publica*, it would have been hard to conceive of Pompey as an equivalent of Scipio as portrayed in *De Re Publica* book 6. While he wrote, politics moved from utter turmoil to a new stability and the parallel must have seemed more plausible. Corruption impeded the curule elections for 53 and there were fears that Pompey was hoping this would proceed to the point where drastic solutions would be required. Once again we lose most of the Ciceronian evidence at a critical point. The letters to Quintus cease at the end of 54 and there is a long gap in the correspondence with Atticus. Until the eve of Cicero's departure to his province in 51 we have to make do with a few letters to friends, the most important those to Trebatius and Curio. Later correspondence is on occasion helpful. There are two preserved speeches, the *pro Rabirio Postumo* and *pro Milone* and some fragments of the *De Aere Alieno Milonis*. The limitations of the published defence of Milo as historical evidence have already been discussed (Chs. II and III). Asconius' commentary on the speech is in many ways more valuable to the

---

[81] See *CRR* 226 for the view that the apparent absence of the *rector* from the text of *De Legibus* is because the *rector* is present in Cicero's own person performing the function described in *De Re Publica* book 5.

historian than the speech itself. It is an important period in Cicero's life where his friendship with Milo created friction in his relationship with Pompey, which in due course he forgot through contentment with Pompey's new dispensation in 52.

At the end of 54 there were two main points where the pressure of Pompey was felt, the attempts to condemn Gabinius and the problem of the elections. Gabinius had arrived in the neighbourhood of the city on 19 September to find that his opponents were mounting charges. The younger L. Lentulus Niger had already summonsed him for treason (*maiestas*), while Tiberius Nero and C. Memmius (not the consular candidate, but a tribune that year) were competing to do the same in the court for recovery (*de repetundis*) (*QF* 3. 1. 15). Gabinius actually entered the city on the night of 27 September, the day before he was due to present himself before the tribunal of C. Alfius, the magistrate in charge of the treason court (*QF* 3. 1. 24).[82] A *divinatio* took place on 11 October to see who should undertake the *repetundae* prosecution—Memmius, Nero, or two young Antonii who now joined the field. On 8 October (the tenth day after his arrival) Gabinius had come to the senate to make a return of the number of casualties among the enemy and his own troops. Before he could leave, a group of *publicani* were admitted. In the subsequent debate Cicero made an attack on him, presumably similar to that he made on Piso in 55. Nevertheless, he restrained himself from actually joining in any of the prosecutions because he did not trust current juries and was reluctant to fight with Pompey over Gabinius: he had enough of an impending problem, he comments, over Milo (*QF* 3. 2. 1–2).[83]

There was also a *divinatio* in October over a charge of electoral bribery against Gabinius, which was won by P. Sulla (*QF* 3. 3. 2). The verdict in the *maiestas* trial was delivered on 24 October, the day before the games commemorating Sulla's victory: Gabinius was acquitted by 38 votes to 32. Cicero ascribes this to an incompetent accuser who was suspected of collusion, to the pleas made by Pompey to the jury, and to talk of an *interregnum* and a dictatorship for Pompey.[84] He once more declares his reluctance to get into an unequal fight with Pompey, especially if it led to the latter ending his feud with Clodius, and complains bitterly that, after all his support which left Pompey in his debt, not him in Pompey's, Pompey could not tolerate any

---

[82] Cf. ibid. 3. 3. 3. Alfius had also presided over the trial of Plancius *de sodaliciis* (*Planc.* 43, 104).

[83] In *QF* 3. 2. 2 I follow Watt's OCT against SB *QFBrut* 86, 212 in reading *hostium* rather than *hostiarum*. The latter's argument from Val. Max. 2. 8. 1 does not seem relevant since Gabinius was clearly not demanding a triumph, as he had already entered the city.

[84] *Att.* 4. 18. 1–3; *QF* 3. 3. 3, 3. 4. 1.

political independence from him. It appears that Pompey had urgently asked him to defend Gabinius and he had refused. He had, however, given evidence, passionately but without venom.[85] Cicero's position on Gabinius remained firm until the end of the year.[86]

The imbroglio over the consular elections is a recurring theme of the correspondence of 54. The candidates were two patricians, M. Valerius Messala and M. Aemilius Scaurus, and two plebeians, C. Memmius and Cn. Domitius Calvinus. At the beginning of July—the time when Triarius began the prosecution of Scaurus (Asc. 19 C)—Cicero thought the candidates were running level. Memmius was at the time Pompey's candidate, but was also hoping for support from Caesar's soldiers and might have found a tribune to obstruct the elections until their return from Gaul in the winter (*Att.* 4. 16. 8)—a similar tactic to that used by Clodius and C. Cato in 56 on behalf of Pompey and Crassus.[87] In a letter of 27 July we find that the elections had been delayed till that date but further obstruction was expected. The volume of bribery was reflected in the doubling of the monthly interest rates on 15 July. Memmius, still Caesar's candidate, was now linked with Domitius and the current consuls in a secret pact, while Pompey seemed to be supporting Scaurus and hostile to Messala. The candidates for the tribunate had taken the unusual step of each depositing 500,000 sesterces with M. Cato, then praetor, which would be distributed among their competitors, if Cato decided that they were guilty of bribery.[88]

Before the middle of September Memmius had inexplicably confessed to the secret pact by which both he and Domitius were expected to give the consuls 40,000 sesterces if they did not confirm the latter's provinces by a faked *lex curiata* and a faked financial grant from the senate (presumably on the assumption that they would fail to secure this legally). Quintus had heard that his brother was involved, which Cicero hastily denied.[89] By the beginning of October all the candidates had been charged with electoral bribery. 'What will you be able to say in their defence?', Cicero imagines

---

[85] *QF* 3. 4. 2–3, 3. 5. 5, 3. 7. 1.

[86] *QF* 3. 6 was written a little after 23 November (see 3. 6. 5). *QF* 3. 7. 3 picks up fears expressed by Quintus, now in winter quarters in north-eastern Gaul (Caes. *BG.* 5. 24. 2, 5. 40 ff.), about Cicero making enemies, which were occasioned by what Cicero said in 3. 4 and 3. 5. This later letter must therefore have been written very close to the end of the year and the *interregnum*.

[87] Dio 39. 27–30.

[88] *Att.* 4. 15. 7–8; *QF* 2. 15. 4. On the flagrant bribery at this time see also *Att.* 4. 19. 1.

[89] *QF* 3. 1. 16; *Att.* 4. 17. 2; unlike SB *Att* 122, 213–14 and Gelzer, 1962–4, i. 118 n. 463, I see nothing wrong in the text here with the MS reading *HS quadragena* (40,000 sesterces). Appian's immense figure of 800 talents (19,200,000 sesterces) being staked by candidates (*BCiv.* 2. 19. 69) is far more likely to be the sums promised to the electorate at large, which were huge (*QF* 2. 15. 4; *Att.* 4. 17. 3).

Atticus saying. He replies that he cannot find anything in the three books that Atticus extravagantly praises—the *De Oratore* (*QF* 3. 2. 3; cf. *Att.* 4. 17. 5). The senate had decreed that all those juries appointed for the candidates should deliver a secret verdict before the elections. But certain of the jurors had appealed to the tribunes on the ground that they should not use procedure that had not been approved by the assembly—a reasonable objection, in that they would have been defying statute and liable to the penalties prescribed under the statute.[90] A second decree was passed that the consuls should pass an appropriate statute before the elections. This was vetoed on the day of the legislative assembly. The consuls referred the veto back to the senate, which decreed that the elections could not be held before the new legislation was passed. This decree was also vetoed and, according to its terms, the matter was brought back to the senate afresh. The senate then decreed that the elections should be held as soon as possible (*Att.* 4. 17. 3).

In practice, the elections continued to be obstructed for one reason or another, whether by those who wished the prosecutions to take place or those who wished the effect of the bribery to be exhausted[91] or supporters of Pompey who wanted him to be made dictator. By the end of the year the talk of a dictatorship was persistent. Pompey was openly denying any interest, but his supporter Lucilius Hirrus, tribune elect for 53, spoke otherwise and Pompey's attitude lacked conviction. Milo was by now estranged from Pompey and feared his effect on his own plans to reach the consulship in 52: if he used violence to back a veto on the election of a dictator, he feared this would turn Pompey into his enemy.[92] A number of tribunes, however, were prepared to make such a veto, and this in the end must have been decisive against Pompey's plans at this time, in spite of preparations by Hirrus and machinations by Appius Claudius. Cicero's view that in the long run Valerius Messala would profit from the situation to become consul, whether the elections were held by an *interrex* or a dictator (*QF* 3. 7. 3) was to be borne out, but only after the lapse of over six months.[93]

According to his last letter to Atticus of 54 Cicero was due to leave Rome on 13 January 53 as Pompey's legate.[94] We have no idea whether this was in fact to be on official business or simply an excuse for him to leave Italy for a time—perhaps to revisit his friends and clients in Sicily, perhaps to visit Cisalpine Gaul to canvass support for Milo's candidature for the consulship,

---

[90] *Att.* 4. 17. 3; *CRR* 63 with n. 98.   [91] For persisting bribery see *Att.* 4. 17. 4.
[92] *QF* 3. 6. 4, 6; cf. *Att.* 4. 18. 3, 19. 1.
[93] Dio 40. 45. 1. App. *BCiv.* 2. 19. 71 makes the delay eight months.
[94] *Att.* 4. 19. 2, cf. *QF* 3. 1. 18 for Quintus believing this to be happening in September 54.

as he had done for his own.⁹⁵ In a letter of spring or early summer 53 (*Fam.* 7. 14. 1) he threatens Trebatius with a visit to Transalpine Gaul but in jest. In practice he does not seem to have left Rome for very long. One of the series of letters to Trebatius in Gaul places Cicero at the villa of M. Aemilius Philemon in the Pontine marshes on 8 April 53—during what would have been the regular legal recess (*Fam.* 7. 18. 3). In what seems to Cicero's earliest letter to Trebatius of that year he alludes to the virtual cessation of legal business at Rome as a result of the lack of regular curule magistrates. *Interreges* were now being appointed, who only held office for five days.⁹⁶ So Cicero suggests that a lawyer could advise any of his clients to ask each *interrex* for two adjournments to seek legal advice and thus ensure that his case never came to court (*Fam.* 7. 11. 1). No criminal tribunals (*quaestiones*) could have been functioning as there were no magistrates to draw up the albums of jurors or receive the charges. Indeed, it was an ideal time for Cicero to take an extended vacation.

Apart from this, the letters to Trebatius tell us nothing of what is going on in Rome and this might suggest that more were written outside the city than editors have supposed.⁹⁷ It is the same with a group of letters to Curio (*Fam.* 2. 2–6), who was in the province of Asia as quaestor or proquaestor. He had been under Cicero's instruction as a boy and Cicero had delighted in his leadership of demonstrations against the three dynasts in 59.⁹⁸ Cicero's letters console him for the death in his absence of his father, the consul of 76 and the joint target of the *In Clodium et Curionem*, and anticipate his return to pursue his political career in the present desperate state of the *res publica*.⁹⁹ In particular Cicero stresses his own present concentration on the future consulship of Milo—for him a task not only of duty (*officium*) but of devotion (*pietas*). The good men, Cicero claims, are Milo's supporters because of his tribunate and help to Cicero, the masses because of his games (which were given in late 54 or early 53), the young and the electorally influential because he himself has been outstanding in delivering votes. All they need is Curio as their leader.¹⁰⁰

---

⁹⁵ *Att.* 1. 1. 2; or even Quintus' candidacy (see Wiseman, 1966).
⁹⁶ Livy, 1. 17. 6; 9. 34. 12; Dion. Hal. *AR* 2. 57. 2; App. *BCiv.* 1. 98. 457.
⁹⁷ There was a further possibility that Cicero would leave Rome as Pompey's *legatus* at the time of the argument in the senate, commemorated in the published *De Aere Alieno Milonis* (*Schol. Bob.* 173 St. on fr. 17 P). On his visit to Cisalpine Gaul in March 52 see below.
⁹⁸ *Fam.* 2. 1. 2; *Att.* 2. 18. 1, 2. 19. 3, cf. 2. 24. 2–3 for his alleged leadership of an anti-Pompeian plot.
⁹⁹ See esp. *Fam.* 2. 5. 2 on the *res publica*.
¹⁰⁰ *Fam.* 2. 6, esp. 3–4. On Milo's games see *QF* 3. 6. 6; Asc. 31 C; Lintott, 1974, 65–6, arguing that Milo had exploited his position as *magister* of a *collegium* to do this.

CICERO AND POMPEY: GABINIUS AND THE PRO RABIRIO POSTUMO

It is in the context of Milo's candidature we must place Cicero's *volte face* in defending Gabinius unsuccessfully against the accusation *de repetundis*[101] and his surviving defence of C. Rabirius Postumus, who was charged with possessing some of Gabinius' ill-gotten gains according to the procedure *quo ea pecunia pervenerit*. These can be placed at the earliest in the latter half of 53 for reasons that by now must be largely clear. There is no hint of a change in attitude to Gabinius or indeed of the approach of his trial in any of the letters of 54. Accusations *de repetundis* were complex and required more time than the few available days for lawsuits at the end of 54. Indeed, one would have expected the prosecutors to take a considerable time over the *inquisitio*, investigation in the province, which would have involved both Syria and Egypt: six months would not have been unreasonable, allowing about three months for travelling. Nor could a *quaestio* trial have been held at Rome in the absence of curule magistrates until late July at the earliest. The only reason for the dating of the trial *de repetundis* in 54 is its position in the account of Cassius Dio, who mentions the trials as a coda to Gabinius' proconsulship.[102] However, Dio's account of the late Republic is not strictly chronological but organized by topic with some chronological distortion, in this respect somewhat different to his narrative of the Principate.[103]

C. Rabirius Postumus was brought to court after Gabinius' condemnation under a procedure introduced by C. Servilius Glaucia in his statute *de repetundis*, whereby if the money extracted from the condemned man's estate was inadequate to pay the financial penalty, this money could be pursued from those to whom the condemned man had passed it on.[104] Rabirius was a *publicanus* and businessman with interests in many parts of the Roman empire. The son of C. Curtius Postumus, himself a leading *publicanus*, he

---

[101] *Rab. Post.* 7, 19, 32–4; Dio 39. 63. 5; Val. Max. 4. 2. 4, 8. 1. 3, the last oddly stating that Gabinius was in fact acquitted after an emotional appeal by his son was rejected by Memmius.

[102] Dio 39. 62. 2–63, esp. 63. 5. This has misled most scholars with the partial exception of Meyer, 1918, 206–7.

[103] See Lintott, 1997a, 2503–11; Lintott, 1974, 67–8. Alexander, 2002, 290, tries to save the traditional view without meeting all the objections against this. Note, against his counter-arguments, (i) that the expedited procedure *de repetundis* after 1 September in the epigraphic law (*RS* i. 1, ll. 7–8) cannot be a parallel for the prosecution of Gabinius, as it was a civil procedure, in which those robbed sued simply for recompense and there was no criminal penalty; (ii) although extraordinary *quaesitores* and juries might be appointed, it was the regular magistrates who created the album of jurors.

[104] *Rab. Post.* 8–9, 37; *Fam.* 8. 8. 2, on which see Lintott, 1980.

had acquired a second patrimony from the man whose name he also adopted.[105] Rabirius had accompanied Gabinius to Egypt in pursuit of the money Ptolemy owed him (*Rab. Post.* 6–7, 19 ff.). Appointed *dioiketes*, a senior minister, there he had been unpopular and thrown into the king's prison (22, 39). He had apparently returned with wealth (40), but in what circumstances had he acquired it? What was at issue in the action brought was not whether Rabirius' own actions there were criminal, but simply whether he had received money that Gabinius had improperly appropriated.[106] Cicero, however, treats the case as if Rabirius himself were on trial *de repetundis*, with some moral, if not legal, justification. For, if the jury did decide to exact money from him, this would be a financial penalty. Moreover, there may have been a penalty of *infamia* attaching to those who were forced to disgorge money involuntarily in this way. Nevertheless, Rabirius was not a defendant in a trial *de repetundis* and much of what Cicero says was not strictly relevant.

The scandalous conduct of Ptolemy and his staff at Rome has been discussed elsewhere (Chapter XIII with nn. 32–5 and Appendix 3). Cicero chooses to portray Rabirius' series of loans to the king as foolish rather than criminal, stressing that they had begun before Ptolemy was expelled from Alexandria and continued at Rome after Ptolemy was a recognized as a king and friend of the Roman people. He even points out that the loan agreement before Ptolemy left Rome was made in Pompey's Alban villa (4–6). As to the suit itself, Cicero resorts to juridical arguments. He first claims that no one to his knowledge had ever been sued under *quo ea pecunia pervenerit*, unless they had been mentioned by name in the *litis aestimatio*, the assessment of damages due after the verdict in the main trial (8–11). The suggestion is that those sued in this way should have been people attested as participating in the seizure of money in the province. Cicero ignores the fact that the procedure was designed to obtain money from those with whom the defendant had chosen to cache his improper profits. He then points out at some length that Rabirius was an equestrian and therefore according to a long, though contested, tradition not liable under the *lex de repetundis* (*Rab. Post.* 11–19). We hear of the resistance to the proposal of M. Livius Drusus in 91 BC (15–16),[107] and of a discussion in Pompey's consulship, presumably that of 55 BC, about subjecting the tribunes of the soldiers, prefects, scribes, and other companions on a provincial magistrate's staff to the law (13). The Gracchan

---

[105] *Rab. Post.* 3–4, 38, 45. Rabirius was perhaps also one of Murena's prosecutors (*Mur.* 56). Other possible members of this wealthy family were Q. and Cn. Curtius Postumus (*2Verr.* 1. 100).

[106] On the prosecution case see Alexander, 2002, 110–20.

[107] In Cicero's imagined dialogue in *Rab. Post.* 17 the MS reading *Tam es tu iudex quam ego senator* should be retained: the point is that being a juror is as much an official post as being a senator. The answer is that jury-service was compulsory, senate-membership voluntary.

law *de repetundis* had included close relatives of senators and those who were or had been minor magistrates, including the tribunes of the soldiers elected by the people, but not those selected by the commander or officers of lower rank. This was evidently still the position.[108]

The prosecution case was that Ptolemy had promised Gabinius ten thousand talents (240 million sesterces) for his restoration; he had appointed Rabirius as his minister (*dioiketes*), and while the latter was collecting this money, he had taken a tenth of it for himself: the global sum that the prosecution sought to collect had been approved by the jury in the *litis aestimatio* (21, 30–1). Cicero's counter-argument is that Rabirius' tenth cannot have been an addition to the global sum—otherwise the prosecution would have been suing for that too—nor would Gabinius have allowed any deduction from it (30–1). The weakness of the second part of the dilemma is clear. Cicero also tries to exploit the fact that an Alexandrian embassy originally praised Gabinius but changed their tune, once he had been condemned (31–6)—the praise was admitted by the prosecutor Memmius, but explained by pressure from Pompey similar to that which drove Cicero to appear in Gabinius' defence (32). We may compare as purveyors of extorted praise the embassies from Messana and Syracuse for Verres.[109] In a final argument that develops into a peroration[110] Cicero maintains that Rabirius was actually seeking his own money but in fact had not recovered the money he lost: it was only Caesar's financial support that had sustained him since (38–41). This allows him simultaneously to claim the support of an outstanding commander, not tarnished by suspicions of corruption in this matter to the extent that Pompey was, and to evoke pity for Rabirius (41–7). Almost at the end Cicero mentions a personal connection of his own: Rabirius had given him and his family financial aid at the time of his exile (47).

It is easy to see why Cicero was induced to defend Rabirius—his own debt of *gratia* and the connection with Caesar, apart from any pressure from Pompey. The Caesarian connection may also help to explain the defence of Gabinius. Caesar tells us in his *Bellum Civile* (3. 4. 4) that among the soldiers available to Pompey in 48 were 500 from the Gabiniani, Gauls and Germans that Gabinius had left at Alexandria as a bodyguard. These were evidently Caesar's present to Gabinius' operation. However, if Cicero was seeking to assist Milo's candidature for the consulship in face of Pompey's hostility, as he had pointed out in his letters of 54,[111] as well as that of Clodius,

---

[108] *Lex. rep.* (*RS* i. 1), ll. 2–3. Under the Principate the law was interpreted as applying to anyone on a magistrate's staff (*Dig.* 48. 11. 1), but it must be concluded from what Cicero says here that this was not in the original *lex Iulia*.
[109] *2Verr.* 4. 15, 141–4; 5. 47.
[110] Cf. Winterbottom, 2004, 218.
[111] *QF* 3. 4. 2–3, 3. 6. 6.

he could not afford to offend Pompey. Defence of friends might entail defence of enemies.

MILO, CLODIUS AND POMPEY'S THIRD CONSULSHIP[112]

The consuls of 53, Valerius Messala and Domitius Calvinus, were only elected in either July or August of that year after Pompey had been asked to provide a force to ensure law and order at the elections.[113] Once elected, they were unable to carry out the elections for the following year because of continuing violence and bribery. Milo's competitors for the consulate were Q. Metellus Scipio and P. Plautius Hypsaeus, both supported by Pompey. He was also in physical conflict with Clodius who was a candidate for the praetorship in 52, after having deferred his candidature, originally intended for the year 53.[114] The two consuls were injured while apparently trying to put down a riot between the forces of Hypsaeus and Milo in the via Sacra, an attack mentioned by Cicero in his defence of Milo.[115] The political crisis was brought to a head by the murder of Clodius by Milo's men on the Appian Way on 18 January 52 and the subsequent rioting of his supporters. This led to Pompey first being entrusted with defending the *res publica* by the last decree, though a proconsul with strictly no constitutional authority within the city, and then to his extraordinary election as sole consul, in which capacity he introduced new criminal procedures and regulations about magistracies.

We are well informed about the history of this period by Asconius in his commentary on the *pro Milone* (30–56 C). We have, however, little access to Cicero's own experience of this time. There are fragments of the *De Aere Alieno Milonis*, a speech published on the basis of an argument held in the senate at the end of 53 or the beginning of 52.[116] According to the scholiast,[117]

---

[112] The section following is selectively derived from Lintott, 1974, to which I must refer the reader for a fuller account of the circumstances of Clodius' murder and Milo's trial.

[113] Dio 40. 45. 11–12; Plut. *Pomp.* 54. 3; App. *BCiv.* 2. 19. 71.

[114] Asc. 30 C; *Mil.* 24; *De Aere Alieno Milonis*, fr. 16 P = *Schol. Bob.* 172 St; Lintott, 1974, 66 n. 60.

[115] Asc. 48 C on *Mil.* 37; *Aer. Al. Mil.* 13 P = *Schol. Bob.* 172 St.

[116] The dating results from the Bobbio scholiast's understanding of fr. 16 (172 St.): Cicero asks Clodius if he is going to defer a second time, which the scholiast interprets as even in the present year, that is the canvass for election for 52. Clodius was entitled to hold the office in 53, but probably abandoned candidature in view of the truncated period of office that remained available.

[117] *Schol. Bob.* 169–70 St.; cf. *Aer. Al. Mil.* 6 P.

the speech arose from an attack made by Clodius on Milo and Cicero in the senate, accusing both of using violence and bribery and claiming that it was improper for a man who had admitted debts of 6 million sesterces, as Milo had, to be seeking the consulship. Cicero then took advantage of a senator's right to reply (*interrogatio*). He commented on Clodius' humiliating climbdown in abandoning his independence for subordination to Pompey (*Aer. Al. Mil.* 1–3 P). and reviewed his past illegalities including his attacks on Cicero and Pompey in 58 (*Aer. Al. Mil.* 4–11 P).[118] He then looked ahead to Clodius' future plans, in particular his plan to widen the exercise of franchise by freedmen,[119] and finished the speech with a disdainful review of the character Clodius had displayed during his past career (*Aer. Al. Mil.* 19–25 P).[120] This was Cicero's last verbal assault on Clodius during the latter's lifetime. His bitterness against Clodius had been augmented, rather than diminished, by the latter's new alignment. The circumstances of the speech attest, moreover, the extent of Cicero's commitment to Milo.

Asconius warned his readers about the extent to which our *pro Milone* represents what was said at Milo's trial in April (41–2 C). The earlier argumentation is plausible as a plea of justification by reason of self-defence and we can take it as a fair representation of what Cicero said in court;[121] the later claim that Clodius' murder was *pro re publica* was not made in court (*Mil.* 72 ff.; Asc. 41 C) and the same is surely true of the preceding appeal to Pompey about the forces he had deployed to protect the court and his attitude to Milo (*Mil.* 67 ff.). We discover from a later letter of Balbus' that Cicero himself had requested the military protection that Pompey provided on this occasion (*Att.* 9. 7b. 2). Cicero had every reason to be nervous about the attitude of both Pompey and many other members of the elite to Milo. Milo's relations with Pompey had not been improved by Clodius' murder. He received a cool reply when he approached Pompey for a view on his own continued candidature for the consulship. Pompey was also hostile to Caelius when the latter, as tribune, threatened to veto Pompey's new criminal legislation, arguing that the trials were foreshortened and that the new tribunal specifically dealing with murder on the Appian Way was legislation aimed at an individual (a *privilegium*) (Asc. 35–6 C). Cicero's persistence in defending Milo under these circumstances deserves Asconius' favourable comment (Asc. 38 C). However, in the speech he delivered he chose to depoliticize the trial—probably the only practical course in the circumstances, but one

---

[118] Cf. *Schol. Bob.* 170–2St.
[119] *Schol. Bob.* 172–3 St; *Aer. Al. Mil.* 16–18 P; cf. *Mil.* 87; Asc. 52 C.
[120] Cf. *Schol. Bob.* 173–4 St.
[121] Ch. IX with nn. 41–2; Riggsby, 1999, 105–12.

that also suited Pompey and the prosecution. His performance at the trial was by his standards feeble, but that was not surprising in face of the hostility of the mass of Clodian supporters mourning their hero.[122]

The published defence of Milo may seem to distance Cicero from Pompey, but we can be in no doubt that, once the crisis of Milo's trials was over, Cicero appreciated the effect of Pompey's third consulship. It would not have been so much because of the judicial legislation, even though in the end this led to the condemnation of some of Cicero's enemies as well as Milo, nor because of the measures about provincial government that led to his own departure from Rome, but simply because of the security to the *res publica* that it afforded. In the published defence of Milo he argues that the purpose of Pompey's military powers was to cure and strengthen those parts of the *res publica* that were sick and failing (*Mil.* 68).[123] Pompey had now done what was proposed for Scipio in his dream in *De Re Publica*.

There is, moreover, half hidden in the period between the end of 54 and the beginning of Cicero's proconsulship in 51, a significant political realignment that brought Cicero closer to him. In October 50, with civil war looming, Cicero discussed with Atticus in a letter the question of preventing Caesar being a consular candidate while retaining his army. Could he speak against Caesar, he asks. 'Where are those clasped hands? For I helped him to obtain this concession, when requested to help with the tribune Caelius by the man himself at Ravenna. By the man himself? By my friend Gnaeus also in that divine third consulship.'[124] This letter is our only evidence for an important piece of Ciceronian diplomacy, which must fall between the election of Pompey to his third consulship on the 26th of the intercalary month at the end of February and Caesar's departure to Transalpine Gaul probably by the end of the third week in March—thus before the date of Milo's trial on 4 April.[125]

As Pompey's legate, Cicero conveniently had the right to leave Italy. The matter in question was the tribunician bill granting Caesar the right to stand for the consulship in his absence, which seems to have been a concession by Pompey to Caesar in order to avoid any possibility of his intervention by proxy in the politics of his third consulship. There had apparently been

---

[122] Asc. 41–2 C, cf. Lintott, 1974, 74 with n. 135 on the misleading criticism in the secondary sources. The notion that Cicero panicked in the face of Pompey's troops is surely an error, perhaps an inference from *Mil.* 67. In fact, Cicero himself requested some of Pompey's troops as a bodyguard (*Att.* 9. 7b. 2; *Fam.* 3. 10. 10).

[123] For the medical imagery see also *Att.* 4. 3. 3; 9. 5. 2; Syme, 1986, 448.

[124] *Att.* 7. 1. 4. See also *Att.* 8. 3. 3 on Pompey's urgent recommendation of the Law of the Ten Tribunes.

[125] Asc. 36 C; Caes. *BG* 7. 6. 1, cf. 8. 2; Lintott, 1974, 73.

suggestions that Caesar too should be elected consul.[126] Caelius was supporting Cicero and Milo and might from his current firmly optimate position have used his veto to block the bill. Cicero must have persuaded him not to intervene and as a result the bill was passed in the name of all ten tribunes (App. 4). As for Cicero, there was probably the reward of election to the augurate in place of Crassus' son Publius, killed in the defeat by the Parthians of his father's army at Carrhae, if the election is to be dated in Pompey's third consulship.[127]

By the beginning of 51 Cicero does seem to have achieved that *otium* he so desired. His greatest enemy was safely dead. He went so far as to date his arrival at Ephesus on 22 July 51 as on the five hundred and sixtieth day after the battle of Bovillae (*Att.* 5. 13. 1). Pompey's 'divine third consulship' had apparently brought promise of a stable *res publica*, secure in the optimate interest. Two of the tribunes who had attacked him while he supported Milo, Pompeius Rufus and Titus Munatius Plancus, had themselves been condemned for violence.[128] He had joined in the prosecution of Plancus and in a letter of February to Marcus Marius he expresses delight that the man had been condemned in spite of Pompey's support for him (*Fam.* 7. 2. 2–3).[129] In the same letter he comments on the mass of forensic business that occupied him (ibid. 4). However, within a short time he had been appointed by the senate to govern Cilicia under the new arrangements introduced by Pompey's legislation the previous year.[130] The separation of provincial government from office at home entailed that appointments had to be made from former magistrates who had not taken up provincial commands at the time.[131] There was no excuse through which he could evade this task. If he was to be true to his new position as an elder statesman in the restored *res publica*, where Pompey and his optimate opponents were reconciled, he had both to accept the task and to perform it well.

---

[126] Dio 40. 50. 3–4.   [127] MRR iii. 209.
[128] *Phil.* 6. 10; 13. 27; *Fam.* 8. 1. 4; Val. Max. 4. 2. 7; Dio 40. 55.
[129] See also Dio 40. 55, including (4) criticism of Cicero's oratorical performance.
[130] First attested in a letter to Appius Claudius, which must have swiftly followed the appointment (*Fam.* 3. 2).
[131] *Fam.* 8. 8. 8; Caes. *BCiv.* 1. 85. 9; Dio 40. 56. 1.

XV

The Governor and the Approach of Civil War

THE RELUCTANT GOVERNOR

CICERO's appointment in Cilicia was unwanted and unexpected, as he himself wrote to Appius Claudius early in 51 (*Fam.* 3. 2. 1). Presumably, it had been decided that Cilicia and Syria needed consular governors because of the Parthian threat and there had then been an allotment (cf. *Fam.* 8. 8. 8) leading to the selection of him and Bibulus. Under the *lex Pompeia* the appointment was to be for a year unless there was prorogation. Cicero made no haste to arrive—assisted by the fact that his predecessor Appius was in no hurry to leave—and was continually urging his correspondents to ensure that his command was not prorogued.[1] His world was the forum, the city, and the Italy of his villas and friends.[2] Moreover, he did not wish to be absent when the issue of Caesar's relationship to Pompey's new dispensation had to be decided.

There were potential perils for him in any provincial governorship. After his years pleading in the *quaestio de repetundis*, first against Verres and then for a multitude of defendants, it would have been tempting to a number of his enemies to see him the centrepiece of one of these trials. There were more specific hostages to fortune: he had left a number of pronouncements in his writings, which might be embarrassingly remembered by his friends or, worse, turned against him by a prosecutor. When he first arrived at Ephesus on 22 July and was received by a mass of both Greeks and Roman tax-collectors, he commented: 'I am sure that you realize from this that my professions over many years have now been brought to the test' (*Att.* 5. 13. 1).

First, there were his letters of advice to Quintus (*QF* 1. 1–2), when the latter was governor of Asia during and after his praetorship (61–59 BC). The first was written in mainly general terms and clearly for public consumption; its

---

[1] See e.g. *Att.* 5. 9. 2; 11. 1, 5; 13. 3; 14. 1; 15. 1 & 3; 17. 5; 18. 1; *Fam.* 2. 7. 4, 10. 4; 3. 8. 9; 15. 9. 2, 14. 5.
[2] The classic texts are *Fam.* 2. 12. 2 to Caelius and *Planc.* 65–6. See also *Att.* 5. 11. 1, 15. 1.

artificiality is patent from its admission that it was written when Quintus was already in his third year as governor and that he needed little advice.³ Here Cicero stressed the glory, indeed the quasi-divine status in Greek eyes, of the governor who controlled himself and was firm with others (1. 1. 2–9). This required him to take responsibility for his staff and entourage, in particular controlling his freedman *accensus*, chief secretary (10–14), and being selective in friendship with Greeks (15–16). At the same time he urged Quintus to show *humanitas*, to be approachable and mild in his behaviour, a point, he suggested, on which his brother could be faulted (21–2, 37–9). There was little about the substance of Quintus' conduct. He had maintained security and liberated cities from unnecessary financial burdens, allowing them to revive— the burdens including contributions for games at Rome and a temple celebrating Cicero himself (24–6). The one specific topic over which Cicero showed some urgency was Quintus' treatment of the companies of tax-collectors: he was exhorted to help them as far as and beyond what the law allowed by reconciling them to the tax-payers (32–4).⁴ The second letter to Quintus was clearly a private letter whose material was in part a critical counterpart to the first. Instead of the recommendation to keep the *accensus* under control (1. 1. 13) we find a complaint about the arrogance of Quintus' freedman Statius (1. 2. 1–3). Instead of the advocacy of conciliatory behaviour towards Greeks (1. 1. 21–2) we find a catalogue of both Greeks and Romans whom Cicero has sought to conciliate because Quintus has offended them by combining severity of action with brutality of language (1. 2. 4–7). Quintus' conduct in Asia had fallen short of Cicero's ideal. Would he himself match his earlier professions?

Cicero had more recently tackled the problem of how to treat the allies in the empire in *De Re Publica*—in circulation according to Caelius (*Fam.* 8. 1. 4) about the time of his departure. In a letter to Atticus (6. 1. 8) he says that he has bound himself with these books like guarantors.⁵ In Book 3 Laelius had argued for a justice that was altruistic and made it proper for superior persons to rule the inferior (Ch. XIV with nn. 74–6). Further discussion about just behaviour may have arisen from the portrait of the *moderator* in Book V. The philosophical approach to provincial administration was in fact anticipated in the first letter to Quintus (27), where Cicero urged, following a proposition in Plato's *Republic*, that Quintus should protect and seek the greatest happiness of those entrusted to him.⁶ The reader of the letters may find the frequent

---

³ *QF* 1. 1. 2, 8, 18, 30.   ⁴ Cf. ibid. 6 on the connection of Cicero with their members.
⁵ See also *Att.* 6. 2. 9 on justice to provincials and 7. 3. 2 on the attitude of the supreme statesman to a triumph.
⁶ Plato, *Rep.* 1. 346 E. Note the later reference (*QF* 1. 1. 29) to Plato's doctrine that the truly happy state will require its rulers to be philosophers.

references to Cicero's abstinence and refusal to exploit Rome's allies repetitive, even nauseous in their self-satisfaction. It was not, Cicero claims, a matter of virtue competing with pleasure: he enjoyed his own integrity (*Att.* 5. 20. 6).[7] We should also allow, however, for a genuine nervousness in the minds of both Cicero and Atticus that there should be no material for Cicero's detractors. Cicero's fulsome self-praise may have been in part an expression of relief.

A more immediate threat to both Bibulus and Cicero was the Parthian army, which seemed likely to follow up its success against Crassus at Carrhae. Cicero had had no love for Crassus himself, especially at the time of his departure from Rome, but he had genuine affection for his son Publius.[8] Whatever the deserts of Crassus and his son, neither Cicero nor Bibulus would have welcomed having his head, as Crassus' was, employed as a prop in a concert performance of an extract from Euripides' *Bacchae*.[9] Fortunately the Parthians were slow to follow up their victory and did not immediately commit a major force across the Euphrates.[10] For a time no news was good news (*Att.* 5. 9. 1, 11. 4, 16. 4). When after Cicero's arrival in Cilicia the threat became fact, C. Cassius in Antioch was able first to resist and then to secure a victory.[11] Cicero, accordingly, took with him two *legati* of considerable military experience, C. Pomptinus, who had eventually in 54 secured his triumph for Gallic victories eight years earlier,[12] and his brother Quintus.[13] The latter had recently finished his service with Caesar in Gaul and the strain of his long absences showed in his relations with his wife Pomponia on his return.[14]

Cicero also had the benefit of a three-day consultation with Pompey at Tarentum before he left (*Fam.* 5. 5. 2; 5. 7. 1). The latter no doubt combined briefing about the Parthians and Cilicia, a province which in its present form he had himself created, with commendations of the neighbouring kings who were his clients. Cicero must have later appeared to be Pompey's man to kings like Deiotarus of Galatia and Ariobarzanes of Cappadocia. However, what was more important, Pompey revealed in these discussions his attitude to future

---

[7] Further references to it in 5. 10. 2, 11. 5, 14. 2, 16. 3, 17. 2, 18. 2, 21. 5, 7; 6. 1. 3; *Fam.* 15. 1. 3, 4. 14–15.

[8] *Att.* 4. 13. 2; *Fam.* 5. 8. 4; 13. 16.

[9] Plut. *Crass.* 33. 2–7.

[10] Dio 40. 28–9; *Att.* 5. 18. 1; *Fam.* 15. 1. 2.

[11] *Att.* 5. 20. 3; *Fam.* 15. 14. 5. According to Dio (40. 29), the Parthians were off their guard as they retreated, after failing also to take Antigoneia.

[12] *Att.* 5. 1. 5, 4. 2; cf. 4. 18. 4; *QF* 3. 4. 6; Dio 39. 65.

[13] See e.g. *Att.* 5. 10. 5; 20. 5. The other two were M. Anneius and L. Tullius (5. 4. 2). Q. Volusius was to perform a *legatus*' job, dispensing jurisdiction in Cyprus (5. 21. 6).

[14] Caes. *BG* 7. 90 shows Quintus still in Gaul in autumn 52. For his return and the disastrous lunch-party with his family see *Att.* 5. 1. 3–4. Pomponia had no doubt been managing Quintus' affairs in Italy since his departure in 57, as she had previously from 61 to 58, and unsurprisingly was reluctant to revert to submissiveness.

politics at Rome: 'I am leaving him behind as an outstanding citizen and very well prepared to resist the threats that are feared.'[15] Cicero is enigmatic and so no doubt was Pompey, but it is clear that Pompey showed that he did not wish his settlement of the *res publica* to be put in jeopardy by Caesar's conduct at the end of his command in Gaul. Cicero uses similar language when replying later to a question by Caelius about Pompey's attitude towards the succession to the Gallic provinces (*Fam.* 2. 8. 2; cf. 8. 1. 2–3). It seems that Pompey has already become more hostile to Caesar and that Cicero does not simply acquiesce but approves. He was to face the implications for his own relationship to Caesar on his return to Italy. For the moment he needed to be kept up to date with the political prospects in Rome and commissioned his friend Caelius to do this (*Fam.* 8. 8. 1; 2. 8. 1).

There was, moreover, preparation for his civil administration in Cilicia. For administrative advice Cicero had as his *accensus* Lentulus Spinther's freedman Pausanias (*Fam.* 3. 7. 4–5). Cicero obtained from Atticus in Italy a copy of a previous edict, probably that of P. Servilius Isauricus (*cos.* 79) for Cilicia.[16] He had also read the edict of Q. Mucius Scaevola (*cos.* 95) for the province of Asia and followed this in many of his own provisions, including that of allowing cases between Greeks to be heard by Greeks (*Att.* 6.1.15). A chapter was to be added from Appius Claudius' edict after Cicero met a delegation of tax-collectors on Samos (*Fam.* 3. 8. 4).

CILICIA

Cicero did not find the sea-voyages on his outward journey comfortable (*Att.* 5. 9. 1; 5. 12. 1). He knew Greece from his youth and was fluent in its language; his ten-day stay in Athens was particularly enjoyable (5. 10. 5). However, it was one thing to be travelling as a private citizen, another as a Roman proconsul with *imperium*. Although Greece was not his province, he might have been asked to exercise his power there.[17] He felt it improper to

---

[15] *Att.* 5. 7. 1. For *civis* describing a man devoted to the republic and civic values cf. Caelius on Cicero (*Fam.* 8. 17. 1); Lucan 9. 190 (Cato's elegy of Pompey); Tac. *Ann.* 1. 33; 2. 82 for the *civilia ingenia* of Drusus Caesar and his son Germanicus.

[16] *Att.* 5. 3. 2. The text is corrupt, the majority of the MSS reading *publii* or *publilii*. Editors have restored *P. Licinii* as a reference to the consul of 131 who commanded in the then new province of Asia, but we may wonder if Licinius Crassus Mucianus ever produced an edict before he was killed while seeking to recover the province from Aristonicus, and for Cicero the later Asian edict of Scaevola was more relevant. *P. Seruilii* seems preferable, as Cicero evidently knew Isauricus' methods (*Att.* 6. 1. 16).

[17] Cf. Plut. *Cim.* 1. 6; Val. Max. 8. 1. *Amb.* 2. It is implicit in *RS* i. 12, Cnidos IV. 31–9.

arrive at Patras on small boats without his baggage (5. 9. 1); after his full staff (*cohors*) had joined him at Athens, he needed a small fleet to transport them, their slaves, and other possessions across the Aegean (5. 11. 4). Apart from his quaestor, *accensus*, and *legati*, there were the tribunes of the soldiers and, in theory military, prefects to whom he had given posts.[18] There were also 'companions', including his son and nephew who were on the verge of manhood.[19] He was upset at the arrogant way some of his staff treated the Greeks at Athens (5. 10. 3).

Once the other side of the Aegean, he was surprised by the attention he received. On Samos and at Ephesus, before he even reached his province, crowds gathered to meet him and deputations from communities and individuals visited him. At Ephesus in particular the tax-collectors came about his edict (*Att.* 5. 13. 1, 5. 14. 2; *Fam.* 3. 8. 4). He was already commemorated on Samos by a monument in a prime position in one of the most famous religious precincts of the ancient world—an exedra with bronze statues of himself and his family some 25 metres from the steps at the east end of the temple of Hera, presumably erected during his brother's governorship of Asia.[20] The Samians had special reason to be grateful to Cicero for incorporating Verres' depredation of their shrine in his prosecution of Verres (*2Verr.* 1. 50–2). According to a later letter to Caelius, he was also to find that as a result of the Catilinarian conspiracy he had a reputation as a capable magistrate even in Cilicia (*Fam.* 2. 10. 2).

The letters from the period of Cicero's governorship reveal more about his own concerns than Cilicia. At times Cicero seems to be in a bubble of his own, as he moves from one end of the province to another. The letters to the senate and magistrates and one letter to Cato are the most informative about his military and diplomatic activity.[21] Regarding his judicial and administrative duties we hear about one or two special problems and can draw inferences from the general descriptions of his conduct, but we lack the quantity of detail to be found later in Pliny's correspondence with Trajan: for example, we have no description of any of the numerous court cases which came before Cicero.

Travelling from Ephesus up the Maeander valley, he reached the first city in his province, Laodicea, on 31 July (*Att.* 5. 15. 1). There he obtained from the

---

[18] Prefects in 5. 11. 6, 21. 10; 6. 1. 4; *Fam.* 3. 6. 5, 7. 4. Some prefectures were intended to be sinecures for people who would not even leave Italy, as were those appointed by Pompey (5. 4. 3, 7. 2).

[19] See e.g. *Att.* 5. 17. 3, 18. 4 and on the *cohors* of companions (*comites*) in general, *Imp. Rom.* 51–2.

[20] Dörner and Gruben, 1953. Cicero later presented his translation of Plato's *Timaeus* as a dialogue held at Ephesus with Nigidius Figulus, then on his return from a post as *legatus*, and the Peripatetic philosopher Cratippus (*Tim.* 1–2).

[21] Though not without artifice, see Hutchinson, 1998, 86 ff. on *Fam.* 15. 4.

tax-collectors the cash voted him from public funds by means of a *permutatio*, an instrument of exchange (*Fam.* 3. 5. 4). His province was disjointed and something of a patchwork, combining parts of the old province of Asia—including Pamphylia and Lycaonia—with Isauria, conquered by P. Servilius in the 70s, and at the eastern end, abutting on Syria, Cilicia in the plain. It was divided geographically by the Taurus mountains and politically by the kingdoms of Cappadocia and Derbe through one of which he had to pass if he was to travel from the western to the eastern section by land. The link was the road from the Maeander valley to the pass in the Taurus mountains through the Cilician gates, one of the two main routes to the East, along which Cicero, like his predecessor, spent much of his time moving.[22] His plan had been to devote the summer to military matters, the winter to jurisdiction (*Att.* 5. 14. 2), but the nature of provincial government was such that problems were brought to the governor without his seeking them out. So we find him immediately complaining that he was required to perform jurisdiction in Laodicea while the undistinguished Aulus Plotius had the authoritative post of *praetor urbanus* at Rome (*Att.* 5. 15. 1). In the event, according to a letter to Atticus, though eager to press on to the Taurus he spent three days each at Laodicea, Apamea, and Synnada, five days at Philomelium, and ten at Iconium before moving to a camp nearby on 24 August.[23]

He was immediately confronted with the problems that Appius was leaving behind. These are doubly documented—in his letters to Atticus and the uneasy correspondence he had with his predecessor. While still at Tralles at the end of July he discovered that the contracts with the *publicani* had been fixed, also that Appius had suppressed a mutiny and paid the soldiers up to 15 July.[24] His next two letters to Atticus complain about the two undermanned legions—a contrast with Pompey's forces—and the wounds inflicted by Appius on the province: the cities had already sold the right to collect their taxes (and spent the money), now they were forced to inflict poll-taxes as well; as for Appius, he had gone to the other end of the province (5. 15. 1–2, 5. 16. 2–3).[25]

There is more detail in the correspondence with Appius. Cicero was puzzled to find that the governor, who had suggested through his freedman Phania and L. Clodius his *praefectus fabrum* that Cicero should enter the

---

[22] Syme, 1939*b*, 121–4. There is a helpful map in S. Mitchell, *Anatolia*, 1993, i. 41.
[23] *Att.* 5. 16. 2; 20. 1; *Fam.* 3. 7. 4, 8. 5–6. The sums clearly do not work unless one includes travelling time in the stay as O. E. Schmidt, 1893, 77–9 pointed out.
[24] *Att.* 5. 14. 1. The *pactiones* were probably those for the collection of the *tributum* exacted locally by the cities themselves, see *Imp. Rom.* 77, 207–8.
[25] See *Imp. Rom.* 77–8, 208 on the means used by cities to raise the money they were due to pay the Romans.

province through Laodicea, made at first no effort to meet him, although he was required by a law of Sulla to leave the province within thirty days of his successor's arrival: instead he was at Tarsus holding an assize and three of the best manned cohorts were with him (*Fam.* 3. 6. 1–5, 3. 8. 5).[26] While Cicero was encamped near Iconium, Appius passed near him on his return journey along the main road, but—Cicero claims this was not his fault—he moved on from Iconium before Cicero could meet him (*Fam.* 3. 7. 4). Cicero's first letters are masterpieces of tact, combining assurances of their unity in friendship with expressions of pained surprise at Appius' behaviour.

After Appius had passed him on his way home, he replied to his complaints with greater forthrightness. In a letter of October from near Tarsus he admitted that he had checked the granting of large grants of expenses by the cities to envoys who were to sing Appius' praises at Rome, because these envoys might find their journey useless and their cities were insolvent. He was afraid that these unnecessary expenses might lead the cities to sell their rights to collect taxes, presumably in advance, and to impose poll taxes and taxes on doors (*Fam.* 3. 8. 2–5). As for the provincial gossip about his hostility to Appius, he had done nothing to encourage it, though he was prepared to tolerate criticisms of Appius' subordinates. His rescinding of Appius' measures should not have been taken to indicate a breach between them (ibid. 5–8). The apologia was clearly somewhat disingenuous, given that in an earlier letter to the senate and magistrates which must have been known to Appius, he had complained that the disaffection in Cilicia had been caused by the oppressive behaviour of the Roman administration (*Fam.* 15. 1. 5) and he was repeating this criticism of Appius in a letter to Atticus of February the next year (*Att.* 6. 1. 2).[27]

Appius was not immediately mollified. A letter from him was brought to Cicero by an embassy from the Appiani in Phrygia who complained that their building plans, presumably of a monument honouring Appius, had been hampered by their inability to exact contributions (*Fam.* 3. 7. 2–3).[28] In replying Cicero referred to a conversation that Appius had apparently held with his *accensus* Pausanias at Iconium, protesting that Cicero had omitted the normal courtesy between an incoming and an outgoing governor: 'Appius

---

[26] While still in Italy Cicero had been first advised by Phania to go by sea to Tarsus, but L. Clodius had later overruled this, saying that Appius would meet him at Laodicea. Scaevola, probably one of Appius' *legati*, had apparently anticipated being left in charge on his departure, but Cicero met him at Ephesus (*Fam.* 3. 5. 3–5).

[27] Cf. *Att.* 5. 16. 2 for his initial reaction. He maintained to Atticus that he had no personal enmity with Appius (6. 2. 10) and by this time that may be strictly true.

[28] The Appiani were later in the *conventus* of Synnada (Pliny, *HN* 5. 105). Their name must derive from Appius or an ancestor of his, see Rawson, 1991, 117.

went to meet Lentulus, Lentulus went to meet Ampius, Cicero did not deign to meet Appius.'[29] Cicero took this as an aristocratic assertion of status and ridiculed any talk of 'Appiusness' and 'Lentulusness' in comparison with claims of achievement: he had held the highest office and was Appius' equal (ibid. 4–5).[30] To judge from the rest of the correspondence Appius was henceforth less acrimonious, probably because he was nervous about impending prosecutions and did not wish Cicero to give any support to them.[31] When Dolabella did bring an accusation against him in February 50, he abandoned any hope of a triumph and entered the city to reply to the charge, hoping primarily for support from Cicero.[32]

The vicissitudes of Cicero's military efforts emerge from the official letters he sent to the senate and magistrates and brief comments in letters to Atticus. In the first official letter (*Fam.* 15. 1), written as he entered Cappadocia from Lycaonia, he relays the news sent him by three of Rome's allied kings that the Parthians have in fact invaded Syria: in response he is marching to the Taurus and Cilicia (in the plain) to demonstrate his clemency and integrity and confront those Cilicians who have already taken up arms in anticipation of a general rebellion against Rome (ibid. 1–3).[33] The rest of the letter is a cry of distress, frankly admitting Cicero's fears. The authorities should at long last take a proper interest in the Asiatic provinces, on which the taxes of the Roman people depend. His forces are desperately under strength; he cannot rely on levies from the local Roman citizens (Bibulus has refused to hold a levy in Syria); as for help from the allies, they are either weakened by the harshness of Roman rule or so alienated that their help was either not be expected or not to be trusted (ibid. 4–5). The eloquent passages in the text are worthy of the *Verrines* or the speech in favour of the Manilian law, but Cicero's criticism of Roman imperial methods is here designed to create an escape-route in case of failure for himself, if he survived, or at least for his reputation.

A second official dispatch, written on or shortly before 20 September, was evidently designed to erase any impression of panic that the first might have caused. By this time Cicero was in camp at Cybistra near the pass across the Taurus. His forces were still small, but he was expecting help from Deiotarus (*Fam.* 15. 2. 2). According to a contemporaneous letter to Atticus, this

---

[29] See *MRR* iii. 15 for an explanation of how T. Ampius Balbus, proconsul of Asia in 58, came to be in Cilicia in 57.

[30] It may be thought that Appius' actual words did not necessarily bear Cicero's interpretation, but no doubt Pausanias had described Appius' demeanour as he had said this.

[31] *Fam.* 3. 10. 5, 3. 11. 1–3, 3. 12. 1; cf. 2. 13. 2.

[32] *Fam.* 8. 6. 1; Caelius advised Cicero to provide it.

[33] Cf. *Fam.* 15. 3, written to Cato from Iconium, for the message from Antiochus of Commagene that the Parthians were beginning to cross the Euphrates.

reinforcement would double Cicero's army: Cicero had nonetheless prudently entrusted his son and nephew to Deiotarus' care in Galatia.[34] However, the main theme of the letter was a diplomatic success. Cicero had been urged by a decree of the senate to protect the young Ariobarzanes of Cappadocia (*Fam.* 15. 2. 4, cf. 4. 6). On visiting the king he was first told that there was no threat to Ariobarzanes' life. Then on the following day the king informed him that his brother Ariarathes had now confessed to having being approached by conspirators who wished him to supplant the king. Cicero refused a request to allocate the king infantry and cavalry from his own forces and merely urged him to use his royal authority against the conspirators—we may wonder if he cited his own conduct in 63 (*Fam.* 15. 2. 5–7). In the epilogue he congratulates the magistrates and senate on their foresight and himself for his epiphany at the right moment through an unbelievable and almost divine stroke of fortune (ibid. 8).

It appears from a later letter to Cato about his achievements that Cato had proposed the senate decree about Cappadocia and had personally commended to Cicero two royal advisers; Athenais, the queen dowager, had driven these advisers into exile but, while at Cybistra, Cicero had secured their recall and the removal from the kingdom of the young high priest of Ma-Bellona at Comana who was also a potential threat. Cicero regarded the kingdom as part of Cato's *clientela* and so was particularly anxious to impress Cato with his services there.[35]

By the time Cicero wrote this letter, however, he had much more to celebrate. While at Cybistra he discovered that his praetorian cohort and cavalry at Epiphanea near the Syrian border had cut to pieces an invading force of Parthian cavalry, and he moved immediately across the Taurus to join them. Here there were no longer Parthians but he successively attacked three towns in the Amanus range and then the capital of the 'Free Cilicians', Pindenissus (*Fam.* 15. 4. 7–10). This town succumbed after a siege of 56 days. Cicero's pretexts were their disaffection and sympathy with the Parthians and their reception of runaway slaves (ibid. 10).[36] In fact, apart from making a further demonstration of Roman power to the Parthians, he was not averse to military glory himself and no doubt wished to reward his forces and convince them that they had been recruited to some purpose. This is evident in a letter he wrote to Atticus on the Saturnalia, the day Pindenissus surrendered. The soldiers had enjoyed a happy Saturnalia since Cicero conceded

---

[34] *Att.* 5. 18. 2, 4, cf. 5. 17. 3.   [35] *Fam.* 15. 4. 6, 15; [Caes]. *Bell. Afr.* 66. 3–4.
[36] *Fugitivi* should have its normal meaning of runaway slaves. See *Att.* 5. 15. 3 for Cicero's earlier joke about fighting the Free Cilician leader Moeragenes over one who had run away from Atticus.

them all the booty except the persons captured, whom he later sold as slaves. As for Cicero, he had been hailed 'commander' (*imperator*) after victory at the Amanus and had encamped at Issus where Alexander the Great—'a considerably better commander than you or I'—encamped before his battle with Darius. Meanwhile, he maintains, the news of his arrival had induced the Parthians to retreat and Cassius to break out of Antioch and defeat them; Bibulus on the other hand had lost a cohort in battle on the Syrian side of the Amanus (*Att.* 5. 20. 3, 5).[37]

The portrayal of Cicero's forces varies from letter to letter and even within letters. In the first letter to the senate and magistrates they were weak and unreliable (*Fam.* 15. 1. 5). In this letter to Cato, he writes first that he had collected an adequate force from Roman veterans he had levied and allied volunteers, indeed he had actually sent the bulk of Deiotarus' forces away. However, he later claims credit for defending the province through fair dealing and self-discipline in spite of a weak army (ibid. 4. 3, 14). Here he is clearly appealing to Cato's Stoic belief in control of appetite. In practice, it would have been sensible policy to minimize the burden on allies by avoiding both forced levies and the impact on the civilian population of a large army. If the army was weak, this was in part Cicero's own choice.

After his victory Cicero went back to Laodicea, where he had first entered the province, leaving Quintus to winter the troops in the area just conquered (*Att.* 5. 20. 5; 5. 21. 6). On his return there in February he was already looking forward to the end of his command, with his programme planned until his departure on 28 July (ibid. 9): as he wrote to Caelius in April, 'An amazing longing has come over me for the city, my people, and you especially, at the same time weariness with the province, perhaps because I have achieved such a reputation, that I should not be seeking to supplement it but rather should fear any risk to it, perhaps because the whole task is not worthy of my powers, who can and am accustomed to undertake greater burdens in public affairs, perhaps because the threat of a major war is impending, which I seem likely to escape, if I depart on the date that has been fixed' (*Fam.* 2. 11. 1). He was to hold the assizes of all the dioceses west of the Taurus at Laodicea, finishing by mid-May. He would then make his way back to the east end of the province (the Taurus could not be crossed before June).[38] For the moment Laodicea was conveniently located for communication with Rome and Athens (where Atticus was expected) and also a few miles from the hot springs of Hierapolis

---

[37] See *Fam.* 2. 10 for a progress report in the middle of the siege to Caelius; 15. 14 for Cicero's letter of congratulation to Cassius.
[38] *Att.* 5. 21. 9, 14, 6. 2. 6.

(Pamukkale). It would, however, have been a long journey for the some of the litigants to come there.

Apart from the regular process of jurisdiction, much of which would have been a preliminary hearing of private cases before entrusting them to one or more judges, as with the *praetor urbanus* and *peregrinus* at Rome,[39] Cicero both intervened and refrained from intervening in the administration of the cities. On the way back from his campaign in the winter he dealt with the famine arising from the poor harvest in the province by urging those who held grain-supplies to make them available to the community (*Att.* 5. 21. 8). He did not interfere in the local civil jurisdiction of the cities where only Greeks were involved. 'The Greeks are exultant because they have access to native judges. "Worthless ones surely," you will say. What does it matter? They think they have achieved autonomy. Our citizens, I suppose, have really responsible ones in Turpio the shoemaker and Vettius the contractor' (*Att.* 6. 1. 15). The Greeks, he judged, were happy to have this veneer of independence and to be free of debt.

The cities clearly profited from his intervention as much as from his abstinence. Cicero ascribes their solvency partly to the fact that he did not require them to spend money on him or his staff, partly to a by-product of his jurisdiction at Laodicea, which in public matters to some extent became as much administration or negotiation as the delivery of judgments. He had imposed the standard 12% per annum interest rates for reasonably prompt payment of tax arrears (otherwise the debtors had to pay the extortionate rates in their contracts). Furthermore, while handling the claims of the tax-collectors against the cities Cicero discovered that the city magistrates had been embezzling money over the last ten years (probably through the sale of the rights to farm taxes in their locality). Cicero persuaded these men to return the money and so enable the cities to pay off the tax arrears for the last two five-year periods (*lustra*). 'So I am the favourite of the *publicani*. "Men who know about gratitude," you say. I am well aware of it' (*Att.* 6. 2. 4–5).[40]

While he could do justice to the tax-collectors, it was more difficult to satisfy the avidity of his friends. The story of the people of Salamis on Cyprus is a notorious example of a particular kind of imperial corruption, emerging from a series of letters to Atticus.[41] The Salaminians had sent an

---

[39] *Imp. Rom.* 57 ff. That the civil jurisdiction he had to perform was primarily for cases involving Roman citizens is clear from his account of the despatch of Volusius to Cyprus, 'in order that the few Roman businessmen there could not claim that they had not received jurisdiction' (*Att.* 5. 21. 6).
[40] Cf. *Att.* 6. 1. 16; *Fam.* 2. 13. 3; and on his abstinence *Att.* 5. 20. 6, 5. 21. 5, 7.
[41] *Att.* 5. 21. 10–12, 6. 1. 5–7, 6. 2. 7–9, 6. 3. 5.

embassy to Rome in 56, following Cato's organization of the island as a province, perhaps to plead for some special status. They needed to borrow money, but this was forbidden by a law of Gabinius' designed to prevent provincials being induced to borrow money in order to hand out bribes. Friends of Brutus were nevertheless prepared to oblige—at an extortionate rate of interest, four times the normal rate of 12% with annual compounding—provided they were granted a *privilegium*, immunity from the consequences under Gabinius' law. A first decree of the senate, passed through Brutus' influence, granted them immunity from prosecution; they then realized that they needed exemption from the clause in the law that made any such loan-contract invalid, and this was duly provided by a second decree (*Att.* 5. 21. 10–11).

Six years later the Salaminians owed a sum that they calculated to be 106 talents at the rate of interest set out in the governor's edict (12% with annual compounding), roughly 2.5 million Roman sesterces, but Brutus' friend Scaptius, using the interest rate in the contract, was seeking around 5 million. Scaptius had received the title of *praefectus* and some squadrons of cavalry from Appius, Brutus' father-in-law, in order to force the Salaminians to pay up what they owed (ibid. 10). He had besieged the Salaminian senate in their senate-house until five members died of starvation (*Att.* 6. 1. 5, 6. 2. 8). Cicero stripped Scaptius of his force after hearing a Cypriot embassy at Ephesus (6. 1. 5, 6. 2. 9). Once he had reached Tarsus, he began to negotiate with the parties. The Salaminians were willing to pay up: their debt, they said, was less than the levy they had been paying to the governor (*Att.* 5. 21.10–12). As Cicero had told Atticus earlier, he had put an end to the practice whereby every year before his governorship cities had been paying money to avoid having troops billeted on them; the Cypriots as a whole had paid 200 talents (*Att.* 5. 21. 7). However, Scaptius, though he agreed that the Salaminians' calculation according to Cicero's edict was correct, did not want to accept the sum and asked Cicero to leave the matter as it was, hoping that under another governor he might get the interest laid down in the contract. Cicero permitted this and did not even allow the Salaminians to deposit their repayment in a religious shrine. He recognized that Scaptius' demand was shameless, but felt that he had done as much as he could for Brutus, especially as there had been a recent decree of the senate requiring that an interest rate of 12% without compounding should be preserved: certainly his conduct would be approved by Brutus' uncle Cato (ibid. 12–13).[42]

Cicero is still defending himself at length in the second letter to Atticus written a week after the first. He had now learnt that the money was not owed

[42] Cf. *Att.* 6. 1. 7.

to Scaptius and his associate Matinius, but had actually been Brutus' own. That had not been clear in an original memorandum Brutus had sent Cicero. This also contained instructions about extracting a debt from Ariobarzanes (perhaps contracted after a similar loan to an embassy). Apparently at his meeting with the king Cicero had refused the offer of a gift and recommended that the money should be used to pay Brutus. However, the king had subsequently been assailed by a horde of Pompey's agents seeking a sum of money, besides which the debts to Brutus seem insignificant. Ariobarzanes was currently paying them 33 Attic talents (800,000 sesterces) a month out of the taxes he raised and that was not even enough for the monthly interest. Cicero had allowed both Scaptius and Gavius the post of prefect in the kingdom (it was not in his province, he maintained: so it did not breach his rule about not giving prefectures to businessmen) (*Att.* 6. 1. 3–4). He later told Atticus that he had treated Brutus somewhat more liberally than Pompey in proportion to the sum owed them: Pompey was promised 200 talents over six months; Brutus had been provided with about 100 talents this year (*Att.* 6. 2. 5).

Cicero's final problem was how to manage his departure from the province in the best possible fashion. There was once again a Parthian threat with their king Orodes himself expected: for Cicero the months of June and July were critical. By the spring of 50 Cicero could envisage leading a larger army than before, thanks to the assistance promised by Deiotarus—15,000 infantry armed like Roman legionaries and 2,000 cavalry (*Att.* 5. 21. 2; 6. 1. 14). With his two reinforced legions and the allied auxiliaries he had used the previous year, he had a considerable force, but he hoped not to have to fight. Owing to the obstruction over provincial appointments (see below), no former praetor could succeed him, as had been envisaged on 29 September 51 (*Fam.* 8. 8. 8). According to the decree that appointed him he was expected to leave after a year after appointing a deputy governor. A new quaestor was coming, C. Coelius Caldus (*Att.* 6. 2. 10, 6. 4. 1); the present one, Mescinius Rufus, was unsuitable (6. 3. 1, 6. 4. 1); Pomptinus had departed early according to a previous arrangement; Cicero's brother was therefore the most appropriate as the experienced military man remaining, but hated the province.[43] On June 7 Cicero reached Tarsus and soon received requests from almost everyone on Bibulus' staff, though not Bibulus himself, to march into Syria to provide assistance. He decided to stay put and defend his own frontier (*Att.* 6. 5. 3). Eventually his tenure ran out; by this time the Parthians had withdrawn, and he gratefully appointed the newly arrived Coelius as his

---

[43] *Att.* 6. 3. 1–2; *Fam.* 2. 15. 4, 3. 10. 3.

successor rather than his brother.[44] He left by sea, suffering a protracted sea voyage via Side, Rhodes, and Ephesus to Athens.[45]

One immediate concern on his journey home was his daughter's betrothal to Cornelius Dolabella, who by prosecuting Appius Claudius had increased the latter's suspicions of Cicero's bad faith.[46] Another was his desire for a triumph. While still in Cilicia he had been decreed by the senate a public thanksgiving (*supplicatio*), which Cato had joined in drafting though he had originally voted against it. He was now hoping for a triumph (*Att*. 7. 1. 7),[47] stimulated by rivalry with Bibulus, who with similar ambitions had in Cicero's view claimed far more than he had actually achieved by blockading himself in Antioch (*Att*. 7. 2. 6). The effusive letter Cicero had written Cato about his achievements in 51, in which he attributed his success to moral virtue and sought to appeal to their mutual interest in philosophy (*Fam*. 15. 4. 14, 16), provoked a brief reply, which the writer claimed nonetheless to be more verbose than was his usual custom.

Complimentary to Cicero but at the same time deftly evasive, Cato ironically suggested that Cicero would not want the senate to congratulate the immortal gods instead of thanking him personally for what depended on his own reason and self-discipline rather than chance—so warning him against a philosophical fallacy. The endorsement of his moral virtue was surely better than a triumph won through a combination of the brute force of his soldiers and divine favour (*Fam*. 15. 5, esp. 2). Cicero sent a somewhat grovelling reply, apologizing for what had appeared to be excessive greed and suggesting that a triumph was something normal that he would not reject if it came his way (*Fam*. 15. 6. 2)—in Stoic terms it would have been fundamentally 'indifferent' but nevertheless to be preferred. He could, he said, have received no greater praise than Cato's letter or the speech he had made in the senate, a copy of which he had read. However, he managed one barb of irony of his own, arguing that he derived the greatest honour and pleasure from the fact that Cato had readily conceded to friendship what he would have conceded to the plain facts of his achievement anyhow (ibid. 1). Caesar congratulated

---

[44] *Att*. 6. 6. 3; *Fam*. 2. 15. 4. Cicero complains about Bibulus' attitude to him in a letter to the latter's *pro quaestore* Sallustius (*Fam*. 2. 17. 6–7). See also *Fam*. 2. 19 for Cicero's welcoming letter to Coelius; *Fam*. 5. 20 for a somewhat irritable letter to Mescinius Rufus from near Rome about business matters that had to be completed after his departure, including the concordance with the quaestor of his accounts, which Cicero had ordered to be deposited at Laodicea and Apamea according to the *lex Iulia de repetundis* (1–2, cf. *Att*. 6. 7. 2, *Fam*. 2. 17. 2). From this (9) we also learn about the surplus from his governorship that Cicero deposited with the *publicani* at Ephesus but soon lent to Pompey, cf. *Att*. 11. 3. 3.

[45] *Att*. 6. 7. 2, 6. 8. 4; *Fam*. 2. 15. 4, 3. 11. 4.

[46] *Att*. 6. 6. 1, 6. 9. 5; cf. 3. 10. 5, and 8. 6. 1 for Dolabella's accusation of Appius Claudius.

[47] Cf. *Fam*. 8. 11. 1–2, 15. 4. 11, 15. 5. 2, 15. 6. 1–2.

Cicero on his *supplicatio*, taking what seemed to Cicero indecent satisfaction (he uses the word 'triumphing') over Cato's opposition (*Att.* 7. 1. 7, cf. 9. 16. 2). This presaged how Cicero's hope of military glory would become lost in a much greater political issue.

CAELIUS, ATTICUS, AND CICERO

Cicero began at last to discuss with Atticus the prospect of real conflict between Caesar and Pompey on his way home. At the end of September a certain Batonius told his aide Lepta at Ephesus that Caesar would not let go his army, he had support from many of the magistrates elected for 49, and Pompey was thinking of leaving the city (*Att.* 6. 8. 2). On landing at Athens on 14 October Cicero received a letter from Atticus informing him that Caesar was expected at Placentia with four legions on the 15th (*Att.* 6. 9. 5). We are largely indebted to the letters of Caelius for our knowledge of the earlier stages of the crisis. He had until then lived up to the promises Cicero had made about him to the jury at his trial (*Cael.* 77–8). He had devoted himself to the optimate cause, supporting Cicero in his defence of Milo and being prepared originally to veto the bill granting Caesar the right to stand for the consulship in his absence.[48] Requested by Cicero to keep him informed about political developments, he delegated to another the provision of a compilation of city news—both events and gossip—while himself providing his own perspective on what he considered the most important issues.[49]

In reply to Caelius' first letter Cicero wrote that what he most expected from him was forecasts about the future. The context is made immediately plain by the reference to his own talks with Pompey at Tarentum and the comment on Pompey as an outstanding citizen, excellently prepared to meet future dangers. He recommended Caelius to embrace Pompey's cause: 'he has now the same perception of good and bad citizens as I do' (*Fam.* 2. 8. 1–2).[50] It is not fortuitous then that this correspondence is so illuminating on the outbreak of the civil war. As Caelius relates in his first letter to Cicero, the consul M. Marcellus had postponed discussing the question of succession to Caesar until June 1 (it may have been raised at the time of the provincial

---

[48] Asc. 33, 36 C and see above Ch. XIV with nn. 123–7.
[49] *Fam.* 8. 1. 1–2; cf. 11. 4 for the commentary on urban events compiled by his aide, which included a rudimentary society page.
[50] Caelius had asked about this interview, requesting Cicero to distinguish between what Pompey said and the intention he displayed. 'For he is accustomed to think one thing and say another, but not be clever enough to conceal what he wants' (*Fam.* 8. 1. 3).

allocations that created Cicero's own appointment). There had also been rumours that Caesar had instructed the cities in Transpadane Gaul that were not communities of Roman citizens to elect magistrates as if they were. As a sign of his disapproval Marcellus had a citizen of Novum Comum flogged to demonstrate his lack of citizenship. He was, however, as Cicero pointed out to Atticus, a Transpadane with Latin rights which he owed to the action of Pompey's father (in 89 BC).[51]

In Caelius' letters the crisis over Caesar is presented as a particularly intriguing titbit in a *hors d'œuvre* of political news and gossip. In 51 Caelius was himself a candidate for the curule aedileship, a magistracy for whose games he wanted a supply of panthers from Cicero. When he wrote on 1 August, his own elections had been delayed (*Fam.* 8. 2. 2, 3. 1, 4. 3). One of the tribunes elect, Servaeus, had been condemned for bribery and this had allowed Curio, Caelius' and Cicero's mutual friend, to stand in the supplementary election. He was unpredictable but Caelius believed him at this point a friend of the 'good men' and the senate, especially as Caesar had rejected his overtures to him.[52] On 22 July the senate had discussed the pay for Pompey's troops and in the debate the legion that Pompey had lent Caesar was mentioned. Pompey found himself forced to say that he would take back the legion after barracking from his critics; discussion of the succession to Caesar was postponed until his return from visiting troops at Ariminum (*Fam.* 8. 4. 4).

Caelius already anticipated a veto in the senate and in a subsequent letter of August or September 51 repeated this warning: any debate about the Gallic provinces would lead to a veto and, as a riposte, another tribune would veto any discussion of the other provinces on the ground that all should be discussed together. This would suit Caesar and all those who pursued their own rather than the public interest (*Fam.* 8. 4. 4, 8. 5. 2–3). By 2 September Caelius had been elected at the expense of Lucilius Hirrus and there had been no discussion of the provinces on account of the bribery trial of the consul-designate C. Marcellus. According to Caelius, Pompey was worried that Caesar should wish to become consul while retaining the Gallic provinces—in the same way that he himself had retained those in Spain while consul—but

---

[51] *Fam.* 8. 1. 2; *Att.* 5. 2. 3, 5. 11. 2 cf. Suet. *Jul.* 28. 3, explaining this as a dispute over Caesar's creation of a new citizen colony at Novum Comum according to provisions in the *lex Vatinia*. If the man had not been a local magistrate who would *ipso facto* have acquired Roman citizenship in view of his previous Latin rights, Marcellus' action was not strictly illegal, since as a Latin the man was not protected by *provocatio*, but it was, as Cicero remarks, disgusting.

[52] *Fam.* 8. 4. 2: Caelius thought it charming that Curio, who was incapable of forward planning, was thought to have plotted cunningly in escaping the opposition of powerful men, 'Laelii and Antonii', presumably planned for next year. Antonius was Caesar's man, Laelius on the side of Pompey and the 'good men', cf. Caes. *BCiv.* 3. 5, 7, 40, 100. But there is no need to emend *Laelios* to *Lollios* with Shackleton Bailey. Neither faction wanted a maverick confusing the contest.

was in no hurry for action. His father-in-law Scipio argued that there should be a debate on March 1 the following year about the Gallic provinces and nothing else, much to the displeasure of Balbus who was acting as Caesar's political manager in Rome (*Fam.* 8. 9. 1–2, 5).

Caelius' next letter begins with a number of legal intrigues (*Fam.* 8. 8. 1–3),[53] but its chief purpose is to show how the issue of the Gallic provinces had, following Pompey's wishes, been postponed until the next March. Unusually Caelius incorporates the texts of one *senatus consultum* and three recorded *auctoritates* (decrees that had been vetoed) that resulted from a debate on 29 September. His aim was not only to illustrate the present impasse over Caesar but to explain to Cicero why a successor was unlikely to be appointed to his governorship in Cilicia for some time. The decree instructed the consuls of 50 to give priority from 1 March to debates on the consular provinces, ignoring the restriction on holding senate meetings during days reserved for assembly business, and summoning senators on the jury panels formed from the 300 elite judges appointed by Pompey in 52 (ibid. 5). A decree declaring that any obstruction to the process was against the public interest was vetoed, as was another inviting soldiers of Caesar who had completed their regular service or had some other claim to demobilization to apply to the senate (ibid. 6–7). The third vetoed decree had sought to provide that an allotment should be held for Cilicia and the eight provinces currently governed by former praetors, drawing on former praetors who had not held provincial governorships. The allotment was to begin with those qualified under Pompey's law by a five-year interval from city office and then, if not enough men became available by this method, move down through the boards of praetors by seniority (ibid. 8). This would have left Syria, with the prospect of a war with Parthia, and one or more of the Gallic provinces and Illyricum as provinces for those of consular rank.

According to Caelius, those who wanted a firm stance from Pompey were encouraged by remarks of his. He stated that he could not decide on Caesar's provinces before 1 March without committing an injustice, but after this he would have no hesitation. When questioned about a veto on that occasion he said that, if Caesar organized a veto, it was tantamount to disobeying the senate. 'Well then,' said another, 'what if he wants both to be consul and to have an army?' To which Pompey replied (really kindly!), 'What if my son were to strike me over the head with a stick?' The last comment, with its appeal to *patria potestas*, the traditional power of the paterfamilias over his family, was a strong assertion of authority and something of an insult to Caesar, even if it could be explained away as a declaration that the previous suggestion was ridiculous. In Caelius' view, the upshot was that people

[53] Lintott, 1980, 385–6.

believed that Pompey had a problem with Caesar (*Fam.* 8. 8. 9);[54] as for Caesar, he wanted to fall back on one of two arrangements, either that he should stay in Gaul and his candidature in absence should not be accepted 'this year', i.e. the forthcoming year when the issue would be raised,[55] or, if it should be possible for him to be elected (if he could be exempted from the *leges annales* so as to stand again within ten years of his last consulship), he would leave his province. Caelius was proceeding from the premiss, which may or may not have been erroneous but was in circulation at Rome at the time, that Caesar really wanted to be consul and hold a military command at the same time. It need not have been in Gaul: he might have returned to inaugurate his consulship and then departed immediately to fight the Parthians. Either possibility was anathema to Pompey. However, Caelius thought that Caesar might settle for election to the consulship and a return home. At this point it was Curio who threatened to oppose him.

When Caelius wrote in mid-November, the news of the Parthian threat had confused the issue further. Some were for sending out Pompey, other wished to send out Caesar and 'his own', the Gallic, army, others the consuls. As Caelius remarked, the consuls were reluctant to hold a senate-meeting, afraid that the senate might vote that they should put on their general's cloaks and set off for the war, and also that their command might be humiliatingly transferred to someone else. They were so ineffective in putting through what they did want, that there was no hope of their carrying out what they did not want (*Fam.* 8. 10. 2–3). The consul-designate Paulus had his eye on a province, which might have meant a slow succession to Cicero. As for Curio, he would probably give a little help to Pompey against Caesar, but at the same time, as a further display of independence, he was raising again the topic of the Campanian land (ibid. 3–4).

In the new year some time before 1 March 50 the situation changed. Up to then, perhaps reassured by the dispatches of Cicero and Cassius (*Fam.* 15. 4; *Att.* 5. 21. 2), the new consuls had done nothing, according to Caelius, but pass a decree about the Latin festival. Curio had put forward for discussion shortly after entering on his tribunate an elaborate law about roads like Rullus' agrarian law, apparently involving a tax on users to finance building and repair.[56] He then sought to get an intercalary month inserted in the

---

[54] *Pace* Balsdon, 1939, 175–6 and Gruen, 1974, 469 n. 70, the normal meaning of *negotium esse alicui cum aliquo* is that someone has a problem, not a bargain with another.

[55] For this meaning of *hoc anno* cf. *Att.* 7. 8. 4 (*consulatum hoc anno neglecturum*), written in December 50 and looking forward to 49.

[56] *Att.* 6. 1. 25; *Fam.* 8. 6. 5: Caelius implies that it was only formally proposed at the time of his letter, but Cicero had heard about it in Cilicia by 19 February. Curio is said by App. *BCiv.* 2. 27. 102 to have envisaged a five-year commission for himself.

month February to rectify the discrepancy between the Roman (at this time essentially lunar) calendar and the sun.[57] When this was blocked, he became more dramatically *popularis* and began to deliver speeches in support of Caesar, while proposing both his road bill and a law about the distribution of grain (*Fam.* 8. 6. 5). Appian and Dio Cassius maintain that he had been bribed by Caesar long before, but had concealed this until he had a suitable pretext for a change of allegiance.[58] However, Caelius, who was Curio's friend and close to Roman gossip, says nothing about this. The temporary disappearance of the Parthian threat was a mixed blessing at Rome: it might have seemed convenient to some if Cicero or Bibulus had sustained a major defeat, which would have necessitated the dispatch of either Caesar or Pompey to the East.

Curio now began the obstruction that exacerbated the breach between Caesar and Pompey. Caelius wrote to Cicero at length in the spring about the struggle in the senate that had been required to obtain days of thanksgiving (*supplicationes*) for him and Bibulus. He explains that Curio, who had been unable to put his legislation to the vote, because religious objections had been devised so as to make it improper for assemblies to meet on the days reserved for their business, was reluctant to see any other religious event created that would impede him. However, he withdrew his opposition when the consuls assured him that they would not put the vote into effect during their year of office and he came under pressure from Balbus, who told him that opposition would be an injury to Caesar (*Fam.* 8. 11. 1–2). Caesar was eager to maintain his friendship with Cicero (*Att.* 7. 2. 7) and would not have wanted a precedent for obstruction to further *supplicationes* on behalf of his own achievements. The opposition came openly from Cato (see above), his acolyte Favonius, and Hirrus, and tacitly from aristocrats such as Metellus Scipio and L. Domitius Ahenobarbus.

However, the issue of Caesar's provinces had come to dominate the political agenda. Pompey was now arguing that it was fair for Caesar to leave his provinces on 13 November at the end of the year's campaigning season; Curio was promising last-ditch resistance against this. For Pompey this was a deliberate attempt to pick a fight: he was clearly afraid of Caesar being elected consul before he handed over his army and provinces. This attitude was not well received by Curio, who attacked Pompey's own conduct in his second consulship—presumably on the ground that he had retained his proconsular power over the corn-supply and organized for himself a further five-year extraordinary command to follow the consular year. Caelius was sure that Caesar would come to Curio's rescue, if he became subject to extreme

---

[57] It was needed, see Lintott, 1968.   [58] App. *BCiv.* 2. 26. 100–27. 103; Dio 40. 60–2.

pressure. If Caesar's opponents backed down, he would stay in Gaul as long as he wanted (*Fam.* 8. 11. 3). In Pompey's mind it seems to have been no longer a matter of requiring Caesar to have handed over his provinces before he entered on his consulship, as in the autumn of 51, but of securing this before he even became elected.

Caelius is not considering at this point the possibility of Caesar being allowed to stand in the elections of 50. Perhaps Pompey would only have helped in this regard if Caesar had allowed a successor to be appointed. The otherwise puzzling date of 13 November would have allowed six weeks for Caesar to come to Rome and prepare a triumph before entering office. Caesar on the other hand seems not to have wanted this kind of deal: he already had a favoured candidate for the consulship, his former legate Ser. Sulpicius Galba (*BG* 8. 50. 4), who as a patrician was not permitted to hold a consulship in the same year as Caesar. Pompey had thought it unjust to press for Caesar's succession before 1 March (*Fam.* 8. 8. 9): he now seems to have believed, rightly or wrongly, that Caesar's legitimate tenure had come to an end.[59] What his attitude was to Caesar's right to stand for the consulship in absence is not clear: a brief letter from Caelius towards mid-summer, congratulating Cicero on Tullia's engagement, reveals that instead of a decree threatening Curio, the senate had voted that this right should be respected, even if Caesar had not handed over army or provinces. Pompey was absent because of a bad stomach complaint at the time. Caelius promised to let Cicero know how he reacted to the decree (*Fam.* 8. 13. 2).

Cicero replied to these letters as he began his return voyage. 'I am truly worried about the condition of the republic. I am a supporter of Curio, I desire Caesar to be held in honour, I can die for Pompey; but nothing is dearer to me than the republic itself, in which you are not undertaking any striking activity. For you seem to me to be torn in two directions, because you are both a good friend and a good citizen' (*Fam.* 2. 15. 3). About this time or shortly afterwards Caelius was writing to him from Rome in the aftermath of the elections. He passed over the consular elections, about which Cicero would have been informed by the city news (*acta*) that was being sent him, but joyfully recorded the defeat of L. Domitius Ahenobarbus by Marcus Antonius in the contest for the post of augur left vacant by the death of Hortensius. His view of the elections in general was that they were of major importance and support had depended on party sentiment (i.e. attachment to Caesar or Pompey) rather than the duty (*officium*) resulting from personal connections (*Fam.* 8. 14. 1). Interestingly, Caesar was to complain that Galba had failed to get elected consul for the same reason: 'Galba had his consulship

---

[59] On the legalities surrounding Caesar's command see App. 4.

snatched away, although he had been far superior in influence (*gratia*) and personal endorsements (*suffagia*).'⁶⁰ In fact two Pompeians were elected, Lentulus Crus and C. Marcellus, brother of the consul of 51 and cousin of his namesake, the current consul.

As for the political crisis, 'the issue about which those who control matters are likely to fight is that Gnaeus Pompeius has decided not to allow Caesar to become consul unless he has handed over army and provinces; Caesar is, however, convinced that he cannot be secure if he has left his army; nevertheless he offers this arrangement, that both should hand over their armies. Thus that love-affair and scandalous liaison has not degenerated into secret backbiting but exploded into war' (ibid. 2). For Caelius the problem was that his personal connections were with one side (i.e. Caesar's); he approved the cause (Pompey's) whose personalities he hated. He believed that one could support the party with better moral principles in a contest between civilians, but once it came to arms one should chose the safer side. Pompey would have the senate and the equestrian judges on his side; Caesar would be joined by all those whose lives were ruined or in danger, but his army was incomparable (ibid. 3). After a brief humorous digression, chiefly on the ironies of Appius' severity as censor, Caelius returns to the main theme. If one of the two did not go to fight the Parthians, it would be a contest by armed violence. Both sides were ready. Fortune was promoting a vast and delightful gladiatorial contest for Cicero, if he could find a safe seat (ibid. 4).⁶¹

Caelius is not concerned with constitutional niceties. A power contest was at last coming to the boil. He had indicated the severity of the breach a year before.⁶² However, his letters do seem to show a hardening of Pompey's official position, which may have resulted from a change of attitude in face of what he regarded as Caesar's obstinacy, but equally may be evidence of Pompey feeling free to reveal his true sentiments, when he felt that he could no longer be accused of a breach of faith—that is, once he believed that Caesar's command had exceeded its legal term. Moreover, Caesar's proposal that they should both give up their armies not only threatened the supremacy that Pompey had engineered for himself in 52 but was an open manifestation of Caesar's distrust of his former ally. Pompey seems to have indicated opposition to any repeat of Caesar's consulship of 59 to Cicero at their

---

⁶⁰ Caes. *BG* 8. 50. 4. Cicero heard at Ephesus on 29 September about the result of the elections of magistrates at Rome (*Att.* 6. 8. 2). This helps to date Caelius' letter, which was clearly written in the immediate aftermath of the augural elections that followed the elections of magistrates (*BG* 8. 50. 1–4, see How ii. 298), therefore in August rather than late September.

⁶¹ *Spectaculum* must mean here a show in which blood was spilt. See Antonius' letter in 43 BC (*Phil.* 13. 40) for a more elaborate exploitation of this image.

⁶² *Fam.* 8. 8. 9; cf. 14. 2 'saepe tibi scripsi me <ad>(or <in>) annum pacem non videre'.

Tarentum meeting in 51. This inspired Cicero with confidence at the time. He nevertheless had hoped that Caesar could be accommodated in the political framework created by Pompey's third consulate. We do not have his letters to Caesar from this period, except for two citations attributed to the third book of his letters by the grammarian Nonius: 'If you could only see this, you would be protecting yourself not by retaining your army, but by handing over or disbanding it'; 'several of your friends want the senate to be despised, scorned, and set at naught by you.'[63] Both these remarks would fit well with Cicero's understanding of the situation during his return to Rome.

From Athens Cicero sent a more elaborate reply to the letter he received from Atticus on 14 October. Only the god who had allowed him to escape from the Parthian war could extract the Romans from an immense struggle. However, he wanted advice about his own personal problem in relation to the impending conflict. Atticus had advised him to become friend to both Pompey and Caesar, and he had succeeded in so doing (*Att.* 7. 1. 2). His notion, he claims, had been that as Pompey's ally he would never be compelled to commit a political crime, nor would he have to fight Caesar, since Pompey and Caesar were so closely tied (a somewhat optimistic gloss on the recantation of 56 BC). Each of the two now believed in Cicero's loyalty to him, Pompey perhaps more sincerely, as he judged that Cicero approved of his present political stance (ibid. 3). What should he do now? The question did not relate to civil war, since he realized that defeat with the one (Pompey) would be better than victory with the other, but to his attitude to the political agenda on his return: should he support the proposals that Caesar be not accepted as a consular candidate in his absence and let go his army? Cicero imagines being asked his opinion in the senate: 'Speak, M. Tullius.' He answers, 'Please wait until I consult Atticus.' Could he speak against Caesar? What about the handshakes at Ravenna in 52, when he helped Caesar to secure the privilege of standing in his absence at his request and that of Pompey too? Could he do the opposite? Once again the reminiscence of Hector in the *Iliad* appears. He feels shame in face of Pompey—and the Trojan men and women (ibid. 4).[64]

It would have been easier, he muses, if he had stayed in his province. This leads him to reflect on the difficulty inherent in his virtuous conduct or pretence of virtue in the province, when he left the new quaestor expenses for a year and handed back money to the treasury in spite of the protests of his

---

[63] *Ep. ad Caes.* 3. frr. 9–10 = Nonius Marcellus 286, 436 M = 441, 702 L. See below on Caesar's letters to Cicero at this time.

[64] See on the Ravenna meeting Ch. XIV with nn. 123–7; *Att.* 2. 5. 1 of April 59 for the quotation from the *Iliad*, 6. 442, 22. 100. It was to reappear in the letters of the early civil war, *Att.* 7. 12. 3, 8. 16. 2.

staff. His main concern had been his reputation. He remarks that this was what Thucydides called a digression from the story, an allusion to the historian's account of the Pentekontaetea (ibid. 6).[65] We may wonder if he saw analogies between the impending conflict and the Peloponnesian War and mentally compared Pompey to Pericles standing firm in face of threats to the Athenians' supremacy from their former ally Sparta. That would fit with the conclusion of his previous letter: 'In present circumstances I like my post on the Athenian acropolis'.[66] Nevertheless, he asks Atticus' advice on how to retain Caesar's goodwill and how to obtain a triumph, citing Caesar's letter of congratulation to him, which apparently promised him every support (*Att.* 7. 1. 7; cf. 7. 2. 7).

When he arrived at Brindisi, another letter from Atticus was given him with an account of Atticus' talk with Pompey at Naples. The latter was well disposed to Cicero and his claim for a triumph. At Aeclanum on his journey back through Italy Cicero received the answer to his questions from Athens. Atticus, it appears, suggested that Cicero must have regretted leaving Cilicia so promptly and, while arguing that he had no particular obligation to Caesar, advised him to pursue security and neutrality (*Att.* 7. 3. 1–3). This is implied by Cicero's reference to the consulars Servius Sulpicius Rufus and Volcatius Tullus who in spite of past loyalties were conspicuously inactive when the civil war started.[67] Cicero found this difficult to swallow. He had left Cilicia, hoping to participate in either reconciliation or the victory of the good men. He wished to live up to the image of the statesman that he had shaped in book 6 of *De Re Publica*, that is, of one who would answer the call to save the Republic in a crisis, a course of which he was reminded by the statue of Minerva guardian of the city that he had dedicated on the Capitol before going into exile.[68]

He realized, however, that it was impossible to follow such an ideal course in present circumstances, since this was a power-struggle between two men at the risk of the whole community. This letter develops the exasperation he had expressed earlier over his assistance to Caesar and Pompey in 52. Why had Pompey not defended the republic in Caesar's consulship? Why had he not defended Cicero the next year on behalf of the safety of the republic? Why had he fought to get the ten tribunes to pass a law about Caesar's candidature in absence? Nevertheless the answer to the president of the senate's request to speak was 'I agree with Gnaeus Pompeius.' He would, however, urge Pompey

---

[65] Thuc. 1. 97. 2.
[66] *Att.* 6. 9. 2, immediately following a reference to Caesar bringing four legions to Placentia.
[67] See e.g. *Att.* 8. 1. 3, 9a. 1, 15. 2. Atticus had regarded them as adequate models of conduct (*Att.* 7. 3. 3, 'quibus tu es contentus').
[68] *Att.* 7. 3. 2–3, cf. Ch. XIV with nn. 79 ff.

towards reconciliation because of the threat to the republic from civil war. They were dealing with a most audacious and well-organized man, who had on his side all the condemned, all the disgraced, all those who deserved to be condemned or disgraced, almost all the young men, the whole of the corrupted urban populace, powerful tribunes now joined by Quintus Cassius, and all those in debt.[69] There was, however, one problem to which he adverts at the end of the letter: he was among those who were in debt—to Caesar. What should he do, if, instead of the seductive letters that Caesar and Balbus were now sending him, the man from Tartessus should say 'please see that the money is paid' ?[70]

On 10 December, the day the new tribunes entered office, Cicero met Pompey (*Att.* 7. 4. 2). In recent correspondence there had been no mention of Curio's obstruction and we are dependent on the secondary sources for knowledge of important developments. Curio had apparently generated from his attacks on Pompey great enthusiasm among the urban plebs, who seem to have kept in mind their support of Clodius against Pompey earlier in the decade. Shortly before he demitted the tribunate, after a motion had been passed in the senate recommending that Caesar should lay down his command, he capped this by proposing that both Caesar and Pompey should lay down their commands, a motion that was passed by 370 votes to 22. In a fury the consul C. Marcellus responded to this by placing a sword in Pompey's hands and urging him to save the republic, following which Pompey left the neighbourhood of Rome to take command of the two legions that had been sent back by Caesar from Gaul at the senate's request, ostensibly for potential service against Parthia.[71]

Cicero and Pompey talked for two hours. Pompey was pleased to see him; he urged him to seek a triumph and accordingly to avoid entering the senate in case he should alienate a tribune by the position he took in debates (the senate could be held outside the *pomoerium*, for example in the temples of Apollo and Bellona in the Circus Flaminius, where Cicero could attend without laying down his *imperium*). However, Pompey gave the impression

---

[69] *Att.* 7. 3. 4–5 cf. 7. 7. 6 discussed below. The list of Caesar's supporters in some ways recalls that of the Catilinarians in *Cat.* 2. 17–22, except that in a much briefer compass it ranges more widely and is designed to magnify the danger rather than bring it into contempt. The 'disgraced' will be those especially who had been 'noted' as such by the censors, on the initiative of Appius Claudius (*Fam.* 8. 14. 4; Dio 40. 63. 3–64. 1), including the historian Sallust (Ps. Cic. *Inv. Sall.* 16) and the former tribune C. Ateius Capito (*Div.* 1. 29).

[70] *Att.* 7. 3. 11; Tartessus is Gades (Cádiz), the home town of Balbus. The cash that Cicero had saved from his province, over 2 million sesterces, was at Ephesus (*Fam.* 5. 20. 9; *Att.* 11. 3. 3).

[71] App. *BCiv.* 2. 27. 104–31. 122; Plut. *Pomp.* 58. 4–59. 1; cf. *Caes.* 29. 4–30. 5; Dio 40. 64. 1–4. The last two accounts are less full, Plut. *Caes.* omitting the sword episode and Dio the vote Curio engineered in the senate.

that there was no hope of a settlement, citing the recent embassy of Hirtius. The latter had arrived at Rome on the evening of 6 December, but had set off back to Caesar in the middle of the night, in spite of a meeting that Balbus had arranged for him with Scipio before dawn the next morning. This was for Pompey proof positive of Caesar's alienation (*Att.* 7. 4. 2). It is nonetheless striking that Pompey did not anticipate any immediate action from Caesar. Cicero himself did not believe that Caesar would be mad enough to put at risk his present power and the consulship that even his enemies were prepared to concede him (ibid. 3).

In two brief letters written about a week later from his villa at Formiae Cicero makes clear his own desire for peace at any price, one shared by the knights and senators he met, who were bitterly critical of Pompey's journey to the legions (*Att.* 7. 5. 4–5; 7. 6. 2). It was too late to resist Caesar now. However, whatever his own feelings about peace, he would not disagree with Pompey openly. Three more substantial letters followed before he left Formiae. In the first he reveals to Atticus that Pompey and his advisers have plans to send him to Sicily because he still has *imperium* and the right to command troops (*Att.* 7. 7. 4). Owing to the obstruction to provincial allocations there would have been a vacancy in the governorship that at the time was perhaps filled by a quaestor. Nevertheless, this decision by Pompey's 'cabinet' looked like preparation for war. Cicero thinks it lunacy and points out to Atticus that 'he will use the first gate he sees' (into Rome), if he finds his *imperium* a nuisance. In reply to Atticus' report that none of the good men or quite good men have any doubts about his choice of action, he breaks out into a series of expostulations about the whole concept of good men, which represents a *reductio ad absurdum* of the principle on which he had tried to base his politics. True, there were good individuals but in civil conflict one had to look for orders and classes. Was the senate good, when the provinces had no proper governors? Were the tax-collectors good? They were never reliable but now Caesar's firmest friends. Were the money-lenders and farmers? They had no fear of tyranny provided that they had peace (ibid. 5).

Did he then agree with accepting the candidature of Caesar when he retained his army after the legal term of his command? He did not approve of accepting the candidature of an absentee, but the granting of the latter implied the granting of the former (ibid. 6).[72] Did he agree, he asks ironically,

---

[72] 'Cum id datum est, illud una datum est'. See Shackleton Bailey's translation (SB *Att* iii. 175) of a sometimes misunderstood passage. The indicative in the *cum* clause in historic time shows that the clause does not introduce a temporal relationship but a logical relationship (cf. *Sull.* 81, another sometimes misinterpreted passage): it does not imply that the law of the ten tribunes included a clause specifically permitting Caesar's retention of his army. For Cicero's acceptance of the validity of Caesar's privilege see *Att.* 9. 11A. 2; *Fam.* 6. 6. 5.

with a ten-year command legislated in the way it was, with his own exile, the loss of the *ager Campanus*, the adoption of a patrician (i.e. Clodius) by a plebeian, that of a Gaditane (Balbus) by a Mytilenean (Pompey's friend Theophanes), the wealth of Labienus and Mamurra, Balbus' garden villa at Rome and Tusculan home? They should have resisted Caesar when he was weak. As it was, he had eleven legions, as much cavalry as he wanted, the support of the Transpadane region, the urban plebs, and the young men. They either had to fight him to the death or accept his candidature according to the law (of the ten tribunes). Fighting meant proscription for the vanquished and slavery nonetheless for the victors. What was he himself going to do? Like a lost beast he would follow a flock of his own kind, the so-called 'good men'. This meant voting with Pompey, that is, with Atticus.

The letters have already informed us of Cicero's instinctive support for Pompey and the 'good men'. What we find here is a protest about the existence of the crisis in the first place, a forerunner of many others in the correspondence. There are characteristic features. First, Cicero regards Caesar's first consulship as the decisive moment, a view that was to become firmly established in the later historiography of the civil wars.[73] Secondly, like Caelius, Cicero has no confidence in the likelihood of a Pompeian victory. Thirdly, he does not anticipate that even a Pompeian victory would have desirable consequences: it would simply bring servitude rather than the death and confiscation of property that would follow victory by Caesar.[74] As for the legalities of the present situation, though he believes that Caesar's command has reached its term, he accepts that Caesar's right to be a candidate in absence, undesirable as it is, remains valid.

It is important to emphasize that Cicero did not question this right, which in Cicero's mind left Caesar some room for manoeuvre. The law governing candidature for office permitted Caesar to stand in the summer of 49 for a second consulship in the year 48 (Caes. *BCiv.* 3. 1. 1). Even if he left his command in Gaul, he would not lose his *imperium* until he crossed the *pomoerium*—an action that he would not take until the triumph, one may imagine, he planned for 1 January 48. Pompey had taken over nine months to prepare his Asiatic triumph; Caesar could reasonably have taken a similar time without damaging his prestige. Subsequent correspondence, however, suggests that this loophole was not agreeable to Pompey. Nor, to judge from his actions and writings, did it satisfy Caesar.

---

[73] See Syme, 1950; Lintott, 1971, 493 ff.
[74] Cf. *Att.* 10. 4. 3, 10. 7. 1, cf. 10. 14. 1. For the later history of the view that success in a civil war was a mixed blessing for the victorious side see e.g. Lucan 7. 122–3; Sen. *Ep.* 14. 12–13; Tac. *Hist.* 1. 50; Lintott, 1971, 494 ff.

In the late afternoon of 25 December Cicero had another private meeting with Pompey at Formiae, in which he did not even find the will for peace. Pompey expected a political revolution if Caesar became consul, even if he had already yielded command of his army. He also thought that, 'when Caesar heard that careful preparations were being made against him, he would abandon the consulship in the coming year and in preference hold on to the army and the province: if Caesar did anything crazy, however, he had utter contempt for him and trusted in his own and the republic's forces.' Pompey was happy to provoke Caesar into civil war (*Att.* 7. 8. 4). They read the text of an address to the people that Antonius had delivered a few days earlier, shortly after entering the tribunate. Apart from complaints about those condemned in 52 and threats, it contained a critique of Pompey's life from the time he left boyhood (ibid. 5). We can imagine what this contained: Pompey's desertion of the Marian side for Sulla, his exploitation of illegal commands, the execution of leading Marians both under Sulla and later, his repeated unscrupulous manoeuvring for power, and finally the breach of his alliance with Caesar.[75] At the end of the letter Cicero returns to his nagging worry, he will have to pay off Caesar with money saved to pay for his triumph (*Att.* 7. 8. 5).

The last surviving letter before the outbreak of war followed the next day. It contains an elaborate logical exposition of the possibilities in the current political situation, which neatly illustrates the influence of Greek philosophy on Roman methods of thinking (*Att.* 7. 9. 1–2).[76] There were five possible scenarios for the elections. (1) They might be held with Caesar retaining his army through his tribunes or a concession by the senate. Or (2) Caesar might be persuaded to hand over province and army and so to become consul. Or (3), if he were not so persuaded, he might permit the elections to be held without his candidature, while retaining his province. Or (4), if he should obstruct such an election through tribunes but otherwise remained at peace, matters would come to an *interregnum*. Or (5), if he should bring in an army, because his candidature was not accepted, there would be war with him. As for his resorting to arms, this would happen either immediately when the Pompeians were less prepared or at the time when his candidature at the elections was not accepted in spite of his friends' demand. His motive would either be simply the refusal of his candidature or, additionally, because one of his obstructing and demagogic tribunes took refuge with him after being disgraced or restricted or deposed or expelled or claiming to have been so

---

[75] The flavour of the attack can be gauged from the report of Valerius Maximus (6. 2. 8) of Helvius Mancia's outburst, when accusing Scribonius Libo before the censors, including the phrase *adulescens carnufex*, 'cadet executioner'. See also Sall. *Hist.* 2. 16–17.

[76] *Att.* 7. 9. 2: Cicero calls it a πρόβλημα πολιτικόν.

treated. Once war broke out, the Pompeians would have either to hold the city or abandon it and try to cut Caesar off from supplies and his remaining forces. The problem was, which of these possibilities, one of which certainly had to be undergone, did Atticus think the least evil.

Cicero's anticipates Atticus' reply to be, that Caesar should hand over his army and so become consul. He agrees and is not surprised at his taking this course, if he cannot secure his candidature while retaining his army. But the Pompeians 'have nothing worse to fear than him as consul, as some people think'. 'I prefer it this way', he imagines Atticus' comment, 'to with an army.' 'Yes, but that very "this way" someone thinks a great evil and he has no remedy.' Once again he describes Pompey's reaction to the prospect of Caesar's second consulship and adds that in this case Pompey is determined to go to Spain (ibid. 3). Further expostulations follow about Caesar's 'shameless' demand to have his candidature while retaining his province: they had to concede or fight. However, action in the event of war depended on circumstances. The present question was whether they should give way to Caesar's demand. In fact circumstances rendered Cicero's question vain, since the new consuls precipitated matters by seeking to bring Caesar's command to an end long before the elections in spite of the proconsul's desperate concessions.

XVI

The Mediator and the Partisans

THE FAILURE OF PEACEMAKING

THE first letter of Cicero's to Atticus that we possess from the year 49 was written as he left the outskirts of Rome on 18 January—the day after Pompey's retreat in face of Caesar's invasion of Italy (*Att.* 7. 10). We depend on Caesar and the secondary sources for most of our knowledge of how the crisis was precipitated, though Cicero's correspondence sheds some light on the part he tried to play in it. The manuscripts of Caesar's *Bellum Civile* are also defective since they begin abruptly with what seem to be the events of 5 January. Fortunately, the material in Appian's *Civil War* and Plutarch's *Life of Caesar* is especially rich at this point, probably because it derives ultimately from Asinius Pollio's history.[1] Caesar sent to the senate a letter detailing his achievements and offering to reduce his command to Cisalpine Gaul and Illyricum with two legions. He was prepared to yield his *imperium* completely when Pompey did the same, but he threatened to defend the fatherland and his own interests swiftly, if the latter chose to retain his command.[2] This letter must have contained the remark that he was only defending his *dignitas*, his standing in Roman society.[3] Curio delivered this letter to the senate on 1 January, but Caesar's favoured tribunes Antonius and Q. Cassius could not persuade the consuls to have it read openly and debated there. So Antonius read it out at a *contio* (Caes. *BCiv.* 1. 1; Plut. *Caes.* 30. 3). The senate in the meantime tried to pass a decree that Caesar should release his army by a fixed date or be declared a public enemy (*hostis*), and that Domitius Ahenobarbus should succeed him in Gaul, but this was vetoed.[4]

---

[1] The account of Kornemann, 1896, esp. 610 ff., 678–80, is fundamental.
[2] App. *BCiv.* 2. 32. 126–9; Plut. *Caes.* 30–31. 1. Suetonius (*Jul.* 29. 2) adds an alternative offer of Illyricum with one legion, cf. Plut. *Pomp.* 59. 5 for Illyricum with two legions. In Plut. *Caes.* 31. 2 the reduction to one legion was a suggestion of Cicero's.
[3] See *Att.* 7. 11. 1; cf. Caesar's repetition in the letter to Pompey (*BCiv.* 1. 9. 2), where it was a reply to Pompey's appeal to Caesar's *dignitas* in the letter brought by young L. Caesar, on which see below.
[4] App. *BCiv.* 2. 32. 129; Plut. *Caes.* 30. 4–5: Antonius apparently engineered a vote, like Curio, that both Caesar and Pompey should lay down their arms.

Two days intervened on which the senate could not be held because they were reserved for assembly business (*dies comitiales*) (Caes. *BCiv.* 1. 5. 4.). Finally on 5 January Caesar's letter was read in the senate and the consuls introduced a general debate on public affairs (*de re publica infinite*). Pompey was not present, but the consul Lentulus Crus and Pompey's father-in-law Metellus Scipio both advocated a hard line, Scipio arguing that they could not expect Pompey's support later, unless they took strong measures now; according to Caesar he was thought to be speaking for Pompey (Caes. *BCiv.* 1. 1. 1–4). Caesar describes opposition from M. Marcellus, who advocated delay until they had made better military preparations, and from Calidius and Caelius, who wanted Pompey to leave for his Spanish provinces to avoid giving Caesar a reason to resort to arms. These objections were brushed aside by the consul. It is at this point that, according to Plutarch,[5] Cicero intervened and tried to negotiate a settlement between Pompey and Caesar's friends. He had originally planned to arrive at Rome on his birthday, 3 January, after passing the previous night at Pompey's Alban villa, but, when he discovered that the 2nd was the date of the Compitalia, a festival that would be attended by Pompey's slave-household, he postponed his arrival at Rome until the 4th (*Att.* 7. 5. 3, 7. 3). Pompey, Plutarch alleges, was prepared to yield to the settlement proposed but was overruled by Lentulus' group in the senate. If true, this would have constituted both a considerable change of Pompey's attitude and a remarkable achievement by Cicero.

It is not surprising that Caesar ignores this in *Bellum Civile*. There he was eager to show that Pompey had been a willing accomplice of his optimate opponents, because he desired to maintain his own domination (*BCiv.* 1. 4. 4–5). And there is a fair degree of truth in this. Cicero's correspondence, especially that of December 50, has shown us how reluctant Pompey was to see his settlement of the *res publica* and his present dominance at Rome overthrown by the return of a victorious general who remained *popularis* in his political sympathies. It is possible that Pompey was at this point persuaded that Caesar was only seeking security and had no ambition to combine the consulship with the retention of most of his army, though this is not the impression that we get from a general comment of Cicero later: 'he has given Caesar strength; he has suddenly begun to fear him all the same; he has accepted no terms for peace; he has made no preparation for war....'[6]

---

[5] *Caes.* 31. 2, cf. *Cic.* 37. 1.

[6] *Att.* 8. 8. 1. Cicero continues there, 'he has left the city, through his own fault he has lost Picenum, he has penned himself up in Apulia, he is going to Greece, he is leaving us all without a word, without any part in such a great and unusual strategy....'.

Cicero wrote on 12 January in general terms about his own efforts for peace in a letter to his freedman secretary Tiro, convalescing after an illness in Greece (*Fam.* 16. 11. 2):[7] he had arrived at the city on 4 January and, although he had a magnificent reception, had fallen into the very fire of civil discord or rather war. When he tried to remedy this, the desires of certain men stood in his way (there were men on both sides who wanted to fight). Caesar was shamelessly holding on to army and provinces and had sent menacing letters to the senate. Cicero goes on to claim that after the emergency decree entrusting the safety of the *res publica* to the magistrates (on 7 January), Antonius and Cassius fled with Curio to Caesar, though they had been expelled by no violence. On the other hand, it appears from Caesar's account that 'that last decree' resulted from a debate on the tribunes' veto and effectively recommended that their opposition should be treated as a threat to the *res publica* (*BCiv.* 1. 2. 7–8, 1. 5. 4–5). So the threat was there, even if they were not actually offered violence.

In a following letter to Tiro Cicero talks of the madness (*furor*) that came over not only the 'bad' men but also those believed to be 'good', making them desire to fight in spite of his protests that there was nothing sorrier than civil war.[8] He does not seem to have attended the senate meetings of 5–7 January; neither he nor Pompey could do so if they were held within the *pomoerium*.[9] He was present, however, at one at least of the subsequent meetings outside the *pomoerium*. In May 44 Atticus recalled the speech that Cicero had made in the temple of Apollo in 49, in which he had continued to argue for a peace-settlement and seems to have advocated that the Pompeians should remain in Rome.[10] Nevertheless, the final product of these meetings was the allocation of provinces to both those with *imperium* and those without. Cicero took the region of Capua—presumably with the task of ensuring security, against an uprising by gladiators for example, and defending the area against Caesar—after assurances that the consul Lentulus would deal with the matter of his triumph once preparations for war had been made.[11]

He made one more effort to negotiate. Caelius in his desperate letter to Cicero of 48 refers to their last meeting before he departed to Ariminum to join Caesar, allegedly motivated by affection for Curio and anger with Appius

---

[7] See *Att.* 7. 2. 3; 8. 5. 2, 6. 4–5 on Tiro.
[8] *Fam.* 16. 12. 2. On this 'mad' desire see also *Fam.* 4. 1. 1 to Sulpicius Rufus of April 49.
[9] Caesar's description of the occupation of the *comitium* and the *clivus Capitolinus* with soldiers on 7 January suggests that this meeting was in one of the neighbouring temples, perhaps that of Concord. He contrasts this with the subsequent senate meetings outside the city boundary (*BCiv.* 1. 3. 3, 6. 1).
[10] *Att.* 15. 3. 1, the speech recalled also in *Marc.* 15.
[11] Caes. *BCiv.* 1. 6. 1–7; *Fam.* 16. 11. 3; cf. Dio 41. 3. 3.

Claudius.[12] Cicero had been playing the part of the 'wonderful citizen', the man devoted to the republic and civic values, and had given him a message to carry to Caesar about peace (*Fam.* 8. 17. 2). This may have helped to inspire Caesar's most generous offer of peace, sent from Ariminum after he had crossed the Rubicon. Pompey had also sent a verbal message to Caesar using as intermediaries the young L. Caesar and the praetor L. Roscius Fabatus, apparently apologizing for what must have seemed to Caesar a breach of faith and asserting that the interests of the *res publica* had to come first (Caes. *BCiv.* 1. 8. 2–4). Caesar makes it clear that this was a private message, not an official attempt to negotiate.[13] In his reply Caesar suggested disarmament by both sides and free elections without the threat of arms. To achieve this he wanted a personal meeting with Pompey so that they could exchange oaths (Caes. *BCiv.* 1. 9). According to Cicero, the letter was brought to Pompey at Teanum by L. Caesar, but he later refers to Roscius' participation (*Att.* 7. 14. 1, 8. 12. 2); Caesar says it was brought by L. Roscius to Capua. This was certainly where the proposal was discussed (*Att.* 7. 15. 2). Probably there were two messengers with similar letters: both the men were sent back (*BCiv.* 1. 10. 1–2).

Cicero tells us that Caesar was prepared to hand over Transalpine and Cisalpine Gaul to his allotted successors, Domitius Ahenobarbus and Considius Nonianus, and stand in person at the elections, provided that Pompey went to Spain.[14] He refers contemptuously to the version of the terms which he was told by L. Caesar at Minturnae, but makes it clear that Caesar's offer was taken seriously enough by Pompey's council of war for a reply to be sent on 25 January.[15] This accepted Caesar's proposition as a final outcome, but demanded that Caesar should retire to his province—by now he had occupied not only Ariminum but Pisaurum, Ancona, and Arretium (*Att.* 7. 11. 1)—so that a senate-meeting could be held in Rome to discuss the terms (*Fam.* 16. 12. 3). The composition of the reply was entrusted to the heavy hand of Sestius and included at least one ingratiating compliment.[16] Among the Pompeians even Cato was for peace at this time (*Att.* 7. 15. 2).

There was, however, no trust on either side. Curio, who had now been taken on by Caesar as one of his officers, apparently derided the embassy in a letter to Furnius.[17] In the event Caesar interpreted the refusal of an immediate

---

[12] Caelius also expected Caesar to win, 8. 14. 3, 15. 1.

[13] The young Lucius Caesar was a Pompeian, though his father was Caesar's legate. For a discussion of the messengers in this exchange, exploding modern theories that there was an official embassy to Caesar after the 'last decree', see SB *Att* iv. 441–7 = Shackleton Bailey, 1960.

[14] *Fam.* 16. 12. 3—nothing is said of Illyricum: perhaps Caesar intended to retain this until near election time.

[15] *Att.* 7. 13a. 2, 7. 15. 2, 7. 16. 1–2, 7. 17. 2.

[16] *Att.* 7. 17. 2, 7. 26. 2, 8. 9. 2.   [17] *Att.* 7. 19; cf. 8. 12C. 1 for Curio's recruiting for Caesar.

face-to-face meeting and the Pompeian request that he withdraw to his province as a move to gain time for recruitment without any commitment to the terms proposed: he therefore continued his advance and this effort for peace collapsed (*BCiv.* 1. 10. 2–11). Balbus was to write to Cicero a month later that Caesar wanted nothing more than to live in security with Pompey as the leading man (*princeps*). This might well have been true once; whether it was true any longer was another matter. Cicero was sceptical (*Att.* 8. 9A. 2). As for Pompey, Cicero later commented that he showed affection to Caesar, when everyone else feared him, but after he himself began to fear him, he thought everyone should be Caesar's enemy. This fear led to his refusal of all terms for peace (*Att.* 8. 1. 4, 8. 8. 1).

Cicero himself had mixed feelings about the Pompeian offer. He thought that it was so generous that Caesar must accept it: a second consulship would amount to victory in a less criminal manner than his present course involved (*Att.* 7. 15. 3, 7. 17. 2). However, he found the prospect of a second consulship for Caesar so appalling that he momentarily contemplated going with Pompey to Spain (*Att.* 7. 18. 2). Some light on his fears is shed by a tantalizing passage in a self-justificatory letter to Pompey a month later. He refers to how he was left alone to face Clodius in 58 and argues that if he had offended Caesar in the present situation, when the latter was being offered a second consulship and a magnificent triumph in spite of the fact that a civil war had started, he would be open to the same sort of attacks by *populares* as before. He claims that this was not mere suspicion: such threats had in fact been openly made to him, presumably by former supporters of Clodius.[18] For example, there was Q. Pompeius, the former tribune of 52 who, according to popular gossip, had killed Cicero on his journey through Italy in 51 (*Fam.* 8. 1. 4). Cicero, therefore, continued in correspondence with Caesar, in order to keep their friendship intact both in the interests of a possible peace-settlement (he included generous compliments to Pompey) and, failing that, as insurance for his own security.[19]

His command of the coastal area south of Rome was for the time being convenient but unproductive. The consuls summoned him to a meeting at Capua on 4 February; they arrived late and nothing was achieved. Levies of troops proved impossible; Pompey was away at Luceria seeking to secure the loyalty of legions there;[20] when he sent a message with C. Cassius that the

---

[18] *Att.* 8. 11D. 7. He later identified the Caesarians with his earlier Catilinarian opponents (*Att.* 10. 8. 8).

[19] *Att.* 8. 2. 1, 8. 3. 2, 8. 11. 5; cf. 7. 21. 3 for Caesar's letters from Gaul and 23. 3 on reports of Caesar's favourable reaction to Cicero's.

[20] *Att.* 7. 15. 3, 7. 20. 1; the adjective qualifying 'legions' is uncertain owing to a corrupt text. See SB *Att.* iv. 311, arguing for the traditional emendation *Appianas*, describing the legions that returned from Gaul.

consuls should return to Rome to draw money from the reserve fund in the treasury, they demurred because they thought it unsafe.[21] In fact, there was an immediate general shortage of cash, as private debts were called in. In periods of civil war everyone sought liquidity and tended to hoard coined money if they could.[22] In response to a letter received from Pompey on 15 February Cicero set out to join him in Luceria, but on the 18th he had only got as far as Cales when he changed his mind on receiving information that Domitius Ahenobarbus was not joining Pompey but standing and fighting at Corfinium (*Att.* 8. 3. 7, 8. 11A–D).[23] He told Atticus that Pompey could hardly abandon Domitius in spite of his previous moves towards embarkation at Brindisi, but this was wishful thinking: by the 24th it was reported that Pompey was on his way to Brindisi and Domitius had surrendered (*Att.* 8. 8. 1–2).

TO LEAVE OR NOT TO LEAVE?

Apart from his immediate reaction to events, the almost daily letters of this period are testimony to various kinds of reflection. First, there is exasperation over Pompey's failure in Italy and his retreat abroad, especially as the latter entails that any hope of preventing full-scale civil war is lost; secondly, there is deliberation over his own proper conduct in the circumstances; thirdly, associated with this, there is the recall of past civil war and its potentially horrific consequences. Cicero had of course had lived through the wars of the eighties, which were illustration enough, but, interestingly, he also applies his reading of Greek history.

In a letter written on the night of 18–19 February his exasperation with Pompey burst out. Pompey had done nothing wisely, nothing courageously, nothing that was not against his own advice and recommendation. The list of errors begins with his support for Caesar's legislation of 59, the grant of Transalpine Gaul to Caesar, his marriage, and the adoption of Clodius. Pompey had, moreover, been keener to bring Cicero back from exile than to prevent his exile in the first place. He extended and supported Caesar's proconsulship; then, after becoming the defender of the *res publica* in 52, he had continued to conciliate Caesar by special measures like the law of the ten

---

[21] *Att.* 7. 20. 1, 7. 21. 1–2, 8. 11B. 2.
[22] *Att.* 7. 18. 4, cf. 9. 9. 4. See Frederiksen, 1966.
[23] See SB *Att* iv. 448–59 = Shackleton Bailey, 1956, on the chronology of the letters at this point with an elucidation of Pompey's diplomacy with Domitius and Cicero's with Pompey.

tribunes. Now the retreat to the distant empty spaces of Apulia could only mean that he was planning to sail away (*Att.* 8. 3. 3).[24]

We have already had occasion to mention the letter of 27 February in which he recalls the function of the *moderator* portrayed in book 5 of *De Re Publica* and comments that 'my friend Gnaeus never has had this in mind before and certainly not in his present cause; the pair have both sought domination; they have not acted to make the community happy and virtuous' (*Att.* 8. 11. 1–2). Cicero goes on to accuse Pompey of planning from the start to create a vast army, including foreign kings and savage tribes, to attack Italy, all in order to recreate a form of Sullan tyranny (ibid. 2–4). The theme of foreign fleets and tribes reappears in later letters. In one he lists by their home ports the navies of the eastern Mediterranean and imagines them all being used to blockade the sea-routes to Italy and seize the corn provinces; in another he asks ironically if he, a man whom some called the protector and parent of the city, could lead an army of Getae, Armenians, and Colchians against it?[25] Cicero also returns to the comparison with Sulla. At one point he quotes Pompey saying frequently, 'Sulla was able to, shall I not be able?', which in itself might simply be a reference to the strategy of reinvading Italy from the East (*Att.* 9. 10. 2); elsewhere it is again a matter of a Sullan tyranny, and he coins two new desiderative verbs, *sullaturire* and *proscripturire*, for 'to long to be a Sulla' and 'to long to proscribe'.[26] Similarly, when he mentions the threatening talk of the Pompeians at Brundisium, reported to him by Furius Crassipes, he talks of 'undiluted proscriptions, undiluted Sullas' (9. 11. 3).

In the letter of 27 February he notes Caesar's letters and the message passed on by Balbus' son commending his failure to participate in the war (*Att.* 8. 11. 5). The young Balbus had also letters for the consul Lentulus Crus offering him rewards if he returned to Rome. This may seem astonishing in the light of Lentulus' responsibility for precipitating the war in the first place. However, Balbus' father was bound by *officium* not only to Pompey, who had granted him citizenship, but to Lentulus Crus, who must have been one of Pompey's officers and granted him his *nomen*.[27] He was still looking after all Lentulus' private affairs at Rome, as he wrote later to Cicero, (*Att.* 9. 7B. 2). It was not only Cicero whose private obligations were being stretched by civil war.

Cicero attached to this letter to Atticus his recent correspondence with Pompey, where the general's polite but brief recommendations that Cicero

---

[24] For a similar denunciation of Pompey as the cause of the present disaster because of his errors over ten years see *Att.* 9. 5. 2.
[25] *Att.* 9. 9. 2, 9. 10. 3. The threat of the Getae was not so fantastic. An inscription shows us that Pompey did send an envoy to their king Burebista (*Syll*³. 762, 21 ff.).
[26] *Att.* 9. 7. 3, 9. 10. 6. For Sulla-style rule see also 10. 7. 1; *Lig.* 12.
[27] Syme, 1939a, 44, n. 2.

should join him contrast with Cicero's extensive explanations of why he was not so doing. His two letters are somewhat disingenuous in professing his original ignorance of Pompey's plans to retreat from Italy, when one to Atticus on 16 February shows that it was not so much a question of ignorance as reluctance to leave Italy—for the same reason that earlier he had not wanted to leave the city: he wanted a settlement or at least a quick end to the war.[28] In the second of 27 February he regrets that by the time he knew of Pompey's plans he was cut off from joining him (8. 11D. 2–5) and goes on to assert firmly both his desire for peace at almost any price and his personal devotion to Pompey. In the course of this he replies to the criticisms that he knows are circulating among Pompeians that he was lukewarm about the war and over-friendly to Caesar. He readily admitted the first charge and, as to the second, argued that he had to insure his position if a peace was agreed; he had been no more Caesar's friend than many making these charges against him.[29] Atticus had earlier mentioned the circulation of a letter that Cicero had written in reply to one of Caesar's with a request about the latter's gladiators at Capua, in which Cicero had both showed benevolence for Caesar and respect for Pompey, urging Caesar to make an agreement.[30] Then (17 February), as now, Cicero was unrepentant. Meanwhile the Italian upper class who had been afraid of Caesar's advance were now impressed with his clemency and devoted to him. Cicero contrasts this with their earlier vows to the gods on behalf of Pompey's recovery from illness.[31]

Only an agreement between Caesar and Pompey would have satisfactorily solved Cicero's dilemmas about his own future course. While Pompey was still in Italy, Cicero still on occasion saw hope of peace, at other times he thought it impossible because Pompey was not prepared for any sort of terms. His pessimism was shared by Balbus, who treated any acceptance of terms by Pompey as more wishful thinking than a real expectation.[32] A tantalizing glimmer of hope was provided by the episode of Numerius Magius. Associated in our manuscripts with a letter to Atticus of 13 March are three letters Cicero had received, one from Oppius and Balbus senior in Rome and a second from Balbus alone enclosing a third from Caesar to the pair (*Att.* 9. 7A,

---

[28] *Att.* 8. 11B. 3, 8. 11D. 1; cf. 8. 1. 2–3. See 7. 23. 1 for his previous fear that Pompey planned to leave. This does not mean that his reaction to the news from Corfinium in the letter of the night of 18–19 February from Cales was not genuine (*Att.* 8. 3. 7). See SB *Att* iv. 454–9.
[29] *Att.* 8. 11D. 6–8, cf. 12. 2.
[30] *Att.* 8. 2. 1, cf. on the gladiators 7. 14. 2.
[31] *Att.* 8. 13. 2, 8. 16. 1–2: including the leading *equites* who were Pompey's select group of jurors. See also 9. 13. 4 and 9. 5. 4 for a comparison of the vows for Pompey's health with the decrees of congratulation to Caesar for his victory. These decrees contrasted also with the sympathy of the *municipia* for Pompey just after Caesar's invasion (7. 11. 4).
[32] *Att.* 8. 13. 1, 8. 15. 3, 8. 15A. 1.

B, and C). Oppius and Balbus play with Cicero the role that Rosencrantz and Guildenstern play with Hamlet: they court him respectfully and try to elicit his intentions so that they can communicate them to their master. The first letter begins in a disgustingly ingratiating manner: 'The advice not just of humble people like us, but also of men of great importance tends to be judged in the eyes of the majority by results, not by intentions' (*Att.* 9. 7A. 1). The pair hold out the hope that Caesar will hold discussions on negotiations with Pompey when he comes back to Rome, and recommend that Cicero pursue a policy of neutrality, which Caesar in the light of his sensibility (*humanitas*) and generous spirit (*indulgentia*) will surely approve (ibid. 1–2).

In the following letter Balbus argues that Caesar' desire for reconciliation and his remoteness from any form of brutality (*crudelitas*) is shown by the enclosure (9. 7B. 1). In this short letter of about 5 March Caesar says that he is glad they approve of his policy at Corfinium. He wants to show himself as merciful as possible (*lenissimum*) and so achieve a settlement with Pompey. They should try in this way to win over the support of everyone and enjoy a lasting victory, since all others have failed to escape odium through their brutality nor have any of them maintained their victorious position except Sulla, someone whom he is not proposing to imitate.[33] He then briefly relates that he has captured and, following this principle, released Magius, a *praefectus fabrum* (in effect an aide-de-camp) of Pompey, who is indeed the second *praefectus fabrum* to have been captured and released. According to Caesar, both *praefecti* should show their gratitude by urging Pompey to be his friend, rather than the friends of their former common enemies who have engineered the present predicament of the *res publica* (*Att.* 9. 7C. 2). Caesar's expectation was fulfilled. Cicero received a letter from Balbus on 24 March with an enclosure of a letter of Caesar to Balbus and Oppius. In this Caesar reports his arrival at Brundisium and commencement of a siege, then: '(Pompey) sent me Numerius Magius with a proposal about peace. I replied what I thought fit. I will let you know when I have hopes of progress in an agreement'.[34]

By the time Cicero learnt this, however, it was too late: Pompey had sailed from Brundisium on 17 March.[35] We cannot be sure about how the negotiations broke down. Caesar's own version in *Bellum Civile* is inconsistent with this letter. He claims that after first capturing Magius he sent him to Pompey

---

[33] *Att.* 9. 7C. 1. Caesar's own key words here are *lenissimus, misericordia,* and *liberalitas.* Cf. Caes. *BG* 8. 44. 1; *BCiv.* 1. 74. 7; 3. 98. 2 (*lenitas*), and see n. 52 below.

[34] *Att.* 9. 13A. 1, cf. 9. 15. 4 for Cicero's ignorance of the content of Caesar's reply.

[35] *Att.* 9. 15a from Matius and Trebatius. Earlier letters to Cicero dated this to 4 and 15 March (9. 6. 3, 9. 14. 3).

with a request for a personal meeting, negotiations at a distance through intermediaries being unsatisfactory. Then he relates his surprise that with the siege well advanced Magius had not returned and adds that he sent Caninius Rebilus to approach Scribonius Libo with a request to press Pompey to such a meeting; Libo, however, replied that Pompey could do nothing in the absence of the consuls.[36] Caesar may have been correct about Pompey's desire for the consuls' agreement to any terms, but have suppressed any mention of what Pompey had actually offered.

Cicero's uncertainty about his own proper course is visible when he was intending to join Pompey at Luceria. At this point he thinks that Atticus is advising him to leave Italy, but he believes this neither morally right nor expedient for himself and his children: if Socrates could bear thirty tyrants, he could tolerate one (*Att.* 8. 2. 4). Nevertheless, when he has abandoned this plan and is returning to Formiae from Cales he remarks that he has one ship ready at Caieta and another at Brundisium (*Att.* 8. 3. 6); ten days later he unhappily decides to remain in Italy on moral grounds (*Att.* 8. 11. 4); a few days after this he has changed his mind (8. 14. 2). Later still he reluctantly assents to joining in a war on Italy because of his debt to Pompey and the shame of subjecting himself to Caesar and acquiescing in his criminal actions (*Att.* 9. 1. 4, 9. 2a. 1).

He found relief from some of his anxiety through setting out the issues as topics to be debated in Latin and Greek from either side. These 'theses' were not just rhetorical and dialectical exercises but genuine moral questions for him. We find them in Greek in a letter to Atticus of 12 March: 'Should one remain in one's fatherland when it is subject to a tyranny? Should one use every means when undertaking the overthrow of a tyranny, even if this is bound to hazard the survival of the city? Should one be wary of the man who overthrows a tyrant in case he too elevates himself to this position? Is it politically wise to retire somewhere and do nothing when one's fatherland is subject to tyranny or should every risk be taken in the pursuit of freedom? Should one bring war against one's country and besiege it when it is subject to tyranny? Should one enrol oneself with the best men even if one does not approve the overthrow of tyranny by war? Should one share the dangers of friends and benefactors in politics, even if their general policy seems at fault? Should the benefactor of his fatherland who has suffered irreparable harm and jealousy for that very reason voluntarily risk himself for his fatherland or should he be permitted to look after himself and his nearest and dearest, leaving aside any conflicts with those in power?' The last dilemma in particular expresses Cicero's anguish that he was being forced

---

[36] Caes. *BCiv.* 1. 24. 4–5, 1. 26. 2–5; cf. Rambaud, 1953, 140–1, 147–51.

once again into the battle-line in spite of his former surrender to *force majeure*.[37]

A few days later he reviewed Atticus' advice in earlier letters. Like Cicero, Atticus originally saw no merit in either Pompey's abandonment of the city or his plan to leave Italy. The latter, he thought, would mean a war fought to a finish. He refused to recommend that Cicero should leave Italy with Pompey: it would be risky and politically valueless, whereas he might be of value if he stayed behind.[38] After continuing to discourage departure as useless and dangerous, he modified his attitude in a letter of 22 February, suggesting that Cicero should take his lead from Manius Lepidus and Lucius Volcatius Tullus, the former consuls of 66 BC: if they remained, he should remain with the understanding that, if Pompey escaped safely and found a firm base somewhere, he could leave behind the 'living dead' of Caesar's supporters,[39] and resign himself to defeat with Pompey rather than power amid rubbish like them. He was not sure, however, what Cicero should do, if Lepidus and Tullus left immediately.[40] In early March he was still advocating a policy of wait-and-see, reassuring Cicero that his caution was not dishonourable. Caesar's restraint in victory, moreover, was making him wonder where their best interests lay.[41] As other letters show us, Atticus also advised Cicero to ask Caesar to allow him to absent himself from politics and so avoid being actively associated with hostile measures against Pompey in the same way that before he had taken no active steps against Caesar.[42]

It was contact with Caesar and the Caesarians that seems to have ultimately persuaded Cicero that he must leave Italy. Cicero was at first afraid of Caesar's reaction to his attitude. A particular problem was his triumph. It would be humiliating if he had to beg for it, worse still if it was pressed on him, since acceptance would be disgraceful and refusal would appear to Caesar as total repudiation. Caesar had always blamed him for their previous alienation, because he refused the offer of the post on the agrarian commission in 59.[43] While still advancing to Brundisium Caesar sent with Furnius a brief note to Cicero thanking him for the attitude he had taken and requesting that they meet on his return to Rome, so that he could make use of his 'advice,

---

[37] *Att.* 9. 4. 2; cf. 10. 8. 4. For another 'thesis' see 10. 1. 3: 'Should one join the council of a tyrant if he is going to discuss something good?' On topics and the intertwining of rhetoric and dialectic in Aristotle's teaching in particular see Long in Powell, 1995, 52–8.
[38] *Att.* 9. 10. 4–5 from letters written on 21, 23, 25 January and 7 February.
[39] Atticus seems to have compared them to the ghosts met by Odysseus in *Odyssey* book 11.
[40] *Att.* 9. 10. 7. For Lepidus' considering departure see 9. 1. 2.
[41] *Att.* 9. 10. 8–10, Atticus' letters of 1, 4, and 5 March.
[42] *Att.* 9. 2a. 1 (8 March); 9. 6. 6 (11 March); 9. 7. 3 (13 March).
[43] *Att.* 9. 2a. 1; cf. 2. 19. 4.

influence, standing, and help in everything'.[44] On 19 March Cicero was visited by C. Matius, one of Caesar's friends whom Cicero respected as sensible and unlike the rest of the 'living dead': Matius interpreted the letter as asking for help towards a peace-settlement (*Att.* 9. 11. 2). Cicero accordingly wrote a reply, a copy of which he sent to Atticus.

He begins by saying that he was not surprised that Caesar wanted to use his 'advice (*consilio*)' and 'standing (*dignitate*)', but did not understand the words 'influence (*gratia*)' and 'help (*ope*)'. He was, however, led by hope that 'in the light of his remarkable and incomparable wisdom' Caesar was interested in a peace-settlement and he thought that he himself was well suited to this project (9. 11A. 1). He refers to his previous efforts for peace with Pompey and the senate, his avoidance of involvement in the war, and his opinion that Caesar was being wronged in the war because of the opposition of his enemies to the privilege conceded him by the Roman people (ibid. 2).[45] Just as he had defended previously Caesar's standing, so now he was concerned for Pompey's. Accordingly, he now asked Caesar to spare a little time to considering how he himself might through Caesar's generosity remain virtuous, grateful, and loyal. He was sure that Caesar would grant this not only in Cicero's interest, but because it suited the public interest and Caesar's own good faith that he should be preserved as a mutual friend of Caesar and Pompey and well qualified as a possible mediator. He was impressed by Lentulus Spinther's letter to him about Caesar's generosity, for which he had thanked Caesar. Lentulus had saved him, as he hoped Caesar would. He had been showing his gratitude to Lentulus; he would like to be allowed to do the same to Pompey (ibid. 3). He circulated this letter to many others. Atticus later informed him how widely it was known and clearly suggested that there were adverse comments about its phraseology, to which Cicero replied that this was necessary in order to persuade Caesar.[46] On his return journey from Brundisium after Pompey's embarkation on 17 March Caesar sent a brief reply expressing his delight at Cicero's approval of his rejection of cruelty and urging him to meet him at Rome, clearly at the senate-meeting that he had advertised for 1 April (*Att.* 9. 16. 2, 9. 17. 1).

---

[44] *Att.* 9. 6. 6, 9. 6A; cf. 9. 9. 3 for Cicero interpreting this to mean that he should use his consular rank and influence to get the senate to approve a motion that Caesar wanted.

[45] Strictly this must refer to the privilege of standing for the consulship in his absence but, as Shackleton Bailey rightly suggests (SB *Att* iv. 383), the implication is that Caesar's enemies were opposed to his second consulship. See *Fam.* 6. 6. 5 for Cicero's later claim that he had worked to get Caesar's right to stand in absence accepted.

[46] *Att.* 8. 9. 1, evidently misplaced in the manuscripts. It must belong to the end of March. See SB *Att* iv, no. 188, 394–5.

In fact Cicero met Caesar on his journey north from Sinuessa on 28 March.[47] Cicero assumed correctly that Caesar wanted to legitimize his position by getting consuls or a dictator elected by a praetor with augural approval, something which was improper constitutionally (*Att.* 9. 9. 3, 9. 15. 2). He did not wish to cooperate with this plan nor did he want to go to Rome (9. 17. 1, 9. 18. 1), but was keen to obtain Caesar's acceptance of his neutrality and continuing friendship with Pompey as well as Caesar.[48] At the meeting he was true to his purpose, but provoked an irritable reaction from Caesar, who claimed that he was being tried and condemned by Cicero and that the others would be reluctant to come to the senate if he did not. Cicero's answer was that they were not so committed to Pompey. Caesar then invited him to come to the senate and talk peace. Cicero first asked whether he could say what he liked and, when Caesar replied (somewhat ironically) 'Can I tell you what to say?', said that he would make a motion against the invasion of the Spains and Greece and express deep regret about Pompey. When Caesar said that this was not what he wanted, Cicero answered that he could not come to the senate without speaking in this way and that there was much else that he could not pass over in silence. Caesar's exit line was to ask him to think about it: if he could not employ Cicero's support in the senate he would use that of anyone he could find and stop at nothing—and so they parted. Cicero was sure that Caesar was not pleased with him, but he was pleased with himself for the first time for a long period (9. 18. 1–3).

This meeting seems to have finally convinced Cicero that he must go. When he went to Arpinum to give his son the toga of manhood, he found the townsmen gloomy over the recruitment and billeting of troops. This would have been an indication that the war was going to be long. He would not leave Italy for the sake of the *res publica*, which he thought totally destroyed, but to show his gratitude to Pompey for extracting him from the misfortunes that he himself had created. Above all he could not bear to see Caesar's men in power (*Att.* 9. 19. 1–2). Some of his own friends he still respected: Trebatius was a good man and a good republican (*Att.* 10. 1. 3, 10. 11. 4); Matius desired peace (*Att.* 9. 11. 2). However, he could not resist irony about the mental 'torture' Balbus suffered over the peace negotiations at Brundisium—Balbus, Pompey's preferred intimate who had been given the site for his garden villa

---

[47] Caesar had spent the night of 27 March at Sinuessa (*Att.* 9. 15a, 9. 16. 1).

[48] *Att.* 9. 15. 1. *Contra* SB *Att* iv. 388, this seems to refer to what he had requested in his letter to Caesar rather than, more specifically, the condoning of his absence from the senate. In 10. 3a. 2, when he reports that Caesar had forgiven him for his absence in a letter but had added the comment that Titinius and Servius Sulpicius complained that they had not been released from their obligation, he says that their reluctance to be present was ridiculous when their sons had been with Caesar besieging Pompey.

by Pompey and now had betrayed him (9. 13a, cf. 13A. 2). As for his former client Rabirius Postumus, who was bustling about in Caesar's service, Cicero could not stand the sight of him.[49]

It was another friend who brought him news of what actually happened in the senate at Rome. On 14 April Curio, now on his way to Sicily to secure the province for Caesar, visited Cicero in his villa at Cumae (*Att.* 10. 4. 8). Caesar was by then travelling to Spain after a frustrating three days of senate meetings, culminating in vetoes by the tribune L. Metellus, and obstruction by the same tribune to his withdrawal of money from the treasury.[50] Curio expected that those condemned to exile under Pompey's law about electoral bribery would be restored.[51] What was more important, he described Caesar's fury at the opposition that he had encountered. Caesar had wanted to kill Metellus, and many of his entourage had urged him to do so: nor would the killing have stopped there. As for Caesar's self-restraint, he thought *clementia* was popular, but if he lost public support, he would turn brutal.[52] Curio assumed that Caesar would take the Spanish provinces and then would pursue Pompey to the death, though he feared the potential power of the Pompeian fleet (*Att.* 10. 4. 9, cf. 10. 7. 3). In fact the senate had agreed to Caesar's proposal of an official embassy to Pompey about a settlement but no one wished to be an ambassador either for fear of being treated as a Caesarian by Pompey or through doubts about Caesar's sincerity.[53] The senate decree that had improperly given Curio, a private citizen, his command with six *fasces* had been 'stolen', presumably slipped through rather than forged (*Att.* 10. 4. 9).

Cicero now wished he had received a specific pledge from Caesar to respect his neutrality if he left Italy, as L. Philippus had, but Curio reassured him, saying that he would write to Caesar. He was even prepared for Cicero to go to Greece via Sicily. As for Caesar, according to a letter Curio had received from Dolabella, he was happy that Cicero had not come to Rome (*Att.* 10. 4. 10–11). Cicero was relieved that the reports Quintus' son had been making about his father and uncle's attitudes to Caesar and Hirtius had had no effect (ibid. 6). Tullia wrote to Cicero urging him not to leave before he heard whether Caesar had succeeded in Spain. His reaction, in a letter of 2 May,

---

[49] *Att.* 9. 2a. 23, 9. 3. 2, 9. 6. 2. Cicero calls him by his birth name Curtius. For his later doubly dyed *toga praetexta*, when he had been given *imperium*, see *Fam.* 2. 16. 7.

[50] Caes. *BCiv.* 1. 32–3; App. *BCiv.* 2. 41. 163–4; Plut. *Caes.* 35. 4–11.

[51] This happened late in the year: Caes. *BCiv.* 3. 1. 4.

[52] For Caesar's anger see also *Att.* 10. 8. 6 and Caelius in *Att.* 10. 9A. 1 = *Fam.* 8. 16. 1. Curio may have been unfair, see *VRR* 51; Amm. Marc. 29. 2. 18. *Clementia* seems to be the word Curio used. See n. 33 above for Caesar's vocabulary and on this Griffin, 2003, 159–63.

[53] Caes. *BCiv.* 1. 32. 8–33; Plut. *Caes.* 35. 4–6.

was that, if Caesar failed, his own subsequent arrival at Pompey's side would be shaming and hardly appreciated by Pompey; if, however, Caesar succeeded, it would be a long war and he could not delay for ever (*Att.* 10. 8. 1–2).

It is clear that his talk with Curio of seeking a place of neutral retirement, though probably sincere at the time, was deceptive. He had indeed provisionally accepted an invitation from Atticus to go to Epirus, though he feared that it would be devastated by the war.[54] He was also seriously considering going to Malta, where he had a longstanding guest-friend, A. Licinius Aristoteles.[55] Essentially he could not face living under Caesar's domination, which he feared would produce the same sort of *popularis* measures that he had opposed before—attacks on private fortunes, cancellation of debts as well as the return of exiles like Gabinius and Clodius' friends, Sextus Cloelius and Plaguleius: he would be in effect subject to his former Catilinarian opponents.[56] He even convinced himself on the basis of Plato's account of the demagogic tyrant in *Republic* books 8 and 9 that no Caesarian tyranny could last long, apparently forgetting that Dionysius I, Plato's model, had remained in power for thirty-seven years (*Att.* 10. 8. 6).

Whatever his plans, it was best to pretend that he was going to Malta. Cicero enclosed to Atticus what he, not unfairly, described as an odious letter from Marcus Antonius (*Att.* 10. 8A). The latter claimed to have more affection for Cicero than he could possibly imagine. This led him to fear the stories that Cicero was about to cross the sea, false though they might well be, especially since he valued so highly Dolabella and his daughter Tullia and he was so highly valued by 'us all'—by which Antonius meant presumably the Caesarians—who had almost more concern for Cicero's status and reputation that he had himself. Antonius referred to a breach of friendship between them, arising more from his own jealousy than from any offence by Cicero—perhaps the fact that Antonius had joined in the accusation of Milo (Asc. 41 C). He finished by warning Cicero in the light of both his own and Caesar's regard, to distrust the man who did him an injury first in order to do him a service later, that is Pompey, and not to abandon one who would wish to preserve his security and prestige, even if he, unthinkably, ceased to hold him in affection (*Att.* 10. 8A. 2).[57] Cicero also received a letter from Caesar on

---

[54] *Att.* 9. 12. 1, 10. 7. 3. He had solicited the invitation (9. 7. 7). For the expected plundering of Greece, especially by Pompeians, see 9. 9. 2.

[55] *Att.* 10. 7. 1, 10. 8. 10, 10. 9. 1; cf. *Fam.* 13. 52. He had of course originally considered Malta as a place of exile in 58 (*Att.* 3. 4).

[56] *Att.* 10. 8. 2–3, cf. §8 and 8. 11B. 7 for his earlier fears. See *Dom.* 89 for Plaguleius; for Cloelius, *Pis.* 8; Asc. 7, 33, 47, 55–6 C; *QF* 2. 5. 4.

[57] This sort of jibe about Pompey was first made on Cicero's return from exile—by Clodius (*Dom.* 29).

2 May written in the middle of April. The latter had heard rumours of Cicero's intention to leave and urged him to neutrality. In view of Caesar's success he had no reason to join Pompey for the sake of security and had no honourable excuse either, since he had previously refused to associate himself with Pompey's plans. To leave Italy now was an insult to their friendship and one which suggested he disapproved of Caesar's conduct. He was lucky to have the guarantee of secure neutrality that was not available to others (*Att.* 10. 8B. 1–2).

With this letter came one containing even blunter advice from Caelius, who had visited Cicero at Cumae but was now travelling with Caesar (*Att.* 10. 9A).[58] He had interpreted Cicero's last letter to him as implying that he would join Pompey, had persuaded Caesar to write, and was now making his own plea (ibid. 4). Like Curio he warned Cicero that Caesar's clemency had now been stretched to the limit, especially after the opposition in the senate (ibid. 1). There was no point in following people in defeat, whose battle-line he had been reluctant to join and whom he had offended by his hesitation. Cicero should look after his family and not face friends like Dolabella and Caelius himself with an awkward choice between their own security and endangering his life. He should not be careless in choosing the best course through shame at failing to be sufficiently optimate (a supporter of the best). At least he should wait for the result in Spain (ibid. 2–3). Cicero's son and nephew apparently wept when they read the letter and the references to his family. In his reply Cicero claimed that he was only seeking to hide himself. Caelius should have already known how desperate he was. Hortensius used to pride himself on never having participated in civil war; Cicero hoped for even greater glory from the same thing because in his case it could not be attributed to cowardice (*Fam.* 2. 16. 2–3). If there ever should be a *civitas*, a republican community again, there would be a place for him; if not, he invited Caelius to join him in whatever deserted place he had settled (ibid. 6).

Cicero had clearly written in the same vein but less effusively to Antonius. His answer came on 3 May, shorn of the insincerities of the other's previous letter. In Antonius' view a neutral remained in his fatherland. The man who left proved himself to be making a judgement about one side or the other. But it was not for him to take a legal decision on who could leave or not. The job given him by Caesar was to prevent anyone leaving Italy.[59] If Cicero wished an exemption from this, he should write to Caesar. Antonius was sure that Cicero

---

[58] A less well-preserved text in *Fam.* 8. 16, cf. *Fam.* 2. 16. 3, in Cicero's reply, for Caelius' visit, perhaps about the same time as Curio's.

[59] He told Trebatius that he had in fact specific instructions to prevent Cicero leaving (*Att.* 10. 12. 1).

would receive this, especially as he promised to remember his friendship with the Caesarians (*Att.* 10. 10. 2). Cicero planned to pretend to comply, saying he would write to Caesar, then to slip away (ibid. 3). He was, however, expecting a visit from Antonius. The tribune was travelling around with his mistress Volumnia Cytheris in an open *lectica*, his wife in another; seven more carried his female friends and others his male friends.[60] After being expected for some days he did not in fact come, saying in apology that he was embarrassed because he thought that Cicero was cross with him.[61]

Servius Sulpicius did come on 8 May. He had apparently spoken in the senate in favour of reconciliation and against Caesar's going to Spain. Now he felt vulnerable and sought Cicero's advice in person.[62] He feared the outcome of the civil war, whoever won. Pompey was angry with him and ready for reprisals; Caesar was not his friend and an unscrupulous radical; both needed money. If the condemned exiles returned, he would go into exile himself. Cicero was sure this would happen and in general agreement with him but, because he thought him too nervous, did not confide in him his own plans.[63] Meanwhile Cicero was being watched by Antonius' soldiers.[64] He no longer had confidence in how Curio would treat him in Sicily. At first there had been uncertain news of support for Cato, but he had in fact left Syracuse on 23 April, as Cicero was informed by Curio (*Att.* 10. 12. 1–2, 10. 16. 3). According to Caesar, Cato, who had been energetically refitting old warships and commissioning new ones in Sicily while simultaneously recruiting in both southern Italy and Sicily, made a speech in the Syracusan assembly complaining that he had been betrayed by Pompey and then fled.[65]

Cicero says little positive about his own plans except to allude mysteriously to 'Caelius' and 'that Caelian project' and finally to tell Atticus to present himself in good health when Cicero met him in Greece.[66] He still had hopes that at some time he might once again be a political figure, presumably as a mediator, but it would not be yet.[67] He certainly did not want to raise a revolt in Italy. When on his arrival at Pompeii Ninnius brought him a message that

---

[60] *Att.* 10. 10. 3, 5; cf. 10. 16. 5; *Phil.* 2. 58. See also 10. 13. 1 for his arrogant treatment of municipal embassies.

[61] *Att.* 10. 11. 4, 10. 13. 2, 10. 15. 2–3.

[62] *Att.* 10. 10. 4; *Fam.* 4. 2. 1–3, esp. 1. 1, 2. 3.

[63] *Att.* 10. 14. 1, 3. Antonius' trip to Ischia is jokingly explained as 'to promise a return to the exiles' (*Att.* 10. 13. 1).

[64] *Att.* 10. 12. 1; 10. 12a. 2; 10. 18. 1–2.

[65] *BCiv.* 1. 30. 4–5. See also Plut. *Cato mi.* 53. 2–4; App. *BCiv.* 2. 40. 162 for Pollio leading Curio's advance guard and claiming that Caesar's control of Italy gave him the right to take over the province.

[66] *Att.* 10. 12a. 3, 10. 14. 3, 10. 15. 2, 10. 16. 6.

[67] *Att.* 10. 15. 3 'cuius gravioris personae suscipiendae spes'. The praetor A. Allienus thought that one of the praetorian college, the senior magistrates in Italy, might do this job.

the centurions of three cohorts wanted to hand over themselves and the town to him (taking him still as the magistrate in charge of the area), he took care to leave his villa before dawn (*Att.* 10. 16. 4). The Caelian project might be one of taking over the province of Africa, as Shackleton Bailey has argued, suggesting that this had to be abandoned when it was clear that Cato had not held Sicily.[68] Alternatively, it might be one of returning to Italy to act as a leader of the non-Caesarians and a peacemaker, if Caesar got into difficulties—something that Caelius could have proposed to him at Cumae in April. Cicero's last comment to Atticus as he travels to Formiae on 19 May is that he has come to the point when he can act neither courageously nor prudently (*Att.* 10. 18. 3). His final brief note was to his wife as he embarked at Caieta on 7 June. In this he talks with relief about defending the *res publica* with people like himself (*Fam.* 14. 7. 2). There is a gap in his correspondence when he sails, and we lose detailed knowledge of his life for a long time.

THE LESSONS OF HISTORY

Atticus must have wearied of his agonized deliberations, as most modern readers seem to do. As we have seen, Cicero exploited his rhetorical and dialectical training and his knowledge of philosophy. However, what yielded more practical help was history: the wars between the Marians and Sulla which dominated his youth are a constant background to his thought—and not his alone. Pompey's own words and conduct led Cicero to compare him to Sulla (see above with n. 26). Caesar allegedly was claiming to be seeking revenge for Pompey's murder of the Marians Cn. Carbo and M. Brutus (*Att.* 9. 14. 2). As soon as it seemed likely that Caesar would be left in control of Italy, Cicero compared his future regime to that of Cinna, suggesting that he would slaughter leading optimates.[69] Moreover, the prospect of the return of exiles and the cancellation of debts that he detested had its precedent under the Marian regime (10. 8. 2).

This period also provided him with models for behaviour. Like Hortensius, he had so far managed to avoid taking an active part in civil war (*Fam.* 2. 16. 3). When Cicero thought of the Cinnan regime he also thought of the consulars of that time, who could not hide as easily as Hortensius: L. Marcius Philippus the consul of 91, censor in 86, L. Valerius Flaccus, consul in 86, his mentor

---

[68] SB *Att* iv. 461–9, App. VI. On this view it might also have something to do with the family of M. Caelius Rufus, who had property in Africa (*Cael.* 73).
[69] *Att.* 8. 3. 6, 8. 9a. 2 'crudelitas Cinnana'.

Q. Mucius Scaevola, consul in 95, who, according to Cicero, used to say that he foresaw what did in fact happen but preferred this to approaching the walls of his home city under arms (*Att.* 8. 3. 6).[70] What had Scaevola foreseen? The massacres of the Marian return in 87 or his own murder at the time of the Marian flight in 82?[71] Probably the latter: at one point Cicero wished for a death like Scaevola's; at another he expected either to be killed by Caesar like Scaevola or proscribed by Pompey as L. Scipio was by Sulla (9. 12. 1, 9. 15. 3). When reflecting on the unpredictability of the future he even refers to the failure of Gaius Marius himself, 'the most shrewd of men', to foresee the Sullan march on Rome (10. 8. 7).

He looked back further to the Greek history that he had read. At first he was not sure whether Caesar would be a Pisistratus or Phalaris, craftily conciliatory or brutal, and it is with some exasperation that he terms him later a Pisistratus—appropriately a demagogic tyrant (7. 20. 2; 8. 16. 2). He contrasted those who had cooperated with the Cinnan regime, including his mentor Scaevola, not with the Sullan supporters but with Thrasybulus, who had recovered the Piraeus from the tyranny of the Thirty, after returning from exile at Thebes, action which in due course led to the restoration of Athenian democracy: Thrasybulus 'perhaps (chose) better' (*Att.* 8. 3. 6). This vision would have retained its attraction for Cicero even amid the despair with which he planned his departure.

His knowledge of the tyrants and Thrasybulus could have derived from any general history of Greece. However, when he cited Themistocles' failure to foresee the future, he quoted in Greek Thucydides' encomium on his prudence (*Att.* 10. 8. 7). As he showed later in his dialogue *Brutus*, he knew other more sensational sources on Themistocles, Clitarchus and Stratocles.[72] However, he would have read Thucydides thoroughly as part of his oratorical studies in Greek.[73] Moreover, the precise quotation suggests that he had been recently rereading him. The previous autumn he referred in a letter to Atticus to Thucydides' Greek phrase for the digression on the Pentekontaetea (*Att.* 7. 1. 6). Did he draw parallels between the breakdown of relations between

---

[70] For Scaevola's opposition in the senate to the declaration of Marius to be a public enemy see Val. Max. 3. 8. 5 (which could well derive from a Ciceronian *exemplum*), wrongly ascribed by Valerius to the homonymous augur (*cos.* 117).

[71] See Cic. *de Or.* 3. 8; Livy, *Per.* 80, 86; App. *BCiv.* 1. 71. 326–72. 339; 88. 403; other references to be found in GC, pp. 176–7.

[72] *Brut.* 43. See Ch. XIV with n. 6 on the curious reference in *Fam.* 5. 12. 5 to Themistocles' return from exile.

[73] Cf. *Brut.* 29, 287–8; *De Or.* 2. 56, 93; *Orat.* 30–3. Cicero himself thought that Thucydides was an inappropriate model for oratory (*Brut.* 287–8; *Orat.* 31–2), but it is clear that he was so taken by the Atticists of his time. See Rawson, 1985, 144 for Philodemus' view in his *On Rhetoric* and, on knowledge of Thucydides in this period, Hornblower, 1995, 62–4, 68.

Athens and Sparta and that between Pompey and Caesar? Was for him the truest explanation of the war the growing power of Caesar which instilled fear into Pompey and drove him to fight? Or was Caesar the equivalent not of Sparta but of Xerxes? Cicero certainly compared Pompey's evacuation of Italy with Themistocles' evacuation of Attica.[74]

Ultimately, his historical precedents showed him how difficult it was, even for men of heroic stature, to reconcile conflicting moral claims and to forecast the future. His parting letter to Terentia suggests that after all his intellectual exercises he followed his gut feelings. As he wrote to Atticus in May (*Att.* 9. 12. 4), 'I never wanted to be a partner in his (Pompey's) victory, I would have preferred to share in his defeat.' In the words he used the previous December, like a cow following the herd, he followed the 'good men' or so-called 'good men', even if they were rushing over a precipice (*Att.* 7. 7. 7).

---

[74] *Att.* 10. 8. 4. His remark in *Att.* 6. 9. 5 that in face of the news of Caesar's legions at Placentia he likes his post on the Athenian acropolis may even be seen as a reference to Pericles' strategy in 431. Notice also his knowledge of Thucydides' complimentary description of the oratory of the Athenian oligarch Antiphon (*Brut.* 47). It is interesting too that Caesar in his *Anticato* compared Cicero to Pericles and Theramenes (Plut. *Cic.* 39. 5). Was he suggesting deliberate imitation by Cicero?

XVII

Living with Dictatorship

THE RETURN TO ITALY

THE thirty-eighth chapter of Plutarch's *Cicero*, which deals with Cicero's stay in Greece and presence with the Pompeian army, is remarkable for being largely composed on the basis of Ciceronian jokes, all of them bitter, none very funny—the exception is an anecdote about Cato, who criticized him for uselessly abandoning his neutrality.[1] This indicates the paucity of other material about this period of Cicero's life. There is no correspondence from the latter part of 49, which can be in part explained by his living with Atticus and in part by fears over the security of letters. We do not know how soon Cicero actually attached himself to the Pompeian army. He certainly had no active commission from Pompey—his own decision (*Att*. 11. 4).[2] He may have spent some time with Atticus on his estate in Epirus first, before the arrival of Caesar on the Illyrian shore of the Adriatic on 5 January 48 brought Epirus itself into the front line and hastened Pompey's arrival from Macedonia. At this point Pompey's camp would have offered more security than Atticus' ranch.[3] Owing to the lack of intercalation in the calendar, it was still not yet winter.[4] A desperate note to Atticus, asking him to look after Cicero's private affairs in Italy, seems to belong to the first half of January and implies that by then Cicero was with Pompey's forces.[5]

A sprinkling of letters follows. In one Cicero's excuse for not writing more frequently is that he had nothing worth saying, inasmuch as he did not approve of events and Pompeian policies (*Att*. 11. 4). It was also difficult

---

[1] Plut. *Cic*. 38. 1—probably deriving from a Cato biography, like the story of Cato helping Cicero to escape being killed by Pompey's son and his soldiers when he refused to take command of the Pompeian forces after Pharsalus (ibid. 39. 1–2).

[2] Whether he actually behaved as part of the Pompeian army is uncertain. Note the contrasting claims later in *Marc*. 14 (not to have joined the Pompeian army but Pompey) and *Lig*. 9–10 (L. Tubero and I were both in the same army).

[3] Caes. *BCiv*. 3. 6 for the crossing, ibid. 11–13 on Pompey's journey and 16. 1 on Caesar's march to Buthrotum.

[4] See Caes. *BCiv*. 3. 9. 8—winter 'approaching' when Octavius joined Pompey at Dyrrhachium.

[5] *Att*. 11. 1, esp. 2 'si ii salvi erunt quibuscum sum'. Cf. O. E. Schmidt, 1893, 183–5.

both to find suitable carriers and to get letters through without their being intercepted.[6] In spite of receiving an inheritance Cicero had money problems both in Illyricum and back in Italy. Although he soon moved half of the 2,200,000 sesterces he had deposited at Ephesus, by midsummer it seems that it had largely disappeared in a loan to Pompey.[7] He was miserable with frustration and anticipation, unlike most of his companions in the Pompeian cause; in the summer he was also ill physically; only the presence of Brutus was a comfort.[8] Caelius wrote to him from Italy, expressing disgust at the side he himself had chosen: every one in Italy except the money lenders was now a Pompeian. He promised to secure a Pompeian victory, even if the Pompeians themselves did not want it: Cicero was invited to wait for further news. Meanwhile, Caelius warned prophetically against attempting to defeat a Caesarian army in pitched battle (*Fam.* 8. 17. 2). This is the last letter from Caelius, evidently written on the eve of his unsuccessful attempt to raise rebellion in southern Italy with Milo, after he had been prevented from proposing laws about debt-relief in Rome.[9] Dolabella, who was with Caesar's forces, wrote to Cicero after Caesar's successes outside Dyrrhachium, begging him, not to desert Pompey immediately, but to refuse to follow him when he retreated from the area.[10] It was Caesar who was to retreat from Dyrrhachium but this was only a preliminary to his victory at Pharsalus. On the news of this battle Cicero, who had in fact remained at Dyrrhachium but with the excuse of illness,[11] chose to follow Dolabella's advice unambiguously and, after travelling to Patras, where he parted with Quintus and Quintus' son, returned to Italy.[12]

The first letter to Atticus after Cicero reached Brundisium (*Att.* 11. 5), usually dated about 4 November on the ground that it is parallel to a dated letter to Terentia (*Fam.* 14. 12), shows that Atticus and others in Rome already knew about his journey to Italy and were taking thought about his future (*Att.* 11. 5. 1): they recommended that he should come close to Rome, passing through towns by night (ibid. 2). Cicero was worried both about security of travel for a known Pompeian and the attitude of leading Caesarians to him, should he have succeeded in reaching the neighbourhood of Rome. He wrote to Oppius and Balbus and in a letter of 27 November hoped Atticus would

---

[6] *Att.* 11. 2. 4, 11. 4a; cf. *Fam.* 14. 6.   [7] *Att.* 11. 1. 2, 11. 2. 1–4, 11. 3. 1–3; *Fam.* 14. 6.
[8] *Att.* 11. 2. 2–3, 11. 3. 1, 11. 4a. See *Fam.* 6. 1. 5 for support also from A. Torquatus.
[9] Caes. *BCiv.* 3. 20–2; Dio 42. 22–5.
[10] *Fam.* 9. 9. 2–3, cf. Caes. *BCiv.* 3. 39–53.
[11] For the presence at Dyrrhachium of Varro and Cato also see *Div.* 1. 68, 2. 114 (the story of the prophecy by the praetor C. Coponius in command of the Rhodian fleet); *Fam.* 9. 6. 3. The date of Pharsalus comes from the Fasti of Amiternum (*Inscr. It.* xiii. 2, pp. 190–1, 493).
[12] *Att.* 11. 5. 4, 11. 9. 2, cf. Plut. *Cic.* 39. 1–3.

enlist the support of Trebonius and Pansa (11. 6. 3). There was some confusion when Antonius believed that, in the light of a letter of Caesar regarding Cato and L. Metellus, he should ban Cicero from Italy until Caesar had investigated his attitude. However, Cicero explained through L. Lamia that he had come in response to an invitation by Caesar sent through Dolabella. In consequence Cicero found himself, like Laelius, to be a named exception in Antonius' edict (11. 7. 2).

Cicero still felt it too embarrassing and uncomfortable to come to Rome and its neighbourhood. His arrival in Italy had sprung from impulse rather than reflection (11. 5. 1); he might have done better to hide himself somewhere in Greece like Sulpicius Rufus.[13] He still had his lictors; above all the civil war was not yet over and he felt himself the subject of a whispering campaign among both Pompeians and Caesarians: nor was this paranoia.[14] Although he disliked Brundisium (11. 6. 2, 11. 7. 6), the longer he hesitated to place himself more in the public eye, the less confident he became (11. 9. 1). He was particularly reluctant to commit himself openly to the Caesarian side, while the Pompeians in Africa were undefeated (11. 7. 2). This was not through any remaining affection for what had been the republican cause, as he made clear to Atticus in late November 48. He had never regretted leaving the Pompeian army (by this he seems to mean his remaining at Dyrrhachium when Pompey pursued Caesar into Thessaly). 'There was such cruelty among them, so great was their association with barbarian peoples that they had outlined proscriptions not only of men by name but of whole classes, that it had been established by everyone's judgment that the property of all of you would be the spoils of his (Pompey's) victory. I really mean "of you", for I realized that they only had the cruellest plans for you yourself' (11. 6. 2). Atticus is likely to have been a special target because on his return to Italy in 48 he seems to have allied himself closely to the leading Caesarians there, to judge from Cicero's request that Atticus should join with them to write to Caesar on his behalf.[15] More generally he was a leading example of the equestrians who had gone over to Caesar in droves in 49.[16]

By then Cicero knew of Pompey's murder in Egypt and claimed that it did not surprise him: 'such a despair in his cause had overtaken the minds of all the [sc. barbarian] kings and peoples... I cannot fail to grieve for his fate, for I knew him as an upright, decent, and responsible man' (*Att.* 11. 6. 5). In this

---

[13] *Att.* 11. 7. 4; cf. *Brut.* 156.   [14] *Att.* 11. 6. 2, 11. 7. 3, 5, 11. 8. 1, 11. 9. 2.
[15] *Att.* 11. 8. 1, cf. 11. 5. 1 for his joint letters with Caesarians to Cicero, 11. 7. 5 for his pleading Cicero's cause to them. Atticus may also have had a particular quarrel with the Pompeians, when he was in Epirus. Nepos' comment that Atticus did not offend Pompey (Nepos, *Att.* 7. 2) perhaps leaves unsaid more than it says.
[16] See Chapter XVI with nn. 31 and 41.

bleak obituary Cicero stresses moral virtues rather than political principles and judgement. He has not changed his mind about Pompeian policy. Just as Pompey's non-Roman allies had helped to turn what might have been a fight for the republic into a projected raid on the propertied classes of Italy, so they had proved true to form in his defeat, sacrificing their leader in pursuit of their own interest. Distrust of foreign allies also helped him later to justify his failure to join the Pompeians in Africa: 'the *res publica* was not to be defended by barbarian auxiliary forces from a most treacherous nation, especially against an army with so many victories behind it'.[17] Of course a large number of 'good men' were there. Cicero hoped that they would in whole or part surrender to Caesar: if they stuck to their cause and were victorious, his own prospects would be disastrous; so would theirs, should they be defeated, but at least their fate would be more honourable.[18] Meanwhile Quintus and his son, who had gone to make their peace with Caesar, were taking every opportunity to denounce Cicero both to Caesar and to others.[19] Cicero's magnanimous response was to write to Caesar—some time before 8 March 47—saying that Quintus had done nothing to alienate him from Caesar and had not been responsible for his departure to Greece: rather he had followed Cicero (*Att.* 11. 12. 2).

A LITERARY FAREWELL TO THE REPUBLIC

Cicero finally received an 'adequately generous letter' from Caesar in early August 47.[20] He waited till September to greet Caesar after his landing in Italy and then left Brundisium for his villa at Tusculum.[21] There 'he resumed good relations with his former friends, his books', as he wrote to Varro (*Fam.* 9. 1. 2). It is probably from this time that we can date the composition of his survey of past and present orators, dedicated to Brutus.[22] Unlike *de Oratore* and *de Re Publica* it is set in the immediate past. Cicero begins with the death of Hortensius in 50—a source of grief at the time, especially because the political

---

[17] The idea that Curio's expedition to Africa was a war against a successor to the Carthaginians was to be developed in Lucan's *Bellum Civile* 4. 736–7, 788–93.

[18] *Att.* 11. 7. 3 of December 47. Cf. *Fam.* 15. 15. 1–2 for Cicero's opposition to the continuation of the war. Atticus and Cicero received diametrically opposed accounts of the strength of the Pompeians in Africa (*Att.* 11. 9. 2).

[19] *Att.* 11. 7. 7, 11, 8. 2, 11. 9. 2, 11. 10. 1, 11. 13. 2, 11. 16. 4, 11. 22. 1.

[20] *Fam.* 14. 23 to Terentia, of 12 August; *Lig.* 7.

[21] Plut. *Cic.* 39. 4–5; *Fam.* 14. 20; cf. *Att.* 12. 1.

[22] On the time of writing of the *Brutus* see Douglas, 1966, pp. iv–x, pointing to signs that it was not finally completed until after the news of Caesar's victory at Thapsus.

situation required his wisdom and authority, but now to be regarded as fortunate because he did not see the present state of the *res publica* when oratory was at a discount and the forum was deprived of speaking of any sophistication. On the other hand, Cicero argues, the potential influence of a good speaker was highlighted at a time when men shut their ears to the advocates of peace through error or fear.[23] The parallel with the evocation of L. Crassus in *De Oratore* book 3 is obvious: the great speaker dies, fortunately for him, on the eve of a disaster for the *res publica* which arises because oratory has not received the respect that it merits. At the same time Cicero takes the first steps in an interpretation of the civil war, which reappears in his correspondence and his speech for Marcellus (13, 20, 30)—tactful to the aims of both victor and vanquished, but not without plausibility—that it was not caused by greed and ambition but by confusion and mistaken fears. As to Hortensius, Cicero claims that their rivalry did not obstruct his own reputation but added lustre to it through the very competition (*Brut.* 2–3). This presages how later in the dialogue he will describe at length both the development of Hortensius' career as a parallel to his own and the nature of his oratory, which provided a contrast with the current Atticist tendency and absolved Cicero from discoursing at length on what was special about his own oratory.[24]

In the *mise en scène* Cicero portrays himself being visited at home by Atticus and Brutus and thanking them for the comfort they had brought him by encouraging him to resume his earlier studies. Brutus has sent him a letter from Asia,[25] while Atticus has given him a copy of his recently produced chronography.[26] Atticus asks Cicero to resume a conversation he had begun in his Tusculan villa on the history of oratory, which had arisen from his hearing of Brutus' successful defence of King Deiotarus before Caesar in Asia and his despair at the thought that Brutus would never have a suitable field for his talents (20–2). Brutus comments that the study and practice of oratory is conducive to wisdom, which no one can do without, even amid the greatest

---

[23] *Brut.* 1–7, cf. 21, 157 on the emptiness of the courts and the Forum, where there is no place for Brutus and Servius Sulpicius Rufus.

[24] *Brut.* 301–4, 317–33. The digression on Atticism is at 284–91. See Douglas, 1966, pp. xiii–xviii. The argument there that Lysias' Atticism was currently in vogue because under Caesar political activity was eclipsed by lawsuits runs counter to Cicero's view that all forms of oratory were at a discount at the time.

[25] *Brut.* 11–12. The letter is argued by Hendrickson, 1939, to be Brutus' poorly attested *De Virtute* (cf. Douglas, 1966, p. xi). See *Fin.* 1. 8, *Tusc.* 5. 12; Sen. *ad Helv.* 8. 1, 9. 4–7. Hendrickson compares the references in Seneca to M. Marcellus with that in *Brut.* 250, arguing that the latter derives from Brutus' work.

[26] On Atticus' *Liber Annalis* see *Brut.* 11–14, cf. 44; *Orat.* 120; Nepos, *Att.* 18. 1–4; Peter, *HRR* ii, pp. xxi–xxix, 6–8; Douglas, 1966, p. xii.

wars. To which Cicero rejoins approvingly that at the moment all the nobodies think that they have gained or can gain what were once held to be the finest prizes in the community, but no one has been made eloquent by victory (23–4). This sets the tone for the work: admiration for the past is to be mixed with regret for the rift that now separates it from a present dominated by Caesarian *arrivistes*, while oratory itself is to be set on a pedestal as high as philosophy: indeed the participants take their seats on a lawn next to a statue of Plato (24).

Cicero's discourse anchors itself on his previous work in *De Oratore*. The praise of oratory, undertaken there by Cicero in his own person and in the personae of Crassus and Antonius,[27] is swiftly completed. Oratory is the most difficult art because it is a composite of five arts, each important in itself;[28] it was invented in Greece, later than the other arts from the Greek point of view though early in relation to Roman history (*Brut.* 39 ff., esp. 49). The review of the great Greek orators here (26–52) is more elaborate than Antonius' brief list of Greek models in *de Oratore* (2. 93–5): like its predecessor, it includes Thucydides (*Brut.* 29; cf. *de Or.* 2. 93) but no other historian; the sophists appear as teachers of rhetoric with their opponent Socrates, who is at the same time the founder of both dialectic and ethical philosophy (30–1).[29] Finally, Cicero addresses the history of the Roman republic (52 ff.). The catalogue of more or less distinguished orators that follows was perhaps to some extent a compliment to Atticus by imitation. The annotation, however, renders it more than a collection of data.

As soon as Cicero reaches the period for which he has evidence through writings or oral tradition received from his elders, he gives opinions on the strengths and weaknesses of the orator concerned and an overall estimate of his ability (the written speeches that the orator has left behind are treated as an important contribution to his reputation).[30] The orators are judged both in a judicial and a political context, if the latter is appropriate, and allowance is made to for the type of speaking they practised. Thus Cicero distinguishes a *popularis* style in oratory, both its more elevated form in the persons of men like the Gracchi and C. Carbo and that used by effective rabble-rousers;[31] although his partisanship for the *optimates* is obvious, he tries to do justice to

---

[27] *De Or.* 1. 11. 19, 30–4; 2. 2. 30–8.
[28] *Brut.* 25. Presumably the five elements of eloquence in *Brut.* 215 and *De Or.* 2. 79. In *De Or.* 1. 16–17 Crassus enumerates six skills.
[29] This is a rather different appreciation from that voiced in *De Or.* 3. 59–61, that it was Socrates who separated philosophy from oratory by removing it from public life.
[30] On the significance of written speeches, mainly produced after the event, see *Brut.* 91–4.
[31] C. Carbo and the Gracchi 103–5, 125–6. Contrast 136 (Thorius), 178 (Afella), 223–4 (Cn. Carbo, M. Marius, L. Quinctius, Lollius Palicanus, Saturninus, and Glaucia). Even L. Crassus could deploy *popularis* diction (165).

the abilities of their opponents. In the judicial field he notices the rise of the professional accuser with an aggressive style appropriate to his task—not a career for someone of good breeding.[32] At one point he turns aside to point out the orators from the Latin and allied towns of Italy before the Social War (169–70); similarly there were eloquent equestrians from Italy in the period after Sulla (246, 271). The account becomes tedious at times through Cicero's insistence on getting on record every orator he can remember, good, bad, or indifferent. Atticus is made to comment to the effect that in some orators the main quality for their inclusion is that they are dead.[33] Cicero's comprehensiveness is perhaps intended to rival Atticus' chronography. The *Brutus* also, however, has the nature of a multiple funeral *laudatio*, which is also a *laudatio* for the Republic.

It is no surprise after *De Oratore* that L. Crassus and M. Antonius are singled out as the supreme orators of the age before the Social War (138–65) and that Q. Scaevola is associated with them as the best juriconsult who also had genuine oratorical ability (145–52). As in the earlier dialogue we get the impression of a golden age, one which survived in the persons of C. Cotta and Hortensius during Cicero's earlier years as an orator,[34] but had been blighted by the violence begun by the Social War. Cicero's account of his forensic apprenticeship during that period is the more important, because the rest of his surviving writing provides tantalizingly little light on his attitude and conduct then. As we have seen, the letters of early 49 reveal the horror of civil war that the experience of his youth had instilled and his pride over his own abstinence from arms. If his family connections with the Marii allowed him to survive the domination of Cinna, the fate of his mentors Antonius and Scaevola probably allowed him to transfer his allegiance to Sulla with convincing sincerity. However, precisely how he survived the Sullan restoration remains obscure.

In the dialogue Cicero is urged by Brutus and Atticus for a long time to talk about his own career and he gives way to the extent that he discusses Hortensius and himself in parallel (232, 279, 292–7). After a brief appreciation of Hortensius' talents Cicero begins with his own arrival in the Forum in the first year of the Social War (90 BC), when many orators, including Hortensius, were absent on military duty,[35] Cotta was in exile, and the only judicial activity was the trials under the *lex Varia*—the law providing for criminal charges against those who had abetted the Italian revolt.[36] We hear

---

[32] *Brut.* 130–1, 136, 168, 221, 304. Cf. Lintott, 2001–3, 105–22.
[33] *Brut.* 297, cf. 244, 269 for earlier complaints.
[34] *Brut.* 189, 203–4, 228–9.
[35] See *Phil.* 12. 27; *Div.* 1. 72 for Cicero's own appearances on the battle front.
[36] *Brut.* 301–4, cf. 228–9 for Hortensius' first speech in 95; *GC* 136–7 for the *lex Varia*.

of Cicero's apprenticeship to the jurisconsult Scaevola in 89 and his study of philosophy the next year under Philo, at Rome as a refugee from the Academy at Athens owing to Mithridates' invasion of Greece. In 88 Cicero could listen to the *contiones* of one of his models, the tribune P. Sulpicius, but by the end of the year Sulpicius was dead and this was followed in 87 by the 'cruel' deaths of Catulus, Antonius, and C. Iulius Caesar Strabo—Cicero passes over how the first had been ordered by Sulla and the others brought about by Marius and Cinna (305–7). There followed the 'three years without arms' under the domination of the Marians. Earlier in the dialogue, when discussing the oratory of Antistius, Cicero referred to this as a period when the *res publica* was without law and dignity and so Antistius had little competition (227). He now argues that Hortensius was the leading orator, while he himself studied dialectic and practised declamation in Latin and Greek under the Stoic Diodotus (308–10).

The violence when the *res publica* was recovered caused the deaths (in 82) of Scaevola, C. Carbo, and Antistius.[37] However, the return of men like Cotta and Curio and the re-establishment of law and the courts led to Cicero undertaking both private and public cases, while taking the opportunity to study oratory under Molon, the ambassador from Rhodes (311–12, cf. Ch. IV and App. 1). By focusing on his rhetorical education Cicero keeps the account almost, but not quite, sterile of political implications: in the end it is clear that Sulla did restore the Forum to its former importance—a contrast with the time of writing. As for Cicero himself, the impression is that he carefully remained a neutral spectator in the troubled times, taking advantage of his opportunities for study, until the situation was ripe for entry into forensic practice. This might have seemed an encouraging precedent for a young orator who read the *Brutus*, if the dialogue did not have the general atmosphere of the end of an era.

Cicero then describes his journey to the East for further study and his return to compete with Hortensius, which led to the successful prosecution of Verres (313–19, cf. Ch. VII). Hortensius' consulship the next year (69 BC) was the beginning of a temporary decline in his powers, ascribed here to luxurious living and a relaxation from study and rhetorical practice (320), while Cicero himself kept up his hard work and created a new, more refined, style of oratory. He defines this by listing the qualities that other orators did not possess: a more thorough study of literature than the average; knowledge of philosophy, Roman law, and history (including the capability of citing

---

[37] On the orders of the younger Marius, App. *BCiv*. 1. 88. 403; Vell. 2. 26. 2. In *Rosc. Am*. 89–90 Cicero treats the massacre of *accusatores*, including the old man Antistius, in a light-hearted fashion, an appropriate attitude before a Sullan audience.

witnesses from the dead); the ability to use humour against his opponent, to broaden an issue from the particular to the general, to make amusing digressions, to move a judge to anger, grief, or whatever emotion was required (321–2).[38] As for Hortensius, Cicero's consulship revived his competitive instinct and for the next twelve years they lived in friendly rivalry, which culminated in their pleading similar cases under the restricted conditions of Pompey's legislation of 52, just as Brutus had himself. If Hortensius was less successful in his old age, it was because the two styles of Asiatic oratory in which he excelled—the one full of elegant and charming constructions, the other a flood of elaborate and recherché language—suited a young man better than an old, from whom something more imposing and authoritative was required. Both their careers, Cicero claims, ended in 50, the one with Hortensius' death, the other with the death of the republic (323–9).

Finally, Cicero turns to the addressee of the dialogue. Brutus had consoled him in a letter, arguing that his past achievements would speak for themselves about him, when he could no longer, and would live when he was dead: Cicero's political policy would be justified by the preservation of the *res publica*, if things went as they should, if not, by its death. Cicero, however, grieved for Brutus, whose career had been knocked sideways by the impact of politics. 'I am your supporter; I want you to make best use of your talent. I wish for you a *res publica* in which you can renew and expand the reputation of two most distinguished families. Yours was the Forum, yours that career...' (330–1) Cicero goes on to talk of Brutus' rhetorical studies and urges him to continue them in order that he should stand out of the mill of orators (the incomplete end to the dialogue argues that there have never been more than one or two outstanding in any period). On the surface we have a wish for the return of republican politics and the republican law-courts. However, the two families, that of Brutus' birth and that of his adoption, were the Iunii Bruti, descended from L. Iunius Brutus who was the enemy of tyranny and founder of the republic, and the Servilii, among whom had been Ahala, the assassin of the would-be tyrant Maelius. Brutus had placed both L. Brutus and Ahala on his coins.[39] The cryptic message could be disowned but it must have been obvious, not least to Brutus himself.

---

[38] These qualities largely correspond to the description of the art of oratory by Crassus in *De Or.* 1. 17–18. For citing witnesses from the dead see Appendix 3.

[39] *RRC* i. 433. 1–2, dated by Crawford to 54, in this context springing from suspicions of Pompey. See *VRR* 54–6; Balsdon, 1958, 91.

THE NEW ORDER

The ample correspondence with Atticus during Cicero's dictatorship, though it occasionally contains allusions to current politics, is largely void of political comment: instead it is centred on Cicero's private life and his studies. Cicero's attitude to Caesar's dictatorship emerges more clearly from letters to his friends. A number of themes recur—consolation for their present fortunes, reflection on the civil war, Cicero's attitude to the new regime, which ranged from resignation to exasperation, and the new life he has adopted.

Even before his return to the neighbourhood of Rome he wrote to C. Cassius, who had now returned to Italy after making his peace with Caesar in the aftermath of Pharsalus, recalling the conversations that they had at the outbreak of the civil war. They both had hoped that one battle would decide the issue: in that event, Cicero thought, the remains of the republic could be put together again. Unfortunately Caesar's delay in Alexandria had recreated hope among the Pompeians (*Fam.* 15. 15. 1–2). Cicero wrote to Varro near the end of 47 about his return to Rome and the resumption of his studies (*Fam.* 9. 1); a number of letters followed the following year. In these he lamented the suspicions that still surrounded former Pompeians like Varro and himself: the exultant victors treated them as beaten men, those who grieved over the Pompeian defeat were annoyed that they were still alive (9. 2. 2). At the time of this letter (April 46) the news of Caesar's victory over the Pompeians in Africa at Thapsus had just arrived: Cicero was embarrassed at the thought of taking the usual spring holiday in Campania (9. 2. 1, cf. 9. 3, 1). An earlier letter to Atticus refers to various dubious rumours about the conduct of the war. Cicero comments: 'Meanwhile there are games at Praeneste. Hirtius is there and all that lot. And indeed the games are eight days. What dinners, what entertainments! Meanwhile the issue has perhaps been decided. Amazing men! Yet Balbus is building: what does he care?'[40] The Caesarians had been so confident that they celebrated even before the victory. Cicero now advised Varro to keep his head down until the fervour of mutual congratulation among the Caesarians had cooled off (*Fam.* 9. 2. 4). Yet he regularly dined with the new rulers (*Fam.* 9. 7. 1).

In a later letter to Varro, written on the eve of Caesar's return from Africa in late June, Cicero returns to the civil war in Greece. He says that he realized that the Pompeians wanted war, while Caesar did not so much desire it as have no fear of it. Hence one side was bound to suffer calamitous defeat and the other side the greatest of evils, victory in civil war. The last was also true of

---

[40] *Att.* 12. 2. 1–2. See SB *Att* v. 298 for a reassertion of the traditional dating of this letter.

the Pompeians who were making the direst threats even to those who wanted peace like Varro and himself.⁴¹ A more studied piece of self-justification is to be found in a letter to M. Marius (*Fam.* 7. 3). Cicero begins with their meeting at his Pompeian villa on 12 May 49—at the time when he was offered command of the garrison of Pompeii.⁴² His self-respect had then driven him to decide to join Pompey. In Greece he was so revolted at the bloodthirstiness and the rapacity of the Pompeians, especially in the light of their debts, that he shuddered at the thought of their victory. 'There was nothing good except the cause'. Accordingly, he first tried to persuade Pompey to make peace and then to draw out the war. Unfortunately, success at Dyrrhachium gave Pompey confidence in his army and henceforward he was no commander. After Pharsalus Cicero could not contemplate war further; exile was preferable to the risks of continued fighting, but Cicero chose rather to be at home with his own family in order to live, if any form of *res publica* returned, as in his fatherland, if not, as in exile.⁴³

The letters to Papirius Paetus reveal how Cicero is learning to live with the present. In one probably written before Caesar's return from Africa, a response to Paetus' concern that Cicero may have caused offence in Caesarian circles, Cicero reassures him about his own popularity among Caesar's friends.⁴⁴ 'As for the man, in whose power is all power, I see nothing to fear, except that everything is insecure, once the rule of law has been abandoned, nor can the future nature of anything be guaranteed, which depends on another's will, not to say, whim.'⁴⁵ Cicero encapsulates the revolution that had struck the aristocracy of the republic. Formerly, allowing for foreign enemies, dangerous political opponents like Clodius, and natural mortality, they had a secure dominance of the world—*otium cum dignitate* indeed. Now they were always looking over their shoulders, as the new aristocracy was to do under the Principate. Like them, Cicero had to watch his tongue. His reputation for humour meant that a number of witticisms were being attributed to him. If he disowned them, it was at the cost of losing that reputation, which he was happy to do, if he could. Fortunately, he was told that Caesar

---

⁴¹ *Fam.* 9. 7. 2–3, cf. *Att.* 10. 4. 3, 10. 7. 1, 10. 14. 1. See also Ch. XV with n. 74 for his holding this view even before the war.

⁴² *Fam.* 7. 3. 1, cf. *Att.* 10. 16. 4.

⁴³ *Fam.* 7. 3. 1–4. See *Att.* 9. 11. 4 for Cicero anticipating the rapacity of Scipio, Faustus Sulla, and Scribonius Libo in view of their debts; Caes. *BCiv.* 1. 4. 2 on Lentulus Crus. Cicero also obliquely criticises Pompey for failing to support his search for peace (*Fam.* 5. 21. 2 of early 46 to Mescinius Rufus and 4. 7. 2 to M. Marcellus).

⁴⁴ *Fam.* 9. 16. 2; cf. 4. 13. 5 (to Nigidius Figulus); 6. 6. 13 (to Caecina); 6. 10a. 2 (to Trebianus); 6. 12. 2 (to Ampius Balbus) 6. 14. 3 (to Ligarius).

⁴⁵ *Fam.* 9. 16. 3. See *Fam.* 4. 8. 2, 4. 13. 5, 7. 28. 3 for other descriptions of Caesar as the man with supreme power, who controls everything.

had a critical ear for what was Ciceronian and non-Ciceronian, thanks to the way Cicero's Caesarian friends were ordered to relay to Caesar any good remarks that Cicero made at parties (*Fam.* 9. 16. 3–4). All he could do was to avoid stupid or imprudent remarks: he could not guarantee what might be reported to Caesar as his, or Caesar's reception of what he heard, or the good faith of the Caesarians with whom he spent his time. Greek histories were full of stories of how philosophers managed to live under tyrants at Athens and Syracuse. He could surely expect to maintain his status without giving offence.[46]

In a lighter mood Cicero jokes about the declamation lessons he had been giving to Hirtius and Dolabella, while receiving in return lessons in eating dinners. In this he was rivalling the epicure Paetus.[47] He compared himself in his next letter of late July to the tyrant of Syracuse Dionysius II, who in exile had become a schoolmaster. It was a protection against the present political climate. The alternative was death—at least in one's bed. The deaths of Pompey, Lentulus Crus, Afranius, and Scipio had been filthy. Cato's suicide had been glorious. That was still open to him, if he wanted, but he was taking measures to make it unnecessary. The second advantage of the declamation school was that he was regaining fitness and renewing his rhetorical ability by exercises. The final one was the new style of eating.[48]

He made a general defence of the dignity of this sort of teaching in his work on the ideal orator (*Orator*), which he composed after the *Brutus* and Atticus was reading before the end of the year.[49] His day, as portrayed to Paetus, began in the morning with the customary greetings (*salutatio*) from gloomy 'good men' and cheerful Caesarians; he then wrapped himself in his studies, reading or writing.; next came his classes; after that he devoted the rest of the time to his body (*Fam.* 9. 20. 2–3).[50] His interest in good food led to a new friendship with Volumnius Eutrapelus, whose freedwoman, the actress Volumnia Cytheris, had been travelling around as Antonius' mistress in 49: he actually dined in their company towards the end of 46 and felt no shame.[51] His one surviving letter to Volumnius reassures him for missing his declamations, apologizes for his present preoccupations, and promises that, once these are

---

[46] *Fam.* 9. 16. 5–6. Tacitus advocated a similar policy under the Principate (*Agric.* 42. 4; *Ann.* 4. 20).

[47] *Fam.* 9. 16. 7–9. How Epicurean Paetus was philosophically is not quite clear. He was later attending a lecture from an Epicurean philosopher (9. 26. 1, 3), but not taking it very seriously.

[48] *Fam.* 9. 18. 1–3—about the time of Caesar's return (cf. 1). For the date of this see *Bell. Afr.* 98.

[49] *Or.* 142–4; *Att.* 12. 6a. 1.

[50] There is a similar account in a contemporary letter to Curius, where the *salutatio* is said to be better attended, because it was unusual for the visitors to see a decent citizen (*Fam.* 7. 28. 2).

[51] *Fam.* 9. 26. 1–2, cf. *Att.* 10. 10. 5; *Phil.* 2. 58–9.

over, he will say goodbye to Forum and Senate-House and devote himself to the delights of literature with Volumnius and their fellow devotees like Cassius and Dolabella.[52]

Cicero had not, however, lost all contact with politics. The death of Cato led him to write an obituary memoir. His problem was that it was difficult to write anything acceptable to the Caesarians, whether he gave a detailed account of Cato's expressed views and political policy or he simply wrote a trite panegyric of his high principle and constancy. Cicero believed that justice could not be done unless the memoir were sufficiently elaborate, because Cato foresaw the present regime and its likely development, strove to prevent it, and finally died to escape seeing it in place. He was pleased with what he eventually produced (*Att.* 12. 4. 2, 12. 5. 2). According to Plutarch, Caesar treated the author with respect in the reply he composed, the *Anticato* (*Cic.* 39. 5). Cicero must have somehow managed a denunciation both of the corruption that characterized the last years of the Republic and of its overthrow by violence, without pinning the blame exclusively on the Caesarians. Some idea about how this was done can be gleaned from considering the speech he produced about the recall of Marcus Marcellus, which was delivered in the senate in September or October and probably circulated by Cicero soon afterwards.

HELPING FRIENDS: THE PRO MARCELLO AND PRO LIGARIO

Cicero wrote conciliatory letters to Marcellus some time before the debate, in which he pointed to their shared distrust in the Pompeian cause, once it became a question of war. Marcellus was right to retire, as he had after Pharsalus, to exile in Greece, but it was time now to put an end to it, as his friends under the leadership of his cousin Gaius were pressing for his recall: Cicero himself was not in a strong enough position to plead with Caesar, but he was lending his support (*Fam.* 4. 7, cf. 9). The senate meeting itself is described in a letter to Servius Sulpicius Rufus, who had recently accepted from Caesar the position of proconsul of Achaia.[53] For Cicero it is the first time since men had begun to settle constitutional problems by violence that

---

[52] *Fam.* 7. 33. This perhaps belongs to the period when the issue of the recall of Marcellus was being raised in the senate (see below).

[53] See *Fam.* 4. 4. 2, 4. 12. 1 and the letters of recommendation to Sulpicius in his post (*Fam.* 13. 17–28a).

anything had been done 'with dignity'. He describes how, when the matter had been raised by Caesar's father-in-law L. Piso and C. Marcellus had thrown himself at Caesar's feet, the whole senate rose and approached Caesar as suppliants (*Fam.* 4. 4. 3). In reply, Caesar spoke of Marcellus' bitterness and compared him unfavourably with his consular colleague Sulpicius. He reached, however, the unexpected conclusion that he would not deny the senate's request in spite of the bad omen (for the senate's future attitude to him).

Cato would have questioned the term 'dignity', when applied to this senate debate, but the day seemed to Cicero 'so beautiful that I seemed to see some sort of vision (*species*) of a *res publica* that was, as it were, breathing again.' All the consulars asked their opinion on the decision before Cicero thanked Caesar, apart from Volcacius Tullus (ibid. 4).[54] Cicero then decided to change his policy of remaining silent in the senate and thanked Caesar at length. He was afraid that this might have brought to an end his policy of respectable retirement (*honestum otium*), but was pleased that he had avoided giving offence to Caesar, who might have thought Cicero's silence an indication that he thought that there was no *res publica*. Nevertheless, he intended only to involve himself in public life within strict limits, so that he could satisfy both Caesar and his studies. Caesar was the only good thing in public life in Rome; for the rest, Sulpicius did better to hear of this by report than see it with his own eyes (ibid. 4–5).[55] Cicero writes in similar terms to Cornificius, who was at that time governing Syria, and goes on to talk of his thick skin when he saw Titus Plancus at Caesar's games and heard what was said in the plays of Laberius, an *eques* who was forced to appear on the stage,[56] and of Publilius Syrus (*Fam.* 12. 18. 2).

There is no reason to doubt the presentation of the senate debate in the letter to Sulpicius Rufus. Caesar's response was not predictable. If it had been negative, Cicero would have remained silent. His ability to improvise what was no doubt a polished speech was once more in evidence, made easier by the fact that he had already rehearsed many of the themes in previous writing (see below). As for the speech that he circulated, this must have borne some relation to what he said at the time but have been composed *ex post facto*, and

---

[54] Of the consulars only Tullus (*cos.* 66), M'. Lepidus(*cos.* 66), if alive and present, and L. Caesar (*cos.* 64) were senior to Cicero by year of office. The dictator probably privileged Piso and C. Marcellus (*cos.* 50) in the order of speakers because of their kinship with him and their involvement in the petition.

[55] A similar comment in a contemporary letter to Cornificius, the governor of Syria—'Many things would not please you, things on the other hand which do not even please Caesar himself' (*Fam.* 12. 18. 2).

[56] Macr. 2. 7. 4 = Laberius 125 Rib.

Cicero would have taken the opportunity to improve it further. Since Cicero's aim in speaking was to find an acceptable position for himself in relation to Caesar (*Fam.* 4. 4. 4), an early circulation was desirable.[57] What we possess in our manuscripts goes beyond thanks to Caesar over this issue, becoming an apologetic reflection on the civil war and a speech of advice to a ruler.[58]

In the *prooemium* we find the same self-justification that Cicero gave to Sulpicius: he has broken silence because Caesar has subordinated his own feelings to the authority of the senate (1–3). Cicero then contrasts Caesar's military success, in which he needed the physical support of his forces and, above all, the help of fortune, with the self-control and forgiveness that Caesar has just displayed (4–12). He claims that there is no force that cannot be weakened or broken by the force of iron (8). This argument is similar to that of Cato's letter to Cicero explaining why he did not support the proposal for a *supplicatio* for Cicero's success in Cilicia: the exercise of virtue is superior to military success, which depends of the strength of the army and divine favour.[59] Cicero, however, talks not of the gods but fortune (6–7)—appropriately, given Caesar's claim to have a fortune of his own.[60]

Caesar's decision about Marcellus is then interpreted as confirming a view of the civil war that Cicero has already expressed as his own in the *Brutus*: it had been undertaken by the majority through ignorance and unsubstantiated fears rather than through greed or cruelty (13).[61] Cicero goes on to point out his own continued belief in negotiation and his despair that 'not only peace but the speeches of citizens demanding peace were rejected' (14)—another echo of sentiments in the *Brutus* (7): he had never joined an army in civil war; his adherence to Pompey was through private, not public duty; he had spoken for peace before the civil war and continued to do so during it.[62] That his support for Pompey was through personal loyalty is attested by a number of texts in the letters.[63] Similarly, when he goes on to contrast Caesar's clemency

---

[57] Kerkhecker, 2002, 99. *Contra* Dyer, 1990, 19, 30, who believes in a date in 45 after Caesar's return from Spain. This is necessary for him in order to sustain his interpretation of the speech as an implied advocacy of tyrannicide. One may wonder, however, whether Cicero would consider circulating the speech after the news of Marcellus' murder in Athens at the end of May 45 reached Rome, as this would have appeared tasteless.

[58] Cf. *Att.* 12. 40. 2, 13. 27. 1, 13. 28. 1 for Cicero's later attempt to write a parallel to Aristotle's letter to Alexander the Great. On the rhetoric of the *pro Marcello* see Kerkhecker, 2002, with a useful bibliography; Dyer, 1990.

[59] *Fam.* 15. 5. 2, cf. Ch. XV.

[60] See e.g. Caesar in *Att.* 10. 8B. 1; *BCiv.* 3. 10. 6, 3. 26. 1, 3. 73. 3 and other texts assembled and discussed by Weinstock, 1971, 112–27.

[61] Cf. *Marc.* 20, 30; *Brut.* 7.

[62] Similar statements about his absence from the civil war in *Fam.* 2. 16. 3–4; about speaking for peace cf. Ch. XVI with nn. 5, 10, 46.

[63] See e.g. *Att.* 8. 11D. 6, 9. 4. 2, 9. 11. 2; Ch. XVI *passim*, Kerkhecker, 2002, 109–111.

with the Pompeian 'anger' and threats to all who had not joined them, he is merely making public what he had been saying in letters since before Pompey left for Greece in 49.[64] Caesar is urged to keep in mind this clemency and generosity as a form of true wisdom, and this idea generates a transition from gratitude for the past to an appeal for the future, by virtue of which the speech becomes a senator's advice to a supreme magistrate (19 ff.).[65]

The subject of threats to Caesar's life is delicately broached. Who, Cicero asks, can want Caesar dead? Hardly his old friends, nor those whose lives he has saved and turned from enemies into friends. The safety of everyone depends on Caesar's. It is a cause of fear and sorrow to Cicero that the *res publica*, which should be immortal, is established in the life of one mortal (21–2). Caesar is briefly recommended to re-establish civil society—the law-courts, the soundness of credit (*fides*), the decency of family life, and the breeding of children (23). We may cynically wonder whether Cicero was seriously expecting Hirtius, Volumnius, and Paetus to cut down on their dinners. However, it was probably true generally that the atmosphere of civil war had led to the search for instant pleasure, and financial uncertainty would not have encouraged the propertied classes to settle down to raise families. The wounds of civil war, Cicero continues, must be healed. For this reason Caesar must not be careless with his own life—at this point Cicero quotes his remark that he had lived long enough for either nature or glory—but continue his policies in order to recreate stability (24–9). The conclusion returns to the theme of the confusion and uncertainty about motives and policies in the civil war. The forgiving commander has won, which should be an argument against further resort to arms and for concord among all sane men. Everyone should now be Caesar's bodyguard; everyone is grateful to Caesar, not least Cicero, both for Marcus Marcellus and himself (30–4).

The question arises how we should treat a speech that at times seems to be outrageous flattery of the dictator, yet by its emphasis on the threat to Caesar's life is interpretable as an invitation to murder Caesar by innuendo? Dyer has argued that the very praise of clemency was intended to arouse indignation among Cicero's senatorial audience, because it pointed to despotism, citing the attitude of Cato (Plut. *Cato mi.* 66. 1).[66] M. Marcellus himself, to judge from the tone of his letter of thanks to Cicero (*Fam.* 4. 11) also thought that clemency implied servitude. However, a large number of the senators were Caesarians and even pardoned Pompeians were not necessarily so sensitive to indignity, when they considered the alternative. We can compare Cassius'

---

[64] Ch. XV with nn. 25, 26, 31.
[65] For Caesar as *dictator rei publicae constituendae* see CRR 113 n. 88.
[66] Dyer, 1990, 20–2.

remark in a letter of early 45 (*Fam.* 15. 19. 4). Cicero makes it clear in his letter to Sulpicius Rufus that part of his object was to satisfy Caesar that he believed some form of *res publica* still existed and was co-operating with it (*Fam.* 4. 4. 4); he also thought at the time that Caesar himself was the best thing in a disagreeable regime (ibid. 5).[67] He would not, therefore, have been intending positively to advocate tyrannicide either in the original debate or in a speech circulated in the aftermath of the event.[68]

The comment that there was no force that could not be weakened or broken by the force of iron was a conventional sentiment, if anything a warning against relying on force rather than conciliation, not a threat from Cicero (8). As a sentiment, it can be linked with Cicero's call to restore the rule of law (23): they are both pleas for a restoration of a genuine *res publica*. The repeated allegation that the civil war was an unfortunate mistake (13, 20, 30) is also an argument that at bottom there was nothing wrong with the old system. Cicero argues that this restoration (23, 29) is the reason for which Caesar himself and all around him must work to preserve his life. He carefully does not say that, if Caesar does not fulfil this function, his life does not matter. The speech was probably produced more in hope than expectation, but in any case it had at the time of its production the function of expressing an attitude to Caesar's dictatorship to which Caesar could not reasonably object, even if he did suspect it. By the same token it would have contributed to Cicero's good relations with the friends of Caesar whom he was cultivating. This would have been helpful in the efforts he was making to secure pardon or reinstatement into Roman society for Pompeian friends.

At the time he delivered *pro Marcello* Cicero had probably already decided to approach Caesar on behalf of his friend Q. Ligarius. He had been left to govern Africa when a *legatus* of Considius Longus in 50, had joined the Pompeian side there, and after Thapsus had been spared by Caesar but apparently not permitted to return to Italy.[69] Cicero promised Ligarius to help his brothers in their efforts to get him recalled, offering 'the ghost of my former standing (*dignitas*) and the remains of my influence'.[70] In a later letter he talks of coming to Caesar on the morning of 26 November with Ligarius' brothers, 'withstanding all the indignity and unpleasantness of approaching him and addressing him, with Ligarius' brothers and kinsmen lying at his (Caesar's) feet'. He had made a speech to fit the case and circumstances and

---

[67] Cf. *Fam.* 9. 17. 2 to Paetus on the restrictions placed on Caesar by his partisans.
[68] The scholiast (*Schol. Gron.* 295–6 St.) is therefore right in rejecting the interpretation of the majority of commentators that this is an *oratio figurata*.
[69] *Lig.* 2–5; 11; *Bell. Afr.* 89. 2.
[70] *Fam.* 6. 13. 2–4 'imago meae dignitatis... reliquiae gratiae', also, more conventionally, 'studium, consilium, opera, gratia, fides'.

was pleased with Caesar's friendly words and expression (*Fam.* 6. 14. 2). However, Ligarius was then accused of treason by Q. Aelius Tubero, a former Pompeian[71] in a trial which seems to have taken place before Caesar in the Forum (*Lig.* 6)—evidently an *ad hoc* procedure, not a trial before the established tribunal for treason, the *quaestio de maiestate*, in which Caesar could have no place. The point of Tubero's accusation was that Ligarius had sided with an enemy of Rome, King Juba.[72] Pansa, who spoke first for the defendant, admitted that Ligarius had been involved in the African war (*Lig.* 1), which left Cicero only room to make a plea for mercy (*deprecatio*). According to Plutarch, Caesar is supposed to have said to his friends who were assessors, 'What prevents us spending some time listening to Cicero speaking, since it has been established long ago that the man is criminal and an enemy?', but was then so moved by Cicero's speech that he acquitted.[73] Cicero was therefore pleading for someone who on his own advocate's admission had sided with a foreign king against a Roman magistrate.

Cicero first describes carefully how Ligarius happened to be in Africa at the time of the civil war, but leaves somewhat vague, attributing it to necessity, how he came to stay there when P. Attius Varus came and on his own authority seized command of the province. He passes over the fact that Varus had prevented Tubero's father Lucius, then the Pompeian appointee, and Tubero himself from landing.[74] At this delicate point Cicero digresses into a eulogy of Caesar's clemency towards himself (6–8), after he had joined the same side as Ligarius.[75] This is then developed into an attack on Tubero's accusation (10–19). Caesar's clemency should not inspire cruelty from those he had pardoned. Tubero is accusing some one who has admitted his guilt, someone whose case for pardon is somewhat better than Tubero's own. The man is already in exile, so Tubero can be only intending to get him executed.[76] No one had ever tried that even at the time of the Sullan proscriptions, those cruel actions for which Caesar himself had at last taken revenge.[77] It was not as if Tubero were trying to refute a dubious defence which Cicero was using to obtain Ligarius' pardon, he was telling Caesar not to pardon (16). Furthermore, he called adherence to the Pompeian cause a crime. This brings Cicero back to a theme of the *pro Marcello* that the resort to civil war sprang from

---

[71] *Lig.* 2, 10–11, 17; Caes. *BCiv.* 1. 30. 2, 1 31. 3.   [72] Quint. 11. 1. 80.
[73] Plut. *Cic.* 39. 6.   [74] *Lig.* 2–5, esp. 4 (*necessitas*); cf. 23, Caes. *BCiv.* 1. 30. 2, 1. 31.
[75] *Lig.* 9–10. In *Marc.* 14 he had argued that he had not joined the Pompeian army but Pompey himself. Here, he admits participation in order to link himself to Tubero.
[76] *Lig.* 11. Exile, not execution, was the penalty under Caesar's own laws against public violence and treason and this seems to have been true of the law governing the *quaestiones* in the late Republic (*Phil.* 1. 23; cf. Sall. *Cat.* 51. 22, 40).
[77] *Lig.* 12. Cicero deliberately admits in public here the Sullan associations of the Pompeian cause cf. Ch. XVI with n. 26.

error and fear[78]—or at worst from hope, greed, hatred, and obstinacy (17–19). In any case a weakness sent by fate had overtaken men's minds.[79] Just as Caesar was protecting his *dignitas*, so were the Pompeians—Cicero had already argued this to Caesar in a letter of 49 (*Att.* 9. 11A. 2). It was a dispute between citizens, not a war against the *res publica* by enemies who wanted its destruction.

After arguing from Caesar's clemency, the inappropriateness of Tubero as a prosecutor, and the nature of the civil war, Cicero now compared his client's conduct with that of his prosecutor's father, suggesting, more than a little ingenuously, that it had been no easier for Ligarius to leave Africa than for L. Tubero to disobey his commission from the senate to take over the province. As for their being excluded, it was not Ligarius who was responsible, it was Varus. What had the two Tuberones then done? They went to complain to Pompey, whose partisans Varus and King Juba claimed to be (20–7). Cicero is happy to accept that Africa was a threat, 'the citadel of all the provinces, created for making war against this city' (22), and stress the influence of Juba, a most powerful enemy of Caesar's cause, and that of the Roman citizens in Africa (24).[80] This implicitly excuses Ligarius by suggesting that he was no longer free to follow his own inclination. In Macedonia, Cicero continues, the Tuberones received no satisfaction for their expulsion from Africa; they nevertheless remained with the Pompeian army, not because they believed in the cause, but because they wanted to be on the winning side when a fight was inevitable (25–8). The orator makes no comparison with Ligarius here, he suggests it by implication: the Tuberones remained Pompeian by choice.

The peroration is relatively long. Cicero claims that he is not pleading this case as he would before a judge but asking for pardon as from a parent. Pardon will be welcome among Caesar's own friends but also among Ligarius' family and connections in Sabine territory who—like most of municipal Italy—had gone over to Caesar's side in 49 (32–6). The final comparison is with M. Marcellus. Caesar had achieved glory by conceding his life to the senate; he should win similar glory with the people by showing mercy to Ligarius (37–8). The *pro Ligario* is in more than one way a pendant to *pro Marcello* and Cicero had a similar interest in publishing it—to stake out openly his relationship to Caesar. We know that it was in circulation in June of 45: Oppius and Balbus were so pleased about it that they sent it to Caesar (*Att.* 13. 19. 2, 13. 20. 2).

---

[78] Cf. *Marc.* 13, 20, 30 and *Deiot.* 10.
[79] *Fatalis calamitas* seems to mean the mental blindness called ἄτη in Greek literature.
[80] For Cicero's distrust of Juba see *Att.* 11. 7. 3. Juba had been Pompey's guest-friend and enraged by Curio's attempt to confiscate his kingdom in 50 (Caes. *BCiv.* 1. 25. 4); he had been recognized as a friend and ally of the Roman people by the senate in January 49 (ibid. 1. 6. 4).

Another beneficiary of Cicero's pleas was T. Ampius Balbus, a diehard Pompeian whom the Caesarians called 'the trumpet of the civil war' (*Fam.* 6. 12. 3).[81] From what Cicero says, it appears that he made a formal plea before Caesar, in which he was greatly helped by Cicero's friendships with Hirtius, Pansa, Balbus, Oppius, Matius, and Rabirius Postumus. The pleas of Ampius' kinsman Tillius Cimber were also effective. Cicero tries to minimise, when writing to Ampius, any humiliation that might have been involved. He pleaded the case 'more frankly than his circumstances permitted'. He had not used any method that he would not have used for himself. He had not made himself a slave to the situation: his connections with the leading Caesarians were longstanding—that is, not a product of toadying to the victors (ibid. 1–2). The letter implies that Ampius was still truculent and uneasy about Caesar's clemency. He needed reassurance, in particular that he would get a *diploma*, a warrant entitling him to travel at public expense. Cicero had not offered him much hope before and consoled him on his fortitude in exile. He now urged him to show the virtue he commemorated in his historical writing, although the need for it would be less when he returned (ibid. 3–5). Three letters to an otherwise unknown exile Trebianus suggest a similar story to that of Ampius. The first two letters promise help, finding encouragement in Caesar's tendency to be more equitable, the likely revival of the *res publica*, and Cicero's own good relations with Caesar's friends and, to an extent, the man himself (*Fam.* 6. 10a. 2, 6. 10b. 2). A later letter (6. 11), perhaps to be dated in June of 45,[82] shows that Trebianus had obtained his repatriation, thanks to help from Dolabella.

In fact pleading with Caesar was an inevitably humiliating business for a consular. After Caesar's murder Cicero was told an anecdote by Matius about the time when Cicero approached Caesar on behalf of Sestius (*Att.* 14. 1. 2)— an event that cannot be precisely dated during Caesar's stays in Rome.[83] Matius must have been in Caesar's council on the occasion, as he probably had been for the case of Ampius. Cicero was sitting waiting outside the room used for the audience and Caesar commented, 'Should I be in any doubt that I am supremely hated, when Marcus Cicero is sitting and cannot meet me at his own convenience? Yet if anyone is easygoing, he is. Nonetheless I have no doubts that he really hates me.' The anecdote illustrates how it had been a characteristic of the republic that any of the leading men (*principes*) would

---

[81] See *HRR* ii, pp. lxix f. and 45; Suet. *Iul.* 77; Caes. *BCiv.* 3. 105 on his failure to extract money from the temple at Ephesus.

[82] Cf. O. E. Schmidt, 1893, 317, associating it with *Att.* 13. 9.

[83] It might have had nothing to do with Sestius' own problems but concerned his patronage of Ariarathes of Cappadocia (*Att.* 13. 2a. 2), with whose family Cicero had a connection since his governorship.

normally make themselves available immediately to those of similar status. Now Cicero was in a similar situation to someone who in the present era wants to see the chief executive of a major company and has to wait in an ante-room.

To his old friend Aulus Caecina, however, Cicero could offer no more than consolation and assistance in his exile.[84] In a letter written shortly after the *pro Marcello* he is still optimistic, remembering with gratitude how Caecina, an expert on Etruscan augury, had apparently forecast Cicero's recall from exile (*Fam.* 6. 6. 2). Here he refers to his own expulsion in 58 as a preliminary to an attempt to overthrow the republic. With similar precision to Caecina's, Cicero had predicted the disastrous consequences of Pompey's alliance with Caesar: the alliance broke the power of the senate, the divorce stirred up civil war (ibid. 3). Apart from prediction Cicero had offered good advice to both parties. His recall of his efforts to secure peace seems to be not quite accurate. He certainly did not urge Pompey to go to Spain, as he maintains here,[85] though of course this formed part of the terms Caesar sent to Capua after the outbreak (*Fam.* 16. 12. 3). As for his struggle for the acceptance of Caesar's right to stand in absence for the consulship, this might have been part of the package that he was trying to negotiate in the first week in 49: he seems to be suggesting something of this sort in his letter to Caesar in March.[86] However, his letters of 50, while they show his own acceptance of this right, show no evidence that he was insisting on it with others.[87] The account of the civil war is one familiar to us. He had tried to remain neutral but eventually self-respect got the better of fear and he had left Italy to join Pompey; he had predicted all the disasters (*Fam.* 6. 6. 6).

Having established his augural credentials Cicero goes on to prophesy that Caesar, although he has been unmoved by Caecina's pleas so far, will in time give way. He is naturally mild and clement, as Caecina's book of 'Complaints' makes clear, and, although so far he has been angry at the criticisms there, will soon absorb the praises. He will also be strongly influenced by a united Etruria, in whose aristocracy, as in that of Italy as a whole, Caecina is so

---

[84] Caecina is surely the man for whom Cicero delivered *pro Caecina* (*Fam.* 6. 7. 4–*veterem tuum.... clientem*). It is no problem that Cicero knew his father also (6. 9. 1), cf. How, ii. 410. Rawson, 1991, 297, n. 43 prefers a son of Cicero's client, on the ground that the correspondent was apparently coeval with or younger than Cicero, while the client had married in the 70s a widow with a grown-up son. However, marriages with older women for financial reasons are not unthinkable and the widow need only have been in her thirties herself. Rawson, infers more plausibly (ibid. 298) a Sullan allegiance, which would help to explain the current implacable hostility between Caesar and Caecina.
[85] *Fam.* 6. 6. 5, cf. *Att.* 5. 11. 3, 7. 9. 3, 7. 18. 2; *Fam.* 3. 8. 10 for his attitude to the possibility.
[86] Ch. XVI with nn. 5 and 45; *Att.* 9. 11A. 2.
[87] *Att.* 7. 7. 6, 7. 9. 3. Ch. XV with nn. 72–4.

distinguished (ibid. 8–9).[88] There was encouragement too in the treatment of Pompeians: they were not treated as criminals. Caesar always referred to Pompey with respect; Cassius had been his legate, Brutus had been made governor of Gaul, Sulpicius Rufus of Greece, while Marcellus, with whom he was most bitter, had been recalled. So had a number of villains, but that should be an argument for helping a good man (ibid. 10–11). Cicero ends by moral encouragement and assuring Caecina that he has promised help to his son, the more valuable because of his influence with Caesar's friends (ibid. 12–13).[89] Caecina, for his part, was not mollified but intransigent. In a letter written at the time of Caesar's departure to fight the sons of Pompey in Spain he assumed that everyone was hoping for Caesar's defeat (*Fam.* 6. 7. 2). So far from obtaining his return, Cicero had to work hard to get him support on a business journey to Asia, after he was no longer permitted to stay in Sicily (*Fam.* 6. 5, 8–9). Similarly, Cicero could do no more than console Aulus Torquatus, who had given him moral support while they had been in Pompey's camp, (*Fam.* 6. 1–4, esp. 6. 1. 5) and the polymath Nigidius Figulus, who had been at his side in 63.[90]

One of the most interesting examples of Cicero's patronage was his contact with his one-time enemy Vatinius. The latter had supported Cicero when in charge of Brundisium in 48–7 (*Att.* 11. 5. 4, 11. 9. 2), served with Caesar in Africa (*Bell. Afr.* 10. 1) and in July 45 was proconsul in Illyricum fighting brigands, who perhaps included Pompeian rebels. Vatinius now approached Cicero as a former client, who had been saved by him at this trial, asking him to support his efforts to be rewarded for his successful campaigns (*Fam.* 5. 9. 1). He expressed dismay over Cicero's request for pardon for a certain Catilius who had been responsible for murder, rape, and devastation and was now on trial. He was prepared to oblige but wished for Cicero's help over a decree of thanksgiving (*Fam.* 5. 10a). Cicero seems to have done what he asked and was repaid: in particular Vatinius recaptured a runaway slave called Dionysius, whom Cicero had used as a reader (*Fam.* 5. 9. 2, 5. 11. 3). In the last surviving letter of 5 December 45 we find Vatinius, inspired by receiving the thanksgiving decree, relating a further successful campaign in Dalmatia, which had only been terminated by the cold (5. 10b). More generally, 55 of the 79 letters of commendation collected in book 13 of the *Letters to Friends* can be assigned to the period of Caesar's dictatorship. They are mostly in favour of businessmen and show that Cicero still had a role as a patron of the equestrian order, whose importance was growing under the new regime.

---

[88] A brief reference to the bitterness of the *Querelae* in Suet. *Iul.* 75. 5.
[89] See n. 44 above for references to this repeated theme.
[90] *Fam.* 4. 13. esp. 2. On Figulus see Rawson, 1985, 123, 291, 309.

PHILOSOPHICAL RETIREMENT

Towards the end of the year 46 Cicero was already disillusioned once again with the new regime. In one letter to Paetus he mentions the surveying of the land of Veii and Capena, clearly imagining possible land confiscations but claiming philosophical indifference. If Caesar wanted there to be the sort of *res publica* that he perhaps wanted and they all should hope for, he had no means of achieving it; he had tied himself to so many people. Neither Cicero nor even the 'princeps' could foresee the future: Cicero was Caesar's slave and Caesar was slave to circumstances (*Fam.* 9. 17. 2–3). He consulted Paetus about buying a house in Naples and, when the latter was clearly surprised that Cicero could abandon most of his life at Rome, referring to the behaviour of senior statesmen like Catulus—presumably the consul of 78, who remained active in the sixties BC—Cicero replied that he himself had not wanted to be too long away from his post as watchman over the *res publica* then. 'I was sitting at the stern and holding the tiller, but now I have hardly a place in the bilge. Do you think that there will be any fewer decrees of the senate, if I am at Naples? When I am at Rome and a regular visitor to the forum, decrees of the senate are drafted at the home of your devotee, my friend; and indeed, when it occurs to him, I am put down as present at the drafting and I hear that a decree has been transmitted to Armenia and Syria, which is said to have been passed on my motion, before the matter has been raised for discussion in the first place.' Cicero has been thanked by foreign kings totally unknown to him for proposing that they should be recognized as kings by the Romans (*Fam.* 9. 15. 4). The forger of decrees was probably Balbus,[91] but the ultimate responsibility must rest with Caesar himself. In a note to Atticus shortly before Caesar's departure to fight Pompey's sons, Cicero wonders if he will hold the elections in the Campus or, in defiance of the constitution, in Spain (*Att.* 12. 8).

While Caecina hoped for a Pompeian victory in Spain, Cicero was uncommitted. Writing to Torquatus, he commented that the size and training of forces on either side made the result unpredictable. However, he also remarked that the general attitude in Italy was that, although there was some difference between the causes on either side, there would not be much difference in the result of victory for either side. People knew about Caesar; as for the young Gnaeus Pompeius, everyone was thinking how terrifying a victorious army with a grudge would be (*Fam.* 6. 4. 1). About the end of

---

[91] Cf. *Fam* 9. 17. 1, 9. 19. 1 on his closeness to Paetus. The forger is not Caesar, who is given his title of *praefectus moribus* in 9. 15. 5, cf. Suet. *Iul.* 76. 1. See How ii. 418. Oppius and Balbus were to act for Caesar while he was in Spain (*Fam.* 6. 8. 1). See Malitz, 1987, 54 ff. on Caesar's cabinet of non-senatorial friends.

the year Cicero was exchanging letters with C. Cassius, the later tyrannicide. He refers briefly to the lack of news from Spain (15. 18. 2, 15. 17. 3), but his main object seems to be to make fun of Cassius' new adherence to Epicureanism, with references to current events. Humour, he writes in one letter, is the only relief from their troubles. 'Where, you will say, is philosophy? Yours is in the kitchen, mine is harassing me; for I am ashamed to be a slave' (*Fam.* 15. 18. 1). In another he refers to the death of his former client, P. Sulla. 'Some said it was brigands, others over-eating.' Cassius, he suggests, would bear his death philosophically, although they had lost the 'face of the city'. Caesar would miss his bidding in the auctions of the property of the proscribed. Pansa, however, who had just set out for Spain with good wishes from everyone (30 December), illustrated how virtue should be pursued for its own sake (*Fam.* 15. 17. 2–3). By the third letter Cicero has nothing to say about politics but jokes about Epicurean theories of sense-perception, especially as they were propounded by a certain Catius (15. 16. 1–2).

Cassius replied from Brundisium that for every Catius he could hurl back quantities of insensitive practitioners of Stoicism. As for Epicurean ethics, while it was difficult to convince men that what was morally good should be chosen for its own sake, it was both true and probable that pleasure and freedom from pain were achieved by virtue, justice, and by morally good behaviour. This was why an Epicurean like Pansa was virtuous. 'For this reason Sulla (Cassius now becomes jocular too) amidst the disagreement of philosophers did not ask what was the good, but bought up all the goods.' He had borne bravely the news of Sulla's death, but Caesar would soon find substitutes for him. Cassius now begged for further news from Spain. 'Damned if am not worried and prefer to have an old and clement master rather than try a new and cruel one. You know what an idiot Gnaeus is; you know how he thinks cruelty a virtue; you know how he thinks that we have always despised him; I am afraid that he may crudely want to take reprisal with a sword' (15. 19. 1–4).

For most of the following year Cicero's writings shed little light on politics. In the midst of his disillusionment the death of his daughter Tullia, shortly after she gave birth to a son to Dolabella (by now divorced from her) cast him into deeper despair.[92] As he said in his reply to the letter of consolation Servius Sulpicius sent him, Tullia had been the one consolation he had, after abandoning through distaste his forensic life and the senate house; now she was gone, he could not take refuge in public affairs.[93] Atticus even

---

[92] *Fam.* 4. 5–6, cf. 6. 18. 5 (to Lepta). On the chronology of this period of Cicero's life see O. E. Schmidt, 1893, 270–8.

[93] *Fam.* 4. 6. 2, cf. *Att.* 12. 21. 5, 12. 23. 1.

assumed that he would not be interested in news from Spain (*Att.* 12. 23. 1). When he received news from Hirtius about the Caesarian victory at Munda and the flight of Pompey's son Sextus from Corduba, he professed little interest.[94] The letters also shed little light on his divorce and remarriage, which must have occurred about the end of 46. There is one reference to his new young wife Publilia; when he mentions Terentia, it has something to do with money.[95]

He was at the time finding it impossible to write a letter of advice to Caesar on the model of those of Aristotle and Theopompus to Alexander, because what it would be honourable to write would not please Caesar. This task had perhaps been suggested by men like Oppius and Balbus as a response to Caesar's praise of him in his *Anticato*.[96] By the end of May he had produced a text, which seems to have showered praise on Caesar's victories and suggested that (on the model of Alexander) he should turn his victorious arms against Parthia, but Caesar's friends, who vetted the draft, suggested so many changes that he was glad to drop it (*Att.* 13. 27. 1). They seem to have objected to anything that suggested that Caesar's current measures were defective (13. 28. 1–2). One political matter that stirred Cicero's interest came from the more remote past. Brutus had written a *Cato*, which had in Cicero's view overstressed the contribution of the hero to the debate on the fate of the leading Catilinarians. In fact, Cicero complains, almost all the consulars had spoken in favour of execution. He had chosen Cato's motion because Cato had praised his own contribution in brilliant language. However, Brutus had given him no credit either for detection of the conspiracy or his advocacy of execution, simply calling him 'the excellent consul' (*Att.* 12. 21. 1). It is hardly surprising that in his depression Cicero was so sensitive about his past moment of glory.

He sought positive comfort for Tullia's death by seeking to buy a garden estate, in order to erect a shrine to her there—in fact unsuccessfully.[97] Another resource was to write a *Consolatio*, perhaps in the form of a letter addressed to himself.[98] The basic nature of this genre of writing can be seen in the letter that Servius Sulpicius sent him. Servius began by pointing to the misery that fortune had inflicted on 'us', that is, the Roman aristocracy by

---

[94] *Att.* 12. 37a (5 May); cf. *Bell. Hisp.* 31–4. The news had arrived in Rome on the day before the Parilia, 20 April (Dio 43. 42. 3).

[95] Publilia and the divorce *Att.* 12. 32. 1; cf. Quint. 6. 3. 75; Plut. *Cic.* 41. 2–6; *Fam.* 4. 14. 3 (on Terentia's domestic treachery); Terentia—*Att.* 12. 18a. 2, 12. 19. 4, 13. 46. 3.

[96] *Att.* 12. 40. 1–2. For Caesar's letter of consolation to Cicero, received in July and containing references to his plans see *Att.* 13. 20. 1.

[97] *Att.* 12. 18. 1, 12. 23. 3, 12. 38a. 2, 12. 41. 4, 12. 43. 2. See SB *Att* V, App. 3, 404 ff.

[98] *Att.* 12. 14. 3, 12. 28. 2; *Div.* 2. 3. Fragments and *testimonia* in *Div.* 2. 22; *Tusc.* 1. 65, 76, 83, 3. 71, 76, 4. 63.

depriving them of the position of respect that was as dear to them as their children. What sort of life lay before Tullia? Could she have found a suitable young man for an alliance to raise children, who could maintain the family property, ascend the ladder of public office, and enjoy their freedom in assisting their friends in their affairs (*Fam.* 4. 5. 2–3)? Servius then appealed to history. When returning from Asia to Greece, he looked at the cities round about the Saronic Gulf, once of considerable importance but now desolate, and meditated on the impermanence of human achievement. Amid the deaths of so many distinguished men and the losses inflicted on the Roman world, was he troubled by the death of one little woman? She had at least enjoyed the republic while it lasted. Finally, he turned philosophical. Cicero, who spent so much time philosophically consoling others, should take his own medicine and by recognizing that his grief would pass overcome it. If the dead had any feelings, Tullia would not want her father to grieve (ibid. 4–6). In his reply Cicero turned back the argument from the fall of the republic: its very collapse made him inconsolable; in this way he was unlike the historical exemplars he cites—previous consular fathers who had lost children (*Fam.* 4. 6. 1–2).

Such exemplars formed one of the themes of his own, now lost, *Consolatio* (*Div.* 2. 22; *Tusc.* 1. 70). However, much of it was philosophical argument (n. 98 above). Cicero had certainly been returning to philosophy before Tullia's death but this gave him further impetus. He began his series of philosophical works with the *Hortensius*, of which we only have fragments. It was an invitation (protreptic) to philosophy in the form of a dialogue between Hortensius, Catulus, and Lucullus, set in the latter's luxurious villa[99]—somewhat ironical in view of Cicero's denunciation of the 'fish-tank men' (*piscinarii*) in letters of the late 60s.[100] The question seems to have been, how a statesman or general should relax. Lucullus advocated reading history (F11–15); Hortensius attacked philosophy (*Fin.* 1. 2) and presumably advocated reading oratory, while Catulus advocated philosophy: one small book on duty was better than a long speech for the seditious fellow Cornelius, that is, Cicero's *pro Cornelio* (F 21). However, philosophy was not for women or slaves, who were busy with other tasks (F 89). One wonders whether Tullia would have agreed.

Cicero originally intended to use the same cast for his first philosophical dialogue proper, the *Academica*, though for Book II the location was Hortensius' villa at Bauli.[101] However, we learn from letters to Atticus of late June 45

---

[99] *Div.* 2. 1. For the fragments see Grilli, 1962. F2 and 64 describe the location; for the participants see e. g. F 4, 11, 21, 54.
[100] *Att.* 1. 18. 6, 1. 19. 6, 1. 20. 3, 2. 1. 7.   [101] *Acad.* 2. 9; *Att.* 13. 16. 1, 13. 19. 5.

that Cicero became convinced of the inappropriateness of presenting these characters discussing philosophy in a technical way; he then decided to ascribe the dialogue to Cato and Brutus, but finally, on the suggestion of Atticus, transformed it into one between himself and Varro, someone genuinely learned in Academic philosophy, with a further contribution from Atticus.[102] Curiously, the book 2 that we possess is from the original draft, which can only have had a limited circulation (*Att.* 13. 13/14. 1), while the long extract from book 1 is from the revised version. The topic was appropriate for a foundation work—the theory of knowledge. It allowed Cicero to sketch the philosophical tradition in which he worked, that of the Old and New Academy with their relatives, the Peripatos and the Stoa. It also enabled him to defend the value of writing Greek philosophy in Latin and the propriety of coining Latin technical terms (*Acad.* 1. 10–12, 24–5). However, it becomes clear in the dialogue that theory of knowledge and the appropriate parts of physics and metaphysics are ultimately important as the basis for ethics.

'Varro' is portrayed as claiming that he undertakes the study of philosophy in order to acquire a consistent way of life and intellectual pleasure,[103] while in his reproduction of Antiochus' attack on New Academic scepticism 'Lucullus' asks how the wisdom manifesting itself in a consistent way of life can come into being without a sure basis in perception and knowledge (*Acad.* 2. 23). In the sketch of the history of the philosophical schools Socrates is praised as the man who brought philosophy down from the obscurities of nature to ordinary life, as well as for the introduction of dialectic and scepticism (*Acad.* 1. 15–17). Later the chief feature of the difference between the Peripatetics and the Stoic Zeno is said to lie in their treatment of virtue. Theophrastus is said to have stripped virtue of its glory and strength by denying that it was sufficient for happiness (in fact the doctrine of the *Nicomachean Ethics*),[104] while Zeno thought happiness lay in virtue alone (*Acad.* 1. 35–8).[105] At the end of book 2 we find Cicero portraying himself in his own person defending New Academic scepticism against the dogmatism of Antiochus. In the course of this he touches on moral philosophy and argues that scepticism allows him the flexibility to choose a preferred view, in his case

---

[102] *Att.* 13. 12. 1, 13. 13/14. 1, 13. 16. 1–2, 13. 19. 3, 5. *Fam.* 9. 8 is Cicero's letter of explanation to Varro. See Inwood and Mansfeld, 1997, on this work, in particular on the various versions, Griffin, 1997*a*.

[103] *Acad.* 1. 7; *constantia vitae* seems to be here a life according to stable moral principles (cf. Ar. *EN* 1. 1100^{b}11–13 βεβαιότης) and not simply resistance to pain or pleasure.

[104] *Acad.* 1. 33–4; cf Ar. *EN* 1. 1099^{a}31 ff.

[105] Cicero had been trying to impress on Cassius the corollary of this—that virtue should be chosen for its own sake (*Fam.* 15. 17. 2–3). On the philosophic importance of the letters see Griffin, 1995.

the Stoic view that moral behaviour was the only good for man, while allowing him some susceptibility to alternative views, even that of Epicurus (*Acad.* 2. 129 ff., esp.138–41).

The *Academica*, therefore, are in a number of ways a preparation for Cicero's first major work on ethics, the *De Finibus*, which Cicero had finished about the time he was revising the *Academica* (*Att.* 13. 12. 3, 13. 19. 4). Atticus started to publish both the books, in Cicero's view prematurely, about the end of June (*Att.* 13. 21a. 1–2). The *De Finibus* concerned the ultimate purposes in life which acted as standards by which conduct could be chosen and judged (1. 11). In the introduction, addressed to Brutus, which defends his project, Cicero stresses that devotion to philosophy, because of the very nature of philosophy, cannot be half-hearted (1. 2–3). Furthermore, he once again justifies his writing in Latin: he was not trying to translate the Greek philosophers, except for some passages, but to give support to those whom he approved, with his own judgement and his own organization of their ideas (1. 4–10, esp. 5). Nothing could be more important that the 'ends', the ultimate aims of human behaviour, the standards by which all conduct should be judged (1. 11–12). The work consists of three separate dialogues, two of which are set in the late fifties and the third in Cicero's youth: apart from Cicero, the participants had since died (*Att.* 13. 19. 4). In the first, consisting of books 1 and 2, L. Torquatus, Pompeian praetor of 49, defends Epicureanism in the presence of Cicero and another Pompeian, C. Valerius Triarius, and Cicero replies. In books 3 and 4, Cato, who is portrayed in Lucullus' library at Tusculum 'surrounded by many Stoic books' (3. 7), defends Stoicism and Cicero replies.[106] In book 5, set in Athens during Cicero's studies in Greece in the early seventies, M. Piso expounds traditional Academic and Peripatetic philosophy, as revived by Antiochus, for the benefit of Cicero's cousin Lucius, with an audience of Cicero, Quintus, and Atticus.

Cicero does his best to make Epicureanism attractive and convincing. His Epicurean friends, especially Atticus, who is portrayed expressing his devotion to Epicurus and his teacher Phaedrus (5. 3, cf. 1. 16), would have complained if he had done otherwise. It was also important to stress the seriousness of the philosophical contest with Epicureanism. Cicero mentions the large number of Epicureans (1. 25, 2. 44) and their devotion: they have his image on their cups and their rings (5. 3). At Athens, following his will, his school celebrated his birthday on the twentieth of each month (2. 101). He concedes that their arguments have the advantage of accessibility and intelligibility, thanks to the

---

[106] The dramatic date is clearly the beginning of April 52, as Cato refers to the new law of Pompey that gives the defence counsel only three hours to reply (*Fin.* 4. 1, cf. Asc. 39 C), that prescribed for the trial of Milo. The Megalensia had just begun, implying 5 April (3. 8).

non-technical language in which they are couched.[107] In his argument Torquatus is made to equate pleasure, something which everyone knows from experience and therefore needs no definition, with absence from pain, from which a policy of virtuous conduct can be derived.[108] This, according to another Epicurean, Cassius in the letter discussed above, was why Pansa pursued virtue (*Fam.* 15. 19. 2).

In Cicero's rebuttal, however, the move from pleasure to absence of pain is seized on as a vulnerable point. Absence of pain is something different and more complex than the simple pursuit of animal pleasure and should not be linked with it (2. 6–26). Nor is pleasure self-evidently the ultimate end towards which even animals strive: they aim for self-love and survival (2. 31–4). In fact, it is more plausible to deduce from animal behaviour the old Academic and Peripatetic ideal of living in accordance with nature (2. 34, cf. 40). Furthermore, the avoidance of pain is not self-evidently an adequate explanation of how people make choices in every situation. Once we accept the existence of the concept of what is honourable (*honestum*, τὸ καλόν), it is far more convincing as the aim of people who act altruistically and patriotically (2. 45–66). People do their duty for its own sake (2. 72); people love their friends for themselves (2. 78–83)—an anticipation of the doctrine of true friendship in the later *De Amicitia*. This brief summary does not do justice to the passion and the rhetoric that Cicero deploys in expounding his case, which sometimes make the logic of his actual argument obscure.[109] It is important too that he does not question the practical morality of his interlocutor: he knows that Torquatus himself did pursue virtue in his friendships and in prosecuting his father's enemy (2. 62, 80). He abhors, however, a theoretical basis that justifies a very different kind of morality, especially in men like Crassus, who pursued his own interest, and Pompey, who refrained from injustice although he could have been unjust with impunity (2. 57).

There is a change of tone in books 3 and 4. As Cicero points out in the introduction, the simplicity of the Epicurean argument facilitated a transparent exposition; the Stoic form of discourse was, however, precise or rather thorny (*spinosum*) (3. 3). The argument follows naturally from the point that Cicero was arguing at the end of book 2. Cato undertakes to persuade him that there are important differences between the Stoic and Academic views of moral worth as a good, between the conception of it as the only good and as

---

[107] *Fin.* 1. 15, 2. 15–16, 3. 3. See also *Acad.* 1. 5, *Tusc.* 4. 3. 6 on the popular Epicurean writers Amafinius and Rabirius.
[108] *Fin.* 1. 29–54, 65–9 (on friendship).
[109] Book 2 begins with Socratic questioning, for which Cicero is invited by Torquatus to substitute a continuous discourse, more rhetorical rather than philosophical (2. 17).

the supreme good (3. 10–14).[110] There follows an exposition of regular Stoic doctrine—the aim of living in accordance with nature (3. 20 ff.), the equation of the good with what is morally worthy (*honestum*) and praiseworthy, and hence of the moral life with the happy life, in which the supreme good will be achieved in the mind (3. 26 ff.). The crucial difference between the Stoics and the Peripatetics is the view of the latter that pain is an evil. The Stoics believe that the good man can be happy when tortured on a rack, the Peripatetics not: for the Peripatetics the good things of the body and external goods make a person happier; for the Stoics this is anathema (3. 41–4). Cato then explains the doctrine that, although only moral worth is good and moral evil is bad, certain things are to be promoted in men's estimation, such as health and wealth, and others not, such as illness and poverty (3. 51–4).[111] The consequences for conduct are then explored. The wise man performs his duties, including those in the intermediary field between good and evil, that is, those not in themselves conducive to virtue, which are according to nature. This leads on to specific topics: the propriety of suicide in certain circumstances (60–1), the love of children (62), the unity of mankind under divine providence, including those of future generations (63–9), friendship, justice, and truthfulness (70–2).

Cicero begins his reply by criticizing the Stoics for minimizing their dependence on Peripatetic thought (4. 3 ff.) and developing a new and less satisfactory mode of argument, which neglected rhetorical presentation. He then turns to ethics and attacks the limitations that Stoics set on the concept that they inherited of living according to nature: they argued that matters like health and the absence of pain could not be classed as good (only as something to be promoted) and they restricted what was good to the operations of the mind, which took away the moral value of the majority of human choices (4. 14 ff., esp. 23, 27, 40–2). It was not true that everyone except the wise was equally unhappy: there were grades of moral achievement (4. 63–8).

Cicero ends by re-emphasizing what he has been regularly saying throughout his discourse—that the Stoics had unnecessarily separated themselves from the philosophic tradition in which they worked by insisting on over-subtle distinctions in terminology and pressing apparently logical argument to implausible conclusion (68 ff.).[112] In this he appeals to his now dead friend

---

[110] This also involves explaining why the view of Pyrrho and Aristo, that it was the only good, is wrongly formulated. Pyrrho and Aristo's views were not in fact precisely the same. See Long and Sedley 1987, i. 20–2 and more generally on Stoic ethics Wright, 1991.

[111] We also find another highly technical distinction between constituent goods and productive goods (3. 55).

[112] Notice his earlier rejection (49–50) of the Stoic equation of the good with the praiseworthy. Some goods were praiseworthy, but others like health and wealth were not (since they involved no moral achievement).

M. Piso (4. 73) and to the arguments he had himself used in the *pro Murena*, which, he admits, were light-hearted and designed for the Forum audience (74).[113] On the other hand he rejects the tactics of the speech in favour of a subtler attack. Were all moral failings equal? Strings out of tune were indeed equally out of tune, inasmuch as they were out of tune (as a Stoic would argue). However, they were not out of tune equally, and the same was true of moral failings. His final move is to invoke Panaetius' gentler and less thorny mode of argument, which acknowledged his debt to the Academy and the Peripatetics, in response to which Cato is made to acknowledge that the differences between Stoicism and these schools lay more in language than thought (4. 78–80).

In book 5 the tone is more relaxed, the exposition smooth, and the language simpler. The persona of M. Piso undertakes an exposition of the approach of the Old Academy and the Peripatetics, which serves to show both Stoic dependence on their thought and the differences to which Cicero has already drawn attention. It is appropriate that Cicero himself, though present in the dialogue, does not take a leading role, given his criticism of Antiochus' dogmatism in the second book of the *Academica*. Piso begins with a sketch of the development of Peripatetic philosophy with special attention to its interest in the supreme good (5. 9–14). The old Academics and Peripatetics understood this to be living according to nature, a principle that, he maintains, cannot be reconciled with either pleasure or absence of pain (5. 17–23). Seeking to live according to nature is a natural consequence of our self-love (27–37). This implies desiring the fullest development of our corporeal and mental faculties, the more distinguished of which are mental, which in turn implies the pursuit of virtue (37–40). We naturally seek to discover our own nature and this provides us with moral education (41–4).

There is nothing wrong in seeking good things for the body, such as beauty, health, and freedom from pain, but mental excellence is superior (46–54). This is cultivated by action, and it is actions that produce virtue (55–60). The actions in question are those of moral worth, which are pursued for their own sake, not for utilitarian reasons, as is shown in men's intuitive reactions to the behaviour of others and their own conduct (61–4). The greatest moral worth is seen in relationships with others—in families, friendships, neighbourhoods, and civic communities, where justice is the product of individual moral worth. These relationships are to be pursued for their own sake, although they are external to the nature of the individual, whose supreme good is the development of his own nature, because they are cultivated through the performance of duties that are the expression of virtue (65–70).

[113] Cf. *Mur.* 61–3.

The goods of the body complete a most happy life, but a happy life can exist without them (71–2).

Piso's exposition ends with remarks on some variations of doctrine and a complaint about the Stoics for stealing Peripatetic ideas and placing them under their own flag (72–4). Cicero then in his dramatic persona contrasts what they have heard with the views of another Peripatetic, Staseas of Naples, who put more weight on good or bad fortune and the good or bad condition of the body. He then raises the problem that, once these are admitted as relevant, the wise man cannot be always happy (75–7). This leads Cicero to expound a slight modification of the Stoic view that virtue is the only good—which, he argues here, has the merit of logical coherence. His own, he admits, is somewhat logically inconsistent, that virtue is so far the supreme good that it completely outweighs any misery: in consequence, the truly wise man with outstanding virtue is always happy (71–95, esp. 91, 95). He ends, nevertheless, by admitting the attractiveness of Piso's presentation (95).

The dialogue finishes with a core of agreement, surrounded by some uncertainty. In a piece of byplay Cicero emphasizes his alignment with the New Academy in so far as he only approves views as probable rather than certainly true (5. 76). Virtue has certainly won over pleasure. However, although the philosopher Cicero would like to believe that virtue is enough for happiness, he cannot ignore external goods. And this of course reflects Cicero the man in 45 BC. He would have liked to have obtained happiness through what, he believed, had been his recent pursuit of virtue, but he was still the victim of his external circumstances.

The immediately succeeding work, the *Tusculan Disputations*, show him once again gnawing the bone of the problem of happiness (*Div.* 2. 2). Like the *De Finibus*, it is dedicated to Brutus and is presented as a suitable rejoinder to the latter's book *de Virtute* which he had sent to Cicero (*Tusc.* 1. 1, 5. 1). The work has a setting, the Academy in Cicero's Tusculan villa (2. 9, 3. 7), but no named participants, only an anonymous group of friends (*familiares*) (1. 7, 2. 9).[114] After the introduction in book 1 Cicero begins tackling the problem posed—whether death is an evil—with a brief piece of Socratic dialectic, which soon tires his interlocutor, and he is invited to deliver a discourse (1. 9–17); a similar pattern is followed in subsequent books, the dialectic becoming often almost perfunctory.[115] Cicero says that great eloquence is required to for men to desire death or at least not to fear it (1. 117). He saw the books as a form of declamation on philosophy (1. 7), and their

---

[114] In *Att.* 13. 19. 3 he told Atticus that he was on the whole avoiding having living persons in his dialogues, but had made an exception for Varro in the *Academica*.
[115] *Tusc.* 2. 14–15, 3. 7–8, 4. 8–10, 5. 12–18.

discourses are more exercises in rhetoric than philosophical exploration. Gelzer rightly points out that this can be justified in the light of the scepticism of the New Academy, which held no assertions to be certain but only more or less probable.[116]

In book 1 Cicero asserts the immortality of the soul and, without repeating Plato's argumentation, reaches a Platonic conclusion that we only really live after death (esp. 1. 74–5), appealing to Cato as a recent witness. In the next book the question is whether pain is the greatest of evils or indeed an evil at all (2. 14), which Cicero answers from the Stoic position in the negative. In book 3 the topic is sickness (3. 7–9) and Cicero adopts a similar Stoic approach: the only real sickness is sickness of the soul, which can be cured by a form of cognitive therapy, in other words σωφροσύνη (translated by Cicero as *frugalitas*) (3. 14 ff., esp. 16). Next he considers whether the wise man is free from any form of mental agitation (πάθος or *perturbatio*). After an exposition of Stoic psychology (4. 14 ff.), he makes some concession to the plausibility of the Peripatetic case that a modicum of some passions, such as anger and pity, may be useful (4. 43 ff.), but finally maintains the view that virtuous action is based on reason rather than passion (51 ff.). In the final book he comes back to the question treated in the last book of *De Finibus*, whether virtue is enough for the happy life (5. 2, 12), but with a different outcome. Here he maintains the strict Stoic position that it is enough, dismissing the counter-arguments of the Peripatetics (5. 22–31).[117]

The rigid adherence to Stoic dogma lacks conviction, when compared with the more flexible Academic position he advocated in *De finibus*, which was in fact that espoused by Brutus in his own treatise (*Tusc.* 5. 1, 21–2). There is, moreover, an air of unreality about much of this work in spite of the fact that it purports to have a practical purpose—well illustrated by the story of the Carthaginian Academic philosopher Clitomachus (Hasdrubal), who after the destruction of Carthage in 146 sent to the enslaved Carthaginians in Italy a consolatory homily about the wise man not being miserable about the capture of his country (3. 52–4). At one point Cicero admits that philosophy cannot cure the minds of everyone and that this was true of all but a few philosophers. The majority used their teaching to display knowledge rather than as a rule for life; they did not order their life according to reason but were slaves of their desires (2. 11–12). On occasion Cicero leaves philosophy for more conventional wisdom. At the end of book 1 (82 ff.) he talks of the advantages of death over life for many men; the end of book 3 (74 ff.) gives practical

---

[116] 1969, 305. See Douglas, 1995, and White, 1995.

[117] He admits that there is a vital difference between the two, contrary to what was said in *De Finibus* 4 (*Tusc.* 5. 32): in his view the wise man is not only happy but most happy (5. 34).

advice on forms of consolation. In the philosophical works that were to follow, *De Natura Deorum* and *De Divinatione*, the sceptical Academic in Cicero returned and the author seems more comfortable in this persona.

THE CLIMAX OF THE DICTATORSHIP

Caesar's long-awaited return from Spain did not occur until late summer.[118] The adulation that followed his final defeat of the Pompeians had been manifest for some time—to Cicero's displeasure. As early as mid-May he commented on the proposal that Caesar's statue, dedicated to The Unconquered God, should be erected in the temple of Quirinus (near Atticus' house on the Quirinal): 'I prefer that he should share a temple with Quirinus than with Salus (Safety)'. The story was that Romulus (deified as Quirinus) had been murdered by senators.[119] In July Cicero found disagreeable the procession at the games in which Caesar's ivory image was carried.[120] In mid-August he is surprised at a remark of Brutus to Atticus that Caesar was going over to the 'good men': 'where will he find them, unless perchance he hangs himself?' He then asks about the stemma Atticus had constructed for incorporation in Brutus' 'Parthenon', depicting his descent from L. Brutus and Servilius Ahala.[121] He refers to Caesar as a king (*rex*), when discussing how Quintus' son had been denouncing both his father and Cicero for disloyalty, and talks of 'royal' shows, when apologizing to Lepta for being unable to get him a job as one of their supervisors: there was no room for Lepta among Caesar's intimates, especially one who would be a beneficiary without making a corresponding contribution to Caesar's welfare (*Att.* 13. 37. 2–3; *Fam.* 6. 19. 2). Meanwhile he exchanged compliments with Caesar about their writing. Caesar commented that frequent reading of Cicero's *Cato* had enriched his own vocabulary, while Brutus' *Cato* made him think himself eloquent (*Att.* 13. 46. 2). Cicero for his part had expressed admiration to Oppius and Balbus

---

[118] See *Att.* 13. 46. 2 for Caesar's plan to return before the *ludi Romani* in early September, 13. 47a. 1 for his request that Cicero should attend the senate on 1 September. He did not in fact hold his triumphs before October (Vell. 2. 56. 1–3).

[119] *Att.* 12. 45. 2 cf. Dio 43. 45. 3. SB *Att* v. 338 doubts whether Cicero had the last point in mind, but the remark is sinister in any case. See also Weinstock, 1971, 169 ff., with references to previous scholarship, who raises the possibility of a cult of *Salus Caesaris*.

[120] *Att.* 13. 44. 1; cf. Dio 43. 45. 2; Suet. *Iul.* 76. 1. For a convincing restatement of the view that these games were the *ludi Apollinares* in the first half of July and not the *ludi victoriae Caesaris* at the end of the month see Ramsey and Licht, 1997, 25–40; Ferrary, 1999, 224–5.

[121] *Att.* 13. 40. 1, cf. Nepos, *Atticus* 18. 3. Brutus had gone to meet Caesar on his journey home (*Att.* 13. 23. 1, 13. 39. 2, cf. 13. 44. 1).

for Caesar's two invectives against Cato, presumably for their rhetorical qualities, and on Atticus' advice expanded them in a letter addressed to Caesar himself, which was vetted by Oppius and Balbus and passed on (*Att.* 13. 50. 1; Suet. *Iul.* 56. 5).

Probably not long after Caesar's return he found himself once more defending a Pompeian. It was, however, a rather different trial from that of Ligarius. King Deiotarus of Galatia had been accused by his grandson Castor of plotting to murder Caesar, when Caesar stayed with him on his way from fighting Pharnaces in 47. Deiotarus had been already tried by Caesar at Nicaea in 47—the occasion on which Brutus spoke for him.[122] It was perhaps as a result of this trial that Deiotarus lost his tetrarchy over the Galatians.[123] Cicero was indebted to him for his friendship and help during his governorship of Cilicia. Deiotarus was not a Roman and therefore unprotected by *provocatio*, nor would his trial have been limited by the rules governing the treason court (*quaestio de maiestate*).[124] It was held not in the Forum but *in camera*: Cicero complains about the limitations imposed by speaking between walls of a private house without the background of the buildings surrounding the Forum (*Deiot.* 5–7).[125] Caesar was judging a case in which he was the alleged victim. It is not surprising, therefore, that in the introduction Cicero appeals to his fairness and clemency, especially as Caesar was well known to have borne a grudge against Deiotarus for actually appearing in Pompey's battle line at Pharsalus (*Deiot.* 7–9).

Cicero links his client with other Pompeians by referring to the 'widely shared mistake' (*error communis*) (*Deiot.* 10)—a theme of his in the speeches for Marcellus and Ligarius.[126] This leads him into a narrative of Deiotarus' participation in the civil war, which, Cicero argues, was affected by the fact that he only heard one side of the story—the ultimate decree against Caesar and the flight of the consuls and senate from Italy—not of Caesar's desire for reconciliation and the conspiracy of 'certain men' against his dignity. Above all he was moved by the authority of Pompey who was both his guest-friend and friend, and this outweighed any connection to Caesar.[127] After Pharsalus he changed sides, supporting first Domitius Calvinus, Caesar's appointee in the Asiatic provinces, and Caesar himself in their war against Pharnaces, for which Caesar rewarded him by maintaining his royal title (13–14).[128] All this

---

[122] *Brut.* 21; *Att.* 14. 1. 2; Tac. *Dial.* 21. 5.   [123] *Bell. Alex.* 78. 5.
[124] Cicero treats it as a capital trial, *Deiot.* 1.
[125] Note 'intra domesticos parietes' (5). Trials *intra cubiculum* were to become a scandal under the emperor Claudius, Tac. *Ann.* 11. 2, 13. 4; Suet. *Claud.* 15.
[126] *Marc.* 13, 20, 30; *Lig.* 17–20.
[127] *Deiot.* 9–13; *Schol. Gron.* 300 St.
[128] In fact hardly surprising, as Pharnaces had occupied some of Deiotarus' territory (*Bell. Alex.* 34–5).

is used as an argument from probability against the accusation that Deiotarus then planned to violate the laws of hospitality at his palace at Blucium by having Caesar, although his guest, assassinated by armed men when on the way from bath to dinner (15–17).[129]

Cicero then turns to the evidence from a royal slave, the doctor Phidippus, asking, if a doctor was involved, why they did not try to poison Caesar (17–18). The story the doctor told was complex. Caesar's fortune saved him first when he did not visit the place appointed for him to receive gifts before dinner. Then the following day, when he had left Deiotarus' palace for a fortress, a further attempt failed, because Caesar decided he would vomit after dinner not in the bath but in his bedroom (19–21). After the failure, Phidippus' brothers were imprisoned, while Phidippus himself was sent with an embassy to Rome. Here he revealed the plot to Castor, whom Caesar was keeping there, presumably as a hostage for Deiotarus' good behaviour (2–3, 21–2). There was an arguably more serious charge: Deiotarus had sent troops to 'some Caecilius or other' and imprisoned those who did not want to go. Cicero brushes this aside, pretending ignorance of Caecilius Bassus, the one survivor of the Pompeian cause in the East, still in arms in Syria (ibid. 22–5).[130] He similarly dismisses allegations of Deiotarus' alienation from Caesar, including one that he had danced naked, while drunk, when hearing news that Caesar was in trouble in Africa (ibid. 24–8).[131] As for Castor, he was over-enthusiastic for battle, even after Pharsalus, in spite of Cicero's attempt to dissuade him (28–9). Granted, however, that Deiotarus was alienated from Caesar, this was not enough to induce him to commit such a crime. The slave who was source of the evidence had been corrupted to make accusations—a complete violation of Roman tradition. Here Cicero claims that Phidippus had actually tried to escape from Castor and revealed his corruption to Cn. Domitius Calvinus, when Servius Sulpicius Rufus and Titus Manlius Torquatus were dining with him (30–2). Calvinus, Caesar's commander in Asia in 48–47, was among Caesar's assessors.[132] So this allegation by Cicero cannot have been totally unfounded.

One particularly delicate allegation is reserved to last. Blesamius, an envoy of Deiotarus, had been briefing the king on Caesar's unpopularity. Caesar was thought to be a tyrant; men were offended at seeing his statue placed among those of the kings; they had not been applauding him. Cicero claims that this was simply city gossip, not in Blesamius' letter, and pointed to Caesar's

---

[129] For Deiotarus' palace see S. Mitchell, 1993, i. 55–7.
[130] Cf. *Att.* 14. 9. 3; *Fam.* 11. 1. 4, 12. 18. 1; Dio 47. 26. 2–27.
[131] Cicero does admit that these rumours had inspired Caecilius' revolt (*Deiot.* 25).
[132] 'Hunc Cn. Domitium' (*Deiot.* 32).

clemency: he did not use violence outside battle; there were no executions, torture, or attacks on households—in other words no proscriptions—the forum was not filled with soldiers. What was one statue more (the most distinguished place was after all the Rostra)? The lack of applause did not matter to Caesar and could be explained by sheer stupefaction—or perhaps the desire to avoid commonplace approbation?[133]

Cicero devotes his peroration to reconciling Caesar with Deiotarus and takes the opportunity to play with the concept of kingship. Caesar gave everything to Deiotarus, when he granted him the name of king. Deiotarus is content with the title and the reputation he has acquired among Roman commanders, confirmed by decrees of the senate. He even keeps in mind the doctrine of the philosophers that virtues are the only goods and sufficient for the happy life (Cicero manages to slip in here a reference to the major theme of his recent philosophical writing) (35–8). Cicero is working for his friend, but at the same time for all those men Caesar has pardoned who may otherwise worry that their status may be in question (39). Caesar, urges Cicero, should keep in mind two kings. We may wonder who these are: Deiotarus and his potential successor Castor? That would be what Cicero would have said to Caesar, but his audience could not have helped thinking of Caesar himself. Cicero goes on to say that the royal name has always been *sanctum* at Rome, that of kings who were friends and allies most sacred (*sanctissimum*) (40). The word *sanctum* has a double meaning, 'sacred through respect' and also 'forbidden under penalty'. The office of kingship had been under a curse since the beginning of the Republic.[134] Cicero's concluding plea, after invoking the loyalty of the royal ambassadors, is that Caesar should remember that his sentence today will either bring disaster on kings or an untarnished reputation and security (41–3).[135]

The speech had an immediate reputation. Dolabella wanted a copy, and Cicero sent it to him with the deprecation that it was an unimportant case where he was doing a favour to an old friend (*Fam.* 9. 12. 2). Caesar must have realized what Cicero had been saying to him about the precariousness of kingship but ignored it. In a letter to Atticus written two months after Caesar's murder Cicero remarked that 'it was less dangerous to speak against that nefarious faction when the tyrant was alive than after his death' (*Att.* 14. 17. 6). In December Caesar was prepared to take dinner with Cicero during the Saturnalia holiday (*Att.* 13. 52). He was travelling with a guard of 2,000

---

[133] *Deiot.* 33–4. Cf. Dio 43. 45. 3–4 for the statue in the temple of Jupiter Capitolinus.
[134] Livy, 2. 8. 2.
[135] This section of the speech best merits the description, *oratio figurata*, which most commentators applied to the *pro Marcello* (*Schol. Gron.* 295–6 St.), discussed by Dyer, 1990, 26–30.

soldiers. When Caesar came, they were accommodated in the grounds and the villa was cordoned off. Caesar was still on a regime of emetics and could eat without restraint; he also enjoyed the conversation over dinner. Three extra *triclinia* were for his entourage, and entertainment was provided for the less important freedmen and slaves—an anticipation of the imperial court. 'In short', Cicero told Atticus, 'we seemed human beings.[136] He was not, however, the sort of guest to whom one could say, "Please look in on me again on your return journey." Once is enough. There was nothing serious in the conversation, but plenty about literature.' That last remark is revealing. One cannot imagine two Romans of consular rank having dinner under the Republic and never talking about politics, their lifeblood. This too was probably not lost on Caesar.

Cicero's correspondence gives us one last glimpse of Caesar before the Ides of March. In January 44 he wrote to his friend M'. Curius at Patras, reassuring him that he had been commended to the incoming governor Acilius Glabrio and suggesting that there was no reason for him to return to Rome.[137] He himself was embarrassed at participating in public affairs.[138] An illustration follows (*Fam.* 7. 30. 1). On 31 December Caesar was planning to hold, in the presence of the consul Q. Fabius Maximus, the election of quaestors in the Campus, a procedure involving the tribal assembly (*comitia tributa*). Early in the morning with the election beginning, the death of Fabius was announced, his curule chair was removed, and Caesar moved directly to hold an assembly of the military assembly (*comitia centuriata*), which an hour after midday returned C. Caninius Rebilus as consul suffect for the rest of the year, that is until the following morning. Cicero has fun over this: 'In Caninius' consulship no one had lunch. However, there was no crime, for he had such marvellous vigilance that he did not sleep throughout his consulship.' However, he adds, if Curius were at Rome, he would not be able to refrain from weeping: there were countless other things of this kind. Cicero's consolations were philosophy and their mutual friend Atticus (ibid. 2) and, one might add, his surviving importance as patron.

---

[136] Shackleton Bailey translates 'homines visi sumus' as 'I showed him I knew how to live', comparing a deliberately precious remark of Nero's (SB *Att* v. 259, 396; Suet. *Nero* 31. 2). But Cicero is more worried about seeming inferior through being forced to treat Caesar as a superhuman being, not just as another senior senator, than on account of his domestic lifestyle.

[137] *Fam.* 7. 30. 1, 3, cf. 13. 50.

[138] *Fam.* 7. 30. 1; cf. *Att.* 13. 42. 3 for his assisting the master of horse Lepidus as an augur in early January.

XVIII

The Ides of March and After

THE PASSIONATE SPECTATOR

CICERO had been planning to speak in the senate on the Ides of March 44 about Antonius' dubious claim that the election of Dolabella as suffect consul under his presidency was vitiated by a fault in the auspices. The speech was never to be delivered. Instead Cicero witnessed the murder of Caesar, which, he wrote in his work on divination, left the body in such a state that neither friends nor even slaves approached it.[1] Antonius was later to claim in his speech of 19 September that Cicero instigated the murder. Cicero's reply, clearly true but disingenuous, was that he was not a member of the conspiracy.[2] He had, however, in the *Brutus* left a heavy hint to its dedicatee that tyrants should be assassinated, there had been pointed remarks in the speech for Deiotarus about tyranny and kingship, and he had no doubt let fall in conversation remarks like that in a letter to Atticus about preferring Caesar to share a temple with Quirinus, i.e. Romulus, than with *Salus* (Safety).[3] Antonius backed up his accusation with the statement that Brutus waved his bloody dagger in the air and congratulated Cicero on his recovery of liberty (*Phil.* 2. 28). If we had found a remark like this in an invective of Cicero's, we would have treated it with suspicion. Cicero, certainly, does not deny that Brutus called his name, but we may wonder if the gesture was as dramatic as Antonius represented it. Cicero did indeed join the conspirators when they took position on the Capitol, but refused to go on an embassy to Antonius with other consulars, arguing that they could not trust any agreement that might be reached (*Phil.* 2. 89). Two days later on the day of the festival of Liber Pater/Bacchus, the Liberalia, he spoke in the senate in favour of an amnesty for the conspirators and accepted the compromise whereby this amnesty and the abolition of the dictatorship were linked with recognition of Caesar's *acta*.[4]

---

[1] *Phil.* 2. 88, cf. 83–4; *Div.* 2. 23. Cicero was probably in the course of writing this last work at the time.
[2] *Phil.* 2. 25. Cf. his remarks to Trebonius and Cassius, *Fam.* 10. 28. 1; 12. 3. 1; 4. 1.
[3] *Brut.* 331; *Deiot.* 33–4, 40–1; *Att.* 12. 45. 2 (see Ch. XVII with n. 119).
[4] The evidence can be found in Appendix 7.

The period from the Ides of March 44 to July 43 is especially richly documented in Cicero's works. The correspondence with Atticus recommences the month after Caesar's assassination and continues till November 44. There are also many letters to and from the conspirators and others who were important in the political and military manoeuvring that was to follow. In the *Philippic* speeches we have the largest item of political oratory that Cicero ever committed to writing. Moreover, he was still producing philosophical and rhetorical works, some of which were highly relevant to his political thinking.

Two letters at most are evidence of immediate reactions to the assassination. A brief note to the conspirator Minucius Basilus has been taken by many commentators as the ancient equivalent of a greetings telegram: 'I congratulate you; I rejoice for myself. I give you my affection and protection of your interests. I wish to receive your affection and discover what you are doing and what is being done' (*Fam.* 6. 15). The letter, the only one to Basilus in the surviving correspondence, has no date and no specific reference to the conspiracy: it could refer to some other momentous event in Basilus' career.[5] However, the very fact that it has survived suggests that those who first edited Cicero's letters thought it worth including precisely because they took it to be a reference to the conspiracy.

Of certain relevance is a letter of Decimus Brutus to Marcus and Cassius, which must have been passed on to Cicero by one of its recipients (*Fam.* 11. 1).[6] Decimus had been visited the previous evening by Hirtius who had revealed the hostile and (in Decimus' view) treacherous attitude of Antonius. The latter stated that not only could he not grant Decimus his province (of Gallia Cisalpina, as provided in Caesar's arrangements),[7] but he did not think any of the conspirators could remain safely in the city owing to the hostility of the soldiers and the plebs (ibid. 1). Decimus did not believe this, but rather that Antonius feared that any recognition of the conspirators would lead to the exclusion of the Caesarians from politics. His reaction was to ask for a 'free embassy' (*legatio libera*) to cover the conspirators' withdrawal from the city. Antonius promised to secure this from the senate, but Decimus doubted

---

[5] For doubts see SB *Fam.* ad loc.

[6] Commentators have placed this either in the interval between the murder and the debate on the Liberalia or after the debate and the funeral. I prefer the earlier date, following Schmidt and How (see How ii. 479), because there is reference neither to the agreement on the amnesty, nor to the apparent reconciliation between Antonius and the leading conspirators following it, nor to the funeral as a source of popular hostility. It is clear from the defensive posture assumed by the conspirators on the Capitol on the Ides that the reaction to the murder among the soldiers and plebs was immediate.

[7] That is, he could not, as consul, preside over a senate meeting in which the province was approved and money voted towards its administration by Decimus Brutus.

whether he would obtain it and, even if he did, feared that it would be simply the first step to their being declared public enemies and exiles (ibid. 2). He went on to reflect that the reason for not taking further drastic action now, rather than later when they were exiles, was that in the present situation that they had no secure base except Sextus Pompeius and Caecilius Bassus (ibid. 3–4). He notes at the end of the letter that he had made a further request for the conspirators to remain in the city with an official bodyguard, but did not think that this would be granted (ibid. 6).

No text illustrates better the powerlessness of the conspirators and their failure to think through the consequences of their action. Their opponents had access to over 30 legions, while Caecilius Bassus in Syria had one and Sextus Pompeius in Spain eventually seven;[8] Caesarians controlled also the public finances. Cicero's own letters, though reflecting enormous relief that Caesar was gone, are equally full of helplessness and foreboding. On 7 April Cicero was outside Rome, profiting from the usual legal and senatorial vacation.[9] He was staying with C. Matius, one of Caesar's former inner circle, but excluded from the councils of state since the murder. Matius thought the situation desperate: if Caesar could not solve Rome's problems, who would do so now? He was expecting with glee an uprising (*tumultus*) in Gaul. This would normally mean one mounted by the subject peoples, but there was also a question of the Caesarian legions and veterans (*Att.* 14. 1. 1).[10] Cicero was appalled and contrasted Matius with Oppius who missed Caesar just as much but said nothing to offend any of the 'good men', that is, republicans. Matius related two remarks of Caesar's, one relating to Cicero's inability to see Caesar at his own convenience, which has already been mentioned,[11] the other about Brutus: 'What this man wants, is a major problem, but whatever he does want, he really wants' (ibid. 2).

At the beginning of April Cicero still has no suspicions of Antonius' ambitions (*Att.* 14. 3. 2), but is unhappy about the general hostility of Caesarians: liberty has been recovered but not the *res publica* (*Att.* 14. 4. 1). By this last term he seems to mean the normal functioning of republican government. He recognizes that, however glorious the assassination was, the job was only half done and could not be completed without money and men

---

[8] Sextus Pompeius had apparently seven two months later, but how many men were Roman citizens is doubtful (*Att.* 16. 4. 1) See on this and the numbers and loyalties of legions Brunt, 1971, 478–80; Botermann, 1968, esp. 181 ff.

[9] Cf. *Att.* 14. 5. 2 'res prolatae'.

[10] Cf. 14. 5. 1, 14. 6. 1 for the rumoured threat from the Gallic legions; *Att.* 14. 9. 3 for the passivity of the subject peoples; *VRR* 153–4 for the term *tumultus*. Note that Matius had spoken to no leading Caesarian but Lepidus since the Ides of March.

[11] Ch. XVII with n. 83.

(ibid. 2). The satellites of the tyrant are still the magistrates and in command of Caesar's armies, they have veteran bodyguards, while the conspirators are penned up in their houses. He himself should have taken advantage of the offer of a *legatio*, a 'free embassy', before the senatorial vacation (*Att.* 14. 5. 2).[12] He was in fact planning to leave Italy for Greece in July to see at first hand the progress his son was making in his studies in Athens (*Att.* 14. 7. 2). The news on 12 April of a meeting of Antonius with Brutus and Cassius was welcome, but Cicero regretted the effect of the terms agreed in the senate on 17 March, whereby Caesar's *acta* were to be respected: this entailed that the pre-election of the next two years' consuls and tribunes, undertaken by Caesar before his Parthian campaign, was to remain valid.[13] Meanwhile men from the *municipia* who visited Cicero at Fundi were overjoyed and wanted to hear his appreciation of the political situation (*Att.* 14. 6. 2). It is not clear what determined the attitude of these local worthies whose class had on the whole profited from Caesar's regime. It may be that they had feared Caesar's plans for land-division.[14] or had been worried about the potential consequences of any failure by Caesar in the East.

By April 16–17 the news from Gaul was reassuring, less so the news about the shops Cicero owned in Rome: two had collapsed, the rest had cracks, and so not only the tenants but the mice had moved out (*Att.* 14. 9. 1–2). Cicero's philosophic studies, he claimed with some irony, enabled him to consider it not even an inconvenience: they would have to be rebuilt, in such a way that some profit would accrue from the operation, presumably in the shape of higher rents. A few days later Cicero heard of the result of the negotiations between Antonius and the conspirators: D. Brutus, Trebonius, and Tillius Cimber were to go straight to their provinces.[15] However, he was not happy, because this was in effect to ratify Caesar's arrangements. We find here, for the first time in the letters we possess, expression of serious regret over the missed opportunity on the Ides of March. He had urged at the time that Brutus and Cassius, as praetors, should have summoned the senate to the Capitol: by the Liberalia on 17 March it was too late. Then Atticus had loudly proclaimed that it would be a disaster if Caesar had a funeral procession. Instead Caesar had been cremated in the forum and a tear-jerking panegyric had led to the poor and the slaves attacking the houses of Caesar's opponents with fire (*Att.* 14. 10. 1). Cicero goes on to point out that all those who had profited

---

[12] The offer had been made by Caesar (*Att.* 14. 13. 4). On *legationes liberae* see Ch. XII with n. 31.
[13] *Att.* 14. 6. 1–2. In fact the magistrates for the first year had been pre-elected *in toto* (Dio 43. 51. 5).
[14] Cf. *Att.* 14. 6. 1. Cicero himself seems to have been worrying about encroachments by settlers on his property later (*Att.* 15. 3. 1).
[15] Cf. App. *BCiv.* 3. 2. 4–5, 3. 6. 18.

from the confiscation of the property of Pompeians, whether ex-centurions like Scaeva and Fuficius Fango or those from the ranks of senators and knights, must inevitably be afraid for their gains (ibid. 2).[16]

The same letter tells us of the arrival (18 April) of Caesar's heir Octavius at Neapolis. The next morning Octavius was visited by Balbus, who went on to tell Cicero at Cumae that the young man would enter on his inheritance—something which, as Atticus had foreseen, would cause problems with Antonius (ibid. 3).[17] Two days later Octavius was staying in the villa next door to Cicero, that of his stepfather Philippus. Cicero found him deferential and friendly, completely devoted to him. However, like Philippus, he did not greet him as Caesar and he did not believe he could be a 'good citizen'.[18] The massive entourage of Caesarians who surrounded him were threatening death to the conspirators and complaining that the present situaion was intolerable (the group no doubt included later known adherents like Agrippa and Maecenas but for the moment the power in it would have lain with men like Balbus, Hirtius, and Pansa).[19] Cicero wondered about the impact the 'boy' would have when he came to Rome, seeing that 'our liberators' could not be there in safety. He was also unhappy about the consuls designate Hirtius and Pansa who still forced him to give declamations, as they had in 46 (*Att.* 14. 12. 2).

Meanwhile there were further indications of Antonius' exploiting the agreement to accept Caesar's *acta* (*Att.* 14. 12. 1): he had actually posted up a law, claiming that it had been passed by Caesar as dictator in an assembly, making all Sicilians Roman citizens. Cicero alleges that it was in return for a huge bribe. However, Antonius could no doubt have argued that it was a logical development of Caesar's extension of the franchise, for example to those beyond the Po in Cisalpine Gaul. In any event it would have secured Antonius immense support in the island. Cicero's attitude is that he had not been happy when Caesar granted Latin rights *en bloc* to the Sicilians, whom Cicero still regarded as his clients (that would have allowed their magistrates to become Roman citizens), but this was intolerable. As for another of his clients, Deiotarus, he deserved to be recognized as king, but not after a bribe to Antonius' wife Fulvia. Nevertheless, in the light of the overturning of

---

[16] Cf. *Att.* 14. 6. 1 on a particular farm at Fundi.

[17] Cicero had anticipated Octavius' approach with some qualms (*Att.* 14. 5. 3, 14. 6. 1). If we follow Nicolaus of Damascus (*FGH* 90 F 130. 57) and Appian (*BCiv.* 3. 12. 40–13. 43), Octavius went first to Rome and this is in itself perfectly plausible. See Toher, 2004. However, in *Att.* 14. 12. 2 Cicero seems to talk as if the boy had not yet reached Rome.

[18] The generally accepted supplement 'quem nego posse <esse> bonum civem' in *Att.* 14. 12. 2 seems necessary in view of the explanation that follows in the next sentence.

[19] *Att.* 14. 11. 2, 12. 2.

Caesar's decisions, there was hope for the people of Buthrotum (Atticus and his friends) who were due to suffer confiscation of land after failing to pay the taxes imposed on them.[20]

Cicero himself felt directly the impact of Antonius' manoeuvres. The consul wrote to him from Rome stating that he had secured from Caesar a decision to bring back from exile Sex. Cloelius, Clodius' lieutenant and legal draftsman, condemned for violence in 52.[21] He would not, however, put Caesar's memorandum into effect without Cicero's agreement. It was especially in the name of Clodius' son, P. Claudius Pulcher, that he asked Cicero to set aside his hostility and make it plain that his dispute with the boy's father was political and not motivated by a desire to humiliate the family.[22] Like the letter Antonius wrote to Cicero in 49,[23] the apparently deferential letter contained a none-too-delicate threat. Antonius asked to be allowed to advise the boy not to perpetuate the family feud. Although he was sure that Cicero's fortune was secure, he thought he would prefer to pass a respected and tranquil old age rather than an anxious one (*Att.* 14. 13A. 3).

Cicero was sure that Antonius would bring back Cloelius anyway (*Att.* 14. 13. 6, 14. 14. 2). He therefore replied in a letter which is a masterpiece of insincerity and must have been recognized as such by Antonius. If only they had been able to deal with this in person, Antonius could have seen in Cicero's face his affection for him. As it was, Antonius' letter had been most kind and respectful and Cicero was responding in kind by yielding both to it and to his own essentially kind nature. In fact he had no personal hatred for Cloelius and thought it wrong to attack the friends of his enemies. As for the young Clodius, he had no wish to perpetuate a family feud; the quarrel had been political. At his age he had no fear of the boy, but rather hoped that the concession would create good relations between himself and Antonius (*Att.* 14. 13B).[24]

At the end of April he complained to Atticus about the persistence of tyranny with the tyrant removed. Indeed it was worse: things were being done which Caesar himself would never have done, such as recalling Cloelius. They were slaves to Caesar's documents, although they had not been slaves to Caesar. The root of the problem was the senate-meeting on the Liberalia, which senators had been forced to attend and then could not

---

[20] Their story is told in a letter to L. Plancus, a copy of which Cicero sent to Atticus perhaps in early July (*Att.* 16. 16A. 4–5, cf. 15. 29. 3). See also 12. 6a for Atticus' plea to Caesar.

[21] *Att.* 14. 13. 6 with 14. 13A–B; Asc. 33, 55–6 C.

[22] *Att.* 14. 13A. 3: 'pro re publica videri gessisse simultatem cum patre eius, non <quod> contempseris familiam'; 'honestius enim et libentius inimicitias rei publicae susceptas nomine quam contumaciae'. On this Claudius see Wiseman, 1968.

[23] Cf. *Att.* 10. 8A. 1.

[24] Cf. *Att.* 14. 19. 2 for Antonius' thanks and Pansa's fury over the concessions.

give voice to their views freely because of the armed veterans in attendance (*Att.* 14. 14. 2).[25] This was not the fault of the Bruti but of those stupid people (*bruti*) who showed their appreciation of Caesar's assassination but did not stay true to their beliefs. And then the funeral had ruined everything (ibid. 3). Atticus had just written that Antonius would hold a meeting of the senate on 1 June to discuss the provinces, in which he would seek the command of both Cisalpine and Transalpine Gaul, to be extended beyond the now normal two years—in effect a re-creation of Caesar's great command.[26] There were rumours that a force of veteran soldiers was being secretly organized, in particular to attack the conspirators, and Cicero was later advised not to attend (*Att.* 14. 22. 2). These rumours led Brutus and Cassius to write a letter to Antonius protesting that, if true, this amounted to a breach of their understanding with him (*Fam.* 11. 2). Cicero was also informed by Balbus that Antonius was going round the veteran settlements extracting oaths that they would uphold Caesar's measures and ordering that they should maintain their arms ready for inspection by the local magistrates every month (*Att.* 14. 21. 2).

Cicero was, however, genuinely impressed, when he heard on 1 May about Dolabella's participation in the suppression of a movement among the urban plebs led by Amatius, a man claiming to be the grandson of the great C. Marius.[27] This man had first come to Cicero's notice in 45, when he unsuccessfully sought Cicero's help as a defence-advocate, perhaps in a suit over his claim to Roman citizenship (*Att.* 12. 49. 2). After Caesar's death he had led a movement among the urban plebs which set up a statue and altar to the dead man, and harassed the conspirators. The disturbances, if anything, would have assisted the cause of Caesar's heir and were an unwelcome distraction for the consuls, even if they tacitly approved of the pressure brought on the conspirators to leave Rome.[28] Cicero's letter to Dolabella was fulsome, but perhaps irritating to the recipient in that it dwelt on the glory that had reflected on Cicero himself and compared Dolabella to Brutus as an example of virtue (*Att.* 14. 17A. 1–5). Cicero wrote this letter on 3 May; six days later he was furiously complaining that Dolabella had not paid a debt

---

[25] There is an untranslatable pun: *Liberalia* and 'libere potuimus sententiam dicere?'
[26] *Att.* 14. 14. 4, cf. *Phil.* 1. 19; Dio 43. 25. 3.
[27] *Att.* 14. 15. 1, 14. 16. 1, 14. 17A, 14. 19. 1; cf. *Phil.* 1. 5, where both Antonius and Dolabella are given the credit for executing Amatius; *Phil.* 2. 107 for Dolabella alone overthrowing Amatius' altar to Caesar.
[28] Earlier references are *Att.* 14. 6. 1, 7. 1, 8. 1; also 5. 1, assuming that we identify the movement with the 'conspiracy of Caesar's freedmen'. The Marius was otherwise called Amatius or Herophilus. See further Val. Max. 9. 15. 1; Livy, *Per.* 116; App. *BCiv.* 3. 3, 6–8; Nic. Dam. (*FGH* IIA 90 F128) *Vita Caesaris* 14; Yavetz, 1969, 58–61, 70–2. Appian ascribes the repression to Antonius alone.

to him that had been due on 1 January, in spite of the fact that he had paid off other debts and had sought help from Caesar's funds in the temple of Ops.[29]

By this time Cicero was in gloom over the exclusion of Brutus and Cassius from political life and thinking more and more about going to Greece (*Att.* 14. 18. 4, 14. 19. 1). He wrote to Cassius that Dolabella's action was the one source of confidence amid the manifold dangers to the *res publica*. 'For after the king has been killed, we are putting into effect every royal nod... Enactments are being posted, immunities are being given, vast sums of money are being disbursed, exiles are being allowed home, forged decrees of the senate are being put on record...'. It was up to the liberators to do something more (*Fam.* 12. 1. 1–2). On 11 May he told Atticus that he had dedicated to Brutus his essay on the best style of speaking (*De Optimo Genere Dicendi*), with which he knew Brutus would disagree. His only hope was that Brutus would be able to deliver a political speech safely in the city. If this happened, the republicans had won: the other side would either find no leader for a civil war or would be easily defeated.[30] He himself was trying to convert his Caesarian friends to a favourable attitude towards the conspirators. Hirtius was making the right noises, but he was living with Balbus, who also made the right noises. Cicero, it seems, feared the latter's loyalty to Caesar's memory and association with Octavius. Pansa was certainly eager for peace, but Cicero assumed other Caesarians were looking for a pretext for civil war (*Att.* 14. 20. 4).[31]

There was, however, an encouraging sign of dissension among Caesarians: after Antonius' brother Lucius, one of the tribunes, had delivered a frightening harangue, Dolabella opposed him. The republicans now seemed to have a political leader. Presumably L. Antonius, who was about to give Octavius a platform to address the people, had argued for vengeance, Dolabella for reconciliation (*Att.* 14. 20. 1, 4). In a later letter the same day, written after a visit from Balbus. Cicero stressed the latter's eagerness for war and his account of M. Antonius' military preparations.[32] A bitter complaint follows: 'That action was performed with the courage of men but the strategy of boys. For who has not recognized this? An heir to the kingship has been left behind' (*Att.* 14. 21. 3). The heir is Antonius, but in a context where there is another bid for Caesar's legacy—or perhaps more than one since Cleopatra was

---

[29] *Att.* 14. 18. 1; cf. 14. 19. 4–5.
[30] *Att.* 14. 20. 3. *De optimo genere dicendi* (now thought authentic) is a brief essay in which Cicero seeks to convert an Atticist orator into what was for him the true Atticism of Aeschines and Demosthenes.
[31] See *Att.* 14. 21. 4 for further attempts by Cicero to convert Hirtius.
[32] *Att.* 14. 21. 2, cf. 15. 2. 3.

advertising her claim that her son Ptolemy was Caesar's child.³³ The attitude of Caesarians is well summarized in a subsequent letter: 'A most distinguished man has been murdered; the whole of public affairs have been thrown into chaos by his death; all his actions will be rendered void, as soon as we (the republicans) cease to be afraid; he was ruined by his clemency: if he had not employed this, nothing like this would have happened to him.' Even Hirtius was as afraid of a coup d'état by republicans as of one by Antonius (*Att.* 15. 1. 3). Cicero expects war if Sextus Pompeius arrives with a strong army, and realizes with discomfort that his pleasure at Caesar's death rules out neutrality. Should he join an army? It is a thousand times better to die, especially at his age (*Att.* 14. 22. 1–2).

Brutus' answer to *De Optimo Genere Dicendi* was to send Cicero his written version of the speech he delivered on the Capitol on 17 March. The language and arguments were beautifully chosen but Cicero felt that it lacked the passion of Demosthenes (*Att.* 15. 1a. 2).³⁴ On 19 May came news of Octavius' first *contio* which displeased both Atticus and Cicero. Cicero was equally unhappy about Matius and Rabirius Postumus undertaking to mount the games celebrating Caesar's Victory (*ludi victoriae Caesaris*) in July.³⁵ He felt that he could achieve nothing by attending the senate and was nervous about the potential threat from the veterans.³⁶ On June 2 there was further bad news. Antonius was going to propose in the senate that Brutus and Cassius were to be sent as commissioners to buy grain in Asia and Sicily respectively (*Att.* 15. 9. 1) Brutus himself also wrote, explaining that he would not perform his normal duty as *praetor urbanus* of celebrating the *ludi Apollinares*.³⁷ Cicero's profound despondency, as well as a genuine element of fear, is displayed in his letter of 24 May: 'I get no joy from the Ides of March. For he would never have returned (sc. from Parthia), panic would not have forced us to ratify his decisions; alternatively . . . I would have been so influential with him (whom I pray the gods may destroy, dead as he is) that at my age, since I am not free after my master has been killed, he would not have been a master to be avoided' (*Att.* 15. 4. 3).

---

³³ *Att.* 14. 20. 2; cf. 15. 1. 5, 15. 4. 4 for an obscure rumour about her; 15. 15. 2 for Cicero's displeasure at her method of approaching him for some literary service.

³⁴ Appian (*BCiv.* 2. 137. 570–141. 591) places the original speech clearly after the senate debate of the Liberalia, which he wrongly dates to the day after the murder (2. 126. 525). It seems most likely that he has got the sequence of events right but the date of the senate debate wrong, *contra* e.g. SB *Att* vi. 378, Syme, 1939*a*, 99. See *Att.* 15. 2. 2, 15. 3. 2 for Atticus' attempts to get Cicero to write his version of the speech.

³⁵ *Att.* 15. 2. 3. One of the Hostilii Sasernae was to be their colleague, cf. *MRR* ii. 324–5 and Supp. 29. Cicero finally heard from Atticus in late May about Antonius' proposals for the assembly on 1 June. These entailed stripping D. Brutus of the province of Cisalpine Gaul (*Att.* 15. 4. 1). See Appendix 7 for the legislation.

³⁶ *Att.* 14. 22. 2, 15. 3. 1, 15. 4. 4.   ³⁷ *Att.* 15. 10; cf. 15. 11. 2.

In reaction to Antonius' measures Brutus had a family conference at Antium about 8 June. His mother Servilia, half-sister Iunia Tertulla (who was Cassius' wife), and wife Porcia were all present, as were Cassius, Favonius, and Cicero. For the women of the family this must have been one of the last times they saw Brutus and Cassius (*Att*. 15. 11. 1).[38] Cassius was determined not to accept the insult of the corn-commission in Sicily and planned to go to Greece; Brutus was still wondering if he should return to Rome. Cicero was not in favour of Brutus going to a province either immediately or when his praetorship ended. There was then much talk of lost opportunities, Cassius apparently believing that Decimus Brutus should have acted, presumably with his army. Cicero first remarked that they should not go over old ground but then turned this into a rhetorical *praeteritio* by doing precisely the same himself. He had not reached the point of saying that they should have stabbed Antonius but was merely arguing that they should have summoned the senate themselves on the Ides, when Servilia exclaimed, 'I have never heard anyone make that suggestion', so achieving the unusual distinction of silencing Cicero (ibid. 1–2).[39] The outcome was that Cassius seemed committed to going to Greece, while Brutus gave up any idea of going to Rome and seemed to be planning to go to Asia. Servilia still had enough influence with the Caesarians for her to promise to get rescinded the senate's decision about the corn-commissions (ibid. 2).[40] As for Cicero, though he had satisfied his conscience by meeting Brutus, he was even more convinced that he should leave Italy, which he could now conveniently do, as Dolabella had made him his legate on 3 June, a post which could last five years, the length of Dolabella's command (ibid. 4).[41]

Cicero was still thinking about Octavianus, as he now called him after he had entered on his inheritance. The latter had enough talent and courage, and, Cicero believed, his attitude to the conspirators was likely to be as Cicero wished. However, there were great problems: he was young, a Caesar, Caesar's heir, and bound to be influenced by the talk he heard around him. His stepfather Philippus felt that this made him untrustworthy. Nevertheless, Cicero believed that he should be cultivated and, if nothing else, kept apart from Antonius.

---

[38] Another family conference without Brutus and Cassius was to be held in July 43 (*Ad Brut*. 26. 1). Iunia lived on until AD 22 (Tac. *Ann*. 3. 76).

[39] Cicero claimed that he had made this proposal at the time in an earlier letter to Atticus (*Att*. 14. 10. 1).

[40] Cf. *Att*. 15. 12. 1. See 14. 21. 3 for Cicero's comment on the irony that the mother of a tyrannicide should possess a villa at Naples confiscated from a Pompeian.

[41] Caesar had put restrictions on *liberae legationes* for the performance of vows at shrines. So they were less convenient. Moreover, Cicero felt it grotesque that he should perform a vow made on condition that the *res publica* should have stood firm, when it had been overthrown.

Octavianus was devoted to his brother-in-law C. Marcellus—whose advice, Cicero hoped, was in the republican interest—but had no great faith in Hirtius and Pansa (*Att.* 15. 12. 2). The young man was evidently continuing to be deferential to Cicero and his hostility to Antonius was genuine. Cicero was more confident in his sincerity than Philippus, but could not get over the fact that he was Caesar's heir and at an age, where his views and loyalties were unstable. These themes return in later letters. In fact Octavianus was more stable than Cicero feared, but no more reliable on this account for Cicero.

For the rest of June and July Cicero's letters to Atticus are for the most part a tissue of brief comments and answers to Atticus' questions, which often leave the present-day reader bewildered. There is an occasional reference to politics. Cicero continues to anticipate civil war (*Att.* 15. 18. 2). Any sensible man, he writes, would ascribe his planned journey to desperation rather than the duties of a *legatus* (*Att.* 15. 20. 1). According to Atticus, even 'good men' were talking in extreme terms about the *res publica*: they thought it was lost. Cicero himself had begun to lose confidence from the time he heard the tyrant called 'a most distinguished man' in an address to the people.[42] The news that Sextus Pompeius had been welcomed at Carteia reinforced Cicero's fears about the imminence of fighting since he believed that neutrality was impossible (*Att.* 15. 20. 3).[43] There was some excitement in the family when Quintus' son detached himself from Antonius—with a strange story that the consul had asked him to gather a force of armed men in order to make him dictator—and said that he was joining Brutus and Cassius (*Att.* 15. 21. 1, 15. 22. 1). The young Quintus' story seems to have been deliberately exaggerated. Possibly he had been asked to gather together veterans for the assembly meetings at the beginning of June.[44] Brutus left the area of Rome on 25 June (*Att.* 15. 24), after sending a letter to ask Cicero to watch 'his games' (that is, the *ludi Apollinares* that were to be held on his behalf in his absence). Cicero thought this unsafe, but was interested in their outcome (*Att.* 15. 26. 1, 15. 28, 15. 29. 1). He was with Brutus on Nesis (modern Nisida near Pozzuoli) when Atticus's letter arrived informing him of a demonstration in Brutus' favour by the crowd watching Accius' *Tereus*.[45]

---

[42] *Att.* 15. 20. 2. This seems to me to be more probably a reference to speeches in the immediate aftermath of the Ides of March actually heard by Cicero than a more recent event, though of course the theme was repeated (*Att.* 14. 11. 1, 14. 22. 1; SB *Att* vi, p. 397).

[43] Cf. *Att.* 14. 22. 2, 15. 22. 1, 16. 4. 2. Any idea that Sextus would resort to arms was exploded by 8 July (*Att.* 16. 1. 4, 16. 4. 1–2).

[44] He seems to have been given a quaestorship beginning 5 Dec. 44 under Caesar's arrangements (*Att.* 16. 14. 4).

[45] *Att.* 16. 2. 3; cf. *Phil.* 1. 36; App. *BCiv.* 3. 23. 87; 3. 24. 90. Appian maintains that Octavian's supporters broke up the demonstration.

Apart from making representations about the land of the Buthrotans,[46] Cicero was largely preoccupied with organizing money and making travel arrangements for his visit to Greece.[47] He was not in a positive frame of mind. He was unhappy, he told Atticus while still in his Puteolan villa, to be leaving him for an uncomfortable journey which did not suit a man of his age and rank. Moreover, it seemed odd to be leaving an Italy in peace, while planning to return when it might be at war. Finally, he was wasting time that could have been spent in his nicely built and agreeable properties, in travelling to foreign parts. He hoped at least to be of some use to his son.[48] When staying at Vibo with Sicca, shortly before he had to decide how to make the actual crossing to Greece, he was still lamenting his absence from Atticus and his 'sweet little villas, the darlings of Italy.' The danger at home seemed to have evaporated. He was glad that his departure was approved, provided that he came back before 1 January, which is what he planned, for he preferred to be at home under threat than secure in Atticus' Athens (*Att*. 16. 6. 2).[49]

FURTHER PHILOSOPHICAL CONSOLATION

De Natura Deorum, De Divinatione, De Fato

During the previous six months Cicero had had ample opportunity to pursue his philosophical projects. His works on *The Nature of the Gods* and *Divination* form a pair.[50] The latter was completed after Caesar's murder (*Div.* 1. 119, 2. 23), but the combined project was probably begun in 45.[51] Indeed the former portrays itself as having been written 'when ... the state of the *res publica* is such that it must inevitably be governed by the policy and management of one man' (*ND* 1. 7). One cannot imagine Cicero leaving this sentence in a work published after the Ides of March. However, it is not clear if and when these works were circulated. We have no mention of this in the

---

[46] *Att*. 15. 14. 2–3, to Dolabella; 16. 16A–F, to L. Plancus, Cupiennius, and Capito. The latter is identified by Shackleton Bailey with Ateius Capito (SB *Att* v. 375), but the C. Fonteius Capito who a few years later moved the *lex Fonteia* (*RS* i, no. 36) for Antonius' benefit, would be more appropriate as one of the Antonian land commission. See also *Att*. 15. 29. 3, 16. 4. 3 for rumours that the land commission had been expelled from Buthrotum.

[47] See *Att*. 15. 20. 3, 15. 25, 15. 26. 3–4, 16. 1. 3, 5, 16. 4. 4, 16. 5. 3.

[48] *Att*. 16. 3. 4; cf. 6. 2 for the time of return.

[49] The *villulae* were Cicero's *ocelli*, just as the peninsula of Sirmio, where Catullus had his *villula*, was his *ocellus* (*Cat*. 31. 2, cf. 26. 1).

[50] There are references to *ND* in *Div*. 1. 7–9, 33, 117; 2. 3, 148.

[51] See *Att*. 13. 39. 2 for Cicero seeking in August a relevant work of the Epicurean philosopher Phaedrus, mentioned by 'Cotta' in *ND* 1. 93.

surviving correspondence and there are signs of lack of revision in *De Natura Deorum*: the three books recount a dialogue that Cicero must have imagined taking place over a number of days,[52] but after the introduction in Book 1 the dialogue is in fact continuous. This would no doubt have been noticed by a critical reader like Atticus.

The *De Natura Deorum* has a setting in a garden villa of C. Aurelius Cotta (cos. 75), who like Cicero was an adherent of the sceptical Academy and whose oratory Cicero admired.[53] Cicero portrays himself visiting there during the Latin festival at a time in the seventies BC after his own return from Greece (*ND* 1. 15).[54] The preface (1. 1–14), addressed to Brutus, defends the importance both of this much-debated topic, on the ground that it is the basis of religion and piety, and of Cicero's own authority as an expounder of philosophy. He has studied this from his youth and his adherence to the sceptical Academy, for whom no perception is absolutely true but nevertheless probability is an adequate standard of conduct, will, he suggests, be justified in the light of the variety of views he is about to relate (1. 12–14). The persona of Cicero himself is no more than a reporter of the dialogue, a link between the participants and the reader. The protagonists, apart from Cotta, are the Epicurean C. Velleius and the Stoic Q. Lucilius Balbus, men otherwise almost unknown to us.[55]

The Stoic is made almost immediately to declare the division between his school and the Peripatetics, arguing that the latter do not distinguish properly the right and the expedient (1. 16), a topic to which Cicero will return in *De Officiis*. Then Velleius embarks on a diatribe against all who interpret the universe and construct deities without taking into account *physiologia*, natural science (1. 20). Cicero portrays this as delivered with the usual Epicurean confidence (1. 18). He probably gives a fair reproduction of the scorn exponents of Epicureanism had for rival philosophies, including an element of knockabout humour, though the detail of this may be his own—for example the riposte to the Stoic view that deity is spherical: the result will be that he will rotate with unimaginable speed, which will preclude any intellectual stability or happiness (1. 24, cf. 2. 46). Some serious philosophical problems are touched on, for example that of relating the infinity of time to a doctrine of creation (1. 20–1). The brief review of the varied conceptions of

---

[52] See the references to 'yesterday' and 'the day before yesterday' in *ND* 2. 73 and 3. 18.
[53] Points stressed at *ND* 1. 17, 2. 1. Cotta is described as one of the leading orators of the Republic in the *Brutus* (182–3 and then *passim*, finally at 333).
[54] Probably before Cotta's consulship and his subsequent departure to Gaul as proconsul (*Brut.* 318; Sall. *Hist.* 2. 98 (D)).
[55] Apart from a mention in *De Or.* 3. 78 which suggests that they were established figures before the Social War.

god held by philosophers (1. 25–43), including the scornful reference to Democritus (1. 29), matches that in Philodemus *De Pietate* and may derive from statements by Epicurus himself.[56]

The sum of Velleius' criticism is that both the traditional accounts of the poets and the theories of the majority of philosophers are unacceptable, the former because they present the gods as unworthy of reverence, the latter because they are far from normal human conceptions and are inconsistent with the notion that deity is animate. For the Epicurean the existence of gods is proved by our common innate perception that gods exist.[57] Their beautiful, intelligent, anthropomorphic, but unemotional nature is deduced partly from human conceptions, partly from the implications of divine immortality. Their happiness precludes toil or involvement in human affairs: it is in other words an ideal version of Epicurean happiness (1. 46–53).

In reply Cotta raises immediately the question whether gods exist at all, only to leave it unanswered. As a priest whose duty it was to maintain public religious ceremonies and rules, he would like to be convinced of their existence, not merely as opinion but an established truth. Many experiences shake this opinion, causing him from time to time to disbelieve in their existence. However, for the purposes of the discussion he will accept it, since this is the common view of all philosophers (1. 61–2).[58] He cannot, however, accept that the existence of gods is proved by human perceptions, for which the evidence is far from universal. He is not convinced by Epicurean physics nor can he accept Epicurean metaphysical belief in a quasi-corporeal substance for the gods, but, even if this belief were true, that would be no reason to believe that the divine substance has human form (1. 65–77). Cotta introduces here Xenophanes' argument that animals would imagine deities in their own shape (1. 77–8).[59]

He goes on to discourse at some length on the variety of human perceptions of divinity, the difficulties consequent on endowing gods with human faculties, and the inadequacy of the Epicurean argument that a reasoning deity must have human form (1. 79–102). In the latter part of his attack other elements in Epicurean argument provide targets—Epicurean theories of sense-perception, on which their apprehension of divinity was based (1. 103–10), the Epicurean concept of happiness (111–14), and the Epicurean claim to have encouraged piety combined with freedom from superstition (115–23). Instead, argues

---

[56] See *PHerc.* 1428, re-edited by Henrichs, 1974; Dyck, 2003a, 8.
[57] *ND* 1. 44 'firma consensio'; 'insitas eorum vel potius innatas cognitiones', called by Cicero *praenotio* (as a translation of the term πρόληψις).
[58] Cf. *ND* 3. 5 for his later acceptance of Roman authority in religious matters.
[59] Cf. Xenophanes 172–3 Kirk–Raven. This will of course also be an argument against God's having made men in his own image.

Cotta, Epicurus overthrew human morality, removing among other things the basis of true human friendship (121–3):[60] in short Poseidonius was right when he argued that Epicurus was a crypto-atheist (1. 123–4).

In the next book Cotta persists in refusing to put forward a positive argument, in spite of Lucilius Balbus' comment that a philosopher, a *pontifex*, and a Cotta should have firm view of his own to propound (2. 2). Instead, Balbus embarks on an exposition of the Stoic view, which, in spite of his promise to keep it short (2. 3), turns out to be more prolix and rambling than Velleius' speech. After listing the heads under which Stoic discussion took place he begins with the first, arguments for the existence of gods (2. 3–4). He briefly mentions the argument from the magnificent design of the world and the evidence of divine epiphany (2. 4–7), before moving on to prediction, premonition, and augury. The examples from Roman history here anticipate material that appears later in *De Divinatione*.[61] These arguments are summed up in the four reasons given by Cleanthes for human belief in divinity (2. 13–15): prediction; the benefits provided by the earth; the awe inspired by portentous events; the regular movements of heaven and earth.

There follow some exceedingly bogus arguments seeking to prove the Stoic view that the world itself is animate, sentient, and rational, in fact a supremely rational being, whose fiery essence is shared by the sun and stars (2. 16–44). The rest of the book elaborates on the nature of divinity. Granted that the world is a sentient rational being, it is not difficult to argue that divinities govern the world and have concern for mortals, the traditional names given to the gods concealing divine powers who work for the benefit of mankind (2. 62–72). Once the argument from design is accepted, it is a short step to Stoic providence ($\pi\rho\acute{o}\nu o\iota a$) (2. 73 ff.).[62] Lucilius Balbus is portrayed as someone as dogmatic as Velleius, but even more pedantic and humourless.[63] At the end of his immense disquisition he tells Cotta that it is wicked and impious to argue against the existence of the gods, whether sincerely or as a devil's advocate (2. 168).

Cotta prefaces his answer Socratically by saying that it is not so much a refutation as a series of questions about ideas that he cannot grasp (3. 1). As to Balbus' reminder that he is a priest, he has defended, and will always defend, Roman religion—consisting as it does in ritual, auspices, and the predictions made by the *haruspices* and those in charge of the Sibylline books—but for

---

[60] The reference to the Peripatetic ideal of disinterested friendship here anticipates the doctrine of the *De Amicitia*.

[61] e.g. Flaminius (*ND* 2. 8; *Div.* 1. 77; 2. 21, 67; Ti. Gracchus the elder (*ND* 2. 10–11; *Div.* 1. 33). The story of Vatinius' grandfather and the news of Pydna (*ND* 2. 6, cf. 3. 13) serves also as a compliment to the current holder of the name.

[62] The coherence of Stoic views with their basic tenets is conceded at *ND* 3. 4.

[63] See e.g. *ND* 2. 46–7, 73.

these his authorities are Roman chief priests and the augur Laelius, not any philosopher. He is bound to believe in ancestral religion, but a philosopher owes him proof (3. 4–6). He then expresses scepticism about Balbus' basic proofs. No one really believes in divine epiphanies; even if we accept divination, we do not know how it works; as for popular belief, the question is not, are there people who believe in the gods, but do gods exist (3. 11–19). Next Cotta attacks some particular arguments of Balbus (3. 20–39) including the argument from design (23–4): in the end he suggests that philosophers' theories are no better than the beliefs of the uneducated in the divinity of fish, animals, human beings, and even inanimate objects like stars (3. 39–41). He draws attention to the different myths told by different peoples about one and the same of the traditional divinities, and to the inconsistencies between peoples in the ascription of divine status (3. 42–64). During this he remarks that he has received better instruction about divine worship from *mos maiorum* and pontifical law, allegedly bequeathed by Numa, than from Stoic arguments (3. 43). Nevertheless, he specifically rejects one largely Roman tradition of worshipping divinized values such as Intelligence, Hope, and Good Faith.[64]

The final main section of the work is an attack on the Stoic notion of divine providence, in which Cotta essentially proceeds by listing everything that has gone wrong in the world (3. 65–95). At the beginning he criticizes the idea that reason is a divine gift, on the ground that it often is used in pursuit of criminal purposes: to the argument that reason is a gift that can be beneficial but also can be misused by men, he replies that the very fact that it can be misused shows that the gift is not an inheritance intended to be helpful (70–1). The catalogue of crimes and misery has both Roman and Greek examples: those most relevant to Cicero and Cotta are the exile of P. Rutilius and the assassinations of Livius Drusus, Scaevola, Catulus, and the others murdered by Cinna (80–1).[65] At the end of the dialogue the issue is left in the air. Balbus asks for a day to reply on behalf of Roman religion (not Stoicism) and Cotta says that his only aim was to be refuted. Cicero's own final comment is that Velleius preferred Cotta's views, while he himself thought those of Balbus were 'more inclined to a semblance of the truth' (95).[66]

Cicero, then, though he must have sympathized with the acceptance of Roman religious tradition which he ascribes to Cotta, was reluctant to follow

---

[64] *ND* 3. 61 'mentem, fidem, spem, virtutem, honorem, victoriam, salutem, concordiam, ceteraque eius modi'. See on what Cicero calls the *utilitates* Clark, forthcoming.

[65] C. Marius is described as 'the most treacherous of men', more disparagingly than elsewhere in Cicero's works, but this is appropriate to Cotta's *persona*.

[66] Cf. *Div.* 1. 8–9.

his persona's argument in divorcing it completely from philosophy and intellectual justification. What part of Stoic notions he found attractive, is hard to define: he certainly had some sympathy with the idea of a supreme rational being in the universe (cf. *Div.* 2. 148), but he must have had doubts about the workings of providence in view of his despair over recent developments in Rome's history, not to mention his own life. The intellectual argument for a personal atheism or agnosticism is strong, but Cicero retains a sentiment that would like to protest against this. This attitude can also be discerned in the sequel to *De Natura Deorum*, *De Divinatione*.

In the introduction to the work Cicero reviews the place divination had not only in the public practice of various civilizations but in philosophic thought, noting that, although most philosophers down to the earlier Stoics had granted it some recognition, more recent Stoics, especially Panaetius, had raised doubts, as had the Academic Carneades. Accordingly Cicero states that it is good Academic procedure to go over the arguments, as he had done in *De Natura Deorum* (*Div.* 1. 1–7). The medium he chooses is a dialogue in his Tusculan villa between himself and his brother Quintus. The latter who is portrayed as one who had recently read *De Natura Deorum* and, though shaken by Cotta's arguments which seemed to him to overthow not only Stoic theology but religion itself, still retained his belief in the gods (1. 8–9).[67] Quintus says incorrectly that divination was passed over in these books,[68] but in any case his reason for discussing it is to support belief in the existence of gods (1. 9–10).

The argument of the first book is essentially that divination works, even if we cannot explain exactly how it does. Quintus compares it to the science of herbal medicine, which cures even though its exponents are unable to give a rational account of the operation of their drugs (1. 12–13, 16), and to the ways in which the behaviour of birds and animals foretells changes in the weather and the seasons, quoting here Cicero's translation of the $\Delta\iota o\sigma\eta\mu\iota\alpha$ of Aratus, the *Prognostica* (1. 13–15). The evidence cited begins with Cicero's own account in the poem on his consulship of the portents that foretold the Catilinarian conspiracy (17–22). It goes on to deal with divination by augurs and *haruspices* (25–36), Greek oracles (37–8), dreams (39–63), deathbed predictions and other forms of clairvoyance (64–9). There is a brief reference to the theory of the human soul being derived from a world soul (70), and then Quintus returns to some reinforcing examples of prophesy, both according to ritual methods and unsolicited signs (71–108). Finally, Quintus returns to the point he touched on before, the derivation of the human soul from

---

[67] 'Quintus' adduces Cicero's final statement in *ND* 3. 95.
[68] In fact it is part of Lucilius Balbus' argument in *ND* 2. 7–12.

some divine soul and nature (109–10). This enables it to predict in various ways, some rational, some through divine inspiration (111–17). In this we find again the Stoic doctrine of divine providence and divine control over the universe which is manifest in a determined succession of events, called *fatum* (118–31). The portents of Caesar's death noted by the Etruscan *haruspex*, Spurinna, are mentioned here with the comment that they were sent to forewarn him, not to enable him to evade death (119). The book ends with Quintus dismissing professional fortune-tellers and necromancers, who, it is implied, do not have the divine route to the truth, and Cicero praising him for the preparation behind his discourse (132).

The preface to the second book begins with a review of Cicero's philosophic work to date (2. 1–7). Cicero says that the flow of books has been interrupted by a *causa gravior*, a more serious issue, clearly Caesar's murder and its consequences. He regards his project as educating Romans in order to improve their morality. He uses Latin to make the work accessible and because it will bring glory on the Roman people, if they can study philosophy without knowing Greek (4–5). The project had been begun when in the midst of civil wars he could not protect the *res publica* as he had in the past nor could he do nothing. Rome had fallen into the power of one man. However, now he was being drawn back into politics and could only spare so much time on philosophy (6–7).

In the dialogue proper Cicero begins his reply to Quintus by an argument taken from Carneades that divination deals with matters that are outside the usual sciences—such as astronomy, ethics, politics, medicine, and navigation—and depend on chance (cf. 1. 9). How then, he asks, can prediction be valid in such matters (9–17)? And how is this reconcilable with the belief that matters are controlled by *fatum* (18–19)? Either everything is determined, in which case divination by auspices is of no value, or obedience to the indications of auspices will invalidate the originally predicted outcome, in which cases Stoic determinism is proved wrong (20–1). Quintus could object here that he argued in the first book (1. 119) that the portents received by Caesar were to forewarn him not to enable him to escape his fate, but this was not the usual Roman attitude to the use of auspices and divination. This is shown, for example, by their reaction to the neglect of auspices by C. Flaminius and P. Claudius Pulcher that Cicero goes on to mention (2. 21–2). According to the Stoic view, Cicero continues, knowledge of the future would be of no advantage: would Priam, Crassus, and Pompey have been helped by foreseeing their deaths? 'What do we think about Caesar? If he had foreseen that he would be slaughtered in the senate which for the most part he himself had co-opted, in Pompey's senate-house before the statue of Pompey, with so many of his own centurions looking on, at the hands of most noble citizens, some of whom owed their position entirely to him, and then lie in such a state that not only no friend, not even a slave would approach him, what mental torture would he have felt throughout his life?' (2. 23).

Cicero now proceeds with a review of Quintus' examples, pointing out the implausibility of some reports, the unreliability of deductions made, and the lack of clear connection between portent and event, except for close precedence in time (2. 26–69). Events, believed strange, on examination are found to have natural causes (58–60). As for formal divination, Cicero in his capacity as augur states that the augural science, even though established for the purpose of divination, has not as its object the prediction of the future but is maintained for the sake of public opinion and political expediency (2. 70–5). The current scepticism about divine guidance is illustrated by the fact that pro-magistrates who undertake wars have no right to take the auspices (2. 76–7). Cicero's next subject is foreign types of divination, including substantial sections on astrology (85–99) and on clairvoyance and oracles (100–18).[69] Cicero mentions the Sibylline books here, treating them as something outlandish and dangerous, only to be consulted with prior political approval: they cannot be regarded as the product of a frenzied seer, because they are artistically constructed (110–12).[70]

The final topic is dreams (119–48), a section whose very length suggests the importance in which they were held. Here Cicero explains the dream that while in exile he had had about Marius, by the fact that he frequently thought at that time about Marius' courage in exile; similarly Quintus' dream about Cicero reflected his waking worries about his brother.[71] As a conclusion to the dialogue Cicero draws a distinction between superstition, such as is manifested in the interpretation of dreams, and true religion. The latter involves the maintenance of traditional religious rites. He himself accepts, moreover, the argument from the beauty and order of the universe and believes in a supreme eternal nature. True religion is thus to be combined with the understanding of nature. The destruction of superstition does not entail the destruction of religion (2. 148–9).

In the second book of *De Divinatione* Cicero's endorsement of conventional religion and of a vague deism is combined with scepticism about any

---

[69] This includes an attack on Stoic logic for assuming the propositions about the gods it seeks to prove (2. 101–3), comparing the correct method of the Epicurean proof that the universe is infinite.

[70] He refers here to the rumour that L. Cotta, whom he does not name, would produce a text urging that Caesar should be given the title of king (2. 110, cf. Suet. *Iul.* 79. 3).

[71] *Div.* 2. 140–2, cf. 1. 59. Cicero apparently dreamt that Marius in triumphal attire encouraged him and led him to the temple of Honos and Virtus, where in fact his recall was voted (cf. *Sest.* 116 ff.).

rational basis for divination. Nevertheless, the examples he collects of successful prediction in the first book make a powerful impression.[72] The Ides of March may have made him wonder if divine providence existed. However, what followed would have cast him once more into doubt: indeed predictions about destiny unfavourable to the conspirators seem to have made him even more eager than before to argue against determinism.[73] This he did in a work on destiny, *De Fato*, of which we possess a substantial fragment.

Cicero staged this as a dialogue held between himself and Hirtius in his Puteolan villa, where we know that Hirtius met him on 14 and 16 May 44.[74] They were 'searching for policies which related to peace and concord between citizens... since every sort of pretext for new upheavals was being sought after the death of Caesar and we believed that these should be countered' (*Fat.* 1–2). Cicero rejects here the view that the disbelief in destiny means accepting the total dominance of chance. There is no need to press the claim of destiny, since without it everything can be explained either by nature or fortune (6). One's general character may be conditioned by birth or climate, but that is insufficient to determine the minutiae of behaviour (7–9). There is then a review of philosophers' opinions—the Stoic argument for determinism deriving from their logic (20–1); Carneades arguing that there can be both a general acceptance of causation and belief in uncaused free will without the need to postulate the Epicurean swerve (23–31); the various classical determinists (39); Chrysippus' differentiation between first causes, subsidiary causes, and proximate causes (41 ff.). When this long fragment ends, Cicero seems to be exploring the possibilities for gaps in causation. What his ultimate conclusion was, we cannot say, except that the practical aim of the dialogue was, to judge from the introduction, to suggest that there was nothing inevitable about the demise of republican government.

---

[72] See Beard, 1986, Schofield, 1986.

[73] See on the portents following Caesar's murder Weinstock, 1971, 370 ff. Dio places the appearance of the comet, treated as *sidus Iulium*, at games celebrating Venus Genetrix combined with funeral honours to Caesar, which he seems to place in May 44 (45. 6. 4–7. 1), *contra* Suet. *Iul.* 88 which places it at those following Caesar's first consecration as a god. Recently, scholars have generally believed that it was first seen at the *ludi victoriae Caesaris* (in July). Ramsey and Licht, 1997, have argued for a new solution to the problem, arguing that the games in July were officially for Venus Genetrix and that the comet should be identified with one seen in China in May–June. They also draw attention to the likely atmospheric disturbances earlier resulting from the eruption of Etna (13, 99 ff.). See their app. 1, 155 ff. for a collection of the ancient sources on the comet.

[74] *Att.* 14. 22. 1; 15. 1. 3.

THE DE AMICITIA AND CICERO'S CORRESPONDENCE WITH MATIUS

Shortly before Cicero left for Greece he was circulating the lost work *De Gloria* (*Att.* 15. 17. 2). The *Topica Aristotelea* on the art of creating rhetorical proofs was written on his voyage and sent to Trebatius Testa on 28 July (*Fam.* 7. 19; *Top.* 5).[75] The remaining two works that we must consider discuss practical ethics, *De Amicitia* (On Friendship) and *De Officiis* (On Duties), which occupied him on and after his return in the later months of 44.[76] The work on friendship has a particular interest since it deals with the same issues as an exchange of letters between Cicero and C. Matius (*Fam.* 11. 27, 28), which followed Cicero's return from his abortive voyage in the direction of Greece. Cicero's letter has been traditionally placed in late August 44 and, in spite of more recent controversy, this dating remains preferable.[77] The precise relationship between the letters and the dialogue is unclear. Was Cicero inspired to write *De Amicitia* by the correspondence? Was Matius reacting not only to Cicero's letter but to a draft of the *De Amicitia*?[78] The first proposition is possible but unprovable, the second cannot be substantiated by Matius' letter. As will appear, the *De Amicitia* approaches the topic of conflict of loyalties even more delicately than Cicero's letter to Matius. A blunter answer was to be given in the *De Officiis* (3. 19).

Cicero's letter to Matius is a reply to a complaint that Matius had made through Trebatius as his intermediary. It clearly concerned the unfriendly criticisms that Cicero had been heard to make of Matius' conduct in support of the Caesarian cause (*Fam.* 11. 27. 1, 7);[79] Matius probably also suggested that Cicero's support for the conspirators was itself a breach of the friendship that had existed between Caesar and Cicero. For Cicero embarks on a review of the course of his own friendship with Matius, which embraces the

---

[75] Roman illustrations are used, for example the definitions of *ius civile* and *gentiles* (*Top.* 28–9).

[76] The *De Amicitia* is mentioned in *Off.* 3. 31. Cicero was consulting Atticus about a point of chronology relevant to the former in November (*Att.* 16. 13a), shortly after he reported that he had finished two books of *De Officiis* (ibid. 11. 4–5).

[77] *Fam.* 11. 27 follows the allegation that Matius voted first on one of Antonius' pieces of legislation and his curatorship of the *ludi victoriae Caesaris* in July (7). Trebatius is said to have visited Cicero as soon as he could, in spite of illness, when Cicero returned to his Tusculan villa (1). This suggests the date in late August 44. A later date in October is less likely since by then Cicero's relationship to the young Caesar would surely have been raised, at least by Matius. For other arguments see Gilboa, 1974, refuting the case for the late date made by Kytzler, 1960.

[78] See Griffin, 1997b, with the earlier bibliography in Barnes and Griffin, 1997, 275–7; Brunt, 1988, ch. 7, esp. 351–61 and 379–81.

[79] Our evidence for these is the (usually cryptic) comments in the letters to Atticus, see *Att.* 14. 1. 1, 14. 4. 1, 14, 5. 1, 15. 2. 3.

connection it brought with Caesar. Cicero and Matius had apparently been friends in their youth. Then, when Caesar was in Gaul, Matius had brought Caesar and Cicero together (ibid. 2).[80] He had tried to advise Cicero in 49 before the latter's departure to Greece,[81] and then assisted and advised him on his return to Italy, suggesting his programme of philosophical writing (ibid. 3–5). All Matius' qualities, maintains Cicero, give him joy, especially his loyalty in friendship, wise advice, sense of responsibility, constancy, combined with charm, humanity, and knowledge of literature (ibid. 6). For these reasons in the first place he did not believe that Matius had been the first voter 'on that law' (presumably one of Antonius' in June), secondly, if he had believed it, he would never have supposed that Matius had done so without good reason. Matius' importance leaves his actions open to malicious interpretation, but, Cicero claims, he defends Matius—in the same way as, he is sure, Matius is accustomed to defend him against his enemies—either by outright denial, as with the voting, or by calling the action loyal and humane, as with the curatorship of the games (ibid. 7).

So far the impression we have is of an exercise in limiting damage in face of what had been a serious complaint—one where Cicero was clearly disingenuous about his reaction to Matius' actions. At the end of the letter, however, Cicero turns to counter-attack, using as a weapon the philosophy that he has already highlighted as a link between them (ibid. 5): 'But the point does not escape you, versed as you are in philosophy, that, if Caesar were a tyrant (my opinion), two different positions could be argued about your duty, either the one which I usually employ, that your loyalty and humanity should be praised for maintaining your affection for a friend even when he is dead, or the one that several people use, that the liberty of the fatherland takes precedence over the life of a friend. I only wish you had heard my arguments in these discussions (ibid. 8).' Cicero then softens the delicately implied rebuke by remarking how he regularly praises Matius for having done his best to dissuade Caesar from the civil war in 49 and then encouraged him to be moderate in victory.

Matius in reply commences by taking Cicero's letter at its face value. He had been sure that Cicero still had a good opinion of him: he had done nothing to offend any good man (*Fam.* 7. 28. 1).[82] Similarly he could not believe that a man well educated in moral behaviour like Cicero, who had been the object of his sustained benevolence, could have without due consideration thought

---

[80] Cf. *Fam.* 7. 15. 2.   [81] See above Ch. XVI n. 35 and *Att.* 9. 11. 2.
[82] Matius seems to have used *bonus* here in a simple sense of 'morally good', knowing well that it might also be interpreted in its specific sense of 'politically conservative', hence 'republican', and not caring if on that interpretation others might contest his claim.

otherwise. What follows is a vigorous and formal defence of his conduct, ostensibly against third parties—'they' have made charges against him' (ibid. 2)—but, because it is a riposte to the implied reproof at the end of Cicero's letter, directed also at Cicero himself. 'They' criticize him for his outrage at the death of a man with whom he was closely connected and held in affection; 'they' say that he should have put his fatherland before friendship, assuming that they have proved that his death was in the public interest. He, Matius asserts, would not go in for clever pleading; he had not reached that grade of philosophical education.[83] By this time the connection with Cicero's own letter is patent and so is the contrast Matius makes between himself and Cicero, the clever advocate.

The essence of Matius' self-defence is that he has supported a friend, not 'Caesar', that is a political cause. Picking up the praise at the end of Cicero's letter, he expands on it. He was against the civil war; he did not profit from the victory (indeed Caesar's legislation diminished his wealth);[84] he worked for clemency to be extended to the defeated. His indignation at the death of a friend was only natural, especially since the same men created odium for Caesar and killed him (ibid. 4). It was outrageous that some should be permitted to rejoice in a crime, others forbidden to grieve. The self-styled creators of liberty were not allowing people the freedom of emotion normally permitted even to slaves. He would not be terrified by them nor would he avoid an honourable death, but he hoped that they would all soon regret Caesar's death.[85]

As for the charge that he ought to desire the preservation of the *res publica*, Matius continues, it was obvious from his whole career that he had nothing to do with the bad men (*improbi*)—that is the radicals and subversives. His curatorship of the games was a private duty owed to a distinguished close friend and a young man of outstanding promise fully worthy of Caesar. His frequent morning visits to the house of the consul Antonius were something which his critics did also, in their case in the pursuit of some favour. Caesar had never prevented him cultivating anyone he wanted, even if they were Caesar's enemies (ibid. 5–7). In any case he was the sort of discreet and loyal man that even his enemies would prefer as a friend to people like themselves. He would be happy to retire to Rhodes, but, if that were impossible, he would always support the right solution at Rome. He was grateful to Trebatius for

---

[83] *Gradum sapientiae* (*Fam.* 11. 28. 2) refers to *hominem doctissimum* (11. 27. 8).

[84] This is generally assumed to be Caesar's law or laws about debt. However, if Matius was, as seems likely, a creditor, he would have simply acquired property at reasonable, though not knockdown, prices.

[85] One may compare Matius' modest remarks with the more flamboyant approach allegedly taken by Octavius, when he quoted to his mother Achilles' words about the necessity of avenging Patroclus (App. *BCiv.* 3. 13. 46–7; Hom. *Il.* 17. 98–9).

revealing Cicero's sincere and friendly attitude to him and giving him more reason for holding Cicero in affection (ibid. 8).

Matius' letter, in spite of the persona of bluff simplicity that he adopts, is itself a masterpiece of rhetoric.[86] In elite Roman society it was impossible to separate entirely private life from politics. Matius' friendship with the dictator had meant that he was one of his inner circle of advisers (*Fam.* 6. 12. 2). His connection with the young Caesar places him among the friends who supported and financed the young man's rise to power in spite of Antonius' obstruction.[87] His frequent visits to Antonius, with whom he had no connection in the month after Caesar's murder,[88] probably contributed to the negotiations between the two leading Caesarians. We can well believe that he was uncomfortable about Caesar's more *popularis* measures, but he had associated the preservation of the *res publica* with the preservation of Caesar (cf. *Att.* 14. 1. 1). The splendidly defiant tone of Matius' letter, therefore, masks a degree of disingenuousness comparable to that displayed by Cicero. The latter's friendship with Matius seems to have been less close than his link with Trebatius, to whom he had been a patron and could write in a much more relaxed fashion. A textual indication may be found in the use of the word *conglutinare* ('glue together') in Cicero's letter (*Fam.* 11. 27. 2): Cicero says here that Matius' absence prevented their friendship being glued together by regular acquaintance (*consuetudo*), but the phrase itself suggests a relationship that has to be cemented artificially, as in *De Amicitia* (see below).[89] We should therefore allow a greater distance between Cicero and Matius than is at first sight suggested by the intimacy described in Cicero's letter.[90]

It is not difficult to see in the *De Amicitia* echoes of the effect of political divisions, especially the civil wars, on personal relations. It is set in the same year as *De Re Publica* (129 BC), but a few days after Scipio's death, and purports to be what Q. Mucius Scaevola the Augur, when in extreme old age in the nineties BC, told Cicero about a conversation with Scipio's great friend Laelius. Atticus, the dedicatee of the dialogue, is asked to certify what Cicero recalls. He is expected to remember the topic, because he had been close to the tribune of 88 BC, P. Sulpicius, and knew the sensation and indignation that had been caused by the breach in friendship between Sulpicius and the consul of that

---

[86] It resembles in this respect Antonius' letter in *Phil.* 13. 22 ff.   [87] Syme, 1939, 130–2.
[88] See above at n. 10.
[89] In *Amic.* 32 the friendships which *utilitas* glues together come unstuck, when interests diverge. The *concordia* of 63 was *conglutinata* (*Att.* 1. 17. 11). *Ars* is required to glue together the parts of oratory (*de Or.* 1. 188). See also Ter. *Andr.* 913; Plaut. *Bacch.* 693.
[90] See Heldmann, 1976, 91 ff.

year Q. Pompeius Rufus (*Amic.* 2–3).[91] This somewhat involved construction places the dialogue at a time of both political and personal crisis for Laelius, the centre of the dialogue, and furthermore introduces a notorious instance where, rightly or wrongly, a political clash not only dissolved a friendship but brought on a civil war.

The dialogue takes its starting-point from Laelius' loss of his great friend. His son-in-law Fannius comments on his reputation for a philosophic wisdom, which allows him to regard human fortunes of secondary importance compared with virtue, and asks how he was coping with Scipio's death in the light of a recent social engagement he had missed (ibid. 6–7). His other son-in-law Scaevola then rapidly interjects that he ascribes Laelius' absence to ill-health and Laelius agrees. He does grieve but there are consolations. Scipio had not suffered by death. He had achieved everything he could and further life would only have brought on decline (ibid. 8–12). Laelius mentions how on his last evening Scipio had been escorted home from the senate by senators, Roman citizens, allies, and Latins. The occasion envisaged is presumably the day when he successfully proposed in the senate that there could be appeal from the decisions of the Gracchan land-commission.[92] Cicero also makes Laelius refer to Scipio's dream about immortality (ibid 13–14), his own creation in *De Re Publica* book 6. Urged to discuss friendship, Laelius begins by disclaiming the philosophical wisdom which Stoics claim is the only title to virtue. This is too strict for mortals: he himself is content to think those men judged in the past to have been good men to have been also wise (17–19).[93] As for friendship, it is something natural created by proximity, but the proximity arising from birth and race is not enough without benevolence. The term friendship is inappropriate in the absence of benevolence, while the term kinship remains valid.[94]

Laelius' definition of friendship is 'the sharing of sentiment (*consensio*) about all things divine and human combined with benevolence and affection'. It was the best thing in life, since it created and maintained virtue—provided that virtue was understood in the everyday fashion and not by strict philosophical standards (20–1).[95] He develops this view by considering two different explanations of the origin of friendship: the one which sees it as compensation for

---

[91] *Capitali odio*, 'mortal hatred' (*Amic.* 2), is an especially appropriate phrase because the feud led to Pompeius' and later Sulpicius' death.

[92] App. *BCiv.* 1. 19. 79.

[93] This is similar to the distinction that Aristotle drew between wisdom (σοφία) and practical wisdom (φρόνησις), *Eth. Nic.* 6. 1141^{a}9 ff.

[94] On the Peripatetic origin of Cicero's views see Gell. 1. 3. 10–20, referring to Theophrastus' work on friendship; Griffin, 1997*b*, 86–8; Bringmann, 1971, 220 ff.

[95] For the only true friendship being the friendship of the good for each other on account of their goodness see Ar. *Nic. Eth.* 8. 1157^{a}20 ff.

individual weakness and lack of resources, the friends making up for each other's failings; the other, more ancient and finer, which acknowledges mutual help as a feature of friendship but argues that this relationship derives from nature itself. Exchanges of services (*utilitates*) occur even in pretended friendships (26). On the other hand there was the natural affection of animals for their offspring, while men loved all those who seem to be 'lamps' of virtue. The love of a good man may be confirmed by mutual benefits, but is not dependent on them. We are not liberal and beneficent in order to receive favours in return: for a benefit is not a loan at interest. The Epicurean approach, which bases everything on pleasure, is inappropriate for something noble and divine. Any friendship that is glued together by expediency would be dissolved whenever this changes (27–32).[96] Cicero is of course dismissing here not only Epicureanism, but the traditional Roman attitude to political and business friendships, which has played a large part in his own life.

The discussion now moves to the dangers to friendship—political differences, changes in character through the effect of age or misfortune, rivalries arising from avarice or ambition. The great problem comes when a friend asks you to do something immoral, for example to lead an army against your fatherland like Coriolanus or seek a tyranny like Spurius Cassius or Sp. Maelius (35–6). The dramatic date of the dialogue prevents any reference to Sulla, Marius, or Caesar, but the contemporary relevance is the more powerful for being unstated and the answer seems the more inevitable. The dialogue's own contemporary example is the followers of Tiberius Gracchus. Notoriously C. Blossius of Cumae, when defending himself before the tribunal of the consuls Popillius Laenas and Rupilius (among whose council of assessors Cicero's Laelius claims to have been), asserted that through friendship he would have done anything that Gracchus wanted. 'Even burn down the temple of Jupiter Capitolinus?', he was asked. 'He would never have wanted that', was the reply, 'but if he had, I would have obeyed.' This remark is used to show the wickedness of Blossius, who is described as an instructor rather than a follower of Gracchus and a subsequent participant in the Aristonicus rebellion in Asia (37). Cicero in a later aside directs the same criticism of improper loyalty against C. Carbo, C. Cato, and C. Gracchus (39).

The correct approach is not to deviate from virtue for the sake of a friend, since this in itself will dissolve a true friendship. To do whatever a friend wants or expect to obtain whatever you want is only acceptable between men who have perfect wisdom, not those whom we know in ordinary life (37–8). The danger of following a friend in shameful action is illustrated by the actions of

[96] Cf. *Amic.* 51 and see Gellius' defence of the argument (17. 5). The end of *Amic.* 32 echoes Ar. *Nic. Eth.* 8. 1157^{a}14–15.

the friends of Ti. Gracchus: they have prolonged the threat posed by Gracchus through dividing the people from the authority of the senate. More lessons will be learnt from this about performing subversive actions than about resistance to them. Laelius mentions C. Gracchus twice here, anticipating with foreboding his tribunate. Good men must be instructed not to persist in friendship with such men, and the bad must be punished, whether leaders or followers. It was lack of support that rendered traitors like Themistocles and Coriolanus no danger (39–43). Cicero thus criticizes by implication all Caesar's friends who supported him when he embarked on civil war, and those who continued to sustain his cause after his death, even if, like C. Gracchus, they thought this an act of piety. There is no separate ethic for public and private friendship. Of course the conflict between friendship and political morality was nothing new: this is brought out in the reference to Pompeius Rufus and Sulpicius at the beginning of the dialogue. Nor was it new to Cicero personally: it was one of the problems that he was posed in 49.[97] The setting of the *De Amicitia* enables Cicero to handle the subject without self-exposure and with the minimal offence to potential readers.

The succeeding discussion of the modalities of friendship includes a denunciation of tyrants as essentially friendless—a passage which would have seemed hollow to loyal Caesarians like Matius (52–5). Cicero rejects the notion of complete parity in our attitudes to ourselves and our friends, likewise parity of services exchanged, and parity of self-esteem among friends (56–9).[98] In general, the superior friend should strive to bring the inferior friend up towards his own level, but only to the level his friend can sustain (69–73). We may have to do for our friends what we would not consider on our own behalf—beg from someone unworthy, be a suppliant, or make an excessively rancorous accusation of someone else (57). He surely had in mind occasions like the senate debate about M. Marcellus' recall. He himself had managed to avoid violent denunciation of the Pompeians in public, as far as we can tell. However, in order to retain his influence with men like Oppius and Balbus, he may have expressed himself at dinner-parties in the sort of terms that we find in his intimate letters. He sums up such concessions to friendship by arguing that one should deviate from the path of rectitude in order to forward the less than just desires of a friend, if his life or reputation is at stake, provided that what we do is not too disgraceful (61). This exception would also have excused his past defences in court of less reputable friends.[99]

---

[97] See Ch. XVI with nn. 29, 37, and 46; Heldmann, 1976, 99 ff.
[98] *Contra* Ar. *Nic. Eth.* 8. 1158^{b}1 ff.
[99] Gellius criticized this passage for not giving a more precise definition of the seriousness of the injustice or the extent of the concession to friendship that should be made (1. 3. 13–18). He

Among the warnings Cicero gives we find a caution against excessive hastiness in breaking off a friendship through change in a friend's character or a political disagreement (76–8), and a denunciation of obsequiousness and flattery, the latter extended to cover currying popular favour with oratory (88–96). The discourse ends with an appeal to virtue and the memory of Scipio's friendship (100–4). As a whole *De Amicitia* is an exposition of Cicero's republican values, to some extent idealized but with a strong element of practicality. Free and honest friendship is to be combined with, and if necessary subordinated to, optimate political opinions. A similar testament to the morality of the elite of the Republic is to be found in his next, much larger, work.

Practical Ethics for a Republican: The De Officiis

Cicero did not succeed in delivering paternal advice to his son in person at Athens. The *De Officiis* is an elaborate substitute for this,[100] being described in Cicero's introduction as a complement to his son's Greek philosophical studies, since it will provide a similar Peripatetic approach to that of Cratippus and be at the same time an exemplar of Latin discourse (*Off.* 1. 1–3).[101] It is also a convenient addition to the programme of Cicero's philosophical works, since it complements the discussion of ethical principles in the *Academica*, *De Finibus*, and *Disputationes Tusculanae*. Cicero presents it as part of the philosophic activity that he was been forced to undertake through the loss of the Republic (2. 2–5, 3. 2–3): he does not visualize a return to politics. At the outset he refers briefly to issues of principle, dismissing the Epicurean position as something rejected by him in these earlier writings. No consistent rules about what he terms *officia*—normally translated as 'duties'[102]—can be laid down except by those for whom moral excellence (*honestas*) is either the sole or the principal aim.[103] This was the common tradition of Stoics, Academics, and Peripatetics (ibid. 1. 4–7).

His own discussion is based on Panaetius' work (1. 7–8, 152, etc.). In a letter to Atticus of early November (16. 11. 4) he writes of having finished the

---

quotes Chilon's solution to the conflict between friendship and justice of persuading his fellow judges to condemn a friend, while tacitly acquitting him himself (ibid. 4–7). See Griffin, 1997*b*, 87–8.

[100] Cf. *Att.* 15. 13a. 2 of late October: 'exstabit opera peregrinationis huius'.

[101] Cratippus is also mentioned in the prooemium to Book 3 (6).

[102] Cicero discussed the translation with Atticus (*Att.* 16. 14. 3). 'Appropriate actions' is a more accurate rendering of the Stoic term τὸ καθῆκον he is translating, on which see Dyck, 1996, 3–8. However, what we read is a treatise on what Romans conceived as 'duties', see Griffin and Atkins, 1991, p. xlv.

[103] Cf. e.g. *Fin.* 2. 59; *Rep.* 3. 38.

De Officiis, as far as covered by Panaetius, in two books. The latter had divided the subject into three topics—firstly deliberations about the honourable and the base, secondly about the expedient and inexpedient, and thirdly how to choose, when the first two questions gave inconsistent answers—but had failed to tackle the third topic. Poseidonius had discussed this, and Cicero was trying to obtain both a summary and a copy of the work itself.[104] Panaetius' division is elaborated further in Cicero's introduction, where he argues that he ought also to have considered choices between two honourable and two expedient options (*Off.* 1. 10). The structure of the first two books at least, therefore, depends on Stoic philosophy. The examples, such as that of Regulus mentioned in the letter, are mainly Roman. What is not so clear is how far the specific recommendations are simply a reproduction of Panaetius' and Poseidonius' doctrines or are contaminated by ideas from other sources including Cicero himself. He says himself that for this inquiry he will follow the Stoics especially, not as a mere translator, but as usual will use his own discretion over how much and how he draws on these sources (ibid. 6).

The first topic of the work proper is what is morally good, termed by Cicero the honourable (*honestum*).[105] He argues that man, as a rational animal, in addition to providing for himself and his family, has a natural appreciation of what is true, beautiful, and well-ordered (1. 11–14). This resolves itself into four parts: the first is wisdom and understanding the truth, the second is the preservation of society through just distribution and the fulfilment of contracts, the third is courage, the fourth is self-discipline in word and deed (1. 15). Cicero elaborates on this classification at some length. The second topic, justice, rapidly becomes a discussion of injustice, which is created partly by fear, partly by excessive desire for wealth, high office, power, and glory. A remark of Crassus' is used to illustrate the man who desires wealth in order to have the resources to do what he likes for himself and others: 'No wealth is sufficient for whoever wants to be a leading man (*princeps*) in the *res publica*, if he cannot support an army on the income from it' (1. 25). Caesar for his part is described as someone who perverted all human and divine justice to achieve *principatus*, pre-eminence (26). Cicero further discusses occasions when one is not bound to keep promises and agreements (31–2).[106] There is an important section on treating enemies justly, including the theory of the just war (34–41). Here Cicero recommends mercy towards defeated enemies

---

[104] See also *Off.* 3. 7–10, where it appears that Poseidonius in fact wrote little. Cicero argues here that Panaetius cannot have thought conflicts between the honourable and the expedient impossible (9–10).

[105] Evidently a translation of τὸ καλόν (Dyck, 1996, p. 69).

[106] Here he refers to the exceptions made in praetorian law for those made under duress or through deception, *metus* and *dolus*.

who have not been cruel (35), and draws a distinction between wars for survival against enemies and wars for glory against rivals for power (38). The latter in particular had to be waged after proper formal declarations and required the maintenance of good faith with opponents.[107] The distinctions Cicero makes between opponents and between wars overlap to some extent. The idea that one should take different attitudes to savage and civilized opponents has been regularly found more recently in imperial powers: it is not so clear that it was the normal Roman attitude then, which was based, rather, on expediency. The Romans, moreover, were prepared to spare any defeated enemy—once: they were merciless against rebels.[108]

The second topic, according to Cicero's classification, also includes beneficence and generosity (*liberalitas*) (42–60, cf. 20). This must be just, unlike the gifts of the property of the proscribed by Sulla and Caesar (45). The argument turns to the part of benevolence in friendship, the rules for exchange of services (47–52),[109] and then to the relative importance of social bonds. Of these a man's tie with his fatherland is said to be the most important (57). The third topic, bravery (62–92), leads Cicero to discuss once again attitudes to war. Bravery must be combined with justice, and for this reason military ambition in the pursuit of pre-eminence or glory must be avoided (62–9). Thus Cicero in effect rejects what he argued in the persona of Furius Philus, following Carneades, to have been the characteristic of all empires (*Rep.* 3. 20–32). This allows him also the opportunity to reassert his belief that achievement in civilian life is frequently superior to that in war (74–8).

The treatment of the last topic, self-discipline, covers over a third of the book (93–151) and is taken to embrace the choice of fitting behaviour in all aspects of ordinary life (93–9). Here we find a theoretical discussion about what it is to live according to nature (100–7):[110] this involves acting consistently both with the rational nature we share with other human beings and with our own individual persona, which varies according to our age and position in the community (122–3). Cicero goes on to talk of modes of dress, behaviour, and speech, this last varying according to its context, public or private (132–7); the appropriate type of house (138–40), and those arts and

---

[107] This is to some extent a reprise of the defence of the justice of the Roman empire by the persona of Laelius in *Rep.* 3. 33 ff. See on the fetial procedure Dyck, 1996, 133–6; Rich, 1976, 56–104, and from a philosophical point of view Barnes, 1986.

[108] See *VRR* 42–4. For expediency being the Roman standard compare Cicero's comment on the destruction of Corinth with Sallust's on Marius' destruction of Capsa (*Iug.* 91. 6–7).

[109] A subject briefly treated in *Amic.* 69–73.

[110] For possible conflict between this and self-discipline see 1. 159 referring to Poseidonius' work.

commercial pursuits which were liberal and which degrading. People hated occupations such as those of moneylenders and customs officers. All wage-earning was degrading, if only labour but no special skill was bought, since the price was paid for servitude; the same was true of retail trading, manual labour, and the trades that gratified pleasure. Medicine, architecture, and the teaching of honourable subjects were honourable for those of the appropriate rank. Small-scale commerce was degrading, but vast and varied trading was not to be criticized, especially when it migrated from the port to an estate. Of all the forms of acquisition nothing was better than agriculture (150–1). Cicero concludes the book by assigning more importance to social virtue than intellectual virtue (153–60).[111]

Cicero certainly derived the basic structure of the book and probably some more theoretical formulations from Panaetius, but the work reads less as a connected philosophical argument than as a collection of his own ideas about morality discursively presented under any heading that conveniently offered itself. It is better organized than table-talk or a collection of maxims, but the appearance of philosophic grounding is often deceptive: Cicero does not consider objections to his point of view, as he does in dialogues argued from both sides of the case, according to Academic practice.[112]

At the beginning of book 2 we find another defence of Cicero's philosophic activities. He contrasts the time when the *res publica* was managed by those to whom it had entrusted itself, that is regularly elected magistrates, and the period under the domination of one man (2. 2). During the former period he wrote about his own actions and had no time to do more than read philosophy. Now he had time to put down in writing philosophy, the study of wisdom, which is both a source of pleasure and the supreme *ars*, branch of knowledge (3–6). He also justifies his sceptical Academic position in contenting himself with believing what is more probable (7–8; cf. 3. 20).

The main discussion of how one should behave to one's best advantage takes as its starting point the fact that the resources a man needs for life depend largely on the existence of society, especially if he is a political leader or general (2. 11–16).[113] It therefore must be reckoned virtuous to have the capacity to win over other men to assist you to obtain your needs—a third fundamental virtue to complement intellectual ability and self-discipline (17–8). After a brief digression on fortune (it is extremely important but its effects are combined more usually with those deriving from human resources

---

[111] This complements an earlier digression on the need for those with intellectual ability to participate in politics (1. 70–3).

[112] Specifically mentioned as Cicero's philosophic practice in *Off.* 2. 8.

[113] The last sentiment is ascribed specifically to Panaetius (2. 16), from which it is evident that the central train of thought in this book must be his.

and inclinations), Cicero lists six reasons for the assistance that human beings give to another of their kind, three good, three bad: benevolence towards someone they love; respect for someone of whose virtue they are in awe and whom they think worthy of the greatest success; trust in someone they believe will look after their interests; then fear of another's power, the expectation of benefits, and the actual receipt of bribes (19–21). In the text we possess Cicero proposes to discuss next 'those matters closer to virtue', and then a second, briefer list follows, which does not quite correspond with the first (22).[114]

Cicero in fact continues by discussing the inadequacy of rule through fear, at first with examples of Greek tyranny—Dionysius I of Syracuse, Alexander of Pherae, Phalaris, Demetrius the Besieger, and the Spartans in the early fourth century (2. 23–6). The reference to the Spartan empire encourages a further passage on the Roman empire, this time an expression of regret for the change that it had suffered. Once it had depended on benefits, not injuries; wars were undertaken either in defence of allies or to settle who should rule; reprisals after wars were only taken when necessary; the senate was a haven for kings, republics, and peoples. It was not so much *imperium*, rule, as *patrocinium*, patronage. This tradition slipped away until the consequences of Sulla's victory caused men to regard no treatment of the allies unjust, once they had seen such atrocities against citizens. Moreover, there was a continuity between Sullan methods and those undertaken in an impious cause, through an even more disgusting victory, resulting in ruin for whole provinces and regions—this last allusion to Caesar is made clearer by the example of Massilia, an old ally, forming part of a Roman triumph (26–9). Cicero says that he himself has added the Roman examples (26), but it should be remembered that the portrayal of the effect of moral decline on the Roman empire is found in sources of the second century.[115]

The interest in the rest of the book lies particularly in the examples. Cicero picks out justice as the common root of the good sources of popularity (2. 38). In his discussion he remarks on the reputation for popularity of certain brigands, bracketing the Lusitanian Viriatus with Bardulis the Illyrian (40),[116] and compares the Gracchi unfavourably with their father (43). Following this, Cicero's discourse turns to how a young man like his son can make a good public impression of the virtues he possesses (44 ff.). This

---

[114] Editors normally bracket this as dubiously Ciceronian. However, if it is removed, it is hard to explain how Cicero can move straight on to compare the effect of affection and fear, after saying that he is about to discuss those attitudes closer to virtue. It is more likely that this is an example of an alternative formulation by Cicero that has led the subsequent discussion in a different direction to that originally anticipated. See Dyck, 1996, 287 ff.

[115] See Lintott, 1972*b*.

[116] Bardulis, who was most powerful in the early 4th c., was presumably Panaetius' example.

embraces eloquence: Cicero advises young Marcus not to become a professional accuser like M. Brutus, the son of the jurisconsult: at all costs he must not accuse the innocent (2. 50; cf. *Brut.* 130). However, one should not scruple to defend a guilty man, provided that he is not a criminal. A judge must pursue the truth; an advocate should defend what is plausible, even if not strictly true: Panaetius himself thought so (51). It is defences that above all that create glory and influence. At this point Cicero cites his defence of Sextus Roscius as a supreme example of how one can win a reputation for defending someone who appears to be being unjustly oppressed by a powerful man.

The two sides of generosity, the good *liberalitas* and the bad *largitio*, are treated in parallel (2. 52 ff.). The latter is denounced for its corrupting effect on the receiver and the damage it does to a man's own family wealth. Here Cicero distances himself from the lavish public shows praised by Theophrastus (56), who seems to have reflected in his work *On Wealth* the Greek ideal of euergetism; he was also cautious about the Roman tradition of splendid aedileships (57–8). Spending money on the public was only justifiable in pursuit of a greater good. Cicero manages to include under this heading Milo's purchase of gladiators to resist Clodius (58). One may help out either someone who has fallen onto hard times or poor individuals in general (61–3); hospitality towards distinguished foreigners is also proper (64). It is important to assist others with legal advice and advocacy, or, when lacking these skills, in the search for jurisconsults and advocates and in seeking help from judges and magistrates (65–7). Cicero then inserts a general warning against expecting swift returns from giving help to the wealthy and powerful who cannot tolerate the idea of being clients. He returns to the subject of public generosity with an attack on *popularis* methods on the ground that they damage the principle of private property (72 ff.). The targets include the grain law of C. Gracchus—contrasted with the moderate one of M. Octavius (72)—agrarian legislation both at Rome and in Greece (73, 78–83), and the cancellation of debts (84–6). The important thing was to avoid selfish greed but to preserve one's own property so that one did not need to rob others (75–6, 87).

In the introduction to book 3 he suggests that, while it was clear that Panaetius did in fact think that conflicts between the honourable (morally correct) and expedient could occur, it might be argued that he was wrong to do so, since on his principles only the honourable was expedient in the first place (*Off.* 3. 13). His answer is that this is only true for the honourable actions of those with perfect wisdom (he means those who are sages by Stoic standards). He himself was discussing duties that Stoics classed as 'intermediate' (*media*). It is for the performance of duties in this sense that men like the Decii, the Scipiones, Fabricius, Aristides, Cato the Censor, and Laelius were renowned (14–17).[117] However, although men commonly called good, like those mentioned, do not find the honourable in conflict with the expedient in their performance of 'intermediate' duties, this is a characteristic of those who measure everything by expediency.

Panaetius, therefore, must be interpreted to the letter as saying that men customarily are uncertain about such a conflict, not that they should be (18). This occurred when what seemed dishonourable was not in fact so, as when men thought that it was a criminal act to kill a man, even a friend, who was a tyrant (19). Essentially it was contrary to man's social nature to pursue one's own interest at the expense of another's, both within one's own society, where this was enjoined by law, and outside it. This was a divine and human law (20–5). Those who violated this rule either did not understand that they were acting against nature, or thought that misfortunes like death, poverty, pain, or the loss of children, family, or friends were more to be avoided than inflicting unjust harm (*iniuria*) on another (26). It was against nature to inflict harm on another in one's own self-interest because it was a violation of the common humanity shared not just with fellow-citizens but with foreigners also (27–8) (Cicero says nothing specific about slaves). However, it was acceptable to do harm to someone of no value to the community, such as a tyrant, for your own benefit, if your own life was valuable to the community (29–30).

For the rest of the book Cicero proceeds to hammer home his message about the identity of the honourable with the truly expedient through examples, many of which are Roman. L. Brutus was right to depose Tarquinius Collatinus from the consulate in order to eliminate the tyrant's family from the fatherland; Romulus wrong to kill his brother (40–1). Though friendship was more important than personal advantages, a judge must act in accordance with good faith and his oath, even if that was against his friend's interest (43–4). It was right to prevent non-citizens acting as citizens, as Crassus and Scaevola did in 95; it was inhuman to ban foreigners from the city as Pennus did in 126 and Papius in 65 (47).[118] There is a long section on honesty in commercial transactions, dealing especially with the selling of estates (54–72). The real proof of the principle that only the honourable was expedient, however, came with extreme examples where the rewards were enormous and the fault comparatively minor. Cicero discusses here the dishonest accusations brought by C. Marius against Metellus Numidicus and the sharp practice of Marius Gratidianus (79–82), but soon returns to the theme of

---

[117] This is the same standard that Cicero adopts in *Amic.* 20–1.
[118] The *lex Iunia* and the *lex Papia* provided, like the *lex Licinia Mucia*, for the challenging of men of doubtful Roman citizenship, such as Archias and Balbus (*Arch.* 10; *Balb.* 52), but seem to have gone further by expelling aliens who made no claims to be Roman.

tyranny. He refers obliquely to Pompey's maintenance of his own power by exploiting the unscrupulous and unpopular behaviour of Caesar and to the latter's fondness for the lines in Euripides' *Phoenissae*: 'If you have to break the law, you should do so to obtain a tyranny. Otherwise you should observe morality' (82).[119]

In the latter part of the book there is some pretence of logical organization,[120] but it seems to be a pretext for Cicero to tell the stories he thinks relevant We find again the classic *exemplum* of Fabricius and the deserter from king Pyrrhus (86–7, cf. 1. 40) and some rather more confusing cases: Philippus imposing taxation on cities which had secured immunity by bribing Sulla, without returning the bribes; Cato's opposition to the requests for the tax-collectors; Curio arguing that Roman interests should prevail while advocating the justice of citizenship for the Transpadane Gauls (87–8). Regarding the importance of keeping oaths, Regulus is cited and the surrender to the enemy of those whose treaties the senate repudiated, the consuls defeated at the Caudine Forks and Hostilius Mancinus (99–111).[121] The book ends somewhat breathlessly with an attack on the Epicureans and others who espoused the principle of pleasure (116–20), and an *envoi* to his son (121).

If, Cicero says, he had reached Athens, young Marcus would at last have heard something from his father. These volumes were a substitute, since his country had recalled Cicero in a loud voice from the middle of his voyage. What the young man received was an attempt to integrate Stoic and Peripatetic moral theory with the lifestyle of the Roman upper class in order to create a practical ethic that was in harmony with the best of Roman tradition. The political background implied is republican, one in which the main restraints on young Marcus will be the laws and his own scruples.[122] Cicero lost no opportunity to reiterate in this work the moral rectitude of the assassination of Caesar. He also rejected imperial conquest in pursuit of personal glory, not only because this was unjust to those conquered (1. 34–41), but because it was dangerous to republican government at home (1. 62–9; 3. 82). Moreover, the very composition of the work indicates a hope that the republic would return.

---

[119] Eur. *Phoen.* 524–5; cf. Suet. *Iul.* 30. 5.

[120] See *Off.* 3. 96 and 116, where Cicero claims that he is considering in turn the conflict of the various aspects of virtue with expediency.

[121] These are contrasted with Q. Pompeius opposing his own surrender and the deceitful behaviour of one of the ten envoys from Hannibal's Roman captives after Cannae (3. 109, 113).

[122] *Off.* 3. 61 neatly illustrates the way Cicero thought the first reinforced the second. Here the laws have stigmatized the vice of deceit (*dolus malus*) and embraced the concept of good faith (*fides bona*).

XIX

Answering the Republic's Call

THE FIRST TWO PHILIPPICS

CICERO tells Atticus in a letter of 19 August how he came to abandon his voyage to Greece.[1] His ship had tried to sail eastwards from Leucopetra (at the toe of Italy) but had been driven back by an adverse wind. At the villa of his friend P. Valerius he met some notables from Rhegium, who brought news from Rome and from Brutus in Naples. L. Piso had attacked Antonius in the senate on 1 August; there was to be a plenary session on 1 September which Brutus and Cassius had asked by letter all former consuls and praetors to attend: the issue they wanted raised was whether they should be allowed to return to their praetorships at Rome. Cicero was also provided with the texts of an edict of Antonius and a reply to it by Brutus and Cassius. From Cicero's elaborate explanation of his decision it appears that before 19 August Atticus too had changed his mind, advising Cicero to return, and that the decision had been further reinforced by Cicero's meeting with Brutus near Velia on the voyage back up the coast of Italy. In Brutus' view Cicero had now escaped two charges, first that he was abandoning the *res publica* in despair, secondly that he was going to Greece to see the Olympic Games (16. 7. 2–5). Cicero thought this would have been disgraceful at any time, sharing the general Roman revulsion from Greek athletics in the nude.[2]

We can read the letter of Brutus and Cassius in Cicero's collection (*Fam.* 11. 3). They expressed regret over the tone of Antonius' edict, saying that there was nothing insulting in praetors making a demand from the consul. Antonius had apparently stated that he made no complaints about their attempts to raise armies overseas and had bitterly reproached them for their murder of Caesar. They denied any approach to the armies and in the name of concord and liberty deprecated his threat of military force. It would not cow them; nor should Antonius claim to treat as subjects those whose action allowed him now his freedom. Their position was that they desired him to be

---

[1] *Att.* 16. 7. 1, 5, 7. Cf. *Phil.* 1. 7–10.
[2] *Att.* 16. 7. 5. Augustus, when he introduced Greek athletic contests, barred women from watching them (Suet. *Aug.* 43. 1, 44. 3).

a great and renowned man in a free *res publica*; they were not challenging him to a feud but they valued their liberty more than his friendship. At the end the conciliatory tone is abandoned: Antonius should consider carefully whether his ambitions could be sustained and should keep in mind not the length of Caesar's life but the short time he had ruled as a tyrant.

Antonius' agenda in the senate on 1 September was in fact *supplicationes* (days of thanksgiving). Cicero was absent, claiming exhaustion after his journey, but by his absence (probably forewarned) he avoided voting for a motion which, though directed at the recent achievements of a living commander, apparently comprised an extra day of thanksgiving for the dead Caesar. Antonius noted his absence and delivered a fierce denunciation of him, threatening to destroy his house (*Phil.* 1. 11–13). The honorand of the decree of 1 September was probably L. Munatius Plancus, who had recently been victorious over the Raeti and to whom Cicero wrote two successive apologetic letters, promising support for the future.[3] He came to the senate the next day in Antonius' absence (*Phil.* 1. 16)—Dolabella was presiding— and delivered the first speech of what he was to term his *Philippics*.[4]

The first part of this speech is a defence of his departure and return, portraying it as a response to Antonius' own behaviour: he had been waiting and hoping for the *res publica* to return at long last to the authority of the senate.[5] He reviews Antonius' conduct, beginning with the senate-meeting in the temple of Tellus on 17 March and Antonius' reaction to his own advocacy of reconciliation in which he had recalled the Athenian amnesty after the return of the democracy in 404 BC. Antonius' early actions are disingenuously presented as admirable, especially his alleged refusal to exploit Caesar's *commentarii* relating to immunities and the restoration of exiles. Cicero is more sincere when he praises the suppression of the pseudo-Marius.[6] However, he portrays the legislation of early June, with the senate threatened by veterans and the expulsion of the liberators from the city, as a drastic change of Antonius' course (1. 6). Cicero attributes his own return to a belief that Antonius would once more follow the authority of the senate (1. 7–10, esp. 8). He then protests about the attack on him the day before: Antonius would not have wanted him present if he knew that he would denounce the proposal for

---

[3] *Fam.* 11. 1–2. Cf. *Inscr. It.* xiii. 1. 567. I follow here the convincing reinterpretation of the texts by Ferrary (1999), who argues that what Antonius had done was to put in to effect the proposal of 45 BC (Dio 43. 44. 6, 45. 7. 2) that a day should be added in honour of Caesar to every *supplicatio*.

[4] *Ad Brut.* 3. 4; 4. 3. See Wooten, 1985, for the Demosthenic characteristics of the speeches, e.g. the disjunctions, especially between freedom and slavery (62 ff.).

[5] On the first two *Philippics* see Ramsey, 2003.

[6] *Phil.* 1. 1–5. See Chap. XVIII with nn. 27–8.

a *supplicatio* on the ground that it combined thanks to the immortal gods with honours to a dead man (11–13).[7] He also complains about the lack of support for Piso's speech in favour of Brutus and Cassius on 1 August (14–15, cf. 10).

The second half of the speech is couched as a proposal,[8] but rapidly becomes a denunciation of both the contents and the methods of Antonius' recent legislative activity and of the cooperation of the presiding consul Dolabella in this. Cicero argues that the preservation of the *acta Caesaris* are essential for peace and concord, but that these *acta* are not to be found in handwritten notes in books and papers, but engraved on bronze as laws commanded by the people.[9] Such were the *acta* of Gracchus, Sulla, and Pompey in his third consulship.[10] Antonius in his legislation had overthrown the law of Caesar that limited consular provinces to two years and praetorian to one (19). Antonius' proposal for a third panel (*decuria*) of jurors without the previous census qualification violated Caesar's judiciary laws.[11] A second proposal was that those condemned for violence or treason should have the right to appeal to the assembly. Cicero argues that this would simply confirm the current reluctance to bring charges against those who used armed violence in politics. From one point of view it was otiose, as such men were not being accused. From another it was disgraceful, since it would simply allow such men to appeal to an assembly where they could use violence and so deter any future accuser or any judge who dared to condemn. It directly contradicted Caesar's laws about violence and treason, which required those condemned to be sent into exile.[12]

Cicero then proclaims that he is prepared to accept the *acta Caesaris*, including those sanctioning return for exiles, grants of citizenship, and immunity from taxation produced after his death. Consistency means, however, that Caesar's laws must be respected—not changes to them by Antonius—but how can men like him oppose Antonius' new proposals when Antonius was prepared to force them through by violence even in face of tribune's veto or any religious obstruction (24–5)? His peroration is an appeal, first mainly to Dolabella, then to Antonius himself. The consuls should not be angry with him for speaking his mind on politics, in spite of

---

[7] See n. 3 above. [8] *Phil.* 1. 16 'primum igitur acta Caesaris servanda censeo'.

[9] Ibid. 16–18: those 'in commentariolis et chirographis et libellis' are contrasted with 'quae ille in aes incidit, in quo populi iussa perpetuasque leges esse voluit' (16).

[10] Cicero seems to choose these persons, not only on account of the number of their laws but because they had changed constitutional and criminal law. The Gracchus is surely Gaius.

[11] Ibid. 19–20. See Ramsey, 2005.

[12] Ibid. 21–3. On the relation of Antonius' proposal to previous legislation about *provocatio*, see Lintott, 1972a, 239–40; on Caesar's law about violence see *VRR* 106–8.

the threat of violence. People told him that an opponent of Caesar, such as he was, could not speak as freely as Piso, who was Caesar's father-in-law; he was also warned that there was no fairer an excuse for absence from the senate on account of illness than the excuse of death.[13] Nevertheless, Cicero's plea to Dolabella was to pursue his grand aim—not money, as some suspected, but the traditional aim of the *nobilis*, glory and the affection of his fellow citizens—by virtuous action (29–30).

As for Antonius, he reminded him of his actions to secure peace after Caesar's murder and his abolition of the dictatorship, which was as much a condemnation of Caesar as the ban on the use of the *praenomen* Marcus by the family of the patrician Manlii after the attempt on tyranny by Manlius Capitolinus (31–2). Why had Antonius changed? Not for a sordid reason like money, surely? More probably he had been tempted by the prospect of absolute power sustained by fear. Instead, he should imitate his grandfather (the orator), who was equal in liberty to all others, but a leading man though his worth.[14] His death at the hands of Cinna was peferable to Cinna's own domination. Above all, he should be moved by Caesar's example. No one was happy, when his death would bring great glory to the killer. If he wanted to be popular, he should be guided by the applause given to Brutus at the games or, alternatively the good reputation of Hirtius. We have in effect a polemical version of what he was to say to his son in the third book of *De Officiis* (79–83). At the end, Cicero expressed gratitude to the senate for their attention to his speech and hope that he will have other opportunities to enjoy this. He then adapted for himself the remark that was attributed to Caesar: 'My life has been long enough to fulfil my years and my glory. Any increment is not so much for my benefit as for you and the *res publica*.'[15]

Cicero's speech was directed as much towards moderate Caesarians as to any supporters of the liberators. There is the polite reference to Hirtius and the recognition of Caesar's laws as part of the corpus of Roman law. However, the implication of his speech is that the traditional *res publica*, guided by the senate's authority, must return and there could be no question of a reimposition of the rule of one man. The venality of both Antonius and Dolabella is

---

[13] Ibid. 27–8. The translation here of the pregnant sentence, 'nec erit iustior in senatum non veniendi morbi causa quam mortis' (28) is an attempt to bring out the grim humour. *Morbus sonticus*, serious illness, was a standard excuse, with *vadimonium, iudicium, funus familiare feriaeve denicales*; see *lex Col. Gen.* (*RS* i, no. 25) 95, col. ii, ll. 21–3. See also *XII Tab.* (*RS* ii, no. 40), ii. 2. Notice also the story of a litigant before the emperor Claudius excusing the absence of a witness: 'mortuus est: puto, licuit' (Suet. *Claud.* 14. 3).

[14] Ibid. 34 'libertate...parem ceteris, principem dignitate'. See on the relation between Cicero's arguments in the *De Officiis* (see esp. 2. 31 ff.) about the correct pursuit of *gloria* and those in *Philippics* 1 and 2, Long, 1995a.

[15] Ibid. 35–8; cf. *Marc.* 25.

hinted at by *praeteritio*; Antonius' dynastic ambition is openly denounced. This clearly provoked Antonius even further. The *Ludi Romani* followed and on the last day, 19 September, Antonius delivered a counterattack in the senate, in which he claimed that Cicero had been behind the plot to kill Caesar. Cicero recounted this to Cassius, saying that Antonius' object had been to stir up hostility among the veterans and in consequence neither Piso nor he himself nor Servilius Isauricus, who had spoken after Cicero in the same terms, could come safely to future meetings.[16] The rest of the leading consulars were either unsympathetic to the liberators or absent from the senate for a variety of reasons.[17] Cicero's first attempt to return to public life after his voyage had proved abortive. As a substitute for politics, he spent his time composing a written answer to Antonius which embodied the most powerful invective of his that survives—the *Second Philippic*. In the same period he was writing the *De Officiis* with its many references to Caesar's tyranny and the correctness of his murder,[18] *De Amicitia*, and the letter to Matius (*Fam.* 11. 27). He was also probably revising the *De Consiliis Suis*, a secret memoir begun in 59, which argued that Caesar had been planning tyranny since the sixties.[19]

When the *Second Philippic* was first widely circulated, is not clear; Cicero had consulted Atticus about a first draft at the end of October, leaving to him the choice of the right time to publish. He was still incorporating Atticus' suggestions in early November.[20] The broadside would not have been allowed to emerge until Antonius had left Rome for Cisalpine Gaul at the end of the month and perhaps not until the senate had decided to act against him in January of the next year. The bitterness of the attack seems to be a reaction not so much to the charge that Cicero was behind the plot to kill Caesar, which could be regarded as a compliment, but the way that Antonius had presented this as treachery and ingratitude. His speech of 19 September was comparable to the attack he made in December 50 on Pompey's career from the time he took the toga of manhood (*Att.* 7. 8. 5). It probably contributed to the portrait of Cicero as envious, malicious, and treacherous, which we can find in later invective.[21]

A number of Antonius' charges can be discerned in the *Second Philippic*. He claimed that Cicero had violated his friendship by appearing against him

[16] *Phil.* 2. 25, 28–30, 5. 19–20; *Fam.* 12. 2. 1–2; Cassius had received a text of the first *Philippic* (ibid. 1).
[17] Hostile L. Aemilius Paulus (*cos.* 50), C. Marcellus (*cos.* 50), L. Philippus (*cos.* 56); absent L. Cotta (*cos.* 65), L. Caesar (*cos.* 64), and Ser. Sulpicius Rufus (*cos.* 51).
[18] *Off.* 1. 26, 43, 2. 2, 29, 3. 19, 29, 82.
[19] *Att.* 16. 11. 3; cf. 2. 6. 2, 14. 17. 6; Asc. 83 C; Plut. *Crass.* 13. 4.
[20] *Att.* 15. 13. 1, 15. 13a. 3; 16. 11. 1–2.   [21] See Lintott, 1997a, 2514–7; Gabba, 1957.

in a lawsuit, in spite of the fact that he had been Cicero's pupil. For his part he had done Cicero a favour by not standing against him for the augurate, and protected him in 48, when he returned from Greece to Brundisium (*Phil.* 2. 3–6). Antonius denounced the execution of the Catilinarian conspirators and Cicero's commemoration of this in verse (10–20), and charged Cicero with plotting Clodius' death (21–2), dividing Pompey from Caesar (23–4), and plotting Caesar's murder (25–8).[22] He also tried to depict Cicero as someone who was a poor friend and companion, dwelling on his unhappy time in Pompey's camp and the fact that no one wanted to leave Cicero a legacy (37–41).

The *Second Philippic* is a riposte in kind. The first third is a reply to Antonius' charges—or at least to those charges to which Cicero could find some answer. The remainder is a vituperative review of Antonius' career not merely from his first arrival at manhood but from the time he was a boy, culminating in an exhortation to change his ways similar to that in the *First Philippic*. Cicero begins with Antonius as a boy in a *toga praetexta*, sitting in the fourteen rows reserved for equestrians in the theatre in spite of the fact that his father was bankrupt. Once officially a man, Antonius is said to have become a male prostitute before being taken as a lover by Curio. Cicero claims that he had to intervene on Curio's behalf with his father, asking him to cover the debts that Curio had sustained in order to bail out Antonius (44–6).[23] Antonius had been close to Clodius during the latter's tribunate, had accompanied Gabinius to Egypt, but then, after joining Caesar in Gaul and returning to Italy to seek the quaestorship, he had been reconciled with Cicero through Caesar's influence: indeed, alleges Cicero, he had tried to kill Clodius, perhaps when seeking to bring him to trial.[24] After being quaestor to Caesar in Gaul by special appointment, Antonius returned to be tribune and by his opposition to the senate to provide Caesar with a pretext for civil war (50–5).

In his account of Antonius' behaviour during the civil wars Cicero minimizes his political and military services to Caesar and highlights his debauchery and corruption. He had at the time been disgusted by Antonius' processions with mistress and wife in 49.[25] Antonius' behaviour both then and on his return from the victory at Pharsalus is depicted as a continuous orgy of wine, sex, and robbery (55–63). His actions became even more

---

[22] See *Fam.* 12. 3. 1 (to Cassius) for confirmation that Antonius did bring this last charge.

[23] Unless the elder Curio had emancipated his son, as a *pater* he was liable for these debts anyhow.

[24] *Phil.* 2. 48–9; *Mil.* 40. For Antonius being elected in 52 quaestor for the year 51 see *MRR* iii. 19–20, following Linderski and Kaminska-Linderski, 1974.

[25] Cf. Ch. XVI with n. 60–1.

outrageous when, on his return from Alexandria, Caesar entrusted him with selling the property of the proscribed. He missed the African campaign and set out late for that in Spain, only reaching Narbo. His conduct while returning to Rome, and on the way canvassing for the consulship in Cisalpine Gaul, was undignified and revolting (64–78).[26]

Cicero in this passage sets up a contrast between Antonius and Dolabella: the latter actually fought in Thessaly, Africa, and Spain, and was wounded in this last campaign (75). On Caesar's return to Rome, Cicero continues, Antonius induced Dolabella to stand for the consulship, but he found himself overwhelmed by a combination of Antonius and Caesar himself (78–9). That Dolabella was disaffected towards Caesar at that time is not implausible: it might explain his interest in Cicero's speech *De rege Deiotaro* with its ambiguous hints about kingship.[27] We must also accept as true Cicero's claim that Dolabella criticized Antonius bitterly in a speech on 1 January 44—something which apparently provoked Caesar to promise to give him a suffect consulship before he left for the East and Antonius to declare that in his capacity as augur he would obstruct it or declare it invalid (79–81).

Cicero exploits this alleged assertion to show Antonius' ignorance of augural law compared with his own. As an augur Antonius could only report unsolicited omens seen on the occasion to the magistrate presiding over an assembly; it was as a consul that he could actively seek out unfavourable omens before the event.[28] He interweaves Antonius' machinations against Dolabella with evidence of his servility towards Caesar in the days before the Ides of March: he was always putting his head round the back of Caesar's sedan to seek consent for the sale of some privilege. When the day for Dolabella's election came, Antonius did not look for evil omens beforehand but waited for enough votes to be cast and reported for the election to be complete, before adjourning the assembly (82–4).[29] Then he offered Caesar the diadem at the Lupercalia and, when Caesar refused it, ordered that an entry should be made in the *fasti*, that (in Cicero's ironical formulation) 'the consul Marcus Antonius had conferred with popular approval a kingship on Gaius Caesar, *dictator perpetuus*; Caesar did not want to take it up.' Were Tarquinius banished, asks Cicero, and Cassius, Maelius, and Manlius killed

---

[26] For a revaluation of Antonius' position in Caesar's eyes during the years 47–45 see Ramsey, 2004.

[27] *Fam.* 9. 12. 2. See Ch. XVII with n. 135.

[28] *Phil.* 2. 81. The last point is illustrated by Bibulus' conduct as consul in 59. See Chap. XII with nn. 5, 6, and 19.

[29] On procedure in the *comitia centuriata* and the use of omens see CRR 56–7, 60–2, 102–4, VRR 144–5. What Antonius seems to have done, to judge from *Phil.* 2. 84, was to announce the popular verdict but to state that he would not declare Dolabella formally elected until he had reflected on the validity of the procedure.

only for Antonius to set up a king at Rome?[30] In fact he had prepared to defend his conduct over the auspices against an attack by Cicero in the senate on the Ides of March.

The death of Caesar should not have invalidated his decision on the auspices as well as eliminating this debate, but, it is implied, the bar on Dolabella's election was forgotten. Cicero turns instead to Antonius' conduct after Caesar's assassination (88), using a very different tone from that used in the *First Philippic*. Antonius, he claims, panicked and fled. He advised the liberators that Antonius would promise anything while he was afraid, but subsequently would return to type: accordingly, he made no attempt to involve himself with the negotiations conducted by other consulars. Then came the senate meeting in the temple of Tellus (17 March), when Antonius was admirable through fear. The good impression was first overthrown by the funeral speech, then restored by the decree passed on Antonius' proposal preventing new privileges and immunities being granted and that abolishing the dictatorship, then dispersed again by what followed—to others' surprise, but not Cicero's (88–91). Antonius used the money in the temple of Ops to pay his own debts and raised more through the sale of privileges. The recognition of Deiotarus is cited, similarly the liberation of Crete from provincial status, and the return of exiles. The importance of Antonius' visit to Campania is seen here not so much in the preparation of a military base, which is what chiefly disturbed Cicero at the time (*Att.* 14. 21. 2), as in its benefits for Antonius' more dubious friends (100–3).[31] Its climax was Antonius' party on the return journey in the Casinum villa of Varro that he had acquired during the civil wars (103–5). Following this there was the reversal of Caesar's legislation on Antonius' return to Rome. His neglect of Caesar's memory could also be seen in his refusal to take up his priesthood of Julius the divine and his failure to add a fifth day to the circus days of the *ludi Romani* in honour of Caesar. Cicero was against these honours, but Antonius, to be consistent, should have defended them (107–11).

Finally, Cicero challenges Antonius to speak and show he could rival his eloquent grandfather: could he defend his use of a bodyguard? He should abandon the threat of arms and seek the goodwill of the people. The use of arms merely exposed him to the threat of the noble young men who would defend the republic.[32] There was a great gulf between peace, which was liberty enjoyed in tranquillity, and servitude. The liberators had excelled those who

---

[30] *Phil.* 2. 84–7. On the tyrant-demagogues see *VRR* 55–7; Lintott, 1970, 12 ff.

[31] However, Cicero does mention Antonius consulting him about the legalities of creating a new colony at Capua (*Phil.* 2. 102), something unmentioned in the surviving letters.

[32] On *adulescentes nobiles* see Ch. XIII n. 53; Lintott 1970, 24 ff.

had either expelled a king or killed an incipient tyrant: they had killed a tyrant in power—an unprecedented action. Antonius should compare the day on which he abolished the dictatorship with his present conduct. He would never be free from fear. Caesar had devoted his immense talents and resources to establishing a monarchy by a mixture of war and conciliation, assisted by a subservient community; Antonius could not match him. In conclusion, as in the first *Philippic*, Cicero says that his own life did not matter—no more than it had done in his consulship—provided that the Roman people was free and its citizens did their duty by the community.

Whereas the first *Philippic* had a definite political purpose—it was a piece of persuasion adapted to the occasion on which it was given—the second *Philippic* is written to salvage Cicero's own *dignitas* by attacking that of Antonius. It was traditional among Romans to respond to what they regarded as libel not by protest but by counterattack.[33] Its writing gave Cicero pleasure[34] and this appears in the lightness of touch and humour with which Cicero treats Antonius' amours, drinking, even his conduct of an election. However, in the conclusion, where Cicero appeals to Antonius to change his ways, he displays his full power and gravity, most strikingly in his evocation of Caesar's mephistopholean abilites (116). Cicero knew that Antonius would not change. So this persuasion was not so much advice to him but a warning—and a recommendation to Republicans to do their duty and send him to join Caesar.

ANTONIUS, OCTAVIANUS, AND THE LAST SURVIVING LETTERS TO ATTICUS

Cicero, once again in temporary political retirement, could do no more than write invective against Antonius at this time, but in his correspondence he kept in touch with those who commanded, or might soon command, armies. He reported to Q. Cornificius, now in Africa, that Antonius was not only at war with him, but also attacking Cornificius in his speeches. The 'good men' had no leader; the tyrant-slayers were at the other end of the world; Pansa had the right sentiments and spoke bravely; Hirtius was not recovering quickly enough from an illness (*Fam.* 12. 22. 1–2). In the first week of October he wrote to Cassius of the dedication inscribed on the statue Antonius had erected of Caesar on the *rostra*, 'To an Excellent Father'.[35] This entailed, he

---

[33] See Crook, 1976.   [34] Obvious in *Att.* 16. 11. 1–2.

[35] *Parenti optime merito*, implying that Caesar had performed to the full his duty as a father (*Fam.* 12. 3. 1). The evidence for the award of the title of *parens patriae* to Caesar is assembled by

remarked ironically, that not only the tyrannicides but now he himself would be judged parricides as well. If only he had been in the plot, Antonius would not have been troubling them now.[36]

On 2 October the tribune Cannutius asked Antonius about the tyrannicides at a public meeting and received a reply that treated them as if they were public enemies (*Fam.* 12. 3. 2; cf. 12. 23. 3). A little later Cicero informed Cornificius of Antonius' claim to have discovered assassins in his house who had been instructed by Caesar Octavianus. While the public thought this was an invention to discredit Octavianus, sensible and 'good' men believed that the story was true and it gave them hope. Meanwhile Antonius had left Rome on 9 October for Brundisium to meet and win over the Macedonian legions (*Fam.* 12. 23. 1–2). Cicero professed himself in despair at the prospect of civil war. This now seemed indicated to him by Antonius' remark to Cannutius that the tribune was looking for a position with those who could have no part in the community while he (Antonius) was alive, viz. the tyrannicides (ibid. 3). Meanwhile, he was in contact with the governor of what the Romans called 'long-haired Gaul' (from Lyon northwards), L. Plancus (*Fam.* 10. 1, 2). In Cisalpine Gaul Decimus Brutus was exercising his troops by fighting a war against Alpine tribes. Cicero was to receive in early December a letter from him asking for support in the senate for a motion recognizing his victories (*Fam.* 11. 4).

At the end of October Cicero, at his Puteoli villa (see *Att.* 16. 14. 1), had heard rumours of trouble among the legions at Alexandria, who were expecting support from Caecilius Bassus and Cassius (*Att.* 15. 13. 4). A letter from Octavianus in the evening of 1 November brought more solid news: he had won over the veterans settled by Antonius at Casilinum and Calatia by offering them 500 denarii a man (about double the annual salary of a common soldier). He was now moving on to the other colonies and wanted a secret meeting with Cicero at or near Capua. The imminent prospect of war left Cicero in a dilemma: whom was he to follow? 'Look at his name; look at his age' (*Att.* 16. 8. 1). As in the summer Cicero found it hard to associate himself with someone who was proud of being the son of a tyrant; he replied that a secret meeting was neither necessary nor possible. A further message came through one of the Caecina family from Volaterrae (not Cicero's client): Antonius was marching the (Fifth) legion of Alaudae in battle order towards Rome, demanding money from the *municipia* on the way. He had meanwhile

---

Weinstock (1971, 200–4, 274–5). However, Antonius may have also been claiming Caesar *in loco parentis* for himself.

[36] Similar sentiments in *Fam.* 12. 4. 1 to Cassius and 10. 28. 1 to Trebonius of the following year.

sent the three now disaffected Macedonian legions north along the Adriatic coast. Octavianus hoped that these would join him. He asked Cicero whether he should go to them or hold Capua or lead his 3,000 veterans to Rome. Cicero advised the last course, as he expected that Octavianus would find support both among the humbler plebeians and possibly even among the 'good' men. Cicero's regret was that Brutus was missing this glorious opportunity (ibid. 2). Octavianus next invited Cicero to come to Rome to speak in the senate on his behalf. Cicero made the excuse that nothing could be done while Antonius was still consul; he did not trust the intentions of the boy and wanted Pansa's support. Moreover, Antonius might still prevail. Yet, unlike Varro, Cicero did not disagree with Octavianus' project; he even thought that the boy might get Brutus' support (*Att.* 16. 9).

On 5 November Cicero replied to Atticus' comments on the second *Philippic* and *De Officiis*. At the end of the letter he remarked that he was receiving letters every day from Octavianus, urging him first to come to Capua, then to Rome, in order to save the *res publica* a second time (the young man knew how to appeal to Cicero's *amour-propre*). Cicero still had his doubts but he was now more inclined to go to Rome, especially in the light of the reception that Octavianus was receiving in the towns on his way (*Att.* 16. 11. 6). Three days later he was hastening on the journey north, but diverting from the Via Appia inland towards Arpinum in order not to be overtaken by Antonius' swift march. Atticus urged him in a letter to turn to writing history and he was agreeable, but this project was to be lost amid the distractions of politics.[37] He believed that if there was a stalemate between Antonius and Octavianus, he and Atticus should do nothing; if the conflict spread and affected them, they should take a decision in common (16. 13. 4). He agreed with Atticus that, if Octavianus' power became strong, this would ratify Caesar's decisions more irrevocably than the senate's decree on 17 March, against the interests of Brutus. If, however, he was defeated, Antonius was already intolerable. The choice was impossible (16. 14. 1).

The last letter to Atticus of Cicero's that we possess was written after Cicero in Arpinum had received news of Octavianus' arrival in Rome about 10 November. The text of his speech to the people had been sent to Cicero and confirmed his doubts (*Att.* 16. 15. 3). Octavianus had been given an opportunity to speak by the tribune Cannutius.[38] He swore an oath 'as surely as I hope that I may be allowed to attain the high offices of my father', and simultaneously stretched out his right hand towards Caesar's statue on the *rostra*. 'I would not want even my life saved by a man like that,' commented Cicero. Oppius had urged him to embrace the cause of the young man and the

---

[37] *Att.* 16. 10, 16. 12, 16. 13, esp. 1, 16. 13a. 2.   [38] App. *BCiv.* 3. 41. 167–9.

veterans, but he was unwilling to do so unless he was assured that Octavianus would be not only no enemy but a friend of the tyrannicides. Oppius had reassured him on that account, whereupon Cicero had procrastinated by saying that Octavianus would not need help before 1 January: they could test his attitude before the Ides of December by seeing his reaction to the commencement of the tribunate of Servilius Casca (10 December). For the future, Atticus would have letter-carriers and something to write every day. Nevertheless, what really worried Cicero at the time were his finances: in particular Dolabella had set off for Syria without repaying him, and Cicero was unable to pay what he had promised Terentia on behalf of Montanus. There were other unresolved problems. Not only his property but his good name was at stake. He needed to talk to Atticus and was therefore coming to Rome.[39]

It is tantalizing that for us this correspondence stops where it does. We have no direct evidence about what made him choose to align himself decisively with Octavianus, as he had by the time of the third *Philippic* (20 December),[40] nor do we know why we possess no more letters to Atticus. The correspondence cannot have suddenly stopped in the middle of November and, even if they were in Rome together at the end of 44, they would have been separated for periods in the following year. One cannot discount the possibility that Atticus or his heirs suppressed the later correspondence between the two, because it showed either Cicero in a bad light or Atticus himself.[41]

THE PERIOD OF THE REMAINING PHILIPPICS

It is difficult to interpret Cicero solely from his speeches. Fortunately, even if we have no more letters to Atticus, there are many letters to friends surviving from the period from December 44 to the end of the following July. These are often interesting examples of persuasion and informative about public matters. However, both Cicero's private life and for the most part Cicero's more intimate thoughts about his public actions disappear from view. The most intimate letter is the last surviving one to Papirius Paetus of early 43, where Cicero jokes about Paetus abandoning his philosophical pursuit of dinners and tells him that the *res publica* will be in peril if he fails to return to

---

[39] *Att.* 16. 15. 1–2, 5–6. It should be noticed that 'adsum igitur', the last words in the letter, were in the context of his financial problems and did not relate to the *res publica*.

[40] For the date see *Fam.* 11. 6. 2.

[41] See Ciaceri, 1926–30, i. 166; Gelzer, 1969, 406–7 for the first possibility. Cornelius Nepos (*Atticus* 16. 3) had seen 'eleven rolls (of correspondence with Atticus) from his consulship right up to the end'.

former habits in the spring. However, at the end Cicero warns his reader not to think that this jesting means that he has given up politics. He is doing nothing else night and day but working for the survival and freedom of his fellow-ctizens.[42] We must accept his devotion to the *res publica*, but we cannot take completely at face value the apparently bold front to be found in the *Philippics* and in the correspondence with others than Atticus. This may be misleading about his actual attitudes, about his confidence in what he was doing, and even about his importance in the scheme of things.

In spite of what he wrote to Atticus in mid-November, Cicero did not return to Rome until 9 December (*Fam.* 11. 5. 1). He missed seeing Antonius' brief and unsatisfactory stay in Rome at the end of November and the failure of his plan to declare Octavianus a public enemy.[43] He had received a letter from Decimus Brutus (*Fam.* 11. 4) and was further briefed by Pansa about Decimus' intentions to resist Antonius' occupation of Cisalpine Gaul (*Fam.* 11. 5. 1–3). Decimus wanted to be backed by the senate's authority and, Cicero seems to imply, was highly dubious about the boy Caesar's incitement of the consuls' legions to mutiny. However, for the moment Cicero could only urge him not to wait on the senate, when the senate was not free to express a view, nor to impugn the young Caesar's action as 'ill judged' (i.e. illegal), when the same criticism could be made of Caesar's assassination.[44] Some light on Cicero's reasons for hesitancy is shed by a letter sent by his brother to Tiro in December (*Fam.* 16. 27). Cicero himself, we are told, had written to Quintus briefly and in a restrained fashion, but Tiro had revealed the unflattering truth, especially about the consuls designate Hirtius and Pansa. Quintus had no opinion of them, considering them pleasure-loving and effeminately feeble, judging from their behaviour on campaign in Gaul. Antonius would have no difficulty in tempting them to share his self-indulgent life, if they did not receive some stiffening from the tribunes or those without magistracies.

The new tribunes summoned a meeting of the senate on 20 December, apparently intending to obtain a decree granting a bodyguard to Hirtius and Pansa, the consuls designate. Cicero claimed to Decimus that he attended in order to ensure that the latter's achievements were not forgotten (*Fam.* 11. 6. 2). The agenda proposed by the tribunes was that measures should be taken to ensure that the meeting on 1 January should be secure and senators free to express their opinions (*Phil.* 3. 37). Cicero used the occasion to justify the actions of Decimus Brutus and Octavianus and prepare the senate for a later

---

[42] *Fam.* 9. 24. 2–4. Note the use of the word *proficiebas* (2), a technical term for making progress towards Stoic wisdom. The plots at Aquinum and Fabrateria (1) about which Paetus had warned Cicero remain obscure.

[43] *Phil.* 3. 21, 5. 23, 13. 19 and see App 7.

[44] *Fam.* 11. 7. 2. The word used is the adverb *temere*.

attack on Antonius. As he later wrote to Trebonius, 'I embraced the whole of public affairs, *totam rem p(ublicam)*, and delivered an energetic speech in which I recalled a previously enfeebled and exhausted senate to its traditionally virtuous ways more by force of spirit than intellect' (*Fam.* 10. 28. 2).

Cicero began by claiming that a state of war prevailed in which Antonius' entry into D. Brutus' province was merely a preliminary to an attempt to occupy the city (*Phil.* 3. 1–3). Logically, this was an immense *petitio principii*: Antonius' final intentions were unclear. Cicero here, as in later *Philippics*, argued for war by maintaining that it already existed. His evidence for this lay first in Octavianus' efforts to resist Antonius, by raising an army at his own expense (ibid. 3–5), secondly in the desertion of Antonius in favour of Caesar (Octavianus) by the Martian legion and the Fourth under the quaestor L. Egnatuleius (6–8).[45] Thirdly, there was Decimus Brutus' edict expressing loyalty to the senate and people. This allowed Cicero to compare him to his ancestor who expelled the kings and Antonius unfavourably with the proud but law-abiding Tarquinius (8–12). Cicero then interpreted the tribune's motion about security for the meeting as an opportunity to speak about the whole of public affairs (*tota res publica*)—as was indeed the custom on 1 January (13).[46] His own object was to give authority to commanders and to reward soldiers, thus showing that Antonius was no consul but an enemy. Otherwise the legions deserved to be decimated by *fustuarium*[47] and both Decimus Brutus and the young Caesar were criminals (14).

Next Cicero in a long digression defended Octavianus against the attacks on his pedigree made by Antonius and dismissed libels on his own nephew Q. Cicero (now quaestor) and himself (15–18). By contrast he poured scorn on Antonius' threatening edict summoning the senate to the abortive meeting on 24 November[48] and the ineffectual attacks the latter made against opponents on the 28th, when Lepidus was voted a *supplicatio* and various provinces were allocated (19–27). He reviewed in his usual fashion Antonius' corrupt behaviour after Caesar's death and pictured this being relocated to Gaul with the passage of Antonius' army there (29–32). Meanwhile in Rome this was the first day of freedom and Cicero himself was going to exploit it in service to the senate and people (28, 33–6).

His motion was fourfold (37–9): first, that the incoming consuls Pansa and Hirtius should ensure a secure session for the senate on 1 January; secondly, that it was the senate's view that Decimus Brutus' retention of Cisalpine Gaul

---

[45] Cicero interprets this action as a judgement that Antonius was an enemy (*hostis*) (8, cf. 14).
[46] *CRR* 75 with n. 46.
[47] On which see *VRR* 41–2.
[48] Antonius claimed that absentees would be treated as plotters against his life and revolutionaries.

was in the public interest; thirdly, that D. Brutus, L. Plancus, and the other holders of provinces according to Caesar's law should retain them until the senate chose to have them replaced and keep their armies and provinces loyal to the senate and people; fourthly, that in view of the defence of the Roman people by the veterans of Caesar (Octavianus), and the loyalty of the Martian and Fourth legions to the senate and people, they should be granted privileges and thanks and this should be the business of the new consuls when they entered office. It seems likely that what induced Cicero to come out so decisively in favour of Octavianus was his loyalty to Decimus Brutus. He realized that he could not help the one without the other and this decision was to determine his policy in the months following. In his view the only protection for the liberators, at least for the foreseeable future, was to link them (improbably) with the anti-Antonian Caesarians.

His speech to the people the same day in some ways resembled the second *In Catilinam*: it was an exhortation before a campaign with the enemy already in retreat.[49] He claims that the decree of the senate made on his motion amounted in fact to a declaration that Antonius was a public enemy (*hostis*) (*Phil.* 4. 1).[50] Praise follows of the young Caesar and the legions for protecting the liberty of the people. There are subtle variations from the speech to the senate: Cicero speaks here not merely of Octavianus' *patrimonium*, but of his father's soldiers,[51] and invokes the support of the gods.[52] D. Brutus is treated in a more delicate manner (ibid. 7–9). His ancestry, divinely provided, is linked with the liberty of the Roman people, not tyrannicide. His resistance to Antonius (associated with that of the towns of Italy and Gaul) is used to demonstrate the illegitimacy of Antonius' consulship: 'if Antonius is a consul, Brutus is an enemy; if Brutus is the saviour of the *res publica*, Antonius is an enemy.' There is an outrageously sophistic argument—whose premiss is, regrettably, taken seriously by distinguished modern scholars—that the resistance of the province to Antonius' entry showed that he was not consul, because all provinces ought to be within the consul's authority.[53] The climax of the speech is an exhortation to the citizens to display the traditional *virtus* of the Roman people against someone who is no more than a brigand, not even a match for Catiline (ibid. 11–15).

---

[49] See esp. *Phil.* 4. 11–13.
[50] His motion, see *Phil.* 4. 4; *hostis*, ibid. 4. 1–2, 5, 8; *Phil.* 3. 8, 14.
[51] *Phil.* 4. 2–4, cf. 3. 3, where the veterans are discreetly described as *invictum genus*.
[52] *Phil.* 4. 5, cf. 7, 10. However, on 1 January he is prepared to talk to the senate too of the divine capacities of Octavianus and the divine providence behind him (ibid. 5. 23, 43).
[53] *Phil.* 4. 9. This neglects the fact that in the late Republic the root of the Roman conception of *provincia* was the separation of the fields of action of magistrates, when they were not specifically required to cooperate, cf. *Imp. Rom.* 114 with n. 20.

By 1 January Antonius was besieging D. Brutus in Mutina (*Phil.* 5. 24), the first actual military operations in the long-threatened civil war in the West. There was news from Lepidus of a different kind: he had come to terms with Sextus Pompeius (ibid. 39–41). In the senate-meeting it was unusually both consuls who made prefatory speeches—about the present situation and the agenda referred from the debate on 20 December—before opening the debate to the house (*Phil.* 5. 1, cf. 53). They had spoken to Cicero's liking but the speech immediately following, by the consular called first, worried him.[54] Although the speaker accepted the senate's approval of the actions of Octavianus and Brutus and the principle of rewards for the veterans and the legions that deserted Antonius, he had proposed an embassy to Antonius (*Phil.* 5. 1–4). Speaking second, Cicero suspected that this motion would find favour among other consulars: one was even considering giving Antonius the province of Plancus, which Cicero thought mad, given the resources that this province would provide (5–6).

Cicero plunged into a powerful but somewhat incoherent denunciation of Antonius' political actions of 44 (5. 7–25). Most of it is familiar, but Cicero specifically impugned the legitimacy of the statutes enacted at the beginning of June 44 about land and the provinces on the ground that they violated the *leges Caecilia Didia* and *Licinia Iunia*, since the former was passed in a thunderstorm, the latter without due notice, and both with the aid of armed violence. Cicero proposed that because the laws were passed by violence and in contravention of the auspices they did not bind the people. Any laws about land, the confirmation of Caesar's decisions, and the abolition of the dictatorship should be ratified afresh without violating the auspices.[55] He also criticized the judiciary law, which Antonius seems to have passed before he left Rome in October, attacking the 'gamblers, exiles, and Greeks', who were now jurors.[56] In two passages, somewhat awkwardly separated by a denunciation of Antonius' behaviour towards him in September, he called for the laws, not to be abrogated, but to be declared invalid by the senate—a procedure introduced by the *lex Caecilia Didia* in 98 BC.[57]

Eventually we find Cicero reverting to the military crisis. Embassies are futile, he argues: there is no parallel with those sent to Hannibal before the

---

[54] This has been generally assumed to be Fufius Calenus, who might have owed his selection to being Pansa's father-in-law (*Phil.* 8. 19) and was clearly called first in a debate in early February (*Phil.* 10. 3). However, Servilius Isauricus was frequently called before Cicero. If seniority were followed, the likely person would be L. Caesar (*cos.* 64), Antonius' maternal uncle (*Phil.* 8. 12–2), but he is probably the *cognatus* yet to speak, who was prepared to grant Antonius the province of Plancus (5–6).

[55] *Phil.* 5. 7–10, cf. 16, 21; 11. 13; 12. 12; CRR 61–3; VRR 132–48.

[56] *Phil.* 5. 12–15; cf. 1. 20; Ramsey 2005, especially about who the jurors really were.

[57] On the *lex Caecilia Didia* see n. 55.

Second Punic War, since, if Antonius ignores them, the envoys cannot go on to his city to seek satisfaction, Antonius is a Roman attacking a Roman commander and colony (25–7). Even if he abandons the siege, on past behaviour he is still an enemy; otherwise the rewards for Caesar, the veterans, and D. Brutus are inappropriate. How can one levy troops satisfactorily, if still negotiating (28–31)? Cicero's motion follows. First a military emergency (*tumultus*) should be declared, the city should put on *saga* (military cloaks), and levies should be held without exemptions being valid.[58] He dismisses here Antonius' argument that this is a civil war between factions (that is a Caesarian and Pompeian faction): one side was defeated, the other side—Hirtius, Pansa, Caesar's son—are from the heart of Caesar's party. Next Cicero proposes the 'last' decree of the senate, accompanied by an indemnity for Antonius' soldiers if they left him before 1 February, an echo of what had been decreed against Caesar in 49.[59] As for the honours that were on the agenda, D. Brutus should receive approval for his action (35–7), so should Lepidus for his successful negotiations with Sextus Pompeius (38–41).[60]

Most of the final part of the speech, over ten paragraphs, is devoted to Caesar Octavianus and his army. His action is compared with that of the young Pompey, joining Sulla with a private army in 83—to Octavianus' advantage (42–5). Cicero's motion gives him *imperium pro praetore*, a seat in the senate with praetorian rank, and the right to pursue higher offices as if he had been quaestor in 45 (an acceleration of thirteen years in the *cursus honorum*). Such acceleration, Cicero argues, could be justified by the careers of great commanders before the introduction of the *leges annales* that controlled the ascent through the magistracies (45–8).[61] There was no danger in it, as a comparison with the dead dictator showed. If only it had been Caesar's fortune as a young man to have been dear to the senate and all the best men. Lacking this, he chose populist irresponsibility (*popularis levitas*) and a path to power irreconcilable with the freedom of the people (48–9). Octavianus by contrast was prudent. He pursued liberty and the respect of good men. Cicero pledges to his audience that Octavianus has given up personal enmities for the cause of the *res publica*: his expedition to liberate D. Brutus showed that the safety of the community weighed more with him than family grief (50–1). The conclusion is a slight anti-climax but important: the quaestor Egnatuleius should receive a three-year acceleration in the *cursus honorum*. The veterans

---

[58] *Phil.* 5. 31; cf. 6. 2, 8. 2–3; *VRR* 153–5. These procedures were used, for example, on the outbreak of the Social War in 90, in 49, and in 63.

[59] *Phil.* 5. 34, cf. Caes. *BCiv.* 1. 2. 6.

[60] Cicero provides elaborate phraseology for each. The language provides an interesting comparison with that of Greek honorific decrees.

[61] Octavianus was in fact to receive consular rank in the senate (*RG* 1. 2).

are to receive land from that distributed contrary to Caesar's laws or from the Campanian land. The Fourth and Martian legions and those who deserted Antonius' other legions are to receive immunity from military service outside emergencies and demobilization after the present hostilities together with the rewards in money and land that Octavianus promised them (53–4).

In many ways this *Philippic* resembles the earlier political speeches of Demosthenes. It is designed to mobilize opinion and hence military forces against a man who is not universally recognized as an enemy—before it is too late. Structure seems sometimes neglected in order to raise the emotional pitch of the speech. Concrete proposals, some of which are controversial, are mixed with fervent denunciation. We find here even more strikingly than in the third *Philippic* two themes that are the leitmotifs of the series: there can be no peace with Antonius; the preservation of liberty entails acceptance of, and cooperation with, the tyrannicides.

Three days after the fifth *Philippic* Cicero was invited by the tribune P. Apuleius to address the people about the conclusion reached by the senate that day (*Phil.* 6. 1, 3). Cicero complains that, although the motion for the declaration of a *tumultus* that he had proposed on 1 January seemed to have majority opinion on its side, in the end the senate weakened and opted for an embassy (ibid. 3). He briefly repeats his criticism of this policy, but takes encouragement from an earlier resolution that Antonius should return over the Rubicon into Italy but remain at least 200 miles from Rome (3–5). Not that Antonius would comply with it, but his disobedience would make the situation clear. D. Brutus must be rescued: the people should prepare for fighting (6–9, cf. 16).

The speech could have ended there, but Cicero introduces a variation into his regular theme, inspired perhaps by the venue of the meeting. There had recently been erected three gilded equestrian statues—one dedicated by the thirty-five tribes, another by the cavalry with the public horse (*equites equo publico*), a third by *Ianus medius*, the location of the moneylenders in the Forum—to L. Antonius, Antonius' brother and the head of the seven-man land-commission, as their patron (12–15).[62] 'What had Antonius done for the dedicators?' asks Cicero. The *equites* should have chosen him instead. No moneylender would have ever lent L. Antonius 1,000 sesterces: if it was in return for the land he had distributed, then these assignations had been rescinded by the recent motion of L. Caesar (14). This suggests that Cicero's

---

[62] Only the first is described as gilded and equestrian, but it is likely that they were similar. Cicero would have been speaking from the Caesarian *rostra*, which would permit these 'on the left' to be on the Republican *rostra*. The statues suggest that L. Antonius had found favour not only for distributing land but for putting more money in circulation through purchases and so maintaining liquidity, which would have assisted the payment of debts.

proposal, that Antonius' legislation of June should be declared invalid, had been taken up and passed by the senate.[63] Finally, Cicero exhorts the citizens a second time to prepare patiently for the return of the embassy, which would settle the issue of peace or war those (15–17). He calls on them to remember his own constant concern for them, revives a vision of the unity of all ranks at Rome and all the colonies and municipalities of Italy—once deployed against Catiline,[64] this time against Antonius—and tells them that this is their chance. Previously they had lost their liberty by a malignant stroke of fate ('aliquis fatalis casus'). Slavery now will be self-inflicted. Other nations could endure slavery; liberty was the possession of the Roman people (18–19).[65]

The following, seventh, *Philippic* was spoken some time before the return of the embassy towards the end of January.[66] It is a classic illustration of the right of a senator to digress from the topic under discussion.[67] The consul Pansa had consulted the senate about the via Appia and the mint, a tribune had raised the topic of the Luperci. Servilius Isauricus had already spoken (*Phil.* 7. 1, 27). Cicero took the opportunity to criticize those who were in his view giving comfort to Antonius by making public his demands, including the consul Pansa on whom he heaps mitigating praise (ibid. 1–2, 4–6). There had been some developments since 4 January. C. Antonius had been recalled from Macedonia, presumably on the ground that this province might provide M. Antonius with an alternative base (3). Furthermore, levies were being held throughout Italy with no immunities valid, a consequence normally of a decree of *tumultus*.[68] Cicero states roundly that, although his career has been sustained throughout by peace, he does not want peace with Antonius (7–8). He repeats his arguments from consistency—the approval given to Octavianus and D. Brutus, the military preparations (11–15). It would be shameful to back down, also dangerous, given the character of Antonius and his associates, especially L. Antonius (9, 16–20). Ultimately, it would be impossible, since Antonius could never be reconciled with the senate, equestrian order, and the people in Rome and Italy (21–5).[69] For the present, Antonius had to submit to the demands he had already received. It was a matter of the liberty of the Roman people (26–7).

---

[63] See *Phil.* 5. 16, 21, 11. 13, 12. 12. The ground for annulment was the use of violence.
[64] Cf. *Cat.* 1. 27, 2. 24–5.
[65] Cf. *Phil.* 10. 20.
[66] Two letters belong to this period: *Fam.* 11. 8 to D. Brutus, in which Cicero calls Octavianus 'Caesar meus', and *Fam.* 12. 24. 1–2 to Cornificius.
[67] Cf. *CRR* 80.
[68] *Phil.* 7. 12–13. See above, n. 58 and Appendix 7.
[69] There is another allusion to Cicero's consulship in his description of the *equites* guarding the senate on the steps of the temple of Concord, cf. *Phil.* 7. 21 with *Cat.* 3. 21; Sall. *Cat.* 49. 4.

At the end of January the embassy returned. Cicero prefaces two letters at this time—one to Cassius, the other to Trebonius—with a wish that he had been invited to the dinner on the Ides of March: there would have been nothing left over. His exasperation with Antonius was at a peak. He thought the weakness of the envoys L. Philippus and L. Piso disgusting and disgraceful.[70] One could not blame Servius Sulpicius Rufus, as he had died on the journey, and L. Caesar was ill and tied by his kinship with Antonius.[71] Antonius had not only rejected the senate's ultimatum but produced 'intolerable demands' of his own. These can be extracted from the speech Cicero delivered criticizing them, the eighth *Philippic* (*Fam.* 12. 4. 1; *Phil.* 8. 25–7). Antonius was prepared to give up any claim to Cisalpine and Transalpine Gaul, if he was given in exchange 'Long-Haired Gaul' with six legions brought up to strength by men from D. Brutus' army for as long as M. Brutus and Cassius retained provincial commands or a quinquennium at least.[72] He also required a promise in advance of land for his army, the confirmation of the grants of land made by Dolabella and himself and of the decrees made on the basis of the alleged *acta* of Caesar, no investigation of the accounts of the Temple of Ops, immunity for his brother's land-commission and for his own followers, and no repeal of his judiciary law. Antonius' aim for security for himself and his followers against both the conspirators and the other Caesarians is patent. Arguably, however, he had pitched his demands too high: Cicero alleged that because of this he himself was more popular than before (*Fam.* 12. 4. 1).

When Cicero spoke on 3 February, it was after what Cicero regarded as an over-lenient motion, proposed by L. Caesar, had been passed the previous day. Without speaking of a war, the senate had decreed that *saga* (military cloaks) should be worn from the 4th.[73] In Cisalpina the relief of Mutina had already begun with Hirtius dislodging an Antonian outpost at Claterna on the via Aemilia east of Bononia. Octavianus was a little way behind at Forum Cornelii. Antonius allegedly controlled Regium Lepidi and Parma on the via Aemilia west of Mutina, but nothing else.[74] However, the senate had also decided that a last attempt should be made to negotiate. Antonius' envoy, L. Varius Cotyla, was to return, and a senatorial embassy to follow.[75] Cicero

---

[70] *Fam.* 12. 4. 1, 10. 28. 1; *Phil.* 8. 28.   [71] *Phil.* 8. 22; *Fam.* 10. 28. 3.

[72] 'Utramque provinciam', 'both provinces', seems best explained by an original grant to Antonius in June of Gallia Cisalpina and Transalpina (the later Narbonensis), *Phil.* 8. 25, cf. 1. 8, thus depriving Lepidus of the latter (cf. Dio 43. 51. 8). One cannot take too seriously Cicero's allegation that Antonius also claimed Macedonia, after the recall of his brother (*Phil.* 7. 3).

[73] *Phil.* 8. 6; cf. *Ad Caes. iun.* I. fr. 16, which provides the date.

[74] *Phil.* 8. 6; cf. *Fam.* 12. 5. 2; *Ad Caes. Iun.* II. fr. 23a.

[75] *Phil.* 8. 20–4, 28–9, 33; cf. Plut. *Ant.* 18. 8 for his name.

proposed to put a time-limit of the Ides of March on grants of immunity to Antonian soldiers who deserted him and to reject any further attempt to negotiate after the return of Cotyla to Antonius (ibid. 33).

His arguments are designed to show that they are already at war and that peace is impossible, given the nature of their opponent. The first is from language: a *tumultus* is a war, indeed a more threatening war than usual.[76] Moreover, there is already fighting in Cisalpina with D. Brutus under siege and Hirtius advancing (ibid. 4–6). Unlike other civil wars, this has not arisen from a political clash, but because Antonius, in pursuit of plunder for his followers, has decided to disturb a consensus (7–10). Cicero now turns on Fufius Calenus, who has been speaking for peace with Antonius: it is fine to argue for the preservation of citizens' lives, but only if the citizens are good and honourable (11–13). From this he develops his well-known argument about *hostes*, linking Antonius with the Gracchi, Saturninus, Catiline, and Clodius, in order to prove that it was right that certain people should be eliminated from the body politic (14–16). The rest of the speech is largely an expression of outrage at the way Antonius had treated the senate's embassy—not only his demands (25–7) but his continuance of the siege of Mutina (20–1)—and the passiveness of the *consulares* (22, 28–30). Here Cicero alleges that there are people who are jealous of a certain person's constancy, industry, and devotion to the interests of senate and people (there are no prizes for guessing who this is). He calls up the figure of Quintus Scaevola the augur, who, though old and weak, continued to give audiences and attend the senate during the Marsic (Social) War. He himself would not use the pretext of his consular status to remain in a toga, but through shame at the timidity of others of his rank, would put on a military cloak (30–2).

Shortly afterwards the consul Pansa raised the question of honours for the dead Servius Sulpicius, suggesting in a long panegyric that he should have both a statue on the *rostra* and a funeral at public expense; Servilius Isauricus demurred, arguing that a statue was inappropriate, as in the past they had only been granted to those actually killed by the enemy, the envoys to the king of Veii and, much later, Cn. Octavius while on his mission to Antiochus IV (*Phil.* 9. 3–5, 14). Following him, Cicero in his ninth *Philippic* argued that the honour should depend on the cause, not the manner, of death. It was the embassy, and indeed the pressure on Sulpicius in the senate to undertake it, that had killed the envoy (5–9). The statue would be a monument to the embassy and to Sulpicius' distinction as a jurist (10–12). From what he knew of Sulpicius, a bronze statue on foot would please him most, as he disliked excessive display (*insolentia*)—Cicero adds, 'if there is any perception in

---

[76] *Phil.* 8. 2–3; cf. 5. 31, 6. 2 and see n. 58 above.

death', echoing a phrase of Sulpicius' in the consolation letter he wrote to Cicero about Tullia.[77] He did agree with Servilius about the funeral honours. Few had received a tomb at public expense, and, unlike statues, tombs were protected by the holy ground on which they stood, whose sacredness was reinforced by time (14–15). His elaborate and honorific decree granted not only the statue on the *rostra*, but a space of five feet around it from which Sulpicius' children and descendants could view gladiatorial games; his funeral should not limited by the normal restrictions on expenditure in the edict of the curule aediles, and he should have a space for a tomb, thirty foot square, in the *campus Esquilinus* or elsewhere, according to choice (15–17).

A new impetus was given to Cicero's actions by an official despatch from M. Brutus announcing that he had taken control of Macedonia 'on behalf of the senate and Roman people', assisted by, among others, Cicero's son. Pansa brought this immediately before the senate.[78] His reaction was favourable, but the most determined supporter of peace with Antonius among the *consulares*, Fufius Calenus, was more cautious, when called first to speak (*Phil.* 10. 2–6). In a carefully worded speech (he spoke from a prepared text, *de scripto*) he seems to have approved Brutus' actions so far (*Phil.* 10. 5) but wished to put the Macedonian legions under someone else's command (ibid. 6). Inasmuch as the senate had apparently already stripped C. Antonius of his Macedonian command,[79] it would have been reasonable to condone Brutus' unofficial action, especially as he had the cooperation of properly appointed magistrates—Hortensius, the outgoing governor of Macedonia, and Vatinius, the proconsul of Illyricum (*Phil.* 10. 13). However, Calenus and others were arguing the assignment of a military command to Brutus would alienate the Caesarian veterans fighting for the senate against Antonius (ibid. 15–19, cf. 11. 37).

Cicero's strategy of seeking to link the conspirators with the Caesarian opponents of Antonius had now reached a crisis. His tenth *Philippic* was spoken in order to propose that M. Brutus should be confirmed in the governorship of Macedonia. He first suggested that Calenus was isolated from the consul and senate in his prejudice against Brutus and favour for Antonius (ibid. 3–6). He then dwelt on Brutus' patience at his lack of recognition after the Ides of March and his timely intervention in order to deprive M. Antonius of military support from his brother (ibid. 7–11). What had Brutus to do with the Macedonian legions? They belonged to the *res publica* and Brutus was the saviour of the *res publica*. Cicero, just as when he defended emergency measures after the last decree of the senate, argued that

[77] *Phil.* 9. 13; cf. *Fam.* 4. 5. 6.   [78] *Phil.* 10. 1, 13, 25; *Fam.* 12. 5. 1.
[79] *Phil.* 7. 3, 10. 10–11, 13.

the preservation of the republic justified any unconstitutional action (12–14). As for the veterans, Cicero said that they had no more reason to be hostile to Marcus, than to Decimus Brutus or those fighting to rescue him. It was the enemies of Antonius who were preserving Caesar's *acta*. He then suddenly abandons the pose of sweet reasonableness to give a cry of exasperation. If everything was directed according to the veterans' wishes, it would be better to be dead.[80] Once more Cicero appealed to the contrast between liberty and servitude and between the villains on Antonius' sides and the loyalty of Brutus to the republic (21–4), finally producing a motion which, after an honorific preamble, placed Brutus in overall command of Macedonia, Illyricum, and Greece, with the army he now commanded; Q. Hortensius with his pro-quaestor and *legati* was to be the regular governor of Macedonia (25–7).

The senate on this occasion followed Cicero. More news from the East came about the end of February. Dolabella, on his way to take over Syria according to the law of June 44 which the senate had declared invalid,[81] landed with a legion near Smyrna and, after holding unsuccessful talks with Trebonius in which he presumably sought to march through Asia to Syria, sent men into the town by night to seize him, torture him, and assassinate him (*Phil.* 11. 4–9).[82] The story outraged even Fufius Calenus, who successfully proposed that Dolabella should be declared an enemy (ibid. 14–15). The following day Cicero was called after L. Caesar and Servilius Isauricus[83] and spoke the eleventh *Philippic*. He recounted the story with horror—with an unconvincing apology at the end for not having noticed Dolabella's faults, when he was his father-in-law (ibid. 10)—and compared the pro-Antonian 'brigands' in Dolabella's entourage with those in that of Antonius (11–14). If Dolabella was an enemy, who was to fight him (16)? L. Caesar had proposed to confer the command through a popular assembly on an eminent man currently without a magistracy, a procedure for which there was good precedent (19). Caesar had in mind Servilius Isauricus, but he was apparently not eager for the task (20, 25). An alternative was to entrust the war to the consuls (21–5).

Cicero prepares the ground for his own proposal by a review of exceptional commands (*extraordinaria imperia*)—the two Scipiones, the *pontifex maximus* P. Licinius Crassus, Pompey, and Caesar Octavianus (17–20). Isauricus was reluctant; the consuls could not manage both tasks without delays to one of them (20–5). Cicero first suggests either or both of Brutus and Cassius (26). However, he then argues that it is better that Brutus should remain in Macedonia as potential support for operations in Italy. Brutus and Cassius

---

[80] *Phil.* 10. 15–19, esp. 'erumpat enim aliquando vera et me digna vox...' (19). Cf. 11. 38.
[81] *Phil.* 6. 14, 11. 13, 12. 12.
[82] Cf. App. *BCiv.* 3. 26; for other sources *MRR* ii. 349–50. [83] *Phil.* 11. 18–20.

had been their own senate out of necessity. If they thought that this was their duty to pursue Dolabella, they would be doing so without waiting for a decree from the senate. Brutus had already deprived him of some of his cavalry (26–7). However, Cassius, Cicero alleges, had set out for Syria, with the intention of keeping Dolabella from his province. His justification was Jupiter's law that everything that was salutary for the *res publica* should be considered legitimate and just: this law was nothing less than right reason drawn from the power of the gods. Cicero has no qualms here about enlisting the Stoic supreme principle as an ally in civil war (28).[84]

The senate had ratified one command seized illegally that was popular at Rome, that of Octavianus; it had ratified another that would not have been so popular but seemed desirable in the fight against Antonius, that of Marcus Brutus. Cicero's present proposal was even more extreme. Cassius should have a proconsular command in Syria with the armies of Q. Marcius Crispus, Staius Murcus, and Allienus in order to fight Dolabella. He should have the right of gathering ships, crew, money, and military supplies, where he saw fit; his command should extend over Syria, Asia, Bithynia, and Pontus, and his power should be greater (*maius imperium*) than the provincial governors in the area;[85] aid from King Deiotarus and from the other kings, dynasts, and tetrarchs in the area would be appreciated and remembered by the senate and people (29–31). The speech ends with praise of Cassius' potential allies and Cassius' own military ability, and an anticipation of objections. People were saying that Cicero had privileged M. Brutus excessively and was giving Cassius domination and a supreme position (*principatus*). Yet they were glories of the *res publica* like D. Brutus and a contrast to Antonius' supporters (32–6). As for the veterans, Cicero had a duty to look after them, if they were on the right side, not to fear them. Those who were seeking to liberate D. Brutus from siege could not be offended. In any case the veterans were too arrogant: they should not be choosing commanders. The senate should be paying more respect to the new troops who were liberating their fatherland (37–40).

Cicero's proposal, as he explained to Cassius in a letter, was vigorously opposed by Pansa and failed. He was, however, invited to address the people by the tribune M. Servilius and had a good reception, though Cassius' mother-in-law Servilia was uneasy about the potential offence to Pansa.[86] He was unrepentant and urged Cassius to defend the *res publica* without the benefit of a senatorial decree (*Fam.* 12. 7. 1–2). Not long afterwards Antonius' friends at Rome, especially Piso and Fufius Calenus, urged with support from

---

[84] For the principle see *ND.* 1. 39; *Rep.* 3. 33; *Leg.* 1. 33.   [85] Cf. Ch. XIII with n. 4.
[86] Cassius' *frater* was also unhappy, presumably his brother-in-law Servilius Isauricus. Cassius was not charged with war against Dolabella until 27 April after the battle of Mutina (*Ad Brut.* 13. 1).

the consul Pansa that negotiations with him should be resumed. A further embassy was proposed—Servilius Isauricus, L. Caesar, Piso, Calenus, and Cicero.[87] Servilius, who spoke before Cicero, was reluctant; Cicero was embarrassed, and his speech declining participation, the twelfth *Philippic*, betrays both frustration and fear at the prospect. He alleged that the hope that had been expressed of peace was fraudulent: there was no new proposal from Antonius and no evidence of a change in his position (*Phil.* 12. 3–4). His political reasons are not new. Negotiations would take the edge off the campaign already in progress, in which their forces and the towns that supported them in Italy and Gaul were expecting victory.[88] To judge by his last proposals, Antonius has not changed. Could the *res publica* survive, if he and his friends were once more part of it (11–16)?

Cicero then introduces himself into the equation. His belief that Antonius was a public enemy would be an impediment to the embassy. How could he confront the man who claimed that he was giving Cicero's property to Petusius of Urbino, or L. Antonius, from whom he had been forced to hide behind the walls of Arpinum? Or men like Bestia, Trebellius, and Titus Plancus?[89] His own personal security would be in peril on the journey, whichever road he took to the north. His best route, he remarks ironically, was the via Aurelia which would take him past the property of Clodius, from whose staff he could expect hospitality because of their close acquaintance. In fact, he says, he had been vulnerable on the road since the Catilinarian conspiracy.[90] He would be no better off when he got close to Antonius. It would not be a gentlemanly colloquy like the parleys in the Social and Civil Wars. His determination to take a strong line would make him unpopular among the troops on the senate's side. Cicero concluded by pleading with the senate to let him stay safely at home (26–30). This ignominious posture shows how desperately he wished not to go to the battlefront. It was unlikely that he would have been killed, but he might well have been humiliated and would have lost his position at the centre of things at Rome.

On 19 March, the Quinquatria festival of Minerva, Cicero spoke in the senate on behalf of Q. Cornificius, the governor of Africa, after Pansa had read official letters to the senate and people from him, confirming his loyalty to the Republic. The senate decreed its approval, confirming him in his position

---

[87] *Phil.* 12. 1–4; embassy 12. 4–6, 11, 16–19.

[88] Ibid. 5, 9–10, where the action of Patavium is singled out.

[89] Ibid. 16–21. Petusius reappears in the catalogue in *Phil.* 13. 3. We do not know what evidence Cicero had for the story about him, nor when himself he had escaped Lucius Antonius in Arpinum—perhaps in September 44.

[90] Ibid. 23–5. For obscure plots against him recently at Aquinum and Fabrateria see *Fam.* 9. 24. 1.

vis-à-vis the Antonian appointee Calvisius Sabinus (*Fam.* 12. 25. 1–2). Cicero took the occasion to tell Cornificius about his determination in undermining Calvisius Sabinus since 20 December (Calvisius had been forced to return to Rome) and his general policy of attacking Antonius with the aid of Octavianus. He claims that the 'excellent boy' had first protected him from Antonius before protecting the Republic (ibid. 2–4).[91] The proposal for the embassy to Antonius had evidently not found favour in the senate and foundered. It was Pansa and his army of recruits who set out for Gaul, seemingly directly after this debate. The following day, 20 March, both consuls, according to Cicero, were away on military service.[92] The president of the senate would have been the *praetor urbanus*, M. Caecilius Cornutus.[93] A further debate was occasioned by letters from two proconsuls in the West, Lepidus and L. Plancus, advocating a reconciliation.[94] Servilius Isauricus, again speaking before Cicero, rejected this suggestion. Cicero's thirteenth *Philippic* was delivered in support of him, and was perhaps more explicit in denouncing any attempt by Lepidus to intervene in Italy.[95] Cicero exploited both the tone of Lepidus' letter and that of a letter, sent by Antonius to Hirtius and Octavianus, that had been passed on to him. Its text can be recovered from the lemmata in the speech and is itself a powerful piece of rhetoric.[96]

In the *prooemium* Cicero yet again contrasts the claims of peace and liberty (*Phil.* 13. 1–7). Nothing was fouler than the man who had a craving for civil war (ibid. 2). However, by contrast to the earlier leaders in civil war who would have been open to a peaceful settlement, it was impossible to live in peace with Antonius and his supporters. Hence conflict was not only courageous but prudent. Cicero then turns to Lepidus himself, paying tribute to his family, his career, and in particular his negotiations with Sextus Pompeius. Lepidus was deceived if he thought that he could negotiate with Antonius as he had with Pompeius (7–10). Cicero now digresses with a proposal. Inasmuch as the *acta* of Caesar are ratified, Pompeius will have to buy back his own house (at Rome) at no smaller a price than its cost to Antonius, but he can use the money that was voted to him by the senate in compensation.[97] He should also be allowed to buy back the villa at Tusculum from Antonius, those at Formiae and the Alban Lake from Dolabella, that in the *ager Falernus* from the poet Anser, and other properties. Anyone who did not co-operate should

---

[91] Cicero had told Cornificius originally about his efforts in late December (*Fam.* 12. 22a).
[92] *Phil.* 13. 16; cf. *Fam.* 10. 6. 3.
[93] Cf. *Fam.* 10. 12. 3, 10. 16. 1; *Ad Brut.* 5. 3.
[94] *Phil.* 13. 7–9; *Fam.* 10. 6. 1.
[95] *Phil.* 13. 50; cf. 13–14; *Fam.* 10. 27. 2.
[96] See App. 8.
[97] 50 million *denarii* = 200 million sesterces according to App. *BCiv.* 3. 4. 11.

be regarded as an enemy (10–12).[98] Sextus Pompeius, when he met a Roman embassy at Massilia, had been willing to join the forces at Mutina, Cicero alleges, but was reluctant to offend the Caesarian veterans there. Lepidus should avoid being arrogant and think he could invade Italy. His army belonged to the senate and people and should be used to keep off foreign enemies and extend the empire (13–15). The forces round Mutina were ready for battle. Lepidus could not want to impose on Rome the rule of Antonius, given his past behaviour (15–21).

Having dwelt on Antonius' tyrannical actions before and after Caesar's death and his final subversion by Octavianus, Cicero turns to Antonius' letter to Hirtius and the young Caesar (22 ff.). Antonius by now knew of the death of Trebonius, the senate's reaction, and the support for Marcus Brutus. He rejoiced in the deserved punishment of Trebonius, regretted that Dolabella had been declared a public enemy. He was most deeply pained that Hirtius, who owed his position entirely to Caesar, and the 'boy who owed everything to his name' should be depriving Dolabella of his status, freeing 'this hag-witch' (Decimus Brutus) from siege, and giving the greatest possible power to Marcus Brutus and Cassius. What they called the senate was Pompey's camp. Cicero was their leader in spite of his defeat (ibid. 22–6, 30). Antonius now bitterly reviewed the decisions taken to revoke his own measures and Caesar's, in particular the annulment of his veteran settlements (31). He finally came to the crisis at Mutina. They had assembled an army to kill their own former commanders or fellow-soldiers: it was as if Pompey or his son had come back to life (33–4). As for the embassy, he could not expect decent treatment from it on their past behaviour (36). Hirtius and Octavianus had to decide between avenging the death of Trebonius or that of Caesar, between a conflict destined to reanimate the Pompeian cause, or an agreement to avoid giving a certain profit to their enemies, whoever won. This was a spectacle that Fortune had so far avoided, to see two battlelines belonging to the same body fighting it out with Cicero as their coach (38–40). He would not desert the Caesarian cause, the veterans, his pledge to Dolabella, or his associations with Lepidus and Plancus.[99] If he died, it would be for his opponents to discover what Pompeians, insolent in defeat, were like when victorious (44–5). He would let bygones be bygones, if they would or at least join in avenging Caesar's death. He did not think the embassy would come. When they did, he would discover their demands (46–7).

One may question Cicero's wisdom in reading this to the senate. The expostulations which punctuate his reading do not match the pungency of

---

[98] For the poet Anser see Ovid, *Trist*. 2. 435; Serv. ad Verg. *Ecl*. 9. 35.

[99] Lepidus, to judge from his correspondence (below) seems to have been taking Antonius' side at the time; Plancus, to judge from his, was keeping his options open.

Antonius' allegations. The long digression on the quality of men in Pompey's camp in Greece (29–30), which is in total contrast to his comments in his correspondence, would have only stressed his Pompeian loyalties before a largely Caesarian audience. For Cicero the letter proved that Antonius was an irreconcilable enemy to the *res publica*, as indeed he was to Cicero. For others the letter must have been uncomfortable to hear, nor were the references to Lepidus and Plancus as Antonius' allies encouraging to those pursuing war. After the debate Cicero wrote a chilly letter to Lepidus. He reminded him that he should have thanked the senate for the honours they had conferred on him—the *supplicatio* voted on 23 November and the gilded statue proposed by Cicero on 1 January.[100] He was glad that Lepidus was in favour of peace, but this could not be combined with servitude and Lepidus would serve the senate and people best by not intervening in the 'pacification'.

Cicero's other letter that evening, to Plancus, expressed more disappointment than disapproval. Plancus' dispatch to the senate urging peace was not consistent with the verbal message he had sent through his *legatus* Furnius. His ascent through the ranks of magistrates would only have meaning if he linked it with republican values, the liberty of the people and the authority of the senate (*Fam.* 10. 6). Plancus wrote back to Cicero a brief note reassuring him about his devotion to the *res publica* and his consular ambitions:[101] Cicero would learn more from another emissary, M. Varisidius, and Plancus' own official letter (*Fam.* 10. 7). Cicero replied encouragingly on 31 March, pointing out at the same time that the fate of the *res publica* now depended on one battle (*Fam.* 10. 10). Plancus' official dispatch was a long-winded justification of his apparent slowness to declare support for the senate. He had needed to ensure not only the support of his army but the loyalty of the Gallic communities. Antonius had already bid high for the legions' support and during his consulship made concessions to the communities. Plancus had now built up his army to five legions whose loyalty to him had been secured by generous donatives. He was ready now either to defend his province against invaders or lead his army where the *res publica* called him.[102] This produced an effusive response from Cicero, who reported that he had eventually succeeded in getting a motion of thanks to Plancus passed in the senate after a two-day debate on 8–9 April, in spite of religious obstruction and a veto made by the tribune P. Titius on Servilius Isauricus' request (*Fam.* 10. 12. 2–4).

---

[100] *Fam.* 10. 27; cf. *Phil.* 3. 23, 5. 40–1.
[101] D. Brutus and he had been selected by Caesar for the consulship in 42.
[102] *Fam.* 10. 8, esp. 3 and 6. 'Ut ab re p. potius moderata quam ab uno infinita speraret' (3) is surely a reference to solicitation by Antonius.

On 9 April Cicero was handed in the senate a letter from Cassius' quaestor Lentulus Spinther—son of the consul who promoted Cicero's recall from exile—which informed him of his commander's entry into Syria on the invitation of Staius Murcus and Marcius Crispus. Allienus had handed over to Cassius the four legions from Egypt and that of Caecilius Bassus had also joined him. This was to be confirmed in a few days by a note from Cassius himself.[103] Cicero immediately exploited the information to attack Servilius Isauricus for his attitude to Cassius.[104] Two days later Cicero had just written to M. Brutus about this news when he received a letter from him sent on 1 April from Dyrrachium. In this he asked what he should do about his prisoner C. Antonius and gave the news about Cassius, telling Cicero that his own family had been told not to spread the news before they had talked to him.[105] After delicately congratulating him on the fifth and tenth *Philippics*, whose texts he had received, he pointed out that he needed new troops and money, especially as Asia was lost to Dolabella, and hoped that Cicero could send him some by subterfuge or an open motion in the senate. Meanwhile Cicero's son had been earning a good reputation in his army.[106]

Cicero answered that Brutus should continue to detain C. Antonius until the issue of the siege of Mutina was decided, and he should only invade Asia if Dolabella took up position there. There was no money available apart from the loans which the senate had decreed that he could raise from cities, nor were men available from Pansa's army or a new levy. The consul was annoyed that so many volunteers were going to join Brutus (*Ad Brut.* 4. 3–4). Cicero sent Brutus a further letter, perhaps on 14 April, expressing surprise, that, when letters from Brutus and C. Antonius were read in the senate four days earlier, the latter was still styled proconsul and it was clear that Brutus was treating him with respect.[107] Cicero here displays in private the same attitude that we have found in the speeches. Liberty is a greater priority than peace.[108] He admits to having had a more aggressive attitude than Brutus, wanting to liberate the *res publica* not only from a tyrant but from tyranny. Brutus had

---

[103] *Ad Brut.* 2. 3; 3. 2; *Fam.* 12. 11. The details are from Cassius' note.

[104] The 'breaking' of Servilius seems to have come on the second day of debate (*Fam.* 10. 12. 4; *Ad Brut.* 2. 3).

[105] *Ad Brut.* 3. 2–3. Cicero replied that the story had been circulated before Brutus' letter arrived.

[106] *Ad Brut.* 3. 4–6. SB *QFBrut*, p. 228 points out that *adversus Pansam* (5) may mean simply 'vis-à-vis Pansa', not 'against Pansa'. Cicero understood it to mean the diversion of the consul's troops (*Ad Brut.* 4. 4), but it is not clear if this is what Brutus meant.

[107] *Ad Brut.* 5. 4–5. The letter seems to have been written before the agitation that preceded the news from Forum Gallorum. This casts doubt on the date of dispatch in the MSS (6), 19 April. See SB *QFBrut*, p. 229.

[108] *Ad Brut.* 5. 1; cf. *Phil.* 4. 14–16; 7. 7–9, 25–7; 13. 1–7, 15–16.

thought otherwise, and in consequence they would have been in Antonius' power, unless Caesar Octavianus had been inspired by some god (*Ad Brut.* 5. 1–2). At the end of the letter he tells Brutus in effect that he should kill C. Antonius: no distinction can be made between any of the three Antonii and Dolabella. This is not the time for clemency. People do not expect him to be casual or cruel. Moderation means that he should be severe with leaders but merciful to soldiers (ibid. 5). A further letter from Brutus, lost to us, argued that more zeal was to be displayed in preventing civil war than in exercising wrath on the defeated. To this Cicero replied that salutary severity was superior to an empty display of clemency; 'if our wish is to be clement, there will never be a shortage of civil wars'.[109]

By early April Cicero would also have received news from Asinius Pollio, the governor of Further Spain, who had been asked by Pansa to inform the senate of his readiness to obey their instructions. He told Cicero, and had apparently pointed out in an official dispatch, that he could not help in Italy while Lepidus, who was openly admitting his alliance with Antonius, barred his route in Gaul.[110] Nevertheless he had publicly announced at Corduba that he would surrender his province to no one who had not been properly appointed by the senate, and he had refused to send Lepidus the Thirtieth Legion.[111] His instinctive desire was for both peace and liberty. He had regretted the original civil war. With enemies on both sides he had avoided the Pompeians, because he would have been exposed to an enemy there. Although he had joined Caesar reluctantly, he had been warmly received and gave Caesar in return his loyalty. However, the compulsion under which he had been to obey Caesar's orders had taught him the value of liberty and the misfortune of subjection to one man. Hence he was an enemy of anyone with this ambition. He claimed simultaneously a wish to spare the lives of citizens and a readiness to defend the liberty of the *res publica* by force.[112]

On 20 April Cicero got news of the battle of Forum Gallorum, which had been fought about five days before.[113] His informant was Servius Sulpicius

---

[109] *Ad Brut.* 8. 2, sent on 20 April, according to the MSS; if so, before the news of Forum Gallorum arrived.

[110] *Fam.* 10. 31. 4, 6. The letter was written on 16 March, immediately after the arrival of Pansa's.

[111] As he had earlier refused Antonius the Twenty-Eighth Legion (ibid. 5, cf. *Fam.* 10. 32. 4).

[112] *Fam.* 10. 31. 2–3, 5. On the phrase *vindicare in libertatem*, already used by Caesar (*BCiv.* 1. 22. 5) and to be used by his son (*RG* 1. 1) see VRR 29–31, 52. In the twenties BC Augustus was to celebrate both being *vindex libertatis* and saving citizen's lives (*EJ*² 18, 19; *RG* 34. 2).

[113] *Ad Brut.* 9. 2 gives the date of the news arriving at Rome. The MS text of the date of dispatch of *Fam.* 10. 30 is corrupt. It should be either 15 April (a.d. XVII K. Mai) or 16 (a.d. XVI. K. Mai.), not a.d. XII kal. Mai. Octavianus was first hailed *imperator* on a day after the victory

Galba (*Fam.* 10. 30). Galba had been escorting Pansa's legions of recruits to Hirtius' camp. The force of veterans he led included the Martian legion which had mutinied from Antonius. When the latter sent some cavalry and light-armed troops to harass Galba's force, his men could not be restrained from counter-attacking, and after they had made their way though a gap between woods and a marsh, Galba drew them up in line-of-battle. Pansa was bringing his two legions of recruits to join him, when Antonius brought his legions out of the village of Forum Gallorum. The battle was bitterly fought on either side of the via Aemilia. From Galba's description it appears that their left and centre were eventually pushed back by Antonius, while he himself on the right advanced too far in his attack and was nearly cut off. However, Antonius in turn overstretched himself with an attack on his opponents' camp and suffered further serious loss during his return to his own, eventually losing two legionary eagles and sixty standards.

The following day, the festival of the Parilia associated with Romulus (*Phil.* 14. 14), the senate met and Cicero delivered the last of the speeches published as the *Philippics* and the last of his speeches that we actually possess. The news had led to a proposal that the city should return to civilian clothing on the ground that the military threat was over. Cicero opposed this, suspecting that it was a plot by those who wished to diminish the significance of the liberation of D. Brutus, which, he maintained, had been the whole object of the war (*Phil.* 14. 1–5). A further proposal had been made by Servilius Isauricus for thanksgiving to the gods. Cicero declared his wish that the 'wicked and lawless men' over whom the victory had been won should be called by their true name, 'enemies' (ibid. 6–11).[114] The number of days of thanksgiving should be increased and the victorious leaders should be given the title of *imperator*, especially as he himself had been escorted to the Capitol and back the day before in a quasi-triumphal procession (ibid. 11–12).

Why was he talking about himself? It was reluctantly, because over the last three or four days, when gloomy rumours from Mutina were circulating, there had also been a maliciously manufactured story that he would take up the *fasces* on the Parilia (that is, as consul or dictator). The conspirators would have given him the *fasces* and then arranged that he and the senate should be

---

(*Feriale Cumanum*, *Inscr. It.* xiii. 2, pp. 279, 442); the two days are restored in that text as 15 and 16 April, following the date (*xvii K.*) in Ovid, *Fasti*, 4. 673.

[114] He tendentiously describes the terms *improbi* and *audaces*—which he had used himself for political opponents, including Antonius and his supporters (*Phil.* 12. 15, cf. 6. 6.), Catiline, and Clodius—as suitable for urban lawsuits against those who forge wills, expel neighbours by force, or defraud minors (7). On the terms *audaces/audacia* see Wirszubski, 1961, who has shown their association with radicalism, demagogery, and revolution, a usage which was already established when Cicero was a young man.

assassinated. Cicero had squashed the story about the *fasces* in an address to the people, made possible by the tribune P. Apuleius; the people believed him, not the story, and within two or three hours the arrival of the messengers turned the event into a celebration (ibid. 13–16).[115] It all showed the dangers of envy and the wrong kind of political rivalry. True judgement would lead men to recognize that this was a war and Antonius was an enemy (ibid. 17–22). Cicero returns briefly to his argument about *hostes* before moving on to praise the commanders in an account of the battle. Galba had no doubt written to Cicero in search of commendation from the senate, and in this he failed. Cicero's narrative, deriving as it did from Hirtius' despatches, enhanced the heroism of the three commanders—Pansa for leading the assault and suffering serious wounds, Hirtius for retrieving the earlier defeat by counter-attack, and Octavianus for defending the camp (ibid. 25–9). As for the soldiers, their bravery would be best commemorated first by a war-memorial, secondly by bounties to the survivors and the relatives of the dead (29–35). These proposals are finally summed up in a formal *sententia* (36–8).[116]

On 27 April Rome knew of the battle of Mutina. Antonius was in flight but Hirtius had died in the battle and Pansa was dead of his wounds at Forum Gallorum—'good consuls but no more than good' (*Ad Brut.* 10). The senate reacted by declaring that Antonius' followers were public enemies and military action should be taken against them: Cicero at last had his wish. Servilius Isauricus added to his motion two proposals, one specifically about Ventidius Bassus (on his way to join Antonius with fresh troops) and another, that Cassius should make war on Dolabella. Cicero added a rider that Marcus Brutus should have the option of undertaking this war, if he thought it in the public interest; as for C. Antonius, Brutus should make a report to the senate about him (*Ad Brut.* 10, 13. 1) In the meantime Cicero wanted Brutus' support for the cooption of his son into the priesthood of *pontifices* (*Ad Brut.* 13. 3). Cicero's contributions either to the debate on the 27th or to any subsequent debate are not preserved and seem never to have been circulated by Cicero or Atticus. Was this because Cicero thought that there was no need, now that Antonius had been defeated? Did Cicero delay and then give up through despair over the fruitlessness of the victory? Or did the prudent

---

[115] Most of this colourful story is missing in a letter to Brutus, probably written just after the debate on the 21st (*Ad Brut.* 9. 2).

[116] The proposal for a war-memorial (30) was, as Cicero admits, contrary to Roman practice (33), and seems to be an attempt to imitate what had been Greek practice since the end of the Archaic period. Cicero had certainly seen such memorials at Athens (note the walk from the Dipylon gate in *Fin.* 5. 1), but he may also have been influenced by reading Pericles' funeral speech in Thucydides.

Atticus, whose reaction to Mutina was to protect Antonius' family and friends, decide that enough had been done to offend Antonius and put an end to their circulation?[117] The somewhat desperate defiance that we see in Cicero's last letters is perhaps in favour of the last possibility.

It is appropriate here to review the historical importance of the *Philippics* as a whole. Their survival can easily induce the historian to see the political campaign against Antonius as a personal crusade by Cicero. Of course he played an important part. That can be inferred from Antonius' letter and the attempt to discredit Cicero before the news of Forum Gallorum arrived (*Phil.* 14. 13–16). However, political initiative in the Republic centred on the consuls—without their leadership, especially that of Pansa after Hirtius had left Rome in January, the siege of Mutina would not have been lifted—nor were senate decisions formed for the most part by Cicero's proposals. His motion on 20 December secured the official recognition of Decimus Brutus as governor of Cisalpine Gaul and was a pathfinder for some of the decisions taken at the beginning of January (*Phil.* 3. 37–9). However, his proposal on 1 January for an immediate recognition of a state of war with Antonius was not accepted (*Phil.* 5. 31–4, 6. 2–3). Later his outstanding success was to secure the confirmation of Marcus Brutus' command in Macedonia in February (*Phil.* 10. 25–6). His attempt at the end of that month to secure Cassius a supreme command in the East (*Phil.* 11. 30–1) failed at the time: a more modest form of recognition for Cassius was only obtained after Mutina on Servilius Isauricus' motion (*Ad Brut.* 13. 1). If we look for minor sucesses, it may well be that Cicero's amendment to Isauricus' motion about funeral honours for Servius Sulpicius Rufus was carried (*Phil.* 11. 15–17), likewise the amendment to increase the number of days of thanksgiving after Forum Gallorum (*Phil.* 14. 36–7). Other minor successes—the votes of thanks for Cornificius and Plancus, and the rider to Isauricus' proposal on 27 April—are recorded in letters but not in preserved speeches.[118]

An obvious restriction on his leadership was the order of debate. In December he seems to have been called first by the tribunes. After the New Year there is no evidence that that he was ever in that position. On 1 January he spoke second after a supporter of peace; the seventh and ninth *Philippics* followed motions by Isauricus. The eighth *Philippic* came the day after a debate in which L. Caesar seems to have taken the lead. Cicero may have spoken first the second day but we cannot tell. The tenth *Philippic* overthrew a

---

[117] Nepos, *Att.* 9. 3–7. If it is thought that some sort of artistic reason determined the conclusion of the published corpus of speeches (the proposal for a war-memorial being a suitable coda), then this is unlikely to be Cicero's own decision. He would surely have wanted to end with a celebration of Antonius' second defeat and the liberation of D. Brutus.

[118] *Fam.* 12. 25. 1; 10. 12. 2–4; *Ad Brut.* 13. 1.

motion by Fufius Calenus; the eleventh followed speeches by L. Caesar and Servilius Isauricus; on the occasions of the twelfth and thirteenth orations Cicero again spoke after Isauricus, and the fourteenth was a response to contributions by Isauricus and at least one other senator.[119] It is hard to resist the conclusion that the consuls and later the urban praetor M. Caecilius Cornutus took care to avoid giving him the chance to lead the debate, for an obvious reason. The majority of senators owed their position to the dead dictator. Not many would have approved of Caesar's murder, even if they had some affection for the republic. A significant group supported the young Caesar. Although there were few open supporters of Antonius, the consuls did not want Cicero's strongly republican language to offend the majority in the senate and so prevent them from getting senatorial approval for a policy that would keep Rome free from Antonius' domination. Nevertheless, fear of Antonius and hostility to Dolabella enabled Cicero and Servilius Isauricus to secure more recognition at Rome for the leading conspirators than might have been expected. Cicero did indeed fight for the Republic, but this fight was but one component of a complex of political and military manoeuvring which was largely out of his control.

[119] See *Fam.* 10. 28. 2; *Phil.* 5. 1, 7. 1, 27, 9. 14, 10. 3–6, 11. 19, 12. 3–5, 13. 50, 14. 2, 11.

XX

Epilogue

The death of the consuls at Mutina left a vacuum at the summit of the administration at Rome, which in the short term gave more scope to those like Cicero who were pursuing the interests of the conspirators and wished to maintain the fight with Antonius. However, the issue of filling the empty places of the consuls with suffects was divisive, while the lack of consuls restricted the possibilities of any serious initiative from Rome.[1] We possess Cicero's correspondence for three more months. It largely consists of campaign reports by commanders of armies and Cicero's replies, sometimes encouraging, sometimes revealing the fragility of the situation in Italy.

THE PROCONSULS IN THE WEST

A series of letters from Decimus Brutus documents his vain pursuit of Antonius into Transalpine Gaul. On 29 April he was at Regium Lepidi, intending to drive Antonius out of Italy and cut him off from Ventidius. He was hoping for help from Lepidus, Pollio, and Plancus. He had no illusions about Lepidus' reliability but seems to have expected him to abandon his former alliance with Antonius after the latter's defeat. Hence he wanted Cicero to write to Lepidus dissuading him from linking with Antonius.[2] On 4 May he was at Dertona, but Antonius had linked with Ventidius at Vada Sabatia on the Tyrrhenian coast: Brutus expected that he would either make for Lepidus or use the Appennines and Alps as a base for raiding. He commented bitterly that Caesar Octavianus had not listened to him or crossed the Appennines, but one could not give orders to Caesar nor could Caesar give orders to his army. The opposition at Rome to any honours for him did not worry him, but he wanted a solution to his money problems. He was trying to maintain seven legions, but had already spent the 40 million sesterces he possessed and was borrowing on his own security and that of his

---

[1] Cf. D. Brutus' comment in *Fam.* 11. 10. 2.
[2] *Fam.* 11. 9. 1–2. Lepidus (1) is *ventosissimus*, changeable like the wind.

friends (*Fam.* 11. 10). Two days later on his way to the Alps he knew that Antonius was going to join Lepidus (*Fam.* 11. 11). A week later he was at Pollentia, hoping that Antonius would strike north: there was a report that Antonius had asked his soldiers to follow him across the Alps since he had an agreement with Lepidus, but Ventidius' reinforcements (who outnumbered Antonius' forces in spite of the latter's desperate measures of conscription) had booed the suggestion.[3] In fact Antonius and Ventidius did not turn inland but proceeded with their journey to Transalpine Gaul, while Brutus gave up the pursuit.

A letter of Cicero in return, written in early May, would have given him little encouragement. If Antonius gained a position of strength, Cicero wrote, Decimus Brutus' resistance to him would have been in vain. If it was dangerous to meet him in battle, this was not a flight but a change of theatre of war. Public opinion had changed at Rome; people were complaining that Brutus should have finished him off (*Fam.* 11. 12). In fact a thanksgiving was made for Brutus' achievements in the middle of May, but a motion in the senate by Livius Drusus Claudianus and Paullus Lepidus, with Cicero's support, to assign the Fourth and Martian legions to Brutus, unsurprisingly did not succeed.[4] Writing to Brutus in late May (*Fam.* 11. 14), Cicero complained in that he was getting nowhere in the senate: it was no longer his instrument: Brutus would never secure the Fourth and Martian legions, but he might receive some money. Cicero shared his view that Octavianus should garrison Italy and Marcus Brutus should be summoned from Greece. They were also expecting legions from Africa.[5]

On May 24 Brutus was at Eporedia, about to cross the Alps to join Plancus (*Fam.* 11. 20. 2). He wrote to Cicero, worried at the story he had heard from Segulius Labeo about his conversation with Octavianus. The latter had been told of a remark of Cicero's that 'the young man should be praised, loaded with honours, and uplifted (removed)', and commented that he had no intention of allowing himself to be removed (*Fam.* 11. 20. 1).[6] Brutus thought that Labeo himself had retailed the remark to Octavianus or invented it. In any case there was bad feeling towards Cicero among the veterans, who resented the fact that neither Brutus nor Octavianus were on the new land-commission which had been established. Brutus believed that the veterans could be satisfied with land taken from Antonian veterans, while the four new

---

[3] *Fam.* 11. 13. Brutus seems to be replying apologetically to a now lost letter of Cicero's (cf. 1).
[4] *Fam.* 11. 18. 3, 11. 19. 1.
[5] Cf. D. Brutus' letter of early June, *Fam.* 11. 26.
[6] 'Laudandum adulescentem, ornandum, tollendum', where *tollere* means both 'to lift' and 'to take away'.

legions could be settled in the *ager Campanus* or elsewhere.[7] Monetary bounties would have to be decided by the senate after due consideration. Meanwhile he had not received from Octavianus the legion promised him from Pansa's army (ibid. 4). Cicero had reproved Brutus in a letter of 19 May for being too critical of the senate's timidity in his dispatches, when he himself appeared fearful also (*Fam.* 11. 18). Replying to Brutus' letter about Segulius Labeo on 4 June, he complained that Segulius had passed on this remark about Octavianus to everyone but did not deny that he himself had said it. He only wished that he was not on the land commission. Nevertheless he thought Brutus' advice good and had informed his colleagues that nothing should be decided before the commanders returned.[8]

Plancus had sent the senate a dispatch offering military aid which arrived two days before the victory at Mutina.[9] In successive letters Cicero urged him to complete Antonius' defeat. It appears from that of 11 May that he made a further motion about honours for Plancus from a prepared text (*Fam.* 10. 13). Before the news of Mutina reached him, Plancus had headed south across the Rhône with the intention, he implied to Cicero, of joining in that battle. When the news came, it was clear that Antonius' last hopes were Lepidus himself and his army. Plancus was nevertheless holding back, fearful of the reaction of that army, especially the veteran Tenth Legion, which he himself had recalled to the standards and was now with Lepidus (*Fam.* 10. 11. 2). His plan was to put an end to Cicero's worries by an alliance with Lepidus. His brother Titus, M. Iuventius Laterensis, and C. Furnius would be his agents (ibid. 3). A letter of early May reveals the negotiations in progress with Laterensis the important intermediary.[10] Plancus asserted—apparently sincerely, but we do not know with what confidence—that he hoped to control 'the part of Lepidus' army that was corrupted and alienated from the *res publica*'. Hence on 9 May he crossed the river Isère southwards and two days later, when he heard that L. Antonius had arrived with the Antonian advanced guard at Forum Iulii, sent his brother Titus with 4,000 cavalry to block his path.[11]

The situation changed almost immediately. Lepidus sent him an orderly telling him not to come. He was going to press on regardless, but a desperate letter from Laterensis followed, complaining about Lepidus' breach of trust

---

[7] *Fam.* 11. 20. 1–3. The earlier MSS refer to the 'agris Silani' before the Campanian land; later MSS and early editors to the 'agris Sullanis'. 'Sullan land' may well mean land confiscated in Sullan proscriptions, such as that of Volaterrae and Arretium, cf. *Fam.* 13. 4; *Lib. Colon.* 214L; and see above, Ch. XI with n. 50.

[8] *Fam.* 11. 21. 1–2, 5, reading in 5 *vobis*, not *nobis* as in the older MSS.

[9] Or perhaps before the *news* of the victory at Mutina, *Fam.* 10. 14. 1.

[10] It is interesting that ten of Lepidus' small force of cavalry joined Plancus. These may have not been allies but upper-class Romans (*Fam.* 10. 15. 2).

[11] *Fam.* 10. 15. 3–4, following the emendations of Watt's OCT to the dates in the MSS.

which had left him in the lurch: when Lepidus had been addressing his troops, soldiers, who had been corrupted by their officers (men like Canidius and Rufrenus), cried out that they wanted peace, now that two consuls and many of their fellow citizens had been killed and the rest had been treated as public enemies. Plancus' first reaction to this was to hold back and guard his own province (*Fam.* 10. 21). However, on 18 May, after leaving forts and guards to protect the crossing of the Isère for D. Brutus when he arrived, he decided to move further south himself. The army of Lepidus was of critical importance; Plancus claimed to be confident that he could have defeated Antonius' and Ventidius' forces (*Fam.* 10. 18. 3–5). However, his cavalry seem to have failed in their mission of impeding the Antonian advance. We hear in a later letter that he was sending his brother back to Rome, on the ground that he had not sufficiently recovered from a previous illness. By then he had learnt that Antonius and the advanced guard were at Forum Iulii with Ventidius two days march behind, while Lepidus was at Forum Voconii, 24 miles from Antonius (*Fam.* 10. 17. 1–2).

Lepidus sent to Cicero about the same time a formal dispatch explaining that he had advanced beyond Forum Voconii to the river Argens near Forum Iulii, where he faced the Antonian army. Two of his officers, Silanus and Culleo, who had previously joined Antonius, had returned to him, but his infantry and cavalrymen were deserting in numbers (*Fam.* 10. 34).[12] This letter was suitable to be read aloud in the senate, if need be. On May 22 Lepidus followed this with a more personal letter, asking him in the light of their previous good relationship to defend him against his critics (*Fam.* 10. 34a). By 30 May it was all over. In a formal letter to the senate, people, and plebs Lepidus confessed that, although he had tried to make the lives and liberty of the people as a whole his priority, fortune had wrenched from his grasp his personal autonomy. By means of a mutiny the army had maintained its customary attitude to the preservation of citizens' lives and peace in the community and, to tell the truth, had compelled him to support the cause of the safety and security of Roman citizens. He asked the senate not to treat the clemency he and his army were showing in a civil war as a crime. It would be far better for them to protect the safety and status of everyone (*Fam.* 10. 35).

Plancus' version of what happened was sent to Cicero on 6 June. He began by apologizing for trusting Lepidus. He had advanced to a good defensive position forty miles away from the forces of Lepidus and Antonius.[13] Lepidus,

---

[12] M. Iunius Silanus had commanded a unit at Forum Gallorum (*Fam.* 10. 30. 1); Terentius Culleo had been in charge of the passes through the Maritime Alps (App. *BCiv.* 3. 83. 340). See *MRR* ii. 353, 356.

[13] *Fam.* 10. 23. 1–2. Plancus calls this position 'almost in view of Lepidus and Antonius'.

having given up hope of Plancus' support, made an alliance with Antonius on 29 May and immediately advanced towards Plancus. Plancus realized this when Lepidus was twenty miles away and immediately retreated (he congratulates himself in the letter on the good order with which this was done). On 4 June he crossed back over the Isère and broke his bridge. He was waiting for D. Brutus, whom he expected to arrive in three days (*Fam.* 10. 23. 2–3). Meanwhile, Laterensis, whose patriotism was in Plancus' view counterbalanced by naivety in relation to Lepidus, had tried to commit suicide but had been prevented from so doing. Plancus proudly professed that he had rejected all contact with the 'parricides' who were as hostile to him as their fatherland. He ended the letter by requesting Cicero to continue to support those who stood in the battleline. Caesar should come with the strongest forces he had, or, if the man himself was prevented, he should send his army, which was in great peril on its own account (ibid. 4–6). Shortly after this Plancus and Brutus sent a joint letter to the senate and people. Its beginning is missing, but it appears that Antonius and Lepidus had had an unsuccessful skirmish with the cavalry and auxiliaries of Plancus and Brutus south of the Isère. The writers of the letter were, however, afraid of their opponents' crossing the Isère and requested further support (*Fam.* 11. 13a).

Plancus' correspondence does not inspire trust. He desperately seeks to defend himself for any decision and always has half an eye on how his actions would be interpreted afterwards. It would have been more prudent, he says, to wait for Brutus at the Isère, but if he had failed to help Lepidus, who was his personal enemy, when he was taking the right course, it would have been put down to obstinacy or cowardice (*Fam.* 10. 18. 2). He had been credulous about Lepidus, in spite of the fact that he knew the man. It was a sense of shame that his critics might believe that he was too embittered towards Lepidus, which had led him to take the risk of approaching him (10. 23. 1). Plancus also over-dramatizes: Lepidus' orderly forbade him to come the moment he crossed the Isère, yet he pressed on (10. 21. 2). However, it appears that he had time to secure the bridge with forts and move forward beforehand (10. 18. 4). Forty miles away he claims that he was almost in sight of Lepidus and Antonius (10. 23. 2). Nevertheless, in spite of Antonius' claim in the letter to Hirtius and Octavianus,[14] it is clear that, given a choice, Plancus preferred the position of someone loyal to senate and people to that of an ally of Antonius and Lepidus.

Lepidus evidently inspired little trust at the time.[15] He seems to have been prepared to abandon Antonius at the news of Mutina, but was soon brought back to his former loyalty. One should not underestimate the pressure

---

[14] *Phil.* 13. 44.   [15] *Fam.* 11. 9. 1; 10. 23. 1.

brought to bear on him. Silanus must have brought back horrific reports of the casualties at Forum Gallorum and Mutina, which would have produced a bitter reaction among the former soldiers of Caesar who believed in the solidarity of old comrades. What happened at the bridge over the Argens is a genuine turning-point in history. Serving soldiers, not their commanders, did take control of politics—not to make war, but to avoid it.[16]

By the middle of June Cicero had heard the news about Lepidus. He wrote a brief note to Decimus Brutus, telling him that all hopes now depended on him and Plancus. There was a real sickness in the city, which only the arrival of Marcus Brutus could cure.[17] Decimus Brutus had already sent dispatches to the senate and Cicero, reiterating his need for money and arguing that the senate should decide from where they should summon reinforcements (*Fam.* 11. 26). We have no more correspondence from Plancus until a last despairing letter at the end of July.[18]

One important player remained on the fringe of these events, the governor of Further Spain, Asinius Pollio. He wrote to Cicero when the news of Mutina reached him at the beginning of June. He explained that he had not realized how much he would have helped, if he had come to Italy: he could have prevented the battle. Anyone who took pleasure in the fact that Caesar's commanders and veterans had perished would regret in the future the devastation inflicted on Italy. Both sides seemed so eager for battle that it appeared that their greatest fear was a settlement that did no harm to the *res publica* (*Fam.* 10. 33. 1–3).[19] Pollio carefully lists later in the letter (4) the destruction of the Martian legion and the deaths among the officers (there was even a distressing rumour that Octavianus had died). He clearly has no great opinion of Lepidus, who had held back the messengers travelling to him for nine days, but mentions his friendship with both Antonius and Plancus. The final paragraph contains a suggestion that he may be leading his army to Italy without waiting to hear from the senate (ibid. 3, 5).

A second letter sent on 8 June first describes the cruel and corrupt behaviour of his quaestor, the younger Balbus, especially at Gades: Balbus had now fled to Mauretania with his ill-gotten gains (*Fam.* 10. 32. 1–3).[20] Pollio then

---

[16] This was an important precedent for the reconciliation between the troops of Octavianus and Antonius at Brundisium in 40 BC (App. *BCiv.* 5. 59. 246–8).

[17] *Fam.* 11. 25 (18 June). On 6 June Cicero was still ignorant of developments in Gaul (ibid. 24. 1).

[18] *Fam.* 10. 24 is discussed below. Cicero writes a brief note explaining the difficulty in making provision for land for Plancus' soldiers (*Fam.* 10. 22).

[19] The delay was caused by the time taken by the messengers to reach the south of Spain (*Fam.* 10. 31. 5).

[20] On Balbus' disregard of the status of Roman citizen and the right of *provocatio* see VRR 14; Lintott, 1972a, 231, 251–2. Balbus had shown his self-importance by commissioning a *fabula*

asked Cicero's advice. He had three legions, one of which Antonius had tried to tempt at the beginning of the campaign by an offer of 500 *denarii* a soldier immediately and bounties after service: he was still being urged by Antonius and Lepidus to put all three under their command. He took pride in the fact that he had not allowed his soldiers either to sell themselves in the military auction or to desert in face of possible dangers. His reward had been the preservation of the *res publica*, but the *res publica* and the senate majority had not known how to use his loyalty (ibid. 4–5). Pollio combined a devotion to constitutional behaviour with a loyalty similar to that of a Caesarian veteran, which Cicero would not have found comforting.

THE COMMANDERS IN AFRICA AND THE EAST

Africa was securely in the hands of Quintus Cornificius, with whom Cicero had a good relationship. Cicero's last letters to him are more concerned with businessmen who had legal problems than with matters of state.[21] Cornificius was still seeking money for his soldiers. In March Cicero had told him to raise it by exactions or loans; he now talked about the unbelievable shortage of public money and added the opinion that it could be only raised by direct taxation (*tributum*).[22]

The news from the East was more encouraging. In a dispatch sent on 7 May (*Fam.* 12. 12) Cassius thanked Cicero for encouraging him to seize control of the eastern armies and justifying his actions at Rome, and asked him to defend the actions of the soldiers and their commanders Staius Murcus and Marcius Crispus. The army he possessed belonged to the senate and all the best men, and especially Cicero, whom it held in wonderful affection (4). Cassius was about to set off for Cilicia to confront Dolabella. About the middle of the month Cicero passed on the news about Lepidus in brief notes, stressing how much now depended on Cassius and Marcus Brutus (*Fam.* 12. 8–9). At the beginning of July he was able to tell Cassius that by virtue of a decree of 30 June Lepidus and all those 'who had defected from the *res publica* with him' had been declared public enemies. The senate had been courageous but in the hope of Cassius' support. Cicero was awaiting news of a

---

praetexta to celebrate an embassy he had made during the civil war, a copy of which was with Pollio's friend Cornelius Gallus (*Fam.* 10. 32. 3, 5).

[21] *Fam.* 12. 26–7, 29–30; esp. 30. 1 on the businessmen themselves conveying the letters. One of those whose agents were involved was L. Aelius Lamia, now a senator, who as an *eques* had been relegated by Gabinius in 58 after leading a demonstration on behalf of Cicero (*Fam.* 12. 29. 2).

[22] *Fam.* 12. 28. 2, 30. 4

victory so that he could reward the army in whatever way he could. He therefore hoped to see Cassius in Italy as soon as possible. Lepidus was now more unpopular than Antonius ever was. The consuls designate were drawn up against him, but they might not be enough (*Fam.* 12. 10).

Historians who judge in the light of later events may simply regard this invitation as a sign of Cicero's lack of realism about the civil war. It is more relevant to reflect on the origin of Cicero's hope, which must be Sulla's return from the East in 83—one of the most significant events in his youth. Whereas Cicero was critical of Pompey's adoption of a Sullan policy in the civil war, when Pompey could, in his opinion, have stayed in Italy and either compromised or fought there, these choices had not been open to Cassius and Marcus Brutus. The tyrannicides had been forced to secure the East and militarily such a policy had led to Sulla's victory.

Reports on the campaign against Dolabella came from Trebonius' quaestor, Lentulus Spinther, on 4 June,[23] and from Cassius of Parma, one of the tyrannicides, on 15 June. Lentulus had returned to Asia from his temporary refuge with Marcus Brutus in order to fulfil his function of collecting the taxes and sending them to Rome, but had been distracted by discovering that Dolabella not only had a war fleet but had acquired more than 100 freighters on which to embark his troops: these he intended to sail back to Italy, if he failed to retake Syria.[24] Lentulus had sailed to Rhodes, whose authorities had sent embassies and given aid to Dolabella, and found no cooperation: they had shut their gates and port and denied supplies, refusing to believe that Dolabella was a public enemy (*Fam.* 12. 15. 2–4). It is clear that they had been convinced by Dolabella that he represented the legitimate authority of Rome. Lentulus, writing officially, refers to the treaty sworn in 51, in which it was agreed 'to have the same enemies as the senate and Roman people' and complains about 'the diminution of the majesty' not only of his own authority but of that of the Roman people; to Cicero he refers to the Rhodian embracement of the Caesarian cause after Pharsalus.[25] The Rhodian obstruction did Dolabella no good. His captains fled, his war-ships scattered, and the freighters were recovered in Lycia and returned to their owners (*Fam.* 12. 14. 1, 12. 15. 5). When Lentulus was in Pamphylia he obtained further information from deserters that Dolabella had failed to take Antioch, suffering serious losses, and had moved on towards Laodicea, where Cassius was planning to confront him (*Fam.* 12. 15. 7, 12. 14. 4).

---

[23] *Fam.* 12. 15 was an official letter to the senate, people, and plebs; 12. 14 was sent to Cicero at the same time.
[24] *Fam.* 12. 14. 1, 12. 15. 1–2, 6.
[25] *Fam.* 12. 15. 2–3, 12. 14. 2–3. The language about the treaty is appropriate to one in which there was express subordination to Rome.

Much of Lentulus' letter to Cicero is devoted to advancing his own career with Cicero's assistance. Asia had been intended as the consular province of Hirtius and Pansa (of whose deaths Lentulus was still ignorant) and they had permission to appoint deputies. Lentulus wanted to be the deputy (he would have become a *pro quaestore pro praetore*) until their leisurely, as he hoped, arrival (*Fam.* 12. 14. 4–5). Lentulus expected that they would not leave Rome before their consulships had ended (this is important evidence that even after Sulla consuls could take up provincial commands in their year of office, if they wished).[26] His provincial task had been arduous and dangerous, but he wanted to finish it properly: in particular he wished to collect the tax-money due to be transferred to Rome, since much had been lost to Dolabella and he had used much to support Cassius. He claimed credit for being the first to break Antonius' provincial legislation by diverting Dolabella's cavalry and giving it to Cassius, by raising troops of his own, and generally supporting Cassius with money and soldiers. All this he had done in spite of having been a great friend of Dolabella's and having blood-ties with Antonius (ibid. 6–7).

Cassius of Parma was also interested in obtaining Cicero's recognition and patronage. He began by congratulating Cicero in a way that would have especially pleased him: as a consular he had outdone his achievements as consul; his toga had been more successful than arms; he was the source of their freedom (*Fam.* 12. 13. 1–2). The letter goes on to describe how the writer had collected a fleet from the province of Asia to pursue Dolabella's fleet under L. Figulus, who after offers of defection had eventually penned himself up in Corycus in Rough Cilicia. Cassius of Parma had therefore left him to be dealt with by another fleet under the quaestor Turullius and moved to Cyprus. His news was that after an invitation from Laodicea Dolabella had turned the town into a fortress, but was now under siege by Cassius, who had ten legions, twenty auxiliary infantry cohorts, and four thousand cavalry. The price of grain had soared and, when Cassius had been joined by his fleets, Dolabella would soon be starved out (ibid. 3–4).

MARCUS BRUTUS, CICERO, AND OCTAVIANUS

The correspondence with Marcus Brutus is of a different character. When Brutus heard about the success at Mutina, he was at pains to repeat his view that it was for the senate and people to decide on the fate of opponents who

[26] CRR 106, with further references.

had not died in the battleline: this meant that he would continue to keep C. Antonius in detention. Mercy was a preferable course than granting an infinite discretion to those in power. This led him to warn Cicero not to be too optimistic in making concessions to anyone who had acted correctly once, on the assumption that it was impossible for them to be corrupted by this generosity into undertaking bad policies (*Ad Brut.* 11).[27] By 15 May he knew both that the consuls were dead and that proposals were being made for Octavianus to be elected to one of the vacant places. There was a danger, he argued, that Antonius' defeat would be in vain, and this would be especially Cicero's fault in view of his outstanding authority, since his prudence deserted him when it came to granting honours. Even if the fault lay elsewhere, it was also Cicero's for not having corrected it. A postscript mentions a new rumour that Cicero had been made consul, which Brutus welcomed (*Ad Brut.* 12). For a time subsequent letters are mainly concerned with recommendations.[28] L. Bibulus wanted a suffect consulship; Cn. Domitius Ahenobarbus and M. Apuleius were candidates for priesthoods; Antistius Vetus was seeking a praetorship.[29] Pansa's doctor Glycon, who was married to the sister of Brutus' doctor Achilles, was in prison and needed protection from the unjust charge of murdering his patron. Cicero was to arbitrate at Flavius' request in his dispute with the city of Dyrrachium (*Ad Brut.* 14). For his part Cicero recommended to Brutus a centurion from Suessa Aurunca (*Ad Brut.* 16).

When Cicero learnt of the agreement between Lepidus and Antonius in mid-June, he wrote to complain to Brutus that he showed no sign of coming to Italy (apparently a decree of the senate had been passed encouraging him to do so) (*Ad Brut.* 18. 1–2). There was a disease at the heart of the republic, and the victory at Mutina had slipped from their grasp thanks to the failings of D. Brutus. They still had the armies of Brutus and Plancus reinforced by loyal Gauls, but Octavianus had been encouraged by people at Rome to canvass for the consulship. Cicero had sought to dissuade him by letters, had criticized his friends to their face, and exposed their plan in the senate; for its part the senate had unanimously rejected the idea. However, law and tradition were being threatened by the arrogance of commanders and the wilfulness of soldiers. It was the situation that had induced him to set out for Greece the previous year. Only Brutus and Cassius could retrieve it (ibid. 3–5).

At the news of the death of Marcus Brutus' wife Porcia, Cicero wrote a letter of consolation, and followed this with a political letter, apologizing that he

---

[27] He evidently had not yet heard of the deaths of the consuls.
[28] However, on 19 May Brutus passes on to Cicero news of Dolabella's having suffered a defeat on land at the hands of Tillius Cimber, the governor of Bithynia, and Deiotarus (*Ad Brut.* 14. 3).
[29] *Ad Brut.* 15. 1–2, 19. 1–2. Cf. 22. 1 for the election of priests.

could not comply with the pleas of Servilia and Brutus' sister Iunia (Lepidus' wife) and prevent Lepidus being declared an enemy. It was harsh that this should befall his children, but it would have been the same if he had been condemned for violence after surrendering.[30] Brutus had meanwhile written on 1 July, without knowing for sure that Lepidus had joined Antonius, asking Cicero to protect Lepidus' children (*Ad Brut.* 21). On 14 July Cicero explained once again (some letters had gone astray) that he had engineered the postponement of the election of priests to a later year. In the renewed war the army of Octavianus was of no value; it made the arrival of Brutus necessary (*Ad Brut.* 22). He also sent with Messala Corvinus an elaborate defence of his policies since the Ides of March (*Ad Brut.* 23).[31]

Here he describes his despair over the helplessness of the tyrannicides after the Ides of March, which led him to set sail for Greece (*Ad Brut.* 23. 4–5).[32] Antonius' attack on him had led to him to undertake Brutus-like policies of liberating the *res publica*. The young Caesar, without whom they would not be where they are, had been a product of these policies (ibid. 6–7). The only honour Cicero had conferrred on him had been necessary, *imperium* to command an army. It had been Philippus, Servius Sulpicius, and Servilius Isauricus who had augmented this. After Mutina he had heaped honours on D. Brutus, the dead Hirtius and Pansa, even Pontius Aquila, also Plancus. He had also proposed a triumphal entry into Rome (*ovatio*) for Octavianus. This, for reasons he could not reveal, had been a piece of prudence (ibid. 7–9).[33] As for his harsh attitude to penalties, clemency was dangerous (ibid. 10).[34] This was the first civil war in his memory in which there was not some prospect of a *res publica*, whichever side won: this time it was impossible to say what sort of *res publica* the victors would have, the vanquished would have none. His severity against Antonius and Lepidus was also required as deterrent. The harsh consequences for children of their parent's punishment had been a common feature of societies since ancient times (Cicero cites one of his favourite exemplars, Themistocles). What could anyone complain about Cicero's cruelty, when he would have to confess that he would have been even more cruel to Cicero if victorious? He was in fact doing his best for Lepidus' children as the letters of Servilia and Iunia would attest. (ibid. 11–13)

---

[30] *Ad Brut.* 17; 20. 1–3. The second letter must be dated shortly after the senate's declaration on 30 June that Lepidus was a *hostis* (*Fam.* 12. 10. 1).

[31] Corvinus: *Ad Brut.* 23. 1, cf. 20. 1.

[32] Brutus too had been 'giving way' (*cedere*), since it was not possible, according to the Stoics, for a wise man to flee (*fugere*).

[33] The friends of Brutus who had opposed this (9) were perhaps Paullus Aemilius Lepidus and M. Livius Drusus Claudianus, perhaps also Sex. Quinctilius Varus (cf. *Fam.* 11. 19. 1; Vell. 2. 71. 3).

[34] Cf. his quotation of Solon (ibid. 3) that a community was maintained by rewards and penalties.

Epilogue

There is a final letter to Brutus on 27 July. Servilia had invited Cicero to a conference two days earlier, to which Servilius Casca, Antistius Labeo, and Scaptius also came. The question was, should Brutus return to Italy immediately or stay longer in Macedonia?[35] Cicero argued that Brutus' return was essential to prop up the collapsing *res publica*. We are not told what, if anything, was decided. Cicero then expresses regrets to Brutus over his pledge about the young Caesar. Standing security for someone's intentions was more serious and problematic than standing security for a debt. He nonetheless hoped to hang on to the young man in spite of resistance from many (ibid. 2–3). There was still a desperate shortage of money. A 1% levy on capital based on a grossly inadequate census had only produced enough for bounties to two legions. Infinite amounts were still needed for the armies defending Rome at present and for that of Brutus.[36] Cicero ends by telling Brutus that he had spoken in the senate on behalf of Lepidus' children (ibid. 5–6).[37] The following day Plancus wrote to Cicero from his camp with D. Brutus in Gaul (*Fam.* 10. 24). After thanking Cicero for his efforts and pointing to the need of his soldiers for rewards, he looks at the prospects for military success. Brutus and he had seven legions, four of them veteran, in their combined army. If only they could be joined by veteran soldiers from Africa or by Octavianus' army, they could happily join battle (ibid. 1–4). Octavianus had been deaf to

---

[35] *Ad Brut.* 26. 1: Servilia is treated as the presiding magistrate, 'at illa rettulit'.

[36] In a letter to Octavianus Cicero refers to the possibility of raising 60 million sesterces through a tax on tiles (*Ad Caes. Iun.* I fr. 6). This could be a last desperate measure when the *tributum* proved inadequate. The fragments show that the volumes of this correspondence included letters from Octavianus, e. g. frr. 2, 23, 23a, and were not in strict chronological order. Book I had letters whose dates ranged from January or early February 43 (frr. 9, 12, 16) to after Mutina (10); II had three letters of March–early April (fr. 19, cf. *Phil.* 13. 31; frr. 23, 23a), one letter from after Mutina (22); one which might date as early as late November 43 (25, cf. *Phil.* 5. 24).

[37] I have not tried to take into account the texts containing elaborate accusations of Cicero's conduct in the form of letters by Brutus to Cicero and Atticus (*Ad Brut.* 24 and 25). The case against their authenticity has been well summarized by Shackleton Bailey (SB *QFBrut*, pp. 10–14). Historians needing only to refer to them as evidence have tended to accept them, but they have been impugned by scholars who have had an intimate knowledge of the whole *Ad Brutum* correspondence, especially Shackleton Bailey and Schmidt (1884, 630–5). At a time when the whole corpus of these letters was controversial Schmidt was supporting Gurlitt (1883) in arguing for the genuineness of all except these two. Apart from the inaccuracy of some of the charges in these letters, they are quite unlike the rest of Brutus' correspondence with Cicero. They cannot be explained as final bursts of exasperation when the situation was desperate. The reference to Porcia being ill but alive (25. 7) would place their writing, if by Brutus, before her death (hardly later than early June, if *Ad Brut.* 17 is dated at the end of June), and after the news of the *ovatio* voted to Octavianus (*Ad Brut* 23. 9, inaccurately called a triumph 25. 2), presumably known to Brutus about mid-May. Their tone is completely at variance with that of *Ad Brut.* 12 (15 May), which is critical but in a respectful and encouraging fashion. Moreover, if Brutus had indeed written *Ad Brut.* 24, 25, one cannot imagine that Cicero would have defended himself in the measured terms he used in July (*Ad Brut.* 23).

his requests. Like Cicero, he had tried to show goodwill to the young man. However, and he was writing more with regret than with hostility, the fact that Antonius was still alive, that Lepidus was with him, that they had far from contemptible forces, hope, and courage, those two could regard as a debt they owed to Octavianus. With his help the armies of Plancus and D. Brutus could have finished the war. He could not understand what had made Octavianus change his mind and seek a two-month consulship through demands backed by terror (ibid. 5–6).

In less than a month Octavianus was consul after a coup d'état and a strange election by two quasi-consuls, since in the absence of patricians no *interrex* was available.[38] We have nothing in our surviving Cicero texts about this—or perhaps almost nothing. There is a fragment from Cicero's correspondence with Octavianus which reads, 'I am doubly glad that you grant Philippus and me a vacation. For you both pardon what has happened in the past and allow us a future.'[39] Cicero and Philippus were presumably freed from attendance at the senate. How far Cicero was in fact deluded by this action, we cannot tell. Q. Pedius, Caesar's nephew and Octavianus' consular colleague soon passed a law providing for special prosecutions of the conspirators against the dictator. Three months later Octavianus met Antonius and Lepidus near Bononia and initiated the Triumvirate and the proscription of their opponents. For the circumstances of Cicero's death our fullest source is Plutarch's life, which seems to derive from Tiro's biography.[40] Livy remarked that 'his death could appear on a fair valuation less undeserved, because he was likely to suffer from a victorious enemy nothing more cruel that what he would have done to the vanquished if he had had the same good fortune.'[41] Cicero himself had put this the other way round, writing to Brutus: he was only advocating what men like Lepidus would do to him if victorious (*Ad Brut.* 23. 11). As for his own death at the hands of Antonius, he was already anticipating this when civil war loomed in summer 44.[42] It was not that he was a danger to the Caesarians, either then or now after Octavianus had seized Rome: the experience of the civil wars of his youth had taught him that those in power took reprisals against opponents, not so much for what they had actually done or might do, but for what they represented. Moreover,

---

[38] Fasti, EJ², p. 50; App. *BCiv.* 3. 89. 363–94. 387; Dio 46. 43. 5–45. 4; other sources *MRR* ii. 336.

[39] *Ep. ad Caes. Iun.* II. 23B; Gelzer, 1969, 405.

[40] The chief sources on the *Lex Pedia* are Dio 46. 48. 2–49. 5; App. *BCiv.* 3. 95. 392–3; on the creation of the triumvirate and the proscriptions Dio 46. 54–6, 47. 3–13; App. *BCiv.* 4. 2–30; on Cicero's own death Plut. *Cic.* 47–9, esp. 49. 4 (Tiro). See on the latter Homeyer, 1964, esp. 5–16.; on the proscriptions Hinard, 1985, 227–318.

[41] Sen. *Suas.* 6. 17, 22.   [42] *Att.* 15. 18. 2, 15. 20. 2.

Sulla had shown how proscription was a convenient way of legitimizing the seizure of property.

Cicero had had no illusions about Octavianus in November 44 (*Att.* 16. 15. 3). From his return to Rome in December 44 he supported him with his eyes open, viewing him as a necessary instrument against Antonius.[43] Other consulars for diverse motives promoted Octavianus with even greater enthusiasm—his stepfather Philippus, Servilius Isauricus, even Servius Sulpicius Rufus (*Ad Brut.* 23. 7). We cannot tell how far Cicero trusted Octavianus, nor how much confidence he had in the survival of the republic. One has only to read the letters concerned with support for forthcoming elections to realize that, if the charge of naïve optimism is to be laid, it should be laid against not only Cicero but others.[44] It has already been argued that after December 44 Cicero was not the prime mover in the war against Antonius (Ch. XIX). It of course suited Antonius to represent him as such, because he was a Pompeian (*Phil.* 13. 38, 40). Cicero does, however, seem to have been the senior advocate for the conspirators in the senate, and was clearly regarded by them as a source of patronage for themselves and their supporters, as their letters to him show.

The passion of the *Philippics* was not a rhetorical pose; it reflected the genuine excitement of someone involved in a political and personal crisis, which, however uncertain the outcome, gives a greater significance to life than normal. This can be seen in Cicero's letters to the conspirators, at least until the combination of Lepidus and Antonius became known. Even before this Cicero vainly hoped that Marcus Brutus would come to Italy to rescue the situation: it would have been a replay of the return of Sulla in 83. Neither Brutus nor Cassius in the event imitated Sulla. Strategy and perhaps the principle of not invading the fatherland here converged. Brutus for his part, however, was not realistic in believing that republican government could return in Italy without his help.

CICERO

After, and by virtue of, his death Cicero's life soon became a weapon in the literary struggle between the new Caesar and his opponents. The denigration of Cicero implied a rehabilitation of Antonius and his supporters after the *Philippics*; it also excused the cooperation of Octavianus in his proscription.[45]

---

[43] *Ad Brut.* 23. 7–9; *Fam.* 11. 20. 1.
[44] *Fam.* 10. 25, 10. 26. 2, 12. 14. 5; *Ad Brut.* 13. 3, 15. 1–2, 19, 22. 1.
[45] On the invectives against Cicero see Gabba, 1957; Lintott, 1997a, 2514–17. For Augustan treatment of his death see Sen. *Suas.* 6.

By Tacitus' time Ciceronian eloquence could be used as a symbol of what was wrong with the late Republic (*Dial.* 36–40). Can the texts of Cicero and his correspondents enable us to reach a fairer picture, if read with prudence? The greatest frustration in any biography is our ignorance of Cicero's youth. His account in the *Brutus* of the momentous decade from the outbreak of the Social War to Sulla's dictatorship is, albeit useful for some facts, tantalizing in what it does not reveal.[46] The best indicator we have of Cicero's attitudes at that time is his reaction to the civil wars of the forties. He certainly had a horror of civil war and an admiration for a man like his mentor Q. Scaevola who, in spite of the danger to himself, would not either take sides or abandon his fatherland.[47] On the other hand, events after the Ides of March showed that, when it was clear to him that those on one side were enemies of the republic, he could be as ruthless as the most determined supporter of Sulla.[48] It is likely that the murder by the Marians of Scaevola was for Cicero a turning-point that encouraged him to abandon his connections with Marius' family and espouse Sulla's cause.[49] It can further be conjectured that he must have made a decisive move in order to convince the Sullans that he was no danger to them. He himself claims that after a peace settlement became impossible, he made his small contribution to the victory of the right side (*Rosc. Am.* 136).

His earliest pleading of private cases took place against the backdrop of the Sullan proscriptions with the encouragement of Sulla's favourite, the actor Q. Roscius. He presents the defence of Sex. Roscius the following year as a blow struck against the power of Sulla and his men (*Off.* 2. 51). However, it was not, and could not have been, undertaken as an outsider. He might lament in his conclusion the climate of violence at the time, but he could treat with an almost jesting nonchalance the deaths of those who had been accusers under the Cinnan regime.[50] His subsequent early career shows how he had learnt from his teachers not only to be a powerful and eloquent orator but to be a skilful litigant, well versed in the forensic ringcraft necessary for success in the courts. Through this he made important contacts with businessmen of equestrian and lower than equestrian status who would support him in his political career and look on him with favour when they were returned to service as jurors in criminal courts by the *lex Aurelia* of 70. His upbringing and education would not have encouraged to him to promote his political career through the tribunate and demagogic oratory before *contiones*

---

[46] *Brut.* 305–11.   [47] See Ch. XVI with nn. 70–1.
[48] Brutus on the other hand would have kept in mind what had happened to his father for supporting another Lepidus.
[49] *Rosc. Am.* 33.   [50] *Rosc. Am.* 154, 98–9.

(*Leg.* 3. 34–7). However, he had learnt from L. Crassus and Antonius how and when to deploy *popularis* arguments. His ascent to the consulship could be considered a triumph of political knowhow: at least that was the interpretation that readers could find endorsed in the *Commentariolum Petitionis*.

The consulship changed things. Circumstances required him to defend the traditional Roman order in which the good men of property triumphed over dissident aristocrats and their impoverished followers. Conscious of his achievement and his new status as consular, a new Cicero emerged to stand beside the old one, the man of optimate principle. Almost immediately in the Bona Dea affair he decided after some initial caution that he must ignore the danger of making new political enemies in favour of pursuing what he regarded as the course of political rectitude. Faced with a similar choice, when Caesar was planning his legislation in late 60, he decided not to abandon optimate principle. He saved his conscience at the price of political catastrophe at the hands of Clodius. His exile was painful but temporary. His return, however, though at first it seemed, and he certainly claimed it to be, a triumph of principle, was achieved at the cost of almost irreconcilable obligations resulting in awkward compromises. He therefore gave way to circumstances and recanted on principle in politics. In public life he did what he was required to do; he found a place for his idealism in his works on oratory and philosophy.

The governorship of Cilicia not only permitted him to put principle into practice once again, but necessitated that he did so in order to avoid the humiliation of a prosecution. He tried to carry over the new habit, when confronted with an awkward choice by the civil war. Here the principle of being neutral and a peacemaker turned out not to be as morally clean as he would have liked: if he stayed in Italy, it meant living under a regime that revolted him and abandoning someone whom for all his political disagreement he considered to be fundamentally a good man. So he joined Pompey in Greece and the atmosphere of the Republican camp too disgusted him. His return to Italy was humiliating but eventually he found happiness in a mixture of good living and philosophical writing, supported initially by vague hopes that the republic would return. However, the prospect of any sort of republic became smaller and the death of his daughter, apart from the personal loss, must have reminded him of his own mortality. The assassination of Caesar brought first uncertainty and insecurity and then, with civil war in one form or another looming, if not hope, at least a duty to pursue. Whatever effect he actually had on politics, Cicero set himself up as the standard-bearer of Republicanism and received appreciation for this. His last great works were on friendship and duties. Friendship ultimately failed him; he was left with duties, or what was left of them.

His philosophical books show two sides to him. One is that of the Academic sceptic who believes that certainty of knowledge is impossible: the best that one can hope for is probability. This entails dialogue with the deployment of arguments on both sides of the case and flexibility about ethical and political principle. Hence he can prefer Stoic ethics, where virtue is not only the supreme but the sole good, but still make allowance for the Peripatetic position where the good things of this life, 'external goods', are necessary for happiness. In politics, it allows him to regard a potentially demagogic institution such as the tribunate as a necessary evil in his community governed by the best men. The other side is that of the aspiring Stoic sage, for whom virtue is the sole good and all else indifferent. Cicero has an admiration for this ideal without ever being comfortable with it. His final works show him seeking a compromise between Stoic and Peripatetic duties and between these and the behaviour to be expected of a republican aristocrat.

A philosophical dialogue is a sociable occasion, as was the everyday life of a member of the political elite even under Caesar's dictatorship. The position of a Stoic sage was a lonely eminence; any rigid adherence to principle could be equally lonely. When Cicero aspired to a choice determined by principle, he was driven not so much by philosophy as by the heroic ideal. It is the *Iliad* that he quotes in 60–59 BC and at the onset of the civil war.[51] Cato read Plato's *Phaedo*[52] shortly before his death, but, when his hour came, it was perhaps a memory of Homer that fortified Cicero.

[51] Ch. XI n. 65. [52] Plut. *Cato mi.* 68. 2.

APPENDIX 1

The *Pro Sexto Roscio*

THIS first speech of Cicero's in a *quaestio perpetua* has not been discussed, except in passing, in the section on reading forensic oratory, since in view of the number of recent scholarly treatments, this seemed otiose. A large number of these pieces are revisionist in that they seek to change the traditional picture of Cicero bravely defending an innocent man against the machinations of a powerful satellite of Sulla, Chrysogonus, in the aftermath of the proscriptions. For a review of this work see Dyck, 2003*b* and on the proscriptions Hinard, 1985, 17–143. Towards the end of his life Cicero represented the speech to his son as a stand against the domination of Sulla in the *De Officiis* (2. 51). The fact that it is a moral exemplar for him shows that he at least believed his client innocent and unjustly accused through Sullan influence. This contrasts with his claim to have 'wrapped the jury in a cloud' in his later defence of Cluentius (Quint. 2. 17. 21). Many facts about the case remain obscure. What follows is an attempt to separate what is clear from what is not.

Sextus Roscius *pater* was killed near the Pallacine baths in Rome when returning from dinner (*Rosc. Am.*18, 126, 132) some time after 1 June 81 (128). His son Sextus was apparently not in Rome at the time and the prosecutor did not try to allege that he was (74). The father had slaves with him, none of whom seem to have been suspected of actually killing his master, though all or some of them would have been witnesses to the action and may have known the identity of the assassin. When the family property was proscribed, they passed into the hands of T. Roscius, who refused to produce two of them for questioning by the defence before the trial (77, 119–20). It is possible that they had been liberated, like the slaves of Milo in 52 (Asc. 34 C).

After the news of the murder had reached first Ameria and then Chrysogonus at Volaterrae, the father's name was entered on the list of the proscribed; his property was sold to Chrysogonus as *manceps* with T. Roscius as his partner (*socius in bonis*) (*Rosc. Am.* 21, 98, 105). There had been a terminal date of 1 June 81 in the *lex Valeria* for the proscription of the names of people and the sale of their property (128, cf. 20). However, as Stroh points out (1975, 61 ff.), there was another provision in the *lex Valeria* mentioned by Cicero, which included the property of those who died while in the armies opposing Sulla and apparently had no terminal date (126). This then would have justified the seizure of the property, if it could be pretended that Sex. Roscius *pater* had died a Marian soldier. This claim was implausible, but on the other hand it would have automatically rendered invalid any charge against someone for carrying out his murder.

After the sale of the property, T. Roscius became Chrysogonus' *procurator* (agent) for ten of the Roscian farms, while three were either passed on or sold to T. Roscius

Capito (21–3, 99). Ameria sent an embassy of ten leading men (*decem primi*) to Sulla's camp in order to protest, including Capito—no doubt not only outraged at what had happened to the Roscian estate but worried about any further inroads into Amerian land (if one wealthy local could be declared a Marian, so could others). This embassy is presented by Cicero as fruitless, but may at least have received an assurance from Chrysogonus and the Sullan nobles whom they met that the Roscian estate was an exception (24–6, 109–10). Cicero's client then fled to Rome to the house of Caecilia Metella, the sister of the consul of 98 BC Metellus Nepos and wife of Appius Claudius the future consul of 79 BC (27, 147, 149). He was later accused of parricide by C. Erucius, a man already known as an *accusator* (28, 35 ff.) Before the trial he received help from three young nobles, M. Valerius Messala, P. Scipio, and M. Metellus (77, 119, 149). The case was the first heard in 80 (Gell. 15. 28. 3) in the recently reorganized *quaestio de sicariis* presided over by M. Fannius (11–12), presumably near the beginning of the year.

The prosecution's case was apparently that, since originally it was the younger Sextus Roscius who was going to profit, he was the obvious suspect—Cicero cites the '*cui bono*' dictum of L. Cassius (84)—and that he arranged the killing by proxy through one of either his father's slaves or the professional *sicarii* who existed in abundance at Rome then (77–81). Cicero's tactics as defence advocate was to produce an alternative reconstruction, a counter-accusation—again based on the '*cui bono*' principle—that the murder was arranged by the two T. Roscii with Chrysogonus' backing (83–4, 92–135; Riggsby, 1999, 58 ff.). It is clear that these men exploited the elder Roscius' death for profit, and it must have been they who primed the professional accuser Erucius with material to bring the accusation, which had a double purpose: either Sex. Roscius would be condemned and the one person who could contest their claim to have legally confiscated his father's property would be eliminated, or he would escape the charge by admitting that his father was a Marian under the proscription law and thus liable to be killed, but by the same token lose the property (Stroh, 1975, 61 ff.).

In fact, it is perfectly possible that the elder Sex. Roscius was killed by one of the professional *sicarii*, but not on the instructions of either his son or the T. Roscii. The prosecutor admitted that murder was rife in the city. Cicero argued that the assassins (*sicarii/percussores*) and those who bought the property of the proscribed to resell (*sectores*) were part of the same group (80–1, 93–4). That there were connections between some members of each class, the *sicarii* and the *sectores*, is highly plausible, but a universal link is unlikely. The truth in this case may have been simply that the elder Roscius was killed for some reason we cannot establish, and his death was promptly exploited by the two T. Roscii.

What value has the speech for the historian? First, it shows how the proscription law could be exploited improperly, which must have contributed to the bad name that surrounded proscriptions after Sulla's retirement. Secondly, we discover how much unofficial violence accompanied the violence of the proscriptions (80, 93, 154). Thirdly, we have glimpse of the culture of the *quaestiones inter sicarios et de veneficiis*, which makes them different to the majority of the *quaestiones perpetuae* (89–91).

Murder was for the most part a vulgar, plebeian business, and so was its prosecution. There were countless professional accusers (90, cf. 56–7 for a defence of the principle, and see Lintott, 2001–3).

As for Cicero himself, while the *pro Quinctio* already shows him operating happily in the milieu of wealthy men of equestrian and sub-equestrian status who were seeking to make the best of the change in regime, the *pro Sexto Roscio* brings him into contact also with the nobility, at least its cadet members, and a powerful lady. Cicero is careful to mention Sulla only with respect: he is not responsible for the crimes of his minions (6, 25, 131, 136–9). Cicero regards his victory as the victory of the cause of the nobility and proper hierarchy, respect at home, and authority in public life (135–6). However, he cannot understand how those who could not tolerate the excessive brilliance of *equites* under the Marian/Cinnan regime could now put up with the dominance of a 'most villainous slave' like Chrysogonus (140). Cicero's expressed views were well suited to appeal to one of Sulla's new juries of senators, but his implied appreciation of the effect of Sulla's reforms is likely to be genuine, especially as an immediate reaction.

His flippant attitude in the speech to the killing of the Marian accusers, including P. Antistius (89–90), whom he later mentions with respect in the *Brutus* (225, 308, 311), is a somewhat distasteful Sullan posture. Does the speech help us to understand how, in spite of his family links with the Marii, he found a safe niche in the new regime? He states that, once it became plain that a peace settlement was impossible, he strove as far as he could for the victory of those who in fact won (136). This would date the decision after Sulla's reply to the senate's embassy in 84 BC had been rejected. However the fate of his mentor Scaevola in 82 may have been the real turning-point. Cicero compares the brutality of Roscius' accusers to that of the Marian Fimbria, as shown in the latter's violence against Scaevola and his subsequent prosecution of him in 86, allegedly on the ground that the wound had not been serious enough. Cicero then comments briefly on Scaevola's undeserved death, in spite of his work for reconciliation, at the hands of Marians as they left the city in 82 (see further Ch. XVI, with nn. 70–1). He never explains anywhere in the surviving texts what precisely he himself did before and after that. In the end the *pro Sexto Roscio* leaves the historian with as many unanswered questions about Cicero as about the Roscii.

APPENDIX 2

The *De Imperio Gnaei Pompeii* (*Pro Lege Manilia*)

APART from writings on Cicero, this speech is discussed widely in modern accounts of the period. Two interesting treatments of the rhetoric in its historical context are Steel, 2001, 140–54 (on the panegyric) and 173–81 (other aspects of the rhetoric, including the relationship to the people); Morstein-Marx, 2004, on the nature of the rhetoric in the *contio*, its purpose and effectiveness.

The tribune C. Manilius proposed a bill to entrust the command against Mithridates to Pompey probably after his bill to distribute freedmen throughout the tribes had been annulled by the senate in January 66 BC (Asc. 65, cf.45, 60, 64 C; Dio 36. 42. 2–3). The likely context is the period in the months of January and February when foreign embassies were present and the senate discussed foreign relations. It was Cicero's first address to a popular assembly. He claimed in his *prooemium* that before this he had devoted himself to defending individuals against their perils (passing over the political aspects of his prosecution of Verres): it was the *auctoritas* that he derived from his election in first place to the praetorship that encouraged him now to use his talent among those who had elected him (*Leg. Man.* 1–2). He spoke for the bill after four consulars (68)—P. Servilius Vatia Isauricus (*cos.* 79), C. Scribonius Curio (*cos.* 76), C. Cassius Longinus (*cos.* 73), and Cn. Cornelius Lentulus Clodianus (*cos.* 71). As a curule magistrate in office Cicero would have had a right to speak (Pina Polo, 1989, 43 ff.) but it is likely that Manilius, who would have been presiding over the *contio*, knew beforehand that Cicero was going to support the bill. There is no mention of Manilius in his introduction: indeed the tribune first appears when Cicero appeals to him in the peroration (69). It may be that, in view of the controversy over Manilius' previous bill about freedmen, Cicero preferred, at least initially, to distance the bill as much as possible from its proposer.

In its organization the speech resembles to some extent one pleaded in a lawsuit. The subject is indeed described as a *causa* (3–4). A major difference is that the issue to be decided is established before the narrative—a sort of *constitutio causae* (4–6), which introduces the *divisio* that Cicero plans to use: first, he will deal with the nature of the war, then its magnitude, after that the choice of commander (6). Here also we find the objectives which he believes should guide the assembly's decision, the glory of the Roman people, the security of friends and allies, and finally financial interests: the taxes of the Roman people and the private property of Roman citizens. Following this there is a narrative which tells the story of Mithridates' relations with Rome (6–26), divided into two sections, the first about the nature of the war (6–19), the second about its magnitude (20–6). When Cicero turns to the choice of commander, once again he places his conclusion before the arguments: it must be Pompey (27). A new subdivision is introduced, springing from the qualities by which a commander should be judged: military skill, virtue, authority, and good fortune (28). His military virtue is shown by a narrative culminating in his exploits against the pirates the previous year (29–35) To this Cicero adds a brief review of Pompey's pacific virtues—integrity, self-discipline, good faith, approachability, intelligence, and humanity—which stresses the contrast he makes with the generality of Roman commanders (36–42). This amounts to a denunciation of the behaviour of Rome's ruling class which is as critical, if less severe in tone, as those which he published in the Verrines (*Verr.* 4. 207; 5. 126–7). There also he had praised Pompey's clemency (5. 153). As for Pompey's authority and good fortune, these are neatly illustrated above all by the effect caused by his arrival in the neighbourhood in pursuit of the pirates (43–50).

His own case now stated, Cicero proceeded to the counter-arguments put forward by Hortensius and Catulus. Hortensius' argument that all should not be put in the hands of one supreme commander had been used against Gabinius' pirate bill the previous year and by the same token refuted by Pompey's successes (51–8). As for Catulus' appeal not to break with constitutional precedent, Cicero could refer to the extraordinary commands in the careers of Scipio Africanus and Marius and to those already received by Pompey (59–63). In conclusion he summarizes his previous arguments—only Pompey can win the necessary battles without plundering the allies (63–8); he invokes the consulars who have already advocated the bill (68), and finally appeals to Manilius to remain firm in face of force and threats, offering his own resolute support, made in the public interest, not his own (69–71). Given that Manilius had forced his previous bill through with the aid of slaves and freedmen and there had been violence over Gabinius' bill in 67, this can only have been interpreted as encouragement to Manilius to use violence again if he met with violent obstruction.

The speech, as we read it, is an elegant and effective panegyric of Pompey. Whether the great man paid much attention to it, we do not know. He seems to have had the ability to absorb praise of himself effortlessly and insensibly. Pompey's friends at Rome, however, would have taken notice. What was probably more important for Cicero at the time was the effect of his advocacy among his friends from the equestrian order. Much of the speech is devoted to highlighting the problems of businessmen and tax-collectors and encouraging his audience to identify themselves with them and their interests. The news of the war which is a threat to Rome's allies and revenues is brought to Rome by the letters of Roman knights deeply involved in tax-collection, men connected with Cicero: it is they who ask him to speak on behalf of the *res publica* and their own personal perils (4). To highlight the injury and insult inflicted by Mithridates, Cicero remarks that in the past Rome had gone to war on behalf of traders and shipowners, people of lesser status than tax-collectors (11). After dealing with the attacks on the allies he returns to the threat to tax-revenues, in particular those from the province of Asia (14). The menace inhibits economic activity, agriculture, stock-raising, maritime commerce: hence the tithes, the pasture-tax, and transit-dues are affected. Moreover, the great slave-establishments, used in tax-collecting, agriculture, and the exploitation of salt, are no longer secure (15–16). Cicero then asks his audience to recognize that it is in their interest to defend, first, the 'most respectable and well-endowed men', the *publicani*, who are the sinews of the *res publica*, then from outside the ranks of the *publicani*, the hard-working businessmen in Asia and those who have invested their money in the province (17–18)—this must have included senators, men from the equestrian order,[1] and those below equestrian rank. The collapse of their fortunes will ruin credit in Rome itself (19). The equestrian order

---

[1] It is important to notice the distinctions among the equestrian order. Cicero is appealing to a variety of businessmen and investors, not just to the *publicani*. Berry, 2003, 223 has argued that for practical purposes by this time the distinctions in the order do not matter for us. Certainly, Cicero did his best to appeal to as wide a selection of *equites* as possible, but we cannot assume, whether discussing this issue or a trial *de repetundis*, that all the *equites* in a province shared the interests of the tax-collectors, or those in different forms of business shared interests.

and business then disappears from the speech, apart from passing references to the damage to sea-trade inflicted by the pirates. After seeking to clear away any prejudice that Pompey's new appointment would be merely a concession to private interests, Cicero can suggest in his evocation of the general's career that it would contribute to the power, glory, and justice of the Roman empire. Patriotism was a far safer theme, when an orator was seeking to win over the *contio* as a whole.

APPENDIX 3

Further Notes on the *Pro Caelio*

Date

THE speech took place shortly after the acquittal of Sex. Cloelius (*Cael.* 78, cf. *QF* 2. 5. 4), which occurred in the second half of March 56. It has usually been inferred from the statement in *Cael.* 1 that the trial coincided with a festival, that Cicero spoke on the first day of Megalensia, the festival of the Mater Magna, i.e. 4 April. The days immediately following 4 April are described by Cicero in a letter (*QF* 2. 6) that also refers to a previous letter to Quintus (not preserved in the collection), one which dealt with the engagement of Cicero's daughter Tullia to Furius Crassipes on that day and other public and private business (*QF* 2. 6. 1). It would have been this earlier letter that mentioned the outcome of Caelius trial. Cicero was the last speaker at the trial, but the witnesses still remained to be heard and cross-examined, the orators would have held an *altercatio*, and the jury would have needed time to consider their verdict. So we may legitimately wonder whether Cicero's speech at the trial did in fact overlap the festival, though we may accept that the final stages of the trial did.

It was unusual (*Cael.* 1) to hold a public trial on a day that formed part of a major festival. The *lex de vi* apparently made an exception for this. If Caelius' prosecutors were looking for any convenient stick to beat him with, they may have chosen an accusation *de vi* simply for this reason. The trial also came immediately before one of the major judicial recesses, when senators and other members of the elite would go off to their country or seaside villas—Cicero was going to Anagnia, Arpinum, Pompeii, and Cumae. See *QF* 2. 6. 4, cf. 3. 6. 4, *Att.*14.5.2, and *lex Irnit.* K (González, 1986) for the term *res prolatae*.

The Charges

Caelius was charged under the *lex de vi*—apparently originally the *lex Lutatia* (*Cael.* 70), now the *lex Plautia* (*Sest.* 89, 95; Sall. *Cat.* 31. 4; Asc. 55–6 C). If we trust Cicero in this speech and take into account other known accusations, this charge was originally devised to deal with violent sedition in the city, but was extended to cover any violence that could be construed as against the *res publica* (rather than merely to the detriment of private individuals) (*VRR* 109 ff.). Of the four charges first listed by Cicero (*Cael.* 23–4), two—the attack on the Alexandrian ambassadors and the murder of their leader Dion, allegedly paid for by a loan from Clodia (cf. 53)—were clearly offences against the *res publica* (cf. *Dig.* 48. 6. 7 for the provision of the later *lex Iulia de vi publica* that no one with *imperium* should kill *legatos oratores comitesve*); the uprisings at Naples may well have been connected with the Alexandrian affair and anyhow were of public interest. The property of Palla remains an enigma, though Quintilian (4. 2. 27) connected it with the general charge of *vis* ('Palla' appears to be a Latin *cognomen*). The charge of procuring the poisoning of Clodia would not normally be construed as public and belonged properly to the *quaestio de veneficis*. The prosecution may, however, have given it a public aspect by alleging that Caelius wished to silence an accomplice and hence a witness to his plan to murder Dion (56). See Alexander, 2002, 239–42), who also suggests that the story of the attempted transfer of the poison to murder Clodia may have in fact been true, though hard to prove in court.

Caelius

(*a*) Caelius was of equestrian family from Interamna Praetuttianorum in southern Picenum (*Cael.* 4–5), a town that would have only become Roman after the Social War (*c*.88), but the family presumably had been already honoured with Roman citizenship (the prosecution made play with his equestrian origins but said nothing about his recent citizenship). Moreover, his father was well known in the Roman forum, presumably as a businessman rather than an orator (*Cael.* 3). He may be the M. Caelius who appears in the *pro Flacco* (11) as a *publicanus* and a witness for the prosecution on account of one of Flaccus' judicial decisions, perhaps made when he was *praetor urbanus* at Rome. Caelius' father had business interests in the province of Africa and Caelius spent time there (*c*.62–60) as the *contubernalis* of the governor, Q. Pompeius Rufus (*pr.* 63) (*Cael.* 73). Note that the Caelius who was Faberius' debtor in 46 BC (*Att.* 12. 6. 1, 12. 5a. 1, 13. 33. 2) was at this time in Africa.

(*b*) If Caelius himself was born in 82 (Pliny *HN* 7. 165), his tribunate in 52 is early but not impossible, given that it was not part of the regular *cursus*. However, there is a mystery about his quaestorship, not mentioned in *Cael.*, which, if Caelius was born in 82, he would not have been allowed to hold before 51. It is possible that he was given quaestorian status through his successful prosecution of C. Antonius and with this the right to seek higher office early or simply that the successful prosecution allowed him to stand earlier than was normally permitted by the *leges annales*. See Tac. *Ann.* 2. 32, 3.19, describing this sort of privilege under the Principate and Lintott, 2001–3, 112–3. Caelius' quaestorship could then belong to 55—or 54, if the magistracy was not high enough to protect him from prosecution (cf. *QF.* 2. 12. 2). Cicero's comment that Caelius moved to the Palatine (*c*.59–58) at the time when he could stand for a magistracy may simply refer to the age when he could seek the post of *tribunus militum*—in theory after five years' military service—not the quaestorship (*Cael.* 18).

(*c*) Caelius was subject to the *patria potestas* of his father and so was unable to run up debts in his own name (*Cael.* 17), but in any case he does not seem to have been short of money at the time of the case. What Caelius' father thought of his support for Catiline at the time when the latter was advocating a cancellation of debts is a more open question than might appear at first sight. Some businessmen, including *publicani*, may have been facing a cash-shortage in 63. When Caelius later championed the cause of debtors in 48 during the civil war (Caes. *BCiv.* 3. 20–2; Dio 42. 22–4), it seems to have been out of hostility to moneylenders (cf. *Fam.* 8.17.2) and sympathy with those whose assets had become devalued through the conflict: it does not necessarily mean that he was in deep financial trouble himself, as Velleius thought (2. 68. 1–2), nor does it exclude a continuing interest in business on his own account and that of his family. Furthermore, if, with Shackleton Bailey, we identify him with the Caelius of *Att.* 7. 3. 6, 9, 11, he was himself buying up property on the eve of the civil war. He also seems to have had a personal interest in Puteoli and its business (ibid. 9), including the commerce with Egypt. He was quick to hear of the death of Ptolemy Auletes in 51 (*Fam.* 8. 4. 5) and had a connection with C. Vestorius, the trader from Puteoli (*Fam.* 8. 8. 1; D'Arms, 1981, 49–55). There is, moreover, the link with P. Sittius, the entrepreneur, who had an interest *inter alia* in the corn-supply (*Fam.* 8. 8. 10; cf. 5. 17. 2). It is plausible that Caelius and his father had interests of their own in Egypt that were to some extent contingent on Ptolemy's restoration to the throne and would also be assisted if the restoration was undertaken by a proconsul favourable to them. In that case Caelius would belong to the same milieu of Romans doing business with Alexandria as the Coponii (*Cael.* 21–4), C. (Curtius) Rabirius Postumus (*Rab.Post.* 4, 22 ff.), and Vestorius (Vitr. 7. 11. 1). It would not then have been so much a matter of secret work for the king (so Wiseman, 1985, 67) but a known existing connection that made him a target for the prosecution, as was clearly true of P. Asicius (to judge from Ptolemy's present to him). Caelius was no doubt one of numerous Romans who might have been accused of complicity in the king's nefarious activities. That he was picked out reflected the personal enmity of his accusers.

The Speech

The speech is technically adept but above all has the feeling of a relaxed performance. A likely reason for this lack of tension is that Cicero does not need to discuss his own recent career. The attack on Clodius and Clodia in particular is in a tone that makes a pleasant contast with other speeches after his return. To a certain extent Cicero was drawing on previous tactics. As far as we can judge from the surviving fragments, the invective against Clodius and Curio, delivered in the senate in 61 after Clodius' unexpected acquittal for sacrilege, and the consequent altercation with Clodius gave a foretaste of the *pro Caelio* (see Ch. II with nn. 17–23). We find there irony about Clodius' complaints about senators enjoying themselves at Baiae—inconsistent, Cicero suggests, with the Clodian family's long connection with the place; furthermore, Cicero evokes the image of Clodius dressing himself up as a woman for the Bona Dea ceremony without a thought of his grandfather Appius Claudius (*In Clod. et Cur.* 19,

20, 23; *Schol. Bob.* 88–9 St.). The prosopopoiea in particular has been praised (see Austin, 1960, 90). Apart from the occasions when Cicero had personified the fatherland, there was a closer parallel: in his speech in 57 urging Metellus Nepos to support Cicero's return, P. Servilius Isauricus (*cos.* 79)—not in Cicero's catalogue of orators in the *Brutus*—had raised from the dead the shades of past Metelli (*Red. Sen.* 25). Later Cicero himself in *pro Scauro* (46–50) brought back L. Metellus Delmaticus (*cos.* 119) and M. Aemilius Scaurus (*cos.* 115). In *Brutus* 322 he lists the art of citing the most valuable witnesses from the dead as one of the skills which other orators did not, but he himself by implication did, possess. The suggestion that others did not use this technique is unfair, but Cicero was certainly exceptionally skilful at this.

This was not the only connection with drama. In *pro Sestio* Cicero had used on his behalf the evidence of the theatre, lines spoken at the *ludi Apollinares* of July 57 which were exploited by actor and audience as a complimentary allusion to him (*Sest.* 118–23). More generally, quotations from dramatic poetry were nothing new: they went back at least to the days of Cicero's instructors, L. Crassus and M. Antonius (*cos.* 99) (*de Or.* 2. 257, 274). Cicero here employed quotations and images from plays to give colour to his arguments for Caelius. The previous speakers had provided a lead. The accuser Atratinus had called Caelius a pretty little Jason (*ORF* no. 171, fr. 7) and Caelius in return had called Atratinus a Pelias in curls (*ORF* no. 162, fr. 37, Quint.1. 5. 61); then Crassus had quoted Ennius' *Medea* in describing Ptolemy, providing Cicero with a convenient transition to his own first dramatic citation and the introduction of Clodia as a Palatine Medea (*Cael.* 18).

APPENDIX 4

The End of Caesar's Command in Gaul

This appendix deals purely with constitutional issues. Political issues relevant to the present work are dealt with in the text. The topic has had an immense bibliography since Mommsen (1857). In addition to the works cited below, note Hirschfeld, 1904 and 1905; Elton, 1946; Cuff, 1958; Gruen, 1974, 455–90.

1. Caesar's first command was Cisalpine Gaul and Illyricum, given by the *lex Vatinia* for a *quinquennium*. Transalpine Gaul was added by a decree of the senate, presumably on a year-to-year basis with the intention that it would continue until the Gallic crisis was over (cf. Balsdon, 1939, 170–2). Caesar found excuses for prolonging the Gallic war long after the Helvetii and Ariovistus were defeated (in 58): indeed he decided to conquer all Gaul. After the conference of Luca and Pompey and Crassus' election to their second consulships in 55 (secured by violence), the *lex Pompeia Licinia* extended Caesar's command in all his provinces.

2. The total command is regarded by Cicero as ten years (*Att.* 7. 7. 6, *annorum decem imperium*, cf. 7. 9. 4) and the extension by the *lex Pompeia Licinia* as *a quinquennium* (*Att.* 7. 6. 2 'cum quinquennium prorogabamus'). But it remains a question from which date the second *quinquennium* ran. Arguably, the extension of command in Transalpina started from the date of the *lex Pompeia Licinia* (probably February–March 55). However, the command in Cisalpina and Illyricum under the *lex Vatinia* seems to have laid down a date before which succession would be illegal: March 1, 54 (*Prov. Cos.* 36–7). This would have had to be expressed in the form *ante kal. Mart. quintas*, 'before the fifth 1 March' (Romans had no other way of referring to a future year in this period), cf. the formula for the first *quinquennium* of the triumvirate of Antonius, Lepidus and Caesar Octavianus (EJ^2, p. 32 = *Inscr. It.* xiii/1, p. 273, from the Fasti of Colocci) 'M. Aemilius, M. Antonius, imp. Caesar ex a.d. V kal. Dec. ad pr. kal. Ian. sextas' = 27 November 43–31 December (the sixth 31 December) 38 BC. It is possible that on a strict interpretation Caesar's commands in Cisalpina and Transalpina had different terminal dates. Caesar's final proposals before the civil war were that he should retain Cisalpina and Illyricum (Suet. *Jul.* 29. 2; App. *BCiv.* 2. 32).

3. The situation was ripe for confusion, if it became a political issue. Caesar claimed (i) that M. Marcellus' proposal to discuss his recall in 51 was *contra legem Pompei et Crassi ante tempus*, 'before time contrary to Pompey and Crassus' law (Caes. *BG* 8. 53. 1); (ii) that the attempt to recall him in January 49 snatched from him six months of *imperium* (*BCiv.* 1. 9. 2) and that 48 BC was the proper year for his second consulship (*BCiv.* 3. 1). He thus expected to stay in a province until about the time of the consular elections of 49 for 48. In 51 the Gauls expected Caesar to have one more summer in the Transalpine province (*BG* 8. 39).

Pompey claimed (about 29 September 51) that he could not decide about Caesar's provinces *sine iniuria* before 1 March 50 but afterwards would not hesitate (*Fam.* 8. 8. 9). In April–May 50 (*Fam.* 8. 11. 3) he, with senatorial support, put pressure on Caesar to leave his provinces on 13 November 50.

Cicero in 50 December wrote *praeteriit tempus non legis sed libidinis tuae*, 'the time not fixed by law but by your own inclination has passed' (*Att.* 7. 9. 4), and asked rhetorically *exercitum retinentis cum legis dies transierit rationem haberi placet?*, 'do I agree with accepting the candidature of a man who retains an army, when the date fixed by law has passed?' (7. 7. 6). He seems to have thought that the two *quinquennia* were over by the end of 50, perhaps because he took 1 March 50 (or 13 November) as a terminal date or because he counted nine years inclusively as two *quinquennia*.

4. The *lex X tribunorum* of 52 was passed probably in March, when Pompey was sole consul, just before Caesar returned to Transalpina to suppress the revolt of Vercingetorix. Pompey was behind legitimizing Caesar's candidature in absence, and Cicero was asked by Pompey, and by Caesar at Ravenna, to get Caelius to cooperate by refraining from using a tribune's veto (*Att.* 7. 1. 4): *nam ut illi hoc* [sc. *ratio absentis habeatur*] *liceret adiuvi rogatus ab ipso Ravennae de Caelio tribuno pl. Ab ipso autem?*

Etiam a Gnaeo nostro in illo divino tertio consulatu (cf. 7. 3. 4). For Caesar's attitude see *BCiv.* 1. 32. 3, *qui* [sc. *Pompeius*] *si improbasset, cur ferri passus est? Ratio habenda Caesaris absentis erat,* if Pompey had disapproved, why did he allow it to be passed? The candidature of Caesar in his absence should have been accepted'. (Caesar also referred to Cato's attempted filibuster.) Cicero still regards this law as valid in late 50 and early 49: *Att.* 7. 7. 6 *cum hoc aut depugnandum est aut habenda e lege ratio,* 'we must either fight it out with him or accept his candidature according to the law', and thinks that the *lex Pompeia de iure magistratuum* confirmed it (*Att.* 8. 3. 3): *contendit ut decem tribuni pl. ferrent ut absentis ratio haberetur, quod idem sanxit lege quadam sua,* 'he urged the ten tribunes to pass a law conferring candidature in absence, something which he also confirmed by some sort of law of his own'. The provision to avoid a collision between this *lex Pompeia* (see below) and the *lex X tribunorum* seems to have been inserted (Suet. *Jul.* 28) after Pompey's law was first published (not after it was passed, which would have been blatantly invalid). This perhaps offended against the rules for publicizing legislative proposals (*Schol. Bob.* 140 St, Cic. *Vat.* 33–4). If so, it might have led to the invalidation of the whole *lex Pompeia* and rendered Pompey liable to prosecution, but on Cicero's evidence did not in fact do so.

Did the *lex X tribunorum* do more than grant Caesar the right to stand for the consulship in his absence? Stockton, 1975, 239–40, 249 argued that Caesar believed that it implicitly, but only implicitly, granted him the right to stay in Gaul till the consular elections in 49. 'Exercitum retinentis cum legis dies transierit rationem haberi placet? Mihi vero ne absentis quidem; sed cum id datum est, illud una datum est' (*Att.* 7. 7. 6) is surely Cicero's interpretation of the implications of the law (notice the indicative with *cum* in historic sequence: *cum id datum est*): by virtue of giving Caesar the right to stand in absence, they had given him the right to stand while commanding an army; Cicero is not describing a further provision of the law. We cannot imagine that Caesar foresaw in March 52 the precise problem he would be having three years later (note his compliment to Pompey's conduct in the early months of 52 (*BG* 7. 6. 1 *cum iam ille urbanas res virtute Cn. Pompeii commodiorem in statum pervenisse intellegeret,* 'now that he realized that affairs in the city had reached a more satisfactory state through the virtue of Gnaeus Pompeius'); nor is it easy to see how a reference to consular elections three and a half years ahead could be conveniently drafted.

5. As a result of of the *lex Pompeia de iure magistratuum* of 52, which imposed a five-year interval between urban office and provincial command (not applied to Pompey himself, cf. Tac. *Ann.* 3. 28 'suarum legum auctor idem ac subversor'), the senate was enlisting for provincial duty magistrates who had held office in the distant past but had not undertaken provincial commands then—for example in 51 Cicero himself (for 50 see *Fam.* 8. 8. 8). This meant that a successor could be sent out to replace Caesar as soon as his command ended. Cf. Caes. *BCiv.* 1. 85. 9 *in se iura magistratuum commutari, ne ex praetura et consulatu, ut semper, sed per paucos probati et electi in provincias mittantur, in se aetatis excusationem nihil valere, quod superioribus bellis probati ad obtinendos exercitus evocentur,* 'it was to harm him (Caesar)

that the laws governing magistracies were being changed, in order that men should not be sent from the praetorship and consulship to the provinces, as always, but instead people approved and chosen by a few; it was to harm him that the excuse of age was no longer valid, in that men tested in earlier wars were being called back to command armies'.

APPENDIX 5

The *De Legibus*

CONVENIENT reviews of scholarship are to be found in Rawson (1991, 125–48) and the introduction to Dyck's commentary (2004).

In the text of this work Cicero professes it to be a sequel to the *De Re Publica* (*Leg.* 1. 15, 20, 2.23, 3. 4, 12). There are no clear references to its composition in the *Letters* and it is missing from the list of philosophical works in *De Divinatione* (2. 1). It has a comtemporary setting with Cicero, Quintus, and Atticus meeting in a grove with the 'Marian oak' near the Liris in the territory of Arpinum (*Leg.* 1. 1–2; 2. 2–3; fr. 5 = Macr. *Sat.* 6. 4. 8). There is no reference to the civil war. In the preliminary discussion, in which it is suggested that Cicero should write Roman history, 'Atticus' argues that this should preferably comprise contemporary rather than ancient history, in order that 'Cicero' can deal with the glorious exploits of his very great friend Pompey and also his own consulship (1. 8). Cato is treated as still alive and active in the senate (3. 40). The tone of the work implies that the Republic is still a viable option. Cicero clearly embarked on it before the Civil War. We do not know if it was completed. A large part of the text of three books survives in our manuscripts. One citation in Macrobius (6. 4. 8) shows that at least five books were known in antiquity.

It has been argued that the *De Legibus* results from a reworking of the original nine books of *De Re Publica* (cf. *QF* 3. 5. 1). See Gelzer, 1969, 203, following Häfner, 1928, 95, and Ciaceri, 1926–30, ii. 186. This would probably entail that the original material followed what we possess in *De Re Publica* 5 and preceded the *Somnium* in the present Book 6, something possible but not substantiated by any other evidence. The revision would have needed to be extensive. What divides *De Re Publica* and *De Legibus*, apart from their settings, is atmosphere. The former was deliberately placed at a time of crisis that ends with failure: Scipio will achieve immortality but will not survive to put the *res publica* to rights. In what we possess of the latter the participants are relaxed and confident. The mood suits Cicero in the honeymoon after Pompey's third consulship before the threat of civil war grew too great. It has also been suggested in the light of his remark in a letter to Varro after the battle of Thapsus in 46 that Cicero planned to return to the work then (Gelzer, 1969, 273–4). He says there that he would be happy to be employed if anyone wanted an architect or builder for a new *res publica*; if not, he would read and write constitutions and ask questions about laws and morals in books and literature rather than in the senate and forum (*Fam.* 9. 2. 5). However, we hear nothing about any political writings after this except Cicero's failed attempts to write a letter of advice to Caesar (see Ch. XVII with n. 96). Once again the tone of the discussion of republican institutions, so different from the regretful nostalgia of the *Brutus*, which Cicero was working on in 46, is an argument against any significant alteration of the text of the *De Legibus* in this period.

Whereas in the *De Re Publica* Cicero found the ideal constitution in a product of history, the traditional Roman Republic, in *De Legibus* he claimed to derive his ideal set of statutes from theoretical principles (*Leg.* 2.8–14; 3. 32–5). These were not the rules that guide jurisconsults, whose job it was to give legal opinions (*responsitare*) (1. 14). A similar rejection is made in *De Re Publica* (5. 5), when Cicero is discussing the function of the *moderator*: here too the rare word *responsitare* is used. Instead we have in *De Legibus* 1 a theoretical discussion of law as 'right reason' (*recta ratio*) (1. 32–3; cf. *Rep.* 3. 33), following Stoic ethics. Right reason produces statutes, which in turn produce justice (*Leg.* 1. 33). The discussion considers briefly an issue which will be treated later much more fully in philosophical works—the *Academica*, *De Finibus*, and *Disputationes Tusculanae*—whether virtue is the sole good (*Leg.* 1. 53–6). In conclusion 'Quintus' appeals to Cicero to produce not only a law-code but rules for life and 'Cicero' replies by arguing that philosophy, in particular men's understanding of themselves, should be the origin of law and morality (1. 57–62).

I discuss the political rules put forward in *De Legibus* more fully in *CRR* (225–32) and confine myself here to some significant features. In Books 2 and 3 the structure is similar. There is a theoretical introduction, longer in 2 than in 3; the statutes are baldly set out; finally, there is a debate in which Cicero explains his reasoning on certain controversial points. The statutes that are proposed in Books 2 and 3 are based on Roman practice and to some extent derived from early Roman codes: the religious statutes (2. 19–22) from those ascribed to Numa and from Roman tradition (2. 23), two political statutes from the Twelve Tables (3. 11, 44). However, Cicero dresses up in archaic language both constitutional rules that, as far as we know, were never incorporated into statute, for example that there should be two 'praetores iudices consules' (3.8), and innovations of his own, some of which were more reactionary than the practice of the last two centuries of the Republic. For instance, in Cicero's code it was not an offence to flog a Roman citizen, if no veto was used against it (3. 6), contrary to the explicit ban on such punishment of citizens in the *lex Porcia* of Cato the Censor (Lintott, 1972*a*, 249–53).

The treatment of justice is also archaic. The praetor's jurisdiction is confined to private law (3. 6) and there is no place for the *quaestiones perpetuae*, the courts with which Cicero himself was most occupied. The emphasis is on the magistrate who is a 'talking law' (3. 2) at the expense of the assemblies, where every sort of obstruction is to be valid (3. 11), and also to some extent of the senate. The consuls are ordered to regard the safety of the people as the supreme law (3. 6): there is no mention of the last decree of the senate in an emergency. Cicero does, however, recognize the importance of tribunes as a safety-valve for popular feeling by granting them their authority to legislate and veto (3. 9), though he follows this with a discussion in which in the person of Quintus he airs the objections to tribunician power (3. 19–26). As to the religious provisions, Cicero speaks here as a priest whose duty is to follow the authority of the rules he has inherited. His attitude is similar to that ascribed to Gaius Cotta in *De Natura Deorum* (3. 5–6). There is no place for scepticism: the existence and potential benevolence of the gods is a datum, which lies at the foundation of society (2. 15–16). Traditional ceremonies are to be preserved, innovations forbidden. The ceremony of the Bona Dea should, therefore, continue, but no other nocturnal rite for women, nor should there be initiation (such as was practised by the followers of Bacchus), except for the rites of Ceres (2. 21).

What the other books of *De Legibus* contained must be a matter of pure speculation. One possibility is they contained a codification of Roman civil law and a review of Roman jurists similar to the review of orators in the *Brutus*. Gellius (1. 22. 7) speaks of a book of Cicero concerning the organization of civil law as an *ars*, that is, as a logical system (*de iure civili in artem redigendo*). For Cicero's discussion of this in *De Oratore* see Ch. XIV with n. 50.

Cicero's pronouncements do not seem particularly relevant to the circumstances and problems of the late Republic. They were of course designed to fit the ideal constitution of the *De Re Publica*, which in turn involved an education in political morality imposed by law, probably designed to replace the values predominant in the late Republic with those of an earlier epoch (cf. *Leg.* 3. 30–2). Unsurprisingly, these values were expected to be inculcated from the summit of society downwards. Cicero did not see the difficulty of creating morality by legislation, but that was a mistake also committed by the divine Augustus.

APPENDIX 6

The *De Senectute*

For a helpful guide to this work see the edition of Powell, 1988.

Cicero refers to this work in a letter to Atticus of 11 May 44 as already sent to Atticus and apparently no longer fresh in his own mind (*Att.* 14. 21. 3). In the list of philosophical works in the introduction to *De Divinatione* 2, it is said to have been 'added to the collection' recently (*Div.* 2. 3 'interiectus est nuper...'). Atticus was reading it and Cicero was revising it in mid-July 44 (*Att.* 16. 3. 1). The introduction places it somewhere in the middle of his philosophical writing ('De ceteris et diximus multa et saepe dicemus' (*Sen.* 3) It is a work of a very different style from the *Academica*, *De Finibus*, and *De Natura Deorum*, more akin to the *Disputationes Tusculanae*, in that it is a rhetorical discourse on a philosophical question rather than a dialogue on philosophical theory. The protagonist is the 'elder Cato', the Censor, who ennobled his family in the second century BC. He is portrayed addressing Scipio Aemilianus and Laelius in 150 BC, the year before his death (*Sen.* 14). Cicero remarks that, if the reader finds the work too learned when compared to Cato's other writings, he should attribute this to Cato's well-attested study of Greek literature in his old age (*Sen.* 3). However, the majority of the discourse derives from practical moralizing rather than Greek philosophy, and, like a Ciceronian speech, regularly employs anecdote and example rather than strict reasoning. Use of history leads to a concern, unusual in the Ciceronian dialogues, for accurate and explicit chronology (*Sen.* 14, 19, 30, 41–2, 50, 60), which is perhaps at the same time a compliment both to Atticus' chronography and to Cato's own services to history.

Cato lists four chief reasons to think old age unhappy: first, because it is an impediment to activity, secondly, because it makes the body weak, thirdly, because it deprives one of almost all pleasures, fourthly, because it is not far from death (*Sen.* 15). He has earlier dismissed a reason allegedly pleaded by two contemporary consulars, that old men are spurned by those who used to cultivate them—one which we express now by saying that old people become invisible—arguing that this is the fault of their character, not of their age (*Sen.* 7; he returns to this in 25–6). When Laelius suggests that old age is fine for a man of Cato's wealth and status, but this is not the privilege of many, Cato's answer is that the wise man cannot fail to tolerate old age in poverty but the supremely rich man without wisdom cannot fail to find it burdensome. Exercise of virtue is everything (*Sen.* 8–9). He later cites in his support the behaviour of Ennius when he was old and poor (*Sen.* 14). As to the chief objections to old age, he has no difficulty in finding examples of men who were active when old, including himself (*Sen.* 15–33). According to nature, physical weakness in old age is compensated by mental strength (33–8). Nor is the loss of pleasures significant: one chiefly loses the corrupting pleasures or rather observes them at a distance rather than dangerously close (39–50). Above all, there are the pleasures of agriculture to enjoy (51–60).

Cato finally discusses the proximity of death. He begins by arguing that if it extinguishes the soul, it is to be thought unimportant, while if it leads to an eternal future, it is to be desired: the young die as well as the old, but dying in a mature old age is according to nature (66–72). Finally, he turns to philosophical theory and produces Platonic and Pythagorean ideas about the immortality of the soul (77–85), though for him this does not seem to include a belief in the transmigration of souls, since he argues that in any case no one would want to go though the toils and tribulations of life a second time (83). Cato's career was of course crowned with political eminence, riches, and literary success. At the same time he saw the Romans become masters of the world. The chief sadness was the death of his elder son before him (*c.*152 BC: Plut. *Cato mai.* 27. 9; Astin, 1978, 164–5), whom in the dialogue he hopes to meet in the next world (*Sen.* 84).

The subject of the end of *De Senectute* is also that of *Disputationes Tusculanae* book 1, but they are very different in tone. Writing in character, rather than in his own person, seems to allow Cicero to express a more serene and confident view, which he no doubt would like to share, though one cannot see him taking as much pleasure in agriculture as Cato.

APPENDIX 7
Events after Caesar's Murder

44 BC

15 March: Cicero urged by conspirators on Capitol to be their emissary to Antonius (Cic. *Phil.* 2. 89). Hirtius visits D. Brutus in the evening with warnings about Antonius' attitude (*Fam.* 11. 1. 1–2)

16 March: D. Brutus writes to M. Brutus and Cassius in desperation (ibid.).

17 March: Festival of Liberalia. In a senate meeting in the temple of Tellus Cicero advocates reconciliation with the conspirators. This leads to an amnesty, combined with abolition of dictatorship and recognition of *acta* of Caesar. (*Phil.* 1. 4, 31, 2. 89; *Att.* 14. 11. 1, 14. 2; Dio 44. 22. 2–34. 1). *Contio* held by M. Brutus on Capitol (*Att.* 15. 1A. 2). M. Brutus dines with Lepidus and Cassius with Antonius (Dio 44. 34. 7). Appian's version has no mention of Cicero (*BCiv.* 2. 126. 525 ff.). Plutarch dates the meeting wrongly to the 16th (*Brut.* 19).

c.20 March: Opening of Caesar's will; funeral; Antonius' *laudatio*; raids by *plebs* on houses of conspirators and their friends (*Phil.* 2. 91; *Att.* 14. 10. 1; 14. 11. 1; App. *BCiv.* 2. 143. 596 ff.; Dio 44. 35–50; Suet. *Iul.* 83. 5; Plut. *Brut.* 20)

Late March–mid-April: Dolabella is allocated Syria as province (*Att.* 14. 9. 3). Provinces assigned by Caesar to Trebonius (Asia), D. Brutus (Cisalpine Gaul), and Tillius Cimber (Bithynia) are confirmed (App. *BCiv.* 3. 2. 4–5, 6. 18; *Att.* 14. 10. 1, 14. 13. 2). M. Brutus and Cassius were due to get Macedonia and Syria under Caesar's arrangements (*BCiv.* 3. 2. 5).

?Early April: Antonius proposes recall of Sex. Pompeius (currently in revolt in Spain: *Att.* 14. 13. 2), compensation for his confiscated property (said to be at the level of 200 million sesterces), and a naval command for him (App. *BCiv.* 3. 4. 11). See *Att.* 16. 4. 2 for his return to further Spain from New Carthage on hearing the news of Caesar's assassination, 15. 10. 3 for his rapturous reception at Carteia.

Mid-April: Caesar's heir Octavius arrives in Campania on 18th after crossing Adriatic from Apollonia (*Att.* 14. 10. 3). He visits Cicero at Cumae (14. 11. 2, 12. 2).

Mid–late April (after *Att.* 14. 6. 1, of 12 Apr.): Amatius, the pseudo-Marius, is executed by Antonius and Dolabella; his altar and statue-column to Caesar are destroyed by Dolabella (*Att.* 14. 15. 1, 14. 16. 2; *Fam.* 9. 14; 12. 1. 1; *Phil.* 1. 5, 2. 107; Val. Max. 9. 15. 1; App. *BCiv.* 3. 2. 3, 3. 6).

April–May: Antonius in Campania with veteran escort (cf. *Att.* 14. 5. 2), settles demobilized soldiers (*Phil.* 2. 100–7; cf. *Att.* 14. 21. 2 for his telling soldiers to take an oath to uphold Caesar's *acta* and keep their arms prepared). M. Brutus and Cassius remain outside Rome. While in Lanuvium mid-April–end May, they write to Antonius expressing disquiet over his proposed legislation on 1 June (*Fam.* 11. 2. 1, 3, cf. *Att.* 14. 10. 1, 15. 4. 2).

Early May: Cicero at Pompeii writes to Cassius about Antonius' corruption (*Fam.* 12. 1, cf. *Phil.* 2. 92–7; *Att.* 14. 12. 1). Octavius goes to Rome and holds a *contio*; Cicero wonders whether the tribune L. Antonius gave him a platform (*Att.* 14. 20. 5; 15. 2. 3). Octavius declares acceptance of his inheritance before praetor C. Antonius (App. *BCiv.* 3. 14. 49).

Mid-May: An attempt to display Caesar's golden chair at games is vetoed by tribunes (*Att.* 15. 3. 2, 21 May; cf. App. *BCiv.* 3. 28. 105–7; Plut. *Ant.* 16. 5).

1 June: Antonius' agrarian law and a law assigning provinces are passed by violence and with contravention of auspices (*Phil.* 1. 8, 5. 8–10, 8. 25, 10. 17, 13. 5, 31; cf. *Att.* 15. 4. 1, news of the plan to remove D. Brutus from his province; App. *BCiv.* 3. 25. 92–6). L. Antonius is to head new land-commission; Antonius to get Cisalpine and Transalpine Gaul with Macedonian legions for five years; Dolabella to get Syria for five years (cf. *Att.* 15. 11. 4 for Dolabella inviting Cicero to be his *legatus* on June 3).

?Early June: A law is passed permitting the consuls to investigate all Caesar's decrees, regulations, and enactments (*Att.* 16. 16A. 4, 16. 16C. 3; *Phil.* 8. 26).

5 June: The senate passes a decree giving M. Brutus and Cassius corn-supply jobs in Asia and Sicily respectively (*Att.* 15. 9. 1, cf. 15. 5. 2, 15. 11. 1). For their previous allocation of Crete and Cyrene see App. *BCiv.* 3. 8. 29; Plut. *Brut.* 19. 5.

c.8 June: A conference of Brutus' family and friends is held at Antium (*Att.* 15. 11).

25 June: M. Brutus leaves for Greece (*Att.* 15. 24).

30 June: Cicero sets out from his Tusculan villa for Greece (*Att.* 15. 25).

June–July: Lepidus, now in Spain, negotiates with Sextus Pompeius about his recovery of citizenship and status (*Att.* 15. 29. 1; *Phil.* 5. 39–41; cf. Dio 45. 9. 4).

7–13 July: The *ludi Apollinares* are held by C. Antonius on behalf of M. Brutus, the nominal *praetor urbanus*, in his absence (*Att.* 16. 1. 1, 16. 2. 3, 16. 4. 1); demonstrations and counter-demonstrations (App. *BCiv.* 3. 23. 87–91).

20–30 July: The *ludi Victoriae Caesaris* are held with Matius one of the procurators in charge (*Fam.* 11. 27. 8; 28. 6).

Late July–early August: M. Brutus and Cassius issue an edict as they demit their praetorships and prepare to leave Italy (*Phil.* 1. 8; *Att.* 16. 7. 1). Antonius replies with a hostile letter like an edict, to which Brutus and Cassius reply on 4 August (*Fam.* 11. 3; *Att.* 16. 7. 7).

1 August: L. Piso attacks Antonius in the senate (*Att.* 16. 7. 5–7).

6–7 August: Cicero, at the south-western tip of Italy, hears of Piso's intent to renew his attack on 1 September (*Att.* 16. 7. 1) and turns back from journey: meets Brutus at Velia on 17 August (ibid. 5).

1 September: In the senate Antonius attacks Cicero in his absence (*Phil.* 1. 11 ff.).

2 September: *Philippic* 1.

19 September: Antonius' reply to *Philippic* 1 (*Fam.* 12. 2. 1; *Phil.* 5. 19). *Philippic* 2 is later composed as if it were an immediate reply (on the additional fifth day of games in circus) (*Phil.* 2. 110). Cf. *Att.* 16. 11. 1 for the final polish being applied to it on 5 November.

2 October: After his dedication of Caesar's statue on the Rostra with the title 'Parenti optime merito', Antonius replies to the tribune Cannutius to the effect that the conspirators were traitors; Cicero was the head of the plot, and Brutus, Cassius, and Cannutius were acting on Cicero's advice (*Fam.* 12. 3. 1–2).

9 October: Antonius leaves Rome for the Macedonian legions at Brundisium (*Fam.* 12. 23. 2).

2 November: Caesar Octavianus is collecting veterans—3000, given 500 *denarii* a man (*Att.* 16. 8. 1–2).

***c.*10 November:** Caesar Octavianus marches on Rome (*Att.* 16. 11. 6). At a *contio* given by Cannutius he points to the new statue and prays that his own achievements may be worthy of Caesar (*Att.* 16. 15. 3, cf. 14. 1 on Cicero's doubts about him).

Mid-November: Antonius returns to Rome with *legio V Alaudae* (*Att.* 16. 10. 1, cf. 8. 2).

November 24 : Antonius calls a senate meeting, but *legio Martia* mutinies at Alba (*Phil.* 3. 19, 39; 13. 19; App. *BCiv.* 3. 45. 185).

***c.*26–7 November:** *Legio IV* mutinies; Antonius visits Tibur (*Phil.* 3. 39, 4. 6, 13. 19; App. *BCiv.* 3. 45. 185–7).

28 November: A further senate meeting is held and a new allocation of provinces made. Antonius exacts oath of loyalty (*Phil.* 3. 20–6, 5. 23–4, 13. 19; App. *BCiv.* 3. 46. 188).

29 November: Antonius leaves for Cisalpine Gaul (*Phil.* 3. 32, 5. 24, 13. 20; App. *BCiv.* 3. 46. 189).

20 December: *Philippic* 3 to senate; with his motion in support of D. Brutus and Octavianus Cicero prepares ground for action against Antonius on 1 January (*Fam.* 10. 28. 2, 11. 6. 2–3). *Philippic* 4 to people.

***c.*December–January 43:** M. Brutus enters Macedonia and Cassius Syria (*Fam.* 12. 4. 2), cf. *Att.* 15. 13. 4 (25 October) for Caecilius Bassus anticipating Cassius' arrival in Syria.

43 BC

1 January: *Philippic* 5. Cicero proposes to declare a military emergency (*tumultus*) against Antonius (5. 31) and to confer *imperium pro praetore* with further privileges and praetorian status for C. Caesar (Octavianus) (5. 46).

2–3 January: Further senate debates are held, at the end of which honours for Caesar Octavianus are approved (*Res Gestae* 1. 1–2), but the military emergency is not put to the vote (*Phil.* 6. 2–3). Instead an embassy to Antonius is proposed.

4 January: *Philippic* 6 to the people. The embassy to Antonius is set in motion (*Phil.* 6. 4 ff.).

Mid–late January: The *tumultus* and military levies are decreed, cf. Dio 46. 31. 2. *Philippic* 7, a digression from a debate on other subjects, is a review of this (7. 11 ff.; Dio 46. 29. 5). The 'last decree' of the senate is also passed now or later (*RG* 1. 3). Hirtius and Octavianus set out for Mutina (cf. *Fam.* 12. 5. 2).

Late January: Piso and Philippus return from embassy with 'intolerable demands' from Antonius. Itemized in *Phil.* 8. 25–7, they included Transalpine Gaul with 6 legions, reinforced by men from D. Brutus' army. Rumours about Cassius arrive at Rome and firmer news about M. Brutus. It is also reported that Dolabella is about to take over Syria (*Fam.* 12. 4. 2).

2–3 February: Debates are held in the senate. On the 2nd the motion of L. Caesar urging further negotiation is preferred to that of Cicero advocating immediate war (*Phil.* 8. 1–2). *Philippic* 8 on the 3rd (see §6 and *Ep. Caes. Iun.* 1. 16) is a reply to Caesar and Fufius Calenus (11 ff.), proposing that the senate should make no more offers after the return of Antonius' envoy L. Varius (32–3).

4 February: *Saga*, military cloaks, are put on, in recognition of a military emergency (*Phil.* 8. 6; *Ep. Caes. Iun.* 1. 16).

Shortly after 4 February: *Philippic* 9. Cicero proposes honours, a bronze statue on the Rostra and tomb at public expense in *campus Esquilinus* for Servius Sulpicius Rufus (13–17).

Mid-February: *Philippic* 10. After letter to senate from M. Brutus stating that he had taken over Macedonia from C. Antonius and the Illyrian legions from Vatinius (*Phil.* 10. 6–11, cf. *Fam.* 12. 5. 1), Cicero proposes that Brutus should have *imperium* in Macedonia, Illyricum, and all Greece (25–6).

End February: *Philippic* 11. After news of Dolabella's murder of Trebonius (*Phil.* 11. 5) and rumours of Cassius' success reach Rome (32, cf. *Fam.* 12. 5. 1), Cicero fails to get approval for a grant of *maius imperium* to Cassius with a commission to make war on Dolabella (*Phil.* 11. 30–6; *Fam.* 12. 7. 1–2; *Ad Brut.* 4. 2).

7 March: Cassius writes to Cicero from Syria that he has acquired the support of Caecilius Bassus, Staius Murcus, Q. Marcius Crispus, and A. Allienus (*Fam.* 12. 11. 1).

Early March: *Philippic* 12: Cicero opposes a second embassy to Antonius and declines to be a member himself.

19–20 March: After the senate debate on the 19th Pansa leaves Rome (*Fam.* 12. 25. 1; cf. *Phil.* 13. 16 and below).

20 March: *Philippic* 13 after letters from Lepidus and Plancus urging conciliation (*Phil.* 13. 7 ff.; cf. *Fam.* 10. 6. 1, 3; 10. 27). Cicero reads excerpts from a letter written by Antonius to the consuls and Octavianus (*Phil.* 13. 22 ff.). Aid to Sex. Pompeius is voted (ibid. 8–11). Cf. Dio 46. 40. 3 for his receiving command of all the sea and for the recognition of Cassius and Brutus, the latter mentioned by Antonius (*Phil.* 13. 25).

9 April: Lentulus Spinther's letter about Cassius is read by Cicero in the senate (*Ad Brut.* 2. 3).

11 April: Cicero receives news from Brutus about Cassius' success (*Ad Brut.* 4. 2, 5).

14 or 15 April: Battle of Forum Gallorum (*Fam.* 10. 30, from Galba; *Ad Brut.* 9). See Ch. XIX n. 113.

21 April: After news of Forum Gallorum arrives at Rome (*Phil.* 14. 26–7; *Fam.* 10. 30), Cicero delivers *Philippic* 14 on Parilia (*Phil.* 14. 14). Cicero outbids Servilius Isauricus in proposing days of thanksgiving (*supplicationes*) (ibid. 11 ff., 36–80), and uses the thanksgiving as an argument for declaring the defeated Antonians *hostes* (21–4).

c.21 April: Battle of Mutina, deaths of Hirtius and (shortly after battle) Pansa. News reaches Rome by 27th (*Ad Brut.* 10. 13. 1).

27 April: Antonians are declared *hostes* and Cassius is instructed to hunt down Dolabella (*Ad Brut.* 13. 1, cf. 11. 2).

7 May: Cassius, in receipt of Cicero's letter (*Fam.* 12. 7) of early March, is about to march against Dolabella in Cilicia (*Fam.* 12. 12).

c.10 May: D. Brutus, pursuing Antonius, is 30 miles behind him at Pollentia NW of Genoa (*Fam.* 11. 13).

24 May: D. Brutus tells Cicero that his comment about Caesar Octavianus, 'laudandum adulescentem, ornandum tollendum', has been passed on to Octavianus (*Fam.* 11. 20. 1).

29 May: In Transalpine Gaul Lepidus joins Antonius near Forum Iulii (*Fam.* 10. 23. 2).

30 May: Lepidus writes letter of apology to the senate (*Fam.* 10. 35, cf. *Ad Brut.* 20. 1). See *Fam.* 10. 11. 2 for his enlistment of veterans of *legio X*; 10. 33. 2 for his earlier speeches at Narbo in favour of peace.

End May or early June: Cicero writes to D. Brutus that the senate is no longer his instrument. *Legiones IV* and *Martia* will not join Brutus (*Fam.* 11. 14. 1).

6 June: Plancus, who has been approaching Antonius and Lepidus down the Rhône valley, hears of their alliance, retreats, and asks for help: 'Caesar should come himself with his strongest forces; if he is engaged, his army should be sent' (*Fam.* 10. 23, esp. 6).

ca.10 June: D. Brutus joins Plancus (*Fam.* 11. 13a, 11. 25. 2, 11. 26; cf. 10. 24. 3; *Ad Brut.* 22. 2).

Mid June: Embassy of Octavian's veterans to the senate seeking a consulship for their leader. Cicero is suggested as his colleague (*Ad Brut.* 18. 3; *Fam.* 10. 24. 6; *App. BCiv.* 3. 82. 337–8; Dio 46. 42. 2–43. 4).

27 July: Cicero's last letter to M. Brutus. He still hopes to control Octavianus (*Ad Brut.* 26, esp. 3).

28 July: Plancus' last letter to Cicero, complaining that Antonius' survival in strength is all down to Caesar (Octavianus) (*Fam.* 10. 24, esp. 6).

Mid July–?early August: Octavianus' march on Rome from Cisalpine Gaul (Dio 46. 43. 5–45. 2; App. *BCiv.* 3. 89. 363–94. 387). He reaches Rome after 27 July.

19 August: Octavianus elected consul with Q. Pedius (EJ^2 p. 50; Tac. *Ann.* 1. 9; Dio 46. 45. 3; App. *BCiv.* 3. 94. 388).

27 **November:** After a conference at Bononia, the triumvirate comes into being, created by a *lex Titia* (Fasti of Colocci, *Inscr. It.* xiii. 1, p. 273, EJ² p. 32 for the date). Proscription is set in motion.

7 **December:** Killing of Cicero (Tac. *Dial.* 17. 2 for the date).

APPENDIX 8
Antonius' Letter (CIC. *Phil.* 13. 22 ff.)

Antonius to Hirtius and Caesar

COGNITA morte C. Treboni non plus gavisus sum quam dolui. Dedisse poenas sceleratum cineri atque ossibus clarissimi viri et apparuisse numen deorum intra finem anni vertentis aut iam soluto supplicio parricidi aut impendente laetandum est. Iudicatum hostem populi Romani Dolabellam eo quod sicarium occiderit, et videri cariorem rei publicae filium scurrae quam C. Caesarem, patriae parentem, ingemiscendum est. Acerbissimum vero est te, A. Hirti, ornatum beneficiis Caesaris et talem ab eo relictum qualem ipse miraris, et te, O puer, qui omnia nomini debes, id agere ut iure deminutus sit Dolabella, et ut venefica haec liberetur obsidione, ut quam potentissimus sit Cassius atque Brutus.

Nimirum eodem modo haec aspicitis ut priora. Castra Pompeii senatum appellatis; victum Ciceronem ducem habuistis; Macedoniam munitis exercitibus; Africam commisistis Varo bis capto; in Syriam Cassium misistis; Cascam tribunatum gerere passi estis. Vectigalia Iuliana Lupercis ademistis; veteranorum colonias, deductas lege, senatus consulto sustulistis; Massiliensibus iure belli adempta redditurros vos pollicemini; neminem Pompeianum qui vivat teneri lege Hirtia dictitatis. Apuleiana pecunia Brutum subornastis; securi percussos Petraeum et Menedemum, civitate donatos et hospites Caesaris, laudastis; Theopompum nudum, vi expulsum a Trebonio, confugere Alexandream neglexistis. Ser. Galbam eodem pugione succinctum in castris videtis; milites aut meos aut veteranos contraxistis tamquam ad exitium eorum qui Caesarem occiderant et eosdem nec opinantis ad quaestoris sui aut imperatoris aut commilitonum suorum pericula impulistis. Denique quid non aut probastis aut fecistis, quod faciat, si reviviscat, Cn. Pompeius ipse, aut filius eius, si modo possit?

Postremo negatis pacem fieri posse, nisi aut emisero Brutum aut frumento iuvero. Quid? hoc placetne veteranis istis, quibus adhuc omnia integra sunt, quos iam vos adsentationibus et venenatis muneribus venistis depravaturi. At militibus inclusis opem fertis. Nihil moror eos salvos esse et ire quo libet, si tantummodo patiuntur perire eum qui meruit. Concordiae factam esse mentionem scribitis in senatu et legatos esse consularis quinque. Difficile est credere, eos qui me praecipitem egerint, aequissimas condiciones ferentem et tamen ex his aliquid remittere cogitantem, putare aliquid moderate aut humane esse facturos. Vix etiam veri simile est, qui iudicaverint hostem Dolabellam ob rectissimum facinus, eosdem nobis parcere posse idem sentientibus.

Quam ob rem vos potius animadvertite utrum sit elegantius et partibus utilius Treboni mortem persequi an Caesaris, et utrum sit aequius concurrere nos quo facilius reviviscat Pompeianorum causa totiens iugulata, an consentire ne ludibrio sit inimicis, quibus, utri nostrum ceciderint, lucro futurum est. Quod spectaculum adhuc ipsa Fortuna vitavit, ne videret duas acies lanista Cicerone dimicantis, qui usque eo felix est ut isdem ornamentis deceperit vos quibus deceptum Caesarem gloriatus est. Mihi quidem constat nec meam contumeliam nec meorum ferre, nec deserere partis quas Pompeius odivit, nec veteranos sedibus suis moveri pati nec singulos ad cruciatum trahi, nec fallere fidem quam dedi Dolabellae, nec Lepidi societatem violare, piissimi hominis, nec Plancum prodere participem consiliorum. Si me rectis sensibus euntem di immortales, ut spero, adiuverint, vivam libenter. Sin autem me aliud fatum manet, praecipio gaudia suppliciorum vestrorum. Namque si victi Pompeiani tam insolentes sunt, victores quales futuri sint vos potius experiemini. Denique summa iudici mei spectat huc, ut meorum iniurias ferre possim, si aut oblivisci velint ipsi fecisse aut ulcisci parati sunt una nobiscum Caesaris mortem. Legatos venire non credo. Cum venerint, quae postulant cognoscam.

When I learnt of the death of Trebonius, it did not bring me more joy than sorrow. It is a cause for rejoicing that a criminal has paid his penalty to the ash and bones of a supremely distinguished man and the power of the gods has made itself plain in less than a year, inasmuch as punishment for an act of parricide is already paid or impending. It is a matter for grief that Dolabella has been judged an enemy of the Roman people on the ground that he killed an assassin, and the son of a comedian seems dearer to the Republic than Gaius Caesar, the father of his fatherland. However, what hurts most is that you, Aulus Hirtius, who have been honoured through Caesar's generosity and left by him such a figure that you are amazed at yourself, and that you, boy, who owe all to your name, are attempting to justify the degradation of Dolabella and to liberate this hag-witch from siege, so that Cassius and Brutus should be as powerful as possible.

I suppose you have the same view of these actions as the previous ones. You are calling Pompeius' camp the senate; you have taken the defeated Cicero as your leader, you are building up Macedonia with legions; you have entrusted Africa to Varus, who was twice a prisoner-of-war; you have sent Cassius to Syria; you have allowed Casca to hold the tribunate. You have stripped the Luperci of the Julian revenues; you have abolished by decree of the senate colonies of veterans that had been founded by law; you are promising to return to the Massilians what was taken from them by the law of war; you continually maintain that no living Pompeian is bound by the Hirtian law. You have improperly financed Brutus with Apuleius' money; you have praised his execution of Petraeus and Menedemus, who had been granted Roman citizenship and were guest-friends of Caesar; you have ignored the violent expulsion of Theopompus by Trebonius and his consequent flight without his belongings to Alexandria. You have before your eyes in camp Servius Galba still wearing the same dagger; you have recruited soldiers from either my men or the veterans on the pretext of killing those who had murdered Caesar, and contrary to their expectations you have encouraged these same men to imperil their own quaestor or commander or fellow-soldiers. In short, is there anything that you have not approved or done that Gnaeus Pompeius himself would do, if he could return to life, or his son, if he only had the power?

Finally you say that peace is impossible, unless I either release Brutus or assist him with grain. Well: is this is what those veterans want, who still have a choice about their actions, whom you have now come to corrupt with flattery and poisoned gifts? You claim you are helping the besieged soldiers. I do not mind them being spared their lives and going where they like, if only they allow the death of the man who has deserved it. You write that there has been talk of reconciliation in the senate and there are five consular envoys. It is difficult to believe that those who have driven me to my ruin although I offered the fairest terms and had it in mind nevertheless to relax these with some concessions, have any moderate ideas or will act humanely in anything. It is also hardly probable that the same men who judged Dolabella a public enemy on account of a completely just action can spare us who hold the same views.

For these reasons you should rather take thought yourselves whether it is a nicer choice and more expedient for our party to avenge the death of Trebonius or that of Caesar, and whether it is more equitable that we should meet in battle in order to facilitate the revival of the Pompeian cause whose throat we have so often cut, or to join in agreement, in order to avoid being a mockery to our enemies, who will take the profit, whichever of us falls in battle. This is a spectacle that Fortune herself has so far avoided, not wanting to see two battle lines belonging to the same body fighting to the death with Cicero as the manager, who is so lucky that he has deceived you with the same honours as he once boasted that he had used to deceive Caesar. For my part I am determined not to tolerate any insult to me or my men, nor to desert the party which Pompeius hated, nor to allow the veterans either to be driven from their settlements or dragged off one by one to be tortured, nor to break the pledge I gave to Dolabella, nor to infringe my alliance with Lepidus, a man of the greatest loyalty, nor to betray my partner Plancus. If the immortal gods help me on this correct course, as I hope, I will be delighted to survive. If, however, some other fate awaits me, I am taking pleasure in advance at your punishment. For, if the Pompeians are so arrogant when defeated, it will be for you, not me, to find out what they will be like when victorious. To summarize finally my deliberations, this is my view: I can tolerate the injuries to my own men, if those who have done them are either willing to forget they have done them or prepared to join with us in avenging Caesar's death. I do not believe the envoys are coming. When they have come, I will find out their demands.

Bibliography

ALEXANDER, M. C., 1976, 'Hortensius' Speech in Defence of Verres', *Phoenix*, 30, 46–52.
—— 2002, *The Case for the Prosecution in the Ciceronian Era* (Ann Arbor).
ARANGIO-RUIZ, V., 1964, *Marco Tullio Cicerone. Le orazioni per Publio Quinzio. Per Sesto Roscio Amerino. Per l'attore comico Quinto Roscio. Per Marco Tullio* (Verona).
—— and Pugliese Carratelli, G., 1948, '*Tabulae Herculanenses* II', *PP* 3, 165–84.
ASTIN, A. E., 1964, '*Lex Aelia et Fufia*', *Latomus*, 23, 421–45.
—— 1978, *Cato the Censor* (Oxford).
AUSTIN, R. G., 1960, *M. Tulli Ciceronis pro Caelio Oratio*, 3rd edn. (Oxford).
BADIAN, E., 1964, *Studies in Greek and Roman History* (Oxford).
—— 1965, 'M. Porcius Cato and the Annexation and Early Administration of Cyprus', *JRS* 55, 110–21.
—— 1966, 'Notes on *Provincia Gallia* in the late Republic', in R. Chevallier (ed.), *Mélanges d'archéologie et d'histoire offerts à André Piganiol* (Paris), 901–18.
—— 1969, '*Quaestiones Variae*', *Historia*, 18, 465–75.
—— 1974, 'The Attempt to try Caesar', in J. A. S. Evans (ed.), *Polis and Imperium: Studies in Honour of Edward Togo Salmon* (Toronto), 145–66.
—— 1980, 'A *Fundus* at Fundi', *AJP* 101, 470–82.
—— 1984a, 'Three Non-Trials in Cicero', *Klio*, 66, 291–309.
—— 1984b, 'The Death of Saturninus', *Chiron*, 14, 101–47.
BALSDON, J. P. V. D., 1939, 'Consular Provinces under the Late Republic', *JRS* 29, 57–73 and 167–83.
—— 1957, 'Roman History, 58–56 B.C.: Three Ciceronian Problems', *JRS* 47, 15–20.
—— 1958, 'The Ides of March', *Historia*, 7, 80–94.
—— 1960, '*Auctoritas, Dignitas, Otium*', *CQ*, NS 10, 43–50.
—— 1963, 'The *Commentariolum Petitionis*', *CQ*, NS 13, 242–50.
—— 1966, '*Fabula Clodiana*', *Historia*, 15, 65–73.
BANNON, C. J., 2000, 'Self-Help and Social Status in Cicero's *pro Quinctio*', *Anc. Soc.* 30, 71–94.
BARNES, J., 1986, 'Cicéron et la guerre juste', *Bull. Soc. franç. Phil.* 80, 38–80.
—— and Griffin, M. (eds.), 1997, *Philosophia Togata II: Plato and Aristotle at Rome* (Oxford).
BEARD, M., 1986, 'Cicero and Divination: The Formation of a Latin Discourse', *JRS* 76, 33–46.
BELLEMORE, J., 2005, 'Cato's Opposition to Caesar in 59 BC', in Welch and Hillard (eds.), 2005, 225–57.
BERRY, D. M., 1996, *Cicero.Pro Sulla Oratio* (Cambridge).
—— 2003, '*Equester ordo tuus est*: Did Cicero Win his Cases because of Support from the *equites*?', *CQ*, NS 53, 222–34.
BETHMANN-HOLLWEG, M. A. VON, 1864–6, *Das römische Civilprozess*, 3 vols. (Bonn).

BISPHAM, E., 1997, 'The End of the *Tabula Heracleensis*: A Poor Man's *Sanctio*?', *Epigraphica*, 59, 125–56.
BLEICKEN, J., 1959, 'Ursprung und Bedeutung der Provocation', *ZSS* 76, 324–77.
BOTERMANN, H., 1968, *Die Soldaten und die römische Politik in der Zeit von Caesars Tod bis die Begründung des Zweiten Triumvirats* (Zetemata, 46; Munich).
BRINGMANN, K., 1971, *Untersuchungen zum späten Cicero* (Hypomnemata, 29; Göttingen).
BRUNT, P. A., 1957, 'Three Passages from Asconius', *CR*, NS 7, 193–5.
—— 1971, *Italian Manpower* (Oxford).
—— 1988, *The Fall of the Roman Republic* (Oxford).
BUTLER, S., 2002, *The Hand of Cicero* (London and New York).
CAIRNS, F, and Fantham, E. (eds.), 2003, *Caesar against Liberty? Perspectives on his Autocracy* (Papers of the Langford Latin Seminar, 11; Cambridge).
CAMERON, A., 1976, *Circus Factions* (Oxford).
CAMODECA, G., 1993, 'Per una redazione delle Tabulae Herculanenses I', *CErc* 23, 109–19.
—— 1999, *Tabulae Pompeianae Sulpiciorum (TPSulp)* (Vetera, 12; Rome).
CAMPBELL, G., 2003, *Lucretius on Creation and Evolution: A Commentary on De Rerum Natura Book Five, Lines 772–1104* (Oxford).
CARANDINI, A., 1986, '*Domus* e *insulae* sulla pendice settentrionale del Palatino', *BCAR* 9, 263–78.
CARY, M., 1923, '*Asinus germanus*', *CQ* 17, 103–7.
CIACERI, E., 1926–30, *Cicerone e i suoi tempi*, 2 vols. (Milan, Genoa, Rome, Naples).
CLARK, A., 2007, *Divine Qualities: Cult and Community in Republican Rome* (Oxford).
CLASSEN, C. J., 1998, *Diritto, retorica, politica: la strategia retorica di Cicerone* (Bologna), re-edition of *Recht—Rhetorik—Politik: Untersuchungen zu Ciceros rhetorischer Strategie* (Darmstadt, 1985).
COSTA, E., 1899, *Le orazioni di diritto privato di M. Tullio Cicerone* (Bologna).
—— 1927–8, *Cicerone giureconsulto* (Bologna).
COURTNEY, E., 1963, 'The Date of the *De Haruspicum Responso*', *Philologus*, 107, 155–6.
CRAIG, C. P., 1990, 'Cicero's Strategy of Embarrassment in the Speech for Plancius', *AJP* 111, 75–81.
CRAWFORD, J. W., 1984, *M. Tullius Cicero: The Lost and Unpublished Orations* (Hypomnemata, 80; Göttingen).
—— 1994, *M. Tullius Cicero: The Fragmentary Speeches. An Edition with Commentary*, 2nd edn. (Am. Class. Stud. 37; Athens, GA).
CRAWFORD, M. H., 1977, 'Rome and the Greek World: Economic Relationships', *EHR* 42–52.
CROOK, J., 1976, '*Sponsione Provocare*: Its Place in Roman Litigation', *JRS* 66, 132–8.
—— 1995, *Legal Advocacy in the Roman World* (London).
CUFF, P. J., 1958, 'The Terminal Date of Caesar's Gallic Command', *Historia*, 7, 445–71.
D'ARMS, J. H., 1981, *Commerce and Social Standing in Ancient Rome* (Harvard).
DÖRNER, F. K., and Gruben, G., 1953, 'Die Exedra der Cicerones', *MDAI(A)* 68, 63–76.
DOUGLAS, A. E., 1966, *M. Tulli Ciceronis Brutus* (Oxford).

DOUGLAS, A. E., 1995, 'Form and Content in the Tusculan Disputations', in Powell (ed.), 1995, 197–218.
DYCK, A. R., 1996, *A Commentary on Cicero, De Officiis* (Ann Arbor).
—— 2003a, Cicero, *De Natura Deorum Liber I* (Cambridge).
—— 2003b, 'Evidence and Rhetoric in Cicero's *Pro Roscio Amerino*: The Case against Sex. Roscius', CQ, NS 53, 235–46.
—— 2004, *A Commentary on Cicero, De Legibus* (Ann Arbor).
DYER, R. R., 1990, 'Rhetoric and Intention in Cicero's *Pro Marcello*', JRS 80, 17–30.
ECK, W., CABALLOS, A., and FERNÁNDEZ, F., 1996, *Das senatus consultum de Cn. Pisone patre* (Vestigia, 48, Munich).
ELTON, G. R., 1946, 'The Terminal Date of Caesar's Gallic Proconsulate', JRS 36, 18–42.
FANTHAM, E., 2004, *The Roman World of Cicero's* De Oratore (Oxford).
FERRARY, J.-L., 1988, '*Rogatio Servilia agraria*', Athenaeum, 66, 141–64.
—— 1995, 'The Statesman and the Law in the Political Philosophy of Cicero', in Laks and Schofield (eds.), 1995, 48–73.
—— 1999, 'À propos de deux passages des Philippiques', Archiv für Religionsgeschichte, 1, 215–32.
FEZZI, L., 2003, *Falsificazione di documenti pubblici nella Roma tardoreppublicana (133–31 a.C.)* (Florence).
FRAZELL, D., 2004, 'The Composition and Circulation of Cicero's *In Verrem*', CQ, NS 54, 128–42.
FREDERIKSEN, M. W., 1966, 'Cicero, Caesar, and the Problem of Debt', JRS 56, 128–41.
FRIER, B. W., 1983, 'Urban Praetors and Rural Violence', TAPA 113, 221–41.
—— 1985, *The Rise of the Roman Jurists: Studies in Cicero's pro Caecina* (Princeton).
FRISCH, H., 1948, 'The First Catilinarian Conspiracy: A Study in Historical Conjecture', CM 9, 10–36.
GABBA, E., 1957, 'Note sulla polemica anticiceroniana di Asinio Pollione', RSI 69, 317–39.
—— 1958, *Appiani Bellorum Civilium Liber Primus* (Florence).
GAROFALO, L., 1989, *Il processo edilizio: contributo allo studio dei iudicia populi* (Padua).
GELZER, M., 1962–4, *Kleine Schriften*, 3 vols. (Wiesbaden).
—— 1969, *Cicero: Ein biographischer Versuch* (Wiesbaden).
GILBOA, A., 1974, 'A Further Comment on the Dating of the Cicero–Matius Correspondence (Fam. XI 27/8)', Historia, 23, 217–8.
GONZÁLEZ, J., 1986, '*Lex Irnitana*', JRS 76, 147–243.
GRIFFIN, M. T., 1973, 'The Tribune C. Cornelius', JRS 63, 196–213.
—— 1995, 'Philosophical Badinage in Cicero's Letters to his Friends', in Powell (ed.), 1995, 325–46.
—— 1997a, 'The Composition of the *Academica*: Motives and Versions', in Inwood and Mansfield (eds.), 1997, 1–35.
—— 1997b, 'Cicero and Matius on Friendship', in Barnes and Griffin (eds.), 1997, 86–109.
—— 2001, 'Piso, Cicero, and their Audience', in C. Auvray-Assayas and D. Delattre (eds.), *Cicéron et Philodème: la polémique en philosophie à Rome à la fin de la République* (Paris), 85–99.

—— 2003, 'Clementia after Caesar: From Politics to Philosophy', in Cairns and Fantham (eds.), 2003, 157–82.
—— and Atkins, E. M. (eds.), 1991, *Cicero. On Duties* (Cambridge).
GRILLI, A., 1962, *M. Tulli Ciceronis Hortensius* (Milan/Varese).
GRIMAL, P., 1967, *Études de chronologie cicéronienne (années 58 et 57 av. J-C.)* (Paris).
GRUEN, E. S., 1966, 'P. Clodius: Instrument or Independent Agent?', *Phoenix*, 20, 120–30.
—— 1968, *Roman Politics and the Criminal Courts 149–78 BC* (Cambridge, MA).
—— 1970, '*Veteres Hostes, Novi Amici*', *Phoenix*, 24, 237–43.
—— 1971, 'Some Criminal Trials of the Late Republic: Political and Prosopographical Problems', *Athenaeum*, 49, 54–69.
—— 1974, *The Last Generation of the Roman Republic* (Berkeley and Los Angeles).
GURLITT, L., 1883, 'Die Briefe Ciceros an M. Brutus in bezug auf ihre Echtheit geprüft', *Philologus Supp.* 4, 551–630.
HABICHT, Ch., 1990, *Cicero the Politician* (Baltimore/London).
HÄFNER, S., 1928, *Ciceros literarische Pläne* (Diss. Munich).
HEINZE, R., 1909, 'Ciceros politische Anfänge', repr. in id., *Vom Geist des Römertums*, ed. E. Burck, (Darmstadt, 1960), 87–140.
HELDMANN, K., 1976, 'Ciceros Laelius und die Grenzen der Freundschaft', *Hermes*, 104, 72–103.
HENDERSON, M. I., 1950, '*De Commentariolo Petitionis*', *JRS* 40, 8–21.
HENDRICKSON, G. L., 1939, 'Brutus *De Virtute*', *AJP* 60, 401–13.
HENRICHS, A., 1974, 'Die Kritik der stoischen Theologie in P. Herc. 1428', *CErc* 4, 5–32.
HINARD, F., 1985, *Les Proscriptions de la Rome républicaine* (CEFR 83; Rome).
HIRSCHFELD, O., 1904, 'Der Endtermin der gallischen Statthalterschaft Caesars', *Klio*, 4, 77–88.
—— 1905, 'Nochmals der Endtermin der gallischen Statthalterschaft Caesars', *Klio*, 5, 236–40.
HOMEYER, H., 1964, *Die antiken Berichte über den Tod Ciceros und ihre Quelle* (Deut. Beitr. z. Altertumswiss. 18; Baden-Baden).
HORNBLOWER, S., 1995, 'The Fourth-Century and Hellenistic Reception of Thucydides', *JHS* 105, 47–68.
HUMBERT, J., 1925, *Les Plaidoyers écrits et les plaidoiries réelles de Cicéron* (Paris).
HUTCHINSON, G. O., 1998, *Cicero's Correspondence: A Literary Study* (Oxford).
INNES, D. C., 1986, 'Theophrastus and the Theory of Style', in W. W. Fortenbaugh (ed.), *Theophrastus of Eresus: On his Life and Work* (Rutgers Studies in Classical Humanities, 2; New Brunswick, NJ), 251–69.
INWOOD, B., and Mansfield, J. (eds.), 1997, *Assent and Argument: Studies in Cicero's Academic Books. Proceedings of the 7th Symposium Hellenisticum (Utrecht, August 21–25, 1995)* (Leiden, New York, and Cologne).
KERKHECKER, A., 2002, '*Privato Officio, Non Publico*: Literaturwissenschaftliche Überlegungen zu Ciceros "pro Marcello" ', in J. P. Schwindt (ed.), *Klassische Philologie inter disciplinas* (Heidelberg), 93–149.
KINSEY, T. E., 1971, *M. Tulli Ciceronis Pro P. Quinctio Oratio* (Sydney).

KINSEY, T. E., 1985, 'The Case against Sextus Roscius of Ameria', *Ant. Class.* 54, 188–96.
KYTZLER, B., 1960, 'Beobachtungen zu den Matius-Briefen', *Philologus,* 104, 48–62.
KORNEMANN, E., 1896, 'Die historische Schriftstellerei des C. Asinius Pollio', *JbClPh,* Supp. 22, 557–691.
KUMANIECKI, K., 1961, 'De Oratione Tulliana in Toga Candida Habita', *Atti del I congresso internazionale di studi ciceroniani* (Rome), i. 157–66.
—— 1970, *Les Discours égarés de Cicéron Pro Cornelio* (Meded. Kon. Vlaam. Acad. België, Kl. der Lett. 32/8, Brussels).
LABRUNA, L., 1970, *Vim fieri veto* (Naples).
LAKS, A., and SCHOFIELD, M. (eds.), 1995, *Justice and Generosity: Studies in Hellenistic Political Philosophy. Proceedings of the 6th Symposium Hellenisticum* (Cambridge).
LINDERSKI, J., and KAMINSKA-LINDERSKI, A., 1974, 'The Quaestorship of Marcus Antonius', *Phoenix*, 28, 213–23.
LINTOTT, A., 1965, '*Trinundinum*', *CQ*, NS 15, 281–5.
—— 1967, 'P. Clodius Pulcher—*Felix Catilina*?', *G&R*, NS 14, 157–69.
—— 1968, '*Nundinae* and the Chronology of the Late Roman Republic', *CQ*, NS 18, 189–94.
—— 1970, 'The Tradition of Violence in the Annals of the Early Roman Republic', *Historia*, 19, 12–29.
—— 1971, 'Lucan and the History of the Civil War', *CQ*, NS 21, 488–505.
—— 1972a, '*Provocatio*: From the Struggle of the Orders to the Principate', *ANRW* I 2. 226–67.
—— 1972b, 'Imperial Expansion and Moral Decline in the Roman Republic', *Historia*, 21, 626–38.
—— 1974, 'Cicero and Milo', *JRS* 64, 62–78.
—— 1980, 'M. Caelius Rufus and Pausanias', *CQ*, NS 30, 385–6.
—— 1981, 'The *leges de repetundis* and Associate Measures under the Republic', *ZSS* 98, 162–212.
—— 1990a, 'Electoral Bribery in the Roman Republic', *JRS* 80, 1–16.
—— 1990b, 'Le procès devant les recuperatores d'après les données épigraphiques jusqu'au règne d'Auguste', *RHDFE* 68, 1–11.
—— 1997a, 'Cassius Dio and the History of the Late Roman Republic', *ANRW* II 34. 3, 2497–2523.
—— 1997b, 'The Theory of the Mixed Constitution at Rome', in Barnes and Griffin (eds.), 1997, 70–85.
—— 2000, 'Aristotle and the Mixed Constitution', in R. Brock and S. Hodkinson (eds.), *Alternatives to Athens* (Oxford), 152–66.
—— 2001–3, '*Delator* and *Index*: Informers and Accusers at Rome from the Republic to the Early Principate', *Accordia Research Papers*, 9, 105–22.
—— 2006, 'La violenza della lotta degli ordini', in G. Urso (ed.), *Terror et Pavor* (I convegni della fondazione Niccolò Canussio, 5; Pisa), 13–19.
LOMAS, K., 2004, 'A Volscian Mafia? Cicero and his Italian Clients', in Powell and Paterson (eds.), 2004, 97–116.

LONG, A. A, 1995a, 'Cicero's Politics in De Officiis', in Laks and Schofield (eds.), 1995, 213–40.
—— 1995b, 'Cicero's Plato and Aristotle', in Powell (ed.), 1995, 37–61.
—— and Sedley, D. N., 1987, *The Hellenistic Philosophers* (Cambridge).
McDERMOTT, W. C., 1977, 'The Verrine Jury', *RhM*, NF 120, 64–75.
MACK, D., 1937, *Senatsreden und Volksreden bei Cicero* (Kieler Arbeiten zu klassicher Philologie, 2; Würzburg, repr. Hildesheim 1967).
MALITZ, J., 1987, 'Die Kanzlei Caesars—Herrschaftsorganisation zwischen Republik und Prinzipat', *Historia*, 36, 51–72.
MARINONE, N., 2004, *Cronologia ciceroniana* (Collana di studi ciceroniani, 6), 2nd edn. by E. Malaspina (Bologna).
MARSHALL, B. A., 1985, *A Historical Commentary on Asconius* (Columbia, MO).
MARTIN, J., 1970, 'Die Provokation in der klassischen und späten Republik', *Hermes*, 98, 72–96.
MAY, J. M. (ed.), 2002, *Brill's Companion to Cicero: Oratory and Rhetoric* (Leiden).
MEIER, C., 1961, 'Zur Chronologie und Politik in Caesars ersten Konsulat', *Historia*, 10, 68–98.
—— 1966, *Res Publica Amissa* (Wiesbaden).
METTE, H.-J., 1965, 'Der junge Zivilanwalt Cicero', *Gymnasium*, 72, 10–27.
METZGER, E., 1997, *A New Outline of the Roman Civil Trial* (Oxford).
—— 2005, *Litigation in Roman Law* (Oxford).
MEYER, Ed., 1918, *Caesars Monarchie und das Principat des Pompejus* (Berlin and Stuttgart).
MITCHELL, S., 1979, 'R.E.C.A.M. Notes and Studies No. 5: A Roman Family in Phrygia', *AS* 29, 13–22.
—— 1993, *Anatolia*, 2 vols. (Oxford).
MITCHELL, T. N. 1979, *Cicero: The Ascending Years* (New Haven).
—— 1991, *Cicero: The Senior Statesman* (New Haven).
MOMMSEN, Th., 1857, *Die Rechtsfrage zwischen Caesar und dem Senat* (Breslau) = *Gesammelte Schriften* (Berlin, 1905–13) iv. 92–145.
MOREAU, Ph., 1982, *Clodiana Religio: un procès politique en 61 av. J.-C.* (Paris).
MORSTEIN-MARX, R., 2004, *Mass Oratory and Political Power in the Late Roman Republic* (Cambridge).
MUSTAKALLIO, K., 1994, *Death and Disgrace: Capital Penalties with Post Mortem Sanctions in Early Roman Historiography* (Annales Academiae Scientiarum Fennicae, Dissertationes Humanarum Litterarum 72, Helsinki).
NARDO, D., 1970, *Il Commentariolum petitionis: la propaganda elettorale nella ars di Quinto Cicerone* (Padova).
NICOSIA, G., 1965, *Studi sulla 'deiectio'* (Milan).
NISBET, R. G. M., 1961a, *Cicero: In L. Calpurnium Pisonem Oratio* (Oxford).
—— 1961b, 'The *Commentariolum Petitionis*: Some Arguments against Authenticity', *JRS* 51, 84–7.
OGILVIE, R. M., 1965, *A Commentary on Livy Books 1–5* (Oxford).
OOST, S. I., 1955, 'Cato Uticensis and the Annexation of Cyprus', *CPh* 50, 98–112.

PAILLIER, J.-M., 1988, *Bacchanalia: la répression de 186 av. J.-C. à Rome et en Italie* (*BEFRA* 270; Rome).
PINA POLO, F., 1989, *Las contiones civiles y militares en Roma* (Zaragoza).
PLATSCHEK, J., 2005, *Studien zu Ciceros Rede für P. Quinctius* (Münch. Beitr. z. Papyrusf. u. ant. Rechtsgesch. 94; Munich).
POCOCK, L. G., 1924, 'Publius Clodius and the Acts of Caesar', *CQ* 18, 59–64.
—— 1926, *A Commentary on Cicero In Vatinium* (London).
POWELL, J. G. F., 1988, *Cato Maior de Senectute* (Cambridge).
—— 1994, 'The *rector rei publicae* of Cicero's *De Re Publica*', *SCI* 13, 19–29.
—— (ed.), 1995, *Cicero the Philosopher* (Oxford).
—— and Paterson, J. (eds.), 2004, *Cicero the Advocate* (Oxford).
RAMBAUD, M., 1953, *L'Art de la déformation historique dans les commentaires de César* (Ann. de l'univ. Lyon, 3ème sér. 23, Paris).
RAMSEY, J. T., 2003, *Cicero: Philippics I–II* (Cambridge).
—— 2004, 'Did Julius Caesar Temporarily Banish Antony from his Inner Circle?', *CQ*, NS 54, 161–73.
—— 2005, 'Mark Antony's Judicial Reform and its Revival under the Triumvirs', *JRS* 95, 20–37.
—— and Licht, A., 1997, *The Comet of 44 B.C. and Caesar's Funeral Games* (American Classical Studies, 39; Atlanta).
RAWSON, E., 1983, *Cicero. A Portrait*, 2nd edn. (Bristol).
—— 1985, *Intellectual Life in the Roman Republic* (London).
—— 1991, *Roman Culture and Society* (Oxford).
RICH, J. W., 1976, *Declaring War in the Roman Republic in the Period of Transmarine Expansion* (Coll. Latomus, 149, Brussels).
RICHARDSON, J. S., 1971, ' The *Commentariolum Petitionis*', *Historia*, 20, 436–42.
—— 1987, 'The Purpose of the *lex Calpurnia de repetundis*', *JRS* 77, 1–12.
RIGGSBY, A. M., 1999a, 'Iulius Victor on Cicero's Defenses *de Repetundis*', *RhM*, NF 142, 427–9.
—— 1999b, *Crime and Community in Ciceronian Rome* (Austin, TX).
—— 2002, 'The *Post Reditum* Speeches', in May (ed.), 2002, 159–93.
ROBBE, U., 1941, 'L'autonomia dell'*actio certae creditae pecuniae* e la sua distinzione dalla *condictio*', *SDHI* 7, 35–111.
RODGER, A., 1996, 'Postponed Business at Irni', *JRS* 86, 61–74.
SHACKLETON BAILEY, D. R., 1956, '*Exspectatio Corfiniensis*', *JRS* 46, 57–64.
—— 1960, 'The Credentials of L. Caesar and L. Roscius', *JRS* 50, 80–3.
SCHMIDLIN, B., 1963, *Das Rekuperatorenverfahren* (Fribourg).
SCHMIDT, O. E., 1884, 'Zur Kritik und Erklärung der Briefen Ciceros an M. Brutus', *JbClPh* 30, 617–44.
—— 1893, *Der Briefwechsel des M. Tullius Cicero* (Leipzig).
SCHMIDT, P. L., 1973, 'Cicero De Re Publica', *ANRW* I 4. 262–333.
SCHOFIELD, M., 1986, 'Cicero For and Against Divination', *JRS* 76, 47–65.
SEAGER, R. J., 1964, 'The First Catilinarian Conspiracy', *Historia*, 13, 338–47.
—— 1965, 'Clodius, Pompeius and the Exile of Cicero', *Latomus*, 24, 519–31.

—— 2002, *Pompey the Great: A Political Biography*, 2nd edn. (Oxford).
SERRAO, F., 1954, *La 'iurisdictio' del pretore peregrino* (Milan).
—— 1956, 'Appunti sui *patroni* nei processi *repetundarum*', *Studi in onore di Pietro de Francisci* (Milan), ii. 473–511.
SHERWIN-WHITE, A. N., 1973, *The Roman Citizenship*, 2nd edn. (Oxford).
SMITH, R. E., 1957, 'The *Lex Plotia Agraria* and Pompey's Spanish veterans', *CQ*, NS 7, 82–5.
STEEL, C., 2001, *Cicero: Rhetoric and Empire* (Oxford).
STEVENSON, T., 2005, 'Readings of Scipio's Dictatorship in Cicero's *De Re Publica* (6.12)', *CQ*, NS 55, 140–52.
STOCKTON, D. L., 1962, 'Cicero and the *Ager Campanus*', *TAPA* 93, 471–89.
—— 1971, *Cicero: A Political Biography* (Oxford).
—— 1975, '*Quis iustius induit arma*', *Historia*, 24, 222–59.
STONE, A. M., 2005, '*Optimates*: An Archaeology', in Welch and Hillard (eds.), 2005, 59–94.
STRACHAN-DAVIDSON, J. L., 1912, *Problems of the Roman Criminal Law*, 2 vols. (Oxford).
STRASBURGER, H., 1965, 'Poseidonius on Problems of the Roman Empire', *JRS* 55, 40–53.
STROH, K. W., 1975, *Taxis und Taktik: Die advokatische Dispositionskunst in Ciceros Gerichtsreden* (Stuttgart).
—— 2004, '*De Domo Sua*: Legal Problem and Structure', in Powell and Paterson (eds.), 2004, 313–70.
SUMNER, G. V., 1963, '*Lex Aelia, Lex Fufia*', *AJP* 84, 337–58.
—— 1964, 'Manius or Mamercus?', *JRS* 54, 41–8.
—— 1973, *The Orators in Cicero's Brutus: Proposopography and Chronology* (Phoenix Supp. 11; Toronto).
SYME, R., 1939*a*, *The Roman Revolution* (Oxford).
—— 1939*b*, 'Observations on the Province of Cilicia', *Anatolian Studies Presented to W. H. Buckler* (Manchester, 1939), 299–332; repr. *Roman Papers*, i (Oxford), 120–48.
—— 1950, 'A Roman Post-Mortem', *Todd Memorial Lecture no. 3* (Sydney); repr. *Roman Papers*, i (Oxford, 1979), 205–17.
—— 1964, *Sallust* (Berkeley and Los Angeles).
—— 1986, *The Augustan Aristocracy* (Oxford).
TAYLOR, L. R., 1951, 'On the Chronology of Caesar's First Consulship', *AJP* 72, 254–6.
—— 1961, *Party Politics in the Age of Caesar* (Berkeley and Los Angeles).
TATUM, W. J., 1993, 'The *Lex Papiria de dedicationibus*', *CPh* 88, 319–28.
—— 1999, *The Patrician Tribune* (Chapel Hill and London).
THOMAS, D. F. C., 2005, 'Priests and Politicians: Reflections on Livy and Cicero's *De Domo Sua*', in Welch and Hillard (eds.), 2005, 119–40.
THOMPSON, L. A., 1962, 'The Relation between Provincial Quaestors and their Commanders-in-Chief', *Historia*, 11, 339–55.
TOHER, M., 2004, 'Octavian's arrival in Rome, 44 BC', *CQ*, NS 54, 174–84.
TYRRELL, R. Y., and Purser, L. C., 1904–33, *The Correspondence of Cicero*, 7 vols. (Dublin).
ULLMAN, B. L., 1942, 'History and Tragedy', *TAPA* 73, 25–53.

VENTURINI, C., 1969, 'La repressione degli abusi dei magistrati romani ai danni delle popolazioni soggette fino all lex Calpurnia del 149 a.C.', *BIDR* 72, 19–87.

—— 1979, *Studi sul crimen repetundarum nell'età repubblicana* (Milan).

WALBANK, F. W., 1955, 'Tragic History: A Reconsideration', *BICS* 2 (1955), 4–14.

—— 1957, *A Historical Commentary on Polybius*, i (Oxford).

—— 1960, 'History and Tragedy', *Historia*, 9, 216–34; repr. in id., *Selected Papers: Studies in Greek and Roman Historiography* (Cambridge, 1985) 224–41.

WATSON, A., 1965, *The Law of Obligations in the Later Roman Republic* (Oxford).

—— 1967, *The Law of Persons in the Later Roman Republic* (Oxford).

—— 1971, *The Law of Succession in the Later Roman Republic* (Oxford).

WEINSTOCK, S., 1971, *Divus Julius* (Oxford).

WELCH, K., and HILLARD, T. W. (eds.), 2005, *Roman Crossings: Theory and Practice in the Roman Republic* (Swansea).

WHITE, S. A., 1995, 'Cicero and the Therapists', in Powell (ed.), 1995, 219–46.

WINTERBOTTOM, M., 2004, 'Perorations' in Powell and Paterson (eds.), 2004, 215–30.

WIRSZUBSKI, C., 1954, 'Cicero's *Cum dignitate otium*: A Reconsideration', *JRS* 44, 1–13.

—— 1961, '*Audaces*: A Study in Political Phraseology', *JRS* 51, 12–22.

WISEMAN, T. P., 1966, 'The Ambitions of Quintus Cicero', *JRS* 56, 108–15.

—— 1968, 'Pulcher Claudius', *HSCP* 74, 207–13.

—— 1971, *New Men in the Roman Senate 139 B.C–14 A.D.* (Oxford).

—— 1974, *Cinna the Poet and Other Essays* (Leicester).

—— 1985, *Catullus and his World* (Cambridge).

WOLFF, J. G., 1997, ' "Intertium", und kein Ende?', *BIDR* 100, 1–36.

WOOTEN, C. W., 1985, *Cicero's Philippics and their Demosthenic Model* (Chapel Hill, NC, and London).

WRIGHT, M. R., 1991, *Cicero: On Stoic Good and Evil* (Warminster).

YAVETZ, Z., 1969, *Plebs and Princeps* (Oxford).

ZETZEL, J. G., 1995, *Cicero, De Re Publica: Selections* (Cambridge).

ZULUETA, F. de, 1953, *The Institutes of Gaius*, ii (Oxford).

Index

A. PERSONS

M'. Acilius Glabrio (*cos.* 67) 85, 90
Sex. Aebutius 73–9
Q. Aelius Tubero (? *tr.pl.* 130) 232, 236
L. Aelius Tubero 318f
Q. Aelius Tubero, his son 318f
L. Aelius Lamia 144, 177, 196
Mam. Aemilius Lepidus (*cos.* 77) 23f, 115
M'. Aemilius Lepidus (*cos.* 66) 115, 291
M. Aemilius Lepidus (*cos.* 46) 338n, 389f, 393n, 399ff, 401, 403, 408ff, 418ff, 440ff
Paullus Aemilius Lepidus (*cos.* 34) 409, 418n
L. Aemilius Paulus (*cos.* 50) 173, 270
M. Aemilius Scaurus (*cos.* 115) 123, 198, 206
M. Aemilius Scaurus (*pr.* 56) 25f, 108f, 205, 243
L. Afranius (*cos.* 60) 8, 160
P. Albinovanus 28f, 195
Statius Albius Oppianicus, father and son 26f
Sex. Alfenus Varus 45, 49, 51, 56
C. Alfius Flavus (*quaesitor*, 54) 242
A. Allienus (*pr.* 49) 297n, 397, 402, 443
Amatius (the pseudo-Marius) 13, 345, 375, 443
T. Ampius Balbus (*pr.* 59) 141, 260, 320
Amyntas of Pergamum 104, 106
Q. Ancharius (*pr.* 56) 167, 210
T. Annius Milo (*pr.* 55) 9f, 28, 33f, 119f, 181, 190, 192, 194, 203, 241f, 244ff, 371, 426
Anser, the poet 399
Antiochus of Ascalon 327
P. Antistius (*tr.pl.* 88) 308, 427

Pacuvius Antistius Labeo 419
C. Antistius Vetus (*suf.* 30) 417
C. Antonius (*pr.* 44) 242, 392, 395, 402f, 417, 441
L. Antonius (*cos.* 41) 242, 346, 391–2, 398, 402, 410f, 441
M. Antonius (*cos.* 99) 26n, 116f, 123, 227ff, 307f, 377, 422, 433
M. Antonius (*cos.* 44) 242, 272, 279, 281, 283, 295–7, 339–50, 360ff, 374–416 *passim*, 420f, 434, 440ff.
C. Antonius Hybrida (*cos.* 63) 108, 131, 133ff, 147, 168, 173, 200
Apollonius of Panhormus 98
C. Appuleius Decianus (*tr.pl.* 98) 123
C. Appuleius Decianus 104, 106
L. Appuleius Saturninus (*tr.pl.* 103) 9, 116, 122, 124, 144, 176, 196, 394
M. Apuleius (*cos.* 20) 417, 445f
P. Apuleius (*tr.pl.* 43) 391, 405
Q. Apronius 97
C. Aquilius Gallus (*pr.* 66) 44, 49, 58
Ariobarzanes III of Cappadocia 164n, 255, 261f
Aristotle, *Ethics* 327, 363–5
  Politics 234, 236
Asclepiades of Acmona 104f
P. Asicius 191, 200, 432
C. Asinius Pollio (*cos.* 40) 281, 297n, 403, 408, 414f
Athenagoras of Cyme 104f
C. Atilius Serranus (*cos.* 106) 123
Sex. Atilius Serranus Gavianus (*tr.pl.* 57) 12, 180n, 189
P. Attius Varus 318
T. Attius of Pisaurum 36

M. Aufidius Lurco (*tr.pl.* 61) ?104, ?106, 160
C. Aurelius Cotta (*cos.* 75) 227, 307f, 351ff
L. Aurelius Cotta (*cos.* 65) 187
P. Autronius Paetus (*cos.des.* 65) 151

C. Blossius of Cumae 364
C. Burrienus (*pr.* 83) 50f, 55ff

Caecilia Metella 426
Q. Caecilius Bassus 336, 341, 383, 402, 442f
M. Caecilius Cornutus (*pr.* 43) 399, 407
L. Caecilius Metellus (*cos.* 68) 73, 96
L. Caecilius Metellus (*tr.pl.* 49) 294
M. Caecilius Metellus (*pr.* 69) 87, 426
Q. Caecilius Metellus (*cos.* 69) 73n, 107
Q. Caecilius Metellus Celer (*cos.* 60) 9, 125, 142, 149f, 157, 164, 167, 181
Q. Caecilius Metellus Nepos (*cos.* 57) 9, 148ff, 180ff, 187, 197, 433
Q. Caecilus Metellus Numidicus (*cos.* 109) 9, 11, 181, 187f, 196, 198, 372
Q. Caecilius Metellus Pius (*cos.* 80) 23f, 115
Q. Caecilius Metellus Pius Scipio Nasica (*cos.* 52) 249, 269, 271, 277, 282, 311n, 426
Q. Caecilius Niger (*q.* 72) 85
A. Caecina 73ff, 321f
M. Caelius 104
M. Caelius Rufus (*pr.* 48) 168, 199ff, 251f, 256, 262, 267ff, 282ff, 296ff, 431ff
Caesennia 74ff, 79
L. Calpurnius Bestia (*tr.pl.* 62) 149, 200, 398
L. Calpurnius Bibulus (*cos.* 59) 28, 165, 170, 172ff, 192ff, 253, 255, 262, 265
L. Calpurnius Bibulus (*suf.* 40) 417

C. Calpurnius Piso (*cos.* 67) 62ff, 79f, 108, 113
C. Calpurnius Piso, Cicero's son-in-law 174, 177
Cn. Calpurnius Piso (*q.* 65) 134
L. Calpurnius Piso (*cos.* 58) 9, 12f, 144, 176f, 196, 204ff, 314, 376ff, 397f, 441
C.Calvisius Sabinus (*cos.* 39) 398
Ti. Cannutius (*tr.pl.* 44) 383f, 442
P. Canidius Crassus (*suf.* 40) 411
L. Caninius Gallus (*tr.pl.* 56) 192f
C. Caninius Rebilus (*suff.* 45) 290
Carneades 236, 355, 368
L. Carpinatius 97
A. Cascellius (*pr ca.* 40) 80n
Sp Cassius (*cos.* 486) 236, 364, 380
C. Cassius Longinus (*cos.* 171) 188
C. Cassius Longinus (*cos.* 73) 88, 94, 429
C. Cassius Longinus (*pr.* 44) 262, 310, 313, 322, 329, 340, 342, 345f, 348f, 374, 376, 378, 383, 396f, 400, 405f, 414ff, 421, 440ff
L. Cassius Longinus Ravilla (*cos.* 127) 198
L. Cassius Longinus (*pr.* 66) 87, 131
L. Cassius Longinus (*tr.pl.* 44) 222
Q. Cassius Longinus (*tr.pl.* 49) 276, 281, 283
C. Cassius Parmensis (*q.* 43) 416
M. Cassius Scaeva 343
Castor of Galatia 335ff
Catiline, see Sergius
P. Cervius 88
M. Cispius (*tr.pl.* 57) 219, 222
C. Claudius Marcellus (*pr.* 80) 84, 87
C. Claudius Marcellus (*cos.* 50) 268, 276, 314, 349
C. Claudius Marcellus (*cos.* 49) 273
M. Claudius Marcellus (*aed.cur.* 91) 84
M. Claudius Marcellus Aeserninus (*cos.* 51) 84f, 145, 267f, 282, 313ff, 319, 322, 365
C. Claudius Nero (*pr.* 81) 95

T. Claudius 195
Ti. Claudius Nero (*pr.* before 63) 147
Ti. Claudius Nero (*pr.* 42) 242
Ap. Claudius Pulcher (*cos.* 54) 173, 181, 189, 197, 205, 224f, 243, 251, 256, 258ff, 264, 266, 273, 276n, 283f
C. Claudius Pulcher (*cos.* 92) 97, 205f
C. Claudius Pulcher (*cos.* 56) 196
P. Claudius Pulcher, son of Clodius 343
Cleanthes 353
Cleopatra 346f
Clitomachus (Hasdrubal), Academic philosopher 333
Clodia (Claudia) 150, 157, 431f
L. Clodius 258
Sex. Clodius Phormio, banker 79
P. Clodius Pulcher (*tr.pl.* 58) 6ff, 13, 18f, 119f, 130, 154ff, 163, 167, 171–82, 185ff, 194ff, 200f, 204, 206f, 210, 224, 248ff, 286, 343, 371, 379, 394, 398, 423, 432
Sex. Cloelius, scribe 199, 295, 343, 430
A. Cluentius Habitus 36f
C. Coelius Caldus (*q.* 50) 265f
L. and P. Cominius 113
Q. Considius 88
M. Considius Nonianus (*pr.* by 50) 284
C. Considius Longus (*pr.* by 54) 317
C. Cornelius (*tr.pl.* 67) 22ff, 29f, 34, 112ff, 125, 326
L. Cornelius Balbus (*suf.* 40) 165, 207, 271, 276ff, 285, 287ff, 293, 302, 319f, 323n, 335, 343, 345f, 365
L. Cornelius Balbus (*q.* 44), his son 287, 413
C. Cornelius Cethegus 9, 150
L. Cornelius Chrysogonus 425ff
L. Cornelius Cinna (*cos.* 87) 298, 307f, 354, 377
Cn. Cornelius Dolabella (*pr.* 81) 95
P. Cornelius Dolabella (*pr.* 69/8) 73, 75, 80
P. Cornelius Dolabella (*suf.* 44) 266, 294f, 313, 324, 337, 339, 345f, 348, 375ff, 380f, 395f, 399f, 402, 405, 407, 415ff, 440ff
Cn. Cornelius Lentulus Clodianus (*cos.* 72) 94, 429
L. Cornelius Lentulus Crus (*cos.* 49) 178, 273, 282f, 287
Cn. Cornelius Lentulus Marcellinus (*cos.* 56) 84, 94, 190, 194
L. Cornelius Lentulus Niger, *flamen Martialis* 173, 242
P. Cornelius Lentulus Spinther (*cos.* 57) 9f, 28, 187, 190ff, 201, 208f, 223ff, 256
P. Cornelius Lentulus Spinther (*q.* ?44), his son 402, 415f, 443
P. Cornelius Lentulus Sura (*pr.* 63) 173
P. Cornelius Scipio Africanus Aemilianus (*cos.* 147) 153, 232ff, 362f, 366, 371, 396, 438
P. Cornelius Scipio Nasica Serapio (*cos.* 138) 145, 187n, 234
L. Cornelius Sisenna (*pr.* 78) 84, 89f
Faustus Cornelius Sulla (*q.* 54) 30, 311n
L. Cornelius Sulla Felix (*cos.* 88) 36, 241f, 287, 307f, 364, 368, 376, 415, 421f, 425, 427
P. Cornelius Sulla (*cos.des.* 65) 150ff, 242, 324
L. Cornificius (*cos.* 35) 314n, 382f, 398, 406
Q. Cornificius (*tr.pl.* 69) 87, 155
Cratippus, Peripatetic philosopher 366
M. Crepereius 87
Q. Croton 124
M'. Curius (*causa Curiana*) 228f, 338
C. Curtius Postumus (father of Rabirius Postumus) 125, 246

P. Decius Mus (*cos.* 340) and son (*cos.* 312) 187, 197, 371
Deiotarus of Galatia 255, 260ff, 265, 304, 335ff, 397, 417n
Democritus 352

Diodorus of Melita 93
Diodotus, Stoic philosopher 308
Dion of Alexandria 199, 431
Dionysius I of Syracuse 295, 370
Diviciacus, Aeduan chief 162
L. Domitius Ahenobarbus (*cos.* 54) 94, 174, 209, 218, 271, 281, 284, 286
Cn. Domitius Ahenobarbus (*cos.* 32) 417
Cn. Domitius Calvinus (*cos.* 53) 167, 243, 249, 335f

L. Egnatuleius 387, 390
C. Erucius 426
Epicurus 328, 351–3
  Epicureanism 324ff
L. Equitius (Sempronius Gracchus) 122

Fabia, Vestal 157
P. Fabius 69ff
Q. Fabius Sanga 178
Q. Fabius Maximus (*suf.* 45) 338
C. Fabricius Luscinus (*cos.* 282) 371, 373
Q .Fabricius (*tr.pl.* 57) 181, 197
C. Fannius (*cos.* 122) 232, 263
C. Fannius (*tr.pl.* 59) 167, 174
M. Fannius (*pr.* 80) 426
C. Fannius Chaerea 61ff
M. Favonius (*pr.* 49) 167, 194, 271, 348
L. Flavius (*pr.* 58) 142, 162ff.
Q. Flavius Tarquiniensis 61ff
M. Fonteius (*pr.* ?75) 24, 101ff
C. Fonteius Capito 350n
C. Fuficius Fango 343
Q. Fufius Calenus (*cos.* 47) 7, 155f, 159, 389n, 395ff, 443
M. Fulcinius, father and son 74f
Fulvia 343
M. Fulvius Flaccus (*cos.* 125) 188
Furius Crassipes (*q.* 51) 430
Furius, expert on property law 80n
L. Furius Philus (*cos.* 136) 232, 236–7, 368
C. Furnius (*pr.* ?42) 284, 291, 401, 410

A. Gabinius (*cos.* 58) 9, 12f, 113f, 125, 156, 174, 176f, 196, 203ff, 210, 218, 225, 242f, 246ff, 295
L. Gavius 265
L. Gellius Publicola (*cos.* 72) 10, 12

Heius of Messana 93, 105
Heraclius of Syracuse 93n, 105
C. Herennius (*tr.pl.* 60) 161, 163
A. Hirtius (*cos.* 43) 277, 294, 320, 325, 340, 343, 349, 357, 377, 386, 390, 393f, 399f, 404ff, 415, 418, 443ff
Homer 166, 274n, 424
Q. Hortensius (*cos.* 69) 23, 30, 45, 83, 89, 95, 102, 106, 115, 121, 129, 150, 155, 161, 173, 177ff, 195, 198, 220f, 296, 298, 304f, 307ff, 326, 429

C. Iulius Caesar (*cos.* 59) 17f, 28, 125, 133, 147f, 152n, 154f, 163–78, 196, 202, 205ff, 218, 243, 248, 267–80, 310–25, 334–45, 356, 360, 364, 367ff, 376ff, 423, 434, 440
C. Iulius Caesar Octavianus 343, 348f, 361, 383–93, 396, 399f, 403, 408ff, 417ff, 434, 440ff
C. Iulius Caesar Strabo (*aed.cur.* 89) 227, 229, 308
L. Iulius Caesar (*cos.* 64) 161n, 389, 391, 393, 396, 398, 406f, 443
L. Iulius Caesar, son of the above 284
Iunia Tertulla 348, 418
D. Iunius Brutus Albinus 340, 342, 383, 386ff, 394, 397, 400, 404, 406, 408ff, 417f, 440ff
L. Iunius Brutus (*cos.* 509) 174, 309, 334, 371
M. Iunius Brutus, notorious prosecutor 371
M. Iunius Brutus (*tr.pl.* 83) 36, 55, 57, 298

M. Iunius (Q.Servilius Caepio) Brutus (*pr.*44) 129, 173, 264f, 304f, 309, 322, 325, 327f, 334f, 339f, 342, 345, 348f, 374, 376, 395ff, , 400, 405f, 409, 414ff, 421, 440ff
D. Iunius Silanus (*cos.* 62) 17f, 147
M. Iunius Silanus (*leg.* 43) 411
M. Iuventius Laterensis (*pr.* 51) 11, 220ff, 410

Juba I of Numidia 318f

Q. Labienus 120ff
T. Labienus (*tr.pl.* 63) 120ff, 141, 278
C. Laelius (*cos.* 140) 26, 153, 232f, 236ff, 362ff, 368n, 371, 438
D. Laelius (*tr.pl.* 54) 103ff
M. Laenius Flaccus 217
Q. Lepta 334
A. Licinius Archias 153
A. Licinius Aristoteles 295
C. Licinius Calvus 7, 195
L. Licinius Crassus (*cos.* 95) 123, 206, 217, 226ff, 305, 372, 422, 433
M. Licinius Crassus (*cos.* 70) 85, 114, 133, 140, 152n, 157, 160f, 164f, 178, 192ff, 200f, 217ff, 223, 225, 251f, 255, 329, 356, 367, 433f
P. Licinius Crassus (?*q.* 55), his son 178, 252, 255
P. Licinius Crassus Mucianus (*cos.*131) 256n, 396
L. Licinius Lucullus (*cos.* 74) 5, 90, 106, 129, 153, 155, 161, 164f, 174, 195, 326
L. Licinius Murena (*cos.* 62) 108, 130, 149
C. Licinius Sacerdos (*pr.* 75) 94
Q. Ligarius 317ff
M. Livius Drusus (*tr.pl.* 91) 188, 226f, 230, 247, 354
M. Livius Drusus Claudianus (?*pr.* 50) 219, 409, 418n
M. Lollius Palicanus (*tr.pl.* 71) 84

L. Lucceius (*pr.* 64) 165
Q. Lucilius Balbus 351ff
C. Lucilius Hirrus (*tr.pl.* 54) 243, 271
M. Lucretius 87
Lucretius (T. Lucretius Carus) 197n, 227
Lurco, see Aufidius
Q. Lutatius Catulus (*cos.* 102) 123, 188, 227, 308, 354
Q. Lutatius Catulus (*cos.* 78) 18n, 23f, 87, 90f, 115, 163, 198, 326

Sp. Maelius 144, 188, 309, 364, 380
N. Magius 288f
C. Malleolus (*q.* 80) 92, 94
C. Manilius (*tr.pl.* 66) 34, 113f, 125, 239, 428
M. Manilius (*cos.* 149) 232
Q. Manlius 87
M. Manlius Capitolinus 188, 377, 380
A. Manlius Torqautus 302n, 323
L. Manlius Torquatus (*cos.* 65) 129, 178, 201
L. Manlius Torquatus (*pr.* 49) 30, 34, 151f, 328f
T. Manlius Torquatus 336
Cn. Marcius Coriolanus 364f
Q. Marcius Crispus (*pr.* 46) 211, 397, 402, 443
L. Marcius Figulus 416
L. Marcius Philippus (*cos.* 91) 45, 230, 298, 373
L. Marcius Philippus (*cos.* 56) 294, 343, 348f, 418, 420f
C. Marius (*cos.* 107) 12f, 84, 121f, 139, 171, 196f, 206, 216, 308, 345, 354n, 357, 364, 372, 429
M. Marius Gratidianus (*tr.pl.* 87) 132, 372
P. Matinius 265
C. Matius 292f, 320, 341, 347, 359ff, 378, 441
C. Memmius (*pr.* 58) 242f
C. Memmius (*tr.pl.* 54) 242
C. Messius (*aed.pl.* 55) 172n, 184, 219
L. Mescinius Rufus (*q.* 51) 265f

L. Minucius Basilus 340
Q. Minucius Thermus (*tr.pl.* 62) 149
Mithridates of Pergamum 104, 106
Mithridates VI of Pontus 123, 140, 153, 429
Q. Mucius Orestinus (*tr.pl.* 64) 133f
Q. Mucius Scaevola (*cos.* 117) 123, 362f, 394
Q. Mucius Scaevola (*cos.* 95) 227ff, 232, 299, 307f, 354, 372, 422, 427
Sp. Mummius 232, 238
L. Munatius Plancus (*cos.* 42) 375, 383, 388, 389n, 399ff, 406ff, 417ff, 443f, 446f
T. Munatius Plancus Bursa (*tr.pl.* 52) 252, 398
T. Munatius Plancus 410

Sex. Naevius 43–59
L. Ninnius Quadratus (*tr.pl.* 58) 176, 180, 297
C. Norbanus (*cos.* 83) 116ff, 227, 229
Numa Pompilius 151, 235, 437

Octavian (C. Octavius), see C. Iulius Caesar Octavianus
Cn. Octavius (*cos.* 165) 394
M. Octavius (*tr.pl.* 133) 118
M. Octavius (*tr.pl.* after 122) 371
L. Octavius Balbus 87
C. Oppius 287f, 302, 319f, 323n, 335, 341, 365
Cn. Oppius 10, 12

Palla 431
Panaetius 233, 355, 366ff
C. Papius (*tr.pl.* 65) 372
C. Papirius Carbo (*cos.* 120) 306, 364
C. Papirius Carbo Arvina (*pr.* by 83) 308
Cn. Papirius Carbo (*cos.* 85) 95, 398
L. Papirius Paetus 311f, 385f
Pausanias, freedman of Lentulus Spinther 225, 256, 259f
Q. Pedius (*suff.* 43) 420, 444
Sex. Peducaeus (*pr.* 77) 88

Phaedrus, Epicurean philosopher 328, 350n
Philo, Academic philosopher 308
Philodamus of Lampsacus 89, 95
Philodemus, Epicurean philosopher 352
L. Pinarius Natta 188
Cn. Plancius, *publicanus* 160n, 221
Cn. Plancius (*aed.cur.* 55), his son 10f, 160n, 219ff
Plato, *Gorgias* 231
 Phaedrus 231
 Republic 163, 232f, 236f, 240, 254, 295
P. Plautius Hypsaeus (*pr.* ?55) 192, 249
A. Plotius (*pr.* 51) 222
Polybius 233f
Pompeia, wife of Caesar 155
Sex. Pompeius Chlorus 84, 92n
Pompey (Cn. Pompeius Magnus) 5, 9, 84f, 90, 102, 114f, 129, 139f, 149, 151ff, 159ff, 189ff, 201, 205, 207ff, 217f, 223f, 239, 242ff, 247ff, 255f, 265–80, 281–93, 301ff, 309, 315f, 329, 356, 373, 376, 378, 396, 423, 427ff, 433ff, 445ff
Cn. Pompeius, son of Magnus 323f
Sex. Pompeius, son of Magnus 325, 341, 347, 349, 389f, 399f, 440, 443, 445ff
Q. Pompeius Rufus (*cos.* 88) 363
Q. Pompeius Rufus (*pr.* 63) 431
Q. Pompeius Rufus (*tr.pl.* 52) 252, 285
Cn. Pompeius Theodorus 84, 92n
Pomponia 262
T. Pomponius Atticus 5ff, 154f, 160ff, 302, 304, 307, 326, 362, 404, 436
C. Pomptinus (*pr.* 63) 262, 265
Pontius Aquila (*tr.pl.* 45) 418
P. Popilius Laenas (*cos.* 132) 11f, 384
C. Porcius Cato (*cos.* 114) 364
C. Porcius Cato (*tr.pl.* 56) 191, 193f, 224, 243
M. Porcius Cato (*cos.* 195) 371, 437ff

Index

M. Porcius Cato (*pr.* 54) 10, 129, 149, 155, 164ff, 171, 178f, 203, 225, 243, 260, 262, 266f, 271, 284, 297, 301, 316, 325, 327ff, 336, 373, 424, 435f
M. Porcius Laeca 144
Posidonius of Apamea 353, 367, 368n
Ptolemy XII Neos Dionysios (Auletes) 167, 169, 191, 208, 247f, 432
Ptolemy, son of Cleopatra 347
Publilia 325
M. Pupius Piso (*cos.* 61) 7, 107, 154f, 160, 165, 328, 331f

Sex. Quinctilius Varus (*pr.* 57) 202
Sex. Quinctilius Varus (*q.* 49) 418n, 445–6
C. Quinctius 47f
L. Quinctius (*pr.* 68) 70ff
P. Quinctius 43–59
C. Quinctius Valgus 141
P. Quinctius Scapula 49

C. Rabirius 120ff
C. Rabirius (Curtius) Postumus 125, 191, 246ff, 293, 320, 347, 432
L. Racilius (*tr.pl.* 56) 193f, 222
L. Roscius Otho (*pr.* ?63) 136, 142
Q. Roscius, the actor 43, 57, 60ff, 422
Sex. Roscius of Ameria 43, 60, 422, 455ff
T. Roscius 425f
T. Roscius Capito 425
L. Roscius Fabatus (*pr.* 49) 284
P. Rupilius (*cos.* 132) 95, 354
Rufrenus (? *tr.pl.* 42) 413
P. Rutilius Lupus (*pr.* 49) 190ff
P. Rutilius Rufus (*cos.* 105) 123, 354

Sallust (C. Sallustius Crispus, *tr.pl.* 52) 276n
Cn.Sallustius 232
Sassia 36f
C. Saufeius (*q.* 100) 122
Scamander, freedman of Fabricii 37

M. Scaptius 264f, 419
C. Scribonius Curio (*cos.* 76) 18f, 173f, 177, 180, 245, 308, 373, 429, 432
C. Scribonius Curio (*tr.pl.* 50) 171ff, 194, 245, 268ff, 276, 281ff, 294ff, 379
L. Scribonius Libo (*cos.* 34) 192, 279n, 290, 311n
Segulius Labeo 409f
L. Sempronius Atratinus (*suff.* 34) 200, 433
C. Sempronius Gracchus (*tr.pl.* 123) 81, 122, 144, 147, 176, 188, 198, 306, 364f, 370f, 376
Ti. Sempronius Gracchus (*tr.pl.* 133) 144, 162, 187n, 198, 238, 240, 306, 364f, 370, 394
C. Septimius 173
P. Septimius 104
L. Sergius Catilina (*pr.* 68) 108, 129, 133ff, 142ff, 157, 200f, 368, 394
Servilia 348, 418f
M. Servilius (*tr.pl.* 43) 397
C. Servilius Ahala 145, 174, 309
P. Servilius Casca Longus (*tr.pl.* 43) 384, 419, 445f
Q. Servilius Caepio (*cos.* 106) 82, 116, 118
Q. Servilius Caepio (*pr.* ?91) 188
C. Servilius Glaucia (*pr.* 100) 92, 95, 122, 144, 246
P. Servilius Globulus (*pr.* 64) 106, 113
P. Servilius Isauricus (*cos.* 48) 194, 378, 389, 392, 396, 398f, 401f, 405ff, 418, 421
P. Servilius Rullus (*tr.pl.* 63) 137ff, 142, 149, 270
P. Servilius Vatia Isauricus (*cos.* 79) 9, 87, 107, 182, 192f, 205, 256, 258, 429, 433
Servius Tullius 151, 235
P. Sestius (*pr.* 57) 9, 27f, 144, 180n, 181, 194ff, 200, 284, 320
A. Sestullius 105f

Socrates 163, 231, 306
Spurinna 356
C. Staienus 37
L. Staius Murcus (*pr.* ?45) 397, 402, 443
Sthenius of Thermae 84, 93, 95, 105
P. Sulpicius Galba (*pr.* by 66) 87, 131
Ser. Sulpicius Galba (*pr.* 54) 272f, 404, 445f
P. Sulpicius Rufus (*tr.pl.* 88) 116, 227, 362
Ser. Sulpicius Rufus (*cos.* 51) 297, 308, 313ff, 322, 336, 394f, 418, 421, 443

Tarquinius Superbus 234f, 380, 387
Terentia 155, 157, 179, 325
Terentius Culleo (*leg.* 43) 411
M. Terentius Varro, the polymath 232, 310f, 327, 381
M. Terentius Varro Lucullus (*cos.* 73) 23, 69f, 72f, 94, 115, 178, 192
M. Terpolius (*tr.pl.* 77) 116
Themistocles 216, 299, 365, 418
Theophrastus 327, 363n, 371
Thucydides 220n, 239n, 275, 299, 366, 405n
L. Tillius Cimber ((*pr.*? 45) 320, 342, 417n, 440
Sex. Titius (*tr.pl.* 99) 123
C. Trebatius Testa 218, 245, 293, 359, 361f
L. Trebellius (*tr.pl.* 67) 114, 118
L. Trebellius (*tr.pl.* 47) 398
M. Trebellius 49
Trebianus 320
C. Trebonius (*suf.* 45) 302, 342, 400, 440, 443ff
Cn. Tremellius 87
M. Tugio, expert on water law 80n
Tullia 294, 324ff, 395, 430
P. Tullio 204
M. Tullius, Cicero's client 69ff
M. Tullius, prosecutor of Sestius 194f
M. Tullius Cicero (*suf.* 30) 296, 343, 350, 366, 373, 405

M. Tullius Tiro 283, 386, 420
Q. Tullius Cicero (*pr.* 62) 103, 224ff, 255, 262, 265, 304, 355ff, 386, 436
Q. Tullius Cicero (*q.* 43) 294, 296, 304, 349, 387
Servius Tullius 151, 235
D. Turullius (*q.* 43) 416

Valerius Aris 26, 109
C. Valerius Flaccus (*cos.* 93) 51, 55, 107
L. Valerius Flaccus (*cos.* 100) 122
L. Valerius Flaccus (*cos.* 86) 69, 107, 298
L. Valerius Flaccus (*pr.* 63) 26f, 103ff, 173
C. Valerius Triarius 328
P. Valerius Triarius 25f, 109, 243
M. Valerius Messala Corvinus (*suf.* 31) 418
M. Valerius Messala Niger (*cos.* 61) 155
M. Valerius Messala Rufus (*cos.* 53) 243f, 249, 426
L. Varius Cotyla (*aed*, ?44) 393f, 443
M. Varisidius 401
P. Vatinius (*cos.* 47) 27ff, 170f, 174, 195, 198, 322, 395, 443
C. Velleius 351f, 354
P. Ventidius Bassus (*suf.* 43) 405, 408f
C. Verres (*pr.* 74) 82ff, 257, 428
C. Vestorius 432
L. Vettius 173ff
C. Vibius Pansa (*cos.* 43) 302, 308, 324, 329, 343, 346, 349, 386, 390, 394f, 397ff, 404ff, 410, 418, 443f
L. Vibullius Rufus 205
M. Vitruvius Vaccus 188
L. Volcatius Tullus (*cos.* 65) 192f, 291, 314
Volumnia Cytheris 297
P. Volumnius Eutrapelus 312f
Q. Volusius 255n, 263n

Zeno of Citium 327

B. TECHNICAL TERMS

Actio certae pecuniae creditae 62, 65f
Altercatio 18ff, 89, 223
Ampliatio 19, 23, 25, 44
Aqua et igni interdictio 187
Arbitrium ex compromisso 62
Audaces 404n

Bonorum possessio, see *missio in possessionem*

Clementia 289, 294, 315ff
Cognitor 61, 63
Collegium 176f
Comperendinatio 19, 23ff, 33, 89, 92, 101, 104, 108
Commiseratio,conquestio 47, 118, 123
Concursus 164
Constitutio causae 49

Damnum (iniuria) 61, 70
Deductio 75, 79
Diei diffisio 44
Divinatio 82ff
Divisio 193
Dolus malus 70ff

Fundus 55

Hostis 143–4, 152

Indignatio 31n, 47
Inquisitio 25, 85f, 103, 109
Interdictum de vi armata 70n, 73ff
   unde vi 71f
Interrogatio 17, 28ff

Largitio/liberalitas 36, 368, 371
Laudatio 31
Legatio libera 172n, 340, 342
Litis aestimatio 90, 92

Maiestas 113ff, 123f
Missio in possessionem 49, 55ff
Moderator, see *rector rei publicae*

Narratio 49, 60
Nominis delatio 85
Nundinae, see *Trinundinum*

Officium 152, 192, 366
Optimates 197ff, 238
Otium (cum dignitate) 198, 215, 225

Partitio 49
Popularis/es 122, 141, 198ff, 238, 371
Praevaricatio 130
Privilegium 113f, 187

Quadruplator 82

Rector rei publicae 153, 235, 239ff, 254
Recuperatores 68, 70, 79
Relegatio 144, 177

Saga 390, 393
Sanctio 167f, 180
Socius, societas, actio pro socio 47ff, 60ff
Sodalitas 132
Sponsio, stipulatio 53, 56, 62ff, 73f
Subscriptor 86
Supplicatio 203

Testatio 52, cf. 50
Testimonium 20f
Trinundinum (nundinae) 121, 170n, 176, 182, 205
Tumultus 161f, 341, 390, 392

Vadimonium 34f, 49ff

C. STATUTES AND BILLS

Lex Aebutia de rogationibus 188
Leges Aelia et Fufia 176, 182
Lex Antonia agraria 389, 391f, 445, 447
   de iudiciis 389, 391f
   de provinciis 345, 389, 391f
Lex Appuleia de maiestate 116ff
Lex Aquilia 70, 72
Lex Aurelia iudiciaria 23, 90, 422
Lex Caecilia Didia 187, 389
Lex Calpurnia de ambitu 113
   de repetundis 81
Lex Cassia de suffragiis 198
Lex Clodia de civibus indemnatis 176, 187
   de collegiis 176
   de exilio Ciceronis 178f, 186ff
   de provinciis 176, 186
Lex Cornelia de edictis praetorum 113
   de privilegiis 113
   de repetundis 87, 90, 96
   de veneficis 36
Lex Cornelia Caecilia de reditu Ciceronis 181f
Lex decem tribunorum 251f, 278, 434f
Lex Fabia de plagio 120
Rogatio Flavia agraria 162ff
Lex Gabinia de piratis 113, 156
Lex Gabinia de pecuniis credendis 113, 264
Lex Iulia agraria 67f
   de agro Campano 169ff, 190, 201ff
   de maiestate 376
   de repetundis 103, 107, 266n
   de vi 376
Lex Iunia de civitate 372
Lex Licinia de sodaliciis 219ff

Lex Licinia Iunia de rogationibus 28, 188, 389, cf.435
Lex Licinia Mucia de civitate 372
Lex Lutatia de vi 430f
Lex Manilia de imperio Gnaei Pompeii 4, 132, 139, 427ff
   de libertinorum suffragiis 428
Lex Papia de civitate 207
Lex Papiria de dedicationibus 188
Lex Plautia de vi 430f
Lex/rogatio Plotia agraria 137, 161
Lex Plotia iudiciaria 115
Lex Pompeia de iure magistratuum 435f
Leges Pompeiae iudiciariae 250
Lex Pompeia Licinia de provinciis Caesaris 209, 433f
   de tribunis plebis 114
Lex Porcia de provocatione 120, 122, 437
Leges Semproniae (agraria, frumentaria) 198, 371
Lex Sempronia de capite civium 122, 147
   de provinciis consularibus 205
Lex Sempronia (Acilia) de repetundis 81f, 87n, 96
Lex Servilia (Caepionis) de repetundis 82, 118
Lex Servilia (Glauciae) de repetundis 246
Rogatio Servilia agraria 137ff, 162, 270
Lex Terentia Cassia 96
Lex Titia de tribus viris 445
Lex Trebonia de provinciis 209f
Lex Tullia de ambitu 28, 222
Lex Valeria de faeneratione 49
Lex Varia de maiestate 307
Lex Vatinia de provincia Gallia 433f
Lex Voconia de hereditatibus 75

D. CICERONIAN WRITINGS

Orationes

De Aere Alieno Milonis 246, 249f
De Domo 185–9; (55) 178, (72) 37
De Haruspicum Responso 204f; (42) 130, (47) 38
De Imperio Cn.Pompei (pro lege Manilia) 14, 139, 427–9
De Lege Agraria 137–42; (1.77–94) 35f, (2.5–7) 139, (3.2ff) 141
De provinciis consularibus 205–8
De Rege Alexandrino 133
Divinatio in Caecilium 82, 84ff
In Catilinam 136, 142–8; (1.4) 142, (1.20) 143, 145, (1.27) 392; (2) 388, (2.18–23) 13, (2.24–5) 392, (2.28) 143f; (3.1, 23) 147; (4.1–6) 17f, 143, (4.7) 17f, 147, (4.10) 145, 147
In Clodium et Curionem 18f, 159, 432f
In Pisonem 210f, (76–7) 177f
In Q. Metellum 20, 149f
In Toga Candida 130–5, 144
In Vatinium 27–30, 195
In Verrem
    Actio 1 84–8, 90–2; (55) 92
    Actio 2 16, 86–9, 92–100; (4.9f) 97, (4.149) 96, (5.1f, 21f) 98, (5.126f) 99
Philippica(1) 375–8, (2) 15f, 378–82, (2.25,88) 339, (3) 386–8, (4) 388, (5) 388–91, (6) 391f, (7) 392, (8) 393f, (9) 394f, (10) 395f, (11) 396f, (12) 397f, (13) 399–401, 445–7, (14) 404f

Post Reditum ad Quirites 8f, 11–14, 183f
Post Reditum in Senatu 8–11, 183f; (25–7) 181f, (32) 37, 178
Pro Archia 153
Pro Balbo 207f
Pro Caecina 35, 68, 70, 73–80
Pro Caelio 199–201, 430–33; (14) 129
Pro Cluentio 20f, 112; (152) 148
Pro Cornelio 22–4, 112–30, 376
Pro Fonteio 101–3; (21, 39) 24
Pro Flacco 103–8; (21–60) 26f, (94–7) 173, (95) 108
Pro Ligario 317–9, 335
Pro Marcello 16, 314–7, 319, 335
Pro Milone 15, 19f, 33f, 250f; (9–11, 24–60) 119f, (67–91) 250
Pro Murena 123, 136; (49–52) 142n
Pro Plancio 219–23; (72–85) 24f, (97–8) 216f
Pro Quinctio 43–59
Pro Rabirio Perduellionis Reo 120–5, 136; (27) 148
Pro Rabirio Postumo 246–8
Pro Rege Deiotaro 335–7, 339, 380
Pro Q. Roscio Comoedo 60–7
Pro Sex. Roscio Amerino 43, 112, 425–7; (32) 142n
Pro Scauro 25f, 108f, 219
Pro Sestio 194–9; (41) 178, 196, (53) 178, (98) 215, (129) 181f
Pro Sulla 30–1, 150–2; (11–14) 34, (65) 142n
Pro Tullio 68–73

Index

Rhetorica

Brutus 42f, 304–9, 315; (331–4) 309, 339
De Inventione 227; (1.30) 3, (1.98ff) 31n
De Oratore 225–30, 438; (2.62) 3, (2.104ff) 117, 164, 167, (2.197) 116
Orator 312
De Optimo Genere Dicendi 346f
Topica Aristotelea 359

Epistulae

Ad Atticum (1.1–2) 4ff, 129, 131,134; (1.12–16) 153–9, (1.16) 6ff; (1.17–2.3) 159–66, (1.19.4, 2.1.7, 19.4)) 37; (2.1.1–2) 136, (2.3) 168, (2.5)169, (2.16.1–2) 169ff, (2.17–20) 171–3, (2.24) 173–5; (3.8–24) 178–81, (3.15) 179f, (3.23) 180f; (4.1) 182, 184f, (4.2) 185, 188f, (4.3) 189f, (4.5) 208, (4.6) 209, (4.13) 217, (4.15) 219, (4.16) 218, (4.19) 219; (5.1–21) 255–64, (5.7) 255–6, (5.13) 252; (6.1–2) 263–5, (6.8–9) 267; (7.1–9) 274–80, (7.1) 251,266,434f, (7.10–20) 281–6, (7.7.6, 9.4) 434; (8.1–15) 286–8, (8.11) 287; (9.2–19) 287–94, (9.10) 291, (9.11A) 292; (10.4–18) 294–8; (11.1–12) 301–4, (11.6) 303; (12.2) 310, (12.4,5) 313–5, (12.21) 325, (12.45) 334; (13.12–16) 327, (13.27–8) 325, (13.37,40,46) 334, (13.52) 337f; (14.1) 320, 341, (14.2–22) 341–7; (15.1–29) 347–9, (15.11) 348, (15.13) 383; (16.7) 374, (16.8–9) 383–4, (16.11) 366, 383–4, (16.14) 384, (16.15) 384f, 421.
Ad Caesarem 274
Ad Caesarem iuniorem 393n; (I,fr.6) 419n, (II,fr.23b) 420
Ad Brutum (2, 3, 5, 8) 402f, (10, 13) 405, (11,12, 14–26) 416–19, (23) 418, (24–5) 419n, (26) 419.
Ad Familiares (1.1) 191f, (1.2) 193, (1.7) 194, 208, 218, (1.8) 209, (1.9) 215, 223–5, (1.9.7) 28, 201–2; (2.2–6) 245, (2.8) 256, 267, (2.10–11) 262, (2.16) 296; (3.2) 253, (3.5–12) 256, 258–60; (4.4,7, 9) 313–7, (4.5–6) 325f, 394n, (4.13) 322; (5.1–2) 149f, 152, (5.7) 152–3, (5.8) 217, (5.9–11) 322, (5.12) 3, 215–7; (6.1–4) 322f, (6.5–7) 321–2; (6.10A,10B,11,12) 320, (6.13–14) 317f, (6.15) 340; (7.1) 211n, (7.2) 252, (7.3) 311) , (7.6–18) 218, 245, (7.30) 338, (7.33) 313; (8.1–15) 267–71, (8.1.4) 285, (8.16) 296, (8.17) 283f, 302; (9.1) 304, 310, (9.2,7) 310, (9.9) 302, (9.12) 337, (9.15,17) 323, (9.16,18) 310ff, (9.24) 385–6; (10.1) 383, (10.10–12) 401, (10.13–23) 410–12, (10.24) 419f, (10.30) 404, (10.31) 403, (10.32) 413f, (10.34–5) 411f; (11.1) 340f, (11.2) 345, (11.3) 374f, (11.4) 383, 386 (11.5) 386, (11.9–20) 408–10, (11.27,28) 359–62; (12.1) 346, (12.2) 378, (12.3) 382–3, (12.4) 393, (12.8–15) 415–6,(12.11) 402, (12.18) 314, (12.22) 382, (12.23) 397f, (12.26–30) 414; (13) 322; (14.1–4) 179; (14.7) 298, (14.23) 304n, (15.1–4) 260–2, (15.5, 6) 266, 315; (15.15) 310 , (15.16–19) 324, (16.11,12) 283f, (16.27) 386

Ad Quintum fratrem (1.1) 131, 253f, (1.2) 253f, (1.2.15) 171, (1.2.16) 175, (1.4) 177; (2.1,3) 190, (2.6.1–3) 202, (2.7) 203, 205, (2.10–14) 218f, (3.1–7) 242–4, (3.5) 232f, 436.
Commentariolum Petitionis 130–3

Philosophica

Academica 326–8, 438
De Amicitia 132, 153, 329, 359, 362–6
De Divinatione 350f, 355–8, 436; (1.90) 162
De Fato 358
De Finibus 328–32, 438; (5.1) 405n
De Legibus 241n, 436–8
De Natura Deorum 350–5, 438
De Officiis 366–72; (2.51) 3, 425
De Re Publica 3, 232–41, 287, 436–8; (2.56–7) 199
De Senectute 438f
Hortensius 326
Tusculanae Disputationes 332f, 438f

Historica

De Consiliis Suis 135, 378
De Consulatu Suo 136f, 139